THE ENCYCLOPEDIA OF
MIDDLE EAST WARS

THE ENCYCLOPEDIA OF MIDDLE EAST WARS

The United States in the Persian Gulf, Afghanistan, and Iraq Conflicts

VOLUME V: DOCUMENTS

Spencer C. Tucker
Editor

Priscilla Mary Roberts
Editor, Documents Volume

Dr. Paul G. Pierpaoli Jr.
Associate Editor

Colonel Jerry D. Morelock, USAR (retired)
Major General David Zabecki, USAR (retired)
Dr. Sherifa Zuhur
Assistant Editors

FOREWORD BY
General Anthony C. Zinni, USMC (retired)

Santa Barbara, California   Denver, Colorado   Oxford, England

Library of Congress Cataloging-in-Publication Data

The encyclopedia of Middle East wars : the United States in the Persian Gulf, Afghanistan, and Iraq conflicts / Spencer C. Tucker, editor ; Priscilla Mary Roberts, editor, documents volume.
    v.   cm.
  Includes bibliographical references and index.
    ISBN 978-1-85109-947-4 (hard copy : alk. paper) — ISBN 978-1-85109-948-1 (ebook)
    1. Middle East—History, Military—20th century—Encyclopedias.   2. Middle East—History, Military—21st century—Encyclopedias.
3. Middle East—Military relations—United States—Encyclopedias.   4. United States—Military relations—Middle
East—Encyclopedias.   5. Persian Gulf War, 1991—Encyclopedias.   6. Afghan War, 2001—Encyclopedias.   7. Iraq War, 2003—
Encyclopedias.   I. Tucker, Spencer, 1937–   II. Roberts, Priscilla Mary.
    DS63.1.E453 2010
    355.00956'03—dc22

                                                                                                            2010033812

13 12 11 10 9   1 2 3 4 5

This book is also available on the World Wide Web as an ebook.
Visit abc-clio.com for details.

ABC-CLIO, LLC
130 Cremona Drive, P.O. Box 1911
Santa Barbara, California 93116–1911

This book is printed on acid-free paper ♾
Manufactured in the United States of America

About the Editors

Spencer C. Tucker, PhD, graduated from the Virginia Military Institute and was a Fulbright scholar in France. He was a U.S. Army captain and intelligence analyst in the Pentagon during the Vietnam War, then taught for 30 years at Texas Christian University before returning to his alma mater for 6 years as the holder of the John Biggs Chair of Military History. He retired from teaching in 2003. He is now Senior Fellow of Military History at ABC-CLIO. Dr. Tucker has written or edited 36 books, including ABC-CLIO's award-winning *The Encyclopedia of the Cold War* and *The Encyclopedia of the Arab-Israeli Conflict* as well as the comprehensive *A Global Chronology of Conflict.*

Priscilla Mary Roberts received her PhD from Cambridge University and is an associate professor of history and an honorary director of the Centre of American Studies at the University of Hong Kong. Dr. Roberts has received numerous research awards and was the documents editor of *The Encyclopedia of the Cold War* and *The Encyclopedia of the Arab-Israeli Conflict,* published by ABC-CLIO. She spent 2003 as a visiting Fulbright scholar at the Institute for European, Russian, and Eurasian Studies at the George Washington University in Washington, D.C.

ABC-CLIO Military History
Advisory Board Members

Contents

List of Documents

Documents

1. British Foreign Minister Palmerston to Viscount Beauvale, British Ambassador in Vienna, June 28, 1839

Introduction

By the 1830s, European powers realized that the Ottoman Empire was in decline. Ottoman Turkey's weakness quickly became a factor in international power politics. After a long and bitter rebellion, in 1832 the Greeks won independence from the Ottoman Empire, an event that encouraged other states to seek to partition the Ottoman Empire. Czarist Russia, which considered itself the spiritual heir of the Byzantine Empire, sought to enhance its position in the Caucasus and the Middle East. Russian leaders cherished designs of regaining the former Byzantine capital of Istanbul (Constantinople), which controlled the strategic Bosporus Straits, the only maritime passage from the Russian-dominated Black Sea to the Mediterranean. France too sought special rights in the Middle East, in Lebanon, Syria, Egypt, and Palestine. The Austrian Empire, whose Balkan provinces shared borders with the Ottoman Empire, also hoped to enhance its territorial position. Alarmed by the ambitions of their European rivals, whose power they did not wish to strengthen, British statesmen decided that the preservation of the Ottoman Empire was in their own country's interests. In an 1839 letter to the British ambassador in Vienna, capital of the Austrian Empire, Lord Palmerston, then British foreign secretary and later a Conservative prime minister, enunciated this position. Protection of the territorial integrity of the Ottoman Empire would remain British foreign policy for at least four decades and was a major reason for Britain's intervention in the 1854–1856 Crimean War.

Primary Source

The general view which Her Majesty's Government, as at present informed, entertain of the affair in question, may be stated as follows:

The Great Powers are justified in interfering in these matters, which are, in fact, a contest between a sovereign and his subject, because this contest threatens to produce great and imminent danger to the deepest interests of other Powers, and to the general peace of Europe. Those interests and that peace require the maintenance of the Turkish Empire; and the maintenance of the Turkish Empire is, therefore, the primary object to be aimed at. This object cannot be secured without putting an end to future chances of collision between the Sultan and Mehemet Ali. But as long as Mehemet Ali continues to occupy Syria, there will be danger of such collision. Mehemet Ali cannot hold Syria without a large military force constantly stationed there. As long as there is an Egyptian force in Syria, there must necessarily be a Turkish army in that part of Asia Minor which borders on Syria. Each party might agree at present to reduce those forces to a given amount, but neither could be sure that the other was not, after a time, secretly increasing his amount of force; and each party would, beyond a doubt, gradually augment his own force; and thus at no distant period, the same state of things which has existed of late, would again recur: for the motives and passions which have led to it would still be in action. Mehemet Ali, or Ibrahim, would still desire to add more territory to their Pashalics; the Sultan would still burn to drive them back into Egypt.

It appears then to Her Majesty's Government, that there can be no end to the danger with which these affairs menace the peace of Europe until Mehemet Ali shall have restored Syria to the direct authority of the Sultan; shall have retired into Egypt; and shall have interposed the Desert between his troops and authorities and the troops and authorities of the Sultan. But Mehemet Ali could not be expected to consent to this, unless some equivalent advantage were granted to him; and this equivalent advantage might be hereditary succession in his family to the Pashalic of Egypt: Mehemet Ali and his descendants being secured in the Government of that Province in the same way that a former Pasha of Scutari and his family were so secured; the Pasha continuing to be the vassal of the Porte, paying a reasonable tribute, furnishing a contingent of men, and being bound like any other Pasha by the treaties which his sovereign might make. Such an arrangement would appear to be equitable between the parties, because, on the one hand, it would secure the Sultan against many dangers and inconveniences which arise from the present occupation of Syria by the Pasha; while, on the other hand, it would afford to the Pasha that security as to the future fate of his family, his anxiety about which, he has often declared to be the main cause of his desire to obtain some final and permanent arrangement.

It appears to Her Majesty's Government that if the Five Powers were to agree upon such a plan, and were to propose it to the two parties, with all the authority which belongs to the Great Powers of Europe, such an arrangement would be carried into effect, and through its means, Europe would be delivered from a great and imminent danger.

Source: United Kingdom, *Parliamentary Papers,* 1841, 29:117–119.

2. British Prime Minister Benjamin Disraeli, Defense of His Action in Buying the Suez Canal Shares in the House of Commons, February 21, 1876 [Excerpts]

Introduction

The Suez Canal linking the Mediterranean Sea with the Red Sea, built with French finances and engineering expertise in the 1860s and completed in 1869, soon became an important British interest. In 1875 Britain bought Egypt's shares in the Suez Canal Company from the financially straitened khedive of Egypt. Although the French government still remained the majority shareholder, Britain effectively controlled the canal. Eventually, in 1882, British troops occupied Egypt and directed its government, maintaining an effective protectorate over that country until after World War II and generating growing nationalist resentment of colonial rule among the Egyptian population. The major reason the British took over Egypt was that British officials soon came to regard the canal as a major national strategic interest of their country, a route that by eliminating the need for ships traveling between Europe and Asia to circumnavigate Africa greatly facilitated sea communications with India, Britain's greatest imperial possession. Speaking in a parliamentary debate in the House of Commons in February 1876, Conservative prime minister Benjamin Disraeli sought to rebut critics who claimed that Britain's purchase of the khedive's Suez Canal shares was an unnecessary waste of government funds, one that would serve primarily to enrich the Jewish banking house of Rothschild and Sons, which had lent the British government 4 million pounds sterling while Parliament was in recess to finance this transaction. Disraeli, a staunch proponent of the British Empire who sought to maintain, strengthen, and protect British imperial interests, argued that his audience should consider the acquisition of the shares not as a commercial undertaking but rather as "a political transaction . . . calculated to strengthen the Empire." British ownership of the Suez Canal shares would give Britain "a great hold and interest in this important part of Africa" and would also secure "a highway to our Indian Empire and our other dependencies." At Disraeli's urging, the House of Commons voted to approve the purchase of the Suez Canal shares, the beginning of a British interest in the waterway that would last until 1956. In a further demonstration of his commitment to his country's imperial position, later in 1876 Disraeli proclaimed Britain's Queen Victoria empress of India.

Primary Source

Sir, although, according to the noble Lord, we are going to give a unanimous vote, it cannot be denied that the discussion of this evening at least has proved one result. It has shown, in a manner about which neither the House of Commons nor the country can make any mistake, that had the right hon. Gentleman the Member for Greenwich been the Prime Minister of this country, the shares in the Suez Canal would not have been purchased. The right hon. Gentleman defies me to produce an instance of a Ministry negotiating with a private firm. . . . The right hon. Gentleman found great fault with the amount of the commission which has been charged by the Messrs. Rothschild and admitted by the Government; and, indeed, both the right hon. Gentlemen opposite took the pains to calculate what was the amount of interest which it was proposed the Messrs. Rothschild should receive on account of their advance. It is, according to both right hon. Gentlemen, 15 per cent; but I must express my surprise that two right hon. Gentlemen, both of whom have filled the office of Chancellor of the Exchequer, and one of whom has been at the head of the Treasury, should have shown by their observations such a lamentable want of acquaintance with the manner in which large amounts of capital are commanded when the Government of a country may desire to possess

2. British Prime Minister Benjamin Disraeli, Defense of His Action in Buying the Suez Canal Shares

them under the circumstances under which we appealed to the House in question. I deny altogether that the commission charged by the Messrs. Rothschild has anything to do with the interest on the advance; nor can I suppose that two right hon. Gentlemen so well acquainted with finance as the Member for Greenwich and the Member for the University of London [Robert Lowe] can really believe that there is in this country anyone who has £4,000,000 lying idle at his bankers. Yet one would suppose, from the argument of the right hon. Gentleman the Member for Greenwich, that such is the assumption on which he has formed his opinion in this matter. In the present instance, I may observe, not only the possibility, but the probability, of our having immediately to advance the whole £4,000,000 was anticipated. And how was this £4,000,000 to be obtained? Only by the rapid conversion of securities to the same amount. Well, I need not tell anyone who is at all acquainted with such affairs that the rapid conversion of securities to the amount of £4,000,000 can never be effected without loss, and sometimes considerable loss; and it is to guard against risk of that kind that a commission is asked for before advances are made to a Government. In this case, too, it was more than probable that, after paying the first £1,000,000 following the signature of the contract, £2,000,000 further might be demanded in gold the next day. Fortunately for the Messrs. Rothschild they were not; but, if they had, there would in all likelihood have been a great disturbance in the Money Market, which must have occasioned a great sacrifice, perhaps the whole of the commission. The Committee, therefore, must not be led away by the observations of the two right hon. Gentlemen, who, of all men in the House, ought to be the last to make them.

[. . .]

Then the right hon. Gentleman the Member for Greenwich [Mr. Gladstone] proceeds in his attack in his own way, and makes a great many objections, but takes up two great positions as grounds of condemnation. "First of all," he says, "I object to this purchase, because it will give you no influence." That is the assertion of the right hon. Gentleman. I might meet it with a counter assertion. I might offer many arguments to show that it will give us a great deal of influence. I might refer to that which has already occurred, and which, though not in its results very considerable, shows some advantage from what has been done, while before a year has elapsed it will possibly show much more. I might refer to the general conviction and the common sense of society that such an investment cannot be treated as absolutely idle and nugatory, as the right hon. Gentleman wishes to treat it. The right hon. Gentleman takes a position from which it is certainly difficult to dislodge him, because it is perfectly arbitrary. He says—"You have no votes." He views the question abstractedly. He says—"Here is a company, and you have a great many shares in it, but you are not allowed to vote, and therefore it follows you can have no influence." But everybody knows that in the world things are not

managed in that way, and that if you have a large amount of capital in any concern, whatever may be the restrictions under which it is invested, the capitalist does exercise influence.

Then the right hon. Gentleman says—"You have no real control over the purchase you have made; and yet that purchase will lead to great complications." Sir, I have no doubt that complications will occur. They always have occurred, and I should like to know the state of affairs and of society in which complications do not and will not occur. We are here to guard the country against complications, and to guide it in the event of complications; and the argument that we are to do nothing—never dare to move, never try to increase our strength and improve our position, because we are afraid of complications is certainly a new view of English policy, and one which I believe the House of Commons will never sanction. I think under these two heads all the criticisms of the right hon. Gentleman are contained. But the noble Lord [the Marquess of Hartington] who has just addressed us says many points were made by the right hon. Gentleman which the Chancellor of the Exchequer did not answer. There is no precedent of a British Ministry treating with a private firm; my right hon. Friend did not answer that. [Mr. Gladstone: I did not say so.] The right hon. Gentleman, however, says he made no observation of the kind. Then the noble Lord says my right hon. Friend never answered the charge about speculations in Egyptian Stock. Well, I have answered that charge. The noble Lord says my right hon. Friend never touched upon the amount of the commission. I have touched upon it. He says that we never thoroughly cleared ourselves from the charge of not buying the 15 per cent shares. I am here to vindicate our conduct on that point. In purchasing the shares we did, we purchased what we wanted, we gained the end we wished, and why we should involve the country in another purchase, when we should thereby only have repeated the result we had already achieved I cannot understand. The noble Lord says my right hon. Friend never expressed what expectations we had of receiving the £200,000 a-year from the Khedive, but we do not suppose that interest which is at the rate of 5 per cent is quite as secure as it would be if it were at the rate of 3¼ per cent. Then the noble Lord says that my right hon. Friend never met the charge of the right hon. Gentleman that our policy would lead to complications with other nations. We believe, on the contrary, that, instead of leading to complications with other nations, the step which we have taken is one which will avert complications. These are matters which to a great degree must be matters of opinion; but the most remarkable feature of the long harangue of the right hon. Gentleman the Member for Greenwich is that it was in a great degree a series of assumptions, abstract reasonings, and arbitrary conclusions, after which he sat down quite surprised that the Vote should be passed unanimously, and requesting his allies to attack us for not answering that which we have felt not to be substantial, but to consist of assumptions which we believe experience will prove to be entirely false.

The right hon. Gentleman charged us, lastly, with not having answered a charge of having abandoned a strong position. The right hon. Gentleman pictured us as having been in a good position before this—a position which he charged us with having abandoned for one of a more doubtful character. Here again, what proof does he bring of the charge he makes? We found ourselves in a position which has been called a strong position, but we could not for a moment think that our position with regard to the Canal was satisfactory. The International Commission sat, as hon. Members know, before the Conservatives acceded to power, and the work it did was greatly assisted by our Predecessors, and by a number of other able and eminent men; but, as I have said, no one who remembers all the circumstances of the case and what has occurred since, can for a moment pretend that our position with regard to the Canal was then satisfactory. At the moment Turkey was in a very different position from that which she occupies at present, as far as authority is concerned. The Khedive himself was in a very good position; and yet those who are familiar with what occurred at that time know the great difficulties which the Government experienced, and the very doubtful manner in which, for a considerable time, affairs looked with regard to the whole business. Therefore I do not agree with the right hon. Gentleman. I feel that at this moment our position is much stronger, and for the reason that we are possessors of a great portion of the capital invested in the Canal.

The noble Lord himself has expressed great dissatisfaction, because I have not told him what the conduct of the Government would be with regard to the Canal in a time of war. I must say that on this subject I wish to retain my reserve. I cannot conceive anything more imprudent than a discussion in this House at the present time as to the conduct of England with regard to the Suez Canal in time of war, and I shall therefore decline to enter upon any discussion on the subject. . . . What we have to do tonight is to agree to the Vote for the purchase of these shares. I have never recommended, and I do not now recommend this purchase as a financial investment. If it gave us 10 per cent of interest and a security as good as the Consols I do not think an English Minister would be justified in making such an investment; still less if he is obliged to borrow the money for the occasion. I do not recommend it either as a commercial speculation although I believe that many of those who have looked upon it with little favour will probably be surprised with the pecuniary results of the purchase. I have always, and do now recommend it to the country as a political transaction, and one which I believe is calculated to strengthen the Empire. That is the spirit in which it has been accepted by the country, which understands it though the two right hon. critics may not. They are really seasick of the "Silver Streak" [the English Channel]. They want the Empire to be maintained, to be strengthened; they will not be alarmed even it be increased. Because they think we are obtaining a great hold and interest in this important portion of Africa—because they believe that it secures to us a highway to our Indian Empire and our other dependencies, the people of England have from the first recognized the propriety and the wisdom of the step which we shall sanction tonight.

Source: *Hansard* CCXXVII (3rd Ser.), 652–661.

3. Treaty of Berlin, 1878 [Excerpt]

Introduction

The Treaty of Berlin settled the Balkan crisis of the 1870s, in the course of which the general European agreement to respect the territorial integrity of the Ottoman Empire had broken down. In 1875 anti-Ottoman rebellion broke out in the largely Slavic and Christian provinces of Bosnia and Herzegovina, quickly spreading throughout most of the Balkans. The autonomous and formerly Ottoman states of Serbia and Montenegro assisted the rebels, and in 1877, as Turkish suppression of the rebellions seemed likely to be successful, Russia too went to war against the Ottoman Empire. Russia promised the Austro-Hungarian government special rights in Bosnia-Herzegovina, thereby ensuring benevolent neutrality from that power. At one stage, Russian troops came close to seizing Constantinople, and British prime minister Benjamin Disraeli dispatched a naval force to provide support for the embattled Turkish sultan. The Congress of Berlin, called by German chancellor Otto von Bismarck in 1878, sought to reestablish the concert of Europe and a new balance of power. Russia retained most of the Asian lands in the Caucasus that it had seized from the Ottoman Empire, Britain received the island of Cyprus, Austria won a protectorate over Bosnia and Herzegovina, Serbia and Montenegro were recognized as independent states, and Bulgaria, where anti-Ottoman rebellion had also broken out, gained autonomous status, eventually becoming fully independent in 1908. From 1878 until the early 20th century, the situation of the fragile Ottoman Empire was once more relatively stable.

Primary Source

[. . .]

Article LVIII. The Sublime Porte cedes to the Russian Empire in Asia the territories of Ardahan, Kars, and Batoum, together with the latter port, as well as all the territories comprised between the former Russo-Turkish frontier and the following line:

The new frontier starting from the Black Sea, and coinciding with the line laid down by the Treaty of San Stefano as far as a point to the north-west of Khorda, and to the south of Artwin, continues in a straight line as far as the River Tchoroukh, crosses this river and passes to the east of Aschmichen, going in a straight line to the south so as to rejoin the Russian frontier indicated in the Treaty of San Stefano, at a point to the south of Nariman, leaving the town of Olti to Russia. From the point indicated near Nariman the frontier turns to the east, passes by Tebrenec, which remains to Russia, and continues as far as the Pennek Tschai.

It follows this river as far as Bardouz, then turns towards the south, leaving Bardouz and Jonikioy to Russia. From a point to the west of the village of Karaougan, the frontier takes the direction of Medjingert, continues in a straight line towards the summit of the Mountain Kassadagh, and follows the line of the watershed between the affluents of the Araxes on the north and those of the Mourad Sou on the south, as far as the former frontier of Russia.

Article LIX. His Majesty the Emperor of Russia declares that it is his intention to constitute Batoum a free port, essentially commercial.

Article LX. The valley of Alaschkerd and the town of Bayazid, ceded to Russia by Article XIX of the Treaty of San Stefano, are restored to Turkey.

The Sublime Porte cedes to Persia the town and territory of Khotour, as fixed by the mixed Anglo-Russian Commission for the delimitation of the frontiers of Turkey and of Persia.

Article LXI. The Sublime Porte undertakes to carry out, without further delay, the improvements and reforms demanded by local requirements in the provinces inhabited by the Armenians, and to guarantee their security against the Circassians and the Kurds.

It will periodically make known the steps taken to this effect to the Powers, who will superintend their application.

Article LXII. The Sublime Porte having expressed the intention to maintain the principle of religious liberty, and give it the widest scope, the Contracting Parties take note of this spontaneous declaration.

In no part of the Ottoman Empire shall difference of religion be alleged against any person as a ground for exclusion or incapacity as regards the discharge of civil and political rights, admission to the public employments, functions and honours, or the exercise of the various professions and industries.

All persons shall be admitted, without distinction of religion, to give evidence before the tribunals.

The freedom and outward exercise of all forms of worship are assured to all, and no hindrance shall be offered either to the hierarchical organization of the various communions or to their relations with their spiritual chiefs.

Ecclesiastics, pilgrims, and monks of all nationalities travelling in Turkey in Europe, or in Turkey in Asia, shall enjoy the same rights, advantages, and privileges.

The right of official protection by the Diplomatic and Consular Agents of the Powers in Turkey is recognized both as regards the above-mentioned persons and their religious, charitable, and other establishments in the Holy Places and elsewhere.

The rights possessed by France are expressly reserved, and it is well understood that no alterations can be made in the status quo in the Holy Places.

The monks of Mount Athos, of whatever country they may be natives, shall be maintained in their former possessions and advantages, and shall enjoy, without any exception, complete equality of rights and prerogatives.

Article LXIII. The Treaty of Paris of March 30, 1856, as well as the Treaty of London of March 13, 1871, are maintained in all such of their provisions as are not abrogated or modified by the preceding stipulations.

Source: United Kingdom, *Parliamentary Papers,* 83: 690–705, 1878.

4. Resolution of the Arab-Syrian Congress at Paris, June 21, 1913

Introduction

Like other ethnic groups around the world, the Arabs demonstrated a new nationalist consciousness and sentiment during the 19th century that may be ascribed in part to that era's new emphasis on identification along the lines of national groupings. By the turn of the century Arab nationalism had developed rapidly, the product in part of a revitalization of national pride and culture encouraged by French and American missionaries in Lebanon. The growing use of the Arabic language and texts in education helped to spread nationalist sentiment throughout Syria, Iraq (then known as Mesopotamia), and Egypt. In much of the Ottoman Empire, Arab nationalism, though centering on opposition to unadulterated Ottoman rule, often advocated greater Arab autonomy within the empire rather than total independence. Such demands were given additional force when modernizing young military officers took over the Ottoman government in 1909 and launched a program of secular reforms. In Egypt, by contrast, Franco-British dual control and the later British occupation became the focus for Arab protests and resentment. In June 1913, 24 Arab delegates from Syria, Lebanon, Iraq, and the United States met in an Arab-Syrian Congress, held in the French capital of Paris, and passed resolutions demanding that the Ottoman government grant the Arabs and Armenians of Syria, Iraq, and Lebanon more autonomy and recognize Arabic as an official language. The meeting was evidence of a burgeoning sense of a specifically Arab identity that transcended the boundaries of particular Arab provinces.

Primary Source

1. Radical and urgent reforms are needed in the Ottoman Empire.

2. It is important to guarantee the Ottoman Arabs the exercise of their political rights by making effective their participation in the central administration of the Empire.

3. It is important to establish in each of the Syrian and Arab *vilâyets* a decentralized regime suitable to their needs and aptitudes.

4. The vilayet of Bayrut having formulated its claims in a special project adopted on 31 January 1913 by an ad hoc General Assembly and based on the double principle of the extension of the powers of the general council of the vilayets and the nomination of foreign councilors, the Congress requests the execution of the above project.

5. The Arabic language must be recognized in the Ottoman Parliament and considered as an official language in Syrian and Arab countries.

6. Military service shall be regional in Syrian and Arab vilayets, except in case of extreme necessity.

7. The Congress expresses the wish that the Ottoman Imperial Government provide the *mutasarriflik* (autonomous provincial district) of Lebanon with the means of improving its financial situation.

8. The Congress affirms that it favors the reformist and decentralizing demands of the Armenian Ottomans.

9. The present resolution shall be communicated to the Ottoman Imperial Government.

10. These resolutions shall also be communicated to the Powers friendly to the Ottoman Empire.

11. The Congress conveys its grateful thanks to the Government of the [French] Republic for its generous hospitality.

Source: J. C. Hurewitz, *The Middle East and North Africa in World Politics: A Documentary Record* (New Haven, CT: Yale University Press, 1975), 566–567.

5. Sir Henry McMahon, Letter to Ali Ibn Hussein, October 24, 1916

Introduction

As the Turkish sultanate lost its hold upon the territories of the Ottoman Empire and exacerbated Muslim sensibilities by allying itself with Christian Germany in World War I, Hussein ibn Ali, the high priest or sharif of the Islamic territory of the Hejaz, which contains the holy cities of Medina and Mecca, moved more aggressively toward independence. He was encouraged by British officials, including Sir Henry McMahon, British high commissioner in Egypt, who promised him and his three sons—Ali, Faisal, and Abdullah—recognition and financial and military assistance if they were willing to rebel against Ottoman rule. Arab nationalists regarded McMahon's pledge as a promise of immediate and complete independence. The territorial delimitations described in McMahon's letter were ambiguous and left unclear whether they included what was then Palestine, present-day Israel. The British later claimed that Palestine, which was not mentioned, was implicitly excluded from the regions promised to Hussein. Arab nationalists argued that the territories pledged to them included Palestine and that the subsequent British Sykes-Picot Agreement with France over the partition of the Ottoman Empire and the 1917 Balfour Declaration promising Jews a national homeland in Palestine contravened the McMahon letter.

Primary Source

The two districts of Mesina and Alexandretta and portions of Syria lying to the west of the districts of Damascus, Homs and Aleppo cannot be said to be purely Arab, and should be excluded from the limits demanded (by the Arabs).

With the above modification, and without prejudice to our existing treaties with Arab chiefs, we accept those limits.

As for those regions lying within these frontiers wherein Great Britain is free to act without detriment to the interests of her ally, France, I am empowered in the name of the government of Great Britain to give the following assurances and make the following reply to your letter.

1) Subject to the above modifications, Great Britain is prepared to recognise and support the independence of the Arabs in the regions within the limits demanded by the Sherif of Mecca.

2) Great Britain will recognise the Holy Places against all external aggression and will recognise their inviolability.

3) When the situation admits, Great Britain will give to the Arabs her advice and will assist them to establish what may appear to be the most suitable forms of government in those various territories.

4) On the other hand, it is understood that the Arabs have decided to seek the advice and guidance of Great Britain only, and that such European advisors and officials as may be required for the formation of a sound administration will be British.

5) With regards to the vilayets of Baghdad and Basra, the Arabs will recognise that the established position and interests of Great Britain necessitate special administrative arrangements in order

to secure these territories from foreign aggression to promote the welfare of the local populations and to safeguard our mutual economic interests.

I am convinced that this declaration will assure you beyond all possible doubt of the sympathy of Great Britain towards the aspirations of her friends the Arabs and will result in a firm and lasting alliance, the immediate results of which will be the expulsion of the Turks from Arab countries and the freeing of the Arab peoples from the Turkish yoke, which for so many years has pressed heavily upon them.

Source: United Kingdom, Parliament, *Husain-McMahon Correspondence,* Miscellaneous No. 3., Cmd. 5957, 1939.

6. Sykes-Picot Agreement, 1916

Introduction

As Turkish power crumbled in the Middle East, British and French officials reached tentative agreement as to how to divide influence within that region between their two nations. On May 9, 1916, Paul Cambon, the French foreign minister, wrote to British foreign secretary Sir Edward Grey and formally proposed a disposition of the Middle East between France and Britain along lines already agreed to by junior French and British diplomats in the area. Grey replied, first briefly and then at greater length. Britain recognized French predominance in Syria, Lebanon, and Palestine (later exchanged for portions of Iraq) in return for French acceptance of British control of Iraq and Jordan. The British and French envisaged permitting Arab states in these former Ottoman provinces but only on the condition that their governments recognize British or French overlordship. At the subsequent 1919 Paris Peace Conference, Britain and France retained control of these regions, which were defined as mandates under the new League of Nations. This was a great disappointment to the Arab nationalists who had hoped to establish independent states free of Western colonial rule. During the 1920s resentment of Anglo-French domination continued to simmer in the newly established kingdoms of Iraq and Transjordan and in the states of Syria and Lebanon.

Primary Source

Sir Edward Grey to Paul Cambon, May 15, 1916

I shall have the honour to reply in a further note to your Excellency's note of the 9th instant, relative to the creation of an Arab State, but I should meanwhile be grateful if your Excellency could assure me that in those regions which, under the conditions recorded in that communication, become entirely French, or in which French interests are recognised as predominant, any existing British concessions, rights of navigation or development, and the rights and privileges of any British religions, scholastic, or medical institutions will be maintained.

His Majesty's Government are, of course, ready to give a reciprocal assurance in regard to the British area.

Sir Edward Grey to Paul Cambon, May 16, 1916

I have the honour to acknowledge the receipt of your Excellency's note of the 9th instant, stating that the French Government accept the limits of a future Arab State, or Confederation of States, and of those parts of Syria where French interests predominate, together with certain conditions attached thereto, such as they result from recent discussions in London and Petrograd on the subject.

I have the honour to inform your Excellency in reply that the acceptance of the whole project, as it now stands, will involve the abdication of considerable British interests, but, since His Majesty's Government recognise the advantage to the general cause of the Allies entailed in producing a more favourable internal political situation in Turkey, they are ready to accept the arrangement now arrived at, provided that the co-operation of the Arabs is secured, and that the Arabs fulfil the conditions and obtain the towns of Homs, Hama, Damascus, and Aleppo.

It is accordingly understood between the French and British governments:

1. That France and Great Britain are prepared to recognize and protect an independent Arab State or a confederation of Arab states (A) and (B) marked on the annexed map, under the suzerainty of an Arab chief. That in area (A) France, and in area (B) Great Britain, shall have priority of right of enterprise and local loans. That in area (A) France, and in area (B) Great Britain, shall alone supply advisers or foreign functionaries at the request of the Arab state or confederation of Arab states.

2. That in the blue area France, and in the red area Great Britain, shall be allowed to establish such direct or indirect administration or control as they desire and as they may think fit to arrange with the Arab State or Confederation of Arab States.

3. That in the brown area there shall be established an international administration, the form of which is to be decided upon after consultation with Russia, and subsequently in consultation with the other Allies, and the representatives of the Shereef of Mecca.

4. That Great Britain be accorded (1) the ports of Haifa and Acre, (2) guarantee of a given supply of water from the Tigres and Euphrates in area (A) for area (B). His majesty's government, on their part, undertake that they will at no time enter into negotiations for the cession of Cyprus to any third Power without the previous consent of the French Government.

5. That Alexandretta shall be a free port as regards the trade of the British Empire, and that there shall be no discrimination in port charges or facilities as regards British shipping and British goods; that there shall be freedom of transit for British goods through Alexandretta and by railway through the blue area, whether those goods are intended for or originate in the red area, or (B) area, or area (A); and there shall be no discrimination, direct or indirect against British goods on any railway or against British goods or ships at any port serving the areas mentioned.

That Haifa shall be a free port as regards the trade of France, her dominions and protectorates, and there shall be no discrimination in port charges or facilities as regards French shipping and French goods. There shall be freedom of transit for French goods through Haifa and by the British railway through the brown area, whether those goods are intended for or originate in the blue area, area (A), or area (B), and there shall be no discrimination, direct or indirect, against French goods on any railway, or against French goods or ships at any port serving the areas mentioned.

6. That in area (A) the Baghdad railway shall not be extended southwards beyond Mosul, and in area (B) northwards beyond Samarra, until a railway connecting Baghdad and Aleppo via the Euphrates valley has been completed, and then only with the concurrence of the two governments.

7. That Great Britain has the right to build, administer, and be sole owner of a railway connecting Haifa with area (B), and shall have a perpetual right to transport troops along such a line at all times.

It is to be understood by both Governments that this railway is to facilitate the connexion of Baghdad with Haifa by rail, and it is further understood that, if the engineering difficulties and expense entailed by keeping this connecting line in the brown area only make the project unfeasible, that the French government shall be prepared to consider that the line in question may also traverse the polygon Banias-Keis Marib-Salkhad Tell Otsda-Mesmie before reaching area (B).

8. For a period of twenty years the existing Turkish customs tariff shall remain in force throughout the whole of the blue and red areas, as well as in areas (A) and (B), and no increase in the rates of duty or conversions from ad valorem to specific rates shall be made except by agreement between the two Powers.

There shall be no interior customs barriers between any of the above-mentioned areas. The customs duties leviable on goods destined for the interior shall be collected at the port of entry and handed over to the administration of the area of destination.

9. It shall be agreed that the French Government will at no time enter into any negotiations for the cession of their rights and will not cede such rights in the blue area to any third Power, except the Arab State or Confederation of Arab States, without the previous agreement of His Majesty's Government, who, on their part, will give a similar undertaking to the French Government regarding the red area.

10. The British and French Governments, as the protectors of the Arab State, shall agree that they will not themselves acquire and will not consent to a third power acquiring territorial possessions in the Arabian peninsula, nor consent to a third power installing a naval base either on the east coast, or on the islands, of the Red Sea. This, however, shall not prevent such adjustment of the Aden frontier as may be necessary in consequence of recent Turkish aggression.

11. The negotiations with the Arabs as to the boundaries of the Arab State or Confederation of Arab States shall be continued through the same channel as heretofore on behalf of the two powers.

12. It is agreed that measures to control the importation of arms into the Arab territories will be considered by the two Governments.

I have further the honour to state that, in order to make the agreement complete, His Majesty's Government are proposing to the Russian Government to exchange notes analogous to those exchanged by the latter and your Excellency's Government on the 26th April last. Copies of these notes will be communicated to your Excellency as soon as exchanged.

I would also venture to remind your Excellency that the conclusion of the present agreement raises, for practical consideration, the question of claims of Italy to a share in any partition or rearrangement of Turkey in Asia, as formulated in article 9 of the agreement of the 26th April, 1915, between Italy and the Allies.

His Majesty's Government further consider that the Japanese Government should be informed of the arrangements now concluded.

Source: *British Documents on Foreign Affairs: Reports and Papers from the Foreign Office Confidential Print; Series H: The First World War, 1914–1918,* Vol. 2 (Bethesda, MD: University Publications of America, an Imprint of CIS, 1989). Reprinted by permission of LexisNexis.

7. Soviet Appeal to Muslim Workers in Russia and the East, December 7, 1917

Introduction

The Bolshevik government that seized power in Russia in late 1917 was committed to the cause of international revolution, seeking to identify itself with the working class around the world. Before its overthrow in early 1917, Russia's czarist government had negotiated secret treaties with the Allies that promised to Russia Istanbul, capital of the Ottoman empire, and control of the strategic Dardanelles straits, the only passage for vessels from the Black Sea to reach the Mediterranean. Britain and France, the other Allied powers, had also made agreements among themselves as to the disposition of the Ottoman Empire's Middle Eastern provinces, Mesopotamia and Palestine. In December 1917, less than a month after taking power, the Russian Bolsheviks issued an appeal specifically directed at Muslims within and beyond Russia. Those inside Russia's borders, in the Caucasus, Turkestan, the Crimea, and Siberia, were promised freedom of worship and customs. Outside Russia's own boundaries, the Bolsheviks appealed to Muslims throughout Asia to rebel against European imperial rule. The new Russian leaders also renounced the czarist empire's claims against Constantinople, which, they proclaimed, "must remain in the hands of the Mohammedans." They likewise repudiated pledges when the war ended that Persia (present-day Iran) would fall under joint British and Russian control. The Soviet declaration was early evidence that on the international stage, Russia's new government intended to encourage and appeal to Muslim nationalist sentiments, presenting itself as the champion of anticolonial opposition to Western domination. For most of the 20th century, Soviet officials would continue to characterize their policies in this light.

Primary Source

Comrades! Brothers!

Great events are occurring in Russia! An end is drawing near to the murderous war, which arose out of the bargainings of foreign powers. The rule of the plunderers, exploiting the peoples of the world, is trembling. The ancient citadel of slavery and serfdom is cracking under the blows of the Russian Revolution. The world of violence and oppression is approaching its last days. A new world is arising, a world of the toilers and the liberated. At the head of this revolution is the Workers' and Peasants' Government in Russia, the Council of People's Commissars.

Revolutionary councils of workers', soldiers' and peasants' deputies are scattered over the whole of Russia. The power in the country is in the hands of the people. The toiling masses of Russia burn with the single desire to achieve an honest peace and help the oppressed people of the world to win their freedom.

Russia is not alone in this sacred cause. The mighty summons to freedom emitted by the Russian Revolution, has aroused all the toilers in the East and West. The people of Europe, exhausted by war, are already stretching out their hands to us, in our work for peace. The workers and soldiers of the West are already rallying around the banner of socialism, storming the strongholds of imperialism. Even far-off India, that land which has been oppressed by the European "torchbearers of civilisation" for so many centuries, has raised the standard of revolt, organising its councils of deputies, throwing the hated yoke of slavery from its shoulders, and summoning the people of the East to the struggle for freedom.

The sway of capitalist plunder and violence is being undermined. The ground is slipping from under the feet of the imperialist pillagers.

In the face of these great events, we appeal to you, toiling and dispossessed Mohammedan workers, in Russia and the East.

Mohammedans of Russia, Volga and Crimean Tartars, Kirgliisi and Sarti in Siberia and Turkestan, Turcos and Tartars in the Trans-Caucasus, Chechenzi and mountain Cossacks! All you, whose mosques and shrines have been destroyed, whose faith and customs have been violated by the Tsars and oppressors of Russia! Hence-forward your faith and customs, your national and cultural departments, are declared free and inviolable! Organise your national life freely and unimpeded. It is your right. Know that your rights, like those of all the peoples of Russia, will be guarded by the might of the revolution and its organs, the Councils of Workers', Soldiers' and Peasants' Deputies!

Support this revolution and its representative Government!

Mohammedans of the East! Persians, Turks, Arabs and Indians!

All you whose bodies and property, freedom and native land have been for centuries exploited by the European beasts of prey! All you whose countries the plunderers who began the war now desire to share among themselves! We declare that the secret treaties of the deposed Tsar as to the annexation of Constantinople, confirmed by the late Kerensky Government—are now null and void. The Russian Republic, and its Government, the Council of People's Commissars, are opposed to the annexation of foreign lands: Constantinople must remain in the hands of the Mohammedans.

We declare that the treaty for the division of Persia is null and void. Immediately after the cessation of military activities troops will be withdrawn from Persia and the Persians will be guaranteed the right of free self-determination.

We declare that the treaty for the division of Turkey and the subduction from it of Armenia, is null and void. Immediately after the cessation of military activities, the Armenians will be guaranteed the right of free self-determination of their political fate.

It is not from Russia and its revolutionary Government that you have to fear enslavement, but from the robbers of European imperialism, from those who have laid your native lands waste and converted them into their colonies.

Overthrow these robbers and enslavers of your lands! Now, when war and ruin are breaking down the pillars of the old world, when the whole world is burning with indignation against the imperialist brigands, when the least spark of indignation bursts out in a mighty flame of revolution, when even the Indian Mohammedans, oppressed and tormented by the foreign yoke, are rising in revolt against their slave-drivers—now it is impossible to keep silent. Lose no time in throwing off the yoke of the ancient oppressors of your land! Let them no longer violate your hearths! You must yourselves be masters in your own land! You yourselves must arrange your life as you yourselves see fit! You have the right to do this, for your fate is in your own hands!

Comrades! Brothers!

Advance firmly and resolutely towards an honest, democratic peace!

We bear the liberation of the oppressed peoples of the world on our banners!

Mohammedans in Russia!

Mohammedans in the East!

We look to you for sympathy and support in the work of renewing of the world!

Source: U.S. Congress, House, *The Communist Conspiracy: Strategy and Tactics of World Communism* (Washington, DC: U.S. Government Printing Office, 1929), 10–11.

8. Great Britain and Iraq, Treaty of Alliance, October 10, 1922 [Excerpts]

Introduction

In 1920 Great Britain was awarded a League of Nations mandate over Mesopotamia (present-day Iraq), essentially a situation in which the British administered the area as a trustee under League of Nations auspices. From June to September 1920 Mesopotamian nationalists staged a revolt against British rule, demanding full independence. In 1920 France drove Emir Faisal of the Hejaz out of his short-lived kingdom of greater Syria, and the following year Britain offered him the monarchy of Iraq as a client king under British supervision. In 1922 Britain and Iraq signed a treaty setting forth the terms of their relationship. The king was restricted and could appoint no non-Iraqi officials without British consent, preventing any other power from gaining influence over his government. The British would provide "support and assistance" to

the Iraqi armed forces. Equally, except for embassies and other diplomatic facilities, no foreign power could lease or acquire territory within Iraq. Faisal and the Iraqis only grudgingly accepted the terms of this treaty, which made Iraq virtually a British protectorate. In April 1923 a separate protocol to the treaty reduced its duration from an original 20 years to "not later than four years after the ratification of peace with Turkey." Even after the treaty expired in 1927 Britain retained special rights in Iraq, some of which remained in effect even after Faisal won full formal independence for his country in 1932.

Primary Source

Article 1

At the request of His Majesty the King of Iraq, His Britannic Majesty undertakes, subject to the provisions of this treaty, to provide the State of Iraq with such advice and assistance as may be required during the period of the present treaty, without prejudice to her national sovereignty. His Britannic Majesty shall be represented in Iraq by a High Commissioner and Consul-General assisted by the necessary staff.

Article 2

His Majesty the King of Iraq undertakes that for the period of the present treaty no gazetted official of other than Iraq nationality shall be appointed in Iraq without the concurrence of His Britannic Majesty. A separate agreement shall regulate the numbers and conditions of employment of British officials so appointed in the Iraq Government.

Article 3

His Majesty the King of Iraq agrees to frame an Organic Law for presentation to the Constituent Assembly of Iraq, and to give effect to the said law, which shall contain nothing contrary to the provisions of the present treaty and shall take account of the rights, wishes and interests of all populations inhabiting Iraq. This Organic Law shall ensure to all complete freedom of conscience and the free exercise of all forms of worship, subject only to the maintenance of public order and morals. It shall provide that no discrimination of any kind shall be made between the inhabitants of Iraq on the ground of race, religion or language, and shall secure that the right of each community to maintain its own schools for the education of its own members in its own language, while conforming to such educational requirements of a general nature as the Government of Iraq may impose, shall not be denied or impaired. It shall prescribe the constitutional procedure, whether legislative or executive, by which decisions will be taken on all matters of importance, including those involving questions of fiscal, financial and military policy.

Article 4

Without prejudice to the provisions of articles 17 and 18 of this treaty. His Majesty the King of Iraq agrees to be guided by the advice of His Britannic Majesty tendered through the High Commissioner on all important matters affecting the international and financial obligations and interests of His Britannic Majesty for the whole period of this treaty. His Majesty the King of Iraq will fully consult the High Commissioner on what is conducive to a sound financial and fiscal policy, and will ensure the stability and good organisation of the finances of the Iraq Government so long as that Government is under financial obligations to the Government of His Britannic Majesty.

Article 5

His Majesty the King of Iraq shall have the right of representation in London and in such other capitals and places as may be agreed upon by the High Contracting Parties. Where His Majesty the King of Iraq is not represented, he agrees to entrust the protection of Iraq nationals to His Britannic Majesty. His Majesty the King of Iraq shall himself issue exequaturs to representatives of foreign Powers in Iraq after His Britannic Majesty has agreed to their appointment.

Article 6

His Britannic Majesty undertakes to use his good offices to secure the admission of Iraq to membership of the League of Nations as soon as possible.

Article 7

His Britannic Majesty undertakes to provide such support and assistance to the armed forces of His Majesty the King of Iraq as may from time to time be agreed by the High Contracting Parties. A separate agreement regulating the extent and conditions of such support and assistance shall be concluded between the High Contracting Parties and communicated to the Council of the League of Nations.

Article 8

No territory in Iraq shall be ceded or leased or in any way placed under the control of any foreign Power; this shall not prevent His Majesty the King of Iraq from making such arrangements as may be necessary for the accommodation of foreign representatives and for the fulfilment of the provisions of the preceding article.

Article 9

His Majesty the King of Iraq undertakes that he will accept and give effect to such reasonable provisions as His Britannic Majesty

may consider necessary in judicial matters to safeguard the interests of foreigners in consequence of the non-application of the immunities and privileges enjoyed by them under capitulation or usage. These provisions shall be embodied in a separate agreement, which shall be communicated to the Council of the League of Nations.

[...]

Article 15

A separate agreement shall regulate the financial relations between the High Contracting Parties. It shall provide, on the one hand, for the transfer by His Britannic Majesty's Government to the Government of Iraq of such works of public utility as may be agreed upon, and for the rendering by His Britannic Majesty's Government of such financial assistance as may from time to time be considered necessary for Iraq, and, on the other hand, for the progressive liquidation by the Government of Iraq of all liabilities thus incurred. Such agreement shall be communicated to the Council of the League of Nations.

Article 16

So far as is consistent with his international obligations, His Britannic Majesty undertakes to place no obstacle in the way of the association of the State of Iraq for customs or other purposes with such neighbouring Arab States as may desire it.

[...]

Source: "Treaty of Alliance between Great Britain and Iraq, October 10, 1922," *Treaties and Other International Agreements of the United States of America, 1776–1949*, Vol. 2 (Washington, DC: U.S. Government Printing Office, 1969), 1003–1007.

9. The United Kingdom and Transjordan, Agreement on Constitutional Structure and the Limits of Autonomy, February 20, 1928 [Excerpt]

Introduction

The emirate of Transjordan was originally a provisional entity that the British government created in 1921 from a portion of the Palestine mandate in order to placate Emir Abdullah, one of the sons of Sharif Hussein of the Hejaz, to prevent him from stirring up a politically inconvenient revolt against the French. In 1923 the arrangement became permanent on the condition that the British government could conclude suitable arrangements for supervision of the new emirate's affairs. In 1928 Great Britain and Transjordan signed an agreement under whose terms the emirate enjoyed substantial domestic autonomy, but its foreign affairs and external relations were handled by Britain. A British resident, together with his staff, would be stationed in Transjordan and would exercise overall supervision of Transjordan's foreign, financial, and military affairs and advise the emir on all economic and commercial matters, including the granting of concessions to exploit mineral resources or construct railroads. Britain was entitled to station troops in Transjordan, and related expenses, together with those of the British resident and his office, would be borne in part or whole by the government of Transjordan. The British agreed to provide financial assistance to Transjordan. Effectively, Transjordan was a British protectorate. In 1934 the agreement was modified to allow the emir to appoint his own diplomatic representatives to other states in place of allowing the British government to handle all such matters on Transjordan's behalf.

Primary Source

ARTICLE 1

His Highness the Amir agrees that His Britannic Majesty shall be represented in Trans-Jordan by a British Resident acting on behalf of the High Commissioner for Trans-Jordan, and that communications between His Britannic Majesty and all other Powers on the one hand and the Trans-Jordan Government on the other shall be made through the British Resident and the High Commissioner aforesaid.

His Highness the Amir agrees that the ordinary expenses of civil government and the administration and the salaries and expenses of the British Resident and his staff will be borne by Trans-Jordan. His Highness the Amir will provide quarters for the accommodation of British members of the staff of the British Resident.

ARTICLE 2

The powers of legislation and of administration entrusted to His Britannic Majesty as Mandatory for Palestine shall be exercised in that part of the area Mandate known as Trans-Jordan by His Highness the Amir through such constitutional government as is defined and determined in the Organic Law of Trans-Jordan and any amendment thereof made with the approval of His Britannic Majesty.

Throughout the remaining clauses of this Agreement the word "Palestine", unless otherwise defined, shall mean that portion of the area under Mandate which lies to the west of a line drawn from a point two miles west of the town of Akaba on the Gulf of that name up the centre of the Wady Araba, Dead Sea and River Jordan to its junction with the River Yarmuk; thence up the centre of that river to the Syrian frontier.

ARTICLE 3

His Highness the Amir agrees that for the period of the present Agreement no official of other than Trans-Jordan nationality shall be appointed in Trans-Jordan without the concurrence of His Britannic Majesty. The numbers and conditions of employment of British officials so appointed in the Trans-Jordan government shall be regulated by a separate Agreement.

ARTICLE 4

His Highness the Amir agrees that all such laws, orders or regulations as may be required for the full discharge of the international responsibilities and obligations of His Britannic Majesty in respect of the territory of Trans-Jordan shall be adopted and made, and that no laws, orders or regulations shall be adopted or made in Trans-Jordan which may hinder the full discharge of such international responsibilities and obligations.

ARTICLE 5

His Highness the Amir agrees to be guided by the advice of His Britannic Majesty tendered through the High Commissioner for Trans-Jordan in all matters concerning foreign relations of Trans-Jordan, as well as in all important matters affecting the international and financial obligations and interests of His Britannic Majesty in respect of Trans-Jordan. His Highness the Amir undertakes to follow an administrative, financial and fiscal policy in Trans-Jordan as will ensure the stability and good organisation of his Government and its finances. He agrees to keep His Britannic Majesty informed of the measures proposed and adopted to give due effect to this undertaking, and further agrees not to alter the system of control of the public finances of Trans-Jordan without the consent of His Britannic Majesty.

ARTICLE 6

His Highness the Amir agrees that he will refer for the advice of His Britannic Majesty the annual Budget law and any law which concerns matters covered by the provisions of this Agreement, and any law of any of the following classes, namely:—

1) Any law affecting the currency of Trans-Jordan or relating to the issue of bank notes.

2) Any law imposing differential duties.

3) Any law whereby persons who are nationals of any States Members of the League of Nations or of any State to which His Britannic

Majesty has agreed by treaty that the same rights should be ensured as it would enjoy if it were a member of the said League, may be subjected or made liable to any disabilities to which persons who are British subjects or nationals of any foreign State are not also subjected or made liable.

4) Any special law providing for succession to the Amir's throne, or for the establishment of a Council of Regency.

5) Any law whereby the grant of land or money or other donation or gratuity may be made to himself.

6) Any law under which the Amir may assume sovereignty over territory outside Trans-Jordan.

7) Any law concerning the jurisdiction of the Civil Courts over foreigners.

8) Any law altering, amending or adding to the details of the provisions of the Organic Law.

ARTICLE 7

Except by agreement between the two countries there shall be no customs barrier between Palestine and Trans-Jordan, and the Customs tariff in Trans-Jordan shall be approved by His Britannic Majesty.

The Government of Palestine shall pay to the Trans-Jordan Government the estimated amount of customs duties levied on the part of the goods entering Palestine from territory other than Trans-Jordan which subsequently enters Trans-Jordan for local consumption, but shall be entitled to withhold from the sums to be paid on this account the estimated amount of custom duties levied by Trans-Jordan on that part of the goods entering Trans-Jordan from other than Palestine territory, which subsequently enters Palestine for local consumption. The trade and commerce of Trans-Jordan shall receive at Palestinian Ports equal facilities with the trade and commerce of Palestine.

ARTICLE 8

So far as is consistent with the international obligations of His Britannic Majesty no obstacle shall be placed in the way of the association of Trans-Jordan for customs or other purposes with such neighbouring Arab States as may desire it.

ARTICLE 9

His Highness the Amir undertakes that he will accept and give effect to such reasonable provisions as His Britannic Majesty may consider necessary in judicial matters to safeguard the interests of foreigners.

These provisions shall be embodied in a separate Agreement, which shall be communicated to the Council of the League of Nations, and pending the conclusion of such Agreement, no foreigner shall be brought before a Trans-Jordan Court without the concurrence of His Britannic Majesty.

His Highness the Amir undertakes that he will accept and give effect to such reasonable provisions as His Britannic Majesty may consider necessary in judicial matters to safeguard the law and jurisdiction with regard to questions arising out of the religious beliefs of the different religious communities.

ARTICLE 10

His Britannic Majesty may maintain armed forces in Trans-Jordan, and may raise, organise and control in Trans-Jordan such armed forces as may in his opinion be necessary for the defence of the country and to assist his Highness the Amir in the preservation of peace and order.

His Highness the Amir agrees that he will not raise or maintain in Trans-Jordan or allow to be raised or maintained any military forces without the consent of His Britannic Majesty.

ARTICLE 11

His Highness the Amir recognises the principle that the cost of the forces required for the defence of Trans-Jordan is a charge on the revenues of that territory. At the coming into force of this Agreement, Trans-Jordan will continue to bear one-sixth of the cost of the Trans-Jordan Frontier Force, and will also bear, as soon as the financial resources of the country permit, the excess of the cost of the British forces stationed in Trans-Jordan, so far as such forces may be deemed by His Britannic Majesty to be employed in respect of Trans-Jordan, over the cost of such forces if stationed in Great Britain, and the whole cost of any forces raised for Trans-Jordan alone.

ARTICLE 12

So long as the revenues of Trans-Jordan are insufficient to meet such ordinary expenses of administration (including any expenditure on local forces for which Trans-Jordan is liable under Article 11) as may be incurred with the approval of His Britannic Majesty, arrangements will be made for a contribution from the British Treasury by way of grant or loan in aid of the revenues of Trans-Jordan. His Britannic Majesty will also arrange for the payment of the excess of the cost of the British forces stationed in Trans-Jordan and deemed by His Britannic Majesty to be employed in respect of Trans-Jordan, insofar and for such time as the revenues of Trans-Jordan are insufficient to bear such excess.

ARTICLE 13

His Highness the Amir agrees that all such laws, orders or regulations as may from time to time be required by His Britannic Majesty for the purposes of Article 10 shall be adopted and made, and that no laws, orders or regulations shall be adopted or made in Trans-Jordan which may, in the opinion of His Britannic Majesty, interfere with the purposes of that Article.

ARTICLE 14

His Highness the Amir agrees to follow the advice of His Britannic Majesty with regard to the proclamation of Martial Law in all or any part of Trans-Jordan as may be placed under Martial Law to such officer or officers of His Britannic Majesty's Forces as His Britannic Majesty may nominate. His Highness the Amir further agrees that on the re-establishment of civil government a special law shall be adopted to indemnify the armed forces maintained by His Britannic Majesty for all acts done or omissions or defaults made under Martial Law.

ARTICLE 15

His Britannic Majesty may exercise jurisdiction over all members of the armed forces maintained or controlled by His Britannic Majesty in Trans-Jordan. For the purposes of this and the five preceding Articles, the term "armed forces" shall be deemed to include civilians attached to or employed with the armed forces.

ARTICLE 16

His Highness the Amir undertakes that every facility shall be provided at all times for the movement of His Britannic Majesty's forces (including the use of wireless and land-line telegraphic and telephonic services and the right to lay land-lines), and for the carriage and storage of fuel, ordnance, ammunition and supplies on the roads, railways and waterways and in the ports of Trans-Jordan.

ARTICLE 17

His Highness the Amir agrees to be guided by the advice of His Britannic Majesty in all matters concerning the granting of concessions, the exploitation of natural resources, the construction and operation of railways, and the raising of loans.

ARTICLE 18

No territory in Trans-Jordan shall be ceded or leased or in any way placed under the control of any foreign Power; this shall not prevent His Highness the Amir from making such arrangements as may be necessary for the accommodation of foreign representatives and for the fulfillment of the provisions of the preceding Articles.

ARTICLE 19

His Highness the Amir agrees that, pending the making of special extradition agreements relating to Trans-Jordan, the Extradition Treaties in force between His Britannic Majesty and foreign Powers shall apply to Trans-Jordan.

[. . .]

Source: Great Britain, *Treaty Series* (1930), no. 7, Cmd., 3488.

10. The Saudi Arabian Government and the Standard Oil Company of California, Oil Concession Agreement, May 29, 1933 [Excerpts]

Introduction

By the early 1930s American oil companies were beginning to explore the possibility of developing oil concessions in the Persian Gulf area. The Turkish Petroleum Company, later renamed the Iraq Petroleum Company, a consortium that included some U.S. oil companies, had a monopoly on exploration in much of the region, and within this grouping only British nationals could develop oil concessions in the small Persian Gulf emirates. In 1932 Standard Oil of California (Socal), a firm outside the consortium that had already broken into this closed shop on oil exploration licenses by establishing a subsidiary—albeit one including a British member on its board—in the small sheikhdom of Bahrain, a British quasi protectorate, applied for an exploratory oil license in the neighboring independent kingdom of Saudi Arabia. Seeking to improve the terms offered him, King Abd al-Aziz encouraged the Iraq Petroleum Company to compete for the concession, and Socal eventually outbid its rival. The American firm obtained a 60-year contract granting it exclusive oil exploration and drilling rights in 360,000 square miles of eastern Saudi Arabia and a preferential option on an adjoining region, territory over whose ownership Saudi Arabia was still in dispute with the neighboring emirate of Kuwait. The Socal-Saudi agreement was the first major oil concession negotiated by a U.S. business in the Middle East.

Primary Source

ART. 1. The Government hereby grants to the Company on the terms and conditions hereinafter mentioned and with respect to the area defined below, the exclusive right, for a period of sixty years from the effective date hereof, to explore, prospect, drill for, extract, treat, manufacture, transport, deal with, carry away and export petroleum, asphalt, naphtha, natural greases, ozocerite, and other hydrocarbons, and the derivatives of all such products. It is understood, however, that such right does not include the exclusive right to sell crude or refined products within the area described below or within Saudi Arabia.

ART. 2. The area covered by the exclusive right referred to in article 1 hereof is all of Eastern Saudi Arabia, from its eastern boundary (including islands and territorial waters), westward to the westerly edge of the Dahana, and from the northern boundary to the southern boundary of the Saudi Arabia, provided that from the northern end of the westerly edge of the Dahana the westerly boundary of the area in question shall continue in a straight line north, 30 degrees west, to the northern boundary of Saudi Arabia, and from the southern end of the westerly edge of the Dahana, such boundary shall continue in a straight line south, 30 degrees east, to the southern boundary of Saudi Arabia.

For convenience this area may be referred to as the "exclusive area."

ART. 3. Within the time agreed in article 16 of this agreement, the Company shall make a payment to the Government of £30,000 gold, or its equivalent.

ART. 4. The Company shall pay the Government annually the sum of £5,000 gold, or its equivalent. For convenience this payment is termed an "annual rental" and it is payable in advance. The first annual rental shall be paid within the time agreed in article 16 of this agreement; thereafter so long as the contract is not terminated, the annual rental shall be due upon each anniversary of the effective date hereof, and shall be payable within thirty days after such anniversary, provided that upon the commercial discovery of oil no further annual rental shall be due or payable.

ART. 5. If this contract has not been terminated within eighteen months from the effective date hereof, the Company shall make a second payment to the Government, amounting to £20,000 gold, or its equivalent. The due date of such payment shall be eighteen months from the effective date hereof, but the Company shall have fifteen days from the due date within which to make the payment.

ART. 6. Upon the effective date of this agreement the Company shall commence plans and preparations for geological work, so planning the work as to take advantage of the cooler season for more efficient work in the field, and of the hotter season for the necessary office work of compiling data and reports. In the event the actual field work shall commence not later than the end of September 1933, and it shall be continued diligently until operations connected with drilling are commenced, or until the contract is terminated.

ART. 7. Within ninety days after the commencement of drilling, the Company shall relinquish to the Government such portions of the exclusive area as the Company at that time may decide not to explore further, or to use otherwise in connexion with the enterprise. Similarly, from time to time, during the life of this contract, the Company shall relinquish to the Government such further portions of the exclusive area as the Company may then decide not to explore or prospect further, or to use otherwise in connexion with the enterprise. The portions so relinquished shall thereupon be released from the terms and conditions of this contract, excepting only that during the life of this contract the Company shall continue to enjoy the right to use the portions so relinquished for transportation and communication facilities, which, however, shall interfere as little as practicable with any other use to which the relinquished portions may be put.

ART. 8. The Company shall commence operations connected with drilling as soon as a suitable structure has been found, and in any event if the Company does not commence such operations within three years from the end of September 1933 (subject to the provisions of article 25 hereof), the Government may terminate this contract. Once commenced, these operations shall be continued diligently until oil in commercial quantities has been discovered or until this agreement is terminated. If the Company should fail to declare so sooner, the date of discovery of oil in commercial quantities shall be the date upon which the Company has completed and tested a well or wells capable of producing in accordance with first-class oil practice, at least 2,000 tons of oil per day for a period of thirty consecutive days.

Operation[s] connected with drilling include the ordering and shipping of materials and equipment to Saudi Arabia, the construction of roads, camps, buildings, structures, communication facilities, &c., and the installation and operation of the machinery, equipment and facilities for drilling wells.

ART. 9. Upon the discovery of oil in commercial quantities, the Company shall advance to the Government the sum of £50,000 gold, or its equivalent, and one year later the further sum of £50,000 gold, or its equivalent. The due date of the first advance shall be the date of discovery of oil in commercial quantities, as provided in article 8 hereof, and the due date of the second advance shall be one year later. In each case the Company shall have sixty days following the due date within which to make the advance. Both of these advances are in account of royalties, which may be due to the Government, and, consequently, the Company shall have the right to recover the amount of these advances by way of deductions from one-half of the royalties due the Government.

ART. 10. Since it has been agreed that the annual rental of £5,000 gold, or its equivalent is payable to the date of the discovery of oil in commercial quantities, and since it has been agreed also that the annual rental is to be payable in advance, it may happen that the last annual rental paid prior to the date of discovery of oil in commercial quantities will cover a period beyond the date of such discovery. In case that this period should be equal to or greater than one-fifth of a year, the proportionate amount of the £5,000 gold, or its equivalent corresponding to such period, shall be treated as an advance on account of royalties due the Government, and consequently it should be recoverable by the Company by way of deductions from one-half of the royalties due the Government.

ART. 11. As soon as practicable (i.e., allowing a reasonable time for ordering and shipping further materials and equipment to Saudi Arabia and commencing further work), after the date of discovery of oil in commercial quantities, the Company shall continue operations connected with drilling by using at least two strings of tools. These operations shall continue diligently until the proven area has been drilled up in accordance with first-class oil-field practice, or until the contract is terminated.

ART. 12. The Company shall pay the Government a royalty on all net crude oil produced and saved and run from field storage, after first deducting—

(1) Water and foreign substance; and

(2) Oil required for the customary operations of the Company's installation within Saudi Arabia; and

(3) The oil required for the manufacturing the amounts of gasoline and kerosene to be provided free each year to the Government in accordance with article 17 hereof.

The rate of royalty per ton of such net crude oil shall be 4s. gold, or its equivalent.

ART. 13. If the Company should produce, save and sell any natural gas, it will pay to the Government a royalty equal to one-eighth of the proceeds of the sale of such natural gas, it being understood, however, that the Company shall be under no obligation to produce, save, sell, or otherwise dispose of any natural gas. It is also understood that the Company is under no obligation to pay any royalty on such natural gas as it may use for the customary operation of its installation within the Saudi Arabia.

ART. 14. The Government, through duly authorised representatives, may, during the usual hours of operations, inspect and examine the operations of the Company under this contract and may verify the amount of production. The Company shall measure, in accordance with first-class oilfield practice, the amount of oil produced and saved and run from field storage, and shall keep time and correct accounts thereof, and of the natural gas it may produce and save and sell, and duly authorised representatives of

the Government shall also have access at all reasonable times to such accounts. The Company shall within three months, after the end of each semester, commencing with the date of commercial discovery of oil, deliver to the Government an abstract of such accounts for the semester, and a statement of the amount of royalties due the Government for the semester. These accounts and statements should be treated as confidential by the Government, with the exception of such items therein as the Government may require to publish for fiscal purposes.

The royalties due the Government at the end of each semester commencing with the date of commercial discovery of oil, shall be paid within three months after the end of the semester, such portion of the amount as may be unquestioned shall be tendered the Government within the period hereinabove, and thereupon the question shall be settled by agreement between the parties or failing that by arbitration as provided in this contract. Any further sum which may be payable to the Government as a result of this settlement shall be paid within sixty days after the date of such settlement.

[...]

ART. 17. As soon as practicable after the date of discovery of oil in commercial quantities, the Company shall select some point within Saudi Arabia for the erection of a plant for manufacturing sufficient gasoline and kerosene to meet the ordinary requirements of the Government, providing, of course, that the character of the crude oil found will permit of the manufacture of such products on a commercial basis by the use of ordinary refining methods, and provided further that the amount of oil developed is sufficient for the purpose. It is understood that the ordinary requirements of the Government shall not include resale inside or outside of the country. Upon the completion of the necessary preliminary arrangements, and as soon as the Company has obtained the Government's consent to the proposed location, the Company shall proceed with the erection of such plant. During each year following the date of completion of this plant, the Company shall offer free to the Government, in bulk, 200,000 American gallons of gasoline, and 100,000 gallons of kerosene, it being understood that the facilities provided by the Government for accepting these deliveries shall not impede or endanger the Company's operations.

[...]

ART. 19. In return for the obligations assumed by the Company under this contract, and for the payments required from the Company hereunder, the Company and enterprise shall be exempt from all direct and indirect taxes, imposts, charges, fees and duties (including, of course, import and export duties), it being understood that this privilege shall not extend to the sale of products within the country, nor shall it extend to the personal require-ments of the individual employees of the Company. Any material imported free of duty may not be sold within the country without first paying the corresponding import duty.

ART. 20. It is understood, of course, that the Company has the right to use all means and facilities it may deem necessary or advis-able in order to exercise the rights granted under this contract, so as to carry out the purposes of this enterprise, including among other things the right to construct and use roads, camps, build-ings, structures and all systems of communication, to instal and operate machinery, equipment and facilities in connexion with the drilling of wells, or in connexion with the transportation, storage, treatment, manufacture, dealing with, or exportation of petroleum and its derivatives, or in connexion with the camps, buildings and quarters of the personnel of the company; to construct and use storage reservoirs, tanks and receptacles; to construct and oper-ate wharves, piers, sealoading lines and all other terminal and port facilities; and to use all forms of transportation of personnel, or equipment, and of petroleum and its derivatives. It is understood, however, that the use of aeroplanes within the country shall be [the] subject of a separate agreement.

The Company shall also have the right to develop, carry away and use water. It likewise shall have the right to carry away and use any water belonging to the Government, for the operations of the enterprise, but so as not to prejudice irrigation or to deprive any lands, houses or watering places for cattle, of a reasonable sup-ply of water from time to time. The Company may also take for use, but only to the extent necessary for the purpose of the enter-prise, other natural products belonging to the Government, such as surface soil, timber, stone, lime, gypsum stone and similar substances.

Government officials and agents, in pursuance of official business, shall have the right to use such communications and transporta-tion facilities as the Company may establish, provided that such use shall not obstruct or interfere with the Company's operations hereunder, and shall not impose upon the Company any substan-tial burden of expense.

In times of national emergency the use of the Company's trans-portation and communication facilities by the Government shall entitle the Company to fair compensation for any loss it may sus-tain thereby, whether through damage to the Company's facilities, equipment or installation or through the obstruction or interfer-ence with the Company's operations.

ART. 21. The enterprise under this contract shall be directed and supervised by Americans who shall employ Saudi Arab nationals as far as practicable, and in so far as the Company can find suitable Saudi Arab employees it will not employ other nationals.

In respect of the treatment of the Saudi Arab nationals as employ-ees, the Company shall abide by the existing laws of the coun-try applicable generally to employees of any other industrial enterprise.

ART. 22. The Government reserves the right to search for and obtain any substance or products, other than those exclusively granted under this contract, within the area covered by this agree-ment, except land occupied by wells or other installations of the Company, provided always that the right thus reserved by the Gov-ernment shall be exercised so as not to endanger the operations of the Company or interfere with its rights hereunder, and provided also that a fair compensation shall be paid the Company by the Government for all damage the Company may sustain through the exercise of the right so reserved by the Government. In any grant of such right so reserved by the Government, the concessionaire shall be bound by the provisions of this article.

ART. 23. The Company is hereby empowered by the Govern-ment to acquire from any occupant the surface rights of any land which the Company may find necessary to use in connexion with the enterprise, provided that the Company shall pay the occupant for depriving him of the use of the land. The payment shall be a fair one with respect to the customary use made of the land by the occupant. The Government will lend every reasonable assistance to the Company in case of any difficulties with respect to acquiring the rights of a surface occupant.

The Company, of course, shall have no right to acquire or to occupy Holy Places.

[...]

ART. 30. The Company may not, without the consent of the Gov-ernment, assign its rights and obligations under this contract to anyone, but it is understood that the Company, upon notifying the Government, shall have the right to assign its rights and obliga-tions hereunder to a corporation it may organise exclusively for the purpose of this enterprise. Any such corporation or organisa-tion, upon being invested with any or all of rights and obligations under this contract, and upon notification thereof to the Govern-ment, shall thereupon be subject to the terms and conditions of this agreement.

In the event that stock issued by any such corporation or organisa-tion should be offered for sale to the general public, the inhabitants of Saudi Arabia shall be allowed a reasonable time to subscribe (upon similar terms and conditions offered to others), for at least 20 per cent of such shares of stock so issued and offered for sale to the general public.

[...]

Letter of Agreement, Addressed by Hamilton to al-Shaykn 'Abdallah al-Sulayman

Referring to the contract which has been signed to-day by you, on behalf of the Saudi Arab Government, and by the undersigned, on behalf of Standard Oil Company of California, relative to an oil concession covering a portion of eastern Saudi Arabia, I am setting forth below the agreement we have also reached on behalf of the two parties to the same contract, which agreement shall be considered as a part of the said contract. For convenience, the two parties in question shall be referred to below in the same manner as designated in the said contract, namely, the "Government" and the "Company," and the said contract shall be referred to as the "Saudi Arab Concession."

1. The Company is granted a preference right to an oil concession covering a certain area described in Article 3 of the Saudi Arab Concession. The preference right so granted the Company shall be a right to acquire an oil concession covering such area, exclusive of the so-called Neutral Zone also referred to in the same Article 3, by equaling the terms of any offer for such concession that may be made [by] the Government by others in good faith and that the Government may be ready and willing to accept. Within thirty days after receiving from the Government written notice, setting forth in full the terms of such offer, the Company shall notify the Government whether or not the Company wishes to acquire the oil concession by equaling the terms so offered. If the Company does not wish to do so, the Government is free to accept the offer made, but if an oil concession should not be granted to others on the same terms as those so offered and so presented to the Company, the preference right of the Company shall continue, at least so long as the provisions of Article 7 of the Saudi Arab Concession remain in force.

2. The Company's preference right to acquire an oil concession covering the so-called Neutral Zone referred to in Article 3 of the Saudi Arab Concession, shall be a right to equal, with respect to the rights of the Government in the Neutral Zone, the terms and conditions which may be obtained by the Shaikh of Kuwait for a concession covering his rights in the Neutral Zone. In the absence of any grant of an oil concession covering such rights of the Shaikh of Kuwait, the Government will endeavor to reach an agreement with the Shaikh of Kuwait whereby the Company will be permitted to acquire an oil concession covering the rights of the Government and of the Shaikh of Kuwait in the Neutral Zone. In either of these two events, the Company shall have a period of thirty days from the date it receives written notice setting forth in full the terms and conditions of oil concession covering the rights of the Shaikh of Kuwait in the Neutral Zone, or covering the terms of the proposed concession embracing the rights of the Government and of the Shaikh of Kuwait in the Neutral Zone, as the case may be within which to decide and to notify the Government whether or not the Company wishes to acquire the oil concession

on such terms. If the Company does not wish to do so, the Government is free to negotiate with others, but if the oil concession should not be granted to others on the same terms as those offered to the Company, the preference right of the Company shall continue, at least so long as the provisions of Article 7 of the Saudi Arab Concession remain in force.

3. Article 22 of the Saudi Arab Concession states that the use of aeroplanes shall be the subject of a separate agreement. One purpose of the present letter is to set forth the agreement as to this point. In view of the restrictions now prevailing in Saudi Arabia as to the use of aeroplanes within the country by anyone other than the Government, it is hereby agreed that so long as such restrictions remain in force, the Government will undertake to provide, at the request and at the expense of the Company, such aeroplane service as the Company may consider advisable for the purpose of its operations within the area covered by the Saudi Arab Concession. Such service shall be limited to the purposes of the enterprise. If any aeroplane photographs should be taken for geological or mapping purposes, the Government and the Company shall each receive copies, also at the expense of the Company.

4. The consent of the Government must be obtained before the Company shall have any right to examine the so-called Neutral Zone referred to in Article 3 of the Saudi Arab Concession.

5. The provisions of Article 35 of the Saudi Arab Concession shall also apply to this agreement.

[. . .]

Source: J. C. Hurewitz, *The Middle East and North Africa in World Politics: A Documentary Record* (New Haven, CT: Yale University Press, 1975), 445–452.

11. The United States and Saudi Arabia, Provisional Agreement on Diplomatic and Consular Representation, Juridical Protection, Commerce, and Navigation, November 7, 1933 [Excerpts]

Introduction

Where American business interests went, the U.S. government often followed close behind. Within six months of the negotiation in July 1933 by Standard Oil of California (Socal) of an exclusive oil concession in Saudi Arabia, the U.S. ambassador in London, Robert Bingham, negotiated an agreement under whose terms his country and Saudi Arabia could exchange diplomatic representatives with each other. Bingham was entrusted with this task because at this time Great Britain was the only European state where Saudi Arabia maintained a permanent diplomatic mission. Although this agreement was made in November 1933, the U.S. government took no immediate action to implement it. In February 1940, as war in Europe seemed likely to involve the Middle East and less than two years after Socal's Saudi subsidiary, the California Arabian Standard Oil Company (Casoc), discovered commercially viable oil fields in Saudi territory, the U.S. government expanded the responsibilities of its minister in British-controlled Egypt to include accreditation to Jiddah, the Saudi capital, as well. Not until April 1942, when the U.S. State Department appointed a resident vice-consul in Jiddah, a post he combined with chargé d'affaires, did the United States have a physical diplomatic presence in Saudi Arabia. In an index of the growing significance of Saudi Arabia to the United States, in April 1943 the American mission in Jiddah was upgraded to a legation.

Primary Source

[...]

The diplomatic representatives of each country shall enjoy in the territories of the other the privileges and immunities derived from generally recognized international law. The consular representatives of each country, duly provided with exequatur, will be permitted to reside in the territories of the other in the places wherein consular representatives are by local laws permitted to reside; they shall enjoy the honorary privileges and the immunities accorded to such officers by general international usage; and they shall not be treated in a manner less favorable than similar officers of any other foreign country.

ARTICLE II

Subjects of His Majesty the King of the Kingdom of Saudi Arabia in the United States of America, territories and possessions, and nationals of the United States of America, its territories and possessions, in the Kingdom of Saudi Arabia shall be received and treated in accordance with the requirements and practices of generally recognized international law. In respect of their persons, possessions and rights, they shall enjoy the fullest protection of the laws and authorities of the country, and they shall not be treated in regard to their persons, property, rights and interests, in any manner less favorable than the nationals of any other foreign country.

ARTICLE III

In respect of import, export and other duties and charges affecting commerce and navigation, as well as in respect of transit, warehousing and other facilities, the United States of America, its territories and possessions, will accord to the Kingdom of Saudi Arabia,

and the Kingdom of Saudi Arabia will accord to the United States of America, its territories and possessions, unconditional most-favored-nation treatment. Every concession with respect to any duty, charge or regulation affecting commerce or navigation now accorded or that may hereafter be accorded by the United States of America, its territories and possessions, or by the Kingdom of Saudi Arabia to any foreign country will become immediately applicable without request and without compensation to the commerce and navigation of the Kingdom of Saudi Arabia and of the United States of America, its territories and possessions, respectively.

[...]

Source: "Saudi Arabia Diplomatic and Consular Representation; Juridical Protection, Commerce and Navigation Agreement," Trade Compliance Center, http://tcc.export.gov/Trade_Agreements/All_Trade_Agreements/exp_005330.asp.

12. Iran, Soviet Union, and Great Britain, Treaty of Alliance, January 29, 1942 [Excerpt]

Introduction

The heavily mechanized warfare that characterized World War II meant that the oil supplies of the Middle East were too valuable an asset for either side to ignore. During the 1930s Reza Shah of Iran, who resented the fact that the British-dominated Anglo-Iranian Oil Company controlled most of Iran's oil revenues and industry, favored Nazi Germany and staffed much of his government with German advisers. From September 1939 Germany was at war with Great Britain, and in June 1941 German chancellor Adolf Hitler's forces also invaded the Soviet Union, which shared a border with Iran and then became a British ally. Anglo-Russian competition for influence over Iran dated back more than a century, but for the war's duration the two nations cooperated there, as they had in the early 20th century when they divided Iran into spheres of influence. Seeking both to deny Iran's oil reserves to Germany and to protect Soviet oilfields in the nearby Caucasus, in the summer of 1941 both British and Soviet officials demanded that the shah expel the 2,000 Germans then resident in Iran. When he refused, military forces of the two Allied powers jointly occupied Iran, replacing the pro-German shah with his youthful son, Mohammad Reza Shah Pahlavi. Russian forces controlled the north of the country, while British forces controlled the south. Iranian nationalist elements feared that the foreign occupation might easily become permanent. Seeking to alleviate such concerns, and in Britain's case also impelled by anxieties that if no agreement to the contrary was concluded Soviet troops might well remain in place when the war was over, in January 1942 the three powers concluded a treaty of alliance against Germany. This permitted British and Soviet armed forces unrestricted use of Iranian military facilities. Although Iranian nationalists resented the alliance, which was forced upon them, at their insistence this agreement included clauses whereby both Britain and the Soviet Union pledged to "respect the territorial integrity, sovereignty and political independence of Iran." In addition, the treaty provided that both British and Russian occupying forces would leave no later than six months after hostilities ended. In an effort to placate Iranian nationalists, this was an improvement on the one-year interval proposed in the original draft treaty that the British government submitted in September 1941. The treaty went into effect on February 1, 1942, three days after it was signed.

Primary Source

ARTICLE 1

His Majesty The King of Great Britain, Ireland and the British Dominions beyond the Seas, Emperor of India, and the Union of Soviet Socialist Republics (hereinafter referred to as the Allied Powers) jointly and severally undertake to respect the territorial integrity, sovereignty and political independence of Iran.

ARTICLE 2

An alliance is established between the Allied Powers on the one hand and His Imperial Majesty The Shahinshah of Iran on the other.

ARTICLE 3

(i) The Allied Powers jointly and severally undertake to defend Iran by all means at their command from all aggression on the part of Germany or any other Power.

(ii) His Imperial Majesty The Shahinshah undertakes—

(a) to co-operate with the Allied Powers with all the means at his command and in every way possible, in order that they may be able to fulfil the above undertaking. The assistance of the Iranian forces shall, however, be limited to the maintenance of internal security on Iranian territory;

(b) to secure to the Allied Powers, for the passage of troops or supplies from one Allied Power to the other or for other similar purposes, the unrestricted right to use, maintain, guard and, in case of military necessity, control in any way that they may require all means of communication throughout Iran, including railways, roads, rivers, aerodromes, ports, pipelines and telephone, telegraph and wireless installations;

(c) to furnish all possible assistance and facilities in obtaining material and recruiting labour for the purpose of the maintenance

and improvement of the means of communication referred to in paragraph (b);

(d) to establish and maintain, in collaboration with the Allied Powers, such measures of censorship control as they may require for all the means of communication referred to in paragraph (b).

(iii) It is clearly understood that in the application of paragraph[s] (b), (c) and (d) of the present article the Allied Powers will give consideration to the essential needs of Iran.

ARTICLE 4

(i) The Allied Powers may maintain in Iranian territory land, sea and air forces in such number as they consider necessary. The location of such forces shall be decided in agreement with the Iranian Government so long as the strategic situation allows. All questions concerning the relations between the forces of the Allied Powers and the Iranian authorities shall be settled so far as possible in co-operation with the Iranian authorities in such a way as to safeguard the security of the said forces. It is understood that the presence of these forces on Iranian territory does not constitute a military occupation and will disturb as little as possible the administration and the security forces of Iran, the economic life of the country, the normal movements of the population and the application of Iranian laws and regulations.

(ii) A separate agreement or agreements shall be concluded as soon as possible after the entry into force of the present Treaty regarding any financial obligations to be borne by the Allied Powers under the provisions of the present article and of paragraphs (ii) (b), (c) and (d) of Article 3 above in such matters as local purchases, the hiring of buildings and plant, the employment of labour, transport charges, etc. A special agreement shall be concluded between the Allied Governments and the Iranian Government defining the conditions for any transfers to the Iranian Government after the war of buildings and other improvements effected by the Allied Powers on Iranian territory. These agreements shall also settle the immunities to be enjoyed by the forces of the Allied Powers in Iran.

ARTICLE 5

The forces of the Allied Powers shall be withdrawn from Iranian territory not later than six months after all hostilities between the Allied Powers and Germany and her associates have been suspended by the conclusion of an armistice or armistices, or on the conclusion of peace between them, whichever date is the earlier. The expression "associates" of Germany means all other Powers which have engaged or may in the future engage in hostilities against either of the Allied Powers.

ARTICLE 6

(i) The Allied Powers undertake in their relations with foreign countries not to adopt an attitude which is prejudicial to the territorial integrity, sovereignty or political independence of Iran, nor to conclude treaties inconsistent with the provisions of the present Treaty. They undertake to consult the Government of His Imperial Majesty the Shahinshah in all matters affecting the direct interests of Iran.

(ii) His Imperial Majesty The Shahinshah undertakes not to adopt in his relations with foreign countries an attitude which is inconsistent with the alliance, nor to conclude treaties inconsistent with the provisions of the present Treaty.

ARTICLE 7

The Allied Powers jointly undertake to use their best endeavours to safeguard the economic existence of the Iranian people against the privations and difficulties arising as a result of the present war. On the entry into force of the present Treaty, discussions shall be opened between the Government of Iran and the Governments of the Allied Powers as to the best possible methods of carrying out the above undertaking.

ARTICLE 8

The provisions of the present Treaty are equally binding as bilateral obligations between His Imperial Majesty The Shahinshah and each of the two other High Contracting Parties.

[...]

Source: A. H. Hamzavi, *Persia and the Powers: An Account of Diplomatic Relations, 1941–1946* (London: Hutchinson, 1946), 65–68.

13. The Tehran Conference, November 28–December 1, 1943

Introduction

From November 28 to December 1, 1943, British prime minister Winston Churchill, Soviet leader Joseph Stalin, and U.S. president Franklin D. Roosevelt met at Tehran to discuss the future prosecution of the war. Privately they agreed to provide support for the communist partisans in Yugoslavia and to launch Operation OVERLORD, the invasion of Western Europe, in May 1944. They also hoped, fruitlessly, that Turkey might be persuaded to abandon its neutrality and join the Allies in war against Germany. When the conference ended, the three leaders also issued various public declarations on the prosecution and objectives of the war and their

future treatment of Iran. At the beginning of World War II, Britain and the Soviet Union had jointly occupied Iran, replacing its monarch, Reza Shah, whom they considered overly sympathetic to Germany, with his young son, Mohammad Reza Shah Pahlavi. The Allies took this action largely because they sought to deny Germany access to Iran's oil resources. From the mid-19th century onward, Britain and Russia each had a lengthy history of seeking to make Iran (then known as Persia) a virtual protectorate, policies that had led Iranian officials to harbor deep suspicions of the good faith of both powers. Britain also had extensive oil concessions in Iran. At Tehran, both Churchill and Stalin affirmed their mutual intention of withdrawing from Iran once the war had ended and providing the country with economic and other aid in special recognition of its wartime assistance to the Allied cause.

Primary Source

(a) Declaration of the Three Powers, December 1, 1943

We the President of the United States, the Prime Minister of Great Britain, and the Premier of the Soviet Union, have met these four days past, in this, the Capital of our Ally, Iran, and have shaped and confirmed our common policy.

We express our determination that our nations shall work together in war and in the peace that will follow.

As to war—our military staffs have joined in our round table discussions, and we have concerted our plans for the destruction of the German forces. We have reached complete agreement as to the scope and timing of the operations to be undertaken from the east, west and south.

The common understanding which we have here reached guarantees that victory will be ours.

And as to peace—we are sure that our concord will win an enduring Peace. We recognize fully the supreme responsibility resting upon us and all the United Nations to make a peace which will command the goodwill of the overwhelming mass of the peoples of the world and banish the scourge and terror of war for many generations.

With our Diplomatic advisors we have surveyed the problems of the future. We shall seek the cooperation and active participation of all nations, large and small, whose peoples in heart and mind are dedicated, as are our own peoples, to the elimination of tyranny and slavery, oppression and intolerance. We will welcome them, as they may choose to come, into a world family of Democratic Nations.

No power on earth can prevent our destroying the German armies by land, their U Boats by sea, and their war plants from the air.

Our attack will be relentless and increasing.

Emerging from these cordial conferences we look with confidence to the day when all peoples of the world may live free lives, untouched by tyranny, and according to their varying desires and their own consciences.

We came here with hope and determination. We leave here, friends in fact, in spirit and in purpose.

ROOSEVELT, CHURCHILL and STALIN

Signed at Tehran, December 1, 1943

(b) Declaration of the Three Powers Regarding Iran, December 1, 1943

The President of the United States, the Premier of the U. S. S. R. and the Prime Minister of the United Kingdom, having consulted with each other and with the Prime Minister of Iran, desire to declare the mutual agreement of their three Governments regarding their relations with Iran.

The Governments of the United States, the U. S. S. R., and the United Kingdom recognize the assistance which Iran has given in the prosecution of the war against the common enemy, particularly by facilitating the transportation of supplies from overseas to the Soviet Union.

The Three Governments realize that the war has caused special economic difficulties for Iran, and they are agreed that they will continue to make available to the Government of Iran such economic assistance as may be possible, having regard to the heavy demands made upon them by their world-wide military operations, and to the world-wide shortage of transport, raw materials, and supplies for civilian consumption.

With respect to the post-war period, the Governments of the United States, the U. S. S. R., and the United Kingdom are in accord with the Government of Iran that any economic problems confronting Iran at the close of hostilities should receive full consideration, along with those of other members of the United Nations, by conferences or international agencies held or created to deal with international economic matters.

The Governments of the United States, the U. S. S. R., and the United Kingdom are at one with the Government of Iran in their desire for the maintenance of the independence, sovereignty and territorial integrity of Iran. They count upon the participation of Iran, together with all other peace-loving nations, in the establishment of international peace, security and prosperity after the war, in accordance with the principles of the Atlantic Charter, to which all four Governments have subscribed.

WINSTON S. CHURCHILL
J. STALIN
FRANKLIN D ROOSEVELT

(c) Military Conclusions of the Tehran Conference

The Conference

(1) Agreed that the Partisans in Yugoslavia should be supported by supplies and equipment to the greatest possible extent, and also by commando operations:

(2) Agreed that, from the military point of view, it was most desirable that Turkey should come into the war on the side of the Allies before the end of the year:

(3) Took note of Marshal Stalin's statement that if Turkey found herself at war with Germany, and as a result Bulgaria declared war on Turkey or attacked her, the Soviet [Union] would immediately be at war with Bulgaria. The Conference further took note that this fact could be explicitly stated in the forthcoming negotiations to bring Turkey into the war:

(4) Took note that Operation OVERLORD would be launched during May 1944, in conjunction with an operation against Southern France. The latter operation would be undertaken in as great a strength as availability of landing-craft permitted. The Conference further took note of Marshal Stalin's statement that the Soviet forces would launch an offensive at about the same time with the object of preventing the German forces from transferring from the Eastern to the Western Front:

(5) Agreed that the military staffs of the Three Powers should henceforward keep in close touch with each other in regard to the impending operations in Europe. In particular it was agreed that a cover plan to mystify and mislead the enemy as regards these operations should be concerted between the staffs concerned.

FRANKLIN D. ROOSEVELT
JOSEPH V. STALIN
WINSTON S. CHURCHILL

Source: U.S. Department of State, *A Decade of American Foreign Policy: Basic Documents, 1941–1949* (Washington, DC: U.S. Government Printing Office, 1985), 21–22.

14. Saudi Arabia and the United States, Agreement on the Construction of a U.S. Military Air Base at Dhahran, August 5–8, 1945 [Excerpts]

Introduction

Official U.S. interest in Saudi Arabia continued to expand during World War II, culminating in the negotiation of an agreement for the construction of a U.S. air base at the Saudi town of Dhahran, a facility that could be used if necessary to afford military protection to American oil interests in the kingdom. Pervasive fears that U.S. domestic oil reserves would be exhausted in the near future had contributed to the U.S. government's new wartime focus on the small desert state. In April 1942 the U.S. State Department appointed a resident vice-consul in Jiddah, a post he combined with chargé d'affaires, the first occasion on which the United States possessed a physical diplomatic presence in Saudi Arabia. Even so, during 1941 and 1942 the U.S. government turned down suggestions by the California Arabian Standard Oil Company (Casoc), which held a major oil concession in Saudia Arabia, that it should give the kingdom official economic aid under the Lend-Lease Program. Matters changed at the beginning of 1943, when the U.S. government began to deliberate whether it might be able to buy out Casoc's Saudi concession and use it as a strategic military and naval oil reserve. In March 1943 the U.S. State Department declared that Saudi Arabia was eligible for Lend-Lease aid on unusually generous terms. As another indication of growing official American interest in Saudi Arabia, in April 1943 the American mission in Jiddah was upgraded to a legation with a minister resident. In 1944 the U.S. government had begun minting coinage for the Saudi government and had also dispatched a military mission to investigate the kingdom's armaments requirements. The new American interest in Saudi Arabia provoked acerbic friction with the British government, whose officials perceived this as an encroachment on a previously British sphere of influence. The British could not, however, come close to matching what the United States could offer Saudi Arabia in terms of economic and military aid and thus had to acquiesce in growing U.S. involvement with the kingdom. American officials themselves admitted that the "generous budgetary aid for 1945" they offered the Saudi government was a major factor in the successful negotiation that summer, by the U.S. Department of Defense, of an agreement permitting the establishment for three years of an U.S. military airbase in Dhahran, Saudi Arabia, an accord that could potentially also be revised to include civilian and commercial aviation. Associated navigational facilities were to be constructed in various isolated Saudi locations. William A. Eddy, the second U.S. diplomatic minister in Saudi Arabia, sent the State Department a frank account of the negotiations of this agreement, which he and

several American military officers concluded with Saudi officials in early August 1945. The agreement was subsequently repeatedly renewed, and in the early 21st century Dhahran still functioned as a major U.S. air base in the Middle East.

Primary Source

The Minister in Saudi Arabia to the Secretary of State

No. 162 JIDDA, August 8, 1945.
  [Received August 18]

SIR: I have the honor to report that, in accordance with instructions in Department's Telegram No. 210, July 21, accompanied by General Giles, I submitted to the King of Saudi Arabia at Riyadh, August 5, 1945, text of a proposed agreement for the construction at Dhahran of a United States military airbase. The text had been largely drafted by Lieut. Colonels Shumate and Ellis, on the basis of instruction from the War Department, and was modified by me at points on which I had been specifically instructed by the Department of State. After considerable minor changes in phraseology made at Riyadh to include points reserved by the King, and to clarify statements not wholly clear in Arabic translation, the text was agreed by the King and signed by the Acting Foreign Minister, Shaikh Yusuf Yassin. A copy of my Notes No. 237 of August 5, and No. 238 of August 6, and an English translation of the Saudi Arabian Government Note No. 17/2/6/83 of August 6, embodying the agreement verbatim, are enclosed with this despatch.

Upon receipt of final technical data from the War Department, Lieut. Colonels Shumate and Ellis and a Captain of A.T.C. flew from Cairo to Jidda, August 3, to discuss with me the draft of the agreement they had prepared, thus providing a day of deliberation and revision before the arrival the next day of General Giles, who had only just returned to Cairo from an extended trip to the Far East. Stormy weather, however, prevented the plane carrying Colonels Shumate and Ellis from landing at Jidda, and they spent the night at Port Sudan where their plane landed only with the greatest difficulty. They arrived at Jidda the next day, only two hours before the arrival of General Giles with Shaikh Yusuf Yassin, recalled by the King from meetings of the Arab League committee. On August 5, the entire party proceeded from Jidda to Riyadh on the King's plane, returning to Jidda August 7. General Giles and his party proceeded immediately to Cairo.

I believe the Department will find that the agreement reserves all the rights and includes all the essential provisions contained in my instructions, including the rights reserved by the Air Transport Command (Deptel. No. 232, August 3), received by me just as we were leaving for Riyadh. In any case, the agreement includes all the concessions we were able to secure, and more than I expected we would carry away. Several points on which I had expected debate and compromise, such as the numbers of foreign workers to be imported and their nationality, were accepted without question.

General Giles took full part in all discussions and concurred in the final form of the agreement.

Reservations and objections raised by the King were almost exclusively concerned with preserving the appearance, as well as the reality, of his sovereignty and jurisdiction: He insisted that the Saudi flag should fly over the inland posts, the emergency landing field and the isolated stations where navigational aids are to be located, though the operation and control of technical services at these posts will belong to the United States Army. As a matter of fact, I am convinced that this will promote the security and efficiency of these posts, as the untamed tribesmen near those inaccessible posts will respect a station which belongs to the King, and will not consider the presence of isolated United States Army personnel as an "invasion." While the King concedes United States Army jurisdiction over all non-Saudi Arabian personnel within the airbase limits, jurisdiction over police court cases and crimes committed outside the airbase, and involving mixed nationals, is to be the subject of agreement reached after full study of the problems involved. It should also be noted that the Agreement is a concession only for military use of the airbase, including Air Transport Command traffic in the national interest.

All civil air-service concessions and rights will be negotiated and granted on a non-discriminatory basis (see Legation's despatch No. 124, May 13, 1945) by the Saudi Arabian Government. Sub-contracts with commercial airlines cannot be negotiated between the commercial company and the United States Army. To clarify this point, the King insisted on an additional note (Legation's Note No. 238) specifying that if the military need for the airbase should terminate before the end of the three post-war years, the operation and maintenance of the airbase would, at such date, revert to the Saudi Arabian Government. It is also understood, however, that negotiations may be opened with the Saudi Arabian Government at any time for the inauguration of commercial air service to begin whenever the military situation permits the use of the field concurrently by civil airlines.

With regard to the provision for "normal facilities for personal recreation and self improvement," I had expected possible objection to pagan dramatics or Christian worship, neither of which was mentioned. The only query raised was whether the clause would be abused to import prostitutes. Oral assurances to the contrary were accepted.

Time did not permit full details to be drawn up and agreed regarding (1) procedure in criminal cases involving mixed nationals, mentioned above; (2) procedure for administration of customs inspection and passport regulations for civilians, at such time as civilian traffic through the airbase will justify the posting of Saudi customs and passport officers there. Both General Giles and I preferred, at almost all costs, to bring away a signed document covering essentials, instead of postponing the Agreement until all minor matters had been studied. While the United States Army has been studying and drafting its requirements for months, the Saudi Government had no advance opportunity to study the proposed agreement. The speedy conclusion of a signed agreement constitutes a remarkable exception to oriental habits of leisurely consultation and bargaining. Another time, as in the case of proposed Agreements for civil air rights, I hope the text can be forwarded for study by me and by the Saudi Government rather than presented abruptly for an immediate decision.

The contrast between the King's willingness to make concessions during this visit and his unwillingness to accept the valuable services of a military mission early in July was very marked. On the former occasion he had heard nothing about economic and financial help for 1945, and had also recently been advised that plans for long-range economic cooperation would be indefinitely postponed. This time, the visit followed closely upon the notification of generous budgetary aid for 1945, more than twice the aid being given by Britain, and closely upon receipt by the King of enthusiastic reports from Amir Faisal regarding his conferences in Washington with the Acting-Secretary and the Director of the Office of Near Eastern and African Affairs, July 31–August 2 [1], 1945.

In conclusion, I would add a word of apology for the execrable style which mars portions of the Agreement: awkward phraseology, *nonsequiturs,* repetitions, and lamentable incoherence. Hurried attempts at joint revision of phraseology, both at Jidda and at Riyadh, during a few crowded hours, are partly to blame; but the original reason is the attempt to cover in the English text elaborations and explications coined in Arabic by the Saudis and inserted at points which, however eloquent they may be in the classical Arabic, disfigure the English text. However, there was no time for final revision of the style.

Respectfully yours, WILLIAM A. EDDY

[Enclosure 1]

The American Minister in Saudi Arabia (Eddy) to the Saudi Arabian Acting Minister for Foreign Affairs (Yassin)

No. 237   RIYADH, August 5, 1945.

YOUR EXCELLENCY: I have the honor to refer to your Note of May 11 [12], 1945 in which the Saudi Arabian Government agreed in principle to the establishment of a United States Military Airbase at Dhahran for the prosecution of our common war against Japan. The Saudi Arabian Government agreed to the construction and operation of this airbase by the United States Army for the duration of the war against Japan, and for its continued use by the United States Armed Forces for a period of three years after the cessation of hostilities against Japan.

I now have the honor to transmit the following proposals of my Government with regard to the details of construction and operation of the airbase, proposals which are hereby submitted to the government of His Majesty, the Great King of Saudi Arabia.

This airbase, not to exceed an area of five (5) miles by five (5) miles, to be located at approximately Longitude 26°20' North, Latitude 50°10' East, which is within the so-called Damman Tracts, will be constructed by the United States Government in accordance with United States Army mobilization type construction policies, making use of pre-fabricated steel buildings for certain structures. The base in general will consist of two runways and the necessary facilities as are usual for the operation of an airbase accommodating five hundred (500) persons. This five hundred (500) man capacity airbase will be so designed to permit the housing and all other pertinent facilities to be increased to any extent up to a two thousand (2000) man capacity. Such expansions will be made at such time and in such manner as and if deemed necessary by the United States Government during the period of time that the base is occupied by United States Armed Forces. In addition, the United States Government will construct on a Saudi Arabian post to be established near Lauqa, Arabia, at approximately Longitude 29°56' North and Latitude 45°71/2' East, an intermediate emergency airfield. This airfield will consist of the very minimum of improvements and facilities to permit efficient and safe aircraft operations from Cairo, Egypt, to Dhahran. In addition, the United States Government will install standard navigational aids, meteorological facilities and housing, as determined necessary, on a Saudi Arabian post to be established in the vicinity of Hafar al Batin, 28°25' North and 45°35' East. Similar aids and facilities will also be installed at the Dhahran and Lauqa fields. The air route for which the above installations are required will extend from Cairo, Egypt, to Dhahran, Saudi Arabia, by way of Ma'an, Trans-Jordan; Lauqa, Saudi Arabia; and Hafar al Batin, Saudi Arabia.

In the event future technical surveys reveal the necessity of installing certain navigational aids at points along the air route which are not mentioned above, the United States Government will construct same. Navigational aids required at points not on the established air route will not be constructed until the approval of the Saudi Arabian Government is obtained. The coordination of radio frequencies to be used in connection with navigational aids and other communications will be accomplished between technical representatives of the Saudi Arabian Government and the United States Government. In this connection, the United States Government is authorized to employ codes as may be necessary for security purposes.

The Saudi Arabian Government will arrange the necessary details for the United States Government to assume immediate entry rights at Dhahran and Ras Tanura and surface reservations to the required land within the Damman Tracts, and to be granted immediate access to the required lands near Lauqa and Hafar al Batin. This is to permit the rapid and unhampered construction of installations. The land for the Dhahran airbase will be reserved for the exclusive use of the United States Government and the installations thereon will be at the disposition of the United States Government who will use, operate, control and maintain same. On the day of cessation of hostilities against Japan, the airbase at Dhahran will be relinquished by the United States Government, and the

fixed installations thereon, as well as at Lauqa and Hafar al Batin, will become the property of the Saudi Arabian Government; however, for a period not exceeding three years following the cessation of hostilities against Japan, the United States Armed Forces will continue to use, operate and maintain the airbase at Dhahran at its expense. The equipment and improvements at Lauqa and Hafar al Batin will be at the disposition of the United States Government, but the installations will be under the command of the Saudi Arabian Government who will rely upon United States Government technicians for the operation and maintenance of all equipment and for supervising technical tasks.

In view of the extensive air traffic activities involved during the redeployment and period of Army occupation, the Saudi Arabian Government grants the right for the United States Army to use, operate, and maintain the installations referred to above for a period of three years after the cessation of hostilities against Japan.

The United States Government will reimburse the Saudi Arabian Government for all damage to personal property caused by the construction or operation of the above named facilities.

In view of the changing requirements and operations of such an airbase, it is agreed that during the time the airbase is being used by the United States Armed Forces, the United States Government has the right to remove, replace, or alter such items of material and equipment not permanently affixed to or installed on the airbase. It is further agreed that the United States Government has the privilege to make minor alterations, additions and improvements to permanently installed property.

On the expiration of the three-year period following the cessation of hostilities against Japan, the United States Government will turn over these installations in sound condition to the Saudi Arabian Government for operation, control and maintenance. However, the Saudi Arabian Government will not turn such responsibilities over to a third national power nor its subjects.

The construction, maintenance and operation of the airbase requiring the entry and exit of large numbers of United States Army personnel, American civilians and employees of the United States Government, all travelling under competent orders of the United States Government, it is agreed, in order to eliminate undue delay, that such orders issued by the United States Government will be accepted and honored by the Saudi Arabian Government in lieu of passports and residence permits. All other persons authorized by the United States Army Air Transport Command to travel in the national interest will have in their possession the required passports and visas.

These Army personnel, representatives and employees of the United States Government, other than Saudi Arabian subjects, will not be subject to the jurisdiction of the civil or criminal courts of Saudi Arabia for unlawful acts committed within the boundaries of the airbase. All Saudi Arabian subjects will be subject to the Saudi Arabian courts.

It being mutually agreed that mechanics, artisans and labor are not available in sufficient quantities among Saudi Arabian subjects to prosecute the construction of the airbase within the time allotted, the Saudi Arabian Government will allow the United States Government to import into Saudi Arabia, during the construction period, approximately 500 Americans, 1500 Italians, 500 Iraqis and Iranians, 1000 from Aden Protectorate, and 25 Egyptians of European descent for the construction work on the airbase. Wage rates for all employees will be uniform in accordance with individual degree of skill and will conform with current wage rates existing within the locality in which the work is being performed.

[. . .]

It is understood the United States Government has assigned the Commanding General, United States Army Forces in Africa-Middle East Theater, the mission of construction of the airbase and installations contained in the area of operations described above.

Detailed agreements on procedure for the administration of justice involving nationals of more than one country, and for customs and passport regulations, will be the subject of additional memoranda.

At a later date, and in connection with civilian use of the airport, the United States Government will discuss with the Saudi Arabian Government terms under which the Saudi Arabian Government might acquire equipment and non-fixed installations remaining on the airbase when relinquished by the United States Army.

Accept, Excellency, the renewed expression of my high regard.

WILLIAM A. EDDY

[Enclosure 2]

The Saudi Arabian Acting Minister for Foreign Affairs (Yassin) to the American Minister in Saudi Arabia (Eddy)

No. 17/2/6/83 [RIYADH,] August 6, 1945.

I have received your letter dated August 5, 1945, specifying the following:-

[Here follows text of letter of August 5, 1945.]

I have the honor to inform you that the Government of Saudi Arabia has agreed to what has been said in your letter, the text of which is mentioned here above.

Please accept my high regards.

YASSIN

[Enclosure 3]

The American Minister in Saudi Arabia (Eddy) to the Saudi Arabian Acting Minister for Foreign Affairs (Yassin)

No. 238   RIYADH, August 6, 1945.

With reference to my letter to Your Excellency, dated August 5, 1945, I wish to explain the purpose of the United States Government in securing the use of the airbase at Dhahran by the armed forces of the United States after the cessation of hostilities against Japan, for a further period of not more than three years. It is understood that, if the United States Government should discover at an earlier date before the end of the three years that the military need for the airbase no longer exists, then at that date the United States armed forces will relinquish to the Saudi Arabian Government the operation and maintenance of the airbase.

Accept, Excellency, the renewed expression of my high regard.

EDDY

Source: U.S. Department of State, *Foreign Relations of the United States: Diplomatic Papers, 1945,* Vol. 8 (Washington, DC: U.S. Government Printing Office, 1964), 943–950.

15. U.S. Government, Note to the Soviet Union Regarding the Retention of Soviet Troops in Iran, March 6, 1946

Introduction

Despite the Soviet Union's reluctance to discuss the presence of its troops in Iran, in January 1946 the Iranian government took the matter to the United Nations (UN), asking the UN Security Council to investigate the matter and make recommendations for an "appropriate" settlement. When the Security Council considered the situation, the Iranian government complained that the Soviet Union was in breach of the 1942 Tripartite Treaty signed by Iran, the Soviet Union, and Great Britain and that the Soviets had refused to resolve this through bilateral negotiations with Iran. Soviet officials responded that on December 1, 1945, Iran and the Soviet Union had reached a settlement whereby Iran accepted the presence of Soviet troops in Iran. Both sides expressed their readiness to continue bilateral negotiations, and the Security Council then passed a resolution asking the two parties to inform the Security Council of the result of any such negotiations. The U.S. government also continued its own correspondence with the Soviet Union on the subject. Four days after the March 2, 1946, deadline for the withdrawal of Soviet troops had expired, with Soviet forces still present in Iran, the U.S. government addressed a public note to Soviet officials requesting the Soviet Union to "do its part" for international peace "by withdrawing immediately all Soviet forces from the territory of Iran." Although polite and nonthreatening in tone, the note's message was firm and unmistakable. One week later, the U.S. State Department followed this up with a further note asking whether reports of movements of Soviet troops within

Iran, toward both Tehran and the country's western border, were accurate and, if so, why these had taken place. The U.S. government was making it clear that it was not prepared to overlook or acquiesce in Soviet acquisition of a sphere of influence within Iran.

Primary Source

The Government of the United States has been informed that the Government of the Soviet Union has decided to retain Soviet troops in Iran after March 2, 1946, that this decision was taken without the consent of the Iranian Government, and that Soviet troops continue to remain on Iranian territory in spite of the protests of the Iranian Government.

It will be recalled that in reply to a note addressed on November 24, 1945 by the Government of the United States to the Government of the Soviet Union suggesting the immediate withdrawal of all foreign troops from Iran, the Soviet Government on November 29 stated that the period of the stationing of Soviet troops in Iran was governed by the Anglo-Soviet-Iranian Treaty of January 29, 1942. The Government of the United States understood from this statement that it was the intention of the Government of the Soviet Union that all Soviet troops would be withdrawn from Iran not later than March 2, 1946, six months after the date of the signing of the instrument of surrender with Japan on September 2, 1945. This understanding was based upon Article Five of the Tripartite Treaty referred to above which states:

"The forces of the Allied Powers shall be withdrawn from Iranian territory not later than six months after all hostilities between the Allied Powers and Germany and her associates have been suspended by the conclusion of an armistice or armistices, or on the conclusion of peace between them, whichever date is the earlier."

So far as the Government of the United States is aware, this commitment was not questioned at the recent meeting of the Security Council in London which agreed that the Soviet Union and Iran should seek a solution of their differences by direct negotiation.

The decision of the Soviet Government to retain Soviet troops in Iran beyond the period stipulated by the Tripartite Treaty has created a situation with regard to which the Government of the United States, as a member of the United Nations and as a party to the Declaration Regarding Iran dated December 1, 1943, can not remain indifferent. That Declaration announced to the world that the Governments of the United States, the Union of Soviet Socialist Republics and the United Kingdom were at one with the Government of Iran in their desire for the maintenance of the independence, sovereignty and territorial integrity of Iran. In the opinion of the Government of the United States, the maintenance of troops in Iranian territory by any one of the three signatories to that Declaration, without the consent and against the wishes of the Government of Iran, is contrary to the assurances contained in

that Declaration. Furthermore it was generally accepted during the various discussions which took place at the meeting of the Security Council in London that the retention by a member of the United Nations of its troops in the territory of a country which is also a member of the United Nations, without the consent of the Government of that country, is not in accordance with the principles of the United Nations and that the withdrawal of such troops should not be made contingent upon other issues.

The Government of the United States, in the spirit of the friendly association which developed between the United States and the Soviet Union in the successful effort against the common enemy and as a fellow member of the United Nations, expresses the earnest hope that the Government of the Soviet Union will do its part, by withdrawing immediately all Soviet forces from the territory of Iran, to promote the international confidence which is necessary for peaceful progress among the peoples of all nations.

The Government of the United States trusts that the Government of the Soviet Union, no less than itself, appreciates the heavy responsibility resting upon the great powers under the Charter to observe their obligations and to respect the sovereign rights of other states.

The Government of the United States requests that it be promptly advised of the decision of the Government of the Soviet Union which it hopes will be in accord with the views herein expressed.

Source: "U.S. Position on Soviet Troops in Iran," *Department of State Bulletin* 14(350) (1946): 435–436.

16. Prime Minister Ahmad Ghavam of Iran and the Soviet Ambassador to Iran, Communiqué Regarding Soviet-Iranian Negotiations, April 4, 1946

Introduction

Negotiations between Soviet and Iranian diplomats over the presence of Soviet forces in Iran continued for several months in early 1946. On March 26, 1946, Andrei Gromyko, the Soviet representative to the United Nations (UN), reported to the UN Security Council that the two countries had reached agreement on the evacuation of Soviet forces, which had begun on March 2, and he anticipated that this would be completed within the next five to six weeks. U.S. secretary of state James F. Byrnes then, on March 29, introduced a Security Council resolution welcoming this development and in particular the fact that Soviet withdrawal was not connected to negotiations on other subjects, namely oil concessions in Iran, then in progress between Iranian and Soviet officials. The resolution recognized that logistical considerations made it difficult, if not impossible, to speed up by much the scheduled timetable for withdrawals and expressed the hope that the continued presence of some Soviet troops would not be used to pressure Iran in other ongoing negotiations. So long as the Soviet Union continued to remove its forces as anticipated, the Security Council therefore decided to defer any further discussion of the situation in Iran until May 6. The 11-member Security Council passed this resolution on April 4, 1946, with 9 affirmative votes and 1 abstention, while the Soviet representative absented himself and therefore could not vote. On that dame day, Iranian prime minister Ahmad Ghavam and the Soviet ambassador to Iran issued a joint communiqué. The two announced that they had reached "complete agreement . . . on all problems." The Red Army would evacuate all Iranian territory by May 6, 1946, while the two countries would establish a "joint Iranian-Soviet oil company." In the previously Soviet-controlled Azerbaijan Province, where an independent socialist republic had been declared, the Iranian government would implement "reforms," but this was an "internal Iranian affair." Soviet forces did leave Iran on schedule, but the Iranian parliament subsequently refused to grant the Soviet Union the oil concession that this communiqué envisaged. After May 6, the Iranian government alleged that some Soviet military personnel masquerading as civilians had remained behind in Azerbaijan and that Azeri rebels against Iranian rule had been given Soviet armaments to prevent the Iranian government from resuming control of the province. On May 21, 1946, however, a UN Security Council investigative team reported that it had found "no trace whatever of Soviet troops, equipment or means of transport" in Azerbaijan and that there as elsewhere in Iran all Soviet forces had been evacuated on or before May 6. The forceful diplomatic support that the Iranian government received from the United States in this crisis undoubtedly emboldened its officials in taking a firm stance against Soviet demands for a continuing presence within Iran. This was evidence of early U.S. interest in excluding the Soviet Union from the economically and strategically important Middle Eastern region.

Primary Source

Negotiations begun by the Prime Minister of Iran in Moscow with leaders of the Government of the Union of Soviet Socialist Republics and continued in Teheran, after the arrival of the Soviet Ambassador, were ended April 4, 1946 and complete agreement was reached on all problems, namely:

1. Red Army troops will evacuate all Iranian territory within one and one-half months from Sunday March 24, 1946.
2. An agreement for the formation of a joint Iranian-Soviet oil company and its terms will be submitted to the fifteenth Majlis for its approval within seven months after March 24.

With regard to Azerbaijan, since it is [an] internal Iranian affair, peaceful arrangements will be made between the Iranian

government and the people of Azerbaijan for carrying out of reforms, in accordance with existing laws and in a benevolent spirit toward the people of Azerbaijan.

Source: U.S.S.R. Embassy, Washington, D.C., *Information Bulletin* 6 (1946): 299.

17. United Nations Security Council, Resolution Adopted at Its 30th Meeting, April 4, 1946

Introduction

Negotiations between Soviet and Iranian diplomats over the presence of Soviet forces in Iran continued for several months in early 1946. On March 26, 1946, Andrei Gromyko, the Soviet representative to the United Nations (UN), reported to the UN Security Council that the two countries had reached agreement on the evacuation of Soviet forces, which had begun on March 2 and, he anticipated, would be completed within the next five to six weeks. U.S. secretary of state James F. Byrnes then, on March 29, introduced a Security Council resolution welcoming this development and in particular the fact that Soviet withdrawal was not connected to negotiations on other subjects, namely oil concessions in Iran, then in progress between Iranian and Soviet officials. The resolution recognized that logistical considerations made it difficult, if not impossible, to speed up by much the scheduled timetable for withdrawals and expressed the hope that the continued presence of some Soviet troops would not be used to pressure Iran in other ongoing negotiations. So long as the Soviet Union continued to remove its forces as anticipated, the Security Council therefore decided to defer any further discussion of the situation in Iran until May 6. The 11-member Security Council passed this resolution with 9 affirmative votes and 1 abstention, while the Soviet representative absented himself and therefore could not vote.

Primary Source

Taking note of the statements of the Iranian Representative that the Iranian appeal to the Council arises from the presence of Soviet troops in Iran and their continued presence there beyond the date stipulated for their withdrawal in the Tripartite Treaty of January 29, 1942:

Taking note of the replies dated April 3rd of the Soviet Government and the Iranian Government pursuant to the request of the Secretary-General for information as to the status of the negotiations between the two Governments and as to whether the withdrawal of Soviet troops from Iran is conditional upon agreement on other subjects; and in particular taking note of and relying upon the assurances of the Soviet Government that the withdrawal of Soviet troops from Iran has already commenced; that it is the intention of the Soviet Government to proceed with the withdrawal of its troops as rapidly as possible; that the Soviet Government expects the withdrawal of all Soviet troops from the whole of Iran to be completed within five or six weeks; and that the proposals under negotiation between the Iranian Government and the Soviet Government "are not connected with the withdrawal of Soviet troops":

Being solicitous to avoid any possibility of the presence of Soviet troops in Iran being used to influence the course of the negotiations between the Governments of Iran and the Soviet Union; and recognizing that the withdrawal of all Soviet troops from the whole of Iran cannot be completed in a substantially shorter period of time than that within which the Soviet Government has declared it to be its intention to complete such withdrawal:

Resolved that the Council defer further proceedings on the Iranian appeal until May 6, at which time the Soviet Government and the Iranian Government are requested to report to the Council whether the withdrawal of all Soviet troops from the whole of Iran has been completed and at which time the Council shall consider what, if any, further proceedings on the Iranian appeal are required;

Provided, however, that if in the meantime either the Soviet Government or the Iranian Government or any member of the Security Council reports to the Secretary-General any developments which may retard or threaten to retard the prompt withdrawal of Soviet troops from Iran, in accordance with the assurances of the Soviet Union to the Council, the Secretary-General shall immediately call to the attention of the Council such reports which shall be considered as the first item on the agenda.

Source: "Security Council: Discussion of Soviet-Iranian Matters," *Department of State Bulletin* 14(354) (1946): 621.

18. President Harry S. Truman, Special Message to the Congress on Greece and Turkey, The Truman Doctrine, March 12, 1947

Introduction

The growing economic and military weakness of Great Britain was one reason why the United States gradually assumed the role of being the major protagonist in the developing Cold War in the Middle East and elsewhere in the world. In February 1947 British officials informed the U.S. government that economic difficulties prevented them from continuing their previous aid to Greece and Turkey, countries bordering the strategically important supply routes for Middle Eastern oil. In Greece a civil war between

communists and noncommunists was in progress, while Turkey faced Soviet pressure to grant the Russians partial control of the Dardanelles straits separating Europe and Asia, the only route that Soviet vessels could take to pass from the Black Sea to the Mediterranean. U.S. president Harry S. Truman responded on March 12, 1947. In an address before the U.S. Congress, he laid out foreign policy guidelines for the United States in the early days of the Cold War that subsequently became known as the Truman Doctrine. At heart, the policy was one that mandated an active role for the United States in containing the spread of communism around the world. Truman specifically requested aid, primarily financial, for Greece and Turkey but placed this in the broader context of a wide-ranging international communist threat around the world, which he argued mandated U.S. assistance to any nation menaced by either internal or external communist forces. He portrayed a world divided between the forces of freedom and democracy and authoritarian totalitarianism and effectively pledged virtually unlimited U.S. assistance to the former. In this case, the aid that Truman envisaged was primarily financial, which Congress granted by appropriating $400 million to the two countries. The Truman Doctrine laid the groundwork for the Marshall Plan, announced three months later, that extended similar aid to all of Western Europe. More broadly, the Truman Doctrine also formed the backbone of America's Cold War policy and led to both financial and military entanglements throughout the world, including the Korean War and the Vietnam War. Truman's speech was drafted in part by future secretary of state Dean Acheson, who later stated that although he might have exaggerated the communist threat and depicted the international situation in overly black-and-white apocalyptic terms, such tactics were necessary to win support for these policies from the somewhat reluctant American people and their representatives in Congress.

Primary Source

The gravity of the situation which confronts the world today necessitates my appearance before a joint session of the Congress. The foreign policy and the national security of this country are involved.

One aspect of the present situation which I wish to present to you at this time for your consideration and decision concerns Greece and Turkey. The United States has received from the Greek government an urgent appeal for financial and economic assistance. Preliminary reports from the American economic mission now in Greece and reports from the American ambassador in Greece corroborate the statement of the Greek government that assistance is imperative if Greece is to survive as a free nation.

I do not believe that the American people and the Congress wish to turn a deaf ear to the appeal of the Greek government.

Greece is not a rich country. Lack of sufficient natural resources has always forced the Greek people to work hard to make both ends meet. Since 1940, this industrious and peace-loving country has suffered invasion, four years of cruel enemy occupation, and bitter internal strife.

When forces of liberation entered Greece they found that the retreating Germans had destroyed virtually all the railways, roads, port facilities, communications, and merchant marine. More than a thousand villages had been burned. Eighty-five percent of the children were tubercular. Livestock, poultry, and draft animals had almost disappeared. Inflation had wiped out practically all savings. As a result of these tragic conditions, a militant minority, exploiting human want and misery, was able to create political chaos which, until now, has made economic recovery impossible.

Greece is today without funds to finance the importation of those goods which are essential to bare subsistence. Under these circumstances the people of Greece cannot make progress in solving their problems of reconstruction. Greece is in desperate need of financial and economic assistance to enable it to resume purchases of food, clothing, fuel, and seeds. These are indispensable for the subsistence of its people and are obtainable only from abroad. Greece must have help to import the goods necessary to restore internal order and security so essential for economic and political recovery.

The Greek government has also asked for the assistance of experienced American administrators, economists, and technicians to insure that the financial and other aid given to Greece shall be used effectively in creating a stable and self-sustaining economy and in improving its public administration.

The very existence of the Greek state is today threatened by the terrorist activities of several thousand armed men, led by Communists, who defy the government's authority at a number of points, particularly along the northern boundaries. A commission appointed by the United Nations Security Council is at present investigating disturbed conditions in northern Greece and alleged border violations along the frontier between Greece, on the one hand, and Albania, Bulgaria, and Yugoslavia, on the other. Meanwhile, the Greek government is unable to cope with the situation. The Greek Army is small and poorly equipped. It needs supplies and equipment if it is to restore the authority of the government throughout Greek territory.

Greece must have assistance if it is to become a self-supporting and self-respecting democracy. The United States must supply this assistance. We have already extended to Greece certain types of relief and economic aid but these are inadequate. There is no other country to which democratic Greece can turn. No other nation is willing and able to provide the necessary support for a democratic Greek government.

The British government, which has been helping Greece, can give no further financial or economic aid after March 31. Great Britain finds itself under the necessity of reducing or liquidating its commitments in several parts of the world, including Greece.

We have considered how the United Nations might assist in this crisis. But the situation is an urgent one requiring immediate action, and the United Nations and its related organizations are not in a position to extend help of the kind that is required.

It is important to note that the Greek government has asked for our aid in utilizing effectively the financial and other assistance we may give to Greece and in improving its public administration. It is of the utmost importance that we supervise the use of any funds made available to Greece in such a manner that each dollar spent will count toward making Greece self-supporting and will help to build an economy in which a healthy democracy can flourish.

No government is perfect. One of the chief virtues of a democracy, however, is that its defects are always visible and under democratic processes can be pointed out and corrected. The government of Greece is not perfect. Nevertheless, it represents 85 percent of the members of the Greek Parliament who were chosen in an election last year. Foreign observers, including 692 Americans, considered this election to be a fair expression of the views of the Greek people.

The Greek government has been operating in an atmosphere of chaos and extremism. It has made mistakes. The extension of aid by this country does not mean that the United States condones everything that the Greek government has done or will do. We have condemned in the past, and we condemn now, extremist measures of the right or the left. We have in the past advised tolerance, and we advise tolerance now.

Greece's neighbor, Turkey, also deserves our attention. The future of Turkey as an independent and economically sound state is clearly no less important to the freedom-loving peoples of the world than the future of Greece. The circumstances in which Turkey finds itself today are considerably different from those of Greece. Turkey has been spared the disasters that have beset Greece. And during the war, the United States and Great Britain furnished Turkey with material aid. Nevertheless, Turkey now needs our support.

Since the war, Turkey has sought financial assistance from Great Britain and the United States for the purpose of effecting that modernization necessary for the maintenance of its national integrity. That integrity is essential to the preservation of order in the Middle East.

The British government has informed us that, owing to its own difficulties, it can no longer extend financial or economic aid to

Turkey. As in the case of Greece, if Turkey is to have the assistance it needs, the United States must supply it. We are the only country able to provide that help.

I am fully aware of the broad implications involved if the United States extends assistance to Greece and Turkey, and I shall discuss these implications with you at this time.

One of the primary objectives of the foreign policy of the United States is the creation of conditions in which we and other nations will be able to work out a way of life free from coercion. This was a fundamental issue in the war with Germany and Japan. Our victory was won over countries which sought to impose their will and their way of life upon other nations.

To insure the peaceful development of nations, free from coercion, the United States has taken a leading part in establishing the United Nations. The United Nations is designed to make possible lasting freedom and independence for all its members. We shall not realize our objectives, however, unless we are willing to help free peoples to maintain their free institutions and their national integrity against aggressive movements that seek to impose upon them totalitarian regimes. This is no more than a frank recognition that totalitarian regimes imposed on free peoples, by direct or indirect aggression, undermine the foundations of international peace and hence the security of the United States.

The peoples of a number of countries of the world have recently had totalitarian regimes forced upon them against their will. The government of the United States has made frequent protests against coercion and intimidation, in violation of the Yalta Agreement, in Poland, Rumania, and Bulgaria. I must also state that in a number of other countries there have been similar developments.

At the present moment in world history nearly every nation must choose between alternative ways of life. The choice is too often not a free one.

One way of life is based upon the will of the majority, and is distinguished by free institutions, representative government, free elections, guarantees of individual liberty, freedom of speech and religion, and freedom from political oppression. The second way of life is based upon the will of a minority forcibly imposed upon the majority. It relies upon terror and oppression, a controlled press and radio, fixed elections, and the suppression of personal freedoms.

I believe that it must be the policy of the United States to support free peoples who are resisting attempted subjugation by armed minorities or by outside pressures. I believe that we must assist free peoples to work out their own destinies in their own way. I believe that our help should be primarily through economic and financial aid, which is essential to economic stability and orderly political processes.

The world is not static and the status quo is not sacred. But we cannot allow changes in the status quo in violation of the Charter of the United Nations by such methods as coercion or by such subterfuges as political infiltration. In helping free and independent nations to maintain their freedom, the United States will be giving effect to the principles of the Charter of the United Nations.

It is necessary only to glance at a map to realize that the survival and integrity of the Greek nation are of grave importance in a much wider situation. If Greece should fall under the control of an armed minority, the effect upon its neighbor, Turkey, would be immediate and serious. Confusion and disorder might well spread throughout the entire Middle East. Moreover, the disappearance of Greece as an independent state would have a profound effect upon those countries in Europe whose peoples are struggling against great difficulties to maintain their freedoms and their independence while they repair the damages of war.

It would be an unspeakable tragedy if these countries, which have struggled so long against overwhelming odds, should lose that victory for which they sacrificed so much. Collapse of free institutions and loss of independence would be disastrous not only for them but for the world. Discouragement and possibly failure would quickly be the lot of neighboring peoples striving to maintain their freedom and independence.

Should we fail to aid Greece and Turkey in this fateful hour, the effect will be far-reaching to the West as well as to the East. We must take immediate and resolute action.

I therefore ask the Congress to provide authority for assistance to Greece and Turkey in the amount of $400 million for the period ending June 30, 1948. In requesting these funds, I have taken into consideration the maximum amount of relief assistance which would be furnished to Greece out of the $350 million which I recently requested that the Congress authorize for the prevention of starvation and suffering in countries devastated by the war.

In addition to funds, I ask the Congress to authorize the detail of American civilian and military personnel to Greece and Turkey, at the request of those countries, to assist in the tasks of reconstruction, and for the purpose of supervising the use of such financial and material assistance as may be furnished. I recommend that authority also be provided for the instruction and training of selected Greek and Turkish personnel.

Finally, I ask that the Congress provide authority which will permit the speediest and most effective use, in terms of needed commodities, supplies, and equipment, of such funds as may be authorized.

If further funds, or further authority, should be needed for purposes indicated in this message, I shall not hesitate to bring the situation before the Congress. On this subject the executive and legislative branches of the government must work together.

This is a serious course upon which we embark. I would not recommend it except that the alternative is much more serious.

The United States contributed $341 billion toward winning World War II. This is an investment in world freedom and world peace. The assistance that I am recommending for Greece and Turkey amounts to little more than one-tenth of 1 percent of this investment. It is only common sense that we should safeguard this investment and make sure that it was not in vain.

The seeds of totalitarian regimes are nurtured by misery and want. They spread and grow in the evil soil of poverty and strife. They reach their full growth when the hope of a people for a better life has died. We must keep that hope alive.

The free peoples of the world look to us for support in maintaining their freedoms. If we falter in our leadership, we may endanger the peace of the world—and we shall surely endanger the welfare of our own nation.

Great responsibilities have been placed upon us by the swift movement of events. I am confident that the Congress will face these responsibilities squarely.

Source: Harry S. Truman, *Public Papers of the Presidents of the United States: Harry S. Truman, 1947* (Washington, DC: U.S. Government Printing Office, 1963), 176–180.

19. Loy Henderson, U.S. Ambassador to Iran, Communiqué to the U.S. Department of State Regarding the Coup in Iran, August 23, 1953

Introduction

By the early 1950s, the United States had taken on commitments that implied that it would oppose the emergence of communist regimes anywhere in the world. Successive Cold War presidents in the United States turned to the Central Intelligence Agency (CIA) to help overthrow foreign governments that appeared unfriendly to the United States, due to either their ideological complexion or their antagonism toward U.S. economic or strategic interests. The first occasion when the CIA was instrumental in successfully ousting another government came in Iran in 1953. Until the early Cold War, Iran had been largely under British and Russian influence.

The British Anglo-Iranian Oil Company controlled Iran's petroleum resources, and during World War II the British and Russians overthrew the Nazi-oriented monarch, Shah Reza Pahlavi, and jointly occupied Iran to deny these to Germany and safeguard supply routes to the Soviet Union. In 1946 British and Russian forces left Iran, the Russians at least reluctantly, as they had hoped to set up a pro-Soviet republic in the north that they had previously controlled. As early as World War II, U.S. diplomats already believed that their own nation, which they felt that the Iranians knew was untainted by past exploitation of Iran, had an opportunity to win that country's loyalties. In 1951 the Iranian government announced its intention of nationalizing the Anglo-Iranian Oil Company; the British, who controlled the refineries, withdrew their technicians and blockaded all exports of Iranian oil, provoking severe economic difficulties within Iran. The government headed by Prime Minister Mohammed Mossadegh stood firm and eventually, after the young shah, Mohammad Reza Pahlavi, had made an abortive attempt to replace him, declared a national emergency and took control of the Iranian military. In alliance with radical Muslims and the leftist Soviet-leaning Tudeh party, in 1952 Mossadegh implemented socialist reforms, especially in agriculture, and broke diplomatic relations with the United Kingdom. Britain turned to the United States for assistance, characterizing Mossadegh as a radical who was turning toward communism and steering Iran into the Soviet orbit. The administration of Republican president Dwight D. Eisenhower, which took office in January 1953, proved sympathetic and authorized the CIA to spend up to US$1 million removing Mossadegh. CIA agents in Tehran spread rumors and disinformation and in some cases acted as agents provocateurs. Economic problems intensified, and Mossadegh suspended parliament and extended his emergency powers. The CIA sought to persuade the indecisive young shah to dismiss Mossadegh, while Mossadegh urged the monarch to leave the country. Eventually, in 1953, the shah dismissed Mossadegh, but the latter refused to step down from office, and the shah took refuge in Italy. Major protests for and against the monarchy were held throughout the country, as Iranians of all political stripes assumed that before long Mossadegh would declare Iran a republic and himself head of state. Promonarchy forces, heavily funded by the CIA, gained the upper hand, and Iranian tanks and troops entered Tehran, the Iranian capital, and besieged the prime minister's residence until Mossadegh surrendered. He was subsequently put on trial for treason and sentenced to three years in prison. General Fazlollah Zahedi, one of the military leaders who arrested Mossadegh, became prime minister, and the shah flew back and resumed power. From then until his overthrow in 1979, Iran would be a key U.S. ally in the Middle East. Speaking to Loy Henderson, the U.S. ambassador in Iran, the shah expressed his fervent gratitude to the Americans for their role in his return, adroitly stressed his wish to carry out social reforms that would benefit the poorest Iranians, and declared that a communist regime was the only alternative to his own. He made it very clear that to carry out such policies he badly needed American aid, and he also discreetly intimated that the Americans should not "interfere in personnel matters of [the Iranian] Government." The shah soon reached an agreement with the British and Americans, under whose terms the foreign oil companies still made substantial profits as large amounts of Iranian oil once more flowed to world markets. These revenues enabled the shah to modernize his country and make it a strong military state, but his authoritarian policies, his persecution of opponents, and the social disruptions caused by his reforms eventually alienated many Iranians and were among the reasons why in 1979 an Islamic fundamentalist revolt ended his rule. Only in the late 1990s did the U.S. government publicly acknowledge the extent of CIA involvement in the overthrow of Mossadegh. The eventual success of this undertaking subsequently emboldened CIA director Allen W. Dulles and other agency officials to try to orchestrate comparable operations against several other foreign governments—in Guatemala, Cuba, the Dominican Republic, and Chile—that U.S. leaders found unpalatable.

Primary Source

At Shah's request that I visit him privately without publicity, I saw him six o'clock this evening. Pirnia, master of ceremonies, who met me rear entrance Palace, said I would find Shah changed man. He was right. Shah showed vigor, decisiveness and certain amount clear thinking which I had not found in him before. Only time will determine whether this change merely temporary result discovery that people of country had deeper sense of loyalty him than he had realized. In any event, I did not find hesitation, brooding, discouragement and air "what can I do" which I had noticed practically all previous conversations.

He greeted me warmly and expressed deep appreciation of friendship which US had shown him and Iran during period. I read oral message from President to which I had taken liberty of adding introductory paragraph as follows: "I congratulate you for the great moral courage which you displayed at a critical time in your country's history. I am convinced that by your action you contributed much to the preservation of the independence and to the future prosperity of Iran." The Shah wept as I read this message and asked me in reply to tell the President how grateful he was for interest which President and Government of US had shown in Iran. He would always feel deeply indebted for this proof of genuine friendship. Miracle of saving Iran which had just been wrought was due to friendship West, to patriotism Iranian people and to intermediation God. It impossible for him believe so many factors could have contributed simultaneously to this salvation his country unless Providence had so willed.

Shah dwelt for some time on part which "common people of Iran" had played. People of poorest classes who were ill-clad and hungry had been willing sacrifice their lives on his behalf. He could never forget this and he would never be satisfied until hunger had

been eliminated from his country. Iran had been saved but victory would be short-lived unless substantial aid came from US immediately. No time could be lost. This was Iran's last chance to survive as an independent country. I said I agreed that if present government should fail, Communism seemed to be only alternative. He said "if I fail, no alternative but Communism. People have shown their trust in me and it rests upon me prove their trust merited. I must help new government live up to expectations and I cannot do that without quick aid from the US. How soon can this aid come and in what quantities and form?"

I replied US prepared extend aid but it must be given in orderly way and in circumstances which would be acceptable US public as well as Iranian public. I had been endeavoring all day to get in touch with financial and economic experts new government in order begin conversations. If he wished quick aid, he should take steps see that conversations begin immediately. He promised talk to Zahedi this evening in effort accelerate.

Shah said he not completely happy re Cabinet which Zahedi had presented him on his arrival. Same old faces which had been rotating in office for years. He had hoped for Cabinet which would stimulate country particularly youth. He had been told Americans had insisted Amini be included as Minister Finance and that Cabinet be selected before his arrival and presented to him as *fait accompli*. I told him information incorrect.

I do not know who had selected Amini. Certainly not Americans. There had been feeling in Embassy that Cabinet should be formed quickly so Government could begin to function earliest possible moment, no idea endeavoring have members selected without consultation with him. He said he relieved hear me say this. He sure Americans would not begin trying interfere in personnel matters of Government. They should know from experience this would be surest way change friendship into suspicion. Particularly important no interference in future in his control armed forces. Neither foreigners nor Iranians should come between him and army. Razmara had been unsuccessful in trying to separate army from Shah. Mosadeq had been able to break down army unity. It was his task and it would be difficult and delicate one to rebuild army as solid block loyal to him. Otherwise there would be no stability in country.

I asked if I to infer he dissatisfied with way Zahedi had been conducting affairs or if he under impression Zahedi attempting exert authority which should be vested in him. He replied negative insisting he had complete confidence in Zahedi. He did not believe Zahedi had ambitions other than serve Iran and its Shah, nevertheless he thought that certain advisers around Zahedi were pressing latter to take actions without proper consultation with him. He had had several discussions with Zahedi and was sure that he had achieved understanding with him re extent consultation in future.

I said Zahedi and many other army officers had risked their lives for Shah and country. I hoped Shah would show in some way his appreciation. He said he intended to do so but he must disappoint many retired army officers expecting resume active service. Most of them outmoded, some corrupt. He could give them decorations and other awards but not jobs.

In discussing failure of plans on night of August 15 he said someone must have betrayed them. Could it have been British agents?

I expressed surprise. I pointed out on various previous conversations he had said if Iran to be saved necessary for British and Americans to have common policy re Iran and work with mutual confidence. This situation had been achieved and I hoped he would never again make either to British or Americans remarks which might tend undermine that mutual confidence. I knew for fact that British were dealing honestly with him and he should get out of his head once for all idea they engaging in double dealing. He said he relieved hear this and believed me. I told him Communists espionage facilities well developed. They had many dangerous hearing devices. He said perhaps they had broken down code telegrams exchanged between Tehran and Ramsar. I agreed this quite possible.

I said if Iran wanted British and US pursue common policy re Iran Government should not expect receive substantial aid from US while it was making British whipping boy. I worried lest when Majlis reassembled there would again take place long tirades against British. I also concerned re Tudeh press in this respect. He said he would endeavor arrange for those members Majlis who had not resigned to meet and vote dissolution Majlis. Elections would then be held in spring so Government could accomplish much without interference Majlis. It was his intention also not to convene Senate until new Majlis elected. He intended taking steps also to reward in some way although not with Cabinet positions small band Majlis members who had at risk lives refused resign. It also his intention completely root out subversive press. He determined completely wreck Tudeh organization while at same time maintaining as correct relations as possible with USSR.

In terminating conversation he again urged me impress on US Government importance receiving substantial and immediate financial and economic aid. In absence Majlis it would be difficult arrange for loan. Therefore most of this aid must be in form grant. I said if this true we might be severely hampered in our efforts. For instance it might be easier quickly to obtain funds for road building and similar programs through loans rather than grants. He promised look into legal aspects this problem but said he feared it might be impossible for Iranian Government to accept loans without consent Majlis.

HENDERSON

Source: U.S. Department of State, *Foreign Relations of the United States, 1952–1954: Iran, 1952–1954,* Vol. 10 (Washington, DC: U.S. Government Printing Office, 1989), 762–765.

20. The Baghdad Pact, February 24, 1955 [Excerpt]

Introduction

The Baghdad Pact was originally a mutual security agreement, modeled on the North Atlantic Treaty Organization (NATO), that Iraq, Turkey, Pakistan, Iran, and the United Kingdom signed in 1955. The United States encouraged the development of this organization by promising military and economic aid and established a military liaison arrangement with it but initially chose not to join itself, fearing that doing so might lose it the goodwill of various other Middle Eastern states that President Dwight D. Eisenhower's administration also sought to cultivate. The objective was to encourage the signatories to collaborate against potential Soviet expansionism in the area by erecting a bastion of anticommunist states along the Soviet Union's southwestern frontier. The alliance was originally known as the Middle Eastern Treaty Organization (METO). After Iraq, the only Arab member, withdrew in 1958 in the aftermath of a bloody revolution led by the leftist and Moscow-oriented Baath Party, the United States joined as a full member, and the grouping became the Central Treaty Organization (CENTO). The organization proved largely ineffective in preventing the spread of Soviet influence in the Middle East. During the 1960s and 1970s, the Soviet Union simply bypassed the CENTO states to develop close military and economic ties with Egypt, Syria, Iraq, Yemen, Somalia, and Libya, establishing bases in Egypt, Somalia, and Yemen. CENTO lacked a single military command structure, and the links between the member states remained relatively loose. The organization did facilitate American access to bases in Iran with useful communications and intelligence capabilities, while from the late 1950s onward Pakistan allowed the United States to utilize airfields on its own soil to launch U-2 espionage and surveillance flights over Soviet territory. At times Great Britain also made use of bases in Pakistan and, like the United States, also on occasion made use of similar Turkish facilities, although the latter arrangements were organized through the NATO alliance. Never a particularly successful alliance, CENTO largely fell into desuetude after Turkey invaded Cyprus in 1974, causing the British to withdraw their forces from CENTO. In 1979 Islamic radicals overthrew the Iranian monarchy, whose collapse brought the formal end of CENTO.

Primary Source

Whereas the friendly and brotherly relations existing between Iraq and Turkey are in constant progress, and in order to complement the contents of the Treaty of friendship and good neighbourhood concluded between His Majesty The King of Iraq and His Excellency The President of the Turkish Republic signed in Ankara on the 29th of March, 1946 which recognised the fact that peace and security between the two countries is an integral part of the peace and security of all the Nations of the world and in particular the Nations of the Middle East, and that it is the basis for their foreign policies;

Whereas Article 11 of the Treaty of Joint Defence and Economic Co-operation between the Arab League States provides that no provision of that Treaty shall in any way affect, or is designed to affect, any of the rights and obligations accruing to the contracting parties from the United Nations Charter;

And having realised the great responsibilities borne by them in their capacity as members of the United Nations concerned with the maintenance of peace and security in the Middle East region which necessitate taking the required measures in accordance with Article 51 of the United Nations Charter;

They have been fully convinced of the necessity of concluding a pact fulfilling these aims and for that purpose have appointed as their Plenipotentiaries … who, having communicated their full powers, found to be in good and due form, have agreed as follows:

Article 1

Consistent with Article 51 of the United Nations Charter the High Contracting Parties will co-operate for their security and defence. Such measures as they agree to take to give effect to this co-operation may form the subject of special agreements with each other.

Article 2

In order to ensure the realisation and effect application of the co-operation provided for in Article 1 above, the competent authorities of the High Contracting Parties will determine the measures to be taken as soon as the present Pact enters into force. These measures will become operative as soon as they have been approved by the Governments of the High Contracting Parties.

Article 3

The High Contracting Parties undertake to refrain from any interference whatsoever in each other's internal affairs. They will settle any dispute between themselves in a peaceful way in accordance with the United Nations Charter.

Article 4

The High Contracting Parties declare that the dispositions of the present Pact are not in contradiction with any of the international obligations contracted by either of them with any third state or states. They do not derogate from, and cannot be interpreted as derogating from, the said international obligations. The High Contracting Parties undertake not to enter into any international obligation incompatible with the present Pact.

Article 5

This Pact shall be open for accession to any member state of the Arab League or any other state actively concerned with the security and peace in this region and which is fully recognised by both of the High Contracting Parties. Accession shall come into force from the date of which the instrument of accession of the state concerned is deposited with the Ministry of Foreign Affairs of Iraq.

Any acceding State Party to the present Pact may conclude special agreements, in accordance with Article 1, with one or more states Parties to the present Pact. The competent authority of any acceding State may determine measures in accordance with Article 2. These measures will become operative as soon as they have been approved by the Governments of the Parties concerned.

Article 6

A Permanent Council at Ministerial level will be set up to function within the frame work of the purposes of this Pact when at least four Powers become parties to the Pact.

The Council will draw up its own rules of procedure.

Article 7

This Pact remains in force for a period of five years renewable for other five year periods. Any Contracting Party may withdraw from the Pact by notifying the other parties in writing of its desire to do so, six months before the expiration of any of the above-mentioned periods, in which case the Pact remains valid for the other Parties.

[…]

Source: "Pact of Mutual Co-Operation between Iraq and Turkey, February 24, 1955," *United Nations Treaty Series* 233, no. 3264.

21. Soviet Ministry of Foreign Affairs, Statement on Security in the Middle East and Soviet Reaction to the Baghdad Pact, April 16, 1955 [Excerpts]

Introduction

Soviet reaction when Great Britain, Iraq, Turkey, Pakistan, and Iran signed the Baghdad Pact in February 1955 was predictably hostile. Seeking to discredit the arrangement, the Soviet Union publicly condemned it, together with the Southeast Asian Treaty Organization (SEATO) that the United States had recently established, as a means whereby the Western powers sought to establish or continue their "colonial enslavement" of those regions, in defiance of rising nationalist and independence movements. Soviet diplomats portrayed their own country, by contrast, as a longtime champion of anticolonial struggles throughout the Near and Middle East, a characterization that glossed over Soviet attempts in the mid-1940s to establish its own influence in both Iran and Turkey. In what might have been interpreted as a veiled threat, the Soviet Foreign Ministry, mentioning the Soviet Union's close proximity to the area, urged all states in the region to decline "to take part in aggressive military blocs," a policy that would be "an important prerequisite to the ensuring of their security" and the "best guarantee" that they would not be "drawn into dangerous military adventures." Expressing its own backing for the principles that all states should respect others' sovereignty and independence and refrain from intervention in each other's internal affairs, the Soviet Union promised its own support to those nations in the Near and Middle East that chose to observe these principles. The statement was a clear indication that Middle Eastern countries that rejected close relations with the Western powers could almost certainly expect Soviet assistance in following such a course. Inexorably, and despite each Great Power's declarations to the contrary, by the mid-1950s the Middle East was becoming a focus of Cold War rivalries.

Primary Source

The situation in the Near and Middle East has recently become considerably more tense. The explanation of this is that certain western powers have been making new attempts to draw the countries of the Near and Middle East into the military groupings which are being set up as appendages to the aggressive North Atlantic bloc.

[. . .]

It is not difficult to see that, lying at the basis of the policy of setting military groupings in the Near and Middle East—just as in the establishment of the aggressive military grouping in South-East Asia (the so-called S.E.A.T.O.)—is the desire of certain western powers for the colonial enslavement of these countries. The western powers wish to carry on exploiting the people of the countries of the Near and Middle East so as to enrich their big monopolies which are making greedy use of the natural wealth of these countries. Unable to establish and preserve their domination by the old methods, these powers are trying to involve the countries of the Near and Middle East in aggressive blocs, on the false pretext that this is in the interests of the defence of the countries of this area.

Military blocs in the Near and Middle East are needed, not by the countries of that area, but by those aggressive American circles which are trying to establish domination there. They are also needed by those British circles which, by means of these blocs, are trying to retain and restore their shaken positions, in spite of the vital interests of the peoples of the Near and Middle East who have taken the road of independent national development.

[. . .]

As has frequently happened in the past, now, too, efforts are being made to cloak the aggressive nature of the Near and Middle Eastern plans of the United States and Britain with ridiculous fabrications about a "Soviet menace" to the countries of that area. Such inventions have nothing in common with reality, for it is a matter of record that the underlying basis of the Soviet Union's foreign policy is an unalterable desire to ensure peace among the peoples, a peace founded on observance of the principles of equality, non-interference in domestic affairs, and respect for national independence and state sovereignty.

From the very first days of its existence, the Soviet state has decisively condemned the policy of imperialist usurpations and colonial oppression; and it annulled all the unequal treaties which the tsarist government had concluded with the countries of the east.

Regarding the national aspirations of the peoples of the east with full understanding and sympathy, the Soviet government was the first to recognise the independence of Afghanistan and helped her to restore her state sovereignty.

The Soviet government cancelled the tsarist government's unequal treaties with Iran, and transferred to her great material wealth which Russia owned in Iran.

During the years of Turkey's hard struggle for national independence, the Soviet Union stretched out the hand of friendship and gave her all-round assistance—a fact which played a decisive part in the struggle of the Turkish people against the foreign interventionists.

The Soviet government was the first to recognise Saudi Arabia as an independent state and supported the struggle for state independence of Yemen, Syria and Lebanon, and Egypt's rightful demands for the withdrawal of foreign troops from her territory.

In international bodies, the Soviet government always supports the legitimate demands of the countries of the Near and Middle East aimed at strengthening their national independence and state sovereignty.

The Soviet Union has unswervingly pursued, and continues to pursue a policy of peace and the easing of international tension.

Proof of this, in particular, can be seen in its proposal to end the arms drive; to prohibit atomic and hydrogen weapons; for an immediate and substantial reduction of armaments and, first and foremost, of the armaments of the five great powers; and for the establishment of a system of collective security in Europe.

[...]

Of course, the Soviet Union cannot remain indifferent to the situation arising in the region of the Near and Middle East, since the formation of these blocs and the establishment of foreign military bases on the territory of the countries of the Near and Middle East have a direct bearing on the security of the U.S.S.R. This attitude of the Soviet government should be all the more understandable since the U.S.S.R. is situated very close to these countries—something which cannot be said of other foreign powers, for instance, of the United States, which is thousands of kilometers from this area.

The refusal of the countries of the Near and Middle East to take part in aggressive military blocs would be an important prerequisite to the ensuring of their security, and the best guarantee of these countries not being drawn into dangerous military adventures.

Striving for the development of peaceful co-operation among all countries, the Soviet government is prepared to support and develop co-operation with the countries of the Near and Middle East, in the interests of strengthening peace in this area. In its declaration of February 9, 1955, the Supreme Soviet of the Union of Soviet Socialist Republics declared that it considered it of exceedingly great importance that relations among countries, large and small, should be based on those international principles which would facilitate the development of friendly co-operation among the nations, in conditions of a peaceful and tranquil life.

The Soviet Union believes that relations among states, and real security can be ensured on the basis of the practical application of the well-known principles enumerated in that declaration—namely: equality; non-interference in domestic affairs; non-aggression and the renunciation of encroachment on the territorial integrity of other states; and on respect for sovereignty and national independence.

The government of the Soviet Union would support any steps by the countries of the Near and Middle East towards putting these principles into practice in the relations between them and the Soviet Union, towards strengthening the national independence of these countries and consolidating peace and friendly co-operation among the peoples.

If the policy of pressure and threats with regard to the countries of the Near and Middle East is continued, the question should be examined by the United Nations Organisation.

Upholding the cause of peace, the Soviet government will defend the freedom and independence of the countries of the Near and Middle East and will oppose interference in their domestic affairs.

Source: *Soviet News*, no. 3146, April 19, 1955, pp. 1–2.

22. Nikita Khrushchev, "We Will Bury You" Speech, November 19, 1956

Introduction

Nikita Khrushchev, who eventually succeeded Joseph Stalin as secretary-general of the Soviet Communist Party and top Soviet leader, was less formidable than his predecessor but at times could be erratic. Khrushchev frequently expressed his hopes for "peaceful coexistence" with the West, believing that nonsocialist countries would either evolve into communist states or experience autonomous revolutions that were not fomented by Soviet operatives. Fearing the devastating potential impact of nuclear war, Khrushchev also sought to reach understandings on arms control. This did not, however, mean that he had abandoned his faith in communism, the political creed that he had embraced as a young factory worker before World War I. Khrushchev was also notorious for somewhat erratic behavior, especially when he had imbibed plentiful quantities of vodka. In mid-1956, shortly after Soviet troops brutally suppressed the Hungarian Revolution and before the resolution of the Suez Crisis that occurred when Israel, Great Britain, and France invaded Egypt, as the result of which the United States exerted economic pressure to force the three powers to withdraw, Khrushchev attended receptions at the Kremlin and the Polish embassy. In remarks at both venues he took the opportunity to condemn the Suez invasion while characterizing Soviet intervention in Hungary as a justifiable exercise in counterrevolution. Warning that "Fascist bands" sought to destroy communist parties in Italy, France, and elsewhere outside the Soviet sphere, Khrushchev proclaimed that "history is on our side" and warned the Western diplomats present that "We will bury you." In practice, the Russian words that Khrushchev used were less menacing than they appeared in translation and in the original meant something close to "We will attend your funeral." Khrushchev, who around this time had also threatened Soviet intervention if the Suez situation should not be swiftly resolved, apparently meant that the Western powers would collapse of their own volition, but the journalists present reported a somewhat sensational version of his remarks. Indeed, some years later Khrushchev himself looked back on this episode and commented that he had "got into trouble for it" when he had only wished to say that the working classes of the Western states would themselves overthrow their rulers. Khrushchev's speech nonetheless impelled all the Western ambassadors to leave, and the episode was widely reported around the world as an instance of Khrushchev's bullying, blustering style and was taken as a threat to the West. In the popular memory, "We will bury you" would become one of Khrushchev's best-remembered utterances.

Primary Source

Nikita Khrushchev

"We Will Bury You"

Reported in *The Times*, November 19, 1956

Sir William Hayter, the British Ambassador, and diplomatic representatives of other North Atlantic Treaty Organization countries, walked out from a Kremlin reception last night in protest at a speech by Mr. Khrushchev, the Soviet Communist Party chairman, in which he used the words "Fascist" and "bandits" in referring to Britain and France and Israel.

The reception was in honour of Mr. Gomulka, who was concluding his visit to Moscow.

Out of courtesy to Mr. Gomulka, the N.A.T.O. ambassadors and representative of Israel waited until Mr. Gomulka had responded with a toast that was devoid of references to Egypt or Hungary and limited to advocating friendly ties with the Soviet Union based on equality and mutual benefit. Immediately on the conclusion of the translation into Russian of Mr. Gomulka's toast, read in Polish, the western diplomatists strode from the long white and gold St. George's Hall.

Mr. Khrushchev declared that the "bandit-like attack by Britain, France, and their puppet, Israel, on Egypt is a desperate attempt by colonializers to regain their lost positions, to frighten the peoples of dependent countries with force. But the time has passed when imperialists could seize weak countries with impunity. The freedom-loving people of Egypt have administered a fitting rebuff to the aggressors, and its just struggle against foreign invaders has evoked warm support all over the world."

Mr. Khrushchev, words tumbling from his lips in rapid fashion, continued by extending his accusations against other Powers besides Britain, France, and Israel. "Feverish activity is now in progress on the part of all the forces of reaction against the forces of Socialism and democracy. Fascist bands are making frenzied attacks on the advanced detachments of the working class, on the Communist parties of France, Italy, and other countries."

At a reception this evening at the Polish Embassy, Mr. Khrushchev delivered himself of a longer but more mildly worded address criticizing the western Powers. However, most western ambassadors, including Sir William Hayter, restricted themselves to wandering to an adjoining room while Mr. Khrushchev spoke.

Moscow, Nov. 18.—In his speech Mr. Khrushchev, who appeared to be directing his remarks to the western diplomatists, said: "We say this not only for the socialist States, who are more akin to us. We base ourselves on the idea that we must peacefully co-exist. About the capitalist States, it doesn't depend on you whether or not we exist. If you don't like us, don't accept our invitations and don't invite us to come to see you. Whether you like it or not, history is on our side. We will bury you."

There was applause from Mr. Khrushchev's colleagues, and Mr. Gomulka, who had been standing at one side rather glumly, laughed.

Mr. Khrushchev said that many mistakes had been made in building socialism in the Soviet Union because of the lack of examples and the lack of personnel. He continued: "If we could have the revolution over again we would carry it out more sensibly and with smaller losses; but history does not repeat itself. The situation is favourable for us. If God existed, we would thank him for this.

"We had Hungary thrust upon us. We are very sorry that such a situation exists there. We are sure that the Hungarian working class will find the strength to overcome the difficulties. But most important is that the counter-revolution must be shattered."

Turning to Mr. Gomulka, he said: "I am sorry to be making such a speech on the territory of a foreign State. The western Powers are trying to denigrate Nasser. He is not a Communist. Politically, he is closer to those who are waging war on him and he has even put Communists in gaol.

"We sent sharp letters to Britain, France, and Israel—well, Israel, that was just for form, because, as you know, Israel carries no weight in the world, and if it plays any role it was just to start a fight. If Israel hadn't felt the support of Britain, France, and others, the Arabs would have been able to box her ears and she would have remained at peace.

"The situation is serious and we are realists. The fire must be put out. I think the British and French will be wise enough to withdraw their forces, and then Egypt will emerge stronger than ever. We must seek a *rapprochement*. We must seek a settlement so that coexistence will be peaceful and advantageous."

Referring to the Soviet Government's latest disarmament plan, he said: "You say we want war, but you have now got yourselves into a position I would call idiotic. (Mr. Mikoyan interjected: "Let's say delicate.") But we don't want to profit by it.

"If you withdraw you[r] troops from Germany, France, and Britain—I'm speaking of American troops—we will not stay one day in Poland, Hungary, and Rumania. But we, Mr. Capitalists, we are beginning to understand your methods. You have given us a lesson in Egypt. If we had a quarter of our present friendship for the Poles, Czechs, and Slovaks before the war, the war would never have started.

"Nobody should pretend to know the best methods of socialism. The Bulgarians, Poles, Yugoslavs, Rumanians, Czechs, and Soviets—all have their own; but, comrades, it is really better to hawk one's own wares, and if they are good, they will find a buyer on their own. So when our enemies try to bring us into conflict over which is the best method of socialism we reject this. It is not in the interests of socialism."

Source: "Ambassadors Walk Out," *London Times,* November 19, 1956. Reprinted with permission.

23. The Eisenhower Doctrine, January 5, 1957 [Excerpts]

Introduction

On January 5, 1957, U.S. president Dwight D. Eisenhower addressed a special joint session of the U.S. Congress regarding unfolding events in the Middle East. During the Suez Crisis the previous November when Britain, France, and Israel invaded Egypt and tried to retake the Suez Canal, only to retreat under U.S. financial and diplomatic pressure, the Soviet Union had threatened to intervene unless the attackers withdrew. Soviet leader Nikita Khrushchev had also recently intervened in the East European Soviet satellite nation of Hungary to prevent its secession from the Warsaw Pact, and Khrushchev had recently indulged in somewhat threatening utterances as to how his country would prevail in the Cold War. The Middle East had the world's most substantial oil reserves, strategic resources that were increasingly vital to the heavily energy-dependent U.S. domestic economy as well as to its war-making capacity. Convinced that the tumultuous political situation in the Middle East, where rising anti-Western nationalism and Arab resentment of Israel compounded other difficulties, had become a battleground of the Cold War, Eisenhower demanded that Congress grant him the military and financial resources to aid those Middle Eastern powers attempting to fend off communism, advocating a high level of U.S. involvement in the Middle East that became known as the Eisenhower Doctrine. Congress complied, thus initiating a period of extensive U.S. involvement in the Middle East that continues to this day. Ironically, American support for relatively conservative Arab and Middle Eastern regimes would win the United States the distrust of radical elements in the region.

Primary Source

To the Congress of the United States:

First may I express to you my deep appreciation of your courtesy in giving me, at some inconvenience to yourselves, this early opportunity of addressing you on a matter I deem to be of grave importance to our country.

In my forthcoming State of the Union Message, I shall review the international situation generally. There are worldwide hopes which we can reasonably entertain, and there are worldwide responsibilities which we must carry to make certain that freedom—including our own—may be secure.

There is, however, a special situation in the Middle East which I feel I should, even now, lay before you.

[. . .]

I. The Middle East has abruptly reached a new and critical stage in its long and important history. In past decades many of the countries in that area were not fully self-governing. Other nations exercised considerable authority in the area and the security of the region was largely built around their power. But since the First World War there has been a steady evolution toward self-government and independence. This development the United States has welcomed and has encouraged. Our country supports without reservation the full sovereignty and independence of each and every nation of the Middle East.

The evolution to independence has in the main been a peaceful process. But the area has been often troubled. Persistent crosscurrents of distrust and fear with raids back and forth across national boundaries have brought about a high degree of instability in much of the Mid East. Just recently there have been hostilities involving Western European nations that once exercised much influence in the area. Also the relatively large attack by Israel in October has intensified the basic differences between that nation and its Arab neighbors. All this instability has been heightened and, at times, manipulated by International Communism.

II. Russia's rulers have long sought to dominate the Middle East. That was true of the Czars and it is true of the Bolsheviks. The reasons are not hard to find. They do not affect Russia's security, for no one plans to use the Middle East as a base for aggression against Russia. Never for a moment has the United States entertained such a thought.

The Soviet Union has nothing whatsoever to fear from the United States in the Middle East, or anywhere else in the world, so long as its rulers do not themselves first resort to aggression.

That statement I make solemnly and emphatically.

Neither does Russia's desire to dominate the Middle East spring from its own economic interest in the area. Russia does not appreciably use or depend upon the Suez Canal. In 1955 Soviet traffic through the Canal represented only about three fourths of 1% of the total. The Soviets have no need for, and could provide no market for, the petroleum resources which constitute the principal natural wealth of the area. Indeed, the Soviet Union is a substantial exporter of petroleum products.

The reason for Russia's interest in the Middle East is solely that of power politics. Considering her announced purpose of Communizing the world, it is easy to understand her hope of dominating the Middle East.

This region has always been the crossroads of the continents of the Eastern Hemisphere. The Suez Canal enables the nations of Asia and Europe to carry on the commerce that is essential if these countries are to maintain well-rounded and prosperous economies. The Middle East provides a gateway between Eurasia and Africa.

It contains about two thirds of the presently known oil deposits of the world and it normally supplies the petroleum needs of many nations of Europe, Asia and Africa. The nations of Europe are peculiarly dependent upon this supply, and this dependency relates to transportation as well as to production! This has been vividly demonstrated since the closing of the Suez Canal and some of the pipelines. Alternate ways of transportation and, indeed, alternate sources of power can, if necessary, be developed. But these cannot be considered as early prospects.

These things stress the immense importance of the Middle East. If the nations of that area should lose their independence, if they were dominated by alien forces hostile to freedom, that would be both a tragedy for the area and for many other free nations whose economic life would be subject to near strangulation. Western Europe would be endangered just as though there had been no Marshall Plan, no North Atlantic Treaty Organization. The free nations of Asia and Africa, too, would be placed in serious jeopardy. And the countries of the Middle East would lose the markets upon which their economies depend. All this would have the most adverse, if not disastrous, effect upon our own nation's economic life and political prospects.

Then there are other factors which transcend the material. The Middle East is the birthplace of three great religions—Moslem, Christian and Hebrew. Mecca and Jerusalem are more than places on the map. They symbolize religions which teach that the spirit has supremacy over matter and that the individual has a dignity and rights of which no despotic government can rightfully deprive him. It would be intolerable if the holy places of the Middle East should be subjected to a rule that glorifies atheistic materialism.

International Communism, of course, seeks to mask its purposes of domination by expressions of good will and by superficially attractive offers of political, economic and military aid. But any free nation, which is the subject of Soviet enticement, ought, in elementary wisdom, to look behind the mask.

Remember Estonia, Latvia and Lithuania! In 1939 the Soviet Union entered into mutual assistance pacts with these then independent countries; and the Soviet Foreign Minister, addressing the Extraordinary Fifth Session of the Supreme Soviet in October 1939, solemnly and publicly declared that "we stand for the scrupulous and punctilious observance of the pacts on the basis of complete reciprocity, and we declare that all the nonsensical talk about the Sovietization of the Baltic countries is only to the interest of our common enemies and of all anti-Soviet provocateurs." Yet in 1940, Estonia, Latvia and Lithuania were forcibly incorporated into the Soviet Union.

Soviet control of the satellite nations of Eastern Europe has been forcibly maintained in spite of solemn promises of a contrary intent, made during World War II.

Stalin's death brought hope that this pattern would change. And we read the pledge of the Warsaw Treaty of 1955 that the Soviet Union would follow in satellite countries "the principles of mutual respect for their independence and sovereignty and non-interference in domestic affairs." But we have just seen the subjugation of Hungary by naked armed force. In the aftermath of this Hungarian tragedy, world respect for and belief in Soviet promises have sunk to a new low. International Communism needs and seeks a recognizable success.

Thus, we have these simple and indisputable facts:

1. The Middle East, which has always been coveted by Russia, would today be prized more than ever by International Communism.

2. The Soviet rulers continue to show that they do not scruple to use any means to gain their ends.

3. The free nations of the Mid East need, and for the most part want, added strength to assure their continued independence.

III. Our thoughts naturally turn to the United Nations as a protector of small nations. Its charter gives it primary responsibility for the maintenance of international peace and security. Our country has given the United Nations its full support in relation to the hostilities in Hungary and in Egypt. The United Nations was able to bring about a cease-fire and withdrawal of hostile forces from Egypt because it was dealing with governments and peoples who had a decent respect for the opinions of mankind as reflected in the United Nations General Assembly. But in the case of Hungary, the situation was different. The Soviet Union vetoed action by the Security Council to require the withdrawal of Soviet armed forces from Hungary. And it has shown callous indifference to the recommendations, even the censure, of the General Assembly. The United Nations can always be helpful, but it cannot be a wholly dependable protector of freedom when the ambitions of the Soviet Union are involved.

IV. Under all the circumstances I have laid before you, a greater responsibility now devolves upon the United States. We have shown, so that none can doubt, our dedication to the principle that force shall not be used internationally for any aggressive purpose and that the integrity and independence of the nations of the Middle East should be inviolate. Seldom in history has a nation's dedication to principle been tested as severely as ours during recent weeks.

There is general recognition in the Middle East, as elsewhere, that the United States does not seek either political or economic domination over any other people. Our desire is a world environment of freedom, not servitude. On the other hand many, if not all, of the nations of the Middle East are aware of the danger that stems from International Communism and welcome closer cooperation with the United States to realize for themselves the United Nations goals of independence, economic well-being and spiritual growth.

If the Middle East is to continue its geographic role of uniting rather than separating East and West; if its vast economic resources are to serve the well-being of the peoples there, as well as that of others; and if its cultures and religions and their shrines are to be preserved for the uplifting of the spirits of the peoples, then the United States must make more evident its willingness to support the independence of the freedom-loving nations of the area.

V. Under these circumstances I deem it necessary to seek the cooperation of the Congress. Only with that cooperation can we give the reassurance needed to deter aggression, to give courage and confidence to those who are dedicated to freedom and thus prevent a chain of events which would gravely endanger all of the free world.

There have been several Executive declarations made by the United States in relation to the Middle East. There is the Tripartite Declaration of May 25, 1950, followed by the Presidential assurance of October 31, 1950, to the King of Saudi Arabia. There is the Presidential declaration of April 9, 1956, that the United States will within constitutional means oppose any aggression in the area. There is our Declaration of November 29, 1956, that a threat to the territorial integrity or political independence of Iran, Iraq, Pakistan, or Turkey would be viewed by the United States with the utmost gravity.

Nevertheless, weaknesses in the present situation and the increased danger from International Communism, convince me that basic United States policy should now find expression in joint action by the Congress and the Executive. Furthermore, our joint resolve should be so couched as to make it apparent that if need be our words will be backed by action.

VI. It is nothing new for the President and the Congress to join to recognize that the national integrity of other free nations is directly related to our own security.

We have joined to create and support the security system of the United Nations. We have reinforced the collective security system of the United Nations by a series of collective defense arrangements. Today we have security treaties with 42 other nations which recognize that our peace and security are intertwined. We have joined to take decisive action in relation to Greece and Turkey and in relation to Taiwan.

Thus, the United States through the joint action of the President and the Congress, or, in the case of treaties, the Senate, has manifested in many endangered areas its purpose to support free and independent governments—and peace—against external menace, notably the menace of International Communism. Thereby we have helped to maintain peace and security during a period of great danger. It is now essential that the United States should manifest through joint action of the President and the Congress our determination to assist those nations of the Mid East area, which desire that assistance.

The action which I propose would have the following features.

It would, first of all, authorize the United States to cooperate with and assist any nation or group of nations in the general area of the Middle East in the development of economic strength dedicated to the maintenance of national independence.

It would, in the second place, authorize the Executive to undertake in the same region programs of military assistance and cooperation with any nation or group of nations which desires such aid.

It would, in the third place, authorize such assistance and cooperation to include the employment of the armed forces of the United States to secure and protect the territorial integrity and political independence of such nations, requesting such aid, against overt armed aggression from any nation controlled by International Communism.

These measures would have to be consonant with the treaty obligations of the United States, including the Charter of the United Nations and with any action or recommendations of the United Nations. They would also, if armed attack occurs, be subject to the overriding authority of the United Nations Security Council in accordance with the Charter.

The present proposal would, in the fourth place, authorize the President to employ, for economic and defensive military purposes, sums available under the Mutual Security Act of 1954, as amended, without regard to existing limitations.

The legislation now requested should not include the authorization or appropriation of funds because I believe that, under the conditions I suggest, presently appropriated funds will be adequate for the balance of the present fiscal year ending June 30. I shall, however, seek in subsequent legislation the authorization of $200,000,000 to be available during each of the fiscal years 1958 and 1959 for discretionary use in the area, in addition to the other mutual security programs for the area hereafter provided for by the Congress.

VII. This program will not solve all the problems of the Middle East. Neither does it represent the totality of our policies for the area. There are the problems of Palestine and relations between Israel and the Arab States, and the future of the Arab refugees. There is the problem of the future status of the Suez Canal. These difficulties are aggravated by International Communism, but they would exist quite apart from that threat. It is not the purpose of the legislation I propose to deal directly with these problems. The United Nations is actively concerning itself with all these matters, and we are supporting the United Nations. The United States has made clear, notably by Secretary Dulles' address of August 26, 1955, that we are willing to do much to assist the United Nations in solving the basic problems of Palestine.

The proposed legislation is primarily designed to deal with the possibility of Communist aggression, direct and indirect. There is imperative need that any lack of power in the area should be made good, not by external or alien force, but by the increased vigor and security of the independent nations of the area.

Experience shows that indirect aggression rarely if ever succeeds where there is reasonable security against direct aggression; where the government disposes of loyal security forces, and where economic conditions are such as not to make Communism seem an attractive alternative. The program I suggest deals with all three aspects of this matter and thus with the problem of indirect aggression.

It is my hope and belief that if our purpose be proclaimed, as proposed by the requested legislation, that very fact will serve to halt any contemplated aggression. We shall have heartened the patriots who are dedicated to the independence of their nations. They will not feel that they stand alone, under the menace of great power. And I should add that patriotism is, throughout this area, a powerful sentiment. It is true that fear sometimes perverts true patriotism into fanaticism and to the acceptance of dangerous enticements from without. But if that fear can be allayed, then the climate will be more favorable to the attainment of worthy national ambitions.

And as I have indicated, it will also be necessary for us to contribute economically to strengthen those countries, or groups of countries, which have governments manifestly dedicated to the preservation of independence and resistance to subversion. Such measures will provide the greatest insurance against Communist inroads. Words alone are not enough.

VIII. Let me refer again to the requested authority to employ the armed forces of the United States to assist to defend the territorial integrity and the political independence of any nation in the area against Communist armed aggression. Such authority would not be exercised except at the desire of the nation attacked. Beyond this it is my profound hope that this authority would never have to be exercised at all.

Nothing is more necessary to assure this than that our policy with respect to the defense of the area be promptly and clearly determined and declared. Thus the United Nations and all friendly governments, and indeed governments which are not friendly, will know where we stand.

If, contrary to my hope and expectation, a situation arose which called for the military application of the policy which I ask the Congress to join me in proclaiming, I would of course maintain hour-by-hour contact with the Congress if it were in session. And if the Congress were not in session, and if the situation had grave implications, I would, of course, at once call the Congress into special session.

In the situation now existing, the greatest risk, as is often the case, is that ambitious despots may miscalculate. If power-hungry Communists should either falsely or correctly estimate that the Middle East is inadequately defended, they might be tempted to use open measures of armed attack. If so, that would start a chain of circumstances which would almost surely involve the United States in military action. I am convinced that the best insurance against this dangerous contingency is to make clear now our readiness to cooperate fully and freely with our friends of the Middle East in ways consonant with the purposes and principles of the United Nations. I intend promptly to send a special mission to the Middle East to explain the cooperation we are prepared to give.

[. . .]

Source: Dwight D. Eisenhower, *Public Papers of the Presidents of the United States: Dwight D. Eisenhower, 1957* (Washington, DC: U.S. Government Printing Office, 1958), 6–16.

24. TASS News Agency, Statement on the Eisenhower Doctrine, January 14, 1957 [Excerpts]

Introduction

The Soviet Union was predictably hostile to the Eisenhower Doctrine on the Middle East, proclaimed by the president in January 1957. The Soviet media, including TASS, the official news agency, attacked Eisenhower's proclamation as a colonialist move on the part of the United States. Soviet officials took particular exception to the possible future American military interventions in the Middle East that Eisenhower's speech anticipated. Soviet critics, using classic Cold War rhetoric, charged that the U.S. government sought to replace British and French imperialism in the area with its own hegemony, in defiance of the aspirations to national independence of the Arab peoples in the region. The real objective of the United States, in Soviet eyes, was to impose "a kind of military protectorate" over the Middle East and protect its petroleum interests there, especially the near-monopolistic position of American oil companies. The Soviet Union reminded Arab countries of its own support for Egypt in the recent Suez Crisis and urged them to look to the Soviet Union for protection against attempts at domination by outside powers. Quite clearly, the two Cold War superpowers now saw the Middle East as a significant arena for strategic and economic competition, its various states constituting a potential sphere of influence from which each sought to exclude the other.

Primary Source

The President of the United States of America, Mr. Dwight D. Eisenhower, on January 5 addressed a special message to Congress on the policy of the United States in the Middle East countries. In his message, which abounds in anti-Soviet remarks, the President, describing the present situation in the Middle East as "critical," demanded the authority to use the armed forces of the United States in the Middle East at any moment he might consider it necessary, without asking for the consent of Congress as is envisaged in the country's Constitution. The President of the United States also demanded that he be empowered to render military and economic "aid" to the countries of the Middle East. It is envisaged, specifically, that 200 million dollars will be spent for "economic support" to countries of that area.

President Eisenhower's message runs counter to the principles and the purposes of the United Nations and is fraught with grave danger to peace and security in the Middle East area. . . .

In his message to Congress the President of the United States speaks of the sympathy which, he claims, the United States entertains for the Arab countries. Life, however, shows that in actual fact the American ruling circles are setting themselves obviously selfish aims in that area. It is a fact that when Egypt, as a result of the military aggression of Britain, France and Israel, was threatened with the loss of her national independence, the United States refused to pool its efforts with the Soviet Union in the United Nations in order to take resolute measures to cut short the aggression. The primary concern of the United States was not the defence of peace and the national independence of the Arab countries, but the desire to take advantage of the weakening of Britain and France in the Middle East to capture their positions.

At present, when a favourable situation has developed in the Middle East and real possibilities for consolidating peace and settling outstanding issues in that area have been created, the government of the United States has come forward with a programme which envisages flagrant interference by the United States in the affairs of the Arab countries, up to and including military intervention. The aggressive trend of this programme and its colonialist nature with regard to the Arab countries are so obvious that this cannot be disguised by any nebulous phrases about the love for peace and the concern claimed to be shown by the United States for the Middle East countries.

It is permissible to ask: Of what love for peace do the authors of the "Eisenhower doctrine" speak when the threat to the security of the Middle East countries emanates precisely from member-states of N.A.T.O., in which the United States plays first fiddle? What concern for the aforementioned countries can be in question when it is the United States and its N.A.T.O. partners that regard those countries merely as sources of strategic raw materials and spheres for the investment of capital, with the object of extracting maximum profits? Is it not clear that the uninvited "protectors" of the Middle East countries are trying to impose on that area nothing else but the regime of a kind of military protectorate, and to set back the development of these countries for many years? . . .

The United States ruling circles consider that the weakening of the positions of the Anglo-French colonialists in the Middle East and the successes of the Arab countries in consolidating their independence have produced a "vacuum," which they would like to fill by their military and economic intervention in the internal affairs of those countries. But what "vacuum" can be in question here? Since when do countries which have liberated themselves from colonial oppression and have taken the road of independent national development constitute a "vacuum"? It is clear that the strengthening of the national independence of the Arab countries, the intensification of their struggle against colonial oppression by no means create some kind of "vacuum," but are a restoration of the national rights of the Middle East peoples and constitute a progressive factor in social development. The United States tries to present its policy as an anti-colonialist one. But it is not difficult to see the falseness of these assertions, clearly designed to blunt the vigilance of the peoples in the Middle East. The programme of the United States insistently stresses that the Middle East must recognise its interdependence with the western countries, that is, with the colonialists—specifically with regard to oil, the Suez Canal, etc. In other words, the United States is stubbornly seeking to impose a "trusteeship" of the colonialists on the peoples of the Middle East countries....

The authors of the colonialist programme try to sweeten it by a promise of economic "aid" to the Middle East countries. Every intelligent person, however, understands that in reality the United States is offering as charity to the peoples of the Arab countries only a small fraction of what the American monopolies have received and are receiving by plundering, by exploiting the natural wealth belonging to those countries. The United States promises the countries of the Middle East 200 million dollars in the financial years of 1958 and 1959, whereas in 1955 alone the American and British oil monopolies extracted 150 million tons of oil in the Middle East at a total cost of 240 million dollars, and made a net profit of 1,900 million dollars on this oil. Such is the real picture of American "philanthropy-."...

Seeking to cover up gross intervention in the internal affairs of the Middle East countries and their aggressive policy with regard to these countries, the United States ruling circles resort to inventions about a threat to the Arab countries emanating from the Soviet Union. These slanderous assertions will deceive no one. The peoples of the Middle East have not forgotten that the Soviet Union has always defended the self-determination of peoples, the gaining and consolidating of their national independence. They have learned from experience that in relations with all countries the Soviet Union steadfastly pursues the policy of equality and non-interference in internal affairs. They also know very well that the Soviet Union is actively supporting the right of each people to dispose of its natural wealth and use it at its own discretion.

It was not the Soviet Union, but Britain and France—the United States' chief partners in the North Atlantic bloc—which committed aggression against Egypt, inflicting great losses and suffering on the Egyptian people. This is borne out by the fresh ruins of Port Said and other Egyptian cities, as well as by the new plans for United States economic, political and military expansion in the Middle East proclaimed by the American President. These aggressive plans of the American imperialists express their striving for world domination, of which they speak now quite shamefully, presenting this aspiration as the need for "energetic leadership" of the world by the United States.

In the days of hard trials for the Arab peoples it was the Soviet Union, and no one else, who came out as their sincere friend and,

together with the peace loving forces of the whole world, took steps to end the aggression against Egypt. All this is well known....

It is well known that the Soviet Union, as distinct from the United States, does not have and does not seek to have any military bases or concessions in the Middle East with the object of extracting profits, does not strive to gain any privileges in that area, since all this is incompatible with the principles of Soviet foreign policy.

The Soviet Union is vitally interested in the maintenance of peace in the Middle East area, situated as it is in direct proximity to its frontiers. It is sincerely interested in consolidating the national independence of those countries and in their economic prosperity and regards this as a reliable guarantee of peace and security in that area.

In our age the national liberation movement of the peoples is a historical force that cannot be repressed.

The Soviet Union, loyal to the great Leninist principles of recognising and respecting the rights of peoples, large and small, to independent development, regards as one of its prime tasks the rendering of every assistance and support to the countries fighting to consolidate their national independence and their sovereignty. That is why it welcomes the growing unity of the peoples of the Arab countries in their struggle for peace, security, national freedom and independence.

The Soviet Union opposes any manifestations of colonialism, any "doctrines" which protect and cover up colonialism. It is opposed to unequal treaties and agreements, the setting up of military bases on foreign territories, dictated by strategic considerations, and plans for establishing the world domination of imperialism. It proceeds from the premise that the natural wealth of the underdeveloped countries is the inalienable national possession of the peoples of those countries, who have the full right to dispose of it independently and to use it for their economic prosperity and progress. The need to strengthen peace and security demands the wide development of political, economic and cultural ties between all countries. The development of these ties is an important prerequisite for using the achievements of contemporary science and technology for the good of mankind. The policy of establishing closed aggressive military blocs, such as N.A.T.O., S.E.A.T.O. and the Baghdad Pact, and the raising of artificial economic barriers hampering normal relations between states seriously impairs the cause of peace. The Soviet Union, striving to render assistance to peoples fighting for the consolidation of their national independence and the earliest elimination of the aftermath of colonial oppression, is willing to develop all-round cooperation with them on the principles of full equality and mutual benefit....

Authoritative Soviet circles hold that the steps with regard to the Middle East area outlined by the United States government, which envisage the possibility of employing United States armed forces in that area, might lead to dangerous consequences, the responsibility for which will rest entirely with the United States government.

Source: *Soviet News,* no. 354, January 14, 1957, pp. 33–34.

25. Ayatollah Ruhollah Khomeini's Islamic Challenge, Sermons, and Writings, 1963–1980

Introduction

The modernizing policies Mohammad Reza Shah Pahlavi of Iran often offended Muslim clerics, who believed that the monarch's emphasis on creating a secular society broke with numerous Islamic tenets. Over time, they also came to resent his close alliance with the United States, particularly given increasingly strong American support for Israel, a country whose total destruction many Muslims as well as Arab states supported. Among Iranians, by the early 1960s the chief focus and leader for Islamic dissent from the shah's rule was the Shiite Muslim Ayatollah Ruhollah Khomeini (1900–1989), a well-known scholar and opponent of secularism who became Iran's leading Islamic cleric in 1963. Khomeini and other Iranian clerics issued a manifesto attacking the shah's White Revolution program, announced early in 1963, that launched land reforms, privatized state assets, introduced profit-sharing schemes, gave women the vote, and launched a major education literacy program. The shah, in return, publicly denounced the Muslim clerics. In June 1963 Khomeini preached a sermon openly attacking the shah's policies as irreligious and subservient to both the United States and Israel, which caused Khomeini's arrest two days later, an event that sparked major riots throughout Iran in which more than 400 people died. Khomeini was placed under house arrest for several months. Once he was released in October 1964, he denounced the legal immunity that American military advisers and their employees enjoyed in Iran. At this juncture the shah exiled Khomeini, who spent most of the next 14 years in neighboring Iraq. Khomeini continued to preach sermons that vehemently condemned the shah and his policies. The ayatollah alleged that the shah's regime was riddled with corruption and that a small elite allied with foreign capitalists were looting the country. Khomeini claimed that the shah allowed the United States to train Israeli pilots in Iran and called upon all good Muslims in Iran to launch a jihad, or holy war, against the shah and his foreign patrons and allies. After domestic discontent forced the shah to flee Iran in early 1979, Khomeini returned from exile and became head of state. He now sought to make Iran the leader in a Muslim revolution against all foreign oppression, aligning the country

with the Palestine Liberation Organization (PLO) opposing Israel and also with the Muslim rebels against Soviet rule in Afghanistan. The foremost among his targets, however, still remained the United States. In November 1979 Muslim militants who were dedicated supporters of Khomeini sacked the American embassy in Tehran, Iran's capital, taking 63 American diplomats and other personnel hostage, an action that Khomeini endorsed. In a message of September 1980, when the hostages were still in Iranian hands, Khomeini issued an inflammatory message characterizing the United States, which had by this time imposed tight economic sanctions on Iran, as the "Great Satan" and "the number-one enemy of the deprived and oppressed people of the world." Khomeini's sermons were illuminating proof of the degree to which, from at least the early 1960s, the United States and its policies, and rulers associated with these, became a major transnational focus for Muslim antagonism.

Primary Source

Ayatollah Ruhollah Khomeini's Islamic Challenge

SERMON DELIVERED IN QUM, IRAN, JUNE 3, 1963

Iranian nation! Those among you who are thirty or forty years of age or more will remember how three foreign countries attacked us during World War II. The Soviet Union, Britain, and America invaded Iran and occupied our country. The property of the people was exposed to danger and their honor was imperiled. But God knows, everyone was happy because the Pahlavi had gone! Shah, I don't wish the same to happen to you; I don't want you to become like your father. Listen to my advice, listen to the 'ulama [learned clergy] of Islam. They desire the welfare of the nation, the welfare of the country. Don't listen to Israel; Israel can't do anything for you. You miserable wretch, forty-five years of your life have passed; isn't it time for you to think and reflect a little, to ponder about where all this is leading you, to learn a lesson from the experience of your father? If what they say is true, that you are opposed to Islam and the religious scholars, your ideas are quite wrong. If they are dictating these things to you and then giving them to you to read, you should think about it a little. Why do you speak without thinking? Are the religious scholars really some form of impure animal? If they are impure animals, why do the people kiss their hands? Why do they regard the very water they drink as blessed? Are we really impure animals?

SERMON DELIVERED IN QUM, IRAN, OCTOBER 27, 1964

A law has been put before the Majlis [parliament] . . . that all American military advisers, together with their families, technical and administrative officials, and servants—in short, anyone in any way connected to them—are to enjoy legal immunity with respect to any crime they may commit in Iran.

If some American's servant, some American's cook, assassinates your marjá in the middle of the bazaar, or runs over him, the Iranian police do not have the right to apprehend him! Iranian courts do not have the right to judge him! The dossier must be sent to America, so that our masters there can decide what is to be done!

. . . If someone runs over a dog belonging to an American, he will be prosecuted. Even if the Shah himself were to run over a dog belonging to an American, he would be prosecuted. But if an American cook runs over the Shah, the head of state, no one will have the right to interfere with him.

. . . The government has sold our independence, reduced us to the level of a colony, and made the Muslim nation of Iran appear more backward than savages in the eyes of the world! . . .

I don't know where this White Revolution is that they are making so much fuss about. God knows that I am aware of (and my awareness causes me pain) the remote villages and provincial towns, not to mention our own backward city of Qum. I am aware of the hunger of our people and the disordered state of our agrarian economy. Why not try to do something for this country, for this population, instead of piling up debts and enslaving yourselves?

LECTURES DELIVERED TO SEMINARY STUDENTS, NAJAF, IRAQ, JANUARY–FEBRUARY 1970

At a time when the West was a realm of darkness and obscurity—with its inhabitants living in a state of barbarism and America still peopled by half-savage redskins—and the two vast empires of Iran and Byzantium were under the rule of tyranny, class privilege, and discrimination, and the powerful dominated all without any trace of law or popular government, God, Exalted and Almighty, by means of the Most Noble Messenger [the prophet Mohammed] (peace and blessings be upon him), sent laws that astound us with their magnitude. He instituted laws and practices for all human affairs and laid down injunctions for man extending from even before the embryo is formed until after he is placed in the tomb. In just the same way that there are laws setting forth the duties of worship for man, so too there are laws, practices, and norms for the affairs of society and government. Islamic law is a progressive, evolving, and comprehensive system of law. . . .

. . . Huge amounts of capital are being swallowed up; our public funds are being embezzled; our oil is being plundered; and our country is being turned into a market for expensive, unnecessary goods by the representatives of foreign companies, which makes it possible for foreign capitalists and their local agents to pocket the people's money. A number of foreign states carry off our oil after drawing it out of the ground, and the negligible sum they pay to the regime they have installed returns to their pockets by other

routes. As for the small amount that goes into the treasury, God only knows what it is spent on. . . .

Our wretched people subsist in conditions of poverty and hunger, while the taxes that the ruling class extorts from them are squandered. They buy Phantom jets so that pilots from Israel and its agents can come and train in them in our country. . . .—Israel, which is in a state of war with the Muslims. . . .

. . . It is our duty to begin exerting ourselves now in order to establish a truly Islamic government. We must propagate our cause to the people, instruct them in it, and convince them of its validity. We must generate a wave of intellectual awakening, to emerge as a current throughout society, and gradually, to take shape as an organized Islamic movement made up of the awakened, committed, and religious masses who will rise up and establish an Islamic government. . . .

. . . So, courageous sons of Islam, stand up! Address the people bravely; tell the truth about our situation to the masses in simple language; arouse them to enthusiastic activity, and turn the people in the street and the bazaar, our simple-hearted workers and peasants, and our alert students into dedicated mujahids [those engaged in jihad or holy struggle]. The entire population will become mujahids. All segments of society are ready to struggle for the sake of freedom, independence, and the happiness of the nation, and their struggle needs religion. Give the people Islam, then, for Islam is the school of jihad, the religion of struggle; let them amend their characters and beliefs in accordance with Islam and transform themselves into a powerful force, so that they may overthrow the tyrannical regime imperialism has imposed on us and set up an Islamic government.

DECLARATION ON THE ANTI-SHAH DEMONSTRATIONS, ISSUED IN PARIS, OCTOBER 11, 1978

Great people of Iran! The history of Iran, even world history, has never witnessed a movement like yours; it has never experienced a universal uprising like yours, noble people!

Today primary school children of seven or eight stand ready to sacrifice themselves and shed their blood for the sake of Islam and the nation; when has anything like that been seen? Our lion-hearted women snatch up their infants and go to confront the machine guns and tanks of the regime; where in history has such valiant and heroic behavior by women been recorded? Today the thunderous cry of "Death to the Shah!" arises from the heart of the primary school child and the infirm old man alike, and it has blackened the days of this vile Pahlavi regime and so shattered the nerves of the Shah that he seeks to calm himself with the blood of our children and young people.

Beloved sisters and brothers! Be steadfast; do not weaken or slacken your efforts. Your path is the path of God and His elect. Your blood is being shed for the same cause as the blood of the prophets and the Imams [recognized religious leaders] and the righteous. You will join them, and you have no cause to grieve, therefore, but every reason for joy....

MESSAGE ON OCCASION OF THE IRANIAN NEW YEAR, ISSUED IN TEHRAN, MARCH 21, 1980

We must strive to export our Revolution throughout the world, and must abandon all idea of not doing so, for not only does Islam refuse to recognize any difference between Muslim countries, it is the champion of all oppressed people. Moreover, all the powers are intent on destroying us, and if we remain surrounded in a closed circle, we shall certainly be defeated. We must make plain our stance toward the powers and the superpowers and demonstrate to them that despite the arduous problems that burden us, our attitude to the world is dictated by our beliefs....

Once again, I declare my support for all movements and groups that are fighting to gain liberation from the superpowers of the left and the right. I declare my support for the people of [Israeli] Occupied Palestine and Lebanon. I vehemently condemn once more the savage occupation of Afghanistan by the aggressive plunderers of the East [the Soviet Union], and I hope that the noble Muslim people of Afghanistan will achieve victory and true independence as soon as possible, and be delivered from the clutches of the so called champions of the working class.

MESSAGE TO PILGRIMS, ISSUED IN TEHRAN, SEPTEMBER 12, 1980

Part of the extensive propaganda campaign being waged apparently against Iran, but in reality against Islam, is intended to show that the Revolution of Iran cannot administer our country or that the Iranian government is about to fall.... But by the blessing of Islam and our Muslim people, in the space of less than two years, we have voted on, approved, and put into practice all the measures necessary for the administration of the country. Despite all the difficulties that America and its satellites have created for us— economic boycott, military attack, and the planning of extensive coups d'etat—our valiant people have attained self-sufficiency in foodstuffs. Soon we will transform the imperialist-inspired education system that existed under the previous regime into an independent and Islamic education system. The armed forces, the Revolutionary Guards, the gendarmerie, and the police stand ready to defend the country and uphold order, and they are prepared to offer their lives in jihad for the sake of Islam. In addition, a general mobilization of the entire nation is under way, with the nation equipping itself to fight for the sake of Islam and the

country. Let our enemies know that no revolution in the world was followed by less bloodshed or brought greater achievements than our Islamic Revolution, and that this is due entirely to the blessing of Islam....

America is the number-one enemy of the deprived and oppressed people of the world. There is no crime America will not commit in order to maintain its political, economic, cultural, and military domination of those parts of the world where it predominates....

Iran has tried to sever all its relations with this Great Satan and it is for this reason that it now finds wars imposed upon it. America has urged Iraq to spill the blood of our young men [in border clashes that preceded the Iran-Iraq War, 1980–1988], and it has compelled the countries that are subject to its influence to boycott us economically in the hope of defeating us.... This is a result of the Islamic content of our Revolution, which has been established on the basis of true independence. Were we to compromise with America and the other superpowers, we would not suffer these misfortunes. But our nation is no longer ready to submit to humiliation and abjection; it prefers a bloody death to a life of shame.

Source: Ruhollah Khomeini, *Islam and Revolution* (Berkeley, CA: Mizan, 1981), 174–176, 181–188, 239–241, 286–294, 300–306.

26. Dwight D. Eisenhower, Address to the Nation Concerning the Landing of Marines in Lebanon, July 15, 1958

Introduction

In July 1958 President Dwight D. Eisenhower demonstrated that despite Soviet protests he was willing to send American military forces to protect U.S. clients in the Middle East. In Lebanon, pro-Western Christian president Camille Chamoun was at odds with his Sunni Muslim prime minister, Rashid Karami. Karami and rebellious Lebanese Muslims demanded that their country should join the newly formed and short-lived United Arab Republic (UAR), a federation of Egypt and Syria, while Lebanese Christians wished to continue their country's existing pro-Western alignment. On July 14, 1958, a bloody military coup in which young King Faisal II, his uncle, the regent of Iraq, and Prime Minister Nuri al-Said all died, brought a radical Arab regime to power in Iraq. Fearing that Lebanon might follow suit or be forced by Egyptian and Syrian pressure to join the UAR, the following day Eisenhower responded to Chamoun's pleas for assistance by dispatching 14,000 troops, including 5,670 U.S. marines, to Lebanon. American forces restored order, first securing the Beirut airport and then spreading out through the capital and quelling internal opposition. By the time they withdrew on October 25, 1958, American diplomats had persuaded Chamoun to resign his office, and General Fuad Chehab, a moderate Christian, replaced him. Only 4 American military personnel died in Lebanon, 3 in accidents and 1 a victim of sniper fire. The episode gave tangible proof that the United States would react forcefully if a Middle Eastern ally was threatened.

Primary Source

Yesterday was a day of grave developments in the Middle East. In Iraq a highly organized military blow struck down the duly constituted Government and attempted to put in its place a committee of Army officers. The attack was conducted with great brutality. Many of the leading personalities were beaten to death or hanged and their bodies dragged through the streets.

At about the same time there was discovered a highly organized plot to overthrow the lawful Government of Jordan.

Warned and alarmed by these developments President Chamoun of Lebanon sent me an urgent plea that the United States station some military units in Lebanon to evidence our concern for the independence of Lebanon, that little country which itself has for about 2 months been subjected to civil strife. This has been actively fomented by Soviet and Cairo broadcasts and abetted and aided by substantial amounts of arms, money, and personnel infiltrated into Lebanon across the Syrian border.

President Chamoun stated that without an immediate show of United States support the Government of Lebanon would be unable to survive against the forces which had been set loose in the area.

The plea of President Chamoun was supported by the unanimous action of the Lebanese Cabinet.

After giving this plea earnest thought and after taking advice from leaders of both the executive and congressional branches of the Government, I decided to comply with the plea of the Government of Lebanon. A few hours ago a battalion of United States Marines landed and took up stations in and about the city of Beirut.

The mission of these forces is to protect American lives—there are about 2,500 Americans in Lebanon—and by their presence to assist the Government of Lebanon to preserve its territorial integrity and political independence.

The United States does not, of course, intend to replace the United Nations, which has a primary responsibility to maintain international peace and security. We reacted as we did within a matter of hours because the situation was such that only prompt action would suffice. We have, however, with equal promptness moved in the United Nations. This morning there was held at our request an emergency meeting of the United Nations Security Council. At this meeting we reported the action which we had taken. We stated the reasons therefor. We expressed the hope that the United Nations would itself take measures which would be adequate to preserve the independence of Lebanon and permit of the early withdrawal of the United States forces.

The Situation in Lebanon

I should like now to take a few minutes to explain the situation in Lebanon.

Lebanon is a small country, a little less than the size of Connecticut, with a population of about 1½ million. It has always had close and friendly relations with the United States. Many of you no doubt have heard of the American University at Beirut, which has a distinguished record. Lebanon has been a prosperous, peaceful country, thriving on trade largely with the West. A little over a year ago there were general elections, held in an atmosphere of total calm, which resulted in the establishment, by an overwhelming popular vote, of the present Parliament for a period of 4 years. The term of the President, however, is of a different duration and would normally expire next September. The President, Mr. Chamoun, has made clear that he does not seek reelection.

When the attacks on the Government of Lebanon began to occur, it took the matter to the United Nations Security Council, pointing out that Lebanon was the victim of indirect aggression from without. As a result, the Security Council sent observers to Lebanon in the hope of thereby insuring that hostile intervention would cease. Secretary-General Hammarskjold undertook a mission to the area to reinforce the work of the observers.

We believe that his efforts and those of the United Nations observers were helpful. They could not eliminate arms or ammunition or remove persons already sent into Lebanon. But we believe they did reduce such aid from across the border. It seemed, last week, that the situation was moving toward a peaceful solution which would preserve the integrity of Lebanon and end indirect aggression from without.

Those hopes were, however, dashed by the events of yesterday in Iraq and Jordan. These events demonstrate a scope of aggressive purpose which tiny Lebanon could not combat without further evidence of support. That is why Lebanon's request for troops from the United States was made. That is why we have responded to that request.

Some will ask, does the stationing of some United States troops in Lebanon involve any interference in the internal affairs of Lebanon? The clear answer is "no."

First of all, we have acted at the urgent plea of the Government of Lebanon, a Government which has been freely elected by the people only a little over a year ago. It is entitled, as are we, to join in measures of collective security for self-defense.

Such action, the United Nations Charter recognizes, is an "inherent right."

Pattern of Conquest by Indirect Aggression

In the second place what we now see in the Middle East is the same pattern of conquest with which we became familiar during the period of 1945 to 1950. This involves taking over a nation by means of indirect aggression; that is, under the cover of a fomented civil strife the purpose is to put into domestic control those whose real loyalty is to the aggressor.

It was by such means that the Communists attempted to take over Greece in 1947. That effort was thwarted by the Truman Doctrine.

It was by such means that the Communists took over Czechoslovakia in 1948.

It was by such means that the Communists took over the mainland of China in 1949.

It was by such means that the Communists attenuated to take over Korea and Indochina, beginning in 1950.

You will remember at the time of the Korean war that the Soviet Government claimed that this was merely a civil war, because the only attack was by north Koreans upon south Koreans. But all the world knew that the north Koreans were armed, equipped, and directed from without for the purpose of aggression.

This means of conquest was denounced by the United Nations General Assembly when it adopted in November 1950 its resolution entitled "Peace Through Deeds." It thereby called upon every nation to refrain from "fomenting civil strife in the interest of a foreign power" and denounced such action as "the gravest of all crimes against peace and security throughout the world." We had hoped that these threats to the peace and to the independence and integrity of small nations had come to an end. Unhappily, now they reappear. Lebanon was selected to become a victim.

Last year the Congress of the United States joined with the President to declare that "the United States regards as vital to the national interest and world peace the preservation of the independence and integrity of the nations of the Middle East."

I believe that the presence of the United States forces now being sent to Lebanon will have a stabilizing effect which will preserve the independence and integrity of Lebanon. It will also afford an increased measure of security to the thousands of Americans who reside in Lebanon.

We know that stability and well-being cannot be achieved purely by military measures. The economy of Lebanon has been gravely strained by civil strife. Foreign trade and tourist traffic have almost come to a standstill. The United States stands ready, under its mutual security program, to cooperate with the Government of Lebanon to find ways to restore its shattered economy. Thus we shall help to bring back to Lebanon a peace which is not merely the absence of fighting but the well-being of the people.

The Purpose of the United States

I am well aware of the fact that landing of United States troops in Lebanon could have some serious consequences. That is why this step was taken only after the most serious consideration and broad consultation. I have, however, come to the sober and clear conclusion that the action taken was essential to the welfare of the United States. It was required to support the principles of justice and international law upon which peace and a stable international order depend.

That, and that alone, is the purpose of the United States. We are not actuated by any hope of material gain or by any emotional hostility against any person or any government. Our dedication is to the principles of the United Nations Charter and to the preservation of the independence of every state. That is the basic pledge of the United Nations Charter.

Yet indirect aggression and violence are being promoted in the Near East in clear violation of the provisions of the United Nations Charter.

There can be no peace in the world unless there is fuller dedication to the basic principles of the United Nations Charter. If ever the United States fails to support these principles, the result would be to open the floodgates to direct and indirect aggression throughout the world.

In the 1930's the members of the League of Nations became indifferent to direct and indirect aggression in Europe, Asia, and Africa. The result was to strengthen and stimulate aggressive forces that made World War II inevitable.

The United States is determined that that history shall not now be repeated. We are hopeful that the action which we are taking will both preserve the independence of Lebanon and check international violations which, if they succeeded, would endanger world peace.

We hope that this result will quickly be attained and that our forces can be promptly withdrawn. We must, however, be prepared to meet the situation, whatever be the consequences. We can do so, confident that we strive for a world in which nations, be they great or be they small, can preserve their independence. We are striving for an ideal which is close to the heart of every American and for which in the past many Americans have laid down their lives.

To serve these ideals is also to serve the cause of peace, security, and well-being, not only for us but for all men everywhere.

Source: "Radio-TV Statement," *Department of State Bulletin* 39(997) (1958): 183–186.

27. Richard Nixon, Address to the Nation on Policies to Deal with Energy Shortages, November 7, 1973 [Excerpts]

Introduction

In retaliation for U.S. shipments of armaments to Israel during the October 1973 Yom Kippur (Ramadan) War, Arab states led by Saudi Arabia cut back on their production of oil and imposed embargos on sales to the United States and other Western nations that had assisted Israel during the conflict. Oil prices quickly quadrupled, fueling already rising inflation and soon contributing to an economic depression that afflicted Europe as well as the United States. As winter approached, fuel oil was in short supply in the United States. In early November, President Richard Nixon addressed the American people, warning that they faced "the most acute shortages of energy since World War II" and that in the coming winter the country would have between 10 percent and 17 percent less oil than it needed. As a short-term measure, he asked all Americans to economize in their use of energy. He also announced a program of government measures to deal with the problem, including the conversion of oil-burning plants and utilities to coal, a reduction in civilian aircraft flights, cutting the consumption of energy by 15 percent in homes and businesses and by 7 percent in federal government offices, accelerating the construction of nuclear power plants, reducing automobile speed limits to 50 miles per hour, and encouraging states, cities, and individuals to introduce other small-scale measures to economize on energy. In addition, he called on Congress to pass a program of specific energy-saving measures, including the introduction of daylight saving time throughout the year, the relaxation of environmental regulations, the introduction of "special energy conservation measures," funding for the faster exploration and development of existing American oil reserves, the introduction of the 50-mile speed limit, and greater governmental authority to regulate transportation to ensure efficient energy use. Warning that Americans were overly reliant upon energy and used it too prodigally, Nixon complained that Congress had failed to pass any of his earlier legislative initiatives to conserve and develop energy resources, and he asked that Congress take effective action in this area so that by 1980 the United States would be self-sufficient in energy. Nixon's program was imaginative, ambitious, and largely fruitless. Even though Americans might admit intellectually that they should economize, conserve energy resources, develop both new and existing resources, and reduce American dependence on foreign supplies, the measures involved would have demanded massive and often painful restructurings of the American economic and fiscal status quo, which proved to be politically impossible for Nixon and his successors as president to introduce.

Primary Source

I want to talk to you tonight about a serious national problem, a problem we must all face together in the months and years ahead.

As America has grown and prospered in recent years, our energy demands have begun to exceed available supplies. In recent months, we have taken many actions to increase supplies and to reduce consumption. But even with our best efforts, we knew that a period of temporary shortages was inevitable.

Unfortunately, our expectations for this winter have now been sharply altered by the recent conflict in the Middle East. Because of that war, most of the Middle Eastern oil producers have reduced overall production and cut off their shipments of oil to the United States. By the end of this month, more than 2 million barrels a day of oil we expected to import into the United States will no longer be available.

We must, therefore, face up to a very stark fact: We are heading toward the most acute shortages of energy since World War II. Our supply of petroleum this winter will be at least 10 percent short of our anticipated demands, and it could fall short by as much as 17 percent.

Now, even before war broke out in the Middle East, these prospective shortages were the subject of intensive discussions among members of my Administration, leaders of the Congress, Governors, mayors, and other groups. From these discussions has emerged a broad agreement that we, as a nation, must now set upon a new course.

In the short run, this course means that we must use less energy—that means less heat, less electricity, less gasoline. In the long run, it means that we must develop new sources of energy which will give us the capacity to meet our needs without relying on any foreign nation.

The immediate shortage will affect the lives of each and every one of us. In our factories, our cars, our homes, our offices, we will have to use less fuel than we are accustomed to using. Some school and factory schedules may be realigned, and some jet airplane flights will be canceled.

This does not mean that we are going to run out of gasoline or that air travel will stop or that we will freeze in our homes or offices anyplace in America. The fuel crisis need not mean genuine suffering for any American. But it will require some sacrifice by all Americans.

We must be sure that our most vital needs are met first—and that our least important activities are the first to be cut back. And we must be sure that while the fat from our economy is being trimmed, the muscle is not seriously damaged.

To help us carry out that responsibility, I am tonight announcing the following steps:

First, I am directing that industries and utilities which use coal—which is our most abundant resource—be prevented from converting from coal to oil. Efforts will also be made to convert power plants from the use of oil to the use of coal.

Second, we are allocating reduced quantities of fuel for aircraft. Now, this is going to lead to a cutback of more than 10 percent of the number of flights and some rescheduling of arrival and departure times.

Third, there will be reductions of approximately 15 percent in the supply of heating oil for homes and offices and other establishments. To be sure that there is enough oil to go around for the entire winter, all over the country, it will be essential for all of us to live and work in lower temperatures. We must ask everyone to lower the thermostat in your home by at least 6 degrees so that we can achieve a national daytime average of 68 degrees. Incidentally, my doctor tells me that in a temperature of 66 to 68 degrees, you are really more healthy than when it is 75 to 78, if that is any comfort. In offices, factories, and commercial establishments, we must ask that you achieve the equivalent of a two-degree reduction by either lowering the thermostat or curtailing working hours.

Fourth, I am ordering additional reductions in the consumption of energy by the Federal Government. We have already taken steps to reduce the Government's consumption by 7 percent. The cuts must now go deeper and must be made by every agency and every department in the Government. I am directing that daytime temperatures in Federal offices be reduced immediately to a level of between 65 and 68 degrees, and that means in this room, too, as well as in every other room in the White House. In addition, I am ordering that all vehicles owned by the Federal Government—and

there are over a half-million of them—travel no faster than 50 miles per hour except in emergencies. This is a step which I have also asked Governors, mayors, and local officials to take immediately with regard to vehicles under their authority.

Fifth, I am asking the Atomic Energy Commission to speed up the licensing and construction of nuclear plants. We must seek to reduce the time required to bring nuclear plants on line—nuclear plants that can produce power—to bring them on line from 10 years to 6 years, reduce that time lag.

Sixth, I am asking that Governors and mayors reinforce these actions by taking appropriate steps at the State and local level. We have already learned, for example, from the State of Oregon, that considerable amounts of energy can be saved simply by curbing unnecessary lighting and slightly altering the school year. I am recommending that other communities follow this example and also seek ways to stagger working hours, to encourage greater use of mass transit and carpooling.

How many times have you gone along the highway or the freeway, wherever the case may be, and see[n] hundreds and hundreds of cars with only one individual in that car? This we must all cooperate to change.

Consistent with safety and economic considerations, I am also asking Governors to take steps to reduce highway speed limits to 50 miles per hour. This action alone, if it is adopted on a nationwide basis, could save over 200,000 barrels of oil a day—just reducing the speed limit to 50 miles per hour.

Now, all of these actions will result in substantial savings of energy. More than that, most of these are actions that we can take right now—without further delay.

The key to their success lies, however, not just here in Washington but in every home, in every community across this country. If each of us joins in this effort, joins with the spirit and the determination that have always graced the American character, then half the battle will already be won.

But we should recognize that even these steps, as essential as they are, may not be enough. We must be prepared to take additional steps, and for that purpose, additional authorities must be provided by the Congress.

I have therefore directed my chief adviser for energy policy, Governor Love, and other Administration officials, to work closely with the Congress in developing an emergency energy act.

I met with the leaders of the Congress this morning, and I asked that they act on this legislation on a priority, urgent basis. It is imperative that this legislation be on my desk for signature before the Congress recesses this December....

[...]

This proposed legislation would enable the executive branch to meet the energy emergency in several important ways:

First, it would authorize an immediate return to daylight saving time on a year-round basis.

Second, it would provide the necessary authority to relax environmental regulations on a temporary, case-by-case basis, thus permitting an appropriate balancing of our environmental interests, which all of us share, with our energy requirements, which, of course, are indispensable.

Third, it would grant authority to impose special energy conservation measures, such as restrictions on the working hours for shopping centers and other commercial establishments.

And fourth, it would approve and fund increased exploration, development, and production from our naval petroleum reserves. Now, these reserves are rich sources of oil. From one of them alone—Elk Hills in California—we could produce more than 160,000 barrels of oil a day within 2 months.

Fifth, it would provide the Federal Government with authority to reduce highway speed limits throughout the Nation.

And finally, it would expand the power of the Government's regulatory agencies to adjust the schedules of planes, ships, and other carriers.

If shortages persist despite all of these actions and despite inevitable increases in the price of energy products, it may then become necessary—may become necessary—to take even stronger measures.

It is only prudent that we be ready to cut the consumption of oil products, such as gasoline, by rationing or by a fair system of taxation, and consequently, I have directed that contingency plans, if this becomes necessary, be prepared for that purpose.

Now, some of you may wonder whether we are turning back the clock to another age. Gas rationing, oil shortages, reduced speed limits—they all sound like a way of life we left behind with Glenn Miller and the war of the forties. Well, in fact, part of our current problem also stems from war—the war in the Middle East. But our deeper energy problems come not from war, but from peace and from abundance. We are running out of energy today because our economy has grown enormously and because in prosperity what were once considered luxuries are now considered necessities.

How many of you can remember when it was very unusual to have a home air-conditioned? And yet, this is very common in almost all parts of the Nation.

As a result, the average American will consume as much energy in the next 7 days as most other people in the world will consume in an entire year. We have only 6 percent of the world's people in America, but we consume over 30 percent of all the energy in the world.

Now, our growing demands have bumped up against the limits of available supply, and until we provide new sources of energy for tomorrow, we must be prepared to tighten our belts today.

Let me turn now to our long-range plans.

While a resolution of the immediate crisis is our highest priority, we must also act now to prevent a recurrence of such a crisis in the future. This is a matter of bipartisan concern. It is going to require a bipartisan response.

Two years ago, in the first energy message any President has ever sent to the Congress, I called attention to our urgent energy problem. Last April, this year, I reaffirmed to the Congress the magnitude of that problem, and I called for action on seven major legislative initiatives. Again in June, I called for action. I have done so frequently since then.

But thus far, not one major energy bill that I have asked for has been enacted....

Our failure to act now on our long-term energy problems could seriously endanger the capacity of our farms and of our factories to employ Americans at record-breaking rates—nearly 86 million people are now at work in this country—and to provide the highest standard of living we or any other nation has ever known in history.

It could reduce the capacity of our farmers to provide the food we need. It could jeopardize our entire transportation system. It could seriously weaken the ability of America to continue to give the leadership which only we can provide to keep the peace that we have won at such great cost for thousands of our finest young Americans.

That is why it is time to act now on vital energy legislation that will affect our daily lives, not just this year, but for years to come.

We must have the legislation now which will authorize construction of the Alaska pipeline—legislation which is not burdened with irrelevant and unnecessary provisions.

We must have legislative authority to encourage production of our vast quantities of natural gas, one of the cleanest and best sources of energy.

We must have the legal ability to set reasonable standards for the surface mining of coal.

And we must have the organizational structures to meet and administer our energy programs.

And therefore, tonight, as I did this morning in meeting with the Congressional leaders, I again urge the Congress to give its attention to the initiatives I recommended 6 months ago to meet these needs that I have described.

Finally, I have stressed repeatedly the necessity of increasing our energy research and development efforts. Last June, I announced a 5-year, $10 billion program to develop better ways of using energy and to explore and develop new energy sources. Last month, I announced plans for an immediate acceleration of that program.

We can take heart from the fact that we in the United States have half the world's known coal reserves. We have huge, untapped sources of natural gas. We have the most advanced nuclear technology known to man. We have oil in our continental shelves. We have oil shale out in the western part of the United States, and we have some of the finest technical and scientific minds in the world. In short, we have all the resources we need to meet the great challenge before us. Now we must demonstrate the will to meet that challenge.

[...]

Today the challenge is to regain the strength that we had earlier in this century, the strength of self-sufficiency. Our ability to meet our own energy needs is directly limited to our continued ability to act decisively and independently at home and abroad in the service of peace, not only for America but for all nations in the world.

I have ordered funding of this effort to achieve self-sufficiency far in excess of the funds that were expended on the Manhattan Project. But money is only one of the ingredients essential to the success of such a project. We must also have a unified commitment to that goal. We must have unified direction of the effort to accomplish it.

Because of the urgent need for an organization that would provide focused leadership for this effort, I am asking the Congress to consider my proposal for an Energy Research and Development Administration, separate from any other organizational initiatives, and to enact this legislation in the present session of the Congress.

Let us unite in committing the resources of this Nation to a major new endeavor, an endeavor that in this Bicentennial Era we can appropriately call "Project Independence."

Let us set as our national goal, in the spirit of Apollo, with the determination of the Manhattan Project, that by the end of this decade we will have developed the potential to meet our own energy needs without depending on any foreign energy sources.

Let us pledge that by 1980, under Project Independence, we shall be able to meet America's energy needs from America's own energy resources.

[...]

Source: Richard Nixon, *Public Papers of the Presidents of the United States: Richard Nixon, 1973* (Washington, DC: U.S. Government Printing Office, 1975), 916–922.

28. OAPEC Member Countries, Communiqué Issued after Meeting in Kuwait, December 25, 1973 [Excerpt]

Introduction

Having inflicted major economic difficulties on the United States and European nations by means of their oil embargo, Arab oil ministers were determined to continue their pressure on Israel's international backers. Meeting at Kuwait in late December 1973, oil ministers of the Organization of Arab Petroleum Exporting Countries (OAPEC) discussed what further measures they should take. They had, they stated, initially planned to cut oil supplies in January 1974 by an additional 5 percent, which would have meant an overall 30 percent cut in supplies since October 1973. Instead, they chose to reduce the overall cut to a mere 15 percent that month. The oil ministers' communiqué, issued at the end of the meeting, stated that since Japanese policy had moved in a pro-Arab direction since the embargo was first imposed, no further cuts would be imposed on supplies to Japan. Belgium received similar treatment. "[C]ertain friendly countries" were promised levels of oil supplies even higher than those they had been receiving in September 1973. Rather complacently, the Arab ministers noted that American public and congressional opinion was becoming less pro-Israeli and more pro-Arab, even though for the time being the Arab ministers still intended to maintain the oil embargo against the United States. They stated their intention of meeting again in February 1974, at which time, they implied, they would reconsider their position on oil exports to various nations. The partial restoration of Arab output may have stemmed in part from a wish to increase oil revenues. The tone of the communiqué also, however, distinctly suggested that the Arab oil ministers were enjoying their power of toying with the various states, favoring those who took a pro-Arab line while punishing those who did not.

Primary Source

Meeting in Kuwait, the Arab Oil Ministers were addressed by His Excellency Sheikh Ahmed Zaki Yamani, Saudi Arabian Minister for Oil and Mining Resources, and His Excellency Belaid Abdesselam, Minister of Industry and Energy of the Algerian Republic. Referring to the results of their visits to certain western capitals, the two Ministers described their impressions and made proposals, taking account of the results and effects of their visits.

The Ministers present considered the real aim of the oil measures they had taken and which was to make international public opinion aware—without however bringing about an economic collapse which might affect one or more of the world's nations—of the injustice done to the Arab nation as a result of the occupation of its territories and the expulsion of an entire Arab people, the Palestinian people.

They again reaffirmed—as stated continuously since 17th October—that the measures taken should in no way affect friendly countries, thus drawing a very clear distinction between those who support the Arabs, those who support the enemy and those who remain neutral.

The Arab Ministers present noted the changes which had occurred in Japanese policy towards the Arab cause as demonstrated in several ways, including the visit by the Japanese Deputy Prime Minister to certain Arab countries. They also took account of Japan's difficult economic situation and decided to accord it special treatment, excluding it completely from the application of the general cut in output in order to protect the Japanese economy and in the hope that the Japanese Government will appreciate this position and persevere in its fair and equitable attitude towards the Arab cause.

The Arab Ministers also considered Belgium's political stand. They decided not to apply the planned cut to its oil supplies and authorised the transit of its supplies through the Netherlands, provided there were full guarantees that all such oil would be delivered to Belgium. Furthermore, they decided to meet the real requirements of certain friendly countries even if such supplies raised their imports above the September 1973 level and provided Arab oil supplied to them was not diverted and did not replace oil from non-Arab sources.

In order to ensure the application of the abovementioned decisions, the Arab Ministers present decided to increase output in their respective countries by 10% as compared with September output, the new cut in output thus being reduced from 25% to 15%.

They also decided not to apply the 5% cut planned for January.

The Arab Ministers present noted with satisfaction the progressive trend emerging in American public opinion. Certain government circles are thus beginning to become aware of Arab problems and expansionist Israeli policy. This has been particularly clear in the objective and neutral positions towards the Arab-Israeli problem adopted by certain members of the American Senate and House of Representatives.

The Arab Oil Ministers hope that the desire of the American Government to help to find a peaceful and fair solution is a positive factor which will allow beneficial results to be achieved for all the nations of the world and for bilateral relations between the American nation and the Arab nations in particular. The embargo will be maintained for the United States and the Netherlands.

[...]

> **Source:** Western European Union, "Communiqué Issued after the OAPEC Ministerial Meeting (Kuwait, 25 December 1973)," *Western European Union Assembly-General Affairs Committee: A Retrospective View of the Political Year in Europe 1973*, April 1974, pp. 323–324.

29. Washington Conference, Final Communiqué, February 13, 1974

Introduction

Western leaders continued to seek coordinated policies to address the energy crisis and the economic difficulties it encouraged and intensified. In an effort to devise a common strategy to deal with these issues, in February 1974 European finance and energy ministers met in Washington, D.C., to review the situation and its implications. The final communiqué they issued called for concerted efforts by all nations, including the oil-producing and oil-consuming countries, to manage supply and demand and address the inflationary consequences of high oil prices and the impact they were likely to have on international transfers and on poorer developing nations. As meetings and leaders had previously done, the communiqué urged measures to conserve energy and restrict demand and the maximal development of both existing and alternative energy sources. The communiqué proposed greater cooperation among governments and such financial institutions as the World Bank and the International Monetary Fund (IMF) to handle the consequences of the disruptions to the existing balance-of-payments situation caused by major increases in oil and energy prices. Taking up one of the major grievances of both Arab states and many consumers, they "agreed to examine in detail the role of international oil companies." In a nod to ecological concerns, the finance ministers affirmed their commitment to protecting the "natural environment." As with many such declarations, much of this communiqué remained a dead letter, and throughout the 1970s oil-consuming governments around the world proved largely ineffective in addressing the damaging economic and political consequences of high oil prices.

Primary Source

Summary Statement

1. Foreign Ministers of Belgium, Canada, Denmark, France, the Federal Republic of Germany, Ireland, Italy, Japan, Luxembourg, the Netherlands, Norway, the United Kingdom, and the United States met in Washington from 11 to 13 February 1974. The European Community was represented as such by the President of the Council and the President of the Commission. Finance Ministers, Ministers with responsibility for Energy Affairs, Economic Affairs and Science and Technology Affairs also took part in the meeting. The Secretary-General of the OECD also participated in the meeting. The Ministers examined the international energy situation and its implications and charted a course of actions to meet this challenge which requires constructive and comprehensive solutions. To this end they agreed on specific steps to provide for effective international cooperation. The Ministers affirmed that solutions to the world's energy problem should be sought in consultation with producer countries and other consumers.

Analysis of the Situation

2. They noted that during the past three decades progress in improving productivity and standards of living was greatly facilitated by the ready availability of increasing supplies of energy at fairly stable prices. They recognized that the problem of meeting growing demand existed before the current situation and that the needs of the world economy for increased energy supplies require positive long-term solutions.

3. They concluded that the current energy situation results from an intensification of these underlying factors and from political developments.

4. They reviewed the problems created by the large rise in oil prices and agreed with the serious concern expressed by the International Monetary Fund's Committee of Twenty at its recent Rome meeting over the abrupt and significant changes in prospect for the world balance of payments structure.

5. They agreed that present petroleum prices presented the structure of world trade and finance with an unprecedented situation. They recognized that none of the consuming countries could hope to insulate itself from these developments, or expect to deal with the payments impact of oil prices by the adoption of monetary or trade measures alone. In their view, the present situation,

if continued, could lead to serious deterioration in income and employment, intensify inflationary pressures, and endanger the welfare of nations. They believed that financial measures by themselves will not be able to deal with the strains of the current situation.

6. They expressed their particular concern about the consequences of the situation for the developing countries and recognized the need for efforts by the entire international community to resolve this problem. At current oil prices the additional energy costs for developing countries will cause a serious setback to the prospect for economic development of these countries.

General Conclusions

7. They affirmed that, in the pursuit of national policies, whether in the trade, monetary or energy fields, efforts should be made to harmonize the interests of each country on the one hand and the maintenance of the world economic system on the other. Concerted international cooperation between all the countries concerned including oil producing countries could help to accelerate an improvement in the supply and demand situation, ameliorate the adverse economic consequences of the existing situation and lay the groundwork for a more equitable and stable international energy relationship.

8. They felt that these considerations taken as a whole made it essential that there should be a substantial increase of international cooperation in all fields. Each participant in the Conference stated its firm intention to do its utmost to contribute to such an aim, in close cooperation both with the other consumer countries and with the producer countries.

9.(1) They concurred in the need for a comprehensive action programme to deal with all facets of the world energy situation by cooperative measures. In so doing they will build on the work of the OECD. They recognized that they may wish to invite, as appropriate, other countries to join with them in these efforts. Such an action programme of international cooperation would include, as appropriate, the sharing of means and efforts, while concerting national policies, in such areas as:

(a) the conservation of energy and restraint of demand;

(b) a system of allocating oil supplies in times of emergency and severe shortages;

(c) the acceleration of development of additional energy sources so as to diversify energy supplies;

(d) the acceleration of energy research and development programmes through international cooperative efforts.

10. With respect to monetary and economic questions, they decided to intensify their cooperation and to give impetus to the work being undertaken in the IMF, the World Bank and the OECD on the economic and monetary consequences of the current energy situation, in particular to deal with balance of payments disequilibria. They agreed that:

(i) In dealing with the balance of payments impact of oil prices they stressed the importance of avoiding competitive depreciation and the escalation of restrictions on trade and payments or disruptive actions in external borrowing.(1)

(ii) While financial cooperation can only partially alleviate the problems which have recently arisen for the international economic system, they will intensify work on short-term financial measures and possible longer-term mechanisms to reinforce existing official and market credit facilities.(1)

(iii) They will pursue domestic economic policies which will reduce as much as possible the difficulties resulting from the current energy cost levels.(1)

(iv) They will make strenuous efforts to maintain and enlarge the flow of development aid bilaterally and through multilateral institutions, on the basis of international solidarity embracing all countries with appropriate resources.

11. Further, they have agreed to accelerate wherever practicable their own national programmes of new energy sources and technology which will help the overall worldwide supply and demand situation.

12. They agreed to examine in detail the role of international oil companies.

13. They stressed the continued importance of maintaining and improving the natural environment as part of developing energy sources and agreed to make this an important goal of their activity.

14. They further agreed that there was need to develop a cooperative multilateral relationship with producing countries, and other consuming countries that takes into account the long-term interests of all. They are ready to exchange technical information with these countries on the problem of stabilizing energy supplies with regard to quantity and prices.

15. They welcomed the initiatives in the UN to deal with the larger issues of energy and primary products at a worldwide level and in particular for a special session of the UN General Assembly.

Establishment of follow-on Machinery

16.(1) They agreed to establish a coordinating group headed by senior officials to direct and to coordinate the development of the actions referred to above. The coordinating group shall decide how best to organize its work. It should:

(a) Monitor and give focus to the tasks that might be addressed in existing organizations;

(b) Establish such ad hoc working groups as may be necessary to undertake tasks for which there are presently no suitable bodies;

(c) Direct preparations of a conference of consumer and producer countries which will be held at the earliest possible opportunity and which, if necessary, will be preceded by a further meeting of consumer countries.

17.(1) They agreed that the preparations for such meetings should involve consultations with developing countries and other consumer and producer countries.

(1) *France does not accept this paragraph.*

Source: "Final Communiqué of the Washington Conference," *Bulletin of the European Communities* 2 (February 1974): 19–22.

30. The Algiers Agreement, March 6, 1975

Introduction

A long-standing territorial dispute over navigation rights in the strategic Shatt al-Arab waterway dividing Iran and Iraq had been a source of contention between the two states ever since the 17th century. After World War I, British advisers in Iraq observed the thalweg principle: that the dividing line between the two states ran along the middle of the river. The controversy burgeoned again after World War II, and under Saddam Hussein Iraq claimed the entire waterway, Iraq's only outlet to the Persian Gulf, as far as the Iranian shore for a length of 200 miles inland. In 1975 Mohammad Reza Shah Pahlavi of Iran and Hussein, then vice president of Iraq's Revolutionary Council, met in Algiers and reached an agreement. Iraq accepted the thalweg principle in return for greater access to the river; Iran also agreed to end its support for Iraqi guerrillas who opposed Hussein's Baathist government. Iraq's decision in 1980 to abrogate this agreement was the immediate cause of the bloody eight-year war between Iran and Iraq.

Primary Source

The two High Contracting Parties have decided to:

First: Carry out a final delineation of their land boundaries in accordance with the Constantinople Protocol of 1913 and the Proceedings of the Border Delimitation Commission of 1914.

Second: Demarcate their river boundaries according to the thalweg line.

Third: Accordingly, the two parties shall restore security and mutual confidence along their joint borders. They shall also commit themselves to carry out a strict and effective observation of their joint borders so as to put an end to all infiltrations of a subversive nature wherever they may come from.

Fourth: The two parties have also agreed to consider the aforesaid arrangements as inseparable elements of a comprehensive solution. Consequently, any infringement of one of its components shall naturally contradict the spirit of the Algiers Accord. The two parties shall remain in constant contact with President Houari Boumedienne who shall provide, when necessary, Algeria's brotherly assistance whenever needed in order to apply these resolutions.

The two parties have decided to restore the traditional ties of good neighbourliness and friendship, in particular by eliminating all negative factors in their relations and through constant exchange of views on issues of mutual interest and promotion of mutual co-operation.

The two parties officially declare that the region ought to be secure from any foreign interference.

The Foreign Ministers of Iraq and Iran shall meet in the presence of Algeria's Foreign Minister on 15 March 1975 in Tehran in order to make working arrangements for the Iraqi-Iranian joint commission which was set up to apply the resolutions taken by mutual agreement as specified above. And in accordance with the desire of the two parties, Algeria shall be invited to the meetings of the Iraqi-Iranian joint commission. The commission shall determine its agenda and working procedures and hold meetings if necessary. The meetings shall be alternately held in Baghdad and Tehran.

His Majesty the Shah accepted with pleasure the invitation extended to him by His Excellency President Ahmad Hasan al-Bakr to pay a state visit to Iraq. The date of the visit shall be fixed by mutual agreement.

On the other hand, Saddam Hussein agreed to visit Iran officially at a date to be fixed by the two parties.

HM the Shah of Iran and Saddam Hussein expressed their deep gratitude to President Houari Boumedienne, who, motivated by brotherly sentiments and a spirit of disinterestedness, worked for the establishment of a direct contact between the leaders of the two countries and consequently contributed to reviving a new era in the Iraqi-Iranian relations with a view to achieving the higher interests of the future of the region in question.

Source: "Algiers Accord—1975," Mideast Web, http://www.mideast-web.org/algiersaccord.htm.

31. President Jimmy Carter, Toast at a State Dinner, Tehran, Iran, December 31, 1977 [Excerpts]

Introduction

Like his predecessors since the 1950s, U.S. president Jimmy Carter regarded Mohammad Reza Shah Pahlavi of Iran as a key U.S. ally and his country as a bulwark of stability in the Persian Gulf region. In the last days of 1977 and the beginning of 1978, the president toured seven European, Middle Eastern, and Asian countries, spending New Year's Eve in Tehran. At a lavish state banquet hosted by the shah and Empress Farah Diva, Carter lauded their accomplishments in Iran, which he described as "an island of stability in one of the more troubled areas of the world." There was, he said, "no other nation on Earth who is closer to us in planning for our mutual security." He hoped that the two would work closely together to solve regional and international problems. Carter also told the shah how impressed he was by the "transformation" of Iran due to the shah's leadership. The president commented especially on the warm and friendly welcome that he himself had received from thousands of Iranian people as his motorcade passed through the streets earlier that day. He reminded his listeners that many young Iranians were at that time studying in the United States, just as 30,000 Americans were working in Iran, and expressed his hopes that such ties would result in generations of friendship and cooperation between the two countries. In light of subsequent events, the president's comments would come to seem particularly ironic. Just over a year later, popular discontent forced the embattled shah to leave Iran, and the country's new Islamic leadership proved itself bitterly hostile to the United States.

Primary Source

Your Majesties and distinguished leaders of Iran from all walks of life: I would like to say just a few words tonight in appreciation for your hospitality and the delightful evening that we've already experienced with you. Some have asked why we came to Iran so close behind the delightful visit that we received from the Shah and Empress Farah just a month or so ago. After they left our country, I asked my wife, "With whom would you like to spend

New Year's Eve?" And she said, "Above all others, I think, with the Shah and Empress Farah." So we arranged the trip accordingly and came to be with you.

[...]

But we do have a close friendship that's very meaningful to all the people in our country. I think it is a good harbinger of things to come—that we could close out [the] Administration of Jimmy Carter, 1977 Dec. 31 this year and begin a new year with those in whom we have such great confidence and with whom we share such great responsibilities for the present and for the future.

[...]

Iran, because of the great leadership of the Shah, is an island of stability in one of the more troubled areas of the world.

This is a great tribute to you, Your Majesty, and to your leadership and to the respect and the admiration and love which your people give to you.

The transformation that has taken place in this nation is indeed remarkable under your leadership. And as we sat together this afternoon, discussing privately for a few moments what might be done to bring peace to the Middle East, I was profoundly impressed again not only with your wisdom and your judgment and your sensitivity and insight but also with the close compatibility that we found in addressing this difficult question.

As we visit with leaders who have in their hands the responsibility for making decisions that can bring peace to the Middle East and ensure a peaceful existence for all of us who live in the world, no matter where our nations might be, it's important that we continue to benefit from your sound judgment and from your good advice.

We also had a chance to discuss another potential troubled area, the Horn of Africa. And here again we live at a great distance from it. But this region, which already sees the initiation of hostility and combat, needs to be brought under the good influence of you and others who live in this region. And we will be glad to cooperate in any way that we can. We want peace to return. We want Somalia and Ethiopia to be friends again, border disputes to be eased and those of us who do have any influence at all to use that influence for these purposes.

We have also known about the great benefits that we derive in our own nation from the close business relationships that we have with Iran.

As I drove through the beautiful streets of Tehran today with the Shah, we saw literally thousands of Iranian citizens standing beside the street with a friendly attitude, expressing their welcome to me. And I also saw hundreds, perhaps even thousands of American citizens who stand there welcoming their President in a nation which has taken them to heart and made them feel at home. There are about 30,000 Americans here who work in close harmony with the people of Iran to carve out a better future for you, which also helps to ensure, Your Majesty, a better future for ourselves.

We share industrial growth, we share scientific achievements, we share research and development knowledge, and this gives us the stability for the present which is indeed valuable to both our countries.

We are also blessed with the largest number of foreign students in our country from your own nation. And I think this ensures, too, that we share the knowledge that is engendered by our great universities, but also that when these young leaders come back to your country for many years in the future, for many generations in the future, our friendship is ensured. We are very grateful for this and value it very much....

[...]

The cause of human rights is one that also is shared deeply by our people and by the leaders of our two nations.

Our talks have been priceless, our friendship is irreplaceable, and my own gratitude is to the Shah, who in his wisdom and with his experience has been so helpful to me, a new leader.

We have no other nation on Earth who is closer to us in planning for our mutual military security. We have no other nation with whom we have closer consultation on regional problems that concern us both. And there is no leader with whom I have a deeper sense of personal gratitude and personal friendship.

On behalf of the people of the United States, I would like to offer a toast at this time to the great leaders of Iran, the Shah and the Shahbanou and to the people of Iran and to the world peace that we hope together we can help to bring.

Source: Jimmy Carter, *Public Papers of the Presidents of the United States: Jimmy Carter, 1977,* Book 2 (Washington, DC: U.S. Government Printing Office, 1978), 2220–2222.

32. President Jimmy Carter, Remarks in an Interview with Barbara Walters Warning the Soviet Union Not to Interfere in Iran, December 14, 1978

Introduction

In November 1978 President Jimmy Carter stated that he did not believe that the Soviet Union was responsible for the growing domestic unrest within Iran. In an attempt to ensure that this continued to be the case, the U.S. government took direct action. In an interview one month later with the well-known television journalist Barbara Walters, Carter confirmed the accuracy of reports that in the previous two weeks he had exchanged letters with Soviet secretary-general Leonid Brezhnev. In this correspondence the president had "made it very clear" that the United States "ha[d] no intention of interfering in the internal affairs of Iran" but that neither would it permit other powers to meddle there. The president told Walters that there was no evidence that the Soviet Union had sought to influence the course of events within Iran. He expressed "support" for the shah's efforts to engage in dialogue with opposition leaders and establish a more broadly based democratic government committed to social change. When pressed by Walters to expand on his words that "We support [the shah] fully" by stating whether this support was "primarily verbal" and what "action" the United States might take should it seems likely that the shah would fall, Carter refused to speculate. Told by her that "if the Shah does fall, it threatens our oil supply, it threatens Israel's oil supply, it threatens Saudi Arabia, it threatens the whole Persian Gulf," Carter declined "conjecturing on something that's hypothetical." He merely expressed the hope that Iran would continue to enjoy fundamental "stability." At this point, the president clearly wished to keep all options open while refraining from any move that might be considered direct intervention in Iranian affairs and could potentially inflame American relations with both Iran and the Soviet Union.

Primary Source

MS. WALTERS. Mr. President, there are reports that you've recently sent messages to the Soviet Union, warning them to keep hands off of Iran. Can you confirm these, and can you tell us if you have any information on Russian involvement in Iran?

THE PRESIDENT. Yes, that's accurate.

MS. WALTERS. You have sent the letters?

THE PRESIDENT. Yes. President Brezhnev and I exchanged messages.

MS. WALTERS. Recently?

THE PRESIDENT. Within the last few weeks, a couple of weeks. And I made it very clear to them, to the Soviets, that we have no intention of interfering in the internal affairs of Iran and that we have no intention of permitting others to interfere in the internal affairs of Iran.

I think it's good to point out, Barbara, that Iran has a 2,500-year history of statecraft, of managing their own affairs properly. Obviously, they've had ups and downs, as we have in our own country. But there's a certain stability there, a certain inclination and capability of the Iranians to govern themselves that I think is a stabilizing factor. We don't know what changes will take place.

MS. WALTERS. Have the Russians been involved, sir, that you know of?

THE PRESIDENT. As far as we know, they have not. We monitor the situation closely. Obviously, there is a Communist party there, the Tudeh party, which perhaps is inclined to encourage violence or disruption in order to change the existing government. But the Shah is communicating with opposition leaders. He is committed to a broader base for the government. He is working toward democratic principles and social change. And he has been embattled lately. And we obviously support him fully.

MS. WALTERS. When we talk about support, what do we mean today, 1978, post-Vietnam, by support? For example, if the Shah does fall, it threatens our oil supply, it threatens Israel's oil supply, it threatens Saudi Arabia, it threatens the whole Persian Gulf. At what point would support turn into action and what kind of action, if any?

THE PRESIDENT. I am not prepared to answer that question.

MS. WALTERS. Because there is no answer, or because—

THE PRESIDENT. Well, the answer is difficult. But I think just conjecturing on something that's hypothetical like that, assuming all the catastrophes that might possibly occur in the Persian Gulf, is something on which I don't want to comment. I don't think it's going to happen. And if I were to surmise that if it happens, we would do this, it would be interpreted by some as an actual prediction by me that it's going to happen, and I don't think it's going to happen.

MS. WALTERS. Is support primarily verbal support?

THE PRESIDENT. No. We have treaty agreements with Iran. We have strong defense agreements with Iran. We look on Iran, as do their neighbors, as being a stabilizing factor. Even the Soviet Union shares a long border with Iran. I'm sure they want stability there on their border. Exactly the formation of the government—I can't speak for the Soviets, but I think that for world peace and for the Soviets, and for us, certainly for the entire Middle East–Persian Gulf region, a stability is desirable, and that's what we want, also.

Source: Jimmy Carter, *Public Papers of the Presidents of the United States: Jimmy Carter, 1978,* Book 2 (Washington, DC: U.S. Government Printing Office, 1979), 2255–2256.

A. [Vance] The Shah was allowed to come into the country for humanitarian purposes when he indicated that there was a possibility that his health was deteriorating. We, of course, worked with him and helped to set up arrangements whereby he could come and receive the tests, treatment, and, eventually, the operation. He obviously will be allowed to remain however long it takes for his recuperation.

Source: "Question and Answer Session in Gainesville," *Department of State Bulletin* 79(2033) (1979): 23.

33. U.S. Secretary of State Cyrus Vance, News Conference Statement on Permission for the Shah of Iran to Come to the United States for Medical Treatment, October 26, 1979

Introduction

One reason Mohammad Shah Reza Pahlavi left Iran in January 1979 was his need for medical treatment for advanced cancer. Initially the U.S. government offered to accept the shah, but he chose to go elsewhere, to Egypt, Morocco, the Bahamas, and Mexico. As his health deteriorated, the shah hoped to visit American medical facilities in New York City. President Jimmy Carter and Secretary of State Cyrus Vance were initially reluctant to permit this. In February 1979 a fundamentalist Islamic regime, whose leader, Ayatollah Ruhollah Khomeini, anathematized the United States, considering it the seat of atheistic irreligion, seized power in Tehran. Carter and Vance did not wish to inflame American-Iranian relations further by offering the shah asylum. In September 1979 Vance told a group in New York that it would not be in the American "national interest" to admit the shah at that juncture. Under pressure from longtime associates of the shah, including former secretary of state Henry Kissinger and Chase Manhattan Bank officials David Rockefeller and John J. McCloy, in late October 1979 the Carter administration reversed this policy. The shah was permitted to make a brief stopover in the United States, solely for medical treatment. His arrival proved the trigger for young Iranian militants to storm the U.S. embassy in Tehran and take its American personnel hostage, the beginning of a lengthy crisis that would not be resolved until January 1981. Unwilling to provoke yet more troubles, U.S. officials pressed the shah to leave the country once his medical treatment was completed, and he did so on December 15, 1979, traveling first to Panama and then on to Cairo, Egypt, where he died in July 1980.

Primary Source

Q. Is the Shah of Iran going to be allowed to stay in this country to receive his chemotherapy treatments, and who made the arrangements to bring him into the country?

34. President Jimmy Carter, Proclamation No. 4702 Prohibiting Petroleum Imports from Iran, November 12, 1979

Introduction

On November 4, 1979, young Iranian militants, infuriated by the decision of President Jimmy Carter to allow the exiled Mohammad Reza Shah Pahlavi of Iran to enter the United States for medical treatment, seized the U.S. embassy in Tehran and took prisoner 63 American diplomats and 3 civilians. This was the beginning of the Iran Hostage Crisis, which lasted 444 days. A few Americans were released fairly expeditiously, mostly for medical reasons, but 52 remained hostages until January 20, 1991, the last day of Carter's presidency. The episode marked the beginning of many years of deep antagonism between the United States and Iran. Carter responded by imposing a wide range of economic sanctions upon Iran. In the previous year Iranian oil exports to the West had already dwindled dramatically, largely due to the prevailing disorder in that country. On November 12, 1979, Carter issued a proclamation formally banning all petroleum imports from Iran to the United States, the beginning of a wide range of sanctions that were expanded in April 1980, when the United States broke diplomatic relations with Iran and forbade virtually all economic dealings between American citizens and companies and Iran, and would last more than a decade and amount to an effective embargo on all trade between Iran and the United States. While these measures damaged Iran economically, they had little or no impact in terms of persuading its fundamentalist Islamic regime to alter its anti-Western policies. Carter, meanwhile, urged Americans to make every effort to use less energy, which would in turn reduce their country's dependence on foreign oil.

Primary Source

Imports of Petroleum and Petroleum Products

By the President of the United States of America

A Proclamation

The Secretary of the Treasury in a memorandum dated November 12, 1979, and the Secretary of Energy in consultation with the Secretaries of State and Defense, have informed me that recent developments in Iran have exacerbated the threat to the national security posed by imports of petroleum and petroleum products. Those developments underscore the threat to our national security which results from our reliance on Iran as a source of crude oil. The Secretaries have recommended that I take steps immediately to eliminate the dependence of the United States on Iran as a source of crude oil.

I agree with these recommendations and that the changes proposed are consistent with the purposes of Proclamation 3279, as amended.

Now, THEREFORE, I, JIMMY CARTER, President of the United States of America, by the authority vested in me by the Constitution and the laws of the United States, including Section 232 of the Trade Expansion Act of 1962, as amended, (19 U.S.C. 1862) do hereby proclaim that:

SECTION 1. Section 1 of Proclamation 3279, as amended, is further amended by the addition of a new paragraph (e) to read as follows:

Sec. l (e). Notwithstanding any other provision of this Proclamation, no crude oil produced in Iran (except crude oil loaded aboard maritime vessels prior to November 13, 1979) or unfinished oil or finished products refined in possessions or free trade zones of the United States from such crude oil, may be entered into the customs territory of the United States.

SEC. 2. Section 11 of Proclamation No. 3279, as amended, is further amended in paragraph (1) to read as follows:

(1) The term "imports", when applied to crude oil other than that produced in Iran, includes both entry for consumption and withdrawal from warehouse for consumption, but excludes unfinished oil and finished products processed in the United States territories and foreign trade zones from crude oil produced in the United States.

Source: Jimmy Carter, *Public Papers of the Presidents of the United States: Jimmy Carter, 1979,* Book 2 (Washington, DC: U.S. Government Printing Office, 1980), 2110–2111.

35. President Jimmy Carter, Executive Order No. 12170 Blocking Iranian Government Assets in the United States, November 14, 1979

Introduction

Two days after issuing Proclamation No. 4702 prohibiting petroleum imports from Iran, President Jimmy Carter followed up with an executive order freezing all Iranian government assets in the United States. This meant that the Iranian government could no longer access any funds, investments, or property it held in the United States. These were to be administered by the secretary of the U.S. Treasury. It was estimated that Iranian government assets in the United States amounted to US$8 billion, a sizable portion of the regime's overseas assets. Denying the government of Ayatollah Ruhollah Khomeini access to these was an important bargaining tool in the Algerian-brokered negotiations that eventually brought the Iran Hostage Crisis to an end.

Primary Source

Blocking Iranian Government Property

Executive Order 12170

November 14, 1979

Pursuant to the authority vested in me as President by the Constitution and the laws of the United States including the International Emergency Economic Powers Act, 50 U.S.C.A. sec. 1701 et seq., the National Emergencies Act, 50 U.S.C. sec. 1601 et seq., and 3 U.S.C. sec. 301, I, JIMMY CARTER, President of the United States, find that the situation in Iran constitutes an unusual and extraordinary threat to the national security, foreign policy and economy of the United States and hereby declare a national emergency to deal with that threat.

I hereby order blocked all property and interests in property of the Government of Iran, its instrumentalities and controlled entities and the Central Bank of Iran which are or become subject to the jurisdiction of the United States or which are in or come within the possession or control of persons subject to the jurisdiction of the United States.

The Secretary of the Treasury is authorized to employ all powers granted to me by the International Emergency Economic Powers Act to carry out the provisions of this order.

This order is effective immediately and shall be transmitted to the Congress and published in the FEDERAL REGISTER.

JIMMY CARTER

Source: Jimmy Carter, *Public Papers of the Presidents of the United States: Jimmy Carter, 1979*, Book 2 (Washington, DC: U.S. Government Printing Office, 1980), 2118–2119.

36. Central Committee, Communist Party of the Soviet Union, Decree Authorizing Introduction of Soviet Troops to Afghanistan, December 12, 1979, and Account by Anatoly Chernyaev of Deliberations Leading Up to This Decision, February 26, 1993 [Excerpt]

Introduction

In December 1979, Soviet leaders decided to send troops to intervene in Afghanistan and issued a decree to this effect. In February 1993 Anatoly Sergeevich Chernyaev of the Soviet Foreign Ministry, who served as Soviet secretary-general and president Mikhail Gorbachev's personal adviser on foreign affairs from 1986 to 1991, reflected on this decision at a conference of top-level Soviet and U.S. decision makers held at Princeton University. Chernyaev, who was serving in the Foreign Ministry at the time, put the blame for the decision squarely upon four individuals: Defense Minister Dmitry Ustinov, Foreign Minister Andrey Gromyko, KGB head Yuri Andropov, and Boris Ponomarev, head of the International Department of the Central Committee of the Communist Party of the Soviet Union (CPSU). The ailing Soviet secretary-general Leonid Brezhnev, the country's nominal supreme leader, apparently had very little to do with choosing this foreign policy option, and those who made the decision were probably jockeying for position in the leadership contest that they knew would follow the declining Brezhnev's death or retirement. Alexander Aleksandrovich Bessmertnykh, who became Soviet foreign minister in 1991 and was also present at the Princeton conference, was as critical as Chernyaev of this decision, describing it as "the complete breakdown of the policy-making standard." Chernyaev detailed how, immediately after the Soviet invasion of Afghanistan, a group of prominent scholars analyzed the situation and concluded that their country had embarked on "a reckless adventure that will end very badly for us." Their report, however, was suppressed for years. Only when Mikhail Gorbachev came to power did the Soviet leadership decide to end the military intervention in Afghanistan, and even then it took him four years to accomplish this.

Primary Source

Central Committee CPSU Decree Authorizing Introduction of Soviet Troops to Afghanistan, 12/12/1979

Chaired by Comrade L.I. Brezhnev

Decree of the CC of the CPSU

On the Situation in "A"

I. To approve the considerations and measures set forth by comrades Andropov Yu. V., Ustinov D. F., and Gromyko A. A.

To permit them, in the course of implementing these measures, to make minor adjustments to them.

Issues requiring decisions of the CC are to be raised in a timely fashion with the Politburo.

Implementation of all these measures is assigned to comrades Ustinov D. F., and Gromyko, A. A. to keep the Politburo informed about the progress of carrying out the projected measures.

Secretary of the CC L. Brezhnev

Account by Anatoly Chernyaev of Deliberations Leading up to the Decision

Mr. Oberdorfer: There was an announcement of the Carter doctrine in 1980: Any threat to the Persian Gulf would be responded to by the United States. Something which didn't come into play that time though it did during the Bush administration.

Mr. Shiltz: That was in Reagan administration, too and it's still out there as far as I know.

Mr. Saunders: It was actually written into a presidential speech at the last minute—again, without broad government consensus. Here is another decision, this one on the American side, in which things happened at high levels without the[m] necessarily thinking through the long-term implications.

Mr. Oberdorfer: Mr. Chernyaev—

Mr. Chernyaev: We really very often are amazed at how much analytical ability goes into explaining why the Soviet leadership decided to invade Afghanistan. There is the assumption that it was a rational decision. The U.S. analysts seem to think for the Kremlin, the KGB, and the Central Committee, and they try to rationally explain what happened and why it happened. But the trouble is that there was nothing of the kind going on in the Central Committee or in the KGB in the way of rational analytical work.

Mr. Bessmertnykh speaks about ideological reasons. I would agree with that, with one correction. It was mostly ideological justification. As far as the initiators are concerned, people like Ustinov—and also, I would say, Gromyko—really did not care much about any ideology. The argument that we were trying to strengthen the security of our southern borders, or even that were pushing toward warm seas, is really total nonsense because everyone understood that we had no need for strengthening security over there at that time, with the overall strategic situation the way it was. Those who initiated the invasion were smart enough to understand that making Afghanistan a socialist country, a part of what was called the socialist community, was utterly absurd; it was totally crazy.

So what was it? It was the manifestation of a totally arbitrary and irresponsible approach to policy making that was typical of the Soviet leadership at that time. There is no document that shows who first had that crazy idea of moving troops into Afghanistan. Of course, in the International Department of the Central Committee we tended to blame Gromyko, and I still do not rule out that he was the one into whose head this kind of idea came. But I know that before that formal meeting of the Politburo, even these that voted, had nothing to do with developing that decision.

It was a decision of four persons: Ustinov, Gromyko, Andropov, and Ponomarev. Ustinov and Gromyko were totally in favor of acting boldly, of moving with troops, sending Karmal down there and installing him in Kabul. The idea was very simple: ["]Well, it's there, why not move in? Why not do it on the cheap?" There had been the assassination of Mr. Taraki, the previous Afghan leader. Amin was behaving in a way that looked like he could not be controlled. So why not install a person with whom it would be easier to deal? That was the entire theory behind that. That was all.

It is said that there were some doubts and hesitation on the part of Andropov. I don't believe that very much, because I feel that a lot of the decision would not have been possible without the reports from his people. So had he had doubts, he would have said so. As for Ponomarev, he knew that even in the Communist parties and the democratic organizations that wouldn't be welcomed, and therefore he rather weakly expressed some doubts. But of course, then he very quickly reoriented himself, saluted, and toed the general line.

Ponomarev was aware of my previous discussion with Mr. Wallace, who was a member of the British Communist Party and who knew the situation in the region very, very well. He was an expert. After the Taraki assassination, Wallace came to see me and we discussed the situation. He asked me, "What are you going to do?" I said, "What should we do? We won't do anything, I think." I said that Taraki had invited Soviet troops to come in thirteen times and we had refused. Then he laughed and said "Well if you choose to do it, ask us, the British, because we have a lot of experience being there."

And a week after the invasion a group of Soviet scholars sent a report to the Ministry of Foreign Affairs. Gorbachev later said in a meeting of the Politburo that he became aware of this report after he became general secretary. The group of scholars who sent that paper was headed by professor Gankovsky. I know him from my university years. He was a major expert on Afghanistan. In that memorandum, a week after the invasion, they analyzed all the possible consequences of the invasion from the standpoint of history, psychology, sociology, politics, national experience, the balance of forces, the surrounding countries, the Muslim world, everything. Their conclusion was that this is a reckless adventure that will end very badly for us, that this is trouble, that this is bad, that this is destructive. And I know that Kornienko afterwards was very much in favor of withdrawing the troops. I heard his reports to the Politburo, and afterwards he stood very firmly for withdrawing the troops from Afghanistan. But Gorbachev, at one point when he was very emotional—he was seething—said to me "You know, Kornienko is withdrawing troops now, but that memorandum from the scholars was in his room, in his desk, locked up, and no one saw that for years and years." It was just sitting there—until the decision was taken to withdraw the troops.

And now about Gorbachev. Right after his election as general secretary on March 16, 1985, Geo[r]giy Arbatov (head of the Institute of the United States and Canada in Moscow) had a talk with Gorbachev. By that time they had already established a good rapport. In the initial years of perestroika, Arbatov was something like a foreign policy confidant of Gorbachev. Arbatov and I had known each other for thirty years, so he also wanted to give me an idea of how to deal with big people and with international affairs. Arbatov told me that when he met with Gorbachev soon after his election as general secretary, Gorbachev had showed him a piece of paper on which there was a list of international questions that he had prioritized (as to) what he wanted to deal with first. Item 7 or 8 was Afghanistan. Arbatov, who was a rather bold man, said "Mikhail Sergeevich, I would place Afghanistan first." Gorbachev said, "Yes, I agree." He said to me afterwards, "This is the number one task that we have to resolve." It would take a long time to discuss why Gorbachev, who from the very outset believed that this was a problem that has to be solved quickly—why still it took four years for us to complete the withdrawal from Afghanistan. I'm trying to [ad]dress that question in the book that I have written.

But as early as the summer of 1985, Gorbachev began to work to educate the members of the Politburo. He brought huge stacks of letters from the mothers of soldiers, from soldiers and officers, to the Politburo. He even brought letters from two generals who were fighting in Afghanistan. He read those letters, which really were very dramatic documents, to the members of the Politburo. The main point made in all of those letters was, why are we there? What are we doing there? In those letters, officers were saying, "We cannot explain to the soldiers why we are in Afghanistan." "How come this is called internationalist duty, when we are destroying villages and killing innocent citizens, and we see terrible things happening?" Those letters also complained that what the newspaper Pravda wrote about Afghanistan was all lies. "The Afghans are not fighting mujaheddin. We are fighting against mujaheddin." At least three times he read out those letter[s] to the members of the Politburo. However, at that time he was not yet saying that the invasion had been a mistake. His conclusion was that Karmal, the Afghan leader, would have to be removed and there would have to be another person with whom you could discuss the withdrawal from Afghanistan.

Mr. Obendorfer: I just want to add something to this. According to conservative estimates, about 1 million of Afghanistan's 12.5 million people had been killed by the time the Soviet troops departed. About 5 million out of 12.5 million people had fled as refugees to neighboring Pakistan or Iran. At least another 1 million had been displaced from their homes within the country. Most of the deaths were civilian, but close to 100,000 resistance fighters, the mujaheddin, were also among the dead. The official Soviet Defense Ministry figure for Soviet military deaths was 13,831, but that included only those who had been killed in action. A more comprehensive estimate of Soviet war deaths from all causes was 36,000. By 1989 it was estimated that three-fourths of Afghanistan's villages had been severely damaged or destroyed, in addition to large sections of the country's few major cities. . . .

Source: William C. Wohlforth, ed., *Witnesses to the End of the Cold War* (Baltimore: Johns Hopkins University Press, 1996), 136–139, 291–292.

37. U.S. Department of State, Statement on Afghanistan, December 26, 1979

Introduction

The American response to the 1979 Christmas Day Soviet military intervention in Afghanistan was swift. Within a few hours, the U.S. State Department issued an official statement deploring the new scale of Soviet involvement in the affairs of that country. State Department spokesman Hodding Carter III read news correspondents a statement describing how Soviet transport planes had made more than 150 flights into Kabul on December 25 and 26. He also mentioned signs that at least five divisions of Soviet troops had massed on the border with Afghanistan and appeared ready to enter the country. The U.S. government strongly condemned this "blatant military interference into the internal affairs of an independent sovereign state." Carter also told newsmen that the United States was making strong direct representations on the subject to Soviet officials.

Primary Source

On December 25–26, there was a large-scale Soviet airlift into Kabul International Airport, perhaps involving over 150 flights. The aircraft include both large transports (AN-22s) and smaller transports (AN-12s). Several hundred Soviet troops have been seen at the Kabul airport and various kinds of field equipment have been flown in. I cannot give you an estimate of numbers.

The Soviet military buildup north of the Afghan border is continuing, and we now have indications that there are the equivalent of five divisions in Soviet areas adjacent to Afghanistan. It appears that the Soviets are crossing a new threshold in their military deployments into Afghanistan. We believe that members of the international community should condemn such blatant military interference into the internal affairs of an independent sovereign state. We are making our views known directly to the Soviets.

Source: U.S. Department of State, *American Foreign Policy, 1977–1980* (Washington, DC: Department of State, 1983), 809.

38. United Nations Security Council Resolution 462, January 7, 1980, and United Nations General Assembly Resolution ES-6/2, January 14, 1980

Introduction

The United States moved quickly to bring Soviet behavior in Afghanistan to the attention of the United Nations (UN) Security Council and General Assembly. On January 7, 1980, the Security Council adopted a resolution, drafted by Bangladesh, Jamaica, Niger, the Philippines, and Zambia, deploring the Soviet armed intervention as inconsistent with the respect for all states' "sovereignty, territorial integrity and political independence" enshrined in the UN Charter. The resolution demanded immediate and unconditional withdrawal of all "foreign" troops, leaving the Afghan people free to determine their own form of government. One week later, by a majority of 104 votes to 18, the UN General Assembly passed a resolution that likewise condemned the situation in Afghanistan. Rather than specifically condemning the Soviet Union by name, the General Assembly resolution followed that of the Security Council in deploring "foreign" intervention in Afghanistan and called for the withdrawal of all "foreign" troops. Besides expressing concern over the broader regional destabilizing impact of armed intervention in Afghanistan, the General Assembly resolution also brought up the problem of the "large outflow of refugees from Afghanistan," which it deplored on humanitarian grounds. All parties involved were asked to restore conditions in Afghanistan, which would facilitate the return home of these refugees, while the international community was requested to provide them with humanitarian assistance.

Primary Source

The Security Council,

Having considered the letter dated 3 January 1980 addressed to the President of the Security Council (S/1374 and Add. 1 and 2),

Gravely concerned over recent developments in Afghanistan and their implications for international peace and security,

Reaffirms the right of all peoples to determine their own future free from outside interference, including their right to choose their own form of government,

Mindful of the obligations of Member States to refrain in their international relations from the threat or use of force against the territorial integrity or political independence of any State, or in any other manner inconsistent with the purposes of the United Nations,

1. Reaffirms anew its conviction that the preservation of sovereignty, territorial integrity and political independence of every State is a fundamental principle of the Charter of the United Nations, any violation of which on any pretext whatsoever is contrary to its aims and purposes;
2. Deeply deplores the recent armed intervention in Afghanistan, which is inconsistent with that principle;
3. Affirms that the sovereignty, territorial integrity, political independence and non-aligned status of Afghanistan must be fully respected;
4. Calls for the immediate and unconditional withdrawal of all foreign troops from Afghanistan in order to enable its people to determine their own form of government and choose their economic, political and social systems free from outside intervention, coercion or constraint of any kind whatsoever;
5. Requests the Secretary-General to submit a report on progress towards the implementation of this resolution within two weeks;
6. Decides to remain seized of this question.

The General Assembly
  Approves the report of the Credentials Committee.
  6th plenary meeting
  January 14, 1980
  ES-6/2.

The General Assembly,

Taking note of Security Council resolution 462 (1980) of 9 January 1980, calling for an emergency special session of the General Assembly to examine the question contained in document S/Agenda/2185,

Gravely concerned at the recent developments in Afghanistan and their implications for international peace and security,

Reaffirming the inalienable right of all peoples to determine their own future and to choose their own form of government free from outside interference,

Mindful of the obligation of all States to refrain in their international relations from the threat or use of force against the sovereignty, territorial integrity and political independence of any State or in any other manner inconsistent with the purposes and principles of the Charter of the United Nations,

Recognizing the urgent need for immediate termination of foreign armed intervention in Afghanistan so as to enable its people to determine their own destiny without outside interference or coercion,

Noting with profound concern the large outflow of refugees from Afghanistan,

Recalling its resolutions on the strengthening of international security, on the inadmissibility of intervention on the domestic affairs of States and the protection of their independence and sovereignty and on the principles of international law concerning friendly relations and co-operation among States in accordance with the Charter of the United Nations,

Expressing its deep concern at the dangerous escalating of tension, intensification of rivalry and increased recourse to military intervention and interference in the internal affairs of States which are detrimental to the interests of all nations, particularly the non-aligned countries,

Mindful of the purposes and principles of the Charter and of the responsibility of the General Assembly under the relevant provisions of the Charter and of Assembly resolution 377 A (V) of 3 November 1950,

1. Reaffirms that the respect for the sovereignty, territorial integrity and political independence of every State is a fundamental principle of the Charter of the United Nations, any violation of which on any pretext whatsoever is contrary to its aims and purposes;
2. Strongly deplores the recent armed intervention in Afghanistan, which is inconsistent with that principle;
3. Appeals to all States to respect the sovereignty, territorial integrity, political independence and non-aligned character of Afghanistan and to refrain from any interference in the internal affairs of that country;
4. Calls for the immediate, unconditional and total withdrawal of the foreign troops from Afghanistan in order to enable its people to determine their own form of government and choose their economic, political and social systems free from outside intervention, subversion, coercion or constraint of any kind whatsoever;
5. Urges all parties concerned to assist in bringing about, speedily and in accordance with the purposes and principles of the Charter, conditions necessary for the voluntary return of the Afghan refugees to their homes;

6. Appeals to all States and national and international organizations to extend humanitarian relief assistance with a view to alleviating the hardship of Afghan refugees in coordination with the United Nations High Commissioner for Refugees;

7. Requests the Secretary-General to keep Member States and the Security Council promptly and concurrently informed on the progress towards the implementation of the present resolution;

8. Calls upon the Security Council to consider ways and means which could assist in the implementation of the present resolution.

Source: United Nations Security Council Official Records, S/13729, January 6, 1980.

39. President Jimmy Carter, "The Soviet Invasion Is the Greatest Threat to Peace since the Second World War," Remarks to a Congressional Group, January 8, 1980 [Excerpts]

Introduction

Speaking to a group of congressional leaders, some of whom were seriously alarmed by the situation two weeks earlier of the Soviet invasion of Afghanistan and the military coup in which President Hafizullah Amin died, President Jimmy Carter expressed his sense of shock and outrage. In somewhat hyperbolic language, he termed the invasion of this relatively small and remote state "the greatest threat to peace since the Second World War." Carter stated that as "the other superpower on earth," the United States had the prime responsibility to take appropriate action that would force the Soviets to "suffer the consequences" of their behavior. He warned that if he as president did not do so, in the future the Soviets would be likely to seek "control over a major portion of the world's oil supplies." While Carter believed that full-scale American military action against the Soviets would constitute overreaction, he detailed the political and economic measures that the United States had already taken. In a striking indication of American displeasure, he had asked the Senate to defer any further consideration of the second Soviet-U.S. Strategic Arms Limitation Treaty (SALT-II), negotiated earlier in his presidency. His government had already presented resolutions to the United Nations (UN) Security Council and General Assembly condemning Soviet actions in Afghanistan and demanding that Soviet forces be withdrawn immediately. The United States had also imposed appreciable economic sanctions on the Soviets, who would no longer be permitted to fish in waters within 200 miles of the American coast or to purchase

high technology, including oil drilling equipment, from the United States. In addition, he had embargoed American grain sales to the Soviet Union in excess of those that his country was bound to supply under existing agreements. He also intended to strengthen the defenses of Pakistan, Afghanistan's neighbor, and if necessary other nations in the region and to maintain American naval forces in the area at a high level. Carter did not anticipate that these measures would persuade the Soviet Union to withdraw its forces from Afghanistan, but he argued that they constituted definite markers indicating the displeasure of the United States and its unwillingness to acquiesce in further Soviet moves against third powers.

Primary Source

In my own opinion, shared by many of the world's leaders with whom I have discussed this matter, the Soviet invasion of Afghanistan is the greatest threat to peace since the Second World War. It's a sharp escalation in the aggressive history of the Soviet Union. Obviously, we all were shocked and deplored publicly and officially the Soviet action in Hungary and then later, in 1968, in Czechoslovakia. Those were two countries which, since the Second World War, were basically subservient to the Soviet Union; they were not independent nations in control of their own affairs. There was an uprising, as you know, and the Soviets brutally stamped the uprising out within those two countries.

This, however, was a sovereign nation, a nonaligned nation, a deeply religious nation, and the Soviets invaded it brutally.

We were informed, other leaders throughout the world were informed, by Soviet Ambassadors and direct messages from Moscow, that the Soviets went into the nation to protect it from some third force that might be threatening Afghanistan. When questioned about where was the third threatening force from, the Soviets have never been able to give a reasonable answer. They claim that they were invited in by the Government to protect Afghanistan. As you know, the leader of Afghanistan, President Amin, who was supposed to have invited them in, was immediately assassinated as soon as the Soviets obtained control over Kabul, the capital city, and several of the members of the President's family were also killed.

We are the other super power on Earth, and it became my responsibility, representing our great Nation, to take action that would prevent the Soviets from this invasion with impunity. The Soviets had to suffer the consequences. In my judgment our own Nation's security was directly threatened. There is no doubt that the Soviets' move into Afghanistan, if done without adverse consequences, would have resulted in the temptation to move again and again until they reached warm water ports or until they acquired control over a major portion of the world's oil supplies.

I talked to the President of Pakistan immediately after this Afghanistan invasion and also talked to many other of the world's leaders and sent them direct messages. The action that we could take was confined to three opportunities. One is to take military action, which I did not consider appropriate. Our country has no desire, nor could we have effectively implemented military action, to drive the Soviet forces from Afghanistan—which left me with two other options, which I chose to exercise. One is political action, and the other one is economic action.

Politically, we joined with 50 other nations to take to the Security Council two propositions: one, to condemn the Soviet Union for the invasion and therefore the threat to world peace; and secondly, to call upon the Soviets to withdraw their troops. The vote was cast after the debates were concluded. The only nations voting against these two propositions were East Germany—again, a Soviet puppet nation—and the Soviets themselves. The permanent members, as you know, have a veto right. And now a move is underway, which I think will be realized, to take this case to the General Assembly for further condemnation of the Soviet Union.

It's difficult to understand why the Soviets took this action. I think they probably underestimated the adverse reaction from around the world. I've talked to many other leaders, our allies and those representing nations that might be further threatened, and they all believe that we took the right action.

It was not done for political reasons; it was not done to implement some foreign policy. It was done in the interest of our national security.

We did take economic action, which I think was properly balanced. It was carefully considered. We will try to impose this action on the Soviet Union in a way that will have a minimal adverse effect on our own country, where the sacrifices will be shared as equitably as you and I together can possibly devise, and at the same time let the Soviets realize the consequences of their invasion.

We will not permit the Soviets to fish in American waters within 200 miles of our land area. They have a very large fishing fleet, involving hundreds of thousands of tons of fish harvested. They will not have those permits renewed. We will not send high technology equipment to the Soviet Union or any equipment that might have a security benefit to the Soviet Union. This will include drilling equipment, for instance, used for the exploration and production of oil and natural gas. We will restrict severely normal commerce with the Soviet Union, which is highly advantageous to them. And of course, I have interrupted the delivery of grain, which the Soviets had ordered, above and beyond the 8 million tons which our Nation is bound by a 5-year agreement to have delivered to the Soviet Union.

We have taken steps to make sure that the farmers are protected from the adverse consequences of this interruption of grain shipments to a maximum degree possible. It will be a costly proposition. I understood this when I took the action. And my estimate is, based on a fairly thorough, but somewhat rapid analysis, that this year the extra cost to purchase this grain and to change the price levels of corn and wheat and to pay the extra storage charges will amount to about $2 billion. That's in fiscal year 1980. In fiscal year 1981 there will be an additional cost of about $800 million.

It may be that as the season progresses and we have more experience in substituting for the Soviet Union as the purchaser of this grain, that there will be an additional 2 or 3 hundred million dollars spent in 1980. If this should take place, then that would reduce by the same amount, roughly, expenditures in 1981 fiscal year. So, the total cost will be in the neighborhood of $2.8 billion. This cost will not fall on the farmers except to the extent that they are taxpayers like every other American. This will be shared by all those in this country who pay taxes to the Federal Government.

This grain will not be permitted to go back on the market in such a way as to depress agricultural prices. . . .

[. . .]

We anticipate that this withholding of grain to the Soviet Union will not force them to withdraw their troops from Afghanistan. We understood this from the beginning. We don't think that economic pressure or even condemnation by the United Nations of the Soviet Union will cause them to withdraw their troops. But we hope that we have laid down a marker and let them know that they will indeed suffer, now and in the future, from this unwarranted invasion of a formerly independent, nonaligned country.

I need the support of the American people. I believe that it's a matter of patriotism, and I believe that it's a matter of protecting our Nation's security. . . .

[. . .]

We want to pursue a long-range analysis and a schedule of actions to strengthen American interests and presence and influence in this troubled area of the world, in Southwest Asia. You know about some of these from news reports that have already been issued. And we will take action, with the Congress' help, to strengthen Pakistan. Our desire is to do this through a consortium of nations; that's also the desire of Pakistan.

I talked since lunch with President Zia of that country. I've talked to him before about this matter. And other nations in the region who might be threatened by the Soviets, from Afghanistan, will also know that we and many other nations on Earth are committed to their adequate defense capability, so that the Soviets will be discouraged from further expansionism in the area.

Because of the Iranian question, we have greatly built up our naval forces in the northern China Sea [and] in the Arabian Sea. Those will be maintained at a higher level than they have been in the past. And as you know, there has been a marshaling of worldwide public opinion, not only in the condemnation of the Iranian terrorists who hold our hostages but also against the Soviet Union for their unprecedented invasion of Afghanistan in this recent few weeks.

[...]

Source: Jimmy Carter, *Public Papers of the Presidents of the United States: Jimmy Carter, 1980–81,* Book 1 (Washington, DC: U.S. Government Printing Office, 1981), 21–24.

40. U.S. Draft of United Nations Security Council Resolution Vetoed by the Soviet Union, January 13, 1980

Introduction

The United Nations (UN) Security Council responded quickly when Iran took several dozen American diplomats hostage. On November 9, 1979, and again on November 27, the president of the Security Council urged Iran to release the hostages immediately. The following month, the Security Council unanimously passed Resolution 457, calling for the release of the hostages and urging the United States and Iran to settle all outstanding issues dividing them peacefully and to their "mutual satisfaction." On December 31 UN Security Council Resolution 461 reaffirmed the earlier resolution. Expressing alarm that the crisis was "a serious threat to international peace and security," the resolution also called on both Iran and the United States to take no action that might "aggravate" the situation and urged the UN secretary-general to "lend his good offices" in the quest to resolve the dispute. Four Security Council members, including the Soviet Union, abstained from voting on this resolution, although none opposed it. On January 13, 1980, the Security Council voted on a resolution submitted by the United States that called on UN member states to impose economic sanctions upon Iran, cutting off official and private trade in everything but food and medicine with that country, denying Iran all loans and credits, and reducing diplomatic contacts to a minimum. Such measures went too far for the Soviet Union, which vetoed the measure, while one other Security Council member voted against it. The Soviet veto meant that even though the vote was 10 to 2 in favor, it automatically failed to pass. The representative of China, a longtime champion of developing Third World nations, absented himself entirely from the vote, while 2 states abstained. The vote defined the limits of the support that the United States could expect from the UN on the Iran Hostage Crisis.

Primary Source

Soviet Veto of Economic Sanctions Against Iran

The Security Council

Recalling its resolutions 457 (1979) of 4 December 1979, and 461 (1979) of 13 December 1979,

Recalling also the appeal made by the President of the Security Council on 9 November 1979 (S/13616) which was reiterated on 27 November 1979 (S/13652),

Having taken note of the letters date[d] 13 November 1979 and 1 December 1979 concerning the grievances and views of Iran (S/13626 and S/13671, respectively),

Having taken into account the order of the International Court of Justice of 15 December 1979 calling on the Government of the Islamic Republic of Iran to ensure the immediate release, without any exception, of all persons of United States nationality, who are being held as hostages in Iran (S/13697) and also calling on the Government of the United States of America and the Government of the Islamic Republic of Iran to ensure that no action is taken by them which will aggravate the tension between the two countries,

Further recalling the letter dated 25 November from the Secretary-General (S/13646) stating that, in his opinion, the present crisis between the Islamic Republic of Iran and the United States of America poses a serious threat to international peace and security,

Bearing in mind the adoption by the General Assembly by consensus on 17 December 1979 of the Convention Against the Taking of Hostages,

Mindful of the obligation of States to settle their international dispute[s] by peaceful means in such a manner that international peace and security, and justice, are not endangered and, to that end, to respect the decision of the Security Council,

Conscious of the responsibility of the States to refrain in their international relations from the threat of use of force against the territory integrity or political independence of any state, or in any other manner inconsistent with the purposes of the United Nations,

Affirming that the safe release and departure from Iran of all those being held hostage is an essential first step in resolving peacefully the issues between Iran and the United States and the other State members of the international community,

Reiterating that once the hostages have been safely released, the Government of Iran and the United States of America should take steps to resolve peacefully the remaining issues between them to their mutual satisfaction in accordance with the purposes and principles of the United Nations,

Further taking into account the report of the Secretary-General of 6 January 1980 (S/13730) made pursuant to resolutions 457 (1979) of 4 December 1979 and 461 (1979) of 31 December 1979,

Bearing in mind that the continued detention of the hostages constitutes a continuing threat to international peace and security,

Acting in accordance with Articles 39 and 41 of the Charter of the United Nations,

1. Urgently calls, once again, on the Government of the Islamic Republic of Iran to release immediately all persons of United States nationality being held as hostages in Iran, to provide them protection and to allow them to leave the country.
2. Decides that, until such time as the hostages are released and have safely departed from Iran, all States Members of the United Nations:
   (a) shall prevent the sale or supply, by their nationals or from their territories, whether or not originating in their territories, to or destined for Iranian government entities in Iran or any other person or body for the purposes of any enterprise carried on in Iran, of all items, commodities, or products, except food, medicine, and supplies intended strictly for medical purposes;
   (b) shall prevent the shipment by vessel, aircraft, railway, or other land transport of their registration or owned by or under charter to their nationals, or the carriage whether or not in bond by land transport facilities across their territories of any of the items, commodities, and products covered by subparagraph (a) which are consigned to or destined for Iranian governmental entities or any person or body in Iran, or to any enterprise carried on in Iran;
   (c) shall not make available to the Iranian authorities or to any person in Iran or to any enterprise controlled by any Iranian governmental entity any new credits or loans; shall not, with respect to such persons or enterprises, make available any new deposit facilities or allow substantial increases in existing non-dollar deposits or allow more favorable terms of payment than customarily used in international commercial transactions; and shall act in a businesslike manner in exercising any rights when payments due on existing credits or loans are not made on time and shall require any persons or entities within their jurisdiction to so likewise;
   (d) Shall prevent the shipment from territories on vessels or aircraft, registered in Iran of products and commodities covered by subparagraph (a) above;

   (e) Shall reduce to a minimum the personnel of Iranian diplomatic missions accredited to them;
   (f) Shall prevent their nationals, or firms located in their territories, from engaging in new service contracts in support of industrial projects in Iran, other than those concerned with medical care;
   (g) Shall prevent their nationals, or any person or body within their territories from engaging in any activity which evades or has the purpose of evading any of the decisions set out in this resolution;
3. Decides that all States Members of the United Nations shall give effect forthwith to the decisions set out in operative paragraph 2 of this resolution notwithstanding any contract entered into or license granted before the date of this resolution;
4. Calls upon all States Members of the United Nations to carry out these decisions of the Security Council in accordance with article 25 of the Charter;
5. Urges, having regard to the Principles stated in Article 2 of the Charter, States not members of the United Nations to act in accordance with the provisions of the present resolution;
6. Calls upon all other United Nations bodies and the specialized agencies of the United Nations and their members to conform their relations with Iran to the terms of the resolution;
7. Calls upon all States Members of the United Nations, and in particular those with primary responsibility under the Charter for the maintenance of international peace and security, to assist effectively in the implementation of the measures called for by the present resolution;
8. Calls upon all States Members of the United Nations or of the specialized agencies to report to the Secretary-General by 1 February 1980 on measures taken to implement the present resolution;
9. Requests the Secretary-General to report to the Council on the progress of the implementation of the present resolution, the first report to be submitted not later than 1 March 1980.

Source: United Nations Security Council Official Records, S/13735, January 10, 1980.

41. President Jimmy Carter, the Carter Doctrine, State of the Union Address, January 23, 1980 [Excerpts]

Introduction

The idealistic Democrat Jimmy Carter, a traditional liberal in international affairs, became president in 1977 and was committed to a foreign policy agenda that envisaged the promotion of traditional

American values, including human rights and peaceable relations with other nations, reductions in military spending, disarmament, and a new emphasis on economic over defense aid. Threatening events in the final years of his one-term presidency caused him to modify these preoccupations and to return to more traditional Cold War strategies. Since 1953 U.S. policy regarding the Middle East had centered upon the powerful oil-rich Iran. In 1978 a radical Islamic regime overthrew the autocratic but Western-oriented government of Mohammad Reza Shah Pahlavi of Iran. The new Iranian leaders were Islamic fundamentalists who, in a major blow to American geopolitical and economic interests, abrogated the existing alliance with the United States, a country they considered the international "great Satan," and cut off oil supplies. In November 1979 radical Islamic Iranians sacked the U.S. embassy in Tehran, holding 52 official American personnel hostage until Carter left office in January 1981. Skyrocketing oil prices caused by the Iranian oil embargo ratcheted up inflation and again reminded American consumers how heavily their way of life depended on alien nations over whom they often had little leverage. To compound American problems in the region, in December 1979 the Soviet Union mounted a major military intervention in previously nonaligned Afghanistan in order to maintain in power a Soviet-backed Marxist regime that had taken power in 1978. Soviet actions were probably primarily due to fears that intensifying Islamic fanaticism in Afghanistan and Iran might infect neighboring Muslim areas of Soviet territory and precipitate separatist movements there. Carter, however, perceived this episode, which he hyperbolically termed "the greatest threat to peace since the Second World War," as part of a calculated Soviet strategy to gain control of the Persian Gulf and the oil-rich states surrounding it. Convinced that Soviet-American détente had become unattainable, he reacted strongly. Addressing Congress and the nation in his January 1980 annual State of the Union address, Carter proclaimed the Carter Doctrine, stating that "business as usual" with the Soviet Union was not possible and that the United States would take all measures necessary to defend the Persian Gulf. The president moved to reinstitute containment policies, demanded annual 5 percent increases in military spending, proposed that young American men be compelled to register for a potential draft, and moved to create a Persian Gulf rapid deployment force. He also called for energy policies that would make his country less dependent on foreign oil. Carter's speech, which effectively reiterated the 1957 Eisenhower Doctrine for the Middle East, also marked a definite break with his earlier efforts toward U.S.-Soviet détente and disarmament, inaugurating several years of deep ideological and strategic antagonism between the two superpowers.

Primary Source

[. . .]

At this time in Iran, 50 Americans are still held captive, innocent victims of terrorism and anarchy. Also at this moment,

massive Soviet troops are attempting to subjugate the fiercely independent and deeply religious people of Afghanistan. These two acts—one of international terrorism and one of military aggression—present a serious challenge to the United States of America and indeed to all the nations of the world. Together, we will meet these threats to peace.

I'm determined that the United States will remain the strongest of all nations, but our power will never be used to initiate a threat to the security of any nation or to the rights of any human being. We seek to be and to remain secure—a nation at peace in a stable world. But to be secure we must face the world as it is.

Three basic developments have helped to shape our challenges: the steady growth and increased projection of Soviet military power beyond its own borders; the overwhelming dependence of the Western democracies on oil supplies from the Middle East; and the press of social and religious and economic and political change in the many nations of the developing world, exemplified by the revolution in Iran.

Each of these factors is important in its own right. Each interacts with the others. All must be faced together, squarely and courageously. We will face these challenges, and we will meet them with the best that is in us. And we will not fail.

In response to the abhorrent act in Iran, our Nation has never been aroused and unified so greatly in peacetime. Our position is clear. The United States will not yield to blackmail.

We continue to pursue these specific goals: first, to protect the present and long-range interests of the United States; secondly, to preserve the lives of the American hostages and to secure, as quickly as possible, their safe release, if possible, to avoid bloodshed which might further endanger the lives of our fellow citizens; to enlist the help of other nations in condemning this act of violence, which is shocking and violates the moral and the legal standards of a civilized world; and also to convince and to persuade the Iranian leaders that the real danger to their nation lies in the north, in the Soviet Union and from the Soviet troops now in Afghanistan, and that the unwarranted Iranian quarrel with the United States hampers their response to this far greater danger to them.

If the American hostages are harmed, a severe price will be paid. We will never rest until every one of the American hostages are released.

But now we face a broader and more fundamental challenge in this region because of the recent military action of the Soviet Union.

Now, as during the last 3½ decades, the relationship between our country, the United States of America, and the Soviet Union is the most critical factor in determining whether the world will live at peace or be engulfed in global conflict.

Since the end of the Second World War, America has led other nations in meeting the challenge of mounting Soviet power. This has not been a simple or a static relationship. Between us there has been cooperation, there has been competition, and at times there has been confrontation.

In the 1940's we took the lead in creating the Atlantic Alliance in response to the Soviet Union's suppression and then consolidation of its East European empire and the resulting threat of the Warsaw Pact to Western Europe.

In the 1950's we helped to contain further Soviet challenges in Korea and in the Middle East, and we rearmed to assure the continuation of that containment.

In the 1960's we met the Soviet challenges in Berlin, and we faced the Cuban missile crisis. And we sought to engage the Soviet Union in the important task of moving beyond the cold war and away from confrontation.

And in the 1970's three American Presidents negotiated with the Soviet leaders in attempts to halt the growth of the nuclear arms race. We sought to establish rules of behavior that would reduce the risks of conflict, and we searched for areas of cooperation that could make our relations reciprocal and productive, not only for the sake of our two nations but for the security and peace of the entire world.

In all these actions, we have maintained two commitments: to be ready to meet any challenge by Soviet military power, and to develop ways to resolve disputes and to keep the peace.

Preventing nuclear war is the foremost responsibility of the two superpowers. That's why we've negotiated the strategic arms limitation treaties—SALT I and SALT II. Especially now, in a time of great tension, observing the mutual constraints imposed by the terms of these treaties will be in the best interest of both countries and will help to preserve world peace. I will consult very closely with the Congress on this matter as we strive to control nuclear weapons. That effort to control nuclear weapons will not be abandoned.

We superpowers also have the responsibility to exercise restraint in the use of our great military force. The integrity and the independence of weaker nations must not be threatened. They must know that in our presence they are secure.

But now the Soviet Union has taken a radical and an aggressive new step. It's using its great military power against a relatively defenseless nation. The implications of the Soviet invasion of Afghanistan could pose the most serious threat to the peace since the Second World War.

The vast majority of nations on Earth have condemned this latest Soviet attempt to extend its colonial domination of others and have demanded the immediate withdrawal of Soviet troops. The Moslem world is especially and justifiably outraged by this aggression against an Islamic people. No action of a world power has ever been so quickly and so overwhelmingly condemned. But verbal condemnation is not enough. The Soviet Union must pay a concrete price for their aggression.

While this invasion continues, we and the other nations of the world cannot conduct business as usual with the Soviet Union. That's why the United States has imposed stiff economic penalties on the Soviet Union. I will not issue any permits for Soviet ships to fish in the coastal waters of the United States. I've cut Soviet access to high-technology equipment and to agricultural products. I've limited other commerce with the Soviet Union, and I've asked our allies and friends to join with us in restraining their own trade with the Soviets and not to replace our own embargoed items. And I have notified the Olympic Committee that with Soviet invading forces in Afghanistan, neither the American people nor I will support sending an Olympic team to Moscow.

The Soviet Union is going to have to answer some basic questions: Will it help promote a more stable international environment in which its own legitimate, peaceful concerns can be pursued? Or will it continue to expand its military power far beyond its genuine security needs, and use that power for colonial conquest? The Soviet Union must realize that its decision to use military force in Afghanistan will be costly to every political and economic relationship it values.

The region which is now threatened by Soviet troops in Afghanistan is of great strategic importance: It contains more than two-thirds of the world's exportable oil. The Soviet effort to dominate Afghanistan has brought Soviet military forces to within 300 miles of the Indian Ocean and close to the Straits of Hormuz, a waterway through which most of the world's oil must flow. The Soviet Union is now attempting to consolidate a strategic position, therefore, that poses a grave threat to the free movement of Middle East oil.

This situation demands careful thought, steady nerves, and resolute action, not only for this year but for many years to come. It demands collective efforts to meet this new threat to security in the Persian Gulf and in Southwest Asia. It demands the participation of all those who rely on oil from the Middle East and who are concerned with global peace and stability. And it demands consultation and close cooperation with countries in the area which might be threatened.

Meeting this challenge will take national will, diplomatic and political wisdom, economic sacrifice, and, of course, military capability. We must call on the best that is in us to preserve the security of this crucial region.

Let our position be absolutely clear: An attempt by any outside force to gain control of the Persian Gulf region will be regarded as an assault on the vital interests of the United States of America, and such an assault will be repelled by any means necessary, including military force.

During the past 3 years, you have joined with me to improve our own security and the prospects for peace, not only in the vital oil-producing area of the Persian Gulf region but around the world. We've increased annually our real commitment for defense, and we will sustain this increase of effort throughout the Five Year Defense Program. It's imperative that Congress approve this strong defense budget for 1981, encompassing a 5-percent real growth in authorizations, without any reduction. We are also improving our capability to deploy U.S. military forces rapidly to distant areas. We've helped to strengthen NATO and our other alliances, and recently we and other NATO members have decided to develop and to deploy modernized, intermediate-range nuclear forces to meet an unwarranted and increased threat from the nuclear weapons of the Soviet Union.

We are working with our allies to prevent conflict in the Middle East. The peace treaty between Egypt and Israel is a notable achievement which represents a strategic asset for America and which also enhances prospects for regional and world peace. We are now engaged in further negotiations to provide full autonomy for the people of the West Bank and Gaza, to resolve the Palestinian issue in all its aspects, and to preserve the peace and security of Israel. Let no one doubt our commitment to the security of Israel. In a few days we will observe an historic event when Israel makes another major withdrawal from the Sinai and when Ambassadors will be exchanged between Israel and Egypt.

We've also expanded our own sphere of friendship. Our deep commitment to human rights and to meeting human needs has improved our relationship with much of the Third World. Our decision to normalize relations with the People's Republic of China will help to preserve peace and stability in Asia and in the Western Pacific.

We've increased and strengthened our naval presence in the Indian Ocean, and we are now making arrangements for key naval and air facilities to be used by our forces in the region of northeast Africa and the Persian Gulf.

We've reconfirmed our 1959 agreement to help Pakistan preserve its independence and its integrity. The United States will take action consistent with our own laws to assist Pakistan in resisting any outside aggression. . . .

In the weeks ahead, we will further strengthen political and military ties with other nations in the region. We believe that there are no irreconcilable differences between us and any Islamic nation. We respect the faith of Islam, and we are ready to cooperate with all Moslem countries.

Finally, we are prepared to work with other countries in the region to share a cooperative security framework that respects differing values and political beliefs, yet which enhances the independence, security, and prosperity of all.

[. . .]

The men and women of America's Armed Forces are on duty tonight in many parts of the world. I'm proud of the job they are doing, and I know you share that pride. I believe that our volunteer forces are adequate for current defense needs, and I hope that it will not become necessary to impose a draft. However, we must be prepared for that possibility. For this reason, I have determined that the Selective Service System must now be revitalized. I will send legislation and budget proposals to the Congress next month so that we can begin registration and then meet future mobilization needs rapidly if they arise.

We also need clear and quick passage of a new charter to define the legal authority and accountability of our intelligence agencies. We will guarantee that abuses do not recur, but we must tighten our controls on sensitive intelligence information, and we need to remove unwarranted restraints on America's ability to collect intelligence.

The decade ahead will be a time of rapid change, as nations everywhere seek to deal with new problems and age-old tensions. But America need have no fear. We can thrive in a world of change if we remain true to our values and actively engaged in promoting world peace. We will continue to work as we have for peace in the Middle East and southern Africa. We will continue to build our ties with developing nations, respecting and helping to strengthen their national independence which they have struggled so hard to achieve. And we will continue to support the growth of democracy and the protection of human rights.

In repressive regimes, popular frustrations often have no outlet except through violence. But when peoples and their governments can approach their problems together through open, democratic methods, the basis for stability and peace is far more solid and far more enduring. That is why our support for human rights in other countries is in our own national interest as well as part of our own national character.

Peace—a peace that preserves freedom—remains America's first goal. In the coming years, as a mighty nation we will continue to pursue peace. But to be strong abroad we must be strong at home. And in order to be strong, we must continue to face up to the difficult issues that confront us as a nation today.

The crises in Iran and Afghanistan have dramatized a very important lesson: Our excessive dependence on foreign oil is a clear and present danger to our Nation's security. The need has never been more urgent. At long last, we must have a clear, comprehensive energy policy for the United States.

As you well know, I have been working with the Congress in a concentrated and persistent way over the past 3 years to meet this need. We have made progress together. But Congress must act promptly now to complete final action on this vital energy legislation. Our Nation will then have a major conservation effort, important initiatives to develop solar power, realistic pricing based on the true value of oil, strong incentives for the production of coal and other fossil fuels in the United States, and our Nation's most massive peacetime investment in the development of synthetic fuels.

[. . .]

Source: Jimmy Carter, *Public Papers of the Presidents of the United States: Jimmy Carter, 1980–1981,* Book 1 (Washington, DC: U.S. Government Printing Office, 1981), 194–200.

42. Islamic Conference, Resolution Condemning the Soviet Invasion of Afghanistan, January 29, 1980

Introduction

The Soviet invasion of Afghanistan, a strongly Muslim nation, won general condemnation around the Islamic world. Meeting in Islamabad, Pakistan's capital, in late January 1980, the 11th conference of Islamic foreign ministers held an extraordinary session to discuss the subject of Afghanistan. Referring specifically to the principles of the movement of nonaligned states, which Afghanistan had helped to found, they roundly condemned the Soviet intervention and occupation as "a flagrant violation of international laws, covenants, and norms." They demanded the immediate departure of all Soviet troops from Afghan territory. Afghanistan's membership in the Organization of the Islamic Conference was suspended. Member states were invited to withdraw diplomatic recognition from Afghanistan and cease all forms of aid to that country and to demonstrate

their "solidarity" with the Afghan people in their struggle for independence. One means by which they could do so, the conference declared, was by boycotting the Olympic Games to be held in Moscow that coming July. The organization also declared its intention of assisting Afghanistan's neighbors in all efforts to safeguard themselves against further Afghan or Soviet encroachments. Islamic states were also urged to provide assistance to the numerous Afghan refugees who had fled their country. The organization's membership included assorted Middle Eastern, Asian, and African states, many of which were radical in outlook and generally reliably pro-Soviet in sympathy. Among them were Algeria, Bahrein, Bangladesh, Burkina Faso, Cameroon, Chad, the Comoros, Djibouti, Egypt, Gambia, Guinea, Guinea-Bissau, Indonesia, Iran, Iraq, Jordan, Kuwait, Lebanon, Libya, Malaysia, the Maldives, Mauritania, Morocco, Oman, Pakistan, Palestine, Qatar, Saudi Arabia, Senegal, Sierra Leone, Somalia, Sudan, Syria, Tunisia, Turkey, Uganda, the United Arab Emirates, and Yemen. The fact that this organization was prepared to condemn the actions of the Soviet Union so forthrightly, mentioning that state by name, which the United Nations (UN) resolutions failed to do, was striking evidence of just how alarming and unacceptable Soviet behavior in Afghanistan appeared to numerous developing nations.

Primary Source

The first extraordinary session of the Islamic conference of foreign ministers meeting in Islamabad, from 7 to 9 Rabi al Awwal, corresponding to 27–29 January 1980;

In pursuance of the principles and objectives of the Organization of the Islamic Conference, and the provisions of resolution adopted by Islamic summit conference, emphasizing the common objectives and destiny of the peoples of the Islamic nation;

Recalling in particular the basic principles of the non-aligned movement of which Afghanistan is a founding member;

Expressing its deep concern at the dangerous escalation of tension, intensification of rivalry and increased recourse to military intervention and interference in the internal affairs of states, particularly the Islamic states;

Expressing the determination of the governments and peoples of member states to reject all forms and types of foreign occupation and expansion and the race for spheres of influence thereby strengthening the sovereignty of peoples and the independence of states;

Seriously concerned over the Soviet armed intervention in Afghanistan and the effect of this interference on the will of the Muslim people of Afghanistan to exercise their right to determine their political future;

Considering that the continuing presence of Soviet troops in Afghanistan, its attempt at imposing the fait accompli and the military operations of these troops against the Afghan people flout international covenants and norms and blatantly violate human rights;

Reaffirming the determination of Islamic states to pursue a non-aligned policy in respect of superpower conflict and to protect Muslim people from the adverse effects of the cold war between these states;

Fully aware of the immense financial burden borne by neighboring countries of Afghanistan, in particular the Islamic Republic of Pakistan, as a result of the asylum it provides to hundreds of thousands of Afghan people, old men, women and children, driven away by the Soviet military occupation;

Affirming that the Soviet occupation of Afghanistan constitutes a violation of its independence, and aggression against the liberty of its people and a flagrant violation of all international covenants and norms, as well as a serious threat to peace and security in the region and throughout the world:

1. Condemns the Soviet military aggression against the Afghan people, denounces and deplores it as a flagrant violation of international laws, covenants, and norms, primarily the Charter of the United Nations, which condemned this aggression in its Resolution No. ES-6/2 of 14 January 1981, 41 and the Charter of the Organization of the Islamic Conference, and calls upon all peoples and governments throughout the world to persist in condemning this aggression and denouncing it as an aggression against human rights and a violation of the freedoms of people, which cannot be ignored.

2. Demands the immediate and unconditional withdrawal of all Soviet troops stationed on Afghan territories, and reiterates that Soviet troops should refrain from acts of oppression and tyranny against the Afghan people and their struggling sons, until the departure of the last Soviet soldier from Afghan territory, and urges all countries and peoples to secure the Soviet withdrawal through all means.

3. Suspends the membership of Afghanistan in the Organization of the Islamic Conference.

4. Invite[s] the member states to withhold recognition to the illegal regime in Afghanistan and sever diplomatic relations with that country until the complete withdrawal of Soviet troops from Afghanistan.

5. Calls upon all member states to stop all aid and all forms of assistance given to the present regime of Afghanistan by member states.

6. Urges all states and people throughout the world to support the Afghan people and provide assistance and succor to the refugees whom aggression has driven away from their homes.

7. Recommends to all member states to affirm their solidarity with the Afghan people in their just struggle to safeguard their faith, national independence and territorial integrity and to recover their right to determine their destiny.

8. Solemnly declares its complete solidarity with the Islamic countries neighboring Afghanistan against any threat to their security and wellbeing and calls upon states of the Islamic Conference to resolutely support and extend all possible cooperation to these countries in their efforts to fully safeguard their sovereignty, national independence and territorial integrity.

9. Authorizes the secretary to receive contributions from member states, organizations and individuals and to disperse the amounts to the authorities concerned on the recommendations of a committee of three member states to be established by him in consultation with the states concerned.

10. Calls upon member states to envisage through appropriate bodies the non-participation in Olympic Games being held.

Source: U.S. Department of State, *American Foreign Policy: Basic Documents, 1977–1980* (Washington, DC: Department of State, 1983), 844–846.

43. President Jimmy Carter, Executive Orders No. 12205, April 7, 1980, and No. 12211, April 17, 1980

Introduction

As the Iran Hostage Crisis entered its sixth month with no resolution in sight, President Jimmy Carter decided to tighten U.S. sanctions against Iran. He did so in part because the Iranian militants holding the hostages had recently offered to hand them over to the custody of the Iranian government, but the Iranian authorities had refused to accept this charge. From the U.S. perspective, this decision made Ayatollah Ruhollah Khomeini's government ultimately responsible for the continuing detention of the hostages. On April 7, 1980, Carter announced that the United States was breaking all diplomatic relations with the government of Iran and expelling all Iranian diplomats. All American trade with Iran was now forbidden, and he stated that even food and medicine shipments were expected to be "minimal or nonexistent." The assets of the Iranian government seized in the United States would be inventoried so that they could be used to pay outstanding claims, including demands for compensation by the hostages and their families. All existing American visas issued to Iranian citizens would be invalidated. Ten days later, the president expanded these sanctions further. The United States barred all Iranian imports, and all "persons subject to the jurisdiction of the United States" were forbidden to transfer funds to any Iranian individual or organization. After a one-week grace period, this provision would apply to American citizens then physically present in Iran. With the exception of journalists, American citizens were forbidden to travel to Iran, and news-gathering organizations were asked to restrict their activities in Iran to a minimum. The U.S. government impounded all military equipment purchased by Iran that was still in American hands. Americans were specifically forbidden to deal with Iran Air, the National Iranian Oil Company, and the National Iranian Gas Company. These sanctions effectively forbade virtually all American dealings with Iran, representing a near total break in relations. By 2010, diplomatic relations between Iran and the United States had still not been resumed.

Primary Source

EXECUTIVE ORDER 12205

PROHIBITING CERTAIN TRANSACTIONS WITH IRAN

By the authority vested in me as President by the Constitution and statutes of the United States, including Section 203 of the International Emergency Economic Powers Act (50 U.S.C. 1702), Section 301 of Title 3 of the United States Code, and Section 301 of the National Emergencies Act (50 U.S.C. 1631), in order to take steps additional to those set forth in Executive Order No. 12170 of November 14, 1979, to deal with the threat to the national security, foreign policy and economy of the United States referred to in that Order, and in furtherance of the objectives of United Nations Security Council Resolution 461 (1979) adopted on December 31, 1979, it is hereby ordered as follows:

1-101. The following are prohibited effective immediately, notwithstanding any contracts entered into or licenses granted before the date of this Order:

(a) The sale, supply or other transfer, by any person subject to the jurisdiction of the United States, of any items, commodities or products, except food, medicine and supplies intended strictly for medical purposes, and donations of clothing intended to be used to relieve human suffering, from the United States, or from any foreign country, whether or not originating in the United States, either to or destined for Iran, an Iranian governmental entity in Iran, any other person or body in Iran or any other person or body for the purposes of any enterprise carried on in Iran.

(b) The shipment by vessel, aircraft, railway or other land transport of United States registration or owned by or under charter to any person subject to the jurisdiction of the United States or the carriage (whether or not in bond) by land transport facilities across the United States of any of the items, commodities and products covered by paragraph (a) of this section which are consigned to or destined for Iran, an Iranian governmental entity or any person or body in Iran, or to any enterprise carried on in Iran.

(c) The shipment from the United States of any of the items, products and commodities covered by paragraph (a) of this section on vessels or aircraft registered in Iran.

(d) The following acts, when committed by any person subject to the jurisdiction of the United States in connection with any transaction involving Iran, an Iranian governmental entity, an enterprise controlled by Iran or an Iranian governmental entity, or any person in Iran:

(i) Making available any new credits or loans;

(ii) Making available any new deposit facilities or allowing substantial increases in non-dollar deposits which exist as of the date of this Order;

(iii) Allowing more favorable terms of payment than are customarily used in international commercial transactions; or

(iv) Failing to act in a businesslike manner in exercising any rights when payments due on existing credits or loans are not made in a timely manner.

(e) The engaging by any person subject to the jurisdiction of the United States in any service contract in support of an industrial project in Iran, except any such contract entered into prior to the date of this Order or concerned with medical care.

(f) The engaging by any person subject to the jurisdiction of the United States in any transaction which evades or avoids, or has the purpose or effect of evading or avoiding, any of the prohibitions set forth in this section.

1-102. The prohibitions in section 1–101 above shall not apply to transactions by any person subject to the jurisdiction of the United States which is a non-banking association, corporation, or other organization organized and doing business under the laws of any foreign country.

1-103. The Secretary of the Treasury is delegated, and authorized to exercise, all functions vested in the President by the International Emergency Economic Powers Act (50 U.S.C. 1701 et seq.) to carry out the purposes of this Order. The Secretary may redelegate any of these functions to other officers and agencies of the Federal government.

1-104. The Secretary of the Treasury shall ensure that actions taken pursuant to this Order and Executive Order No. 12170 are accounted for as required by Section 401 of the National Emergencies Act (50 U.S.C. 1641).

1-105. This Order is effective immediately. In accord with Section 401 of the National Emergencies Act (50 U.S.C. 1641) and Section 204 of the International Emergency Economic Powers Act (50 U.S.C. 1703), it shall be immediately transmitted to the Congress and published in the FEDERAL REGISTER.

JIMMY CARTER

The White House

EXECUTIVE ORDER 12211

FURTHER PROHIBITIONS ON TRANSACTIONS WITH IRAN

By the authority vested in me as President by the Constitution and statutes of the United States, including Section 203 of the International Emergency Economic Powers Act (50 U.S.C. 1702), Section 301 of Title 3 of the United States Code, Sections 1732 and 2656 of Title 22 of the United States Code, and Section 301 of the National Emergencies Act (50 U.S.C. 1631), in order to take steps additional to those set forth in Executive Order No. 12170 of November 14, 1979, and Executive Order No. 12205 of April 7, 1980, to deal with the threat to the national security, foreign policy and economy of the United States referred to in those Orders, and the added unusual and extraordinary threat to the national security, foreign policy and economy of the United States created by subsequent events in Iran and neighboring countries, including the Soviet invasion of Afghanistan, with respect to which I hereby declare a national emergency, and to carry out the policy of the United States to deny the use of its resources to aid, encourage or give sanctuary to those persons involved in directing, supporting or participating in acts of international terrorism, it is hereby ordered as follows:

1-101. Paragraph 1–101 (d) of Executive Order No. 12205 is hereby amended by the addition of a new subparagraph (v) as follows:

(v) Make any payment, transfer of credit, or other transfer of funds or other property or interests therein, except for purposes of family remittances.

1-102. The following transactions are prohibited, notwithstanding any contracts entered into or licenses granted before the date of this Order:

(a) Effective immediately, the direct or indirect import from Iran into the United States of Iranian goods or services, other than materials imported for news publication or news broadcast dissemination.

(b) Effective immediately, any transactions with a foreign person or foreign entity by any citizen or permanent resident of the United States relating to that person's travel to Iran after the date of this Order.

(c) Effective seven days from the date of this Order, the payment by or on behalf of any citizen or permanent resident of the United States who is within Iran of any expenses for transactions within Iran.

The prohibitions in paragraphs (b) and (c) of this section shall not apply to a person who is also a citizen of Iran and those prohibitions and the prohibitions in section 1–101 shall not apply to a journalist or other person who is regularly employed by a news gathering or transmitting organization and who travels to Iran or is within Iran for the purpose of gathering or transmitting news, making news or documentary films, or similar activities.

1-103. The Secretary of the Treasury is hereby directed, effective fourteen days from the date of this Order, to revoke existing licenses for transactions by persons subject to the jurisdiction of the United States with Iran Air, the National Iranian Oil Company, and the National Iranian Gas Company previously issued pursuant to regulations under Executive Order No. 12170 or Executive Order No. 12205.

1-104. The Secretary of the Treasury is delegated, and authorized to exercise, all functions vested in the President by the International Emergency Economic Powers Act (50 U.S.C. 1701 et seq.) to carry out the purposes of this Order. The Secretary may redelegate any of these functions to other officers and agencies of the Federal government.

1-105. The Secretary of the Treasury shall ensure that actions taken by him pursuant to the above provisions of this Order, Executive Order No. 12170 and Executive Order No. 12205 are accounted for as required by Section 401 of the National Emergencies Act (50 U.S.C. 1641).

1-106. The Secretary of State is delegated, and authorized to exercise in furtherance of the purposes of this Order, the powers vested in the President by Section 2001 of the Revised Statutes (22 U.S.C. 1732), Section 1 of the Act of July 3, 1926 (22 U.S.C. 211a), and Section 215 of the Immigration and Nationality Act (8 U.S.C. 1185), with respect to:

(a) the restriction of the use of United States passports for travel to, in or through Iran; and

(b) the regulation of departures from and entry into the United States in connection with travel to Iran by citizens and permanent residents of the United States.

1-107. Except as otherwise indicated herein, this Order is effective immediately. In accord with Section 401 of the National Emergencies Act (50 U.S.C. 1641) and Section 204 of the International Emergency Economic Powers Act (50 U.S.C. 1703), it shall be immediately transmitted to the Congress and published in the FEDERAL REGISTER.

JIMMY CARTER

The White House,

Source: Jimmy Carter, *Public Papers of the Presidents of the United States: Jimmy Carter, 1980–81,* Book 1 (Washington, DC: U.S. Government Printing Office, 1981), 612–614 and 714–716.

44. President Jimmy Carter, Failed Hostage Rescue Speech, April 25, 1980, and Report to Congress on the Operation, April 26, 1980

Introduction

President Jimmy Carter addressed the American nation in a televised speech on April 25, 1980, the day after a U.S. military mission unsuccessfully attempted to rescue 52 Americans being held hostage in the U.S. embassy in Tehran, Iran. Radical Islamic militants had stormed the embassy on November 4, 1979, to protest past American support for the ousted Mohammad Reza Shah Pahlavi of Iran, especially his admission to the United States for medical treatment. Three of the eight helicopters involved developed mechanical problems, and due to a collision between a helicopter and a transport aircraft, eight U.S. soldiers died in the rescue effort, which was eventually called off. The entire episode was widely regarded as a humiliation for the United States, particularly because at no time did any of the forces involved encounter any Iranians, and all the casualties incurred represented self-inflicted damage. On April 26, 1980, the president also submitted a report to Congress on the operation. Three days before the raid, Secretary of State Cyrus R. Vance had resigned in protest over what he considered an ill-advised and futile mission, which the National Security Council had decided to implement during his absence. The ignominious failure of the rescue attempt confirmed Americans in their sense that the Carter administration was ineffective and could not deal with difficult international crises. The Iran Hostage Crisis was not ended until the inauguration of Republican president Ronald Reagan in January 1981, when, in a final snub to Carter, the Iranians released the hostages in return for an agreement that the U.S. government would unfreeze blocked Iranian economic assets. The seizure of the hostages was one of several international events, among them a major oil crisis and the 1979 Soviet invasion of Afghanistan, that, in conjunction with high inflation and unemployment, contributed to a sense of American impotence at this time and were also partly responsible for Reagan's victory over Carter in the 1980 election.

Primary Source

On April 24, 1980, elements of the United States Armed Forces under my direction commenced the positioning stage of a rescue operation which was designed, if the subsequent stages had been executed, to effect the rescue of the American hostages who have been held captive in Iran since November 4, 1979, in clear violation of international law and the norms of civilized conduct among nations. The subsequent phases of the operation were not executed. Instead, for the reasons described below, all these elements were withdrawn from Iran and no hostilities occurred.

The sole objective of the operation that actually occurred was to position the rescue team for the subsequent effort to withdraw the American hostages. The rescue team was under my overall command and control and required my approval before executing the subsequent phases of the operation designed to effect the rescue itself. No such approval was requested or given because, as described below, the mission was aborted.

Beginning approximately 10:30 a.m. EST on April 24, six U.S. C-130 transport aircraft and eight RH-53 helicopters entered Iran airspace. Their crews were not equipped for combat. Some of the C-130 aircraft carried a force of approximately 90 members of the rescue team equipped for combat, plus various support personnel.

From approximately 2 to 4 p.m. EST the six transports and six of the eight helicopters landed at a remote desert site in Iran approximately 200 miles from Tehran where they disembarked the rescue team, commenced refueling operations and began to prepare for the subsequent phases.

During the flight to the remote desert site, two of the eight helicopters developed operating difficulties. One was forced to return to the carrier Nimitz; the second was forced to land in the desert, but its crew was taken aboard another of the helicopters and proceeded on to the landing site. Of the six helicopters which landed at the remote desert site, one developed a serious hydraulic problem and was unable to continue with the mission. The operational plans called for a minimum of six helicopters in good operational condition able to proceed from the desert site. Eight helicopters had been included in the force to provide sufficient redundancy without imposing excessive strains on the refueling and exit requirements of the operation. When the number of helicopters available to continue dropped to five, it was determined that the operation could not proceed as planned. Therefore, on the recommendation of the force commander and my military advisers, I decided to cancel the mission and ordered the United States Armed Forces involved to return from Iran.

During the process of withdrawal, one of the helicopters accidentally collided with one of the C-130 aircraft, which was preparing to take off, resulting in the death of eight personnel and the injury of several others. At this point, the decision was made to load all surviving personnel aboard the remaining C-130 aircraft and to abandon the remaining helicopters at the landing site. Altogether, the United States Armed Forces remained on the ground for a total of approximately three hours. The five remaining aircraft took off about 5:45 p.m. EST and departed from Iran airspace without further incident at about 8:00 p.m. EST on April 24. No United States Armed Forces remain in Iran.

The remote desert area was selected to conceal this phase of the mission from discovery. At no time during the temporary presence of United States Armed Forces in Iran did they encounter Iranian forces of any type. We believe, in fact, that no Iranian military forces were in the desert area, and that the Iranian forces were unaware of the presence of United States Armed Forces until after their departure from Iran. As planned, no hostilities occurred during this phase of the mission—the only phase that was executed. . . .

Our rescue team knew, and I knew, that the operation was certain to be dangerous. We were all convinced that if and when the rescue phase of the operation had been commenced, it had an excellent chance of success. They were all volunteers; they were all highly trained. I met with their leaders before they went on this operation. They knew then what hopes of mine and of all Americans they carried with them. I share with the nation the highest respect and appreciation for the ability and bravery of all who participated in the mission.

To the families of those who died and who were injured, I have expressed the admiration I feel for the courage of their loved ones and the sorrow that I feel personally for their sacrifice.

The mission on which they were embarked was a humanitarian mission. It was not directed against Iran. It was not directed against the people of Iran. It caused no Iranian casualties.

This operation was ordered and conducted pursuant to the President's powers under the Constitution as Chief Executive and as Commander-in-Chief of the United States Armed Forces, expressly recognized in Section 8(d)(1) of the War Powers Resolution. In carrying out this operation the United States was acting wholly within its right in accordance with Article 51 of the United Nations Charter to protect and rescue its citizens where the

government of the territory in which they are located is unable or unwilling to protect them.

Source: Jimmy Carter, *Public Papers of the Presidents of the United States: Jimmy Carter, 1980–81,* Book 1 (Washington, DC: U.S. Government Printing Office, 1981), 777–779.

45. United Nations General Assembly Resolution 35/37, November 20, 1980
Introduction

As the first anniversary of Soviet intervention in Afghanistan approached, the United Nations (UN) General Assembly passed a further resolution demanding withdrawal of all "foreign" troops from Afghanistan. The preamble of Resolution 35/37 affirmed the need to reach "a political solution" of the increasingly violent and bitter Afghan situation, one that would restore Afghan sovereignty and independence and also the state's "non-aligned character." As before, the resolution urged all member states to assist the hundreds of thousands of refugees who had by this time fled Afghanistan while calling upon all parties involved to restore conditions that would induce these exiles to return home. The General Assembly adopted this resolution by 101 to 22 votes, with 12 abstentions. Even though the resolution failed to mention the Soviet Union by name, its passage was further evidence of how Soviet treatment of Afghanistan, a small, poor Islamic country, had alienated many habitual Soviet supporters in the UN. As before, however, the resolution proved ineffective. At approximately one-year intervals throughout the 1980s, the General Assembly continued to reiterate its position on Afghanistan, resolutions that the Soviet Union consistently ignored until close to the end of that decade.

Primary Source

Resolution 35/37, Adopted by the U.N. General Assembly, November 20 1980

General Assembly Call for the Immediate Withdrawal of Foreign Troops from Afghanistan

The General Assembly,

Having considered the item entitled "The situation in Afghanistan and its implications for international peace and security,"

Recalling its resolution ES-6/2 of 14 January 1980 adopted at the sixth emergency special session,

Reaffirming the purposes and principles of the Charter of the United Nations and the obligation of all States to refrain in their international relations from the threat or use of force against the sovereignty, territorial integrity and political independence of any State,

Reaffirming further the inalienable right of all peoples to determine their own form of government and to choose their own economic, political and social system free from outside intervention, subversion, coercion or constraint of any kind whatsoever,

Gravely concerned at the continuing foreign armed intervention in Afghanistan, intervention of the above principles, and its serious implications for international peace and security,

Deeply concerned at the increasing outflow of refugees from Afghanistan,

Recognizing the importance of the continuing efforts and initiatives of the organization of the Islamic Conference for a political solution of the situation in respect of Afghanistan,

1. Reiterates that the preservation of the sovereignty, territorial integrity, political independence and non-aligned character of Afghanistan is essential for a peaceful solution of the problem;
2. Reaffirms the right of the Afghan people to determine their own form of government and to choose their economic, political and social system free from outside intervention, subversion, coercion or constraint of any kind whatsoever;
3. Calls for the immediate withdrawal of the foreign troops from Afghanistan;
4. Also calls upon all parties concerned to work for the urgent achievement of a political solution and the creation of the necessary conditions which would enable the Afghan refugees to return voluntarily to their homes in safety and honor;
5. Appeals to all States and national and international organizations to extend humanitarian relief assistance, with a view to alleviating the hardship of the Afghan refuge[e]s, in coordination with the United Nations High Commissioner for Refugees;
6. Expresses its appreciation of the efforts of the Secretary-General in the search for a solution to the problem and hopes that he will continue to extend assistance, including the appointment of a special representative, with a view to promoting a political solution in accordance with the provisions of the present resolution and the exploration of securing appropriate guarantees for non-use of force or threat of use of force against the political independence, sovereignty, territorial integrity and security of all neighboring States, on the basis of mutual guarantees and strict non-interference in each other's internal affairs and with full regard for the principles of the Charter of the United Nations;

7. Requests the Secretary-General to keep Member States and the Security Council concurrently informed of the progress towards the implementation of the present resolution and to submit to Member States and report on the situation at the earliest appropriate opportunity;
8. Decides to include in the provisional agenda of its thirty-sixth session the item entitled "The situation in Afghanistan and its implications for international peace and security."

Source: U.S. Department of State, *American Foreign Policy: Basic Documents, 1977–1980* (Washington, DC: Department of State, 1983), 884–885.

46. Algeria, Iran, and the United States, Agreements for the Release of the U.S. Hostages, January 19, 1981

Introduction

The crisis in U.S.-Iranian relations sparked by the seizure as hostages in November 1979 of more than 60 American diplomatic personnel continued until the last day of Jimmy Carter's presidency. By late 1980, several factors combined to impel the Iranians to be more accommodating than had initially been the case. The death in July 1980 of Mohammad Reza Shah Pahlavi of Iran removed one source of contention, making it impossible for Iran's new government to demand that he be returned to their custody to stand trial. In September 1980 Iraq invaded Iran, the beginning of a lengthy, costly, and brutal war of attrition that quickly became the focus of most of Iran's national energies. In November 1980 the Republican Ronald Reagan, a staunch conservative and anticommunist who proclaimed himself willing to take forceful action against his country's enemies, won the presidential election. It was widely believed that once he took office in January 1981, Reagan might be prepared to take stronger measures against Iran than Carter had been prepared to contemplate. The government of Algeria served as an intermediary in negotiating a settlement, under whose terms the United States renounced all political or military intervention, direct or indirect, in Iran's internal affairs. Frozen Iranian assets totaling US$8 billion, controlled by U.S. institutions, were to be unfrozen immediately when the hostages were released. All lawsuits that American nationals or institutions had launched against the Iranian government in the United States were to be dropped, with an Iran–United States Claims Tribunal, to be established in The Hague, responsible for awarding appropriate compensation to those who had brought such litigation. The hostages were finally released on the following day a few minutes after Reagan took office, depriving Carter of even the satisfaction of personally announcing their liberation.

Primary Source

Declaration of the Government of the Democratic and Popular Republic of Algeria

(General Declaration), 19 January 1981

The Government of the Democratic and Popular Republic of Algeria, having been requested by the Governments of the Islamic Republic of Iran and the United States of America to serve as an intermediary in seeking a mutually acceptable resolution of the crisis in their relations arising out of the detention of the 52 United States nationals in Iran, has consulted extensively with the two governments as to the commitments which each is willing to make in order to resolve the crisis within the framework of the four points stated in the Resolution of November 2, 1980, of the Islamic Consultative Assembly of Iran. On the basis of formal adherences received from Iran and the United States, the Government of Algeria now declares that the following interdependent commitments have been made by the two governments:

General Principles

The undertakings reflected in this Declaration are based on the following general principles:

A. Within the framework of and pursuant to the provisions of the two Declarations of the Government of the Democratic and Popular Republic of Algeria, the United States will restore the financial position of Iran, in so far as possible, to that which existed prior to November 14, 1979. In this context, the United States commits itself to ensure the mobility and free transfer of all Iranian assets within its jurisdiction, as set forth in Paragraphs 4–9.

B. It is the purpose of both parties, within the framework of and pursuant to the provisions of the two Declarations of the Government of the Democratic and Popular Republic of Algeria, to terminate all litigation as between the government of each party and the nationals of the other, and to bring about the settlement and termination of all such claims through binding arbitration.

Through the procedures provided in the Declarations relating to the Claims Settlement Agreement, the United States agrees to terminate all legal proceedings in United States courts involving claims of United States persons and institutions against Iran and its state enterprises, to nullify all attachments and judgments obtained therein, to prohibit all further litigation based on such claims, and to bring about the termination of such claims through binding arbitration.

Point I: Non-intervention in Iranian Affairs

1. The United States pledges that it is and from now on will be the policy of the United States not to intervene, directly or indirectly, politically or militarily, in Iran's internal affairs.

Points II AND III: Return of Iranian Assets and Settlement of U.S. Claims

2. Iran and the United States (hereinafter "the parties") will immediately select a mutually agreeable Central Bank (hereinafter "the Central Bank") to act, under the instructions of the Government of Algeria and the Central Bank of Algeria (hereinafter "the Algerian Central Bank") as depositary of the escrow and security funds hereinafter prescribed and will promptly enter into depositary arrangements with the Central Bank in accordance with the terms of this Declaration. All funds placed in escrow with the Central Bank pursuant to this Declaration shall be held in an account in the name of the Algerian Central Bank. Certain procedures for implementing the obligations set forth in this Declaration and in the Declaration of the Democratic and Popular Republic of Algeria Concerning the Settlement of Claims by the Government of the United States and the Government of the Islamic Republic of Iran.

(hereinafter "the Claims Settlement Agreement") are separately set forth in certain Undertakings of the Government of the United States of America and the Government of the Islamic Republic of Iran with Respect to the Declaration of the Democratic and Popular Republic of Algeria.

3. The depositary arrangements shall provide that, in the event that the Government of Algeria certifies to the Algerian Central Bank that the 52 U.S. nationals have safely departed from Iran, the Algerian Central Bank will thereupon instruct the Central Bank to transfer immediately all monies or other assets in escrow with the Central Bank pursuant to this Declaration, provided that at any time prior to the making of such certification by the Government of Algeria, each of the two parties, Iran and the United States, shall have the right on seventy-two hours notice to terminate its commitments under this Declaration. If such notice is given by the United States and the foregoing certification is made by the Government of Algeria within the seventy-two hour period of notice, the Algerian Central Bank will thereupon instruct the Central Bank to transfer such monies and assets. If the seventy-two hour period of notice by the United States expires without such a certification having been made, or if the notice of termination is delivered by Iran, the Algerian Central Bank will thereupon instruct the Central Bank to return all such monies and assets to the United States, and thereafter the commitments reflected in this Declaration shall be of no further force and effect.

Assets in the Federal Reserve Bank

4. Commencing upon completion of the requisite escrow arrangements with the Central Bank, the United States will bring about the transfer to the Central Bank of all gold bullion which is owned by Iran and which is in the custody of the Federal Reserve Bank of New York, together with all other Iranian assets (or the cash equivalent thereof) in the custody of the Federal Reserve Bank of New York, to be held by the Central Bank in escrow until such time as their transfer or return is required by Paragraph 3 above.

Assets in Foreign Branches of U.S. Banks

5. Commencing upon completion of the requisite escrow arrangements with the Central Bank, the United States will bring about the transfer to the Central Bank, to the account of the Algerian Central Bank, of all Iranian deposits and securities which on or after November 14, 1979, stood upon the books of overseas banking offices of U.S. banks, together with interest thereon through December 31, 1980, to be held by the Central Bank, to the account of the Algerian Central Bank, in escrow until such time as their transfer or return is required in accordance with Paragraph 3 of this Declaration.

Assets in U.S. Branches of U.S. Banks

6. Commencing with the adherence by Iran and the United States to this Declaration and the Claims Settlement Agreement attached hereto, and following the conclusion of arrangements with the Central Bank for the establishment of the interest-bearing Security Account specified in that Agreement and Paragraph 7 below, which arrangements will be concluded within 30 days from the date of this Declaration, the United States will act to bring about the transfer to the Central Bank, within six months from such date, of all Iranian deposits and securities in U.S. banking institutions in the United States, together with interest thereon, to be held by the Central Bank in escrow until such time as their transfer for return is required by Paragraph 3.

7. As funds are received by the Central Bank pursuant to Paragraph 6 above, the Algerian Central Bank shall direct the Central Bank to (1) transfer one-half of each such receipt to Iran and (2) place the other half in a special interest-bearing Security Account in the Central Bank, until the balance in the Security Account has reached the level of U.S.$1 billion. After the U.S.$1 billion balance has been achieved, the Algerian Central Bank shall direct all funds received pursuant to Paragraph 6 to be transferred to Iran. All funds in the Security Account are to be used for the sole purpose of securing the payment of, and paying, claims against Iran in accordance with the Claims Settlement Agreement. Whenever the Central Bank shall thereafter notify Iran that the balance in the Security Account has fallen below U.S.$500 million, Iran shall promptly make new deposits sufficient to maintain a minimum

balance of U.S.$500 million in the Account. The Account shall be so maintained until the President of the arbitral tribunal established pursuant to the Claims Settlement Agreement has certified to the Central Bank of Algeria that all arbitral awards against Iran have been satisfied in accordance with the Claims Settlement Agreement, at which point any amount remaining in the Security Account shall be transferred to Iran.

Other Assets in the U.S. and Abroad

8. Commencing with the adherence of Iran and the United States to this Declaration and the attached Claims Settlement Agreement and the conclusion of arrangements for the establishment of the Security Account, which arrangements will be concluded with[in] 30 days from the date of this Declaration, the United States will act to bring about the transfer to the Central Bank of all Iranian financial assets (meaning funds or securities) which are located in the United States and abroad, apart from those assets referred to in Paragraphs 5 and 6 above, to be held by the Central Bank in escrow until their transfer or return is required by Paragraph 3 above.

9. Commencing with the adherence by Iran and the United States to this Declaration and the attached Claims Settlement Agreement and the making by the Government of Algeria of the certification described in Paragraph 3 above, the United States will arrange, subject to the provisions of U.S. law applicable prior to November 14, 1979, for the transfer to Iran of all Iranian properties which are located in the United States and abroad and which are not within the scope of the preceding paragraphs.

Nullification of Sanctions and Claims

10. Upon the making by the Government of Algeria of the certification described in Paragraph 3 above, the United States will revoke all trade sanctions which were directed against Iran in the period November 4, 1979, to date.

11. Upon the making by the Government of Algeria of the certification described in Paragraph 3 above, the United States will promptly withdraw all claims now pending against Iran before the International Court of Justice and will thereafter bar and preclude the prosecution against Iran of any pending or future claim of the United States or a United States national arising out of events occurring before the date of this Declaration related to (A) the seizure of the 52 United States nationals on November 4, 1979, (B) their subsequent detention, (C) injury to the United States property or property of the United States nationals within the United States Embassy compound in Tehran after November 3, 1979, and (D) injury to the United States nationals or their property as a result of popular movements in the course of the Islamic Revolution in Iran which were not an act of the Government of Iran. The

United States will also bar and preclude the prosecution against Iran in the courts of the United States of any pending or future claim asserted by persons other than the United States nationals arising out of the events specified in the preceding sentence.

Point IV: Return of the Assets of the Family of the Former Shah

12. Upon the making by the Government of Algeria of the certification described in Paragraph 3 above, the United States will freeze, and prohibit any transfer of, property and assets in the United States within the control of the estate of the former Shah or any close relative of the former Shah served as a defendant in U.S. litigation brought by Iran to recover such property and assets as belonging to Iran. As to any such defendant, including the estate of the former Shah, the freeze order will remain in effect until such litigation is finally terminated. Violation of the freeze order shall be subject to the civil and criminal penalties prescribed by U.S. law.

13. Upon the making by the Government of Algeria of the certification described in Paragraph 3 above, the United States will order all persons within U.S. jurisdiction to report to the U.S. Treasury within 30 days, for transmission to Iran, all information known to them, as of November 3, 1979, and as of the date of the order, with respect to the property and assets referred to in Paragraph 12. Violation of the requirement will be subject to the civil and criminal penalties prescribed by U.S. law.

14. Upon the making by the Government of Algeria of the certification described in Paragraph 3 above, the United States will make known, to all appropriate U.S. courts, that in any litigation of the kind described in Paragraph 12 above the claims of Iran should not be considered legally barred either by sovereign immunity principles or by the act of state doctrine and that Iranian decrees and judgments relating to such assets should be enforced by such courts in accordance with United States law.

15. As to any judgment of a U.S. court which calls for the transfer of any property or assets to Iran, the United States hereby guarantees the enforcement of the final judgment to the extent that the property or assets exist with the United States.

16. If any dispute arises between the parties as to whether the United States has fulfilled any obligation imposed upon it by Paragraphs 12–15, inclusive, Iran may submit the dispute to binding arbitration by the tribunal established by, and in accordance with the provisions of, the Claims Settlement Agreement. If the tribunal determines that Iran has suffered a loss as a result of a failure by the United States to fulfill such obligation, it shall make an appropriate award in favor of Iran which may be enforced by Iran in the courts of any nation in accordance with its laws.

Settlement of Disputes

17. If any other dispute arises between the parties as to the interpretation or performance of any provision of this Declaration, either party may submit the dispute to binding arbitration by the tribunal established by, and in accordance with the provisions of, the Claims Settlement Agreement. Any decision of the tribunal with respect to such dispute, including any award of damages to compensate for a loss resulting from a breach of this Declaration or the Claims Settlement Agreement, may be enforced by the prevailing party in the courts of any nation in accordance with its laws.

Source: U.S. Department of State, *American Foreign Policy: Current Documents, 1981* (Washington, DC: Department of State, 1984), 737–741.

47. Department of State, Daily Press Briefing on U.S. Policy toward the Iran-Iraq War and toward Exports to Iraq, May 14, 1982

Introduction

In September 1980 war broke out in the Persian Gulf when Iran invaded Iraq. Saddam Hussein, who became president of Iraq in 1979 and had largely controlled its government since around 1969, saw the weakness of the Iranian military in the aftermath of the 1979 Revolution as an opportunity to make Iraq the predominant power in the Persian Gulf region. He was motivated in part by long-standing disputes with Iran over control of the Shatt al-Arab waterway, only temporarily resolved in 1975 when the two states signed the Algiers Accord dividing their jurisdiction over the channel along a line running through its center. Hussein now claimed that Iraq should control the entire waterway, up to its Iranian shore. In addition, Hussein resented the encouragement that Iran's new Shiite Muslim ruler, Ayatollah Ruhollah Khomeini, whom Saddam had expelled from Iraq in 1978, gave to Iraqi Shiites in efforts to rise up against his own regime and assassinate members of his cabinet. On September 23 Iraqi forces marched across the Shatt al-Arab waterway into southwestern Iraq, the beginning of eight years of war between the two countries. Officially, as U.S. State Department spokesmen reiterated in repeated statements during those years, the United States remained neutral in this conflict, affirming its support for the "independence and territorial integrity" of both states involved and stating its hopes for the negotiation of an immediate peaceful cease-fire. In practice, for several years the United States welcomed Iran's preoccupation with a lengthy and bloody conflict. In February 1982 the U.S. government also removed Iraq from a list of countries subject to antiterrorism controls, restrictions that had previously prevented Iraq from purchasing American armaments. The administration of

U.S. president Ronald Reagan successfully resisted congressional efforts to restore Iran to that list. Iran, by contrast, remained subject to American antiterrorist export controls, a clear disadvantage to Iran in the ongoing hostilities.

Primary Source

Q. [D]o you have any position on the new developments in the Iran-Iraq war?

A. I don't really have anything on any new developments. I could reiterate for you, though, our attitude towards it which I think might be appropriate as this all progresses.

U.S. policy with regard to the Iran-Iraq war has been clear and consistent since the outbreak of the hostilities 20 months ago. The policy enunciated when Iraqi forces entered Iran remains our policy today. The United States supports the independence and territorial integrity of both Iran and Iraq as well as the other states in the region. In keeping with our policy worldwide, we oppose the seizure of territory by force. We see the continuation of the war, as we have repeatedly said, as a danger to the peace and security of all nations in the Gulf region and we have therefore consistently supported an immediate cease-fire and a negotiated settlement. We have maintained a firm policy of not approving the sale or transfer of American military equipment and supplies to either belligerent, and we have welcomed constructive international efforts to bring an end to the war on the basis of each state's respect for the territorial integrity of its neighbors and each state's freedom from external coercion.

Q. Is there a new turn in the war now that has changed your attitude?

A. No. Our policy remains consistent on this.

Q. Do you have any comment on the action by the House Foreign Affairs Committee refusing to take Iraq off this list of terrorism-banned countries?

A. Yes, I do have something on that. Let me address the amendment as a whole as it was adopted yesterday.

The amendment would impose the controls that were removed by the administration in February. The decisions to remove Iraq from the terrorism list, to exempt civil aircraft for civil airlines from controls for antiterrorism purposes and to adjust the controls for South Africa were made after a lengthy review which is required annually. The review took into account the compatibility of the controls with U.S. foreign policy objectives, the reaction of other countries to the controls, and the likely effect of continuing controls on U.S. export performance. All is required by the Export Administration Act.

We oppose the restrictions the amendment would impose. Fixing controls by legislation reduces our flexibility to respond to changes in the international arena and to insure that export controls further our foreign policy objectives as is required by the Export Administration Act itself. Changing course at this time will also confuse foreign governments and call into question the credibility of the United States as a reliable supplier.

Source: U.S. Department of State, *American Foreign Policy: Current Documents, 1982* (Washington, DC: Department of State, 1985), 783–784.

48. Iraqi President Saddam Hussein, Statement on Israel's Right to a Secure State, January 2, 1983

Introduction

By the 1980s, several Arab leaders were willing to publicly endorse the concept of recognition of Israel. President Saddam Hussein of Iraq, then engaged in a lengthy war with Iran in which he was receiving substantial U.S. support, was among them. Hussein, heading a largely secular government dominated by the socialist Baath Party, was by no means a dedicated Muslim. Interviewed by Democratic congressman Stephen Solarz in 1983, Hussein told him "that the simultaneous existence of an independent Palestinian State acceptable to the Palestinians and the existence of a secure state for the Israelis are both necessary." Hussein's greatest concern over such an arrangement was apparently not the status of Israel but rather his opposition to any potential union of the West Bank and Gaza with the kingdom of Jordan. This would, he claimed, be "unacceptable" to Iraq and other Arab states. Hussein argued that were the Palestinian territories to join Jordan, other Arab states would regard this as threatening "their entire existence" and exposing them to manipulation and menace from "an international conspiracy" or any "big power." Hussein's underlying objection may well have been that a merger of Jordan with the West Bank and Gaza would have enhanced Jordan both territorially and in terms of its international visibility, prestige, and allies, boosting that kingdom's ability to withstand pressure from Iraq.

Primary Source

[Question] Mr. President, I do appreciate your frank answers. I would like to ask you the second question and I would like you to give, with all sincerity, your viewpoint: should Israel agree to return to the pre-1967 borders, but only within an objective framework, giving Jordan the primary responsibility for administrating the West Bank and Gaza Strip. (?Does) this represent an acceptable solution to the problem? Would it be sufficient for Israel to withdraw to the 1967 lines and to accept the establishment of a

Palestinian State in the West Bank and Gaza Strip as a way to solve the conflict?

[Answer] I do not believe that forcing the Palestinians, under the current circumstances, to accept a constitutional formula with any Arab State is a sound action. However, I believe that the simultaneous existence of an independent Palestinian State acceptable to the Palestinians and the existence of a secure state for the Israelis are both necessary.

I believe that you will be committing a grave mistake, unacceptable of course to the Arabs and Iraq, if you think that Jordan is suitable as a Palestinian State. In other words, the state of Palestine would be on the east bank of the Jordan, as some Israeli officials have remarked. The Arabs would feel that their entire existence was threatened and that the political map of their national entity could be threatened any time by an international conspiracy or by the desire of this or that big power.

Source: Saddam Hussein, Interview with Stephen Solarz, January 2, 1983, Foreign Broadcast Information Service, *F.B.I.S.-Daily Report Middle East and North Africa*, January 4, 1983.

49. President Ronald Reagan, Address to the Nation on Events in Lebanon and Grenada, October 27, 1983 [Excerpts]

Introduction

On October 23, 1983, Muslim suicide-bombers drove trucks loaded with explosives into the barracks of peacekeeping forces of U.S. marines and French troops stationed in Beirut, the capital of Lebanon. These troops had been deployed there since late 1982 as part of an international peacekeeping force that was trying to maintain order in Beirut after Israeli forces intent on driving out the Palestine Liberation Organization (PLO) had invaded, triggering a complicated civil war among various Lebanese political factions. The American forces were increasingly perceived as seeking to ensure the victory of Maronite Christian groups linked to Israel. The bombing resulted in the deaths of 241 American servicemen, 58 French paratroopers, and some civilians. The episode was one of the first suicide bombings in the Middle East. Addressing the nation four days later, U.S. president Ronald Reagan affirmed his country's commitment to maintaining order in the Middle East, particularly in Lebanon, and claimed that the attacks were themselves evidence that the marines were succeeding in their mission of restoring stability and normal conditions in Beirut. The United States blamed Syria for the attacks and mounted air strikes and naval bombardments against Syrian, Druze, and Shiite positions

in Lebanon. In practice, nonetheless, shortly afterward the U.S. government, reluctant to face the prospect of further major casualties in such episodes, proclaimed that the marines had accomplished their mission and withdrew them from Lebanon, a decision that hawks later criticized as proving that terrorist tactics were effective. In the same address, Reagan also highlighted the American invasion of the Caribbean island of Grenada, an operation launched two days earlier to overthrow a Marxist government that had murdered socialist prime minister Maurice Bishop and seized power the previous week. Cuban troops and construction workers were present on the island, building an airport that, it was feared, would be used for military purposes, and 1,000 American students were believed to be in danger. In conjunction with forces from seven other Caribbean countries, 5,000 U.S. marines invaded the island and, after some heavy fighting, subdued the Grenadian ground and air forces and the Cuban contingents. They also found a cache of heavy weapons sufficient to arm 10,000 troops. Nineteen American soldiers died and 119 were wounded, while Grenadian casualties were 45 dead and 337 wounded. By mid-December 1983 most resistance had ended, except for some rebels who fled to the hills, and American forces were withdrawn. Parliamentary elections held in 1984 returned the noncommunist New National Party to power. The two near-simultaneous episodes encapsulated the degree to which Reagan's bold rhetoric belied his pragmatic caution in international affairs. Like most American presidents and military men in the aftermath of the Vietnam War, Reagan preferred to keep American military interventions brief and limited and to pick conflicts in which victory would be relatively quick and easy.

Primary Source

Some 2 months ago we were shocked by the brutal massacre of 269 men, women, and children, more than 60 of them Americans, in the shooting down of a Korean airliner. Now, in these past several days, violence has erupted again, in Lebanon and Grenada.

In Lebanon, we have some 1,600 marines, part of a multinational force that's trying to help the people of Lebanon restore order and stability to that troubled land. Our marines are assigned to the south of the city of Beirut, near the only airport operating in Lebanon. Just a mile or so to the north is the Italian contingent and not far from them, the French and a company of British soldiers.

This past Sunday, at 22 minutes after 6 Beirut time, with dawn just breaking, a truck, looking like a lot of other vehicles in the city, approached the airport on a busy, main road. There was nothing in its appearance to suggest it was any different than the trucks or cars that were normally seen on and around the airport. But this one was different. At the wheel was a young man on a suicide mission.

The truck carried some 2,000 pounds of explosives, but there was no way our marine guards could know this. Their first warning that something was wrong came when the truck crashed through a series of barriers, including a chain-link fence and barbed wire entanglements. The guards opened fire, but it was too late. The truck smashed through the doors of the headquarters building in which our marines were sleeping and instantly exploded. The four-story concrete building collapsed in a pile of rubble.

More than 200 of the sleeping men were killed in that one hideous, insane attack. Many others suffered injury and are hospitalized here or in Europe.

This was not the end of the horror. At almost the same instant, another vehicle on a suicide and murder mission crashed into the headquarters of the French peacekeeping force, an eight-story building, destroying it and killing more than 50 French soldiers.

Prior to this day of horror, there had been several tragedies for our men in the multinational force. Attacks by snipers and mortar fire had taken their toll.

I called bereaved parents and/or widows of the victims to express on behalf of all of us our sorrow and sympathy. Sometimes there were questions. And now many of you are asking: Why should our young men be dying in Lebanon? Why is Lebanon important to us?

Well, it's true, Lebanon is a small country, more than five-and-a-half thousand miles from our shores on the edge of what we call the Middle East. But every President who has occupied this office in recent years has recognized that peace in the Middle East is of vital concern to our nation and, indeed, to our allies in Western Europe and Japan. We've been concerned because the Middle East is a powderkeg; four times in the last 30 years, the Arabs and Israelis have gone to war. And each time, the world has teetered near the edge of catastrophe.

The area is key to the economic and political life of the West. Its strategic importance, its energy resources, the Suez Canal, and the well-being of the nearly 200 million people living there—all are vital to us and to world peace. If that key should fall into the hands of a power or powers hostile to the free world, there would be a direct threat to the United States and to our allies.

We have another reason to be involved. Since 1948 our Nation has recognized and accepted a moral obligation to assure the continued existence of Israel as a nation. Israel shares our democratic values and is a formidable force an invader of the Middle East would have to reckon with.

For several years, Lebanon has been torn by internal strife. Once a prosperous, peaceful nation, its government had become ineffective in controlling the militias that warred on each other. Sixteen months ago, we were watching on our TV screens the shelling

and bombing of Beirut which was being used as a fortress by PLO bands. Hundreds and hundreds of civilians were being killed and wounded in the daily battles.

Syria, which makes no secret of its claim that Lebanon should be a part of a Greater Syria, was occupying a large part of Lebanon. Today, Syria has become a home for 7,000 Soviet advisers and technicians who man a massive amount of Soviet weaponry, including SS-21 ground-to-ground missiles capable of reaching vital areas of Israel.

A little over a year ago, hoping to build on the Camp David accords, which had led to peace between Israel and Egypt, I proposed a peace plan for the Middle East to end the wars between the Arab States and Israel. It was based on U.N. resolutions 242 and 338 and called for a fair and just solution to the Palestinian problem, as well as a fair and just settlement of issues between the Arab States and Israel.

Before the necessary negotiations could begin, it was essential to get all foreign forces out of Lebanon and to end the fighting there. So, why are we there? Well, the answer is straightforward: to help bring peace to Lebanon and stability to the vital Middle East. To that end, the multinational force was created to help stabilize the situation in Lebanon until a government could be established and a Lebanese army mobilized to restore Lebanese sovereignty over its own soil as the foreign forces withdrew. Israel agreed to withdraw as did Syria, but Syria then reneged on its promise. Over 10,000 Palestinians who had been bringing ruin down on Beirut, however, did leave the country.

Lebanon has formed a government under the leadership of President Gemayal, and that government, with our assistance and training, has set up its own army. In only a year's time, that army has been rebuilt. It's a good army, composed of Lebanese of all factions.

A few weeks ago, the Israeli army pulled back to the Awali River in southern Lebanon. Despite fierce resistance by Syrian-backed forces, the Lebanese army was able to hold the line and maintain the defensive perimeter around Beirut.

In the year that our marines have been there, Lebanon has made important steps toward stability and order. The physical presence of the marines lends support to both the Lebanese Government and its army. It allows the hard work of diplomacy to go forward. Indeed, without the peacekeepers from the U.S., France, Italy, and Britain, the efforts to find a peaceful solution in Lebanon would collapse.

As to that narrower question—what exactly is the operational mission of the marines—the answer is, to secure a piece of Beirut, to keep order in their sector, and to prevent the area from becoming

1614   49. President Ronald Reagan, Address to the Nation on Events in Lebanon and Grenada

a battlefield. Our marines are not just sitting in an airport. Part of their task is to guard that airport. Because of their presence, the airport has remained operational. In addition, they patrol the surrounding area. This is their part—a limited, but essential part—in the larger effort that I've described.

If our marines must be there, I'm asked, why can't we make them safer? Who committed this latest atrocity against them and why?

Well, we'll do everything we can to ensure that our men are as safe as possible. We ordered the battleship New Jersey to join our naval forces offshore. Without even firing them, the threat of its 16-inch guns silenced those who once fired down on our marines from the hills, and they're a good part of the reason we suddenly had a cease-fire. We're doing our best to make our forces less vulnerable to those who want to snipe at them or send in future suicide missions.

Secretary [of State George] Shultz called me today from Europe, where he was meeting with the Foreign Ministers of our allies in the multinational force. They remain committed to our task. And plans were made to share information as to how we can improve security for all our men.

We have strong circumstantial evidence that the attack on the marines was directed by terrorists who used the same method to destroy our Embassy in Beirut. Those who directed this atrocity must be dealt justice, and they will be. The obvious purpose behind the sniping and, now, this attack was to weaken American will and force the withdrawal of U.S. and French forces from Lebanon. The clear intent of the terrorists was to eliminate our support of the Lebanese Government and to destroy the ability of the Lebanese people to determine their own destiny.

To answer those who ask if we're serving any purpose in being there, let me answer a question with a question. Would the terrorists have launched their suicide attacks against the multinational force if it were not doing its job? The multinational force was attacked precisely because it is doing the job it was sent to do in Beirut. It is accomplishing its mission.

Now then, where do we go from here? What can we do now to help Lebanon gain greater stability so that our marines can come home? Well, I believe we can take three steps now that will make a difference.

First, we will accelerate the search for peace and stability in that region....

Second, we'll work even more closely with our allies in providing support for the Government of Lebanon and for the rebuilding of a national consensus.

Third, we will ensure that the multinational peace-keeping forces, our marines, are given the greatest possible protection....

Beyond our progress in Lebanon, let us remember that our main goal and purpose is to achieve a broader peace in all of the Middle East. The factions and bitterness that we see in Lebanon are just a microcosm of the difficulties that are spread across much of that region. A peace initiative for the entire Middle East, consistent with the Camp David accords and U.N. resolutions 242 and 338, still offers the best hope for bringing peace to the region.

Let me ask those who say we should get out of Lebanon: If we were to leave Lebanon now, what message would that send to those who foment instability and terrorism? If America were to walk away from Lebanon, what chance would there be for a negotiated settlement, producing a unified democratic Lebanon?

If we turned our backs on Lebanon now, what would be the future of Israel? At stake is the fate of only the second Arab country to negotiate a major agreement with Israel. That's another accomplishment of this past year, the May 17th accord signed by Lebanon and Israel.

If terrorism and intimidation succeed, it'll be a devastating blow to the peace process and to Israel's search for genuine security. It won't just be Lebanon sentenced to a future of chaos. Can the United States, or the free world, for that matter, stand by and see the Middle East incorporated into the Soviet bloc? What of Western Europe and Japan's dependence on Middle East oil for the energy to fuel their industries? The Middle East is, as I've said, vital to our national security and economic well-being.

Brave young men have been taken from us. Many others have been grievously wounded. Are we to tell them their sacrifice was wasted? They gave their lives in defense of our national security every bit as much as any man who ever died fighting in a war. We must not strip every ounce of meaning and purpose from their courageous sacrifice.

We're a nation with global responsibilities. We're not somewhere else in the world protecting someone else's interests; we're there protecting our own.

[...]

Let us meet our responsibilities. For longer than any of us can remember, the people of the Middle East have lived from war to war with no prospect for any other future. That dreadful cycle must be broken. Why are we there? Well, a Lebanese mother told one of our Ambassadors that her little girl had only attended school 2 of the last 8 years. Now, because of our presence there, she said her daughter could live a normal life.

With patience and firmness, we can help bring peace to that strife-torn region—and make our own lives more secure. Our role is to help the Lebanese put their country together, not to do it for them.

Now, I know another part of the world is very much on our minds, a place much closer to our shores: Grenada. The island is only twice the size of the District of Columbia, with a total population of about 110,000 people.

Grenada and a half dozen other Caribbean islands here were, until recently, British colonies. They're now independent states and members of the British Commonwealth. While they respect each other's independence, they also feel a kinship with each other and think of themselves as one people.

In 1979 trouble came to Grenada. Maurice Bishop, a protégé of Fidel Castro, staged a military coup and overthrew the government which had been elected under the constitution left to the people by the British. He sought the help of Cuba in building an airport, which he claimed was for tourist trade, but which looked suspiciously suitable for military aircraft, including Soviet-built long-range bombers.

The six sovereign countries and one remaining colony are joined together in what they call the Organization of Eastern Caribbean States. The six became increasingly alarmed as Bishop built an army greater than all of theirs combined. Obviously, it was not purely for defense.

In this last year or so, Prime Minister Bishop gave indications that he might like better relations with the United States. He even made a trip to our country and met with senior officials of the White House and the State Department. Whether he was serious or not, we'll never know. On October 12th, a small group in his militia seized him and put him under arrest. They were, if anything, more radical and more devoted to Castro's Cuba than he had been.

Several days later, a crowd of citizens appeared before Bishop's home, freed him, and escorted him toward the headquarters of the military council. They were fired upon. A number, including some children, were killed, and Bishop was seized. He and several members of his cabinet were subsequently executed, and a 24-hour shoot-to-kill curfew was put in effect. Grenada was without a government, its only authority exercised by a self-proclaimed band of military men.

There were then about 1,000 of our citizens on Grenada, 800 of them students in St. George's University Medical School. Concerned that they'd be harmed or held as hostages, I ordered a flotilla of ships, then on its way to Lebanon with marines, part of our regular rotation program, to circle south on a course that would put them somewhere in the vicinity of Grenada in case there should be a need to evacuate our people.

Last weekend, I was awakened in the early morning hours and told that six members of the Organization of Eastern Caribbean States, joined by Jamaica and Barbados, had sent an urgent request that we join them in a military operation to restore order and democracy to Grenada. They were proposing this action under the terms of a treaty, a mutual assistance pact that existed among them.

These small, peaceful nations needed our help. Three of them don't have armies at all, and the others have very limited forces. The legitimacy of their request, plus my own concern for our citizens, dictated my decision. I believe our government has a responsibility to go to the aid of its citizens, if their right to life and liberty is threatened. The nightmare of our hostages in Iran must never be repeated.

We knew we had little time and that complete secrecy was vital to ensure both the safety of the young men who would undertake this mission and the Americans they were about to rescue. The Joint Chiefs worked around the clock to come up with a plan. They had little intelligence information about conditions on the island.

We had to assume that several hundred Cubans working on the airport could be military reserves. Well, as it turned out, the number was much larger, and they were a military force. Six hundred of them have been taken prisoner, and we have discovered a complete base with weapons and communications equipment, which makes it clear a Cuban occupation of the island had been planned.

Two hours ago we released the first photos from Grenada. They included pictures of a warehouse of military equipment—one of three we've uncovered so far. This warehouse contained weapons and ammunition stacked almost to the ceiling, enough to supply thousands of terrorists. Grenada, we were told, was a friendly island paradise for tourism. Well, it wasn't. It was a Soviet-Cuban colony, being readied as a major military bastion to export terror and undermine democracy. We got there just in time.

[. . .]

The events in Lebanon and Grenada, though oceans apart, are closely related. Not only has Moscow assisted and encouraged the violence in both countries, but it provides direct support through a network of surrogates and terrorists. It is no coincidence that when the thugs tried to wrest control over Grenada, there were 30 Soviet advisers and hundreds of Cuban military and paramilitary forces on the island. At the moment of our landing, we communicated with the Governments of Cuba and the Soviet Union and told them we would offer shelter and security to their people on

Grenada. Regrettably, Castro ordered his men to fight to the death, and some did. The others will be sent to their homelands.

You know, there was a time when our national security was based on a standing army here within our own borders and shore batteries of artillery along our coasts, and, of course, a navy to keep the sea lanes open for the shipping of things necessary to our well-being. The world has changed. Today, our national security can be threatened in faraway places. It's up to all of us to be aware of the strategic importance of such places and to be able to identify them.

[. . .]

Source: Ronald Reagan, *Public Papers of the Presidents of the United States: Ronald Reagan, 1983,* Book 2 (Washington, DC: U.S. Government Printing Office, 1985), 1517–1522.

50. President Ronald Reagan, Address to the Nation Concerning the U.S. Air Strike against Libya, April 14, 1986, and Letter to Congress on U.S. Air Strikes against Libya, April 15, 1986

Introduction

The radical Arab regime of Colonel Muammar Qaddafi, who took power in Libya in 1969, was a constant irritant to U.S. leaders. Though small in population, still under 6 million in the early 21st century, Libya controlled large oil reserves. Qaddafi aligned his country with radical Arab nationalist forces, including the Palestine Liberation Organization (PLO). During the 1970s and 1980s Libya sponsored a wide variety of international terrorist organizations, including the Provisional Irish Republican Army and the breakaway Palestinian Abu Nidal Group. In December 1985 the latter was responsible for armed attacks on ticket counters of the Israeli airline El Al at the Rome and Vienna airports. The United States also held Libyan terrorists responsible for the early April 1986 explosion of a bomb in a West Berlin discotheque that was much patronized by American military personnel. Such incidents and Libyan territorial claims to special rights in the waters of the Gulf of Sidra provoked President Ronald Reagan into ordering a carrier naval task force to the area in March 1986 whose vessels soon clashed with Libyan missile-armed patrol boats. Seeking to send a message that the United States would not tolerate international terrorist operations, in mid-April 1986 Reagan authorized a major long-distance bombing raid by American F-111 warplanes based in Great Britain and A-6, A-7, and F/A-18 aircraft from several aircraft carriers on five Libyan sites, including the airfields and air defense networks at Tripoli and Benghazi. It was widely believed that one target of the

raids was Qaddafi himself, but he escaped harm. His young adopted daughter was killed, and two of his sons were injured. After the raid, Qaddafi apparently increased Libyan support to international terrorist organizations. Arab states, together with the Soviet Union and France, unanimously condemned the operation, whereas the governments of Britain, Australia, and Israel supported it. In most European countries public opinion was strongly opposed to the airstrikes, which many perceived as evidence of the increasingly assertive, militarized, and unilateral character of U.S. foreign policy under the conservative Reagan. While rhetorically condemning the raids, Soviet officials were privately less than enthusiastic toward Qaddafi, who had frequently publicly attacked Soviet policies and ideology and intervened in international situations in ways that undercut Soviet objectives. Soviet leaders therefore did not allow American actions against Libya to disturb the smooth progress of continuing U.S.-Soviet arms control negotiations. In an address to the American people and in a letter to Congress, Reagan justified the air strikes as a preemptive action undertaken in self-defense by the United States.

Primary Source

My fellow Americans: At 7 o'clock this evening eastern time air and naval forces of the United States launched a series of strikes against the headquarters, terrorist facilities, and military assets that support Mu'ammar Qadhafi's subversive activities. The attacks were concentrated and carefully targeted to minimize casualties among the Libyan people with whom we have no quarrel. From initial reports, our forces have succeeded in their mission.

Several weeks ago in New Orleans, I warned Colonel Qadhafi we would hold his regime accountable for any new terrorist attacks launched against American citizens. More recently I made it clear we would respond as soon as we determined conclusively who was responsible for such attacks. On April 5th in West Berlin a terrorist bomb exploded in a nightclub frequented by American servicemen. Sergeant Kenneth Ford and a young Turkish woman were killed and 230 others were wounded, among them some 50 American military personnel. This monstrous brutality is but the latest act in Colonel Qadhafi's reign of terror. The evidence is now conclusive that the terrorist bombing of La Belle discotheque was planned and executed under the direct orders of the Libyan regime. On March 25th, more than a week before the attack, orders were sent from Tripoli to the Libyan People's Bureau in East Berlin to conduct a terrorist attack against Americans to cause maximum and indiscriminate casualties. Libya's agents then planted the bomb. On April 4th the People's Bureau alerted Tripoli that the attack would be carried out the following morning. The next day they reported back to Tripoli on the great success of their mission.

Our evidence is direct; it is precise; it is irrefutable. We have solid evidence about other attacks Qadhafi has planned against the United States installations and diplomats and even American tourists. Thanks to close cooperation with our friends, some of these have been prevented. With the help of French authorities, we recently aborted one such attack: a planned massacre, using grenades and small arms, of civilians waiting in line for visas at an American Embassy.

Colonel Qadhafi is not only an enemy of the United States. His record of subversion and aggression against the neighboring States in Africa is well documented and well known. He has ordered the murder of fellow Libyans in countless countries. He has sanctioned acts of terror in Africa, Europe, and the Middle East, as well as the Western Hemisphere. Today we have done what we had to do. If necessary, we shall do it again. It gives me no pleasure to say that, and I wish it were otherwise. Before Qadhafi seized power in 1969, the people of Libya had been friends of the United States. And I'm sure that today most Libyans are ashamed and disgusted that this man has made their country a synonym for barbarism around the world. The Libyan people are a decent people caught in the grip of a tyrant.

To our friends and allies in Europe who cooperated in today's mission, I would only say you have the permanent gratitude of the American people. Europeans who remember history understand better than most that there is no security, no safety, in the appeasement of evil. It must be the core of Western policy that there be no sanctuary for terror. And to sustain such a policy, free men and free nations must unite and work together. Sometimes it is said that by imposing sanctions against Colonel Qadhafi or by striking at his terrorist installations we only magnify the man's importance, that the proper way to deal with him is to ignore him. I do not agree.

Long before I came into this office, Colonel Qadhafi had engaged in acts of international terror, acts that put him outside the company of civilized men. For years, however, he suffered no economic or political or military sanction; and the atrocities mounted in number, as did the innocent dead and wounded. And for us to ignore by inaction the slaughter of American civilians and American soldiers, whether in nightclubs or airline terminals, is simply not in the American tradition. When our citizens are abused or attacked anywhere in the world on the direct orders of a hostile regime, we will respond so long as I'm in this Oval Office. Self-defense is not only our right, it is our duty. It is the purpose behind the mission undertaken tonight, a mission fully consistent with Article 51 of the United Nations Charter.

We believe that this preemptive action against his terrorist installations will not only diminish Colonel Qadhafi's capacity to export terror, it will provide him with incentives and reasons to alter his criminal behavior. I have no illusion that tonight's action will ring down the curtain on Qadhafi's reign of terror. But this mission, violent though it was, can bring closer a safer and more secure

world for decent men and women. We will persevere. This afternoon we consulted with the leaders of Congress regarding what we were about to do and why. Tonight I salute the skill and professionalism of the men and women of our Armed Forces who carried out this mission. It's an honor to be your Commander in Chief.

We Americans are slow to anger. We always seek peaceful avenues before resorting to the use of force—and we did. We tried quiet diplomacy, public condemnation, economic sanctions, and demonstrations of military force. None succeeded. Despite our repeated warnings, Qadhafi continued his reckless policy of intimidation, his relentless pursuit of terror. He counted on America to be passive. He counted wrong. I warned that there should be no place on Earth where terrorists can rest and train and practice their deadly skills. I meant it. I said that we would act with others, if possible, and alone if necessary to ensure that terrorists have no sanctuary anywhere. Tonight, we have.

Thank you, and God bless you.

Source: Ronald Reagan, *Public Papers of the Presidents of the United States: Ronald Reagan, 1986,* Book 1 (Washington, DC: U.S. Government Printing Office, 1988), 468–469.

51. Soviet Government, Statement on the Persian Gulf Situation, July 4, 1987

Introduction

By the mid-1980s, the Soviet Union viewed continuation of the war that had broken out between Iran and Iraq in 1980 as a destabilizing factor in international affairs. Under Mikhail Gorbachev, who sought peace and stability with other powers in order to concentrate on internal reforms, the Soviet Union had begun to liquidate its own outstanding international entanglements. Already, the Soviets were moving toward withdrawing their forces from the lengthy guerrilla conflict in Afghanistan that they had entered in December 1979. Soviet leaders also sought to de-escalate other disputes in the Middle East. Iran shared a border with the Soviet Union, arousing apprehensions that the ongoing conflict might ultimately spill over into Soviet territory. Soviet leaders viewed the massive deployment of U.S. military forces in the Persian Gulf region during the Iran-Iraq War, especially American interdiction of Iranian air and sea communications and commerce and American attacks on Libya, as efforts to establish U.S. "military-political hegemony in this strategically important area of the world." So long as the conflagration continued, however, American forces were likely to maintain a high profile in the area, with the objective of protecting the vital sea-lanes that transported so much of the world's oil supplies. In mid-1987 an article in the official Soviet newspaper *Pravda* (Truth) called for the withdrawal of "the warships of states not situated in the region" from the Persian Gulf in exchange for agreements by Iran and Iraq that they would "abstain from actions that would threaten international shipping." (Given their own proximity to Iran, the Soviets, of course, might well have argued that their ships should remain there.) The Soviets called upon the United Nations (UN) to negotiate a cease-fire under whose terms the forces of both Iran and Iraq would withdraw behind their respective borders. The fact that both superpowers, which were simultaneously reaching wide-ranging agreements with each other on arms reduction, now favored ending the Iran-Iraq War meant that they could concentrate their efforts on putting additional pressure on both belligerent nations to end hostilities and accept an armistice.

Primary Source

Recently tension in the Persian Gulf has been dangerously growing. A drastically increased number of warships, including those of states located thousands of kilometers away from this important area, are plying international waters traditionally used for trade and other peaceful passage. The continuation of the long senseless war between Iran and Iraq objectively facilitates the aggravation of the situation. As a result, events there are approaching a danger level beyond which exists the risk of the regional conflict developing into an international crisis.

It is absolutely clear that these processes, if not stopped in time and placed under proper control, might pose a serious threat to international peace and security even contrary to the will and intent of the states drawn into them. This turn of events gives rise to the legitimate alarm of the international community. Likewise, this cannot but provoke the concern of the Soviet Union, which is located in the direct proximity of the expanding seat of conflict.

In these conditions there is a pressing need to adopt urgent and effective measures that will promote a radical defusing of tension in the Persian Gulf and an early end to the Iran-Iraq war. Real steps toward attainment of the said aims are needed. Pseudomeasures, supposedly motivated by concern for the safety of shipping or "ensuring stabilization" in the Persian Gulf but in reality prompted by selfish designs, are absolutely impermissible. Such actions are now being undertaken by the United States which wants to exploit the present alarming situation in the Persian Gulf area to achieve its long-harbored plans of establishing military-political hegemony in this strategically important area of the world, an area that Washington is trying to represent as a sphere of American "vital interests." Such is the real explanation of the U.S. policy of building up its military presence, although it tries to cover this up with stereotype contentions about the existence of a "Soviet threat." . . .

Proceeding from the need for radical measures to improve the situation in the region, the Soviet Government suggests that all

warships of states not situated in the region be withdrawn soon from the Gulf and that Iran and Iraq, in turn, should abstain from actions that would threaten international shipping. Such measures, taken in the context of an all-embracing settlement of the Iran-Iraq conflict, would help pacify the situation and eliminate the threat of the spread of an explosive seat of military tension.

The Soviet Union reaffirms its principled stand in favor of ending the Iran-Iraq war and resolving outstanding issues between Iran and Iraq at the negotiating table rather than on the battlefield.

In this connection we attach special importance to political efforts within the framework of the United Nations to find a peaceful solution to the Iran-Iraq conflict.

In agreement with other members of the UN Security Council, we are in favor of effective measures in this direction, specifically an immediate cease-fire and cessation of all hostilities, and a withdrawal of all troops to the internationally recognized borders without delay.

The UN secretary-general can play a substantial role in achieving a fair settlement acceptable to both sides.

The Soviet Union supports the peace-making mission of the UN secretary-general and calls on all other countries to render every kind of assistance to its successful outcome.

The acuteness of the situation in the Persian Gulf area and the need to quickly bring about an end to the Iran-Iraq conflict require that all countries pursue a policy of genuinely constructive deeds, a policy prompted by the overriding interest in preserving peace and effectively strengthening international security, rather than practicing "gunboat diplomacy."

The Soviet Union is ready to cooperate with all those who really share these aims.

Source: *Reprints from the Soviet Press* 40(4) (August 1987): 45–46.

52. President Ronald Reagan, Statement on U.S. Reprisal Raid on Iranian Platforms in the Persian Gulf, October 19, 1987

Introduction

Preoccupation with their war with each other led both Iran and Iraq to make repeated if sporadic attacks on international shipping in the Persian Gulf, as each sought to prevent lucrative overseas oil exports by the other. To ensure safe passage for oil shipments to the West, U.S. naval carrier forces patrolled the Gulf, while oil tankers registered in Kuwait were sometimes reflagged as U.S. vessels. Iranian patrol boats, aircraft, and missile batteries repeatedly launched attacks on military and civilian American ships, which were also vulnerable to mines. The most successful operation against the U.S. military presence was in fact an Iraqi air attack in May 1987, when an F-1 Mirage warplane launched two Exocet missiles against the naval frigate *Stark,* killing 37 sailors. Since the U.S. government leaned toward Iraq in the war, President Saddam Hussein hastily apologized, characterizing the incident as an "accident." President Ronald Reagan was less tolerant when Iranian mines and missiles targeted his country's naval forces and Kuwaiti ships flying American flags. In retaliation, in October 1987 U.S. naval vessels seized and destroyed an Iranian military platform in the central Persian Gulf. The platform was equipped with radar and other communications devices and served as the base for small boat and helicopter attacks against American ships and also as a mine-laying center. To the American people and Congress, Reagan characterized this operation as a measure taken in self-defense to preclude further such incidents. The episode did not, however, end Iranian attacks on American vessels in the Persian Gulf. The following April, an Iranian patrol boat and an Iranian frigate separately launched missiles against U.S. naval craft that were also damaged by mines, once more provoking the U.S. task force to attack Iranian oil platforms in the area. The continuing risk that the Iran-Iraq War posed to U.S. military and civilian vessels in the Persian Gulf was one major reason why in the late 1980s the U.S. government encouraged armistice negotiations between the two belligerent nations. Iran brought suit in the International Court of Justice against these attacks, and in November 2003 the court finally ruled that "the actions of the United States of America against Iranian oil platforms on 19 October 1987 and 18 April 1988 cannot be justified as measures necessary to protect the essential security interests of the United States of America."

Primary Source

Acting pursuant to my authority as Commander in Chief, United States naval vessels at 7 a.m. EDT today struck an Iranian military platform in international waters in the central Persian Gulf. This platform has been used to assist in a number of Iranian attacks against nonbelligerent shipping. Iran's unprovoked attacks upon U.S. and other non belligerent shipping, and particularly deliberate laying of mines and firing of Silkworm missiles, which have hit U.S.-flag vessels, have come in spite of numerous messages from the Government of the United States to the Government of Iran warning of the consequences.

The action against the Iranian military platform came after consultations with congressional leadership and friendly governments. It is a prudent yet restrained response to this unlawful use of force

against the United States and to numerous violations of the rights of other nonbelligerents. It is a lawful exercise of the right of self-defense enshrined in article 51 of the United Nations Charter and is being so notified to the President of the United Nations Security Council.

The United States has no desire for a military confrontation with Iran, but the Government of Iran should be under no illusion about our determination and ability to protect our ships and our interests against unprovoked attacks. We have informed the Government of Iran of our desire for an urgent end to tensions in the region and an end to the Iran-Iraq war through urgent implementation of Security Council Resolution 598.

Source: Ronald Reagan, *Public Papers of the Presidents of the United States: Ronald Reagan, 1987,* Book 2 (Washington, DC: U.S. Government Printing Office, 1989), 1201–1202.

53. The Iran-Contra Report, August 4, 1993 [Excerpts]

Introduction

The Iran-Contra Scandal, one of the most damaging episodes for U.S. president Ronald Reagan, seized Americans' attention during 1985–1987. Revelations came to light that the Reagan administration had secretly negotiated the sale of arms to Iran in the hope of winning the return of American hostages held by the Iranians in Lebanon and in order to finance aid to the Contra rebels, who were fighting the Marxist Sandinista government in Nicaragua. This action was in violation of the Boland Amendment, which prohibited aid to the Contras, and of stated U.S. policies not to negotiate with the Iranians. Such arms sales were particularly embarrassing, since at the time Iran and Iraq were engaged in a protracted and costly war in which the United States favored Iraq and therefore sought to prevent all other countries from exporting armaments to Iran. If nothing else, American diplomacy appeared to lack overall coordination. The matter was eventually turned over to Special Prosecutor Lawrence Walsh, who submitted the final report of his investigation to the U.S. House of Representatives on August 4, 1993. One of the major questions that Walsh had to investigate was the degree of involvement by the Reagan administration. It was White House officials, rather than the State Department, who conceived and implemented these activities. Reagan initially claimed to have been unaware of them but nonetheless took full responsibility for them, while Vice President George H. W. Bush also stated that he himself had been "out of the loop" on the subject. National Security Adviser Robert McFarlane, who had conceived the scheme as a means of improving relations with Iran and made a secret trip to Iran as part of the operation, tried but failed to commit suicide during the investigation. No hostages were freed as a result of these negotiations.

McFarlane and his successor, John Poindexter, were both convicted of lying to Congress, but their sentences were overturned on appeal, as was that of Colonel Oliver North, a National Security Council aide who had been heavily involved in the implementation of these schemes. Most of the other high-ranking officials whom Walsh indicted, including U.S. secretary of defense Caspar Weinberger, who had been accused of lying and withholding information from Congress, were pardoned by Bush after he became president. The Iran-Contra Scandal undoubtedly tarnished Reagan's second term in office, since the president had either deliberately misled the American people and broken various laws or had failed to exercise proper supervision over lower-level officials within his administration. In March 1987 Reagan spoke on national television, telling the American people that he regretted the situation and had been incorrect in stating earlier that the United States had not traded arms for hostages but that he believed that his actions had been right. Reagan's approval ratings at one stage dropped to 46 percent but by the time he finished his presidency had rebounded to 63 percent. Some American politicians have since asserted that in the broader national interest they declined to pursue the Iran-Contra Scandal as aggressively as might have been possible, because they did not wish to bring down the first U.S. president to serve two uninterrupted terms in office since Dwight D. Eisenhower during the 1950s. The executive summary of the report prepared by Walsh was nonetheless a damning catalog of legal violations and abuses of power by a wide range of high-level Reagan administration officials.

Primary Source

Iran-Contra Scandal: Report of the Independent Counsel

Executive Summary

In October and November 1986, two secret U.S. Government operations were publicly exposed, potentially implicating Reagan Administration officials in illegal activities. These operations were the provision of assistance to the military activities of the Nicaraguan contra rebels during an October 1984 to October 1986 prohibition on such aid, and the sale of U.S. arms to Iran in contravention of stated U.S. policy and in possible violation of arms-export controls. In late November 1986, Reagan Administration officials announced that some of the proceeds from the sale of U.S. arms to Iran had been diverted to the contras.

As a result of the exposure of these operations, Attorney General Edwin Meese III sought the appointment of an independent counsel to investigate and, if necessary, prosecute possible crimes arising from them.

The Special Division of the United States Court of Appeals for the District of Columbia Circuit appointed Lawrence E. Walsh as Independent Counsel on December 19, 1986, and charged him with investigating:

(1) the direct or indirect sale, shipment, or transfer since in or about 1984 down to the present, of military arms, materiel, or funds to the government of Iran, officials of that government, persons, organizations or entities connected with or purporting to represent that government, or persons located in Iran;

(2) the direct or indirect sale, shipment, or transfer of military arms, materiel or funds to any government, entity, or person acting, or purporting to act as an intermediary in any transaction referred to above;

(3) the financing or funding of any direct or indirect sale, shipment or transfer referred to above;

(4) the diversion of proceeds from any transaction described above to or for any person, organization, foreign government, or any faction or body of insurgents in any foreign country, including, but not limited to Nicaragua;

(5) the provision or coordination of support for persons or entities engaged as military insurgents in armed conflict with the government of Nicaragua since 1984.

This is the final report of that investigation.

Overall Conclusions

The investigations and prosecutions have shown that high-ranking Administration officials violated laws and executive orders in the Iran/contra matter.

Independent Counsel concluded that:

—the sales of arms to Iran contravened United States Government policy and may have violated the Arms Export Control Act;[1]

—the provision and coordination of support to the contras violated the Boland Amendment ban on aid to military activities in Nicaragua;

—the policies behind both the Iran and contra operations were fully reviewed and developed at the highest levels of the Reagan Administration;

---

1. Independent Counsel is aware that the Reagan Administration Justice Department took the position, after the November 1986 revelations, that the 1985 shipments of United States weapons to Iran did not violate the law. This post hoc position does not correspond with the contemporaneous advice given the President. As detailed within this report, Secretary of Defense Caspar W. Weinberger (a lawyer with an extensive record in private practice and the former general counsel of the Bechtel Corporation) advised President Reagan in 1985 that the shipments were illegal. Moreover, Weinberger's opinion was shared by attorneys within the Department of Defense and the White House counsel's office once they became aware of the 1985 shipments. Finally, when Attorney General Meese conducted his initial inquiry into the Iran arms sales, he expressed concern that the shipments may have been illegal.

—although there was little evidence of National Security Council level knowledge of most of the actual contra-support operations, there was no evidence that any NSC member dissented from the underlying policy—keeping the contras alive despite congressional limitations on contra support;

—the Iran operations were carried out with the knowledge of, among others, President Ronald Reagan, Vice President George Bush, Secretary of State George P. Shultz, Secretary of Defense Caspar W. Weinberger, Director of Central Intelligence William J. Casey, and national security advisers Robert C. McFarlane and John M. Poindexter; of these officials, only Weinberger and Shultz dissented from the policy decision, and Weinberger eventually acquiesced by ordering the Department of Defense to provide the necessary arms; and

—large volumes of highly relevant, contemporaneously created documents were systematically and willfully withheld from investigators by several Reagan Administration officials.

—following the revelation of these operations in October and November 1986, Reagan Administration officials deliberately deceived the Congress and the public about the level and extent of official knowledge of and support for these operations.

In addition, Independent Counsel concluded that the off-the-books nature of the Iran and contra operations gave line-level personnel the opportunity to commit money crimes.

The Basic Facts of Iran/contra

The Iran/contra affair concerned two secret Reagan Administration policies whose operations were coordinated by National Security Council staff. The Iran operation involved efforts in 1985 and 1986 to obtain the release of Americans held hostage in the Middle East through the sale of U.S. weapons to Iran, despite an embargo on such sales. The contra operations from 1984 through most of 1986 involved the secret governmental support of contra military and paramilitary activities in Nicaragua, despite congressional prohibition of this support.

The Iran and contra operations were merged when funds generated from the sale of weapons to Iran were diverted to support the contra effort in Nicaragua. Although this "diversion" may be the most dramatic aspect of Iran/contra, it is important to emphasize that both the Iran and contra operations, separately, violated United States policy and law.[2] The ignorance of the "diversion" asserted by President Reagan and his Cabinet officers on the National Security Council in no way absolves them of responsibility for the underlying Iran and contra operations.

2. See n. 1 above.

The secrecy concerning the Iran and contra activities was finally pierced by events that took place thousands of miles apart in the fall of 1986. The first occurred on October 5, 1986, when Nicaraguan government soldiers shot down an American cargo plane that was carrying military supplies to contra forces; the one surviving crew member, American Eugene Hasenfus, was taken into captivity and stated that he was employed by the CIA. A month after the Hasenfus shootdown, President Reagan's secret sale of U.S. arms to Iran was reported by a Lebanese publication on November 3. The joining of these two operations was made public on November 25, 1986, when Attorney General Meese announced that Justice Department officials had discovered that some of the proceeds from the Iran arms sales had been diverted to the contras.

When these operations ended, the exposure of the Iran/contra affair generated a new round of illegality. Beginning with the testimony of Elliott Abrams and others in October 1986 and continuing through the public testimony of Caspar W. Weinberger on the last day of the congressional hearings in the summer of 1987, senior Reagan Administration officials engaged in a concerted effort to deceive Congress and the public about their knowledge of and support for the operations.

Independent Counsel has concluded that the President's most senior advisers and the Cabinet members on the National Security Council participated in the strategy to make National Security staff members McFarlane, Poindexter and North the scapegoats whose sacrifice would protect the Reagan Administration in its final two years. In an important sense, this strategy succeeded. Independent Counsel discovered much of the best evidence of the cover-up in the final year of active investigation, too late for most prosecutions.

[. . .]

Agency Support of the Operations

Following the convictions of those who were most central to the Iran/contra operations, Independent Counsel's investigation focused on the supporting roles played by Government officials in other agencies and the supervisory roles of the NSC principals. The investigation showed that Administration officials who claimed initially that they had little knowledge about the Iran arms sales or the illegal contra-resupply operation North directed were much better informed than they professed to be. The Office of Independent Counsel obtained evidence that Secretaries Weinberger and Shultz and White House Chief of Staff Donald T. Regan, among others, held back information that would have helped Congress obtain a much clearer view of the scope of the Iran/contra matter. Contemporaneous notes of Regan and Weinberger, and those dictated by Shultz, were withheld until they were obtained by Independent Counsel in 1991 and 1992.

The White House and Office of the Vice President

As the White House section of this report describes in detail, the investigation found no credible evidence that President Reagan violated any criminal statute. The OIC could not prove that Reagan authorized or was aware of the diversion or that he had knowledge of the extent of North's control of the contra-resupply network. Nevertheless, he set the stage for the illegal activities of others by encouraging and, in general terms, ordering support of the contras during the October 1984 to October 1986 period when funds for the contras were cut off by the Boland Amendment, and in authorizing the sale of arms to Iran, in contravention of the U.S. embargo on such sales. The President's disregard for civil laws enacted to limit presidential actions abroad—specifically the Boland Amendment, the Arms Export Control Act and congressional-notification requirements in covert-action laws—created a climate in which some of the Government officers assigned to implement his policies felt emboldened to circumvent such laws.

President Reagan's directive to McFarlane to keep the contras alive "body and soul" during the Boland cut-off period was viewed by North, who was charged by McFarlane to carry out the directive, as an invitation to break the law. Similarly, President Reagan's decision in 1985 to authorize the sale of arms to Iran from Israeli stocks, despite warnings by Weinberger and Shultz that such transfers might violate the law, opened the way for Poindexter's subsequent decision to authorize the diversion. Poindexter told Congress that while he made the decision on his own and did not tell the President, he believed the President would have approved. North testified that he believed the President authorized it.

Independent Counsel's investigation did not develop evidence that proved that Vice President Bush violated any criminal statute. Contrary to his public pronouncements, however, he was fully aware of the Iran arms sales. Bush was regularly briefed, along with the President, on the Iran arms sales, and he participated in discussions to obtain third-country support for the contras. The OIC obtained no evidence that Bush was aware of the diversion. The OIC learned in December 1992 that Bush had failed to produce a diary containing contemporaneous notes relevant to Iran/contra, despite requests made in 1987 and again in early 1992 for the production of such material. Bush refused to be interviewed for a final time in light of evidence developed in the latter stages of OIC's investigation, leaving unresolved a clear picture of his Iran/contra involvement. Bush's pardon of Weinberger on December 24, 1992 pre-empted a trial in which defense counsel indicated that they intended to call Bush as a witness.

The chapters on White House Chief of Staff Regan and Attorney General Edwin Meese III focus on their actions during the November 1986 period, as the President and his advisers sought to control the damage caused by the disclosure of the Iran arms

sales. Regan in 1992 provided Independent Counsel with copies of notes showing that Poindexter and Meese attempted to create a false account of the 1985 arms sales from Israeli stocks, which they believed were illegal, in order to protect the President. Regan and the other senior advisers did not speak up to correct the false version of events. No final legal determination on the matter had been made. Regan said he did not want to be the one who broke the silence among the President's senior advisers, virtually all of whom knew the account was false.

The evidence indicates that Meese's November 1986 inquiry was more of a damage-control exercise than an effort to find the facts. He had private conversations with the President, the Vice President, Poindexter, Weinberger, Casey and Regan without taking notes. Even after learning of the diversion, Meese failed to secure records in NSC staff offices or take other prudent steps to protect potential evidence. And finally, in reporting to the President and his senior advisers, Meese gave a false account of what he had been told by stating that the President did not know about the 1985 HAWK shipments, which Meese said might have been illegal. The statute of limitations had run on November 1986 activities before OIC obtained its evidence. In 1992, Meese denied recollection of the statements attributed to him by the notes of Weinberger and Regan. He was unconvincing, but the passage of time would have been expected to raise a reasonable doubt of the intentional falsity of his denials if he had been prosecuted for his 1992 false statements.

The Role of CIA Officials

Director Casey's unswerving support of President Reagan's contra policies and of the Iran arms sales encouraged some CIA officials to go beyond legal restrictions in both operations. Casey was instrumental in pairing North with Secord as a contra-support team when the Boland Amendment in October 1984 forced the CIA to refrain from direct or indirect aid. He also supported the North-Secord combination in the Iran arms sales, despite deep reservations about Secord within the CIA hierarchy.

Casey's position on the contras prompted the chief of the CIA's Central American Task Force, Alan D. Fiers, Jr., to "dovetail" CIA activities with those of North's contra-resupply network, in violation of Boland restrictions. Casey's support for the NSC to direct the Iran arms sales and to use arms dealer Manucher Ghorbanifar and Secord in the operation, forced the CIA's Directorate of Operations to work with people it distrusted.

Following the Hasenfus shootdown in early October 1986, George and Fiers lied to Congress about U.S. Government involvement in contra resupply, to, as Fiers put it, "keep the spotlight off the White House." When the Iran arms sales became public in November 1986, three of Casey's key officers—George, Clarridge and Fiers—followed Casey's lead in misleading Congress.

Four CIA officials were charged with criminal offenses—George, the deputy director for operations and the third highest-ranking CIA official; Clarridge, chief of the European Division; Fiers; and Fernandez. George was convicted of two felony counts of false statements and perjury before Congress. Fiers pleaded guilty to two misdemeanor counts of withholding information from Congress. The four counts of obstruction and false statements against Fernandez were dismissed when the Bush Administration refused to declassify information needed for his defense. Clarridge was awaiting trial on seven counts of perjury and false statements when he, George and Fiers were pardoned by President Bush.

State Department Officials

In 1990 and 1991, Independent Counsel received new documentary evidence in the form of handwritten notes suggesting that Secretary Shultz's congressional testimony painted a misleading and incorrect picture of his knowledge of the Iran arms sales. The subsequent investigation focused on whether Shultz or other Department officials deliberately misled or withheld information from congressional or OIC investigators.

The key notes, taken by M. Charles Hill, Shultz's executive assistant, were nearly verbatim, contemporaneous accounts of Shultz's meetings within the department and Shultz's reports to Hill on meetings the secretary attended elsewhere. The Hill notes and similarly detailed notes by Nicholas Platt, the State Department's executive secretary, provided the OIC with a detailed account of Shultz's knowledge of the Iran arms sales. The most revealing of these notes were not provided to any Iran/contra investigation until 1990 and 1991. The notes show that—contrary to his early testimony that he was not aware of details of the 1985 arms transfers—Shultz knew that the shipments were planned and that they were delivered. Also in conflict with his congressional testimony was evidence that Shultz was aware of the 1986 shipments.

Independent Counsel concluded that Shultz's early testimony was incorrect, if not false, in significant respects, and misleading, if literally true, in others. When questioned about the discrepancies in 1992, Shultz did not dispute the accuracy of the Hill notes. He told OIC that he believed his testimony was accurate at the time and he insisted that if he had been provided with the notes earlier, he would have testified differently. Independent Counsel declined to prosecute because there was a reasonable doubt that Shultz's testimony was willfully false at the time it was delivered.

Independent Counsel concluded that Hill had willfully withheld relevant notes and prepared false testimony for Shultz in 1987. He declined to prosecute because Hill's claim of authorization to limit the production of his notes and the joint responsibility of Shultz for the resulting misleading testimony, would at trial have raised a reasonable doubt, after Independent Counsel had declined to prosecute Shultz.

Independent Counsel's initial focus on the State Department had centered on Assistant Secretary Elliott Abrams' insistence to Congress and to the OIC that he was not aware of North's direction of the extensive contra-resupply network in 1985 and 1986. As assistant secretary of state for inter-American affairs, Abrams chaired the Restricted Inter-Agency Group, or RIG, which coordinated U.S. policy in Central America. Although the OIC was skeptical about Abrams' testimony, there was insufficient evidence to proceed against him until additional documentary evidence inculpating him was discovered in 1990 and 1991, and until Fiers, who represented the CIA on the RIG, pleaded guilty in July 1991 to withholding information from Congress. Fiers provided evidence to support North's earlier testimony that Abrams was knowledgeable about North's contra-supply network. Abrams pleaded guilty in October 1991 to two counts of withholding information from Congress about secret Government efforts to support the contras, and about his solicitation of $10 million to aid the contras from the Sultan of Brunei.

Secretary Weinberger and Defense Department Officials

Contrary to their testimony to the presidentially appointed Tower Commission and the Select Iran/contra Committees of Congress, Independent Counsel determined that Secretary Weinberger and his closest aides were consistently informed of proposed and actual arms shipments to Iran during 1985 and 1986. The key evidence was handwritten notes of Weinberger, which he deliberately withheld from Congress and the OIC until they were discovered by Independent Counsel in late 1991. The Weinberger daily diary notes and notes of significant White House and other meetings contained highly relevant, contemporaneous information that resolved many questions left unanswered in early investigations.

The notes demonstrated that Weinberger's early testimony—that he had only vague and generalized information about Iran arms sales in 1985—was false, and that he in fact had detailed information on the proposed arms sales and the actual deliveries. The notes also revealed that Gen. Colin Powell, Weinberger's senior military aide, and Richard L. Armitage, assistant secretary of defense for international security affairs, also had detailed knowledge of the 1985 shipments from Israeli stocks. Armitage and Powell had testified that they did not learn of the November 1985 HAWK missile shipment until 1986.

Weinberger's notes provided detailed accounts of high-level Administration meetings in November 1986 in which the President's senior advisers were provided with false accounts of the Iran arms sales to protect the President and themselves from the consequences of the possibly illegal 1985 shipments from Israeli stocks.

Weinberger's notes provided key evidence supporting the charges against him, including perjury and false statements in connection with his testimony regarding the arms sales, his denial of the existence of notes and his denial of knowledge of Saudi Arabia's multi-million dollar contribution to the contras. He was pardoned less than two weeks before trial by President Bush on December 24, 1992.

There was little evidence that Powell's early testimony regarding the 1985 shipments and Weinberger's notes was willfully false. Powell cooperated with the various Iran/contra investigations and, when his recollection was refreshed by Weinberger's notes, he readily conceded their accuracy. Independent Counsel declined to prosecute Armitage because the OIC's limited resources were focused on the case against Weinberger and because the evidence against Armitage, while substantial, did not reach the threshold of proof beyond a reasonable doubt.

[...]

Observations and Conclusions

This report concludes with Independent Counsel's observations and conclusions. He observes that the governmental problems presented by Iran/contra are not those of rogue operations, but rather those of Executive Branch efforts to evade congressional oversight. As this report documents, the competing roles of the attorney general—adviser to the President and top law-enforcement officer—come into irreconcilable conflict in the case of high-level Executive Branch wrongdoing. Independent Counsel concludes that congressional oversight alone cannot correct the deficiencies that result when an attorney general abandons the law-enforcement responsibilities of that office and undertakes, instead, to protect the President.

[...]

Source: Lawrence E. Walsh, *Final Report of the Independent Counsel for Iran-Contra Matters,* Vol. 1 (Washington, DC: Government Printing Office, 1993), xiii–xxii.

54. Mikhail Gorbachev, Soviet Policy Statement on Afghanistan, February 9, 1988 [Excerpts]

Introduction

Intervention in Afghanistan in December 1979 embroiled the Soviet Union in a lengthy, costly, and ultimately unwinnable war in rugged mountainous terrain against tribal Afghan guerrilla forces,

the fundamentalist Islamic mujahideen. Although equipped with armored cars, tanks, and heavy artillery, the Soviet army had little training in guerrilla warfare, and much of its weaponry proved ineffective against these opponents. The war was fought with great brutality on both sides, with the Soviets using helicopters, fighter-bombers, and bombers in a scorched-earth policy designed to raze enemy territory, regardless of civilian casualties. The military situation nonetheless remained one of stalemate. Internationally the Soviet action attracted severe condemnation, as the United Nations (UN) General Assembly—though unable to take any concrete action due to the Soviet veto power on the Security Council—voted repeatedly for resolutions that "strongly deplored" the invasion and called for the Soviets to withdraw, while the foreign ministers of the Organization of the Islamic Conference almost immediately demanded the removal of Soviet forces. The Afghan resistance movement received funding, weaponry (notably FIM-92 Stinger antiaircraft missile systems), and training from the United States, and its members were able to take shelter in camps in neighboring Pakistan. Pakistani special forces quietly took part in the war, and British and U.S. special services were likewise believed to be involved. China, Saudi Arabia, and other Muslim states also contributed funds to the mujahideen. By 1987, resistance forces were launching rocket attacks on the Afghan capital of Kabul and seemed likely to take it and overthrow the government in the near future. The war was expensive and highly unpopular in the Soviet Union, as more than 15,000 young soldiers died in combat, with many more wounded. Nobel Peace Prize winner Andrei Sakharov publicly denounced Soviet policies in Afghanistan and called for peace negotiations. In November 1986 a new Afghan government, headed by Mohammad Najibullah, former chief of the Afghan secret police, took office and announced policies of "national reconciliation." Peace talks were opened between Afghanistan and Pakistan, and in March 1988 Soviet president Mikhail Gorbachev publicly stated that with effect from May 15, 1988, a withdrawal of Soviet troops would begin, to be completed in March 1989. The future of Afghanistan would, he said, now belong to the Afghans, and he would be happy if it chose to become "an independent, nonaligned and neutral state." Gorbachev's declaration effectively represented a defeat for the Soviet Union. In April 1988 Afghanistan and Pakistan finally reached agreement on peace terms, with the Soviet Union and the United States being joint guarantors. Soviet troops left on schedule, with the last departing in March 1989, but bitter civil war continued in Afghanistan. Ultimately the country would fall under the control of the radical Islamic Taliban and provide a haven for the Muslim terrorists linked with the Al Qaeda organization that mounted the successful airborne attacks of September 11, 2001, on landmark American buildings in Washington, D.C., and New York.

Primary Source

The military conflict in Afghanistan has been going on for a long time now. It is one of the most severe and most painful regional conflicts. Now, from all indications, definite prerequisites have been created for its political settlement. In this connection, the Soviet leadership deems it necessary to express its views and to completely clarify its position.

The next round of talks between Afghanistan and Pakistan, through the personal representative of the UN Secretary-General, will take place in Geneva in the near future. There is a significant chance that the coming round will be the final one.

At present, the drafting of documents covering all aspects of a settlement has almost been completed at the Geneva talks. Among these documents are Afghan-Pakistani agreements on noninterference in each other's internal affairs and on the return of Afghan refugees from Pakistan; international guarantees of noninterference in the internal affairs of the Republic of Afghanistan; and a document on the interrelationship of all elements of a political settlement. There is also an accord on creating a verification mechanism.

What remains to be done? A timetable for the withdrawal of Soviet troops from Afghanistan that is acceptable to all sides must be established. Yes, a timetable, since we, in accord with the Afghan leadership, adopted a fundamental political decision on the withdrawal of Soviet troops some time ago, something that was announced at the time.

[. . .]

Seeking to promote a rapid and successful conclusion of the Afghan-Pakistani talks in Geneva, the governments of the USSR and the Republic of Afghanistan have agreed to set a specific date for beginning the withdrawal of Soviet troops—May 15, 1988— and to complete their withdrawal over a period of 10 months. This date has been set based on the assumption that the agreements on a settlement will be signed no later than March 15, 1988, and, accordingly, that they will all go into effect simultaneously two months later. If the agreements are signed before March 15, the troop withdrawal will, accordingly, begin earlier.

[. . .]

Any armed conflict, including an internal one, is capable of poisoning the atmosphere in an entire region and of creating a situation of uneasiness and alarm for the neighbors of the country involved, not to mention the sufferings of and casualties among the people of the country itself. That is why we are opposed to all armed conflicts. We know that the Afghan leadership holds the same position.

As is known, all this led the Afghan leadership, headed by President Najibullah, to a profound rethinking of its political course, a process that resulted in a patriotic and realistic policy of national reconciliation. We are talking about a very bold and courageous action: It is not merely a call to end armed clashes but a proposal to create a coalition government and to share power with the opposition, including those who are waging an armed struggle against the government, and even with those who are abroad directing the actions of the rebels and supplying them with weapons and combat equipment obtained from foreign states. This has been proposed by a government that is invested with constitutional authority and wields real power in the country.

The policy of national reconciliation is an expression of new political thinking on the Afghan side. It shows not weakness but the strength of spirit, wisdom and dignity of free, honest and responsible political leaders who are concerned about their country's present and future.

The success of the policy of national reconciliation has already made it possible to begin the withdrawal of Soviet troops from parts of Afghan territory. At present, there are no Soviet troops in 13 Afghan provinces, because armed clashes there have stopped. It is completely possible to say that the sooner peace is established on Afghan soil, the easier it will be for Soviet troops to leave.

The policy of national reconciliation has provided a political platform for all those who want peace in Afghanistan. What kind of peace? The kind that the Afghan people want. The proud, freedom-loving and valiant Afghan people, whose history of struggle for freedom and independence goes back many centuries, have been, are and will be the masters of their country, which is based, as President Najibullah has said, on the principles of multiple parties in the political field and multiple structures in the economic field.

The Afghans themselves will determine the ultimate status of their country among other states. Most often, it is said that the future, peaceful Afghanistan will be an independent, nonaligned and neutral state. Well, we will be nothing but happy to have such a neighbor on our southern borders.

[. . .]

One final point. When the Afghan knot is untied, this will have a very profound effect on other regional conflicts as well.

If the arms race, which we are so insistently seeking to halt—and with some success—is mankind's insane rush to the abyss, then regional conflicts are bleeding wounds capable of causing spots of gangrene on the body of mankind.

The earth is literally pockmarked with danger spots of this kind. Each of them means pain not only for the peoples directly involved but for everyone, whether in Afghanistan, in the Middle East, in connection with the Iran-Iraq war, in southern Africa, in Kampuchea or in Central America.

Who gains from these conflicts? No one, except arms merchants and various reactionary, expansionist circles who are accustomed to taking advantage of and turning a profit on the misfortunes of peoples.

Carrying through a political settlement in Afghanistan to conclusion will be an important break in the chain of regional conflicts.

Just as the accord on the elimination of medium—and shorter—range missiles sets up a sequence of further major steps in the field of disarmament, steps on which negotiations are under way or are in the planning stage, so behind a political settlement in Afghanistan looms the question: Which conflict will be overcome next? It is certain that more resolutions will follow.

States and peoples have sufficient potential in terms of responsibility, political will and determination to put an end to all regional conflicts within a few years. This is something worth working for. The Soviet Union will spare no effort in this highly important cause.

Source: Mikhail Gorbachev, "Afghan Exit Could Start May 15," *Current Digest of the Soviet Press* 40(6) (1988): 1–3.

55. U.S. Department of State Spokesman Charles E. Redman, Daily Press Briefing, U.S. Condemnation of Chemical Warfare, March 23, 1988

Introduction

From the beginning of the Iran-Iraq War in 1980, there were frequent allegations that Iraq was using chemical weapons. Accusations that Iraq employed these in 1984 were later verified by a United Nations (UN) inspection team. In March 1986 UN secretary-general Xavier Perez de Cuellar formally accused Iraq of chemical warfare, including the use of mustard gas and nerve gas, against Iranian forces. In March 1988 the UN again charged Iraq with using chemical weapons extensively against its opponents, tactics that Iraq continued until accepting a cease-fire in August 1988. The UN Security Council issued several statements condemning the use of such weapons, but neither the Soviet Union nor the United States was willing to support formal resolutions to this effect for fear of alienating Iraq, to which both superpowers were supplying weapons. Official American statements on the

subject were relatively weak and halfhearted, reflecting the continuing U.S. tilt toward Iraq. In a press briefing in March 1988, a State Department spokesman deplored Iraq's use of chemical weapons against Iran and expressed support for past UN Security Council statements condemning such methods of warfare but suggested that "Iran may also have used chemical artillery shells in this fighting." He claimed that both Iran and Iraq were "attempting to stockpile chemical weapons." The only real means of solving this problem, the spokesman suggested, would be a "negotiated peace" settlement under UN Security Council Resolution 598.

Primary Source

Q. Do you have any reaction to the pictures of the apparent nerve gas that was used on the battlefield in Iraq, by Iraq?

A. We've seen these photos and TV pictures showing the results of apparent Iraqi use of chemical weapons in its war against Iran. This incident appears to be a particularly grave violation of the 1925 Geneva Protocol against chemical warfare. There are indications that Iran may also have used chemical artillery shells in this fighting.

We condemn, without reservation, any use of chemical weapons in violation of international law. We call upon Iran and Iraq to desist immediately from any further use of chemical weapons which are an offense to civilization and humanity.

Last year a U.N. team of experts confirmed that Iraq had used chemical weapons. In the past we have supported U.N Security Council statements condemning illegal chemical warfare. We would support similar Security Council action in this instance. There is evidence that both Iran and Iraq are attempting to stockpile chemical weapons, and we have worked to deny both countries access to chemical weapons precursors and the means to manufacture chemical weapons.

And, unfortunately, to end where I always have to end is to say that the root of this tragedy, as of the other tragedies that we have seen, continues to be the war between Iran and Iraq. And so in that context we call upon both sides to reach a negotiated peace in accordance with U.N. Security Council Resolution 598, which calls for an end to the war in all aspects.

I would also note that the Secretary-General of the United Nations has invited the Foreign Ministers of Iran and Iraq to meet with him in New York to discuss implementation of 598, and we urge both sides to give him prompt responses.

Source: U.S. Department of State, *American Foreign Policy: Current Documents, 1988* (Washington, DC: Department of State, 1989), 438.

56. The Geneva Accords on Afghanistan, April 14, 1988 [Excerpts]

Introduction

By the late 1980s, Soviet leaders were desperate to remove their troops from Afghanistan but did not wish to admit the humiliation of defeat there. With assistance from both the United Nations (UN) and the United States, a face-saving formula was found whereby the troops were withdrawn. The solution built on earlier UN-sponsored negotiations of the early 1980s designed to facilitate an end to the conflict in Afghanistan. Afghanistan and Pakistan signed an agreement under the terms of which each promised to withdraw its own military forces from its neighbor's territory, to respect the other's sovereignty and territorial integrity, and to deny the use of its own territory to forces that sought to attack its neighbor. Afghan refugees could return from Pakistan to their own country. All foreign troops were to be withdrawn from Afghanistan within nine months of the signing of the agreements, a clause that meant that the Soviet Union should remove its forces. One original rationale for Soviet military intervention had been that this was to protect Afghanistan against outside pressure. The Geneva Accords could be taken as proof that this pressure had now ended, meaning that Soviet forces had fulfilled their mission and that there was no further need for their presence in Afghanistan. The Soviet Union and the United States each agreed to serve as guarantor of the agreements, although the U.S. government added a rider that, by so doing, it did not agree to recognize the legitimacy of Afghanistan's existing government. Warming U.S.-Soviet relations, especially the close personal ties that had developed since 1985 between U.S. president Ronald Reagan and Soviet secretary-general Mikhail Gorbachev, facilitated the conclusion of the Geneva Accords.

Primary Source

AGREEMENTS ON THE SETTLEMENT OF THE SITUATION RELATING TO AFGHANISTAN

BILATERAL AGREEMENT BETWEEN THE REPUBLIC OF AFGHANISTAN AND THE ISLAMIC REPUBLIC OF PAKISTAN ON THE PRINCIPLES OF MUTUAL RELATIONS, IN PARTICULAR ON NON-INTERFERENCE AND NON-INTERVENTION

The Republic of Afghanistan and the Islamic Republic of Pakistan, hereinafter referred to as the High Contracting Parties,

Desiring to normalize relations and promote good-neighborliness and co-operation as well as to strengthen international peace and security in the region,

Considering that full observance of the principle of non-interference and non-intervention in the internal and external affairs of States is of the greatest importance for the maintenance of international peace and security and for the fulfillment of the purposes and principles of the Charter of the United Nations,

Reaffirming the inalienable right of States freely to determine their own political, economic, cultural and social systems in accordance with the will of their peoples, without outside intervention, interference, subversion, coercion or threat in any form whatsoever,

Mindful of the provisions of the Charter of the United Nations as well as the resolutions adopted by the United Nations on the principle of non-interference and non-intervention, in particular the Declaration on Principles of International Law concerning Friendly Relations and Co-operation among States in accordance with the Charter of the United Nations, of 24 October 1970, as well as the Declaration on the Inadmissibility of Intervention and Interference in the Internal Affairs of States, of 9 December 1981,

Have agreed as follows:

Article I

Relations between the High Contracting Parties shall be conducted in strict compliance with the principle of non-interference and non-intervention by States in the affairs of other States.

Article II

For the purpose of implementing the principle of non-interference and non-intervention, each High Contracting Party undertakes to comply with the following obligations:

(1) to respect the sovereignty, political independence, territorial integrity, national unity, security and non-alignment of the other High Contracting Party, as well as the national identity and cultural heritage of its people;

(2) to respect the sovereign and inalienable right of the other High Contracting Party freely to determine its own political, economic, cultural and social systems, to develop its international relations and to exercise permanent sovereignty over its natural resources. In accordance with the will of its people, and without outside intervention, interference, subversion, coercion or threat in any form whatsoever;

(3) to refrain from the threat or use of force in any form whatsoever so as not to violate the boundaries of each other, to disrupt the political, social or economic order of the other High Contracting Party, to overthrow or change the political system of the other High Contracting Party or its Government, or to cause tension between the High Contracting Parties;

(4) to ensure that its territory is not used in any manner which would violate the sovereignty, political independence, territorial integrity and national unity or disrupt the political, economic and social stability of the other High Contracting Party;

(5) to refrain from armed intervention, subversion, military occupation or any other form of intervention and interference, overt or covert, directed at the other High Contracting Party, or any act of military political or economic interference in the internal affairs of the other High Contracting Party, including acts of reprisal involving the use of force;

(6) to refrain from any action or attempt in whatsoever form or under whatever pretext to destabilize or to undermine the stability of the other High Contracting Party or any of its institutions;

(7) to refrain from the promotion, encouragement or support, direct or indirect, of rebellious or secessionist activities against the other High Contracting Party, under any pretext whatsoever, or from any other action which seeks to disrupt the unity or to undermine or subvert the political order of the other High Contracting Party;

(8) to prevent within its territory the training, equipping, financing and recruitment of mercenaries from whatever origin for the purpose of hostile activities against the other High Contracting Party, or the sending of such mercenaries into the territory of the other High Contracting Party and accordingly to deny facilities, including financing for the training, equipping and transit of such mercenaries;

(9) to refrain from making any agreements or arrangements with other States designed to intervene or interfere in the internal and external affairs of the other High Contracting Party;

(10) to abstain from any defamatory campaign, vilification or hostile propaganda for the purpose of intervening or interfering in the internal affairs of the other High Contracting Party;

(11) to prevent any assistance to or use of or tolerance of terrorist groups, saboteurs or subversive agents against the other High Contracting Party;

(12) to prevent within its territory the presence, harbouring, in camps and bases of otherwise, organizing, training, financing, equipping and arming of individuals and political, ethnic and any other groups for the purpose of creating subversion, disorder or unrest in the territory of the other High Contracting Party and accordingly also to prevent the use of mass media and the transportation of arms, ammunition and equipment by such individuals and groups;

(13) not to resort to or to allow any other action that could be considered as interference or intervention.

[...]

DECLARATION ON INTERNATIONAL GUARANTEES

The Government of the Union of Soviet Socialist Republics and of the United States of America,

Expressing support that the Republic of Afghanistan and the Islamic Republic of Pakistan have concluded a negotiated political settlement designed to normalize relations and promote good-neighbourliness between the two countries as well as to strengthen international peace and security in the region;

Wishing in turn to contribute to the achievement of the objectives that the Republic of Afghanistan and the Islamic Republic of Pakistan have set themselves, and with a view to ensuring respect for their sovereignty, independence, territorial integrity and non-alignment;

Undertake to invariably refrain from any form of interference and intervention in the internal affairs of the Republic of Afghanistan and the Islamic Republic of Pakistan and to respect the commitments contained in the bilateral Agreement between the Republic of Afghanistan and the Islamic Republic of Pakistan on the Principles of Mutual Relations, in particular on Non-Interference and Non-Intervention;

Urge all States to act likewise.

[...]

BILATERAL AGREEMENT BETWEEN THE REPUBLIC OF AFGHANISTAN AND THE ISLAMIC REPUBLIC OF PAKISTAN ON THE VOLUNTARY RETURN OF REFUGEES

The Republic of Afghanistan and the Islamic Republic of Pakistan, hereinafter referred to as the High Contracting Parties,

Desiring to normalize relations and promote good-neighbourliness and co-operation as well as to strengthen international peace and security in the region,

Convinced that voluntary and unimpeded repatriation constitutes the most appropriate solution for the problem of Afghan refugees present in the Islamic Republic of Pakistan and having ascertained that the arrangements for the return of the Afghan refugees are satisfactory to them,

Have agreed as follows:

Article I

All Afghan refugees temporarily present in the territory of the Islamic Republic of Pakistan shall be given the opportunity to return voluntarily to their homeland in accordance with the arrangements and conditions set out in the present Agreement.

Article II

The Government of the Republic of Afghanistan shall take all necessary measures to ensure the following conditions for the voluntary return of Afghan refugees to their homeland:

(a) All refugees shall be allowed to return in freedom to their homeland;

(b) All returnees shall enjoy the free choice of domicile and freedom of movement within the Republic of Afghanistan;

(c) All returnees shall enjoy the right to work, to adequate living conditions and to share in the welfare of the State;

(d) all returnees shall enjoy the right to participate on an equal basis in the civic affairs of the Republic of Afghanistan. They shall be ensured equal benefits from the solution of the land question on the basis of the Land and Water Reform;

(e) All returnees shall enjoy the same rights and privileges, including freedom of religion, and have the same obligations and responsibilities as any other citizens of the Republic of Afghanistan without discrimination.

The Government of the Republic of Afghanistan undertakes to implement these measures and to provide, within its possibilities, all necessary assistance in the process of repatriation.

Article III

The Government of the Islamic Republic of Pakistan shall facilitate the voluntary, orderly and peaceful repatriation of all Afghan refugees staying within its territory and undertakes to provide, within its possibilities, all necessary assistance in the process of repatriation.

[...]

ANNEX III

STATEMENT BY THE UNITED STATES OF AMERICA

The United States has agreed to act as a guarantor of the political settlement of the situation relating to Afghanistan. We believe this settlement is a major step forward in restoring peace to Afghanistan, in ending the bloodshed in that unfortunate country, and in enabling millions of Afghan refugees to return to their homes.

In agreeing to act as a guarantor, the United States states the following :

(1) The troops withdrawal obligations set out in paragraph 5 and 6 of the Instrument on Interrelationships are central to the entire settlement. Compliance with those obligations is essential to achievement of the settlement's purposes, namely, the ending of foreign intervention in Afghanistan and the restoration of the rights of the Afghan people through the exercise of self-determination as called for by the United Nations Charter and the United Nations General Assembly resolutions on Afghanistan.

(2) The obligations under taken by the guarantors are symmetrical. In this regard, the United State has advised the Soviet Union that the United States retains the right, consistent with its obligations as guarantor, to provide military assistance to parties in Afghanistan. Should the Soviet Union exercise restraint in providing military assistance to parties in Afghanistan, the United States similarly will exercise restraint.

(3) By acting as a guarantor of the settlement, the United States does not intend to imply in any respect recognition of the present regime as the lawful Government of Afghanistan.

Source: "Geneva Accords of 1988," Institute for Afghan Studies, http://www.institute-for-afghan-studies.org/Accords%20Treaties/geneva_accords_1988_pakistan_afghanistan.htm.

57. President Ronald Reagan, Letter to Thomas P. O'Neill, Speaker of the House of Representatives and President Pro Tempore of the Senate, on the Destruction of an Iranian Jetliner by the United States Navy over the Persian Gulf, July 4, 1988

Introduction

The United States provoked an embarrassing international incident on July 3, 1988, when the naval cruiser *Vincennes,* part of the American task force in the Persian Gulf, shot down an Iranian civilian airliner, Flight 655 from the coastal city of Bandar Abbas, Iran, to Dubai, killing all 290 passengers and crew, including

66 children and 38 non-Iranian citizens. U.S. naval officers had tracked the plane on sophisticated electronic Aegis radar systems but made no visual contact before launching two surface-to-air missiles that shot it down in the Strait of Hormuz, 11 miles from the *Vincennes*. The U.S. government claimed that those responsible mistakenly believed that the jetliner was an attacking F-14 warplane. Wreckage from the plane fell in Iranian territorial waters, and the Iranian government publicly accused the United States of a deliberate "barbaric massacre" of innocent civilians. In a letter to the Speaker of the House of Representatives, President Ronald Reagan stated that at the time of this incident the *Vincennes* was also responding to attacks by small Iranian patrol boats that were also targeting international shipping, and its crew therefore believed that the approaching aircraft had hostile intentions toward them. He promised a "full investigation" by the Defense Department. Pentagon officials publicly stated that Iran Air Flight 655 had ignored several radioed warnings to change course but later suggested that it was uncertain whether the *Vincennes* had successfully opened radio contact. Three years later, U.S. admiral William J. Crowe publicly admitted that the *Vincennes* had been operating in Iranian territorial waters, something that the U.S. Navy had denied at the time. The failure of the Department of Defense to release portions of its report into the downing of the Iranian flight aroused suspicions that an official cover-up had occurred, although subsequent studies suggest that human error and the aggressive style of the captain of the *Vincennes* were probably responsible for a genuine mistake. The U.S. government expressed its regret for the incident but never apologized for it, admitted any wrongdoing, or accepted responsibility, continuing to blame hostile Iranian actions for its occurrence. Speaking to reporters on August 2, 1988, Reagan said of this incident that "I will never apologize for the United States of America—I don't care what the facts are." The entire crew of the *Vincennes* received combat-action ribbons, and the officers responsible received additional coveted medals. Iranian officials, however, argued that the attack was a deliberate warning to their government that if it continued to decline to reach an armistice agreement with Iraq, the United States would expand its existing naval operations against Iranian vessels and offshore facilities to include direct assaults on land installations and civilians. For many subsequent years, the downing of the jetliner soured U.S.-Iranian relations. Eventually, in February 1996, the U.S. government, while explicitly declining to admit any responsibility or liability for the attack, agreed to pay Iran US$61.8 million as compensation for the lives lost when the airplane was destroyed, in return for which Iran's government dropped the suit over the matter that it had brought against the United States in the International Court of Justice.

Primary Source

On July 3, 1988, the USS VINCENNES and USS ELMER MONTGOMERY were operating in international waters of the Persian Gulf near the Strait of Hormuz. (On July 2, the MONTGOMERY had responded to a distress signal from a Danish tanker that was under attack by Iranian small boats and had fired a warning shot, which caused the breaking off of the attack.) Having indications that approximately a dozen Iranian small boats were congregating to attack merchant shipping, the VINCENNES sent a Mark III LAMPS Helicopter on investigative patrol in international airspace to assess the situation. At about 1010 local Gulf time (2:10 a.m. EDT), when the helicopter had approached to within only four nautical miles, it was fired on by Iranian small boats (the VINCENNES was ten nautical miles from the scene at this time). The LAMPS helicopter was not damaged and returned immediately to the VINCENNES.

As the VINCENNES and MONTGOMERY were approaching the group of Iranian small boats at approximately 1042 local time, at least four of the small boats turned toward and began closing in on the American warships. At this time, both American ships opened fire on the small craft, sinking two and damaging a third. Regrettably, in the course of the U.S. response to the Iranian attack, an Iranian civilian airliner was shot down by the VINCENNES, which was firing in self defense at what it believed to be a hostile Iranian military aircraft. We deeply regret the tragic loss of life that occurred. The Defense Department will conduct a full investigation.

The actions of U.S. forces in response to being attacked by Iranian small boats were taken in accordance with our inherent right of self-defense, as recognized in Article 51 of the United Nations Charter, and pursuant to my constitutional authority with respect to the conduct of foreign relations and as Commander in Chief. There has been no further hostile action by Iranian forces, and, although U.S. forces will remain prepared to take additional defensive action to protect our units and military personnel, we regard this incident as closed. U.S. forces suffered no casualties or damage.

Since March 1987, I and members of my Administration have provided to Congress letters, reports, briefings, and testimony in connection with developments in the Persian Gulf and the activities of U.S. Armed Forces in the region. In accordance with my desire that Congress continue to be fully informed in this matter, I am providing this report consistent with the War Powers Resolution. I look forward to cooperating with Congress in pursuit of our mutual, overriding aim of peace and stability in the Persian Gulf region.

Source: Ronald Reagan, *Public Papers of the Presidents of the United States: Ronald Reagan, 1988–1989*, Book 2 (Washington, DC: U.S. Government Printing Office, 1991), 920–921.

58. Jad al-Haqq, Sheikh al-Azhar, "Fatwa against the Iraqi Invasion of Kuwait," 1990

Introduction

Despite Saddam Hussein's sedulous efforts to present his invasion of Kuwait as a blow for Pan-Arab and Islamic causes, he failed to win the support of most Arab political or clerical leaders. Ten days after the invasion, Jad al-Haqq, the grand imam of al-Azhar University in Cairo, Egypt, the most prestigious institution of learning in the Sunni Muslim world, issued a statement condemning Hussein's action and calling on him to withdraw Iraqi forces from Kuwait and restore its previous government. When Hussein ignored this directive, the grand imam took stronger action, making his behavior the subject of a fatwa, or legal pronouncement. Charging Hussein with "sinful aggression" and an act of "oppression" that set Muslim against Muslim and divided the Arab world in betrayal of Islamic principles, the grand imam declared that according to Muslim precepts, this emergency "requires that armies and forces are sped to surround the ill-doer, so that his harm will not spread; and to contain him as a fire is contained." The grand imam commended the Arab and Islamic states for having taken such actions and proclaimed that their requests "for assistance from [outside] multinational forces" were also justified on the grounds that "[t]hey are Muslim forces or allied to them, and assistance by such troops is permitted in Islam." Following these principles, the grand imam specifically endorsed the presence of "foreign troops" in Saudi Arabia. In conclusion, he once more called on Iraq's leaders to end their occupation of Kuwait and allow the emirate's "legitimate government" to return. The grand imam's fatwa was striking evidence that Hussein's strategy of depicting himself as a champion of Islam and Pan-Arab nationalism had failed to win over many of the Muslim world's most influential leaders.

Primary Source

The Grand Iman Sheikh Jad Al Haq Ali Jad Al Haq, Sheikh Al Azhar announced in his statement released yesterday to the Arab and Islamic world that the Azhar Al Sharif expresses its grave concern over Iraqi insistence on continuing its aggression against our brother Kuwait. He confirmed that the report to Arab, Islamic and foreign troops to defend the sacrosanct in Islam was permitted by religion, and that the responsibility of the Islamic armies was to contain the malefasor so as to prevent his danger from spreading. The statement also called upon President Saddam Hussein and his government to listen to the voice of Islam and of truth, and to desist from the use of force in recognition of their true belonging to the Arab and Islamic nation. The statement reads as follows:

The Azhar Al Sharif has directed an appeal to the peoples of the Arab and Islamic nation and to its leaders, published and broadcast on Friday 19th Muharram 1411 A.H., 10th August 1990 A.D. It coincided with the holding of the Arab summit in Cairo on the same day, at the invitation of President Muhammed Hosni Mubarak, to take cognizance of the nefarious effects on the Arab and Islamic nation resulting from the interference by the leaders of Iraq and their aggression against the State of Kuwait, invading it militarily and occupying its land, and breaching its peoples' rights, as well as all that has been published regarding the pillage of money and the destruction of property. The world has unanimously condemned this grave act, and all international organizations have taken action, such as the Organization of the Islamic Conference, the Conference of Foreign Ministers of Islamic States, the Arab League and the UN Security Council. All this was done on the day the disaster befell, the 2nd August 1990 A.D. Some time has passed since this event that shook the world occurred, and the fleets and armies of different countries, with their arms of terror and destruction, have flocked to our Arab arena where it happened. Yet the leaders of Iraq remain impervious to advice and to the wisdom of Allah in his Book. The Quran calls for aiding the oppressed, and preventing oppression even unto the point of fighting it. For this reason, the Azhar Al Sharif today expresses its grave concern for the future of the Arab and Islamic Nation in light of the insistence on this sinful aggression and its excesses. Al Azhar has called on, and repeats its call to President Saddam Hussein and his government to be true to their membership of the Arab and Islamic Nation, and to desist from this action that has aborted the Arab Nation's abilities to progress and to grow, and trapped it in a cycle of killing that will come from whence they know not, as well as reducing its standing among the nations, leaving it bereft of the spirit of empathy, cooperation and friendliness within it. And all this by its own hand, not by the hands of a stranger: one of its leaders erred and left the path of righteousness. He overran a country and people that had lived in comfort and security, performing their duties to their Nation in all domains, and terrorized women, children and the old in their very homes in the dead of night. This is not the deed of a Muslim. The prophet (pbuh) warns of terrorizing Muslims, saying (according to Abu Daoud): "It is not permitted for a Muslim to terrorize another." In another saying related by Al Bazar and others, he said: "Do not terrorize a Muslim, for the terror of a Muslim is a great oppression." In the saying of Abu Huraira, related by Al Tabarani: "Whomsoever looks at a Muslim so as to frighten him without just cause will be frightened by Allah on the Day of Judgment." The prophet (pbuh) also forbade the terrorizing of Muslims by pointing a weapon towards them, saying as related by Al Shaikhan: "Do not point a weapon at your brother for you know not lest Satan pull at your arm and you fall into a pit of fire." In a saying by Muslim Abu Huraira, "He who points a piece of iron at his brother will be damned by the angels until the end, even if it be his brother to his father or mother." In a saying by Ibn Masoud related by Al Bukhari, "Cursing a Muslim is to stray from the path of righteousness and killing him is to leave the faith." Yet where is all this, regarding what the Iraqi army has done to Kuwait, the destruction, terror, killing, expulsion, plunder and pillage? And what about the Islamic prohibition against terrorizing non-combatants, and killing and torturing them? What happened in terms of the inhumane acts perpetrated by the Iraqi army against Kuwait and its people, as related by the news agencies, is a terrifying and sad thing, refused by Islam and repellent to the conscience of Muslims.

This unenviable situation in which Iraq has placed the Nation, to prepare to face the impending catastrophe that will nigh on annihilate it if the Iraqi leaders continue to the end of their devastating path, requires the Arab and Islamic Nation to respond, and to heed the call to stand against this wrong. Defense of the self and of the Nation requires that armies and forces are sped to surround the ill-doer, so that his harm will not spread; and to contain him as a fire is contained. Allah has permitted fighting the ill-doer: "So fight the malfeasor until it awakens to Allah's commands." And yet the Arab and Islamic forces have heeded the call and come to the aid of the rest of the countries that are exposed to the evil of this catastrophe. They have collaborated in containing the catastrophe in an attempt to stop it until those in charge of it become aware of the extent of the loss caused by this wicked deed; occupying an Arab Muslim people; breaching the sacrosanct relationship that binds neighbors with a military force vastly superior in numbers and equipment. And let those who are attempting to cause the region to explode, and to destroy it, after they have broken the inviolable sanctity of a country and its people, look what good has come to them of this wickedness? And what has the Nation lost? And are the two equal?

This is a great blow that has been dealt to the nation's dignity and its abilities. Even if the Iraqi army has plundered money and committed sins, this is not a gain but more of the same wickedness. It has been forbidden by Allah; he has warned of the penalties, and ordered that it be combated. The force that overran Kuwait had prepared itself and was more than ready. It entered in the dead of night without prior warning, nay in flagrant breach of treaties and promises made by the leaders of Iraq not to do what they have done, and to sit with their neighbor to discuss and debate their differences. It was a terrible surprise for Kuwait and its people then to be viciously attacked with heavy armor, guns and missiles and all the other implements of modern war. This is not of the courage of Arabs and Muslims, nor of the nature of an Arab to raise his sword except against a foe with a sword; for he would never surprise a foe in safety, nor attack an unarmed opponent. Yet how far this is from what happened. Has this attacking army been bereft of the morals of Arabs and of their nature, and all that runs in the teachings of Islam that forbid the stealth and the use of surprise attacks against a foe that has no arms? If the Arab peoples surrounding Kuwait were afraid and surprised by the actions of the Iraqi army, and called on the armies of the Arab and Islamic states, and of other countries that have the weapons to equal those

used by Iraq against Kuwait, there is no wrong in this. Their cry for assistance from these multinational forces is based on the principle of international treaties, and it is their right to defend themselves and to protect their land from this treacherous brother who has heeded no treaty nor promise nor responsibility. Iraq's claim that by doing so, it becomes a mujahid is untrue, for jihad cannot be in doing wrong, nor in aggression against a fraternal Muslim neighbor. In addition, the claim that the incoming troops have denigrated the land and the sacrosanct is untrue also, for they come with the permission of the owners of that land, and to protect them from aggression. They are Muslim forces or allied to them, and assistance by such troops is permitted in Islam, indeed it is one of the foundations of Islam: one of the rights a Muslim has against another is that he require his help and support to counter oppression, and the same applies to the allied forces also. The claim that the sanctity of the holy land has been breached by allowing foreign troops to set foot in the Kingdom of Saudi Arabia is untrue, for the troops are either Muslim or allied to them, and came to counter aggression and fight oppression. Al Azhar Al Sharif, despite this painful reality and our desire to surmount it, and indeed to uncover the harm that has been done to the Nation, calls on the leaders of Iraq to desist from what they have done, and to withdraw their armies to their own borders; calls for the return of Kuwait's legitimate government to its country and people; and this in order to return to the good and repent from evil for the return to righteousness is better than continuing in the path of evil, and the best of the sinners are those that repent. "O ye faithful, respond to Allah and to his prophet if he calls you to that which gives you life, and know that Allah is present between Man and his heart, and that to Him you will come."

Source: Turi Munthe, ed., *The Saddam Hussein Reader* (New York: Thunder's Mouth, 2002), 246–250.

59. Alleged Excerpts from the Saddam Hussein–April Glaspie Meeting in Baghdad, July 25, 1990 [Excerpts]

Introduction

One week before the Iraqi invasion of Kuwait, as tensions between the two states were rising and Iraqi troops were massing on the border with Kuwait, Saddam Hussein and his foreign minister, Tariq Aziz, summoned April Glaspie, U.S. ambassador to Iraq, for a protracted conversation. The Iraqi government later issued a transcript of this meeting. Although Glaspie subsequently told the Senate Foreign Relations Committee that this account was "fabricated," the U.S. State Department neither confirmed nor denied its accuracy. According to the Iraqi transcript, Hussein opened the conversation with a lengthy statement, recounting the past history of U.S.-Iraqi diplomatic relations, which had been resumed in 1984 after a long hiatus following U.S. assistance to Israel during the 1967 Six-Day War. Hussein complained that Kuwait and the other Arab emirates, emboldened by U.S. support, had grown rich at Iraqi expense over the previous years and were treating Iraq with contempt, ignoring Iraqi rights along their joint borders. Hussein also complained that the United States was deliberately keeping the price of oil low, to Iraq's economic detriment, and that the American media were attacking his regime as undemocratic. In response, Glaspie apparently stated that while the United States welcomed relatively low oil prices, these need not be unduly low. She agreed that her country's media were unfair to Hussein. On Kuwait, she stated that the United States had no firm position on the dispute between the two countries but sought to know Hussein's intentions. She did state that the United States hoped that these problems would be speedily resolved, preferably through negotiations among the various Arab states. Hussein then complained to Glaspie that the Kuwaiti government was demanding the repayment of economic assistance it had given Iraq during the Iran-Iraq War, despite the fact that Iraq had effectively been defending Kuwaiti interests as well as its own in that conflict, and that the Iraqi people were suffering. He also told Glaspie that President Hosni Mubarak of Egypt and Saudi Arabian leaders had brokered a meeting between Kuwaiti and Iraqi representatives within a few days, over the coming weekend, that he hoped would reach a settlement of their dispute. Hussein said that Iraqi troops would take no action before this meeting but that "if we are unable to find a solution, then it will be natural that Iraq will not accept death." If this transcript was an accurate account, Glaspie failed to give Hussein any uncompromising warning against invading Kuwait but merely stated that she would fly to the United States the following Monday to meet with President George H. W. Bush. Hussein could have easily interpreted such a response as tacit acquiescence in his plans to use force against Kuwait if no settlement acceptable to him was forthcoming. The episode permanently damaged Glaspie's reputation, and she received no further significant diplomatic postings.

Primary Source

SADDAM HUSSEIN: I have summoned you today to hold comprehensive political discussions with you. This is a message to President Bush. You know that we did not have relations with the U.S. until 1984 and you know the circumstances and reasons which caused them to be severed. The decision to establish relations with the U.S. were taken in 1980 during the two months prior to the war between us and Iran. When the war started, and to avoid misinterpretation, we postponed the establishment of relations hoping that the war would end soon.

But because the war lasted for a long time, and to emphasize the fact that we are a non-aligned country, it was important to reestablish relations with the U.S.

And we chose to do this in 1984. It is natural to say that the U.S. is not like Britain, for example, with the latter's historic relations with Middle Eastern countries, including Iraq. In addition, there were no relations between Iraq and the U.S. between 1967 and 1984. One can conclude it would be difficult for the U.S. to have a full understanding of many matters in Iraq. . . .

[. . .]

Iraqi Policy on Oil

Iraq came out of the war burdened with $40 billion debts, excluding the aid given by Arab states, some of whom consider that too to be a debt although they knew—and you knew too—that without Iraq they would not have had these sums and the future of the region would have been entirely different. We began to face the policy of the drop in the price of oil. Then we saw the United States, which always talks of democracy but which has no time for the other point of view. Then the media campaign against Saddam Hussein was started by the official American media.

The United States thought that the situation in Iraq was like Poland, Romania or Czechoslovakia. We were disturbed by this campaign but we were not disturbed too much because we had hoped that, in a few months, those who are decision makers in America would have a chance to find the facts and see whether this media campaign had had any effect on the lives of Iraqis. We had hoped that soon the American authorities would make the correct decision regarding their relations with Iraq. Those with good relations can sometimes afford to disagree. But when planned and deliberate policy forces the price of oil down without good commercial reasons, then that means another war against Iraq.

Because military war kills people by bleeding them, and economic war kills their humanity by depriving them of their chance to have a good standard of living.

As you know, we gave rivers of blood in a war that lasted eight years, but we did not lose our humanity. Iraqis have a right to live proudly. We do not accept that anyone could injure Iraqi pride or the Iraqi right to have high standards of living. Kuwait and the U.A.E. were at the front of this policy aimed at lowering Iraq's position and depriving its people of higher economic standards.

And you know that our relations with the Emirates and Kuwait had been good. On top of all that, while we were busy at war, the state of Kuwait began to expand at the expense of our territory. You may say this is propaganda, but I would direct you to one document, the Military Patrol Line, which is the borderline endorsed by the Arab League in 1961 for military patrols not to cross the Iraq-Kuwait border.

But go and look for yourselves. You will see the Kuwaiti border patrols, the Kuwaiti farms, the Kuwaiti oil installations—all built as closely as possible to this line to establish that land as Kuwaiti territory.

Conflicting Interests

Since then, the Kuwaiti Government has been stable while the Iraqi Government has undergone many changes. Even after 1968 and for 10 years afterwards, we were too busy with our own problems. First in the north, then the 1973 war, and other problems. Then came the war with Iran which started 10 years ago. We believe that the United States must understand that people who live in luxury and economic security can reach an understanding with the United States on what are legitimate joint interests. But the starved and the economically deprived cannot reach the same understanding. We do not accept threats from anyone because we do not threaten anyone. But we say clearly that we hope that the U.S. will not entertain too many illusions and will seek new friends rather than increase the number of its enemies. I have read the American statements speaking of friends in the area. Of course, it is the right of everyone to choose their friends.

We can have no objections. But you know you are not the ones who protected your friends during the war with Iran. I assure you, had the Iranians overrun the region, the American troops would not have stopped them, except by the use of nuclear weapons.

I do not belittle you. But I hold this view by looking at the geography and nature of American society into account. Yours is a society which cannot accept 10,000 dead in one battle. You know that Iran agreed to the cease-fire not because the United States had bombed one of the oil platforms after the liberation of the Fao. Is this Iraq's reward for its role in securing the stability of the region and for protecting it from an unknown flood?

Protecting the Oil Flow

So, what can it mean when America says it will now protect its friends? It can only mean prejudice against Iraq. This stance plus maneuvers and statements which have been made has encouraged the U.A.E. and Kuwait to disregard Iraqi rights. I say to you clearly that Iraq's rights, which are mentioned in the memorandum, we will take one by one. That might not happen now or after a month or after one year but we will take it all. We are not the kind of people who will relinquish their rights. There is no historic right, or legitimacy, or need, for the U.A.E. and Kuwait to deprive us of our rights. If they are needy, we too are needy.

The United States must have a better understanding of the situation and declare who it wants to have relations with and who its enemies are. But it should not make enemies simply because others have different points of view regarding the Arab-Israeli conflict. We clearly understand America's statement that it wants an easy flow of oil. We understand America saying that it seeks friendship with the states in the region, and to encourage their joint interests. But we cannot understand the attempt to encourage some parties to harm Iraq's interests.

The United States wants to secure the flow of oil. This is understandable and known. But it must not deploy methods which the United States says it disapproves of—flexing muscles and pressure. If you use pressure, we will deploy pressure and force. We know that you can harm us although we do not threaten you. But we too can harm you. Everyone can cause harm according to their ability and their size. We cannot come all the way to you in the United States, but individual Arabs may reach you.

War and Friendship

You can come to Iraq with aircraft and missiles but do not push us to the point where we cease to care. And when we feel that you want to injure our pride and take away the Iraqis' chance of a high standard of living, then we will cease to care and death will be the choice for us.

Then we would not care if you fired 100 missiles for each missile we fired.

Because without pride life would have no value. It is not reasonable to ask our people to bleed rivers of blood for eight years then to tell them, "Now you have to accept aggression from Kuwait, the U.A.E., or from the U.S. or from Israel." We do not put all these countries in the same boat. First, we are hurt and upset that such disagreement is taking place between us and Kuwait and the U.A.E.

The solution must be found within an Arab framework and through direct bilateral relations. We do not place America among the enemies. We place it where we want our friends to be and we try to be friends. But repeated American statements last year make it apparent that America did not regard us as friends. Well the Americans are free. When we seek friendship we want pride, liberty and our right to choose. We want to deal according to our status as we deal with the others according to their statuses. We consider the others' interests while we look after our own.

And we expect the others to consider our interests while they are dealing with their own. What does it mean when the Zionist war minister is summoned to the United States now? What do they mean, these fiery statements coming out of Israel during the past few days and the talk of war being expected now more than at any other time?

I do not believe that anyone would lose by making friends with Iraq. In my opinion, the American President has not made mistakes regarding the Arabs, although his decision to freeze dialogue with the P.L.O. was wrong. But it appears that this decision was made to appease the Zionist lobby or as a piece of strategy to cool the Zionist anger, before trying again. I hope that our latter conclusion is the correct one. But we will carry on saying it was the wrong decision.

You are appeasing the usurper in so many ways—economically, politically and militarily as well as in the media. When will the time come when, for every three appeasements to the usurper, you praise the Arabs just once?

APRIL GLASPIE: I thank you, Mr. President, and it is a great pleasure for a diplomat to meet and talk directly with the President. I clearly understand your message. We studied history at school that taught us to say freedom or death. I think you know well that we as a people have our experience with the colonialists.

Mr. President, you mentioned many things during this meeting which I cannot comment on on behalf of my Government. But with your permission, I will comment on two points. You spoke of friendship and I believe it was clear from the letters sent by our President to you on the occasion of your National Day that he emphasizes—

HUSSEIN: He was kind and his expressions met with our regard and respect.

Directive on Relations

GLASPIE: As you know, he directed the United States Administration to reject the suggestion of implementing trade sanctions.

HUSSEIN: There is nothing left for us to buy from America. Only wheat. Because every time we want to buy something, they say it is forbidden. I am afraid that one day you will say, "You are going to make gunpowder out of wheat."

GLASPIE: I have a direct instruction from the President to seek better relations with Iraq.

HUSSEIN: But how we too have this desire. But matters are running contrary to this desire.

[...]

GLASPIE: Mr. President, not only do I want to say that President Bush wanted better and deeper relations with Iraq, but he also wants an Iraqi contribution to peace and prosperity in the Middle East. President Bush is an intelligent man. He is not going

to declare an economic war against Iraq. You are right. It is true what you say that we do not want higher prices for oil. But I would ask you to examine the possibility of not charging too high a price for oil.

HUSSEIN: We do not want too high prices for oil. And I remind you that in 1974 I gave Tariq Aziz the idea for an article he wrote which criticized the policy of keeping oil prices high. It was the first Arab article which expressed this view.

Shifting Price of Oil

TARIQ AZIZ: Our policy in OPEC opposes sudden jumps in oil prices.

HUSSEIN: Twenty-five dollars a barrel is not a high price.

GLASPIE: We have many Americans who would like to see the price go above $25 because they come from oil-producing states.

HUSSEIN: The price at one stage had dropped to $12 a barrel and a reduction in the modest Iraqi budget of $6 billion to $7 billion is a disaster.

GLASPIE: I think I understand this. I have lived here for years. I admire your extraordinary efforts to rebuild your country. I know you need funds. We understand that and our opinion is that you should have the opportunity to rebuild your country. But we have no opinion on the Arab-Arab conflicts, like your border disagreement with Kuwait. I was in the American Embassy in Kuwait during the late 60s. The instruction we had during this period was that we should express no opinion on this issue and that the issue is not associated with America. James Baker has directed our official spokesmen to emphasize this instruction. We hope you can solve this problem using any suitable methods via Klibi or via President Mubarak. All that we hope is that these issues are solved quickly. With regard to all of this, can I ask you to see how the issue appears to us?

My assessment after 25 years' service in this area is that your objective must have strong backing from your Arab brothers. I now speak of oil. But you, Mr. President, have fought through a horrific and painful war. Frankly, we can see only that you have deployed massive troops in the south. Normally that would not be any of our business. But when this happens in the context of what you said on your national day, then when we read the details in the two letters of the Foreign Minister, then when we see the Iraqi point of view that the measures taken by the U.A.E. and Kuwait is, in the final analysis, parallel to military aggression against Iraq, then it would be reasonable for me to be concerned. And for this reason, I received an instruction to ask you, in the spirit of friendship—not in the spirit of confrontation—regarding your intentions. I simply describe the position of my Government. And I do not mean that the situation is a simple situation. But our concern is a simple one.

HUSSEIN: We do not ask people not to be concerned when peace is at issue. This is a noble human feeling which we all feel. It is natural for you as a superpower to be concerned. But what we ask is not to express your concern in a way that would make an aggressor believe that he is getting support for his aggression. We want to find a just solution which will give us our rights but not deprive others of their rights. But at the same time, we want the others to know that our patience is running out regarding their action, which is harming even the milk our children drink, and the pensions of the widow who lost her husband during the war, and the pensions of the orphans who lost their parents. As a country, we have the right to prosper. We lost so many opportunities, and the others should value the Iraqi role in their protection. Even this Iraqi [the President points to their interpreter] feels bitter like all other Iraqis. We are not aggressors but we do not accept aggression either. We sent them envoys and handwritten letters.

We tried everything. We asked the Servant of the Two Shrines—King Fahd—to hold a four-member summit, but he suggested a meeting between the Oil Ministers. We agreed. And as you know, the meeting took place in Jidda. They reached an agreement which did not express what we wanted, but we agreed. Only two days after the meeting, the Kuwaiti Oil Minister made a statement that contradicted the agreement. We also discussed the issue during the Baghdad summit. I told the Arab Kings and Presidents that some brothers are fighting an economic war against us. And that not all wars use weapons and we regard this kind of war as a military action against us. Because if the capability of our army is lowered then, if Iran renewed the war, it could achieve goals which it could not achieve before. And if we lowered the standard of our defenses, then this could encourage Israel to attack us. I said that before the Arab Kings and Presidents. Only I did not mention Kuwait and U.A.E. by name, because they were my guests.

Before this, I had sent them envoys reminding them that our war had included their defense. Therefore the aid they gave us should not be regarded as a debt. We did not more than the United States would have done against someone who attacked its interests. I talked about the same thing with a number of other Arab states. I explained the situation to brother King Fahd a few times, by sending envoys and on the telephone. I talked with brother King Hussein and with Sheik Zaid after the conclusion of the summit. I walked with the Sheik to the plane when he was leaving Mosul. He told me, "Just wait until I get home." But after he had reached his destination, the statements that came from there were very bad—not from him, but from his Minister of Oil. And after the Jidda agreement, we received some intelligence that they were talking of sticking to the agreement for two months only.

Then they would change their policy. Now tell us, if the American President found himself in this situation, what would he do? I said it was very difficult for me to talk about these issues in public. But we must tell the Iraqi people who face economic difficulties who was responsible for that.

Talks with Mubarak

GLASPIE: I spent four beautiful years in Egypt.

HUSSEIN: The Egyptian people are kind and good and ancient. The oil people are supposed to help the Egyptian people, but they are mean beyond belief. It is painful to admit it, but some of them are disliked by Arabs because of their greed.

GLASPIE: Mr. President, it would be helpful if you could give us an assessment of the effort made by your Arab brothers and whether they have achieved anything.

HUSSEIN: On this subject, we agreed with President Mubarak that the Prime Minister of Kuwait would meet with the deputy chairman of the Revolution Command Council in Saudi Arabia, because the Saudis initiated contact with us, aided by President Mubarak's efforts. He just telephoned me a short while ago to say the Kuwaitis have agreed to that suggestion.

GLASPIE: Congratulations.

HUSSEIN: A protocol meeting will be held in Saudi Arabia. Then the meeting will be transferred to Baghdad for deeper discussion directly between Kuwait and Iraq. We hope we will reach some result. We hope that the long-term view and the real interests will overcome Kuwaiti greed.

GLASPIE: May I ask you when you expect Sheik Saad to come to Baghdad?

HUSSEIN: I suppose it would be on Saturday or Monday at the latest. I told brother Mubarak that the agreement should be in Baghdad Saturday or Sunday. You know that brother Mubarak's visits have always been a good omen.

GLASPIE: This is good news. Congratulations.

HUSSEIN: Brother President Mubarak told me they were scared. They said troops were only 20 kilometers north of the Arab League line. I said to him that regardless of what is there, whether they are police, border guards or army, and regardless of how many are there, and what they are doing, assure the Kuwaitis and give them our word that we are not going to do anything until we meet with them. When we meet and when we see that there is hope, then nothing will happen. But if we are unable to find a solution, then it will be natural that Iraq will not accept death, even though wisdom is above everything else. There you have good news.

AZIZ: This is a journalistic exclusive.

GLASPIE: I am planning to go to the United States next Monday. I hope I will meet with President Bush in Washington next week. I thought to postpone my trip because of the difficulties we are facing. But now I will fly on Monday.

Source: Robert Parry et al., "The USA in Bed with Saddam," The Internet Archive, http://www.archive.org/stream/TheUsaInBedWith-Saddam/USAibwS_djvu.txt.

60. U.S. President George H. W. Bush and British Prime Minister Margaret Thatcher, Joint Press Conference, Aspen, Colorado, August 2, 1990 [Excerpts]

Introduction

One day after he learned of Iraq's invasion and annexation of Kuwait, U.S. president George H. W. Bush flew to Aspen, Colorado, to consult British prime minister Margaret Thatcher. Thatcher, a staunch conservative who believed firmly that Great Powers must use military force when necessary, something she had demonstrated in her own country's earlier war over the Falkland Islands, was later credited with reinforcing Bush's own instincts to take a strong stand over Kuwait. Before taking wing to Aspen, Bush had already issued a statement strongly condemning Iraq's invasion of Kuwait and endorsing the United Nations (UN) Security Council resolution condemning this action. He also signed Executive Order 12723 blocking all property and interests in the United States or controlled by U.S. citizens that belonged to Kuwait's government and its associates, thereby impeding Iraq's ability to seize those assets. In addition, the U.S. government froze all Iraqi assets in the United States. In Aspen, Bush and Thatcher held a joint press conference in which they stated that they were on the "same wavelength": united in condemning the invasion but hoping for the peaceful replacement of the Kuwaiti leaders after a voluntary withdrawal by Iraqi forces. Bush mentioned that he had already held personal consultations on the subject with several major Arab leaders, including King Hussein of Jordan, President Hosni Mubarak of Egypt, and President Ali Abdullah Saleh of Yemen, and that Secretary of State James A. Baker III was also closely in touch with the Soviet leadership. Thatcher was even more forthright than Bush in condemning the invasion, which she described as "totally unacceptable," something that if tolerated

would mean "many other small countries … could never feel safe." She welcomed the Security Council resolution calling for Iraq's withdrawal and stated that if Iraq failed to honor this, the Security Council would need to consider collective action "to see that Iraq withdraws and that the Government of Kuwait is restored to Kuwait." Even at this early stage, Thatcher clearly regarded the episode as a test of "whether the nations of the world ha[d] the collective will" to enforce the Security Council's resolution. At this stage, however, both leaders refused to discuss whether or not military intervention would ultimately be necessary. Bush also hedged when answering a question as to whether, if similar episodes were not to occur in future, it would be necessary to remove Saddam Hussein from power to prevent him from becoming "a constant source of problems" throughout the region.

Primary Source

The President. Let me first welcome Prime Minister Thatcher back to the United States. It's a very timely visit, and as you can well imagine, we have been exchanging views on the Iraq-Kuwait situation. Not surprisingly, I find myself very much in accord with the views of the Prime Minister. I reported to her on contacts that I've had since I left Washington: personal contacts with King Hussein [of Jordan]; Mr. Mubarak of Egypt, President Mubarak; President Salih of Yemen—a long conversation just now. I can tell you that [Secretary of State] Jim Baker has been in close touch with the Soviet leadership, and indeed, the last plan was for him to stop in Moscow on his way back here.

We are concerned about the situation, but I find that Prime Minister Thatcher and I are looking at it on exactly the same wavelength: concerned about this naked aggression, condemning it, and hoping that a peaceful solution will be found that will result in the restoration of the Kuwaiti leaders to their rightful place and, prior to that, a withdrawal of Iraqi forces.

Prime Minister, welcome to Colorado and to the United States. And if you care to say a word on that, then we can take the questions.

The Prime Minister. Thank you, Mr. President, and thank you for the welcome.

We have, of course, been discussing the main question as the President indicated. Iraq has violated and taken over the territory of a country which is a full member of the United Nations. That is totally unacceptable, and if it were allowed to endure, then there would be many other small countries that could never feel safe.

The Security Council acted swiftly last night under the United States leadership, well-supported by the votes of 14 members of the Security Council, and rightly demanded the withdrawal of Iraqi troops. If that withdrawal is not swiftly forthcoming, we have to consider the next step. The next step would be further consideration by the Security Council of possible measures under chapter VII.

The fundamental question is this: whether the nations of the world have the collective will effectively to see the Security Council resolution is upheld; whether they have the collective will effectively to do anything, which the Security Council further agrees, to see that Iraq withdraws and that the government of Kuwait is restored to Kuwait. None of us can do it separately. We need a collective and effective will of the nations belonging to the United Nations—first the Security Council and then the support of all the others to make it effective.

Iraqi Invasion of Kuwait

Q. Mr. President, when Kuwaiti shipping was in danger in the Gulf war, you put those ships under American flags. Now Kuwait itself has been invaded. The Kuwaiti Ambassador says that they're desperate for help and that American intervention is of paramount importance. Will you answer that call, and how will you?

The President. I answer that we're considering what the next steps by the United States should be, just as we strongly support what Prime Minister Thatcher said about collective action in the United Nations.

Q. Are you still not contemplating military intervention?

The President. No. I mentioned at the time we were going to discuss different options, which I did after that first press conference this morning. And we're not ruling any options in, but we're not ruling any options out. . . .

Q. What are the chances of U.S.-Soviet cooperation in restoring peace to the Gulf?

The President. I would say they're very good. I reported to Prime Minister Thatcher on a conversation that I had with Jim Baker on the plane flying out here. And I think you could say that he would not be stopping in Moscow unless there would be a good degree of cooperation between the Soviet Union and the United States. But again, the Soviet Union is a member of the United Nations. They voted with the United Kingdom and with the United States. And so, I think there is a good level of cooperation with the Soviets and, hopefully, with other permanent members and, hopefully, with the rest of the members of the Security Council.

[. . .]

Q. Mr. President, isn't Saddam Hussein [President of Iraq] at the root of this problem? Hasn't he replaced Qadhafi [leader of Libya] as sort of the bad boy of the region? Would you like to see him removed? And what can you do about him?

The President. I would like to see him withdraw his troops and the restoration of the legal government in Kuwait to the rightful place, and that's the step that should be taken. I might say that I am somewhat heartened by the conversations I had with Mubarak and with King Hussein, Mr. Salih—all of whom I consider friends of the United States—and all of them who are trying to engage in what they call an Arab answer to the question, working diligently behind the scenes to come to an agreement that would satisfy the United Nations and the rest of the world. So, there are collective efforts beginning to be undertaken by these worthy countries, and let's hope that they result in a satisfactory resolution of this international crisis.

Q. But, Mr. President, Saddam Hussein has been the source of the most recent mischief in the region—nuclear triggers, missiles, the big gun—as Prime Minister Thatcher knows about. Is he going to be a constant source of problems there in that region?

The President. If he behaves this way, he's going to be a constant source. We find his behavior intolerable in this instance, and so do the rest of the United Nations countries that met last night. And reaction from around the world is unanimous in being condemnatory. So, that speaks for itself.

[. . .]

Q. Prime Minister, is there any action short of military intervention that Britain or the other United Nations countries could take—

The Prime Minister. Yes, of course.

Q.—that would be effective against Iraq?

The Prime Minister. Yes, of course. Yes, of course there is—you know, the whole chapter VII measures. And that, of course—obviously we're in consultation now as to which measures we could all agree on so the Security Council would vote them. And then they'd become mandatory. The question then is whether you can make them effective over the rest of the nations. And obviously, the 14 couldn't do it on their own. And so, there will be a good deal of negotiation as to what to put in the next Security Council resolution if Iraq does not withdraw.

Q. But are you confident that you'd be able to mobilize that kind of international support?

The Prime Minister. I believe that further chapter VII measures would have a good chance of getting through. We certainly would support them.

The President. May I add to that, that the United States has demonstrated its interest in that by the action that I took this morning by Executive order: cutting off imports from Iraq to this country.

Q. Mr. President, can I ask both of you to answer this? How does the fact that they apparently have chemical weapons now affect your decisionmaking and narrow your options?

The Prime Minister. I don't figure it affects it at all. What has happened is a total violation of international law. You cannot have a situation where one country marches in and takes over another country which is a member of the United Nations. I don't think the particular weapons they have affects that fundamental position.

Q. But doesn't it affect what actions we can take? And doesn't it make military action—

The Prime Minister. No, I do not think it necessarily affects what actions we can take.

The President. I would agree with that assessment.

[. . .]

Q. Mr. President, some of the smaller nations in the Persian Gulf—Bahrain, the Emirates, and the others—obviously have reason to worry about what has happened here. What can the United States and Great Britain say to those countries and those people who are feeling very concerned today?

The President. Well, the United States can say that we are very much concerned for your safety. And this naked aggression would understandably shake them to the core. And so, what we are trying to do is have collective action that will reverse this action out and to make very clear that we are totally in accord with their desire to see the Iraqis withdraw—cease-fire, withdraw, and restitution of the Kuwaiti government. And that would be the most reassuring thing of all for these countries who, whether it's true or not, feel threatened by this action.

Q. At the risk of being hypothetical, if Iraq does not move out quickly and has gained a foothold among the smaller Gulf nations, what can the United States and other nations do militarily?

The President. We have many options, and it is too hypothetical, indeed, for me to comment on them. And I'd refer that also to the Prime Minister.

The Prime Minister. That's precisely why you're looking at the next stage in the Security Council; second, what other measures can be put into action mandatorily; and why the very nations to whom you refer—we should also need their cooperation in putting other actions into effect.

[. . .]

Q. Prime Minister, if I could, the President's Executive order this morning established a U.S. embargo on trade with Iraq. When you mentioned chapter VII measures, would you support in the Security Council a call for an international embargo on Iraqi oil?

The Prime Minister. We are prepared to support in the Security Council those measures which collectively we can agree to and which collectively we can make effective. Those are the two tests. We have already frozen all Kuwaiti assets. Kuwaitis have very considerable assets, and it's important that those do not fall into Iraqi hands. Iraq, we believe, has only very, very small assets and rather a lot of debts, so the position is rather different with her.

Source: George H. W. Bush, *Public Papers of the Presidents of the United States: George Bush, 1990,* Book 2 (Washington, DC: U.S. Government Printing Office, 1991), 1085–1088.

61. Joint U.S.-Soviet Statement Calling for the Withdrawal of Iraqi Forces from Kuwait, August 3, 1990

Introduction

When the 1990–1991 Persian Gulf crisis began, U.S. secretary of state James A. Baker III was on his way to Moscow to meet with his opposite number, Russian foreign minister Eduard Shevardnadze. In earlier years, Soviet and U.S. agreement in any such crisis would have been most unlikely, but the dismantling of the Cold War meant that the two big powers were to a considerable degree in accord on the subject. After holding private discussions, Baker and Shevardnadze issued a joint statement in which, on behalf of both their governments, they called for Iraqi troops to withdraw immediately and unconditionally from Kuwait. The statement endorsed United Nations (UN) Security Council Resolution 660 to this effect, passed two days earlier, and called upon Iraq to implement its demands. The Soviet Union agreed to suspend all arms deliveries and sales to Iraq, while the United States had already frozen Iraqi and Kuwaiti assets under its control. The two men called upon the international community to join them not just in condemning Iraq's action but also in taking "practical steps in response," notably by cutting off all supplies of arms to Iraq. They hoped that Arab governments and appropriate regional organizations, particularly the League of Arab States, the Non-Aligned Movement, and the Islamic Conference, would show especially strong support for such measures. Putting the invasion of Kuwait on a footing of broad principle, the statement concluded that "Governments that engage in blatant aggression must know that the international community cannot and will not acquiesce in nor facilitate aggression." To some, the appearance of this joint statement might have seemed to suggest that the two leading Cold War opponents now sought to become partners, setting the basic standards of the "new world order" that President George H. W. Bush would soon proclaim. In fact, it would soon become apparent that the internal fragility of the Soviet Union would debar it from playing any such dominating role in the post–Cold War world.

Primary Source

The Soviet Union and the United States, as members of the United Nations Security Council, consider it important that the Council promptly and decisively condemn the brutal and illegal invasion of Kuwait by Iraqi military forces. The United States and the Soviet Union believe that now it is essential that the Security Council Resolution be fully and immediately implemented. By its action, Iraq has shown its contempt for the most fundamental principles of the United Nations Charter and international law.

In response to this blatant transgression of the basic norms of civilized conduct, the United States and the Soviet Union have each taken a number of actions, including the Soviet suspension of arms deliveries and the American freezing of assets. The Soviet Union and the United States reiterate our call for the unconditional Iraqi withdrawal from Kuwait. The sovereignty, national independence, legitimate authorities, and territorial integrity of the State of Kuwait must be completely restored and safeguarded. The United States and the Soviet Union believe the international community must not only condemn this action, but also take practical steps in response to it.

Today we take the unusual step of jointly calling upon the rest of the international community to join with us in an international cut-off of all arms supplies to Iraq. In addition, the Soviet Union and the United States call on regional organizations, especially the League of Arab States, all Arab governments, as well as the Non-Aligned Movement and the Islamic Conference to take all possible steps to ensure that the United Nations Security Council Resolution is carried out. Governments that engage in blatant aggression must know that the international community cannot and will not acquiesce in nor facilitate aggression.

Source: U.S. Department of State, *American Foreign Policy: Current Documents, 1990* (Washington, DC: Department of State, 1991), 460–461.

62. President George H. W. Bush, Announcement of the Deployment of U.S. Armed Forces to Saudi Arabia for Operation DESERT SHIELD, August 8, 1990 [Excerpt]

Introduction

U.S. president George H. W. Bush responded quickly to the Iraqi takeover of Kuwait. American leaders feared that this was only an opening move in a systematic campaign by Iraqi president Saddam Hussein to make his country the dominant power in the Middle East and that the neighboring oil-rich but small and militarily weak kingdom of Saudi Arabia, a U.S. ally, would be his next target. In an address to the American people six days after Hussein's forces invaded Kuwait, Bush made it clear that the United States would not tolerate such actions and explained his policy toward Iraq and Kuwait. Drawing analogies with the 1930s when European leaders had failed to stand up to aggressive actions by fascist Germany and Italy, he warned that the United States would not yield to Hussein's demands or abandon its allies in the Middle East. Bush called for "the immediate, unconditional, and complete withdrawal of all Iraqi forces from Kuwait" and the removal of the "puppet government" Hussein had installed there. Bush described the broad economic sanctions that the United Nations (UN), at U.S. insistence, had already imposed upon Iraq. He stated that the U.S. government would do all in its power to ensure that these sanctions were effective. Perhaps most important, however, he announced that additional American military forces, including a large airpower component, were being deployed in Saudi Arabia that day to safeguard that kingdom against potential aggression by Hussein. Bush's address marked the first step in the process that would lead, less than six months later, to a full-scale U.S. war to expel Iraq from Kuwait.

Primary Source

In the life of a nation we're called upon to define who we are and what we believe. Sometimes these choices are not easy. But today as President, I ask for your support in a decision I've made to stand up for what's right and condemn what's wrong, all in the cause of peace.

At my direction, elements of the 82nd Airborne Division as well as key units of the United States Air Force are arriving today to take up key defensive positions in Saudi Arabia. I took this action to assist the Saudi Arabian Government in the defense of its homeland. No one commits America's armed forces to a dangerous mission lightly, but after perhaps unparalleled international consultation and exhausting every alternative, it became necessary to take this action. Let me tell you why.

Less than a week ago, in the early morning hours of August 2nd, Iraqi armed forces, without provocation or warning, invaded a peaceful Kuwait. Facing negligible resistance from its much smaller neighbor, Iraq's tanks stormed in blitzkrieg fashion through Kuwait in a few short hours. With more than 100,000 troops, along with tanks, artillery, and surface-to-surface missiles, Iraq now occupies Kuwait. This aggression came just hours after Saddam Hussein specifically assured numerous countries in the area that there would be no invasion. There is no justification whatsoever for this outrageous and brutal act of aggression.

A puppet regime imposed from the outside is unacceptable. The acquisition of territory by force is unacceptable. No one, friend or foe, should doubt our desire for peace; and no one should underestimate our determination to confront aggression.

Four simple principles guide our policy. First, we seek the immediate, unconditional, and complete withdrawal of all Iraqi forces from Kuwait. Second, Kuwait's legitimate government must be restored to replace the puppet regime. And third, my administration, as has been the case with every President from President Roosevelt to President Reagan, is committed to the security and stability of the Persian Gulf. And fourth, I am determined to protect the lives of American citizens abroad.

Immediately after the Iraqi invasion, I ordered an embargo of all trade with Iraq and, together with many other nations, announced sanctions that both freeze all Iraqi assets in this country and protected Kuwait's assets. The stakes are high. Iraq is already a rich and powerful country that possesses the world's second largest reserves of oil and over a million men under arms. It's the fourth largest military in the world. Our country now imports nearly half the oil it consumes and could face a major threat to its economic independence. Much of the world is even more dependent upon imported oil and is even more vulnerable to Iraqi threats.

We succeeded in the struggle for freedom in Europe because we and our allies remain stalwart. Keeping the peace in the Middle East will require no less. We're beginning a new era. This era can be full of promise, an age of freedom, a time of peace for all peoples. But if history teaches us anything, it is that we must resist aggression or it will destroy our freedoms. Appeasement does not work. As was the case in the 1930s, we see in Saddam Hussein an aggressive dictator threatening his neighbors. Only 14 days ago, Saddam Hussein promised his friends he would not invade Kuwait. And 4 days ago, he promised the world he would withdraw. And twice we have seen what his promises mean: His promises mean nothing.

In the last few days, I've spoken with political leaders from the Middle East, Europe, Asia, and the Americas; and I've met with Prime Minister Thatcher, [Canadian] Prime Minister [Brian] Mulroney, and NATO Secretary General [Manfred] Woerner. And

all agree that Iraq cannot be allowed to benefit from its invasion of Kuwait.

We agree that this is not an American problem or a European problem or a Middle East problem; it is the world's problem. And that's why, soon after the Iraqi invasion, the United Nations Security Council, without dissent, condemned Iraq, calling for the immediate and unconditional withdrawal of its troops from Kuwait. The Arab world, through both the Arab League and the Gulf Cooperation Council, courageously announced its opposition to Iraqi aggression. Japan, the United Kingdom, and France, and other governments around the world have imposed severe sanctions. The Soviet Union and China ended all arms sales to Iraq.

And this past Monday, the United Nations Security Council approved for the first time in 23 years mandatory sanctions under Chapter VII of the United Nations Charter. These sanctions, now enshrined in international law, have the potential for denying Iraq the fruits of aggression while sharply limiting its ability to either import or export anything of value, especially oil.

I pledge here today that the United States will do its part to see that these sanctions are effective and to induce Iraq to withdraw without delay from Kuwait.

But we must recognize that Iraq may not stop using force to advance its ambitions. Iraq has massed an enormous war machine on the Saudi border capable of initiating hostilities with little or no additional preparation. Given the Iraqi Government's history of aggression against its own citizens as well as its neighbors, to assume Iraq will not attack again would be unwise and unrealistic.

And therefore, after consulting with King Fahd, I sent Secretary of Defense Dick Cheney to discuss cooperative measures we could take. Following those meetings, the Saudi Government requested our help, and I responded to that request by ordering U.S. air and ground forces to deploy to the Kingdom of Saudi Arabia.

Let me be clear: The sovereign independence of Saudi Arabia is of vital interest to the United States. This decision, which I shared with the Congressional leadership, grows out of the longstanding friendship and security relationship between the United States and Saudi Arabia. U.S. forces will work together with those of Saudi Arabia and other nations to preserve the integrity of Saudi Arabia and to deter further Iraqi aggression. Through their presence, as well as through training and exercises, these multinational forces will enhance the overall capability of Saudi armed forces to defend the Kingdom.

I want to be clear about what we are doing and why. America does not seek conflict, nor do we seek to chart the destiny of other nations. But America will stand by her friends. The mission of our troops is wholly defensive. Hopefully, they will not be needed long. They will not initiate hostilities, but they will defend them-selves, the Kingdom of Saudi Arabia, and other friends in the Persian Gulf.

[...]

Source: George H. W. Bush, *Public Papers of the Presidents of the United States: George Bush, 1990,* Book 2 (Washington, DC: U.S. Government Printing Office, 1991), 1107–1108.

63. United Nations Resolutions on the Gulf Crisis, Nos. 660, 661, 662, 664, 665, 666, 667, 669, 670, 674, 677, 678, August–November 1990

Introduction

Although the United States contributed the bulk of the military forces that waged war against Iraq in 1991, it did so as the leader of a United Nations (UN) coalition fighting to restore the status quo ante in Kuwait. Between August and November 1990, the UN Security Council, urged in particular by the United States and Great Britain, passed a series of resolutions on Kuwait and Iraq. Initially these condemned the Iraqi invasion and takeover of Kuwait and urged Iraq to withdraw immediately and to submit its disputes with Kuwait to UN mediation. On August 6 the Security Council also imposed economic sanctions on Iraq and Kuwait, banning all trade with those countries and freezing the economic assets of both in third countries. Later in August, the maritime forces of all UN member states were enjoined to enforce and facilitate these embargoes where appropriate, a measure that permitted the United States to use its naval vessels in the Persian Gulf for this purpose. When it became clear by September 1990 that the Iraqi government had seized foreign diplomatic personnel in Baghdad and Kuwait and was preventing the free movement of non-Iraqis, intending to use these foreigners as hostages in the hope of precluding any military action against Iraq, the UN demanded their release. Continuing mistreatment of Kuwaiti nationals brought the tightening of sanctions, including the breaking of most aviation links with Iraq and Kuwait. Until the end of October 1990, the Security Council continued to call on Iraq to negotiate a peaceful resolution to the crisis over Kuwait. Finally, as all such exhortations proved fruitless and as it became clear that Iraq had no intention of relinquishing control of the emirate, on November 29, 1990, three weeks after U.S. president George H. W. Bush had announced that coalition forces were beginning to move from a defensive to an offensive basis, the Security Council passed Resolution No. 678, demanding that Iraqi forces leave Kuwait completely prior to January 15, 1991, and, should this not happen, mandating the use of military force if necessary to restore

Kuwait's independence. This resolution provided the legal basis for the eventual coalition military operations against Iraq. The passage of these resolutions was made possible by the harmonious relations between Russia and the Western powers that followed the ending of the Cold War. This meant that the five permanent members of the Security Council—the United States, Great Britain, France, the Soviet Union, and China—all either voted in favor of them or, in the case of China, were at least willing to abstain on the final resolution authorizing forcible intervention against Iraq. The Western powers' need to gain Chinese acquiescence, if not support, meant that their relations with China thawed from the glacial atmosphere that had characterized them in the year after the brutal repression of the June 1989 Tiananmen Square protests in Beijing and elsewhere in China. The decision of the U.S. government to intervene under UN auspices also enabled Bush to argue that coalition powers had made every effort to give Saddam Hussein repeated opportunities to withdraw from Kuwait and that the eventual use of military force was due only to Iraq's intransigence.

Primary Source

No. 660

2 August 1990

The Security Council,

Alarmed by the invasion of Kuwait on 2 August 1990 by the military forces of Iraq,

Determining that there exists a breach of international peace and security as regards the Iraqi invasion of Kuwait,

Acting under Articles 39 and 40 of the Charter of the United Nations,

1. Condemns the Iraqi invasion of Kuwait;

2. Demands that Iraq withdraw immediately and unconditionally all of its forces to the positions in which they were located on 1 August 1990;

3. Calls upon Iraq and Kuwait to begin immediately intensive negotiations for the resolution of their differences and supports all efforts in this regard, and especially those of the League of Arab States;

4. Decides to meet again as necessary to consider further steps to ensure compliance with the present resolution.

No. 661

6 August 1990

The Security Council,

Reaffirming its resolution 660 (1990) of 2 August 1990,

Deeply concerned that that resolution has not been implemented and that the invasion by Iraq of Kuwait continues with further loss of human life and material destruction,

Determined to bring the invasion and occupation of Kuwait by Iraq to an end and to restore the sovereignty, independence and territorial integrity of Kuwait,

Noting that the legitimate Government of Kuwait has expressed its readiness to comply with resolution 660 (1990),

Mindful of its responsibilities under the Charter of the United Nations for the maintenance of international peace and security,

Affirming the inherent right of individual or collective self-defence, in response to the armed attack by Iraq against Kuwait, in accordance with Article 51 of the Charter,

Acting under Chapter VII of the Charter of the United Nations,

1. Determines that Iraq so far has failed to comply with paragraph 2 of resolution 660 (1990) and has usurped the authority of the legitimate Government of Kuwait;

2. Decides, as a consequence, to take the following measures to secure compliance of Iraq with paragraph 2 of resolution 660 (1990) and to restore the authority of the legitimate Government of Kuwait;

3. Decides that all States shall prevent:

(a) The import into their territories of all commodities and products originating in Iraq or Kuwait exported therefrom after the date of the present resolution;

(b) Any activities by their nationals or in their territories which would promote or are calculated to promote the export or trans-shipment of any commodities or products from Iraq or Kuwait; and any dealings by their nationals or their flag vessels or in their territories in any commodities or products originating in Iraq or Kuwait and exported therefrom after the date of the present resolution, including in particular any transfer of funds to Iraq or Kuwait for the purposes of such activities or dealings;

(c) The sale or supply by their nationals or from their territories or using their flag vessels of any commodities or products, including weapons or any other military equipment, whether or not originating in their territories but not including supplies intended strictly for medical purposes, and, in humanitarian circumstances, food-stuffs, to any person or body in Iraq or Kuwait or to any person or body for the purposes of any business carried on in or operated from Iraq or Kuwait, and any activities by their nationals or in their territories which promote or are calculated to promote such sale or supply of such commodities or products;

4. Decides that all States shall not make available to the Government of Iraq or to any commercial, industrial or public utility undertaking in Iraq or Kuwait, any funds or any other financial or economic resources and shall prevent their nationals and any persons within their territories from removing from their territories or otherwise making available to that Government or to any such undertaking any such funds or resources and from remitting any other funds to persons or bodies within Iraq or Kuwait, except payments exclusively for strictly medical or humanitarian purposes and, in humanitarian circumstances, foodstuffs;

5. Calls upon all States, including States non-members of the United Nations, to act strictly in accordance with the provisions of the present resolution notwithstanding any contract entered into or license granted before the date of the present resolution;

6. Decides to establish, in accordance with rule 28 of the provisional rules of procedure of the Security Council, a Committee of the Security Council consisting of all the members of the Council, to undertake the following tasks and to report on its work to the Council with its observations and recommendations:

(a) To examine the reports on the progress of the implementation of the present resolution which will be submitted by the Secretary-General;

(b) To seek from all States further information regarding the action taken by them concerning the effective implementation of the provisions laid down in the present resolution;

7. Calls upon all States to co-operate fully with the Committee in the fulfilment of its task, including supplying such information as may be sought by the Committee in pursuance of the present resolution;

8. Requests the Secretary-General to provide all necessary assistance to the Committee and to make the necessary arrangements in the Secretariat for the purpose;

9. Decides that, notwithstanding paragraphs 4 through 8 above, nothing in the present resolution shall prohibit assistance to the legitimate Government of Kuwait, and calls upon all States:

(a) To take appropriate measures to protect assets of the legitimate Government of Kuwait and its agencies;

(b) Not to recognize any regime set up by the occupying Power;

10. Requests the Secretary-General to report to the Council on the progress of the implementation of the present resolution, the first report to be submitted within thirty days;

11. Decides to keep this item on its agenda and to continue its efforts to put an early end to the invasion by Iraq.

No. 662

9 August 1990

The Security Council,

Recalling its resolutions 660 (1990) and 661 (1990),

Gravely alarmed by the declaration by Iraq of a "comprehensive and eternal merger" with Kuwait,

Demanding, once again, that Iraq withdraw immediately and unconditionally all its forces to the positions in which they were located on 1 August 1990,

Determined to bring the occupation of Kuwait by Iraq to an end and to restore the sovereignty, independence and territorial integrity of Kuwait,

Determined also to restore the authority of the legitimate Government of Kuwait,

1. Decides that annexation of Kuwait by Iraq under any form and whatever pretext has no legal validity, and is considered null and void;

2. Calls upon all States, international organizations and specialized agencies not to recognize that annexation, and to refrain from any action or dealing that might be interpreted as an indirect recognition of the annexation;

3. Further demands that Iraq rescind its actions purporting to annex Kuwait;

4. Decides to keep this item on its agenda and to continue its efforts to put an early end to the occupation.

No. 664

18 August 1990

The Security Council,

Recalling the Iraqi invasion and purported annexation of Kuwait and resolutions 660, 661 and 662,

Deeply concerned for the safety and well being of third state nationals in Iraq and Kuwait,

Recalling the obligations of Iraq in this regard under international law,

Welcoming the efforts of the Secretary-General to pursue urgent consultations with the Government of Iraq following the concern and anxiety expressed by the members of the Council on 17 August, 1990,

Acting under Chapter VII of the United Nations Charter:

1. Demands that Iraq permit and facilitate the immediate departure from Kuwait and Iraq of the nationals of third countries and grant immediate and continuing access of consular officials to such nationals;

2. Further demands that Iraq take no action to jeopardize the safety, security or health of such nationals;

3. Reaffirms its decision in resolution 662 (1990) that annexation of Kuwait by Iraq is null and void, and therefore demands that the Government of Iraq rescind its orders for the closure of diplomatic and consular missions in Kuwait and the withdrawal of the immunity of their personnel, and refrain from any such actions in the future;

4. Requests the Secretary-General to report to the Council on compliance with this resolution at the earliest possible time.

No. 665

25 August 1990

The Security Council,

Recalling its resolutions 660 (1990), 661 (1990), 662 (1990) and 664 (1990) and demanding their full and immediate implementation,

Having decided in resolution 661 (1990) to impose economic sanctions under Chapter VII of the Charter of the United Nations,

Determined to bring an end to the occupation of Kuwait by Iraq which imperils the existence of a Member State and to restore the legitimate authority, and the sovereignty, independence and territorial integrity of Kuwait which requires the speedy implementation of the above resolutions,

Deploring the loss of innocent life stemming from the Iraqi invasion of Kuwait and determined to prevent further such losses,

Gravely alarmed that Iraq continues to refuse to comply with resolutions 660 (1990), 661 (1990), 662 (1990) and 664 (1990) and in particular at the conduct of the Government of Iraq in using Iraqi flag vessels to export oil,

1. Calls upon those Member States co-operating with the Government of Kuwait which are deploying maritime forces to the area to use such measures commensurate to the specific circumstances as may be necessary under the authority of the Security Council to halt all inward and outward maritime shipping in order to inspect and verify their cargoes and destinations and to ensure strict implementation of the provisions related to such shipping laid down in resolution 661 (1990);

2. Invites Member States accordingly to co-operate as may be necessary to ensure compliance with the provisions of resolution 661 (1990) with maximum use of political and diplomatic measures, in accordance with paragraph 1 above;

3. Requests all States to provide in accordance with the Charter such assistance as may be required by the States referred to in paragraph 1 of this resolution;

4. Further requests the States concerned to co-ordinate their actions in pursuit of the above paragraphs of this resolution using as appropriate mechanisms of the Military Staff Committee and after consultation with the Secretary-General to submit reports to the Security Council and its Committee established under resolution 661 (1990) to facilitate the monitoring of the implementation of this resolution;

5. Decides to remain actively seized of the matter.

No. 666

13 September 1990

The Security Council,

Recalling its resolution 661 (1990), paragraphs 3 (c) and 4 of which apply, except in humanitarian circumstances, to foodstuffs,

Recognizing that circumstances may arise in which it will be necessary for foodstuffs to be supplied to the civilian population in Iraq or Kuwait in order to relieve human suffering,

Noting that in this respect the Committee established under paragraph 6 of that resolution has received communications from several Member States,

Emphasizing that it is for the Security Council, alone or acting through the Committee, to determine whether humanitarian circumstances have arisen,

Deeply concerned that Iraq has failed to comply with its obligations under Security Council resolution 664 (1990) in respect of the safety and well-being of third State nationals, and reaffirming that Iraq retains full responsibility in this regard under international humanitarian law including, where applicable, the Fourth Geneva Convention,

Acting under Chapter VII of the Charter of the United Nations,

1. Decides that in order to make the necessary determination whether or not for the purposes of paragraph 3 (c) and paragraph 4 of resolution 661 (1990) humanitarian circumstances have arisen, the Committee shall keep the situation regarding foodstuffs in Iraq and Kuwait under constant review;

2. Expects Iraq to comply with its obligations under Security Council resolution 664 (1990) in respect of third State nationals and reaffirms that Iraq remains fully responsible for their safety and well-being in accordance with international humanitarian law including, where applicable, the Fourth Geneva Convention;

3. Requests, for the purposes of paragraphs 1 and 2 of this resolution, that the Secretary-General seek urgently, and on a continuing basis, information from relevant United Nations and other appropriate humanitarian agencies and all other sources on the availability of food in Iraq and Kuwait, such information to be communicated by the Secretary-General to the Committee regularly;

4. Requests further that in seeking and supplying such information particular attention will be paid to such categories of persons who might suffer specially, such as children under 15 years of age, expectant mothers, maternity cases, the sick and the elderly;

5. Decides that if the Committee, after receiving the reports from the Secretary-General, determines that circumstances have arisen in which there is an urgent humanitarian need to supply foodstuffs to Iraq or Kuwait in order to relieve human suffering, it will report promptly to the Council its decision as to how such need should be met;

6. Directs the Committee that in formulating its decisions it should bear in mind that foodstuffs should be provided through the United Nations in co-operation with the International Committee of the Red Cross or other appropriate humanitarian agencies and distributed by them or under their supervision in order to ensure that they reach the intended beneficiaries;

7. Requests the Secretary-General to use his good offices to facilitate the delivery and distribution of foodstuffs to Kuwait and Iraq in accordance with the provisions of this and other relevant resolutions;

8. Recalls that resolution 661 (1990) does not apply to supplies intended strictly for medical purposes, but in this connection recommends that medical supplies should be exported under the strict supervision of the Government of the exporting State or by appropriate humanitarian agencies.

No. 667

16 September 1990

The Security Council,

Reaffirming its resolutions 660 (1990), 661 (1990), 662 (1990), 664 (1990), 665 (1990) and 666 (1990),

Recalling the Vienna Conventions of 18 April 1961 on diplomatic relations and of 24 April 1963 on consular relations, to both of which Iraq is a party,

Considering that the decision of Iraq to order the closure of diplomatic and consular missions in Kuwait and to withdraw the immunity and privileges of these missions and their personnel is contrary to the decisions of the Security Council, the international Conventions mentioned above and international law,

Deeply concerned that Iraq, notwithstanding the decisions of the Security Council and the provisions of the Conventions mentioned above, has committed acts of violence against diplomatic missions and their personnel in Kuwait,

Outraged at recent violations by Iraq of diplomatic premises in Kuwait and at the abduction of personnel enjoying diplomatic immunity and foreign nationals who were present in these premises,

Considering that the above actions by Iraq constitute aggressive acts and a flagrant violation of its international obligations which strike at the root of the conduct of international relations in accordance with the Charter of the United Nations,

Recalling that Iraq is fully responsible for any use of violence against foreign nationals or against any diplomatic or consular missions in Kuwait or its personnel,

Determined to ensure respect for its decisions and for Article 25 of the Charter of the United Nations,

Further considering that the grave nature of Iraq's actions, which constitute a new escalation of its violations of international law, obliges the Council not only to express its immediate reaction but also to consider further concrete measures to ensure Iraq's compliance with the Council's resolutions,

Acting under Chapter VII of the Charter of the United Nations,

1. Strongly condemns aggressive acts perpetrated by Iraq against diplomatic premises and personnel in Kuwait, including the abduction of foreign nationals who were present in those premises;

2. Demands the immediate release of those foreign nationals as well as all nationals mentioned in resolution 664 (1990);

3. Further demands that Iraq immediately and fully comply with its international obligations under resolutions 660 (1990), 662 (1990) and 664 (1990) of the Security Council, the Vienna Conventions on diplomatic and consular relations and international law;

4. Further demands that Iraq immediately protect the safety and well-being of diplomatic and consular personnel and premises in Kuwait and in Iraq and take no action to hinder the diplomatic and consular missions in the performance of their functions, including access to their nationals and the protection of their persons and interests;

5. Reminds all States that they are obliged to observe strictly resolutions 661 (1990), 662 (1990), 664 (1990), 665 (1990) and 666 (1990);

6. Decides to consult urgently to take further concrete measures as soon as possible, under Chapter VII of the Charter, in response to Iraq's continued violation of the Charter, of resolutions of the Council and of international law.

No. 669

24 September 1990

The Security Council,

Recalling its resolution 661 (1990) of 6 August 1990,

Recalling also Article 50 of the Charter of the United Nations,

Conscious of the fact that an increasing number of requests for assistance have been received under the provisions of Article 50 of the Charter of the United Nations,

Entrusts the Committee established under resolution 661 (1990) concerning the situation between Iraq and Kuwait with the task of examining requests for assistance under the provisions of Article 50 of the Charter of the United Nations and making recommendations to the President of the Security Council for appropriate action.

No. 670

25 September 1990

The Security Council,

Reaffirming its resolutions 660 (1990), 661 (1990), 662 (1990), 664 (1990), 665 (1990), 666 (1990) and 667 (1990),

Condemning Iraq's continued occupation of Kuwait, its failure to rescind its actions and end its purported annexation and its holding of third State nationals against their will, in flagrant violation of resolutions 660 (1990), 662 (1990), 664 (1990) and 667 (1990) and of international humanitarian law,

Condemning further the treatment by Iraqi forces of Kuwaiti nationals, including measures to force them to leave their own country and mistreatment of persons and property in Kuwait in violation of international law,

Noting with grave concern the persistent attempts to evade the measures laid down in resolution 661 (1990),

Further noting that a number of States have limited the number of Iraqi diplomatic and consular officials in their countries and that others are planning to do so,

Determined to ensure by all necessary means the strict and complete application of the measures laid down in resolution 661 (1990),

Determined to ensure respect for its decisions and the provisions of Articles 25 and 48 of the Charter of the United Nations,

Affirming that any acts of the Government of Iraq which are contrary to the above-mentioned resolutions or to Articles 25 or 48 of the Charter of the United Nations, such as Decree No. 377 of the Revolution Command Council of Iraq of 16 September 1990, are null and void,

Reaffirming its determination to ensure compliance with Security Council resolutions by maximum use of political and diplomatic means,

Welcoming the Secretary-General's use of his good offices to advance a peaceful solution based on the relevant Security Council

resolutions and noting with appreciation his continuing efforts to this end,

Underlining to the Government of Iraq that its continued failure to comply with the terms of resolutions 660 (1990), 661 (1990), 662 (1990), 664 (1990), 666 (1990) and 667 (1990) could lead to further serious action by the Council under the Charter of the United Nations, including under Chapter VII,

Recalling the provisions of Article 103 of the Charter of the United Nations,

Acting under Chapter VII of the Charter of the United Nations,

1. Calls upon all States to carry out their obligations to ensure strict and complete compliance with resolution 661 (1990) and, in particular, paragraphs 3, 4 and 5 thereof;

2. Confirms that resolution 661 (1990) applies to all means of transport, including aircraft;

3. Decides that all States, notwithstanding the existence of any rights or obligations conferred or imposed by any international agreement or any contract entered into or any licence or permit granted before the date of the present resolution, shall deny permission to any aircraft to take off from their territory if the aircraft would carry any cargo to or from Iraq or Kuwait other than food in humanitarian circumstances, subject to authorization by the Council or the Committee established by resolution 661 (1990) and in accordance with resolution 666 (1990), or supplies intended strictly for medical purposes or solely for UNIIMOG;

4. Decides further that all States shall deny permission to any aircraft destined to land in Iraq or Kuwait, whatever its State of registration, to overfly its territory unless:

(a) The aircraft lands at an airfield designated by that State outside Iraq or Kuwait in order to permit its inspection to ensure that there is no cargo on board in violation of resolution 661 (1990) or the present resolution, and for this purpose the aircraft may be detained for as long as necessary; or

(b) The particular flight has been approved by the Committee established by resolution 661 (1990); or

(c) The flight is certified by the United Nations as solely for the purposes of UNIIMOG;

5. Decides that each State shall take all necessary measures to ensure that any aircraft registered in its territory or operated by an operator who has his principal place of business or permanent

residence in its territory complies with the provisions of resolution 661 (1990) and the present resolution;

6. Decides further that all States shall notify in a timely fashion the Committee established by resolution 661 (1990) of any flight between its territory and Iraq or Kuwait to which the requirement to land in paragraph 4 above does not apply, and the purpose for such a flight;

7. Calls upon all States to co-operate in taking such measures as may be necessary, consistent with international law, including the Chicago Convention, to ensure the effective implementation of the provisions of resolution 661 (1990) or the present resolution;

8. Calls upon all States to detain any ships of Iraqi registry which enter their ports and which are being or have been used in violation of resolution 661 (1990), or to deny such ships entrance to their ports except in circumstances recognized under international law as necessary to safeguard human life;

9. Reminds all States of their obligations under resolution 661 (1990) with regard to the freezing of Iraqi assets, and the protection of the assets of the legitimate Government of Kuwait and its agencies, located within their territory and to report to the Committee established under resolution 661 (1990) regarding those assets;

10. Calls upon all States to provide to the Committee established by resolution 661 (1990) information regarding the action taken by them to implement the provisions laid down in the present resolution;

11. Affirms that the United Nations Organization, the specialized agencies and other international organizations in the United Nations system are required to take such measures as may be necessary to give effect to the terms of resolution 661 (1990) and this resolution;

12. Decides to consider, in the event of evasion of the provisions of resolution 661 (1990) or of the present resolution by a State or its nationals or through its territory, measures directed at the State in question to prevent such evasion;

13. Reaffirms that the Fourth Geneva Convention applies to Kuwait and that as a High Contracting Party to the Convention Iraq is bound to comply fully with all its terms and, in particular, is liable under the Convention in respect of the grave breaches committed by it, as are individuals who commit or order the commission of grave breaches.

No. 674

29 October 1990

The Security Council,

Recalling its resolutions 660 (1990), 661 (1990), 662 (1990), 664 (1990), 665 (1990), 666 (1990), 667 (1990) and 670 (1990),

Stressing the urgent need for the immediate and unconditional withdrawal of all Iraqi forces from Kuwait, for the restoration of Kuwait's sovereignty, independence and territorial integrity, and of the authority of its legitimate Government,

Condemning the actions by the Iraqi authorities and occupying forces to take third State nationals hostage and to mistreat and oppress Kuwaiti and third State nationals, and the other actions reported to the Council such as the destruction of Kuwaiti demographic records, forced departure of Kuwaitis, and relocation of population in Kuwait and the unlawful destruction and seizure of public and private property in Kuwait including hospital supplies and equipment, in violation of the decisions of this Council, the Charter of the United Nations, the Fourth Geneva Convention, the Vienna Conventions on Diplomatic and Consular Relations and international law,

Expressing grave alarm over the situation of nationals of third States in Kuwait and Iraq, including the personnel of the diplomatic and consular missions of such States,

Reaffirming that the Fourth Geneva Convention applies to Kuwait and that as a High Contracting Party to the Convention Iraq is bound to comply fully with all its terms and, in particular is liable under the Convention in respect of the grave breaches committed by it, as are individuals who commit or order the commission of grave breaches,

Recalling the efforts of the Secretary-General concerning the safety and well-being of third State nationals in Iraq and Kuwait,

Deeply concerned at the economic cost, and at the loss and suffering caused to individuals in Kuwait and Iraq as a result of the invasion and occupation of Kuwait by Iraq,

Acting under Chapter VII of the United Nations Charter,

Reaffirming the goal of the international community of maintaining international peace and security by seeking to resolve international disputes and conflicts through peaceful means,

Recalling also the important role that the United Nations and its Secretary-General have played in the peaceful solution of disputes and conflicts in conformity with the provisions of the United Nations Charter,

Alarmed by the dangers of the present crisis caused by the Iraqi invasion and occupation of Kuwait, directly threatening international peace and security, and seeking to avoid any further worsening of the situation,

Calling upon Iraq to comply with the relevant resolutions of the Security Council, in particular resolutions 660 (1990), 662 (1990) and 664 (1990),

Reaffirming its determination to ensure compliance by Iraq with the Security Council resolutions by maximum use of political and diplomatic means,

A

1. Demands that the Iraqi authorities and occupying forces immediately cease and desist from taking third State nationals hostage, and mistreating and oppressing Kuwaiti and third State nationals, and from any other actions such as those reported to the Council and described above, violating the decisions of this Council, the Charter of the United Nations, the Fourth Geneva Convention, the Vienna Conventions on Diplomatic and Consular Relations and international law;

2. Invites States to collate substantiated information in their possession or submitted to them on the grave breaches by Iraq as per paragraph 1 above and to make this information available to the Council;

3. Reaffirms its demand that Iraq immediately fulfil its obligations to third State nationals in Kuwait and Iraq, including the personnel of diplomatic and consular missions, under the Charter, the Fourth Geneva Convention, the Vienna Conventions on Diplomatic and Consular Relations, general principles of international law and the relevant resolutions of the Council;

4. Reaffirms further its demand that Iraq permit and facilitate the immediate departure from Kuwait and Iraq of those third State nationals, including diplomatic and consular personnel, who wish to leave;

5. Demands that Iraq ensure the immediate access to food, water and basic services necessary to the protection and well-being of Kuwaiti nationals and of nationals of third States in Kuwait and Iraq, including the personnel of diplomatic and consular missions in Kuwait;

6. Reaffirms its demand that Iraq immediately protect the safety and well-being of diplomatic and consular personnel and premises in Kuwait and in Iraq, take no action to hinder these diplomatic and consular missions in the performance of their functions, including access to their nationals and the protection of their persons and interests and rescind its orders for the closure of diplomatic and consular missions in Kuwait and the withdrawal of the immunity of their personnel;

7. Requests the Secretary-General, in the context of the continued exercise of his good offices concerning the safety and well being of third State nationals in Iraq and Kuwait, to seek to achieve the objectives of paragraphs 4, 5 and 6 and, in particular, the provision of food, water and basic services to Kuwaiti nationals and to the diplomatic and consular missions in Kuwait and the evacuation of third State nationals;

8. Reminds Iraq that under international law it is liable for any loss, damage or injury arising in regard to Kuwait and third States, and their nationals and corporations, as a result of the invasion and illegal occupation of Kuwait by Iraq;

9. Invites States to collect relevant information regarding their claims, and those of their nationals and corporations, for restitution or financial compensation by Iraq with a view to such arrangements as may be established in accordance with international law;

10. Requires that Iraq comply with the provisions of the present resolution and its previous resolutions, failing which the Council will need to take further measures under the Charter;

11. Decides to remain actively and permanently seized of the matter until Kuwait has regained its independence and peace has been restored in conformity with the relevant resolutions of the Security Council;

B

12. Reposes its trust in the Secretary-General to make available his good offices and, as he considers appropriate, to pursue them and undertake diplomatic efforts in order to reach a peaceful solution to the crisis caused by the Iraqi invasion and occupation of Kuwait on the basis of Security Council resolutions 660 (1990), 662 (1990) and 664 (1990), and calls on all States, both those in the region and others, to pursue on this basis their efforts to this end, in conformity with the Charter, in order to improve the situation and restore peace, security and stability;

13. Requests the Secretary-General to report to the Security Council on the results of his good offices and diplomatic efforts.

No. 677

28 November 1990

The Security Council,

Recalling its resolutions 660 (1990) of 2 August 1990, 662 (1990) of 9 August 1990 and 674 (1990) of 29 October 1990,

Reiterating its concern for the suffering caused to individuals in Kuwait as a result of the invasion and occupation of Kuwait by Iraq,

Gravely concerned at the ongoing attempt by Iraq to alter the demographic composition of the population of Kuwait and to destroy the civil records maintained by the legitimate Government of Kuwait,

Acting under Chapter VII of the Charter of the United Nations,

1. Condemns the attempts by Iraq to alter the demographic composition of the population of Kuwait and to destroy the civil records maintained by the legitimate Government of Kuwait;

2. Mandates the Secretary-General to take custody of a copy of the population register of Kuwait, the authenticity of which has been certified by the legitimate Government of Kuwait and which covers the registration of the population up to 1 August 1990;

3. Requests the Secretary-General to establish, in co-operation with the legitimate Government of Kuwait, an Order of Rules and Regulations governing access to and use of the said copy of the population register.

No. 678

29 November 1990

The Security Council,

Recalling, and reaffirming its resolutions 660 (1990) of 2 August (1990), 661 (1990) of 6 August 1990, 662 (1990) of 9 August 1990, 664 (1990) of 18 August 1990, 665 (1990) of 25 August 1990, 666 (1990) of 13 September 1990, 667 (1990) of 16 September 1990, 669 (1990) of 24 September 1990, 670 (1990) of 25 September 1990, 674 (1990) of 29 October 1990 and 677 (1990) of 28 November 1990,

Noting that, despite all efforts by the United Nations, Iraq refuses to comply with its obligation to implement resolution 660 (1990) and the above-mentioned subsequent relevant resolutions, in flagrant contempt of the Security Council,

Mindful of its duties and responsibilities under the Charter of the United Nations for the maintenance and preservation of international peace and security,

Determined to secure full compliance with its decisions,

Acting under Chapter VII of the Charter,

1. Demands that Iraq comply fully with resolution 660 (1990) and all subsequent relevant resolutions, and decides, while maintaining all its decisions, to allow Iraq one final opportunity, as a pause of goodwill, to do so;

2. Authorizes Member States co-operating with the Government of Kuwait, unless Iraq on or before 15 January 1991 fully implements, as set forth in paragraph 1 above, the above-mentioned resolutions, to use all necessary means to uphold and implement resolution 660 (1990) and all subsequent relevant resolutions and to restore international peace and security in the area;

3. Requests all States to provide appropriate support for the actions undertaken in pursuance of paragraph 2 of the present resolution;

4. Requests the States concerned to keep the Security Council regularly informed on the progress of actions undertaken pursuant to paragraphs 2 and 3 of the present resolution;

5. Decides to remain seized of the matter.

Source: United Nations Security Council Official Records, S/RES/0660, S/RES/0661, S/RES/0662, S/RES/0664, S/RES/0665, S/RES/0666, S/RES/0667, S/RES/0669, S/RES/0670, S/RES/0674, S/RES/0677, S/RES/0678, August–November 1990.

64. President Saddam Hussein of Iraq, Message to the Iraqi National Assembly, December 6, 1990

Introduction

The holding of Western hostages was one tactical measure that won President Saddam Hussein of Iraq great opprobrium in the aftermath of his invasion of Kuwait. For several months, Hussein refused to permit many Westerners in Iraq and Kuwait to leave those countries, although from August to November 1990 he gradually released most of the women and children. Until December 1990, however, several thousand foreigners still remained under the control of the Iraqi government without freedom of movement even within Iraq and Kuwait. Hussein deliberately placed many of these hostages in strategic locations that were likely to be targets of military operations in the hope that this would deter foreign powers from launching assaults against them. The United Nations (UN) Security Council repeatedly condemned Hussein's action in taking civilians hostage, and eventually, in early December 1990, Hussein decided to release all the remaining Westerners he was still holding. In a speech carried on Baghdad radio he addressed the Iraqi National Assembly, stating that although "denying those people the freedom to travel has rendered a great service to the cause of peace," this had been an exceptional measure, justified only by the special emergency circumstances. Now that Iraq and

Kuwait were fully prepared for war, the time was right to remove such civilians from the cross fire of battle. Moreover, he believed that American public opinion had now turned against the possibility of war against Iraq, while his Arab allies and European leaders were urging him to release the hostages. He therefore urged the National Assembly to rescind its legislation forbidding foreigners to leave, instructions that the rubber-stamp parliament quickly obeyed. Hussein probably hoped that this conciliatory gesture might turn Western public opinion in his favor, but after several months it proved insufficient to cancel out the extremely unsavory impression made by his initial detention of such civilian bystanders.

Primary Source

In the name of God, the merciful, the compassionate. Mr. National Assembly Speaker, members: Peace be upon you. Under difficult conditions, the strength of the believers' affiliation and loyalty is put to the test. Their action in the service of principles is also put to the test. Iraqis in general, and you among them, have proved that on very dark nights, the spark of faith glows in a much nicer way than on ordinary nights. Adherence to the supreme principles governing the relation between man and his Creator and his duty toward Him, as well as the relation between the Iraqis with all peoples, becomes even stronger in the more difficult circumstances.

And, just as the continued endeavor is required on earth, the correct answers to the continuous test are also required, without making the test or success in it dependent on a certain phrase and time.

On the basis of these principles and what we desire—that the influence of the believers expands, and that the knowledge of mankind in general expands with the believers' principles and the truth of their mission—we believe that, this time, the National Assembly is asked to take a decisive and final decision concerning a humanitarian issue, which you, and the whole world, know about.

Some Are Trapped

National Assembly members, the thing that worries the faithful struggler, the honorable struggler, and the brave fighter—who has the values of the chivalrous believer—most is when the trenches in the battle arena get mixed and when some people, who do not want to fight and who are not among the evildoers, get trapped in the space between the two trenches. This worry becomes deep grief when that kind of people are harmed because of the level and type of the conflict.

The foreigners who were prevented from traveling are among those people in the battle between right, led by Iraq's great people and valiant armed forces, and evil, whose failing mass is led by Bush, the enemy of God. As you and my brothers in the leadership know, I realize that despite what they had to put up with, denying those people the freedom to travel has rendered a great service to the cause of peace. And because God has taught us that forbidden things should never be resorted to except in very urgent cases and without any excesses, we must not keep these emergency measures, especially this measure, any longer.

The days, weeks, and months through which our people and nation have passed have been such that our options, even those concerning the nature and form of defense, were not open or without limits in every area and all conditions. For instance, our valiant forces did not have the chance to complete their concentrations in order to confront the possibilities of military aggression against them in the Kuwaiti governorate. So any measure that was taken to delay the war may not have been correct from the humanitarian and practical standpoints and under established norms, but it has provided an opportunity for us to prepare for any eventuality.

Now Fully Prepared

We have now reached the time when, with God's care, our blessed force has become fully prepared, if God wills that we should fight in defense of his values and ideals against the infidels, profligates and traitors, and also in defense of the great national, pan-Arab and humanitarian gains.

Gentlemen: Good people, men and women of different nationalities and political trends have come to Iraq. Dear brothers from Jordan, Yemen, Palestine, Sudan, and the Arab Maghreb have also consulted with us on this issue, as on others. We have felt, guided by our humanitarian feelings, that the time has come to make a firm decision on this subject. We had considered a timing different from the present one; namely, the occasion of Christmas and New Year, which are of special significance to Christians in the world, including Christians in the West.

However, the appeal by some brothers, the decision of the Democratic majority in the U.S. Senate, and the European Parliament's invitation to our Foreign Minister for dialogue; all these have encouraged us to respond to these good, positive changes—changes that will have a major impact on world public opinion in general, and U.S. public opinion in particular, in restraining the evil ones who are seeking and pushing for war as the option they have chosen out of their evil tendencies and premedi[t]ated intentions to do harm.

In view of all this, we have found that the exigencies that permitted the impermissible, and thus prevented the travel of foreigners, have weakened and have been replaced by something stronger; namely, this positive change in public opinion, including the change in U.S. public opinion, which will constitute a restraint on the intentions and decisions of the evil ones, who are led in their evil intentions and steps by the enemy of God, Bush.

Therefore, I call on you, brothers, to make your just decision and allow all foreigners on whom restrictions were placed to enjoy the freedom of travel and to lift these restrictions, with our apologies for any harm done to anyone of them. God, the Almighty, grants forgiveness.

Brothers, I ask you, and th[r]ough you I ask the Iraqi people and our brave armed forces, to maintain your alertness and vigil because the armies of aggression are still on our holy lands, in the Arabian Peninsula, and the evil ones are talking of war. Bush's invitation for talks, as far as we can discern, has continued to bear the possibilities or the inclination toward aggression and war. The buildup is growing.

Therefore, the steadfast believers, both on the level of the public and on the level of our armed forces, should not fall in the trap in which some have fallen in the past.

May God protect you and protect our people and nation, steer humanity from what God hates, help the faithful to carry out what God wishes, and smite the infidels and traitors after exposing them and their shameful deeds. He is the best supporter and backer. God is great, accursed be the infidels and traitors, who gave the oppressors and infidels the opportunity to invade the holy land.

Glory and greatness to the mujahedeen of the occupied land and all the steadfast mujahedeen and fighters of our great Arab nation.

Source: Saddam Hussein, Message, December 6, 1990, Translated by the Foreign Broadcast Information Service, *F.B.I.S.-Daily Report Near East and South Asia,* December 6, 1990, pp. 90–235.

65. Yasser Arafat, The Palestine Liberation Organization and the Gulf Crisis, December 13, 1990

Introduction

Arab-Israeli peace talks remained effectively suspended from June 1990 until the end of the Persian Gulf War in March 1991. In August 1990 Iraqi president Saddam Hussein's army annexed the oil-rich emirate of Kuwait, an ally of the United States, and at the end of February 1991 a U.S.-led military coalition forcibly reversed this. Throughout those months, the Persian Gulf crisis dominated international affairs. Hussein sought to win support from the Arab world by linking his annexation of Kuwait, in defiance of the United States, with his vocal opposition to Israel. During the crisis Hussein threatened to attack Israel, seeking to redefine the conflict as a jihad (holy war) against Israel, and after hostilities began he launched several Scud missiles against Israel.

Emphasizing their joint opposition to Hussein, embattled Israel turned to the United States for protection and offered military assistance and facilities against the common enemy. During the previous year Hussein, seeking to enhance his status and influence within the Arab world, had been increasingly vocal in his opposition to Israel and the United States and in his support for the Palestinian cause, which led to Palestine Liberation Organization (PLO) chairman Yasser Arafat forging an alliance with the Iraqi president. During the Persian Gulf crisis Arafat and the PLO therefore sided with Hussein, a somewhat impolitic choice given the central role that the United States was likely to play in any resumed peace process. In a decidedly rambling interview published in a Croatian newspaper in December 1990, an apparently depressed Arafat sought to justify his position. He highlighted the growing U.S. military presence in the Persian Gulf well before Hussein's invasion as evidence of its unjustified ambitions. Arafat seemingly hoped that war against Iraq might still be avoided. He complained that the recent United Nations (UN) Security Council resolution on Iraq that the United States had obtained was "some kind of declaration of war." Arafat feared that such a conflict would "leave behind nothing but catastrophe" and asked why the Arab states could not have been left to mediate the Iraq-Kuwait dispute among themselves without American intervention. Arafat's interview gave the impression of a man who, watching two of his past partners coming ever closer to outright hostilities, believed that the Palestinian cause was foundering and had almost totally lost his bearings.

Primary Source

Do not forget that I was continually warning about the constant possibility of an escalation in this region. Most specifically, last April I pointed out two possible explosive points: On the one hand this involved increased U.S.-Israeli threats to Iraq and the Palestinians in southern Lebanon, and on the other the mass settlement of Jews into our occupied Palestine—a problem that I was constantly pointing out and to which I was trying to attract the world's attention because it involved a move with unpredictable consequences. I also said that the Arab summit in Baghdad in March this year should be a summit to straighten things out. Anyway, I will give you the letter the Americans sent us at that time through the Arab League. This is the dangerous letter that no one has wanted to talk about. I will give you a copy: go ahead and publish it if you wish. In this letter they openly announce that they will increase their presence in the Gulf and warned the Arabs that they will not tolerate any resistance to their presence. When I spoke about this on 17 May, two lines concerning the U.S. intentions were already apparent among the Arabs. One line approved of their presence and the other did not.

Another issue was the question of Israel and its expansion. The letter itself was a classic ultimatum. They issued a metal coin—here, I will give you one—with a sketch on it of the map of Israel as they see it. This Israel contains half of Iraq, half of Syria, the whole of Lebanon, Jordan, the whole of Palestine, a part of Saudi Arabia, and a good part of Sinai. They have not forsaken this dream. When I left Beirut in 1982, I said that the storm that had overtaken that city would not stop. The storm at that point had one center, one "eye" as we would say: Palestine. Today that storm has two eyes—one in the Gulf and the other in Palestine. . . .

A few days ago, when I was with Saddam Husayn, it seemed to me that the chances of peace were great. What the Americans have prepared through the Security Council, however . . . this is some kind of declaration of war. This is an ultimatum. Really, there is the danger of the Middle East's exploding, not only in the Gulf but on all sides. If Israel is in this war—and it certainly will be—we will fight against it as well as against the Americans. They must know that not one single Arab soldier—neither Egyptian, nor Syrian, nor Saudi—will agree to be in the same trench as Israeli soldiers. This is the reality.

There is no doubt about it. No matter what the outcome of the war, the Arab order as a whole will collapse. . . .

We are the greatest losers even now. Our people in Kuwait were the richest. The total losses of the Palestinian colony in Kuwait amounted to $8.5 billion. Our people had almost $3 billion in the banks there alone. Look what happened. The U.S.-European committee discussed, and to a considerable extent has already paid, compensation to the whole world for the money lost in Kuwait, but the Palestinians did not receive anything. What is this meant to be? A punishment for the Palestinians? Where are the principles here? Are they not ashamed of this? Or do they really only want to ignite a new explosion? Viewed in the long term, perhaps there is cause for optimism. In the shorter term, the situation is exceptionally difficult. It seems that we have definitely come closer to a war which will leave behind nothing but catastrophe. Both Asia and Europe will feel the repercussions. In order for people to come to their senses, it is necessary for a lot of effort to be made throughout the world. But there is no sense. Look at the Security Council—what is its duty? To foment war or to seek peaceful solutions? I cannot accept this. As regards the solution, it is very strange that, for example, it is being demanded of the Palestinians that they talk with the Israelis while they are occupying the Palestinians' country, but at the same time we are not being allowed to ask that the Arabs look for a solution among themselves for the new problem in the Gulf. So one can have negotiations among enemies but not among Arabs. What do they want? That I reject one occupation but accept another, or something like this? I cannot accept a foreign presence in this region. I know that they are literally punishing the Palestinians because of this, but I will not sell my opinion for any sum of money. I could easily say that I support the Saudis or the Americans. You know, however, that I have fought for principles, and I will not betray them.

Source: Walter Laqueur and Barry Rubin, eds., *The Israel-Arab Reader* (New York: Penguin, 2008), 378–380.

66. Joint Congressional Resolution Authorizing Use of Force in the Persian Gulf, January 12, 1991 [Excerpts]

Introduction

With efforts for a negotiated settlement regarding Kuwait at an impasse, on January 12, 1991, the U.S. Congress passed Joint Resolution 77 authorizing the use of military force against Iraq from January 15, 1991, onward. The United Nations (UN) had made this date the deadline for Iraq to comply with the various UN resolutions passed since August 1990 and withdraw from Kuwait. Many in the Democratic-controlled Congress were reluctant to endorse this measure, and voting was substantially along party lines. The Senate voted 52 to 47 in favor of this resolution, with a mere 10 Democrats and all but 2 Republican senators supporting the resolution, while the House passed it by 250 to 183 votes, with 164 out of 167 Republicans and 86 out of 267 Democrats in favor. The resolution stated that before resorting to military measures, the president must demonstrate that all "appropriate diplomatic and other peaceful means" to persuade Iraq to comply with the various UN resolutions had been tried and had proved fruitless. The president was also required to submit reports to Congress at 60-day intervals on the progress of efforts to persuade Iraq to accept the UN resolutions. Passage of the resolution demonstrated that despite the discomfort that many Democrats in particular still felt over the resort to military force, a consensus existed that unless such means were used, Saddam Hussein and Iraq would continue in control of Kuwait. Signing the resolution, President George H. W. Bush thanked its supporters, especially those Democrats who had broken with the majority of their party to provide the necessary margin of support for its passage. While mentioning the long-standing White House position that the 1973 War Powers Resolution was constitutionally invalid and did not affect the authority of the president as commander in chief to deploy U.S. armed forces as he pleased, Bush nonetheless clearly welcomed congressional endorsement of what seemed increasingly likely to be an outright war against Iraq and was unwilling to make the crisis into a test of presidential independence of congressional restraints. Bush also reiterated his hopes that the situation between Kuwait and Iraq, even at this late date, might be peacefully resolved, and he promised to keep Congress fully informed of further developments.

Primary Source

Joint Resolution

To authorize the use of United States Armed Forces pursuant to United Nations Security Council Resolution 678.

Whereas the Government of Iraq without provocation invaded and occupied the territory of Kuwait on August 2, 1990;

Whereas both the House of Representatives (in H.J. Res. 658 of the 101st Congress) and the Senate (in S. Con. Res. 147 of the 101st Congress) have condemned Iraq's invasion of Kuwait and declared their support for international action to reverse Iraq's aggression;

Whereas Iraq's conventional, chemical, biological, and nuclear weapons and ballistic missile programs and its demonstrated willingness to use weapons of mass destruction pose a grave threat to world peace;

Whereas the international community has demanded that Iraq withdraw unconditionally and immediately from Kuwait and that Kuwait's independence and legitimate government be restored;

Whereas the United Nations Security Council repeatedly affirmed the inherent right of individual or collective self-defense in response to the armed attack by Iraq against Kuwait in accordance with Article 51 of the United Nations Charter;

Whereas, in the absence of full compliance by Iraq with its resolutions, the United Nations Security Council in Resolution 678 has authorized member states of the United Nations to use all necessary means, after January 15, 1991, to uphold and implement all relevant Security Council resolutions and to restore international peace and security in the area; and

Whereas Iraq has persisted in its illegal occupation of, and brutal aggression against Kuwait: Now, therefore, be it

Resolved by the Senate and House of Representatives of the United States of America in Congress assembled,

[…]

Section 2. Authorization for Use of United States Armed Forces.

(a) Authorization.-The President is authorized, subject to subsection (b), to use United States Armed Forces pursuant to United Nations Security Council Resolution 678 (1990) in order to achieve implementation of Security Council Resolutions 660, 661, 662, 664, 665, 666, 667, 669, 670, 674, and 677.

(b) Requirement for Determination That Use of Military Force Is Necessary.-Before exercising the authority granted in subsection (a), the President shall make available to the Speaker of the House

of Representatives and the President pro tempore of the Senate his determination that-

(1) the United States has used all appropriate diplomatic and other peaceful means to obtain compliance by Iraq with the United Nations Security Council resolutions cited in subsection (a); and

(2) that those efforts have not been and would not be successful in obtaining such compliance.

[…]

Passed the House of Representatives January 12, 1991.

Source: U.S. Congress, House, *To Authorize the Use of United States Armed Forces Pursuant to United Nations Security Council Resolution 678*, H. J. RES. 77, 102nd Cong., 1st sess., January 13, 1991.

67. American and British Prisoners of War Held by Iraq, Interviews on Iraqi Television, January 20, 1991 [Excerpts]

Introduction

Until the beginning of ground warfare in late February 1991, most of the coalition casualties in the war against Iraq were fliers whose aircraft were shot down by Iraqi planes, missiles, or antiaircraft batteries. Some were killed, but others were taken prisoner by Iraqis. In an effort to strike a propaganda blow, on January 20, 1991, Iraqi television broadcast interviews with seven such American and British prisoners, excerpts of which were later rebroadcast on CNN. In the course of these interviews the prisoners identified themselves, described their missions and how they had been shot down, sent messages to their families, and in several cases stated that they did not support the war against Iraq. The airing of these interviews proved largely counterproductive for President Saddam Hussein of Iraq. The footage of injured men, some of whom had apparently been beaten in order to persuade them to condemn the war, suggested that Iraqi officials were deliberately mistreating prisoners of war in an effort to brainwash them. Hussein also threatened to house prisoners of war close to major Iraqi military targets in the coalition bombing campaign. This practice and the interviews themselves contravened the internationally recognized standards for the treatment of prisoners of war laid down in the Geneva Conventions. Coalition leaders and the United Nations (UN) immediately demanded that Hussein cease exhibiting prisoners of war on television and ensure that their treatment met the Geneva Conventions. Like Hussein's earlier holding of foreign civilians as hostages, his treatment of captured coalition servicemen damaged his image, suggesting that he was both erratic and unscrupulous.

Primary Source

Q. Would you tell us your rank and name?

A. Lieut. Col. Cliff [inaudible; believed to be Lieut. Col. Clifford M. Acree].

Q. What's your age?

A. Thirty-nine.

Q. What's your unit?

A. V.M.O. 2.

Q. You are the commander of that unit?

A. Yes, I am.

Q. Your mission?

A. Observation and reconnaissance.

Q. How your aircraft has been shot down?

A. I was flying a mission in southern Kuwait and was shot down by a surface-to-air missile.

Q. Do you have a message?

A. I would like to tell my wife and family that I'm alive and well.

Second Prisoner

Q. Would you tell us your rank and name?

A. My name is Lieut. Jeffrey Norton Zaun, United States Navy.

Q. Your age?

A. I am twenty-eight.

Q. Your unit?

A. I am from Attack Squadron 35 on the U.S.S. Saratoga, the Red Sea.

Q. Your type of aircraft?

A. I'm flying the A-6E Intruder attack aircraft.

Q. Your mission?

A. My mission was to attack the H3 airfield in southwestern Iraq.

Q. Alone?

A. I flew as part of a formation of four aircraft in order to commit this attack.

Q. What do you think, Lieutenant, about this aggression against Iraq?

A. I think our leaders and our people have wrongly attacked the peaceful people of Iraq.

Q. Do you have a message?

A. Yes, I would like to tell my mother and my father and my sister that I am well treated and that they should pray for peace.

Third Prisoner

Q. Would you tell us about your rank, name and nationality?

A. O.K. My name is Maurice Cocciolone. And I'm a captain from Italian Air Force.

Q. What is your age?

A. I am 30 years old.

Q. Tell us about your unit.

A. My unit is the 155 squadron that is now in the base of Emirates—United Arab Emirates.

Q. What was your mission?

A. To attack the forces of missiles in the southern region of Iraq.

Q. How you have been shot down?

A. We don't know exactly. It was right away fired from the ground. We don't know exactly what was it. There was firing from the ground from Iraq.

Q. What is your opinion about the war and the aggression against Iraq?

A. Well, the war is based on a bad reason . . . to solve a question, political question. War . . . a bad thing in front of you. So I think the best solution of peace . . . would be to find a political peaceful means of bringing this situation to the end.

Q. You have a message to send.

A. O.K. I think the only message would, like to tell my political leaders that to solve question by war is always mad. . . . And also, I have something to tell my parents, to my family. Don't be worried, I am pretty fine here. They are well taking care of me. Thank you.

Fourth Prisoner

Q. About your rank, name and nationality?

A. My name is Guy Hunter Jr. I'm a warrant officer. I am an American.

Q. Your age?

A. Forty-six.

Q. Your unit?

A. D.M.O. 2 in the Marine Corps.

Q. Your type of aircraft?

A. OV-10 Bronco.

Q. What was your mission?

A. Against Iraqi troops in southern Iraq.

Q. How have you been shot down?

A. I am not certain. We were flying, and all of a sudden, a left bang off the left wing, a large bang off the left wing, and the plane began to crash.

Q. What's your opinion of this aggression against Iraq?

A. I think this war is crazy and should never have happened. I condemn this aggression against peaceful Iraq.

Q. Do you have a message to send?

A. Yes, sir, I do. To my wife and children, I miss you very much. I'm in good hands and being treated well. To the children, please study hard in school.

Fifth Prisoner

Q. What is your rank, name and nationality?

A. My name is Flight Lieut. Adrian John Nichols. I'm British.

Q. Your age?

A. Twenty-seven.

Q. Your unit?

A. Fifteenth Squadron.

Q. Type of aircraft?

A. Tornado.

Q. What was your mission?

A. To attack an Iraqi airfield.

Q. How were you shot down?

A. I was shot down by an Iraqi system. I do not know what it was.

Q. What do you think of this war against Iraq?

A. I think this war should be stopped. I do not agree on this war with Iraq.

Q. Do you have a message?

A. Mom and Dad if you are listening, everything is O.K. here. Please pray for me. We shall be home soon.

Sixth Prisoner

Q. Tell us about your rank, name and nationality.

A. My name is Flight Lieut. Peters. I'm British.

Q. Your age?

A. Twenty-nine.

Source: "War in the Gulf: Questioning," *New York Times*, http://www.nytimes.com/1991/01/21/world/war-gulf-questioning-excerpts-interviews-with-men-identified-pilots-downed-over.html?pagewanted=1.

68. Iraqi President Saddam Hussein, "The Mother of All Battles" Speech, January 20, 1991

Introduction

Within days of the beginning of United Nations (UN) coalition air strikes against Iraqi targets, Saddam Hussein addressed the Iraqi people, urging them to rally to their country's defense. He declared that Iraq had not yet used its naval and air forces or its full missile strength against its attackers and that he was waiting until the best moment to do so. Iraqis were, he proclaimed, defending the cause of God, Islam, and the Arab world against "atheism, injustice, and tyranny." Hussein promised that ultimately Iraq would respond and would then win "the mother of all battles," opening the way to the destruction of Israel, the liberation of Lebanon and the Golan Heights from Israeli occupation, and the replacement of the existing pro-American regime in Saudi Arabia. He called on Arabs everywhere to support Iraq and target Western interests in a "holy war." Long on rhetoric and defiance and short on specifics, Hussein's speech was intended not just to rally his own people but also to rally the Arab world around him in his increasingly desperate plight.

Primary Source

In the name of God, the merciful, the compassionate. God hath purchased of the believers their persons and their goods, for theirs in return is the garden of Paradise. They fight in his cause, and slay and are slain—a promise binding on him in truth, through the law, the Gospel, and the Koran. And who is more faithful to his covenant than God? Then rejoice in the bargain which ye have concluded—that is the achievement supreme.

O glorious Iraqis, O holy warrior Iraqis, O Arabs, O believers wherever you are, we and our steadfastness are holding. Here is the great Iraqi people, your brothers and sons of your Arab nation and the great faithful part of the human family. We are all well. They are fighting with unparalleled heroism, unmatched except by the heroism of the believers who fight similar adversaries. And here is the infidel tyrant whose planes and missiles are falling out of the skies at the blows of the brave men. He is wondering how the Iraqis can confront his fading dreams with such determination and firmness.

After a while, he will begin to feel frustrated, and his defeat will be certain, God willing, when he has tangible proof that he [words indistinct]. We in Iraq will be the faithful and obedient servants of God, struggling for his sake to raise the banner of truth and justice, the banner of "God is Great." Accursed be the lowly.

At that time, the valiant Iraqi men and women will not allow the army of atheism, treachery, hypocrisy and [word indistinct] to realize their stupid hope that the war would only last a few days or weeks, as they imagined and declared. In the coming period, the response of Iraq will be on a larger scale, using all the means and potential that God has given us and which we have so far only used in part. Our ground forces have not entered the battle so far, and only a small part of our air force has been used.

"Divine Reinforcement"

The army's air force has not been used, nor has the navy. The weight and effect of our ready missile force has not yet been applied in full. The fact remains that the great divine reinforcement

is our source of power and effectiveness. When the war is fought in a comprehensive manner, using all resources and weapons, the scale of death and the number of dead will, God willing, rise among the ranks of atheism, injustice, and tyranny.

When they begin to die and when the message of the Iraqi soldiers reaches the farthest corner of the world, the unjust will die and the "God is Great" banner will flutter with great victory in the mother of all battles. Then the skies in the Arab homeland will appear in a new color and a sun of new hope will shine over them and over our nation and on all the good men whose bright lights will not be overcome by the darkness in the hearts of the infidels, the Zionists, and the treacherous, shameful rulers, such as the traitor Fahd.

Then the door will be wide open for the liberation of beloved Palestine, Lebanon, and the Golan. Then Jerusalem and the Dome of the Rock will be released from bondage. The Kaaba and the Tomb of the Prophet Mohammed, God's peace and blessings be upon him, will be liberated from occupation and God will bestow upon the poor and needy the things that others owed them, others who withheld from them what they owed them as God had justly ordained, which is a great deal.

"Carry Out Holy War"

Then [words indistinct], the good men, the holy warriors, and the faithful will know the truth of our promise to them that when the forces of infidelity attack the Iraqis, they will fight as they wished them to fight and perhaps in a better way, and that their promise is of faith and holy war. It remains for us to tell all Arabs, all the faithful strugglers, and all good supporters wherever they are: you have a duty to carry out holy war and struggle in order to target the assembly of evil, treason, and corruption everywhere.

You must also target their interests everywhere. It is a duty that is incumbent upon you, and that must necessarily correspond to the struggle of your brothers in Iraq. You will be part of the struggle of armed forces in your holy war and struggle, and part of the multitude of faith and the faithful. If the opposing multitude captures you, you will be prisoners in their hands, even if they refuse to admit this in their communiques and statements.

You will inevitably be released when the war ends, in accordance with international laws and agreements which will govern the release of prisoners of war. In this way you will have pleased God and honored, with your slogans and principles, the trust given to you.

God is great, God is great, God is great, and accursed be the lowly.

Source: Saddam Hussein, "The Mother of All Battles," Baghdad, Iraq, January 20, 1991, cited in Steven A. Yetiv, *The Persian Gulf Crisis* (Westport, CT: Greenwood, 1997), 176–177.

69. Soviet President Mikhail Gorbachev, "The Illogic of Escalation," Statement on the Persian Gulf Conflict, February 9, 1991

Introduction

Although it did not commit troops or funds to the coalition forces, under President Mikhail Gorbachev the Soviet Union supported the U.S. position on Iraq's invasion of Kuwait, voting for the 12 United Nations (UN) Security Council resolutions on the subject passed between August and November 1990. This in itself represented an enormous break with the past, when the Soviet Union had almost automatically opposed any American initiative. Even so, the Soviet president did not welcome the prospect of a major war in the Middle East, fearing especially that in the heat of war the coalition forces might easily expand their mission from the mere expulsion of Iraq from Kuwait to the overthrow of Saddam Hussein and the occupation of his country. Soviet leaders were also apprehensive that any ground war might be immensely destructive, involving the use of chemical, biological, or nuclear weapons of mass destruction. This was particularly the case since, in the case of full-scale hostilities, Hussein had vowed to employ such armaments against Israel, a measure that might inflame an already volatile situation and impel Israel to utilize the nuclear weapons it was widely believed to possess. Following three weeks of allied air strikes against Iraqi positions, Gorbachev therefore appealed to Hussein to reach a negotiated settlement with his opponents and announced that he intended to dispatch to Baghdad a personal representative, Yevgeny Primakov, who subsequently served as Russia's foreign minister and prime minister. Gorbachev hoped that Primakov would be able to open peace negotiations and also lay the groundwork for "a solid and equitable security system" in the region, one that would include a "settlement of the Arab-Israeli conflict and the Palestinian problem." Gorbachev also pledged that Iraq would "hold a worthy place in the postwar settlement." Gorbachev's efforts proved fruitless. The following day, Hussein made a radio address proclaiming his intention to continue resisting all pressure from the United States and its allies to yield over Kuwait. On February 15 the Iraqi Revolutionary Command Council announced that it would accept UN Security Council Resolution 660 of August 1990, calling for negotiations to bring about a withdrawal from Kuwait in exchange for an immediate cease-fire; the repeal of all the 11 following Security Council resolutions condemning Iraq's treatment of Kuwait and imposing sanctions upon Iraq; the withdrawal of all foreign armaments and forces that had entered the Persian Gulf region since August 2, 1990, including those made available to Israel; an Arab-Israeli peace settlement involving Israeli withdrawal from all the territories it had occupied; and the guarantee of Iraq's historic rights, including those within Kuwait. Iraq should also receive financial compensation for all damage it had suffered during the previous months, and its foreign debts would be written off. Such a settlement, which would have effectively given Iraq all it had earlier sought to achieve, was unlikely to be acceptable to the coalition. The same day Bush bluntly rejected these proposals, terming them "a cruel hoax" and stating that unconditional Iraqi withdrawal from Kuwait and the acceptance of all the Security Council resolutions were nonnegotiable prerequisites of any peace settlement.

Primary Source

Statement by the President of the Union of Soviet Socialist Republics concerning the developments in the Persian Gulf

February 9, 1991

Events in the Persian Gulf region are taking an increasingly disturbing and dramatic turn. The largest war in recent decades is gaining momentum. The number of casualties is increasing, *inter alia* among the peaceful population. The military actions have already caused enormous material damage. Entire countries—first Kuwait, then Iraq, and next, perhaps, others as well—are threatened with catastrophic destruction. The discharge of a vast quantity of oil into the Persian Gulf may develop into an extremely serious environmental disaster.

The Soviet leadership confirms once again its principled adherence to the Security Council resolutions which reflect the will of the majority of countries And the hopes of peoples for a new international order which will exclude aggression and encroachment upon other countries' territory and natural resources.

However, the logic of the military operations and the nature of the military actions create a risk that the mandate defined in these resolutions may be exceeded.

The provocative attempts to enlarge the scope of the war by involving Israel and other States in it, thus giving the armed conflict yet another destructive dimension, the Arab-Israeli one, are also extremely dangerous.

To judge from certain statements that have been made at a political level and by influential mass media, an attempt is under way to accustom people on both sides of the conflict to the idea that the use of weapons of mass destruction is possible and permissible. If this happened, the whole of world politics and the entire world community would be shaken to their foundations.

The course this war has taken is a matter of great concern to the Soviet people and to the country's leadership, the more so in that it is raging close to the border of the Soviet Union.

A sense of historical responsibility, common sense and humanity all lead to the same conclusion—that everything possible should be done to bring about a political settlement on the basis of the Security Council resolutions. At this critical juncture, I make a public and urgent appeal to the president of Iraq to weigh once again what is at stake for his country, and to demonstrate the realism which would make it possible to move towards a reliable and just peaceful settlement. I am sending my personal representative to Baghdad immediately for a meeting with President Hussein.

It is our hope that in this way we shall be able, together with the Arab and other Muslim States, with the countries of Europe and Asia, and above all with the United States of America with all the permanent members of the Security Council, not only to help put an end to the state of war as soon as possible but also to pave the way for a strong and equitable system of security in this region that is so vital to the entire world, one which will of course include the settlement of the Arab-Israeli conflict and of the problem of Palestine—with the decisive role in the process being played primarily by the states of the region. A fitting place in the post-war order must be assigned to Iraq, whose people cannot be held responsible for what has happened, but rather deserve our sympathy, compassion and support.

I repeat: In order to effect a breakthrough to peace in the Near and Middle East, the flames of war in the Gulf must be extinguished as soon as possible. At the present juncture, that is what is most important.

Source: United Nations Security Council Official Records, S/22215, February 11, 1991.

70. Soviet Peace Proposal, February 22, 1991

Introduction

On February 22, 1991, U.S. president George H. W. Bush announced a final deadline of noon the following day for unconditional Iraqi withdrawal from Kuwait. He warned that should Iraq fail to remove all its troops from Kuwait by this hour, ground warfare would begin. Still seeking to avert full-scale hostilities, Soviet foreign minister Aleksandr Bessmertnykh and Tariq Aziz, his Iraqi counterpart, were at that time engaged in talks in Moscow. That same day Soviet spokesman Vitaly N. Ignatenko announced, on behalf of President Mikhail Gorbachev, a final peace proposal. This envisaged that Iraqi forces would withdraw from Kuwait "immediately and unconditionally," an operation that would be completed within 21 days. In return, an immediate military cease-fire would be imposed, and all United Nations (UN) sanctions on Iraq would be lifted. The last-ditch proposal represented a major improvement on the terms that Iraq had offered one week earlier, but at this juncture U.S. and coalition leaders found it unacceptable. From Moscow, Aziz issued a statement endorsing this

proposal. He also denied allegations by the U.S. government that in preparation for a possible abandonment of Kuwait, Iraqi forces had instituted scorched-earth policies, intended to destroy the Kuwaiti oil fields and refineries while releasing massive quantities of oil into the Persian Gulf. U.S. president George H. W. Bush quickly rejected this proposal, demanding instead that Iraqi forces begin withdrawing from Kuwait no later than noon on February 23, 1991, and complete their withdrawal within one week. Their failure to do so triggered the beginning of ground hostilities that evening. Although Aziz endorsed the Soviet proposal, his credibility was limited, since even his Soviet interlocutors were by no means certain whether he genuinely spoke for President Saddam Hussein of Iraq. One month later, on March 24, 1991, Hussein demoted Aziz to deputy prime minister, an indication that he felt Aziz had performed poorly as foreign minister.

Primary Source

1. Iraq agrees to carry out Resolution 660 of the United Nations Security Council, that is, to withdraw its forces immediately and unconditionally from Kuwait to positions they occupied on Aug. 1, 1990.

2. The troop withdrawal will start the day after a cease-fire encompassing all military operations on land, sea and in the air.

3. The troop withdrawal will be completed within 21 days, including a pullout from Kuwait City within the first 4 days.

4. Once the withdrawal has been completed, all U.N. Security Council resolutions will no longer be valid because the reasons for them will have been removed.

5. All prisoners of war will be freed and repatriated within three days after a cease-fire and the end of military operations.

6. Control and monitoring of the cease-fire and withdrawal of troops will be carried out by observers or peacekeeping forces as determined by the Security Council.

Source: U.S. Department of State, *United States Policy in the Middle East: September 1956–June 1957* (Washington, DC: U.S. Government Printing Office, 1957), 81–85.

71. Iraqi Order to Withdraw from Kuwait, February 26, 1991

Introduction

The coalition invasion of Kuwait quickly turned into a rout of Iraqi forces. Two days after ground warfare against Iraqi forces in Kuwait began, Iraq's government publicly ordered its forces to withdraw "to the positions in which they were before the 1st of August 1990." Iraq clearly now sought to end hostilities as soon as possible. In this statement, Iraq specifically sought the good offices of Soviet president Mikhail Gorbachev in negotiating a cease-fire with the United Nations (UN). Iraq still clearly hoped that the Soviet peace proposals drafted three days earlier, which Iraq had been willing to accept and to which this statement referred, might become the basis of a peace settlement. Iraq specifically stated that it would accept UN Security Council Resolution 660 of August 2, 1990, calling for Iraq's withdrawal from Kuwait, but made no mention of the numerous other resolutions passed since that date. The text of this order, apparently issued by Iraqi president Saddam Hussein, was read over Baghdad Radio by an official government spokesman. Defiant to the last, Hussein proclaimed that if attacked while retreating, his forces would continue to "fight with force and courage" and that they had "completed their duty of jihad." In his usual grandiloquent rhetoric, he stated that they had "been engaged in an epic, valiant battle which will be recorded by history in letters of light."

Primary Source

In the name of God, the almighty, the compassionate,

Our armed forces have completed their duty of jihad, of rejecting compliance with the logic of evil, force and aggression. They have been engaged in an epic, valiant battle which will be recorded by history in letters of light.

The leadership had stressed its acceptance to withdrawal in accordance with UN Security Council Resolution 660 when it agreed to the Soviet peace proposal. On this basis, and in compliance with this decision, orders were issued to the armed forces for an organized withdrawal to the positions in which they were before the 1st of August 1990.

This is regarded as a practical compliance with Resolution 660.

The spokesman emphasized that our forces, which have proved their fighting and steadfastness ability, will confront any attempt to attack them while implementing the withdrawal order.

They will fight with force and courage to make their withdrawal organized and honorable.

The Iraqi New[s] Agency has learned that the Foreign Minister [Tariq Aziz] informed the Soviet ambassador of this decision, which constitutes a compliance with the UN Security Council's resolution 660. The Foreign Minister asked that a message be conveyed from leader President Saddam Hussein and the Revolutionary Command Council to President Gorbachev requesting him to exert efforts at the UN Security Council to achieve a cease-fire and put an end to the criminal behavior of the United States and its allies and collaborators.

Source: "Orders for a Withdrawal," *Washington Post*, February 26, 1991, A6.

72. Press Secretary Marlin Fitzwater, Statement on the Order for an Iraqi Withdrawal from Kuwait, February 25, 1991

Introduction

Late on February 25, 1991, the United States responded to Iraq's order that all its forces should withdraw from Kuwait. On behalf of U.S. president George H. W. Bush, White House spokesman Marlin Fitzwater indicated that simple Iraqi withdrawal from Kuwait would not suffice to win a cease-fire. Reminding his audience that President Saddam Hussein had repeatedly "broken promises" and that during the Iran-Iraq War his tanks had once pretended to surrender only to then turn and fight, Fitzwater demanded that Hussein himself must "personally and publicly" agree to the terms of the American peace proposal announced on February 22. This included acceptance of all the resolutions that the United Nations (UN) Security Council had passed on Iraq, including those whereby Iraq renounced all claims to Kuwait and promised to provide full compensation to Kuwait and others affected by the war. Until Hussein did so, the coalition forces would continue to fight the retreating Iraqis.

Primary Source

We continue to prosecute the war. We have heard no reason to change that. And because there is a war on, our first concern must be the safety and security of United States and coalition forces. We don't know whether this most recent claim about Iraqi withdrawal is genuine. We have no evidence to suggest the Iraqi army is withdrawing. In fact, Iraqi units are continuing to fight. Moreover, we remember when Saddam Hussein's tanks pretended to surrender at Khafji, only to turn and fire. We remember the Scud attacks today, and Saddam's many broken promises of the past. There are at least an additional 22 dead Americans tonight who offer silent testimony to the intentions of Saddam Hussein. The statement out of Baghdad today says that Saddam Hussein's forces will fight their way out while retreating. We will not attack unarmed soldiers in retreat. But we will consider retreating combat units as a movement of war. The only way Saddam Hussein can persuade the coalition of the seriousness of his intentions would be for him personally and publicly to agree to the terms of the proposal we issued on February 22. And because the announcement from Baghdad referred to the Soviet initiative, he must personally and publicly accept explicitly all relevant U.N. Security Council resolutions, including especially U.N. Security Council Resolution 662, which calls for Iraqi recision of its purported annexation of Kuwait, and U.N. Security Council Resolution 674 which calls for Iraqi compensation to Kuwait and others. That's the end of the statement. I might just add that the President met with his national security advisers for approximately an hour and 15 minutes this evening to consider this matter, and the President has returned to his Residence.

Source: George H. W. Bush, *Public Papers of the Presidents of the United States: George Bush, 1991,* Book 1 (Washington, DC: U.S. Government Printing Office, 1992), 175.

73. President George H. W. Bush, Address to the Nation on the Suspension of Allied Offensive Combat Operations in the Persian Gulf, February 27, 1991

Introduction

United Nations (UN) coalition forces proved more successful than almost anyone had anticipated in driving Iraqi troops out of Kuwait. General Colin Powell, chairman of the U.S. Joint Chiefs of Staff (JCS), had initially feared that American forces might experience up to 30,000 casualties. In fact, 304 American servicemen died in the operation. The ground campaign quickly became a rout of the defeated Iraqi forces, who experienced heavy casualties as they retreated along Highway 80, the coastal road from Kuwait to Basra, that became known as the "Highway of Death." Bush and his advisers resisted the temptation to continue hostilities into Iraq and overthrow Saddam Hussein, a course of action that they feared might lose the coalition the support of its Arab members and leave the United States embroiled in a lengthy and difficult occupation of a potentially unstable nation. On February 27 Bush declared that hostilities would come to an end at midnight, exactly 100 hours after they had begun. The cease-fire's continuation would remain dependent upon Iraq's release of all coalition prisoners, hostages, and Kuwaiti detainees; its compliance with all relevant UN Security Council resolutions; and the suspension of all Iraqi hostilities, including the launching of Scud missiles against third countries. Bush's speech implied that the United States would welcome Saddam Hussein's overthrow or removal by his own people and would be willing to cooperate with an Iraqi government that was not dominated by Hussein and his supporters. Despite these hopes, Hussein successfully suppressed subsequent challenges to his rule and would remain in power in Iraq for another 12 years.

Primary Source

Kuwait is liberated. Iraq's army is defeated. Our military objectives are met. Kuwait is once more in the hands of Kuwaitis, in control of their own destiny. We share in their joy, a joy tempered only by our compassion for their ordeal.

Tonight the Kuwaiti flag once again flies above the capital of a free and sovereign nation. And the American flag flies above our Embassy.

Seven months ago, America and the world drew a line in the sand. We declared that the aggression against Kuwait would not stand. And tonight, America and the world have kept their word.

This is not a time of euphoria, certainly not a time to gloat. But it is a time of pride: pride in our troops; pride in the friends who stood with us in the crisis; pride in our nation and the people whose strength and resolve made victory quick, decisive, and just. And soon we will open wide our arms to welcome back home to America our magnificent fighting forces.

No one country can claim this victory as its own. It was not only a victory for Kuwait but a victory for all the coalition partners. This is a victory for the United Nations, for all mankind, for the rule of law, and for what is right.

After consulting with Secretary of Defense Cheney, the Chairman of the Joint Chiefs of Staff, General Powell, and our coalition partners, I am pleased to announce that at midnight tonight eastern standard time, exactly 100 hours since ground operations commenced and 6 weeks since the start of Desert Storm, all United States and coalition forces will suspend offensive combat operations. It is up to Iraq whether this suspension on the part of the coalition becomes a permanent cease-fire.

Coalition political and military terms for a formal cease-fire include the following requirements: Iraq must release immediately all coalition prisoners of war, third country nationals, and the remains of all who have fallen.

Iraq must release all Kuwaiti detainees. Iraq also must inform Kuwaiti authorities of the location and nature of all land and sea mines. Iraq must comply fully with all relevant United Nations Security Council resolutions. This includes a rescinding of Iraq's August decision to annex Kuwait and acceptance in principle of Iraq's responsibility to pay compensation for the loss, damage, and injury its aggression has caused.

The coalition calls upon the Iraqi Government to designate military commanders to meet within 48 hours with their coalition counterparts at a place in the theater of operations to be specified to arrange for military aspects of the cease-fire. Further, I have asked Secretary of State Baker to request that the United Nations Security Council meet to formulate the necessary arrangements for this war to be ended.

This suspension of offensive combat operations is contingent upon Iraq's not firing upon any coalition forces and not launching Scud missiles against any other country. If Iraq violates these terms, coalition forces will be free to resume military operations. At every opportunity, I have said to the people of Iraq that our quarrel was not with them but instead with their leadership and, above all, with Saddam Hussein. This remains the case. You, the people of Iraq, are not our enemy. We do not seek your destruction. We have treated your POWs with kindness. Coalition forces fought this war only as a last resort and look forward to the day when Iraq is led by people prepared to live in peace with their neighbors.

We must now begin to look beyond victory and war. We must meet the challenge of securing the peace. In the future, as before, we will consult with our coalition partners. We've already done a good deal of thinking and planning for the postwar period, and Secretary Baker has already begun to consult with our coalition partners on the region's challenges. There can be, and will be, no solely American answer to all these challenges. But we can assist and support the countries of the region and be a catalyst for peace. In this spirit, Secretary Baker will go to the region next week to begin a new round of consultations.

This war is now behind us. Ahead of us is the difficult task of securing a potentially historic peace. Tonight though, let us be proud of what we have accomplished. Let us give thanks to those who risked their lives. Let us never forget those who gave their lives. May God bless our valiant military forces and their families, and let us all remember them in our prayers.

Good night, and may God bless the United States of America.

> **Source:** George H. W. Bush, *Public Papers of the Presidents of the United States: George Bush, 1991*, Book 1 (Washington, DC: U.S. Government Printing Office, 1992), 187–188.

74. Iraqi Letters of Capitulation to the United Nations, February 27, 1991

Introduction

With coalition attacks on Iraqi forces continuing, the Iraqi Army in full retreat from Kuwait, and coalition troops entering Iraqi territory, Iraq's leadership was increasingly desperate to negotiate a cease-fire that might leave them still in control of their own country. On February 27, 1991, two days after President George H. W. Bush had rejected Iraq's previous cease-fire offer, Tariq Aziz, Iraq's foreign minister, handed member states of the United Nations (UN) letters expressing Iraq's willingness to comply not just with Security Council Resolution 660, ordering Iraq's withdrawal from Kuwait, but also with Resolutions 662 and 674, those highlighted in

the White House's earlier statement. Under their terms, Iraq would renounce all claims to Kuwait and compensate Kuwait and others for damage inflicted during the crisis. Acceptance of the two latter resolutions was, however, made conditional upon the lifting of the Security Council resolutions imposing economic and military sanctions on Iraq, something that would later become the subject of bitter contention between Iraq and the international community. Iraq also agreed to release all prisoners of war as soon as possible after the cease-fire. In a rather unorthodox procedure, indicative of just how bad Iraq's relations with the UN had become, Aziz asked UN member states to inform Security Council members of this offer and to regard it as an official document of the Security Council.

Primary Source

I have the honor to inform you officially that the Government of Iraq agrees to comply fully with United Nations Security Council resolution 660 and all other U.N. Security Council resolutions.

You are kindly requested to inform the Security Council members and to circulate this letter as an official document of the Security Council.

Signed, Tariq Aziz. The Earlier Letter

I have the honor to notify you that the Iraqi Government reaffirms its agreement to comply fully with Security Council Resolution 660 (1990). The Iraqi armed forces have started to withdraw to the positions which they were in prior to Aug. 1, 1990. It is hoped that the withdrawal will be fully completed in the next few hours, notwithstanding the continued attacks by American and other forces on the Iraqi armed forces during the withdrawal process.

I would like to inform you further that the Iraqi Government agrees to comply with Resolutions 662 (1990) and 674 (1990) if the Security Council adopts a resolution providing for an immediate cease-fire and the cessation of all military operations on land, at sea and in the air and if it is deemed that the bases on which Security Council Resolutions 661 (1990), 665 (1990) and 670 (1990) were adopted no longer exist and that those resolutions consequently are no longer in effect.

The Iraqi Government also affirms its full readiness to release all the prisoners of war immediately after the cease-fire and return them to their home countries within a very short period of time in accordance with the Third Geneva Convention of 1949, under the auspices of the International Committee of the Red Cross.

I should be grateful if you would kindly bring this letter immediately to the attention of the Security Council and have it circulated as a document of the Security Council.

Signed, Tariq Aziz.

Source: United Nations Security Council Official Records, S/22273 and S/22275. February 27, 1991.

75. Cease-Fire Order to Iraqi Troops, February 28, 1991

Introduction

On February 27, 1991, U.S. president George H. W. Bush announced the suspension of coalition combat operations against Iraq, provided that Iraqi troops ceased hostilities and conditional on Iraq's release of all prisoners of war and Kuwaiti nationals, acceptance of all United Nations (UN) Security Council resolutions on Kuwait, and cooperation in identifying land and sea mines in Kuwait. The following day, Iraq's military authorities broadcast over Baghdad Radio a cease-fire order to all Iraqi troops. They proclaimed that Bush had suspended hostilities because he had been impressed by the valor with which their troops had fought around Basra and in other parts of Iraq after withdrawing from Kuwait and feared that if fighting continued, American forces would suffer heavy losses. Even so, the broadcast welcomed the cease-fire, stating that it would preserve the lives of Iraqi soldiers, and ordered Iraqi "units at the battlefront not to open fire."

Primary Source

The aggressors imagined that through the Iraqi command decision to withdraw from Kuwait they were able to put our armed forces in a position that is contrary to the military and manly values for which the men of the mother of battles are reputed in this great showdown.

Many battles occurred in Basra district and other places in our great Iraq's territories after the withdrawal.

Due to faith in our capability that is able to teach the enemy forces lessons that will make them worried militarily and politically if the war continued, Bush announced his decision early this morning.

We are happy for the halt in fighting, which will save the blood of our sons and the safety of our people after God made them victorious by faith against their evil enemies and save the blood of the sons of humanity who suffered due to Bush and his traitorous agents.

Therefore, orders were issued to all our units at the battlefront not to open fire. God is great.

Source: "Transcript of Baghdad's Cease-Fire Order," *New York Times*, http://www.nytimes.com/1991/03/01/world/after-the-war-iraqi-statement-transcript-of-baghdad-s-cease-fire-order.html?page wanted=1.

76. President George H. W. Bush, Remarks to the American Legislative Exchange Council, March 1, 1991, and News Conference on the Persian Gulf Conflict, March 1, 1991 [Excerpts]

Introduction

Two days after he declared a cease-fire of ground hostilities against Iraq, a still euphoric President George H. W. Bush remarked in an impromptu aside to a group visiting the White House that "by God, we've kicked the Vietnam syndrome once and for all." The casual off-the-cuff comment was an indication of how deeply the experience of the Vietnam War had affected American politicians and military men, leading them to believe that the American people would not accept heavy casualties in costly foreign military interventions and therefore making them extremely cautious in deploying forces overseas. Bush's gleeful celebration of victory against Iraq suggested that he anticipated that his country would in the future show less restraint in utilizing its military abroad, although his action in ending the fighting expeditiously, before American troops were forced to engage in extensive combat beyond Kuwait, might have suggested that he still considered a modicum of prudence advisable. Later that day in a press conference on the recent war, Bush expanded on what he envisaged as the future U.S. agenda in the Middle East and, more broadly, around the world. Asked specifically by a journalist whether he anticipated the more extensive use of American military forces in international conflicts, Bush replied that he believed that since the Persian Gulf War had given his country "reestablished credibility," such deployments were unlikely to be necessary in the near future. He also stated that while he intended to maintain a U.S. military presence in the Middle East, he hoped that U.S. ground forces would not "be permanently stationed in the Gulf." Bush warned that he did not intend to provide any American economic assistance for Iraq's reconstruction and suggested that Iraq should utilize its own substantial oil revenues for that purpose. Whether he would maintain this position should Saddam Hussein be deposed from power was left somewhat unclear. Turning to one of the region's most intractable problems, the president did express the hope that in the aftermath of the Persian Gulf War, the United States might be able to move decisively to bring about a lasting settlement of the long-standing Arab-Israeli dispute.

Primary Source

[. . .]

I know you share this wonderful feeling that I have of joy in my heart. But it is overwhelmed by the gratitude I feel—not just to the troops overseas but to those who have assisted the United States of America, like our Secretary of Defense, like our Chairman of our

Joint Chiefs, and so many other unsung heroes—who have made all this possible. It's a proud day for America. And, by God, we've kicked the Vietnam syndrome once and for all. . . .

The President's News Conference March 1, 1991

The President. In the hours since we suspended military operations in the Kuwaiti theater of war, considerable progress has been made in moving towards a cease-fire and postwar planning. As our forces moved into Kuwait City and as the faces of these jubilant Kuwaiti citizens have warmed our hearts, the coalition leaders started the arduous task of addressing the next stages of the Persian Gulf situation.

[. . .]

In the meantime, we are focused on the many diplomatic tasks associated with ending this conflict. General Khalid, General Schwarzkopf, and other coalition military leaders of our forces in the Gulf will meet with representatives of Iraq tomorrow afternoon, March 2d, in the theater of operations to discuss the return of POW's and other military matters related to the ceasefire. We will not discuss the location of the meeting for obvious security reasons. But this is an important step in securing the victory that our forces have achieved.

Work is proceeding in New York at the United Nations on the political aspects of ending the war. We've welcomed here in Washington this week the envoys of several of our close friends and allies. And shortly, Secretary Baker will be leaving for a new round of consultations that I am confident will advance planning for the war's aftermath. Again and as I said Wednesday evening, the true challenge before us will be securing the peace. . . .

Helen [Helen Thomas, United Press International]? Q. Mr. President, you've always said that you were not targeting Saddam under the U.N. mandate and that the coalition has no claim on Iraqi territory. Is that still the case?

The President. We are not targeting Saddam, and we have no claim on Iraqi territory.

Q. Well, will you try to hunt him down for any kind of war crimes trial?

The President. No, I'm not going to say that. Not hunt him down, but nobody can be absolved from the responsibilities under international law on the war crimes aspect of that.

Q. Mr. President, along that line, the reports of atrocities in Kuwait apparently go far beyond the horror stories that you've already described in recent weeks. Who will be held accountable for those,

perhaps, other than Saddam? And do you think that the allied forces will hold any part of southern Iraq as a security zone for any time?

The President. I think on the first question, the first part, I agree that the reports are just sickening that are coming out of Kuwait. We have been concerned about it. Early on in all of this I expressed the concerns that I felt. But I think we'll just have to wait and see because I think the persons that actually perpetrated the tortures and the insidious crimes will be the ones that are held responsible. Now, how you go about finding them—but I think back to the end of World War II. That process took a long time to evolve, but justice was done. I can't say it was complete, can't say everybody that committed a war crime was tried. But it's a very complicated process. But the answer is, the people that did it. Now, a lot of them obviously took off and fled out of Kuwait. But some of the Kuwaitis know who they were, so we'll have to wait and see on that one.

And what was the second part, Terry [Terence Hunt, Associated Press]?

Q. The second part was about a security zone. You've had all this destruction. Is there any thought of establishing a security zone to protect—

The President. On the question of security zone and arrangements out there, these matters will be discussed when Jim Baker is out there with the coalition partners. I don't believe they will be discussed at the military meeting tomorrow.

[. . .]

Q. I know you've heard those reports from the *Le Monde* newspaper. Secretary of State Baker says he knows nothing about the fact that the Algerians have worked out a deal with Saddam that he could come there for political asylum. First of all, have you heard anything about those reports? And if not, do you agree with your Chief of Staff, Mr. Sununu, that it's an unstable situation for him and that you think he might be overthrown?

The President. John [John Cochran, NBC News], I think that subsequent to your discussion with Secretary Baker, the Algerians denied this. I'm seeing General Scowcroft confirm that, that they have denied that. We don't really know about the stability inside. There are rumors, but that—I think it's early. In my own view I've always said that it would be—that the Iraqi people should put him aside, and that would facilitate the resolution of all these problems that exist and certainly would facilitate the acceptance of Iraq back into the family of peace-loving nations.

[. . .]

Q. Mr. President, what can King Hussein do to get himself out of the U.S. doghouse? [Laughter] And if it turns out Jordan was violating the arms embargo against Iraq, can he do so?

The President. I think you know we have had differences with Jordan, and it's going to take some time. I think the Jordanians have to sort out their internal problems, the way they look at this matter. The Jordanians I don't believe have even received the truth as to what has happened to the Iraqi armed forces. From just watching from afar, it seems to me that they have been denied the truth. And the truth is we have destroyed Iraq's armor. And I see people dancing around in the streets still talking about a victory or still saying that we've sued for peace because we were done in by Saddam. So, first thing that has to happen in Jordan, the truth has to hit the streets. And then it will be time to discuss future arrangements. We have no lasting pique with Jordan. As everybody knows, we've had very pleasant relationships with Jordan in the past. But I have tried to be very frank with His Majesty the King and with the Government of Jordan pointing out the certain sense of disappointment that all Americans feel that they moved that close to Saddam Hussein. But I think it's just going to take time, and I can't say how much. But clearly, we do not want to see a destabilized Jordan. I have no personal animosity towards His Majesty the King. So, we'll just have to wait and see.

Q. Sir, a lot of Americans have the impression that Germany and Japan didn't carry their weight in the Persian Gulf crisis. And they find Germany's involvement in the Iraqi chemical weapons and Scud missile operations particularly odious. What can the Germans and the Japanese do to rehabilitate themselves in American public opinion?

The President. Fulfill the commitments that they already have made. I'm told that the Germans have already come in with a substantial—close to 50 percent of their commitment. And I am also told that the Japanese Diet yesterday approved this $9 billion payment. And so, I would simply say Japan and Germany have constitutional constraints—the American people may or may not understand that—constraints that kept them from participating on the ground in the coalition. But I have tried to make clear to the American people that both of them have stepped up and have offered to bear their share of responsibility by putting up substantial amounts of money.

Q. Mr. President, you have mentioned in your speeches third country nationals held by the Iraqis. There have been reports in the last few days of them taking hostages, Kuwaiti hostages, on the way out. May I ask about what seemed to be before a rather optimistic statement by you, why you think they're going to come to the table tomorrow and do the right thing?

The President. Well, the question of third party nationals or Kuwaiti detainees will be presented both at the military meeting on the border, and it is being debated and presented as one of the demands in our Security Council resolution. I'm not sure that that matter will be resolved tomorrow, that part of it. But I hope that we see an undertaking by the Government of Iraq to do that which they should do, and that is to give full accounting and immediate repatriation of these people. I don't know whether they'll do it or not, but there will be, there must be, a full accounting. So we are going to be watching very carefully to see if they are responsive to these concerns.

Q. In the resolution that you are pushing there's a continued push for economic sanctions, continued mention of war reparations. Is that what you're holding over Saddam Hussein's head as leverage for compliance on the prisoners?

The President. No. We just want compliance with the resolutions and compliance with human decency, that is, to release those prisoners and release these that have been kidnapped. And of course, we want the perpetrators brought to justice.

[. . .]

Q. . . . Mr. President, you've talked a great deal throughout these many months and weeks about, at the appropriate time, what you want to see happen in a postwar Middle East. I'd like to ask you two questions. First of all, provided Saddam Hussein is toppled, ousted, and/or leaves—the question—what is your attitude about the U.S. helping to rebuild Iraq? And secondly, how do you feel now about a peace conference for the Middle East and to deal with these larger Arab-Israeli questions that you said would be among the issues on the table once this war was over?

The President. Well, on the second one of the peace conference or the whole concept of trying to bring peace to the rest of the Middle East—and I would say it relates to the Palestinian question; it relates to the Lebanese question. Clearly, it relates to how Iraq is brought back into the family of nations. All of those things are going to be discussed now with our coalition partners by Jim Baker. We are also discussing it, as I said, with those emissaries that have been here.

For example, the Germans don't have forces, but they have some very good ideas on how all of these matters can be brought forward. I want to repeat my determination to have the United States play a very useful role now in the whole question of peace in the Middle East, and that includes all three of these categories. And whether it proves to be a peace conference or some bolder new idea, time will tell. But we are beginning very serious consultations on this.

In terms of rebuilding Iraq, my view is this: Iraq, had they been led differently, is basically a wealthy country. They are a significant oil producer. They get enormous income. But under Saddam Hussein and this Revolutionary Council, they have elected to put a tremendous amount of their treasure into arms. And they've threatened their neighbors. And now they invaded—up to now had invaded a neighbor.

And so, Iraq has a big reconstruction job to do. But I'll be honest with you: At this point I don't want to see one single dime of the United States taxpayers' money go into the reconstruction of Iraq.

Now, you want to talk about helping a child, you want to talk about helping disease, something of that nature, of course, the United States will step up and do that which we have always done—lay aside the politics and help the health-care requirements or help children especially. But not reconstruction—they must work these things out without any help from the American taxpayer.

Q. If I may follow, Mr. President, you've said your argument has never been with the Iraqi people.

The President. Right.

Q. That the United States did not seek the destruction of Iraq.

The President. Exactly.

Q. If Saddam Hussein is gone and the Iraqi people appear to need help because of this crisis in leadership that you spoke about, why not, if not contributing—

The President. Well, we'll give a little free advice. [Laughter] And the advice will be: Use this enormous oil resource that you have, further develop your oil resource and other natural resources, live peacefully, and use that enormous money to reconstruct and do the very questions you're asking about. And in addition to that, pay off these people that you have so badly damaged. They've got a big role ahead of them there. That's the way I look at it.

Q. Mr. President, today you declared an end to the Vietnam syndrome and, of course, we've heard you talk a lot about the new world order. Can you tell us, do you envision a new era now of using U.S. military forces around the world for different conflicts that arise?

The President. No, I think because of what has happened, we won't have to use U.S. forces around the world. I think when we say something that is objectively correct, like don't take over a neighbor or you're going to bear some responsibility, people are going to listen because I think out of all this will be a newfound—put it this way, a reestablished credibility for the United States of America. So, I look at the opposite. I say that what our troops have done over there will not only enhance the peace but reduce the risk that their successors have to go into battle someplace.

Q. But surely, you don't mean that you would be reluctant to do this again.

The President. Do what again?

Q. Send troops if you thought you needed to.

The President. I think the United States is always going to live up to its security requirements.

Q. Sir, I'm struck by—I know these are serious topics, but I'm struck by how somber you feel—you seem, at least here. And I was wondering, aren't these great days? Is this the highlight of your life? [Laughter] How does this compare to being swept out of the ocean a couple of years back?

The President. You know, to be very honest with you, I haven't yet felt this wonderfully euphoric feeling that many of the American people feel. And I'm beginning to. I feel much better about it today than I did yesterday. But I think it's that I want to see an end. You mentioned World War II; there was a definitive end to that conflict. And now we have Saddam Hussein still there, the man that wreaked this havoc upon his neighbors. We have our prisoners still held. We have people unaccounted for. So, I'm beginning to feel that the joy that Americans all feel now is proper. It has to do with a new, wonderful sense of patriotism that stems from pride in the men and women that went over there. And no question about it, the country's solid. There isn't any anti-war movement out there. There is pride in these forces—handful of voices, but can't hear them. And so, I think what happened, the minute we said there will be no more shooting—thousands, hundreds of thousands of families and friends that said, my kids are going to be safe. And I think I was focusing a little more on what's left to be done. But it is contagious. When I walk out of that White House, or when I get phone calls in there from our kids in different States, or when I talk to whoever it is that have just come from meetings—the Vice President's been out around the country, and Barbara's been out around the country, and others here—I sense that there is something noble and majestic about patriotism in this country now. It's there. And so I'll get there, but I just need a little more time to sort out in my mind how I can say to the American people it's over finally—the last "t" is crossed, the last "i" is dotted.

Q. Sir, does that mean that this episode won't be over for you until Saddam Hussein is out of—

The President. No, because I'm getting there. And I'm not gloomy about it. I'm elated. But I just want to finish my job, my part of the job. And the troops have finished their part, in my view. They've done their job. They did it in 100 hours, those ground forces. And the Air Force was superb. And that's what the families sense.

That's what the American people sense. But I still have a little bit of an unfinished agenda.

[...]

Q. Going into the security talks with the countries of the Middle East, are you willing to consider a long-term presence of American troops as a peace-keeping force, or do you think that would be better handled by Arab nations?

The President. I think it would be better handled by Arab nations. There will be a United States presence. There was before this. But there will be—one of the things that Secretary Baker is talking about is all these different security arrangements. Perhaps there will be a role for a U.N. force; perhaps there will be a role for an all-Arab force. Certainly there will be some security role for the United States. But I would repeat here I do not want to send out the impression that U.S. troops will be permanently stationed in the Gulf. I want them back. So, we're still working—we're just beginning to work out these security arrangements, but a part of it will not be a continued presence of substantial quantities of U.S. troops. I'd like to see them all out of there as soon as possible. But there's some shorter-run security problems that I don't want to underestimate.

[...]

Q. Mr. President, clearly, the United States and you have gained a great deal of personal approval and stronger approval in the period of this—in winning the war and in how you have handled this. Do you feel any urgency to use both the heightened respect for the United States and heightened approval of how you've acted in this crisis to press urgently in the Middle East? Or are you more prone to take the prudent and cautious approach and do a lot of consulting and sort of build that approach the way you did leading up to this conflict?

The President. I leave out the polling figures or the renewed—certainly individually, or what I think is a new respect for the U.S.'s credibility. I want to move fast and I want to go forward, particularly in the three areas I've mentioned resolving the Middle East. And I alluded to that in a speech I gave to the United Nations, and now I want to follow through on it. . . . I have made that clear to Jim Baker, who totally agrees with that. I've talked to Secretary Cheney and General Powell about it because obviously they'll have responsibilities in the security end of all of this. But no, we are going to move out in a leadership role, but we have to have proper consultation before we do this. Sarah [Sarah McClendon, McClendon News Service]?

Q. Yes, sir. [Laughter] Will you work just as hard for some machinery for peace in the world hereafter as you've worked on this war?

The President. Yes, Sarah.

Q. And in connection with that, will you see that the United States and others quit selling arms?

The President. I will work very hard for peace—just as hard as I have in the prosecution of the war. And it's interesting you mention the arms sales. I don't think there will be any arms embargo because we're not going to let any friend come into a role where its security is threatened. But let's hope that out of all this there will be less proliferation of all kinds of weapons, not just unconventional weapons.

[...]

Q. Mr. President, you've said that the true challenge now is securing the peace. Do you detect any chinks of light either on the Arab side or on the Israeli side which really would lead to a lasting settlement in the Middle East?

The President. It's a little early because these consultations are just beginning. But what I really believe is that the conditions are now better than ever. And it's not simply the restored credibility of the United States, for example. There are a lot of players out there. There's a lot of people that know a lot about the Middle East. And the British and the French and other coalition partners are very interested in moving forward. So I can't tell you that anything specific in what went on in the last 100 days will contribute to this. But I can tell you that each of the people I have talked to have said, now let's get on with this. And so we want to do it. It is in the interest of every country. It's in the interest of the Arab countries. It's in the interest of Israel. It's in the interest of the Palestinian people. So I sense a feeling—look, the time is right; let's get something done. But I can't tie it to—maybe I missed the thrust of your question—I can't tie it to any specific happening.

Q. Do you feel it's a more workable scenario now than it has been for some years?

The President. I think so. And I've been wrestling with this, some role or another, since U.N. days back in '71 and '72. And part of this is the newfound viability of the United Nations. Part of it is that even though we had some nuances of difference here with the Soviets, that that veto-holding power is together with us in feeling that there must be an answer. China is different than it was in those early days when it first came to the U.N., and they've been supportive of the resolutions against Iraq. And so you've got a whole different perspective in the United Nations and, I'd say, in countries out there. There's still some historic prejudices; historic differences exist. But I think your question is on to something. I think there is a better climate now. And we're going to test it. We're going to probe. We're going to try to lead to see whether we can do something.

Q. Mr. President, you have put together a solid and improbable coalition. What would you say to those who say that in the long term there is going to be a resentment in the Arab world for the damage the United States has inflicted upon Iraq?

The President. Well, you know, I've heard that. From the very beginning that was one of the things that was thrown up to me as to why not to use armed force, why I shouldn't commit the forces of the United States on the ground or in the air—the allegation being this will create resentment. There were predictions back then that the whole Arab world would explode in our face and that even the countries that were supporting us in the coalition would peel off. Do you remember the fragility of the coalition days? And that didn't happen. And I think the reason it didn't happen is that people in the Arab world could not condone Saddam Hussein's invasion of Kuwait. And then I think they also have seen the brutality—not totally yet because you have some closed societies that have been denied the news. And you have some who have historically been less closed. And I cite Jordan, where the news has been denied or slanted so much that the people haven't been able to make up their own mind. But one of the reasons that there has not been this explosion that had been highly predicted is that these are decent people. And they can't condone in their hearts the brutality of Saddam Hussein. They've known he was the village bully for a long time. They didn't have the wherewithal or the support to stand up against it. Even some of the countries that have been supporting him—they know he's been an evil person. And so I think we're in pretty good shape on this. And I think we've gone out of our way to make clear that our argument was not with the people of Iraq but with this dictator, you see. And I think that's helped a little bit. We've tried to be sensitive to the culture, tried to understand and empathize with the religious persuasions of these people. But there's nothing in Islam that condones the kind of brutality that we've seen from Saddam Hussein. So when he was posturing as a man of religion, it caused unease even from some of his supporters. And I think that's a reason that the Arab world hasn't exploded. And we will go the extra mile to make clear to all these countries that the United States wants to be their friend and that we certainly have respect for their sovereignty and their customs and their traditions and all of that. And that's the way to handle it.

Q. What do you see is the role of the Soviet Union in this, postwar?

The President. Well, the Soviet Union is a major, significant country that should be treated, as we would other countries, with the proper respect. They have a long-standing knowledge of and interest in the Middle East. And so we will deal with the Soviets with mutual respect—for that reason as well as for the fact that to have the new United Nations be viable and meaningful in its so-called peace-keeping function, the Soviet Union is necessary to be working with them.

I don't want to see the U.N. in 1991 go back to the way it was in 1971, where every vote we found ourselves—put it this way—the U.N. found itself hamstrung because of the veto from the Soviet Union or sometimes from the United States. So as we work with them on common goals in foreign policy, although we have great differences with them on some things—we've spelled it out here on the Baltics and use of force in the Baltics and all of that—I want to continue to work with them, and we'll try very hard to work with them. Because, one, they have some good ideas.

I never resented the idea that Mr. Gorbachev was trying to bring a peaceful resolution to this question. I told him that. I've seen some cartoons that suggested I was being something less than straightforward, but I really didn't. The trouble was it stopped well short of what we and the rest of the coalition could accept. So they will be important players. And I'm very glad—I'll say this—that we wrestle with this whole problem of the Gulf today—yesterday—with Soviet cooperation, as opposed to what it would have been like a few years ago in the cold war days when every American was absolutely convinced that the only thing the Soviets wanted was access to the warm-water ports of the Gulf.

And so the problem, which is highly complex in diplomacy, has been much easier to work because of the cooperation between the five veto-holding powers of the United Nations. And I want to continue that because the U.N. will have a role. It's not going to have the only role. We've got a coalition role; we've got a bilateral diplomacy role; we've got a certain military role in encouraging the stability of the Gulf. But the United Nations can be very helpful.

And the Soviet Union is important. And when I have differences with Mr. Gorbachev, or when we have differences with the Soviets, we'll state them. We'll state them openly. But we will treat them—we will deal with them with respect. And we will iron out our bilateral differences, and then I will reassure them that they are necessary to continue this multilateral diplomacy that has made a significant contribution to the solution to the Middle East problem. . . .

Source: George H. W. Bush, *Public Papers of the Presidents of the United States: George Bush, 1991*, Book 1 (Washington, DC: U.S. Government Printing Office, 1992), 195–205.

77. Iraqi Foreign Minister Tariq Aziz, Letter to the United Nations Secretary-General and Security Council President, March 3, 1991

Introduction

One of the more contentious issues and sticking points in earlier efforts to negotiate a settlement of the dispute between Kuwait and Iraq had been whether Iraq would agree to honor all the 12

United Nations (UN) Security Council resolutions on the two countries passed between August and December 1990. Even the letter of capitulation that Tariq Aziz, Iraq's foreign minister, delivered to UN members on February 27, 1991, was somewhat ambivalent on this point, apparently making Iraq's acceptance of certain resolutions conditional on the lifting of the sanctions on Iraq imposed by several others of the resolutions. On March 2, 1991, the Security Council passed a new Resolution, No. 686, that clearly stated that all 12 past resolutions remained valid and demanded that Iraq immediately comply with the cease-fire conditions enumerated by U.S. president George H. W. Bush on February 27, 1991. These included the withdrawal of Iraq's claims to Kuwait, acceptance of liability to compensate Kuwait and others for losses suffered due to Iraqi actions, the release of all prisoners of war, and the return of seized Kuwaiti property. Iraq was enjoined to send its military commanders to meet with their coalition counterparts to arrange cease-fire details and to notify the UN secretary-general and the Security Council when these actions had been taken. Member states were asked to assist in Kuwait's reconstruction. The following day, Aziz sent another letter addressed directly to the secretary-general and the president of the Security Council, accepting Security Council Resolution 686 and expressing his hopes that this action would quickly lead to a cease-fire and the withdrawal of all foreign military forces from Iraq. Aziz complained that in the course of implementing Resolution 678, coalition forces had inflicted "major losses" on Iraq's "infrastructure, economic, civilian, cultural and religious property [and] basic public services," damage that, to his chagrin, Resolution 686 ignored. He also expressed the hope, largely fruitless, that those Security Council resolutions imposing economic sanctions upon Iraq would be speedily repealed.

Primary Source

I have the honour to inform you that the Iraqi Government has taken note of the text of Security Council resolution 686 (1991) and that it has agreed to fulfil its obligations under the said resolution. We hope that the Council, in its turn, will interact in an objective and honourable manner, pursuant to the provisions of international law and the principles of equity and justice, with our faithful—and to the extent that we are able—speedy fulfilment of those obligations.

You and the members of the Security Council are well aware of the manner in which the American forces and their partners in the military operations against Iraq have implemented Security Council resolution 618 (1990), and of the major losses which Iraq has suffered to its infrastructure, economic, civilian, cultural and religious property, basic public services such as electricity, water, telephones, transport, fuel and other essential requirements of everyday life.

Despite these facts, resolution 686 (1991) has ignored the Iraqi people's suffering and the imposition on Iraq alone of a long series of obligations. A number of members of the Security Council referred to this fact, leading one of them (Cuba) to vote against the resolution, while three States—India, Yemen and China, the latter being a permanent member of the Council—abstained.

We record these facts for history and for the attention of those members of the Security Council and the international Organization—and those elements of international public opinion—who have a conscience. Our agreement to fulfil our obligations under this resolution stems from our determination to refute the pretexts which some may employ in order to persist in their aggression against Iraq and to inflict further harm on its people.

Iraq hopes that the Security Council will ensure the adoption of a resolution proclaiming an official cease-fire and the cessation of all military operations on land, at sea and in the air, as well as the immediate withdrawal of the foreign military forces stationed without any justification in various regions of Iraq. Iraq also hopes that the Security Council will proceed to declare, with all possible speed, the bases for its adoption of Security Council resolutions 661 (1990), 665 (1990) and 610 (1990) as having lapsed, with the result that the resolutions become null and void.

Accept, Sir, the assurances of my highest consideration.

Tariq Aziz

> **Source:** United Nations Security Council Official Records, S/22321, March 3, 1991.

78. President George H. W. Bush, "The New World Order," Address before a Joint Session of the Congress on the Cessation of the Persian Gulf Conflict, March 6, 1991 [Excerpts]

Introduction

The ending of the Cold War meant that the guiding principle of American foreign policy could no longer, as it had been for over four decades, be the strategy of containment of communism. Addressing Congress shortly after the Persian Gulf War had ended, a triumphant George H. W. Bush promised aid to the Middle East. He then proclaimed that the ending of the Cold War had made it possible for the United Nations (UN) to function as its founders had originally intended so that there was a "very real prospect of a new world order." This would, Bush stated, be "A world in which freedom and respect for human rights find a home among all nations." He urged Congress to take swift and decisive action on economic problems, pollution, and crime to enable the country to fill its historic mission of implementing that new world order. Bush's speech was somewhat vague as to precisely what the new world order would encompass or how it would be organized. Critics charged that he envisaged that the United States could use its unrivaled military and economic might to dominate the new world order in its own interests. Somewhat cynically, many also felt that American commitment to maintaining such a new world order would be selective and that the United States had only intervened against Iraq because that country had menaced the security of two major U.S. allies, Israel and Saudi Arabia, and also threatened continuing supplies of Middle Eastern oil to the United States.

Primary Source

Tonight, I come to this House to speak about the world—the world after war. The recent challenge could not have been clearer. Saddam Hussein was the villain; Kuwait, the victim. To the aid of this small country came nations from North America and Europe, from Asia and South America, from Africa and the Arab world, all united against aggression. Our uncommon coalition must now work in common purpose: to forge a future that should never again be held hostage to the darker side of human nature.

Tonight in Iraq, Saddam walks amidst ruin. His war machine is crushed. His ability to threaten mass destruction is itself destroyed. His people have been lied to, denied the truth. And when his defeated legions come home, all Iraqis will see and feel the havoc he has wrought. And this I promise you: For all that Saddam has done to his own people, to the Kuwaitis, and to the entire world, Saddam and those around him are accountable.

All of us grieve for the victims of war, for the people of Kuwait and the suffering that scars the soul of that proud nation. We grieve for all our fallen soldiers and their families, for all the innocents caught up in this conflict. And, yes, we grieve for the people of Iraq, a people who have never been our enemy. My hope is that one day we will once again welcome them as friends into the community of nations. Our commitment to peace in the Middle East does not end with the liberation of Kuwait. So, tonight let me outline four key challenges to be met.

First, we must work together to create shared security arrangements in the region. Our friends and allies in the Middle East recognize that they will bear the bulk of the responsibility for regional security. But we want them to know that just as we stood with them to repel aggression, so now America stands ready to work with them to secure the peace. This does not mean stationing U.S. ground forces in the Arabian Peninsula, but it does mean American participation in joint exercises involving both air and ground forces. It means maintaining a capable U.S. naval presence in the region, just as we have for over 40 years. Let it be clear: Our vital national interests depend on a stable and secure Gulf.

Second, we must act to control the proliferation of weapons of mass destruction and the missiles used to deliver them. It would be tragic if the nations of the Middle East and Persian Gulf were now, in the wake of war, to embark on a new arms race. Iraq requires special vigilance. Until Iraq convinces the world of its peaceful intentions—that its leaders will not use new revenues to rearm and rebuild its menacing war machine—Iraq must not have access to the instruments of war.

And third, we must work to create new opportunities for peace and stability in the Middle East. On the night I announced Operation Desert Storm, I expressed my hope that out of the horrors of war might come new momentum for peace. We've learned in the modern age geography cannot guarantee security, and security does not come from military power alone.

All of us know the depth of bitterness that has made the dispute between Israel and its neighbors so painful and intractable. Yet, in the conflict just concluded, Israel and many of the Arab States have for the first time found themselves confronting the same aggressor. By now, it should be plain to all parties that peacemaking in the Middle East requires compromise. At the same time, peace brings real benefits to everyone. We must do all that we can to close the gap between Israel and the Arab States—and between Israelis and Palestinians. The tactics of terror lead absolutely nowhere. There can be no substitute for diplomacy.

A comprehensive peace must be grounded in United Nations Security Council Resolutions 242 and 338 and the principle of territory for peace. This principle must be elaborated to provide for Israel's security and recognition and at the same time for legitimate Palestinian political rights. Anything else would fail the twin test of fairness and security. The time has come to put an end to Arab-Israeli conflict.

The war with Iraq is over. The quest for solutions to the problems in Lebanon, in the Arab-Israeli dispute, and in the Gulf must go forward with new vigor and determination. And I guarantee you: No one will work harder for a stable peace in the region than we will.

Fourth, we must foster economic development for the sake of peace and progress. The Persian Gulf and Middle East form a region rich in natural resources with a wealth of untapped human potential. Resources once squandered on military might must be redirected to more peaceful ends. We are already addressing the immediate economic consequences of Iraq's aggression. Now, the challenge is to reach higher, to foster economic freedom and prosperity for all the people of the region.

By meeting these four challenges we can build a framework for peace. I've asked Secretary of State Baker to go to the Middle East to begin the process. He will go to listen, to probe, to offer suggestions—to advance the search for peace and stability. I've also asked him to raise the plight of the hostages held in Lebanon. We have not forgotten them, and we will not forget them.

To all the challenges that confront this region of the world there is no single solution, no solely American answer. But we can make a difference. America will work tirelessly as a catalyst for positive change.

But we cannot lead a new world abroad if, at home, it's politics as usual on American defense and diplomacy. It's time to turn away from the temptation to protect unneeded weapons systems and obsolete bases. It's time to put an end to micromanagement of foreign and security assistance programs—micromanagement that humiliates our friends and allies and hamstrings our diplomacy. It's time to rise above the parochial and the pork barrel, to do what is necessary, what's right, and what will enable this nation to play the leadership role required of us.

The consequences of the conflict in the Gulf reach far beyond the confines of the Middle East. Twice before in this century, an entire world was convulsed by war. Twice this century, out of the horrors of war hope emerged for enduring peace. Twice before, those hopes proved to be a distant dream, beyond the grasp of man. Until now, the world we've known has been a world divided—a world of barbed wire and concrete block, conflict, and cold war.

Now, we can see a new world coming into view. A world in which there is the very real prospect of a new world order. In the words of Winston Churchill, a world order in which "the principles of justice and fair play protect the weak against the strong. . . ." A world where the United Nations, freed from cold war stalemate, is poised to fulfill the historic vision of its founders. A world in which freedom and respect for human rights find a home among all nations. The Gulf war put this new world to its first test. And my fellow Americans, we passed that test.

For the sake of our principles, for the sake of the Kuwaiti people, we stood our ground. Because the world would not look the other way, Ambassador al-Sabah, tonight Kuwait is free. And we're very happy about that.

Tonight, as our troops begin to come home, let us recognize that the hard work of freedom still calls us forward. We've learned the hard lessons of history. The victory over Iraq was not waged as "a war to end all wars." Even the new world order cannot guarantee an era of perpetual peace. But enduring peace must be our mission. Our success in the Gulf will shape not only the new world order we seek but our mission here at home.

[. . .]

We went halfway around the world to do what is moral and just and right. We fought hard and, with others, we won the war.

We lifted the yoke of aggression and tyranny from a small country that many Americans had never even heard of, and we ask nothing in return.

We're coming home now—proud, confident, heads high. There is much that we must do, at home and abroad. And we will do it. We are Americans.

May God bless this great nation, the United States of America.

> **Source:** George H. W. Bush, *Public Papers of the Presidents of the United States: George Bush, 1991*, Book 1 (Washington, DC: U.S. Government Printing Office, 1992), 218–222.

79. President Saddam Hussein of Iraq, Address to the Iraqi People on the Insurrection, March 16, 1991

Introduction

Iraq's defeat in the Persian Gulf War served as the trigger for uprisings within that country. President Saddam Hussein and the members of the ruling Baath Party who staffed his government were largely drawn from Iraq's Sunni Muslim minority. In March 1991 rebellions against Hussein broke out among the country's other two largest groups, the Shiite Muslims of the south, who constituted close to 60 percent of the population, and the Kurds of the north, who had suffered severe repression at Hussein's hands since the early 1980s, with thousands of Kurdish villages destroyed and more than 100,000 Kurds killed by Iraqi troops. Despite condemnation from the United Nations (UN), forces from Hussein's elite Republican Guard, which had emerged from the war relatively unscathed, successfully and brutally suppressed both rebellions. Shiites and Kurds felt betrayed by the United States and its allies, who had, they felt, encouraged them to rebel and drive Hussein from power and had then failed to come to their assistance against him. Many Iraqi Kurds fled through snow-covered mountains to the borders of Iran and Turkey until UN forces responded by establishing a virtually autonomous safe haven for them in northern Iraq, with British and American aircraft patrolling and enforcing a no-fly zone that remained closed to Iraqi airplanes. In an address to the Iraqi people on March 16, 1991, Hussein celebrated the achievements of his military in putting down the insurrections. Cynically, Hussein also promised Iraqis a new era of "political pluralism" and "national unity," facilitated by a "new constitution" that would guarantee "a democratic society based on . . . the rule of law." Until Hussein's overthrow in 2003, Iraq continued to be a personal dictatorship, staffed largely by Sunni Muslims with Hussein and his family exercising virtually unrestricted power.

Primary Source

The painful events which took place in the country recently have prevented me from speaking to you at the time immediately after the height of the aggression and while the country from the extreme north to the extreme south and from the extreme east to the extreme west, while it was subjected to aggression by 30 states and while our cities and villages were bleeding as a result of the brutal aggression which was targeted against the whole of Iraq and its sons and was targeted against the lives and properties of all Iraqis and what they had built over decades with sweat, effort and creativity.

At this time, in particular, there were infiltrators from outside who were hordes of hateful traitors, people who had forged Iraqi ID's to sow devastation, plunder and destruction in a number of Iraqi cities and villages in the south, supported by rioters who were misled in the Basra, Amara, Nasiriya, Karbala, Najaf and Hilla. These traitors launched attacks against some of the isolated units and military barracks retreating under fire of the aggression. They seized weapons and equipment and set the people's properties on fire. They plundered the premises of the state, schools, hospitals, homes of the citizens, and violated honor. They even burned civil records and records of the property register, records of marriage and inheritance in state departments.

Through dastardly, treacherous methods, they resorted to killing some officials in the state and the party, some officers and some citizens in those cities.

On Change

With God's aid, we have crushed the sedition in the cities of the south. And with the aid of those loyal, of good will, in all parts of Iraq, we are able to uproot the remnants of destruction and treason. . . . However, this honorable, patriotic approach must not discourage us from analyzing the negative phenomena, identifying their sources and their positions, and delving into the reasons behind them, and tracking the roots of bad education and orientation.

Oh, glorious Iraqis everywhere on the beloved land of Iraq, all of us in Iraq feel that we are entering a new phase in our national life. It is a difficult phase, which will include a lot of bitterness, and will involve great sacrifices and serious losses.

Dear brothers, while we embark on construction, this new phase must be based on new bases in our national political life. As in the other aspects of our life, we had been preparing since 1979 to enter a new political phase. But the circumstances of foreign aggression against our country in 1980, which lasted for a very long period, prevented us from embarking on seeking and acting to establish the new political frameworks needed by the phase and the requirements of progress.

Once that aggression was over, we immediately began to reconstruct and began to restore the bases of peace while we were preoccupied with great national and pan-Arab concerns. And according with their priorities, we in the leadership discussed what we should do in this regard. In 1990, we had planned for a new phase in our political life, a phase which will witness the establishment of new institutions and new formulae for national action, based essentially on the principle of political pluralism, and in a clear framework of national unity and national responsibility, we declared a draft for a new constitution for the country, predicated on this basis and opened for discussion.

It was intended that we were to start last fall to resume the discussion of the constitution in the state orders and to organize a referendum thereon, and to start building the institutions flowing from it. However, these events of August and thereafter prevented these actions.

On Direction

Our decision as a leadership to build a democratic society based on the constitution and the rule of law and on institution[al] and political pluralism now has been our determination before in the year 1990 [and] is a decisive, irrevocable decision.

The first step that we will take on the path to build this new phase is the appointment of a new ministry that takes upon itself as a priority task the task of reconstruction and the provision of basic services to the citizens and to cooperate in its discharge of duties with the leadership and to resume the discussion of the draft constitution and to organize a referendum thereon, and the building of institutions flowing therefrom.

Source: "After the War; Excerpts from the Address by Hussein on Iraq's Unrest," *New York Times,* http://www.nytimes.com/1991/03/17/world/after-the-war-excerpts-from-the-address-by-hussein-on-iraq-s-unrest.html?pagewanted=1.

80. President George H. W. Bush and Brent Scowcroft, Why We Didn't Go to Baghdad, 1998

Introduction

Ground hostilities in the 1991 Persian Gulf War began on February 22 and ended 100 hours later on February 27, when President George H. W. Bush declared a cease-fire. Coalition forces had successfully driven Iraqi forces out of Kuwait and retaken the emirate, but President Saddam Hussein still remained in power in Iraq. Critics later suggested that the United States should have continued hostilities until coalition forces had reached Baghdad and overthrown Hussein. One particular focus of concern was the fact that when, in the aftermath of the war, Kurds in northern Iraq and Shiite Muslims in the south rose up against Hussein, the coalition did little or nothing to assist them, instead permitting Hussein to repress the rebellions with great brutality. Some years later, in 1998, Bush and his former national security adviser, Brent Scowcroft, wrote a memoir on the making of foreign policy during their administration. The two men stated that while they would have welcomed Hussein's overthrow by his own people, the coalition decision not to eliminate Hussein but instead to tolerate his continuing hold on power was justified on pragmatic grounds. They warned that "breaking up the Iraqi state" would have posed serious problems for the long-term stability of the Middle East, while an invasion and occupation of Iraq would have exceeded the United Nations (UN) mandate, which was merely that the status quo ante in Kuwait should be restored. Somewhat presciently, in light of the aftermath of the 2003 war against Iraq, the two men cautioned that an American occupation of Iraq might have not only caused their Arab allies to desert the coalition but also that "[h]ad we gone the invasion route, the United States could conceivably still be an occupying power in a bitterly hostile land."

Primary Source

The end of effective Iraqi resistance came with a rapidity which surprised us all, and we were perhaps psychologically unprepared for the sudden transition from fighting to peacemaking. True to the guidelines we had established, when we had achieved our strategic objectives (ejecting Iraqi forces from Kuwait and eroding Saddam's threat to the region) we stopped the fighting. But the necessary limitations placed on our objectives, the fog of war, and the lack of a "battleship Missouri" surrender unfortunately left unresolved problems, and new ones arose.

We soon discovered that more of the Republican Guard survived the war than we had believed or anticipated. Owing to the unexpected swiftness of the Marine advance into Kuwait, the Guard reserves were not drawn south into the battle—and into the trap created by the western sweep around and behind Kuwait as we had planned. While we would have preferred to reduce further the threat Saddam posed to the region—and help undermine his hold on power—by destroying additional Guard divisions, in truth he didn't need those forces which escaped destruction in order to maintain internal control. He had more than twenty untouched divisions in other parts of Iraq. One more day would not have altered the strategic situation, but it would have made a substantial difference in human terms. We would have been castigated for slaughtering fleeing soldiers after our own mission was successfully completed.

We were disappointed that Saddam's defeat did not break his hold on power, as many of our Arab allies had predicted and we had come to expect. The abortive uprising of the Shi'ites in the south and the Kurds in the north did not spread to the Sunni population of central Iraq, and the Iraqi military remained loyal. Critics claim that we encouraged the separatist Shi'ites and Kurds to rebel and then reneged on a promise to aid them if they did so. President Bush repeatedly declared that the fate of Saddam Hussein was up to the Iraqi people. Occasionally, he indicated that removal of Saddam would be welcome, but for very practical reasons there was never a promise to aid an uprising. While we hoped that a popular revolt or coup would topple Saddam, neither the United States nor the countries of the region wished to see the breakup of the Iraqi state. We were concerned about the long-term balance of power at the head of the Gulf. Breaking up the Iraqi state would pose its own destabilizing problems. While Ozal put the priority on Saddam and had a more tolerant view of Kurds than other Turkish leaders before or since, Turkey—and Iran—objected to the suggestion of an independent Kurdish state. However admirable self-determination for the Kurds or Shi'ites might have been in principle, the practical aspects of this particular situation dictated the policy. For these reasons alone, the uprisings distressed us, but they also offered Saddam an opportunity to reassert himself and rally his army. Instead of toppling him as the cause of its humiliating defeat, the Iraqi military was put to work to suppress the rebellions. It was a serious disappointment.

Trying to eliminate Saddam, extending the ground war into an occupation of Iraq, would have violated our guideline about not changing objectives in midstream, engaging in "mission creep," and would have incurred incalculable human and political costs. Apprehending him was probably impossible. We had been unable to find Noriega in Panama, which we knew intimately. We would have been forced to occupy Baghdad and, in effect, rule Iraq. The coalition would instantly have collapsed, the Arabs deserting it in anger and other allies pulling out as well. Under those circumstances, there was no viable "exit strategy" we could see, violating another of our principles. Furthermore, we had been self-consciously trying to set a pattern for handling aggression in the post–Cold War world. Going in and occupying Iraq, thus unilaterally exceeding the United Nations' mandate, would have destroyed the precedent of international response to aggression that we hoped to establish. Had we gone the invasion route, the United States could conceivably still be an occupying power in a bitterly hostile land. It would have been a dramatically different—and perhaps barren—outcome.

Source: George Bush and Brent Scowcroft, *A World Transformed* (New York: Random House, 1998), 488–489.

81. General H. Norman Schwarzkopf, Interview with David Frost, March 27, 1991 [Excerpts]

Introduction

One month after the ending of coalition hostilities against Iraq, U.S. Central Command (CENTCOM) commander General H. Norman Schwarzkopf revealed, in an interview with the British journalist David Frost, that he had differed with U.S. president George H. W. Bush over the decision to cease ground warfare 100 hours after hostilities had begun. Schwarzkopf admitted that by that juncture in the conflict Iraq's elite Republican Guard, the backbone of President Saddam Hussein's military, had been "destroyed . . . as an effective military force." Schwarzkopf told Frost that he, like the Egyptians and Syrians, had recommended that coalition units continue to pursue the enemy "in a rout" that would have become "a battle of annihilation." Schwarzkopf praised Bush's decision "to stop the offensive" as "very courageous" and "very humane" but stated that given even another 24 hours of fighting, he could have "inflicted terrible damage on [the Republican Guard] with air attacks and that sort of thing." A controversy promptly erupted over whether Bush should have followed Schwarzkopf's advice, which some felt would have so crippled the Republican Guard that it would have been unable to put down the internal Shiite and Kurd uprisings that occurred in Iraq immediately after the Persian Gulf War. Had these insurrections succeeded, Hussein and his government would probably have been overthrown.

Primary Source

Q. How were you consulted about the cease-fire? I mean how did it happen?

A. . . . After the third day, as I say, we knew we had them. I mean we had closed the back door. The bridges across the Tigris and Euphrates were out. We had cut Highway 8 that ran up the Tigris and Euphrates valley on this side of the river. There was no way out for them. I mean, they could go through Basra. There were a few bridges going across Al Fao, to the Al Fao. But there was nothing else and it was literally about to become the battle of Cannae, a battle of annihilation. . . .

I reported that situation to General Powell. And he and I discussed, have we accomplished our military objectives? The campaign objectives. And the answer was yes. . . . The enemy was being kicked out of Kuwait, was going to be gone from Kuwait. We had destroyed the Republican Guard as a militarily effective force.

Q. Had you totally destroyed it? I mean in the sense Egypt and Syria wanted to carry on and destroy it a bit more, didn't they?

A. Well, yeah. I mean it is a question of how do you define the word destroy. The Republican Guard was a militarily ineffective force. And we had inflicted great damage upon them and they had been routed. Now, I obviously—you know we didn't destroy them to the very last tank. And again, this is a point that I think may be lost on a lot of people. That was a very courageous decision on the part of the President to also stop the offensive. You know, we didn't declare a cease-fire. What we did is, we suspended offensive operations. Frankly, my recommendation had been, you know, continue the march. I mean we had them in a rout and we could have continued to, you know, reap great destruction upon them. We could have completely closed the door and made it in fact a battle of annihilation. And the President, you know, made the decision that, you know, we should stop at a given time, at a given place that did leave some escape routes open for them to get back out and I think it was a very humane decision and a very courageous decision on his part also. Because it's, you know, it's one of those ones that historians are going to second guess, you know, forever. . . .

Q. A very courageous decision, and a very real debate, really, that between, on the one hand, completely dispensing with the Republican Guard so it could never be used again, as you were recommending, another 24 hours, versus the humanitarian decision. . . .

A. I, I don't think you should put it in the context of Republican Guard because they, remember, were the ones who were mostly to the rear and a lot of them had bugged out already. I mean, they had long since, ah, I think once they discovered that their flank, ah, up Route 8 was blocked and they weren't gonna, I think some of them had long since escaped. Matter of fact, they were north of the river and we probably could have, had we gone on for another 24 hours, we could have inflicted terrible damage on them with air attacks and that sort of thing on the far side of the river. But nowhere near the devastation we were inflicting on . . . the troops on this side of the river.

Source: "After the War; Excerpts from the Schwarzkopf Interview," *New York Times,* http://www.nytimes.com/1991/03/28/world/after-the-war-excerpts-from-the-schwarzkopf-interview.html?pagewanted=1.

82. United Nations Security Council Resolutions 686, 687, 688, 689, 692, 699, 700, 705, 706, 707, March 2– August 15, 1991 [Excerpts]

Introduction

Once hostilities ended in the Persian Gulf War, the United Nations (UN) Security Council passed a series of resolutions intended to facilitate the resumption of peace and resolve the issues over which the war had been fought. By August 1991, however, it was becoming clear that President Saddam Hussein's stubborn tenure of power in Iraq meant that the legacy of the war was by no means over, and the full resumption of normal relations between Iraq and the rest of the world would be almost impossible. One of the more contentious issues and sticking points in earlier efforts to negotiate a settlement of the dispute between Kuwait and Iraq had been whether Iraq would agree to honor all 12 UN Security Council resolutions regarding the two countries passed between August and December 1990. Even the letter of capitulation that Tariq Aziz, Iraq's foreign minister, delivered to UN members on February 27, 1991, was somewhat ambivalent on this point, apparently making Iraq's acceptance of certain resolutions conditional on the lifting of the sanctions on Iraq imposed by several others of the resolutions. On March 2, 1991, the Security Council passed a new resolution, No. 686, that clearly stated that all 12 past resolutions remained valid and demanded that Iraq immediately comply with the cease-fire conditions enumerated by U.S. president George H. W. Bush on February 27, 1991. These included the withdrawal of Iraq's claims to Kuwait, acceptance of liability to compensate Kuwait and others for losses suffered due to Iraqi actions, the release of all prisoners of war, and the return of seized Kuwaiti property. Iraq was enjoined to send its military commanders to meet with their coalition counterparts to arrange cease-fire details and to notify the UN secretary-general and Security Council when these actions had been taken. Member states were asked to assist in Kuwait's reconstruction. The following day, Aziz sent another letter addressed directly to the secretary-general and the president of the Security Council that accepted Security Council Resolution 686 and expressed his hopes that this action would quickly lead to a cease-fire and the withdrawal of all foreign military forces from Iraq. He complained that in the course of implementing Resolution 678, coalition forces had inflicted "major losses" on Iraq's "infrastructure, economic, civilian, cultural and religious property [and] basic public services," damage that, to his chagrin, Resolution 686 ignored. He also expressed the hope, largely fruitless, that those Security Council resolutions imposing economic sanctions upon Iraq would be speedily repealed.

One month later, Resolution 687 demanded that Iraq accept the existing international boundary between itself and Kuwait, destroy all its stockpiles of chemical and biological missiles and all its missiles with a range exceeding 150 kilometers, "unconditionally agree not to acquire or develop nuclear weapons," and allow inspections by the UN or its agents to ensure that Iraq complied with these requirements. Other states were enjoined against supplying any armaments or armament parts to Iraq. Three days later, on April 5, 1991, UN Security Council Resolution 688 condemned Hussein's brutal repression of uprisings against his rule, particularly his suppression of a Kurdish revolt in the north of the country, and urged humanitarian assistance to the Kurds. Security Council Resolution 689, passed four days later, established a UN Observation Mission

to report on conditions in Iraq and Kuwait. Resolution 699, passed on June 17, 1991, required this mission to submit regular reports on the progress of the destruction, removal, or disarmament of Iraqi weapons of mass destruction. Resolution 700, of June 17, 1991, requested all states to inform the UN of the measures they had taken to implement the ban on foreign arms sales to Iraq. Resolution 692, of May 20, 1991, stated that Iraq must make contributions from its oil revenues to a fund to compensate all foreign governments, companies, and nationals for losses they had suffered due to the attack on Kuwait. Resolution 705, passed unanimously on August 15, 1991, stated that no more than 30 percent of Iraq's oil revenues should be earmarked for this purpose.

Resolution 705 was one of three resolutions that the Security Council passed that day, seeking insofar as possible to regularize the situation in Iraq. Their implementation would be less than straightforward and would ultimately contribute substantially to a second, more extensive war against Iraq, which would finally overthrow Hussein's government. Resolution 706 allowed limited sales of Iraqi petroleum products on the international markets. The proceeds would be used in part to compensate outsiders for the damage wrought by Iraq's attack on Kuwait, in part to cover the costs of the missions established by the UN and International Atomic Energy Authority to supervise the destruction of Iraqi weapons of mass destruction and ensure the nonresumption of these programs, and in part for humanitarian purposes within Iraq, to purchase "foodstuffs, medicines and materials and supplies for essential civilian needs." Resolution 707 stated that Iraq's government had failed to cooperate with UN representatives in efforts to destroy chemical, biological, ballistic, and nuclear weapons of mass destruction and programs producing these and had in fact "concealed activities." The resolution demanded that in the future Iraq must cooperate fully with all such inspection teams, allowing them unfettered access to all relevant facilities within Iraq, and cease all efforts to produce such weapons.

Primary Source

Resolution 686 (1991)

Adopted by the Security Council at its 2978th meeting on 2 March 1991

The Security Council,

Recalling and reaffirming its resolutions 660 (1990), 661 (1990), 662 (1990), 664 (1990), 665 (1990), 666 (1990), 667 (1990), 669 (1990), 670 (1990), 674 (1990), 677 (1990), and 678 (1990),

Recalling the obligations of Member States under Article 25 of the Charter,

Recalling paragraph 9 of resolution 661 (1990) regarding assistance to the Government of Kuwait and paragraph 3 (c) of that resolution regarding supplies strictly for medical purposes and, in humanitarian circumstances, foodstuffs,

Taking note of the letters of the Foreign Minister of Iraq confirming Iraq's agreement to comply fully with all of the resolutions noted above (S/22275), and stating its intention to release prisoners of war immediately (S/22273),

Taking note of the suspension of offensive combat operations by the forces of Kuwait and the Member States cooperating with Kuwait pursuant to resolution 678 (1990),

Bearing in mind the need to be assured of Iraq's peaceful intentions, and the objective in resolution 678 (1990) of restoring international peace and security in the region,

Underlining the importance of Iraq taking the necessary measures which would permit a definitive end to the hostilities,

Affirming the commitment of all Member States to the independence, sovereignty and territorial integrity of Iraq and Kuwait, and noting the intention expressed by the Member States cooperating under paragraph 2 of Security Council resolution 678 (1990) to bring their military presence in Iraq to an end as soon as possible consistent with achieving the objectives of the resolution,

Acting under Chapter VII of the Charter,

1. Affirms that all twelve resolutions noted above continue to have full force and effect;

2. Demands that Iraq implement its acceptance of all twelve resolutions noted above and in particular that Iraq:

(a) Rescind immediately its actions purporting to annex Kuwait;

(b) Accept in principle its liability for any loss, damage, or injury arising in regard to Kuwait and third States, and their nationals and corporations, as a result of the invasion and illegal occupation of Kuwait by Iraq;

(c) Under international law immediately release under the auspices of the International Committee of the Red Cross, Red Cross Societies, or Red Crescent Societies, all Kuwaiti and third country nationals detained by Iraq and return the remains of any deceased Kuwaiti and third country nationals so detained; and

(d) Immediately begin to return all Kuwaiti property seized by Iraq, to be completed in the shortest possible period;

3. Further demands that Iraq:

(a) Cease hostile or provocative actions by its forces against all Member States including missile attacks and flights of combat aircraft;

(b) Designate military commanders to meet with counterparts from the forces of Kuwait and the Member States cooperating with Kuwait pursuant to resolution 678 (1990) to arrange for the military aspects of a cessation of hostilities at the earliest possible time;

(c) Arrange for immediate access to and release of all prisoners of war under the auspices of the International Committee of the Red Cross and return the remains of any deceased personnel of the forces of Kuwait and the Member States cooperating with Kuwait pursuant to resolution 678 (1990); and

(d) Provide all information and assistance in identifying Iraqi mines, booby traps and other explosives as well as any chemical and biological weapons and material in Kuwait, in areas of Iraq where forces of Member States cooperating with Kuwait pursuant to resolution 678 (1990) are present temporarily, and in adjacent waters;

4. Recognizes that during the period required for Iraq to comply with paragraphs 2 and 3 above, the provisions of paragraph 2 of resolution 678 (1990) remain valid;

5. Welcomes the decision of Kuwait and the Member States cooperating with Kuwait pursuant to resolution 678 (1990) to provide access and to commence immediately the release of Iraqi prisoners of war as required by the terms of the Third Geneva Convention of 1949, under the auspices of the International Committee of the Red Cross;

6. Requests all Member States, as well as the United Nations, the specialized agencies and other international organizations in the United Nations system, to take all appropriate action to cooperate with the Government and people of Kuwait in the reconstruction of their country;

7. Decides that Iraq shall notify the Secretary-General and the Security Council when it has taken the actions set out above;

8. Decides that in order to secure the rapid establishment of a definitive end to the hostilities, the Security Council remains actively seized of the matter.

Resolution 687 (1991)

Adopted by the Security Council at its 2981st meeting, on 3 April 1991

The Security Council,

Recalling its resolutions 660 (1990) of 2 August 1990, 661 (1990) of 6 August 1990, 662 (1990) of 9 August 1990, 664 (1990) of 18 August 1990, 665 (1990) of 25 August 1990, 666 (1990) of 13 September 1990, 667 (1990) of 16 September 1990, 669 (1990) of 24 September 1990, 670 (1990) of 25 September 1990, 674 (1990) of 29 October 1990, 677 (1990) of 28 November 1990, 678 (1990) of 29 November 1990 and 686 (1991) of 2 March 1991,

Welcoming the restoration to Kuwait of its sovereignty, independence and territorial integrity and the return of its legitimate Government,

Affirming the commitment of all Member States to the sovereignty, territorial integrity and political independence of Kuwait and Iraq, and noting the intention expressed by the Member States cooperating with Kuwait under paragraph 2 of resolution 678 (1990) to bring their military presence in Iraq to an end as soon as possible consistent with paragraph 8 of resolution 686 (1991),

Reaffirming the need to be assured of Iraq's peaceful intentions in the light of its unlawful invasion and occupation of Kuwait,

Taking note of the letter sent by the Minister for Foreign Affairs of Iraq on 27 February 1991 and those sent pursuant to resolution 686 (1991),

Noting that Iraq and Kuwait, as independent sovereign States, signed at Baghdad on 4 October 1963 "Agreed Minutes Between the State of Kuwait and the Republic of Iraq Regarding the Restoration of Friendly Relations, Recognition and Related Matters," thereby recognizing formally the boundary between Iraq and Kuwait and the allocation of islands, which were registered with the United Nations in accordance with Article 102 of the Charter of the United Nations and in which Iraq recognized the independence and complete sovereignty of the State of Kuwait within its borders as specified and accepted in the letter of the Prime Minister of Iraq dated 21 July 1932, and as accepted by the Ruler of Kuwait in his letter dated 10 August 1932,

Conscious of the need for demarcation of the said boundary,

Conscious also of the statements by Iraq threatening to use weapons in violation of its obligations under the Geneva Protocol for the Prohibition of the Use in War of Asphyxiating, Poisonous or Other Gases, and of Bacteriological Methods of Warfare, signed at Geneva on 17 June 1925, and of its prior use of chemical weapons and affirming that grave consequences would follow any further use by Iraq of such weapons,

[...]

Aware of the use by Iraq of ballistic missiles in unprovoked attacks and therefore of the need to take specific measures in regard to such missiles located in Iraq,

Concerned by the reports in the hands of Member States that Iraq has attempted to acquire materials for a nuclear-weapons programme contrary to its obligations under the Treaty on the Non-Proliferation of Nuclear Weapons of 1 July 1968,

Recalling the objective of the establishment of a nuclear-weapons-free zone in the region of the Middle East,

Conscious of the threat that all weapons of mass destruction pose to peace and security in the area and of the need to work towards the establishment in the Middle East of a zone free of such weapons,

Conscious also of the objective of achieving balanced and comprehensive control of armaments in the region,

Conscious further of the importance of achieving the objectives noted above using all available means, including a dialogue among the States of the region,

Noting that resolution 686 (1991) marked the lifting of the measures imposed by resolution 661 (1990) in so far as they applied to Kuwait,

Noting that despite the progress being made in fulfilling the obligations of resolution 686 (1991), many Kuwaiti and third country nationals are still not accounted for and property remains unreturned,

Recalling the International Convention against the Taking of Hostages, opened for signature at New York on 18 December 1979, which categorizes all acts of taking hostages as manifestations of international terrorism,

Deploring threats made by Iraq during the recent conflict to make use of terrorism against targets outside Iraq and the taking of hostages by Iraq,

Taking note with grave concern of the reports of the Secretary-General of 20 March 1991 and 28 March 1991, and conscious of the necessity to meet urgently the humanitarian needs in Kuwait and Iraq,

Bearing in mind its objective of restoring international peace and security in the area as set out in recent resolutions of the Security Council,

Conscious of the need to take the following measures acting under Chapter VII of the Charter,

1. Affirms all thirteen resolutions noted above, except as expressly changed below to achieve the goals of this resolution, including a formal cease-fire;

A

2. Demands that Iraq and Kuwait respect the inviolability of the international boundary and the allocation of islands set out in the "Agreed Minutes Between the State of Kuwait and the Republic of Iraq Regarding the Restoration of Friendly Relations, Recognition and Related Matters," signed by them in the exercise of their sovereignty at Baghdad on 4 October 1963 and registered with the United Nations and published by the United Nations in document 7063, United Nations, Treaty Series, 1964;

3. Calls upon the Secretary-General to lend his assistance to make arrangements with Iraq and Kuwait to demarcate the boundary between Iraq and Kuwait, drawing on appropriate material, including the map transmitted by Security Council document S/22412 and to report back to the Security Council within one month;

4. Decides to guarantee the inviolability of the above-mentioned international boundary and to take as appropriate all necessary measures to that end in accordance with the Charter of the United Nations;

B

5. Requests the Secretary-General, after consulting with Iraq and Kuwait, to submit within three days to the Security Council for its approval a plan for the immediate deployment of a United Nations observer unit to monitor the Khor Abdullah and a demilitarized zone, which is hereby established, extending ten kilometres into Iraq and five kilometres into Kuwait from the boundary referred to in the "Agreed Minutes Between the State of Kuwait and the Republic of Iraq Regarding the Restoration of Friendly Relations, Recognition and Related Matters" of 4 October 1963; to deter violations of the boundary through its presence in and surveillance of the demilitarized zone; to observe any hostile or potentially hostile action mounted from the territory of one State to the other; and for the Secretary-General to report regularly to the Security Council on the operations of the unit, and immediately if there are serious violations of the zone or potential threats to peace;

6. Notes that as soon as the Secretary-General notifies the Security Council of the completion of the deployment of the United Nations observer unit, the conditions will be established for the Member States cooperating with Kuwait in accordance with resolution 678 (1990) to bring their military presence in Iraq to an end consistent with resolution 686 (1991);

C

7. Invites Iraq to reaffirm unconditionally its obligations under the Geneva Protocol for the Prohibition of the Use in War of Asphyxiating, Poisonous or Other Gases, and of Bacteriological Methods of Warfare, signed at Geneva on 17 June 1925, and to ratify the Convention on the Prohibition of the Development, Production and Stockpiling of Bacteriological (Biological) and Toxin Weapons and on Their Destruction, of 10 April 1972;

8. Decides that Iraq shall unconditionally accept the destruction, removal, or rendering harmless, under international supervision, of:

(a) All chemical and biological weapons and all stocks of agents and all related subsystems and components and all research, development, support and manufacturing facilities;

(b) All ballistic missiles with a range greater than 150 kilometres and related major parts, and repair and production facilities;

9. Decides, for the implementation of paragraph 8 above, the following:

(a) Iraq shall submit to the Secretary-General, within fifteen days of the adoption of the present resolution, a declaration of the locations, amounts and types of all items specified in paragraph 8 and agree to urgent, on-site inspection as specified below;

(b) The Secretary-General, in consultation with the appropriate Governments and, where appropriate, with the Director-General of the World Health Organization, within forty-five days of the passage of the present resolution, shall develop, and submit to the Council for approval, a plan calling for the completion of the following acts within forty-five days of such approval:

(i) The forming of a Special Commission, which shall carry out immediate on-site inspection of Iraq's biological, chemical and missile capabilities, based on Iraq's declarations and the designation of any additional locations by the Special Commission itself;

(ii) The yielding by Iraq of possession to the Special Commission for destruction, removal or rendering harmless, taking into account the requirements of public safety, of all items specified under paragraph 8 (a) above, including items at the additional locations designated by the Special Commission under paragraph 9 (b) (i) above and the destruction by Iraq, under the supervision of the Special Commission, of all its missile capabilities, including launchers, as specified under paragraph 8 (b) above;

(iii) The provision by the Special Commission of the assistance and cooperation to the Director-General of the International Atomic Energy Agency required in paragraphs 12 and 13 below;

10. Decides that Iraq shall unconditionally undertake not to use, develop, construct or acquire any of the items specified in paragraphs 8 and 9 above and requests the Secretary-General, in consultation with the Special Commission, to develop a plan for the future ongoing monitoring and verification of Iraq's compliance with this paragraph, to be submitted to the Security Council for approval within one hundred and twenty days of the passage of this resolution;

11. Invites Iraq to reaffirm unconditionally its obligations under the Treaty on the Non-Proliferation of Nuclear Weapons of 1 July 1968;

12. Decides that Iraq shall unconditionally agree not to acquire or develop nuclear weapons or nuclear-weapons-usable material or any subsystems or components or any research, development, support or manufacturing facilities related to the above; to submit to the Secretary-General and the Director-General of the International Atomic Energy Agency within fifteen days of the adoption of the present resolution a declaration of the locations, amounts, and types of all items specified above; to place all of its nuclear-weapons-usable materials under the exclusive control, for custody and removal, of the International Atomic Energy Agency, with the assistance and cooperation of the Special Commission as provided for in the plan of the Secretary-General discussed in paragraph 9 (b) above; to accept, in accordance with the arrangements provided for in paragraph 13 below, urgent on-site inspection and the destruction, removal or rendering harmless as appropriate of all items specified above; and to accept the plan discussed in paragraph 13 below for the future ongoing monitoring and verification of its compliance with these undertakings;

13. Requests the Director-General of the International Atomic Energy Agency, through the Secretary-General, with the assistance and cooperation of the Special Commission as provided for in the plan of the Secretary-General in paragraph 9 (b) above, to carry out immediate on-site inspection of Iraq's nuclear capabilities based on Iraq's declarations and the designation of any additional locations by the Special Commission; to develop a plan for submission to the Security Council within forty-five days calling for the destruction, removal, or rendering harmless as appropriate of all items listed in paragraph 12 above; to carry out the plan within forty-five days following approval by the Security Council; and to develop a plan, taking into account the rights and obligations of Iraq under the Treaty on the Non-Proliferation of Nuclear Weapons of 1 July 1968, for the future ongoing monitoring and verification of Iraq's compliance with paragraph 12 above, including an inventory of all nuclear material in Iraq subject to the Agency's

verification and inspections to confirm that Agency safeguards cover all relevant nuclear activities in Iraq, to be submitted to the Security Council for approval within one hundred and twenty days of the passage of the present resolution;

14. Takes note that the actions to be taken by Iraq in paragraphs 8, 9, 10, 11, 12 and 13 of the present resolution represent steps towards the goal of establishing in the Middle East a zone free from weapons of mass destruction and all missiles for their delivery and the objective of a global ban on chemical weapons;

D

15. Requests the Secretary-General to report to the Security Council on the steps taken to facilitate the return of all Kuwaiti property seized by Iraq, including a list of any property that Kuwait claims has not been returned or which has not been returned intact;

E

16. Reaffirms that Iraq, without prejudice to the debts and obligations of Iraq arising prior to 2 August 1990, which will be addressed through the normal mechanisms, is liable under international law for any direct loss, damage, including environmental damage and the depletion of natural resources, or injury to foreign Governments, nationals and corporations, as a result of Iraq's unlawful invasion and occupation of Kuwait;

17. Decides that all Iraqi statements made since 2 August 1990 repudiating its foreign debt are null and void, and demands that Iraq adhere scrupulously to all of its obligations concerning servicing and repayment of its foreign debt;

18. Decides also to create a fund to pay compensation for claims that fall within paragraph 16 above and to establish a Commission that will administer the fund;

19. Directs the Secretary-General to develop and present to the Security Council for decision, no later than thirty days following the adoption of the present resolution, recommendations for the fund to meet the requirement for the payment of claims established in accordance with paragraph 18 above and for a programme to implement the decisions in paragraphs 16, 17 and 18 above, including: administration of the fund; mechanisms for determining the appropriate level of Iraq's contribution to the fund based on a percentage of the value of the exports of petroleum and petroleum products from Iraq not to exceed a figure to be suggested to the Council by the Secretary-General, taking into account the requirements of the people of Iraq, Iraq's payment capacity as assessed in conjunction with the international financial institutions taking into consideration external debt service, and the needs of the Iraqi economy; arrangements for ensuring

that payments are made to the fund; the process by which funds will be allocated and claims paid; appropriate procedures for evaluating losses, listing claims and verifying their validity and resolving disputed claims in respect of Iraq's liability as specified in paragraph 16 above; and the composition of the Commission designated above;

F

20. Decides, effective immediately, that the prohibitions against the sale or supply to Iraq of commodities or products, other than medicine and health supplies, and prohibitions against financial transactions related thereto contained in resolution 661 (1990) shall not apply to foodstuffs notified to the Security Council Committee established by resolution 661 (1990) concerning the situation between Iraq and Kuwait or, with the approval of that Committee, under the simplified and accelerated "no-objection" procedure, to materials and supplies for essential civilian needs as identified in the report of the Secretary-General dated 20 March 1991, and in any further findings of humanitarian need by the Committee;

21. Decides that the Security Council shall review the provisions of paragraph 20 above every sixty days in the light of the policies and practices of the Government of Iraq, including the implementation of all relevant resolutions of the Security Council, for the purpose of determining whether to reduce or lift the prohibitions referred to therein;

22. Decides that upon the approval by the Security Council of the programme called for in paragraph 19 above and upon Council agreement that Iraq has completed all actions contemplated in paragraphs 8, 9, 10, 11, 12 and 13 above, the prohibitions against the import of commodities and products originating in Iraq and the prohibitions against financial transactions related thereto contained in resolution 661 (1990) shall have no further force or effect;

23. Decides that, pending action by the Security Council under paragraph 22 above, the Security Council Committee established by resolution 661 (1990) shall be empowered to approve, when required to assure adequate financial resources on the part of Iraq to carry out the activities under paragraph 20 above, exceptions to the prohibition against the import of commodities and products originating in Iraq;

24. Decides that, in accordance with resolution 661 (1990) and subsequent related resolutions and until a further decision is taken by the Security Council, all States shall continue to prevent the sale or supply, or the promotion or facilitation of such sale or supply, to Iraq by their nationals, or from their territories or using their flag vessels or aircraft, of:

(a) Arms and related materiel of all types, specifically including the sale or transfer through other means of all forms of conventional military equipment, including for paramilitary forces, and spare parts and components and their means of production, for such equipment;

(b) Items specified and defined in paragraphs 8 and 12 above not otherwise covered above;

(c) Technology under licensing or other transfer arrangements used in the production, utilization or stockpiling of items specified in subparagraphs (a) and (b) above;

(d) Personnel or materials for training or technical support services relating to the design, development, manufacture, use, maintenance or support of items specified in subparagraphs (a) and (b) above;

25. Calls upon all States and international organizations to act strictly in accordance with paragraph 24 above, notwithstanding the existence of any contracts, agreements, licenses or any other arrangements;

26. Requests the Secretary-General, in consultation with appropriate Governments, to develop within sixty days, for the approval of the Security Council, guidelines to facilitate full international implementation of paragraphs 24 and 25 above and paragraph 27 below, and to make them available to all States and to establish a procedure for updating these guidelines periodically;

27. Calls upon all States to maintain such national controls and procedures and to take such other actions consistent with the guidelines to be established by the Security Council under paragraph 26 above as may be necessary to ensure compliance with the terms of paragraph 24 above, and calls upon international organizations to take all appropriate steps to assist in ensuring such full compliance;

28. Agrees to review its decisions in paragraphs 22, 23, 24 and 25 above, except for the items specified and defined in paragraphs 8 and 12 above, on a regular basis and in any case one hundred and twenty days following passage of the present resolution, taking into account Iraq's compliance with the resolution and general progress towards the control of armaments in the region;

29. Decides that all States, including Iraq, shall take the necessary measures to ensure that no claim shall lie at the instance of the Government of Iraq, or of any person or body in Iraq, or of any person claiming through or for the benefit of any such person or body, in connection with any contract or other transaction

where its performance was affected by reason of the measures taken by the Security Council in resolution 661 (1990) and related resolutions;

G

30. Decides that, in furtherance of its commitment to facilitate the repatriation of all Kuwaiti and third country nationals, Iraq shall extend all necessary cooperation to the International Committee of the Red Cross, providing lists of such persons, facilitating the access of the International Committee of the Red Cross to all such persons wherever located or detained and facilitating the search by the International Committee of the Red Cross for those Kuwaiti and third country nationals still unaccounted for;

31. Invites the International Committee of the Red Cross to keep the Secretary-General apprised as appropriate of all activities undertaken in connection with facilitating the repatriation or return of all Kuwaiti and third country nationals or their remains present in Iraq on or after 2 August 1990;

H

32. Requires Iraq to inform the Security Council that it will not commit or support any act of international terrorism or allow any organization directed towards commission of such acts to operate within its territory and to condemn unequivocally and renounce all acts, methods and practices of terrorism;

I

33. Declares that, upon official notification by Iraq to the Secretary-General and to the Security Council of its acceptance of the provisions above, a formal cease-fire is effective between Iraq and Kuwait and the Member States cooperating with Kuwait in accordance with resolution 678 (1990);

34. Decides to remain seized of the matter and to take such further steps as may be required for the implementation of the present resolution and to secure peace and security in the area.

Resolution 688 (1991)

Adopted by the Security Council at its 2982nd meeting on 5 April 1991

The Security Council,

Mindful of its duties and its responsibilities under the Charter of the United Nations for the maintenance of international peace and security,

Recalling of Article 2, paragraph 7, of the Charter of the United Nations,

Gravely concerned by the repression of the Iraqi civilian population in many parts of Iraq, including most recently in Kurdish populated areas, which led to a massive flow of refugees towards and across international frontiers and to cross-border incursions, which threaten international peace and security in the region,

Deeply disturbed by the magnitude of the human suffering involved, . . .

[. . .]

Reaffirming the commitment of all Member States to the sovereignty, territorial integrity and political independence of Iraq and of all States in the area,

Bearing in mind the Secretary-General's report of 20 March 1991 (S/22366),

1. Condemns the repression of the Iraqi civilian population in many parts of Iraq, including most recently in Kurdish populated areas, the consequences of which threaten international peace and security in the region;

2. Demands that Iraq, as a contribution to remove the threat to international peace and security in the region, immediately end this repression and express the hope in the same context that an open dialogue will take place to ensure that the human and political rights of all Iraqi citizens are respected;

3. Insists that Iraq allow immediate access by international humanitarian organizations to all those in need of assistance in all parts of Iraq and to make available all necessary facilities for their operations;

4. Requests the Secretary-General to pursue his humanitarian efforts in Iraq and to report forthwith, if appropriate on the basis of a further mission to the region, on the plight of the Iraqi civilian population, and in particular the Kurdish population, suffering from the repression in all its forms inflicted by the Iraqi authorities;

5. Requests further the Secretary-General to use all the resources at his disposal, including those of the relevant United Nations agencies, to address urgently the critical needs of the refugees and displaced Iraqi population;

6. Appeals to all Member States and to all humanitarian organizations to contribute to these humanitarian relief efforts;

7. Demands that Iraq cooperate with the Secretary-General to these ends;

8. Decides to remain seized of the matter.

Resolution 689 (1991)

Adopted by the Security Council at its 2983rd meeting on 9 April 1991

The Security Council,

Recalling its resolution 687 (1991),

Acting under Chapter VII of the Charter,

1. Approves the report of the Secretary-General on the implementation of paragraph 5 of Security Council resolution 687 (1991) contained in document S/22454 and Add. 1–3 of 5 April 1991;

2. Notes that the decision to set up the observer unit was taken in paragraph 5 of resolution 687 (1991) and can only be terminated by a decision of the Council. The Council shall therefore review the question of termination or continuation every six months;

3. Decides that the modalities for the initial six-month period of the United Nations Iraq-Kuwait Observation Mission shall be as set out in accordance with the above-mentioned report and shall also be reviewed every six months.

Resolution 692 (1991)

Adopted by the Security Council at its 2987th meeting on 20 May 1991

The Security Council,

Recalling its resolutions 694 (1990) of 29 October 1990, 686 (1991) of 2 March 1991 and 687 (1991) of 3 April 1991, concerning the liability of Iraq, without prejudice to its debts and obligations arising prior to 2 August 1990, for any direct loss, damage, including environmental damage and the depletion of natural resources, or injury to foreign Governments, nationals and corporations, as a result of Iraq's unlawful invasion and occupation of Kuwait,

Taking note of the Secretary-General's report of 2 May 1991 (S/22559), submitted in accordance with paragraph 19 of resolution 687 (1991),

Acting under Chapter VII of the Charter of the United Nations,

1. Expresses its appreciation to the Secretary-General for his report of 2 May 1991;

2. Welcomes the fact that the Secretary-General will now undertake the appropriate consultations requested by paragraph 19 of resolution 687 (1991) so that he will be in a position to recommend to the Security Council for decision as soon as possible the figure which the level of Iraq's contribution to the Fund will not exceed;

3. Decides to establish the Fund and Commission referred to in paragraph 18 of resolution 687 (1991) in accordance with Part I of the Secretary-General's report, and that the Governing Council will be located at the Offices of the United Nations at Geneva and that the Governing Council may decide whether some of the activities of the Commission should be carried out elsewhere;

4. Requests the Secretary-General to take the actions necessary to implement paragraphs 2 and 3 above in consultation with the members of the Governing Council;

5. Directs the Governing Council to proceed in an expeditious manner to implement the provisions of Section E of resolution 687 (1991), taking into account the recommendations in section II of the Secretary-General's report;

6. Decides that the requirement for Iraqi contributions shall apply in the manner to be prescribed by the Governing Council with respect to all Iraqi petroleum and petroleum products exported from Iraq after 3 April 1991 as well as such petroleum and petroleum products exported earlier but not delivered or not paid for as a specific result of the prohibitions contained in resolution 661 (1990);

7. Requests the Governing Council to report as soon as possible on the actions it has taken with regard to the mechanisms for determining the appropriate level of Iraq's contribution to the Fund and the arrangements for ensuring that payments are made to the Fund, so that the Security Council can give its approval in accordance with paragraph 22 of resolution 687 (1991);

8. Requests that all States and international organizations cooperate with the decisions of the Governing Council taken pursuant to paragraph 5 of the present resolution, and also requests that the Governing Council keep the Security Council informed on this matter;

9. Decides that, if the Governing Council notifies the Security Council that Iraq has failed to carry out decisions of the Governing Council taken pursuant to paragraph 5 of this resolution, the Security Council intends to retain or to take action to reimpose the

prohibition against the import of petroleum and petroleum products originating in Iraq and financial transactions related thereto;

10. Decides also to remain seized of this matter and that the Governing Council will submit periodic reports to the Secretary-General and the Security Council.

Resolution 699 (1991)

Adopted by the Security Council at its 2994th meeting on

17 June 1991

The Security Council,

Recalling its resolution 687 (1991),

Taking note of the report of the Secretary-General of 17 May 1991 (S/22614), submitted to it in pursuance of paragraph 9 (b) of resolution 687 (1991),

Also taking note of the Secretary-General's note of 17 May 1991 (S/22615), transmitting to the Council the letter addressed to him under paragraph 13 of the resolution by the Director-General of the International Atomic Energy Agency (IAEA),

Acting under Chapter VII of the Charter,

1. Approves the plan contained in the report of the Secretary-General;

2. Confirms that the Special Commission and the IAEA have the authority to conduct activities under section C of resolution 687 (1991), for the purpose of the destruction, removal or rendering harmless of the items specified in paragraphs 8 and 12 of that resolution, after the 45-day period following the approval of this plan until such activities have been completed;

3. Requests the Secretary-General to submit to the Security Council progress reports on the implementation of the plan referred to in paragraph 1 every six months after the adoption of this resolution;

4. Decides to encourage the maximum assistance, in cash and in kind, from all Member States to ensure that activities under section C of resolution 687 (1991) are undertaken effectively and expeditiously; further decides, however, that the Government of Iraq shall be liable for the full costs of carrying out the tasks authorized by section C; and requests the Secretary-General to submit to the Council within 30 days for approval recommendations as to the most effective means by which Iraq's obligations in this respect may be fulfilled.

Resolution 700 (1991)

Adopted by the Security Council at its 2994th meeting on 17 June 1991

The Security Council,

Recalling its resolutions 661 (1990) of 6 August 1990, 665 (1990) of 25 August 1990, 670 (1990) of 25 September 1990 and 687 (1991) of 3 April 1991,

Taking note of the Secretary-General's report of 2 June 1991 (S/22660) submitted pursuant to paragraph 26 of resolution 687 (1991),

Acting under Chapter VII of the Charter of the United Nations,

1. Expresses its appreciation to the Secretary-General for his report of 2 June 1991 (S/22660);

2. Approves the Guidelines to Facilitate Full International Implementation of paragraphs 24, 25 and 27 of Security Council resolution 687 (1991), annexed to the report of the Secretary-General (S/22660);

3. Reiterates its call upon all States and international organizations to act in a manner consistent with the Guidelines;

4. Requests all States, in accordance with paragraph 8 of the Guidelines, to report to the Secretary-General within 45 days on the measures they have instituted for meeting the obligations set out in paragraph 24 of resolution 687 (1991);

5. Entrusts the Committee established under resolution 661 (1990) concerning the situation between Iraq and Kuwait with the responsibility, under the Guidelines, for monitoring the prohibitions against the sale or supply of arms to Iraq and related sanctions established in paragraph 24 of resolution 687 (1991);

6. Decides to remain seized of the matter and to review the Guidelines at the same time as it reviews paragraphs 22, 23, 24 and 25 of resolution 687 (1991) as set out in paragraph 28 thereof.

Resolution 705 (1991)

Adopted by the Security Council at its 3004th meeting, on 15 August 1991

The Security Council,

Having considered the note of 30 May 1991 of the Secretary-General pursuant to paragraph 13 of his report of 2 May 1991

(S/22559) which was annexed to the Secretary-General's letter of 30 May 1991 to the President of the Security Council (S/22661),

Acting under Chapter VII of the Charter,

1. Expresses its appreciation to the Secretary-General for his note of 30 May 1991 which was annexed to his letter to the President of the Security Council of the same date (S/22661);

2. Decides that in accordance with the suggestion made by the Secretary-General in paragraph 7 of his note of 30 May 1991, compensation to be paid by Iraq (as arising from section E of resolution 687) shall not exceed 30 per cent of the annual value of the exports of petroleum and petroleum products from Iraq;

3. Decides further, in accordance with paragraph 8 of the Secretary-General's note of 30 May 1991, to review the figure established in paragraph 2 above from time to time in light of data and assumptions contained in the letter of the Secretary-General (S/22661) and other relevant developments.

Resolution 706 (1991)

Adopted by the Security Council at its 3004th meeting, on 15 August 1991

The Security Council,

Recalling its previous relevant resolutions and in particular resolutions 661 (1990), 686 (1991), 687 (1991), 688 (1991), 692 (1991), 699 (1991) and 705 (1991),

Taking note of the report (S/22799) dated 15 July 1991 of the inter-agency mission headed by the Executive Delegate of the Secretary-General for the United Nations inter-agency humanitarian programme for Iraq, Kuwait and the Iraq/Turkey and Iraq/Iran border areas,

Concerned by the serious nutritional and health situation of the Iraqi civilian population as described in this report, and by the risk of a further deterioration of this situation,

Concerned also that the repatriation or return of all Kuwaitis and third country nationals or their remains present in Iraq on or after 2 August 1990, pursuant to paragraph 2 (c) of resolution 686 (1991), and paragraphs 30 and 31 of resolution 687 (1991) has not yet been fully carried out,

Taking note of the conclusions of the above-mentioned report, and in particular of the proposal for oil sales by Iraq to finance the purchase of foodstuffs, medicines and materials and supplies for essential civilian needs for the purpose of providing humanitarian relief,

Taking note also of the letters dated 14 April 1991, 31 May 1991, 6 June 1991, 9 July 1991 and 22 July 1991 from the Minister of Foreign Affairs of Iraq and the Permanent Representative of Iraq to the Chairman of the Committee established by resolution 661 (1990) concerning the export from Iraq of petroleum and petroleum products,

Convinced of the need for equitable distribution of humanitarian relief to all segments of the Iraqi civilian population through effective monitoring and transparency,

Recalling and reaffirming in this regard its resolution 688 (1991) and in particular the importance which the Council attaches to Iraq allowing unhindered access by international humanitarian organizations to all those in need of assistance in all parts of Iraq and making available all necessary facilities for their operation, and in this connection stressing the important and continuing role played by the Memorandum of Understanding between the United Nations and Government of Iraq of 18 April 1991 (S/22663),

Recalling that, pursuant to resolutions 687 (1991), 692 (1991) and 699 (1991), Iraq is required to pay the full costs of the Special Commission and the IAEA in carrying out the tasks authorized by section C of resolution 687 (1991), and that the Secretary-General in his report to the Security Council of 15 July 1991 (S/22792), submitted pursuant to paragraph 4 of resolution 699 (1991), expressed the view that the most obvious way of obtaining financial resources from Iraq to meet the costs of the Special Commission and the IAEA would be to authorize the sale of some Iraqi petroleum and petroleum products; recalling further that Iraq is required to pay its contributions to the Compensation Fund and half the costs of the Iraq-Kuwait Boundary Demarcation Commission, and recalling further that in its resolutions 686 (1991) and 687 (1991) the Security Council demanded that Iraq return in the shortest possible time all Kuwaiti property seized by it and requested the Secretary-General to take steps to facilitate this,

Acting under Chapter VII of the Charter,

1. Authorizes all States, subject to the decision to be taken by the Security Council pursuant to paragraph 5 below and notwithstanding the provisions of paragraphs 3 (a), 3 (b) and 4 of resolution 661 (1990), to permit the import, during a period of 6 months from the date of passage of the resolution pursuant to paragraph 5 below, of petroleum and petroleum products originating in Iraq sufficient to produce a sum to be determined by the Council following receipt of the report of the Secretary-General requested in paragraph 5 of this resolution but not to exceed 1.6 billion United States dollars for the purposes set out in this resolution and subject to the following conditions:

(a) Approval of each purchase of Iraqi petroleum and petroleum products by the Security Council Committee established by resolution 661 (1990) following notification to the Committee by the State concerned,

(b) Payment of the full amount of each purchase of Iraqi petroleum and petroleum products directly by the purchaser in the State concerned into an escrow account to be established by the United Nations and to be administered by the Secretary-General, exclusively to meet the purposes of this resolution.

(c) Approval by the Council, following the report of the Secretary-General requested in paragraph 5 of this resolution, of a scheme for the purchase of foodstuffs, medicines and materials and supplies for essential civilian needs as referred to in paragraph 20 of resolution 687 (1991), in particular health related materials, all of which to be labelled to the extent possible as being supplied under this scheme, and for all feasible and appropriate United Nations monitoring and supervision for the purpose of assuring their equitable distribution to meet humanitarian needs in all regions of Iraq and to all categories of the Iraqi civilian population as well as all feasible and appropriate management relevant to this purpose, such a United Nations role to be available if desired for humanitarian assistance from other sources,

[…]

2. Decides that a part of the sum in the account to be established by the Secretary-General shall be made available by him to finance the purchase of foodstuffs, medicines and materials and supplies for essential civilian needs, as referred to in paragraph 20 of resolution 687, and the cost to the United Nations of its roles under this resolution and of other necessary humanitarian activities in Iraq,

[…]

4. Decides that the percentage of the value of exports of petroleum and petroleum products from Iraq, authorized under this resolution to be paid to the United Nations Compensation Fund, as called for in paragraph 19 of resolution 687 (1991), and as defined in paragraph 6 of resolution 692 (1991), shall be the same as the percentage decided by the Security Council in paragraph 2 of resolution 705 (1991) for payments to the Compensation Fund, until such time as the Governing Council of the Fund decides otherwise,

5. Requests the Secretary-General to submit within 20 days of the date of adoption of this resolution a report to the Security Council for decision on measures to be taken in order to implement paragraphs 1 (a), (b), (c), estimates of the humanitarian requirements of Iraq set out in paragraph 2 above and of the amount of Iraq's financial obligations set out in paragraph 3 above up to the end of the period of the authorization in paragraph 1 above, as well as the method for taking the necessary legal measures to ensure that the purposes of this resolution are carried out and the method for

taking account of the costs of transportation of such Iraqi petroleum and petroleum products,

6. Further requests the Secretary-General in consultation with the International Committee of the Red Cross to submit within 20 days of the date of adoption of this resolution a report to the Security Council on activities undertaken in accordance with paragraph 31 of resolution 687 (1991) in connection with facilitating the repatriation or return of all Kuwaiti and third country nationals or their remains present in Iraq on or after 2 August 1990,

7. Requires the Government of Iraq to provide to the Secretary-General and appropriate international organizations on the first day of the month immediately following the adoption of the present resolution and on the first day of each month thereafter until further notice, a statement of the gold and foreign currency reserves it holds whether in Iraq or elsewhere,

8. Calls upon all States to cooperate fully in the implementation of this resolution,

9. Decides to remain seized of the matter.

Resolution 707 (1991)

Adopted by the Security Council at its 3004th meeting, on 15 August 1991

The Security Council,

Recalling its resolution 687 (1991), and its other resolutions on this matter,

Recalling the letter of 11 April 1991 from the President of the Security Council to the Permanent Representative of Iraq to the United Nations (S/22485) noting that on the basis of Iraq's written agreement (S/22456) to implement fully resolution 687 (1991) the preconditions established in paragraph 33 of that resolution for a cease-fire had been met,

Noting with grave concern the letters dated 26 June 1991 (S/22739), 28 June 1991 (S/22743) and 4 July 1991 (S/22761) from the Secretary-General, conveying information obtained from the Executive Chairman of the Special Commission and the Director-General of the IAEA which establishes Iraq's failure to comply with its obligations under resolution 687 (1991),

Recalling further the statement issued by the President of the Security Council on 28 June 1991 (S/22746) requesting that a high-level mission consisting of the Chairman of the Special Commission, the Director-General of the IAEA, and the Under-Secretary-General for Disarmament Affairs be dispatched to meet with officials at the highest levels of the Government of Iraq at the earliest opportunity to obtain written assurance that Iraq will fully and immediately cooperate in the inspection of the locations identified by the Special Commission and present for immediate inspection any of those items that may have been transported from those locations,

Dismayed by the report of the high-level mission to the Secretary-General (S/22761) on the results of its meetings with the highest levels of the Iraqi Government,

Gravely concerned by the information provided to the Council by the Special Commission and the IAEA on 15 July 1991 (S/22788) and 25 July 1991 (S/22837) regarding the actions of the Government of Iraq in flagrant violation of resolution 687 (1991),

Gravely concerned also by the evidence in the letter of 7 July 1991 from the Minister of Foreign Affairs of Iraq to the Secretary-General and in subsequent statements and findings that Iraq's notifications of 18 and 28 April were incomplete and that it had concealed activities, which both constituted material breaches of its obligations under resolution 687 (1991),

Noting also from the letters dated 26 June 1991 (S/22739), 28 June 1991 (S/22743) and 4 July 1991 (S/22761) from the Secretary-General that Iraq has not fully complied with all of its undertakings relating to the privileges, immunities and facilities to be accorded to the Special Commission and the IAEA inspection teams mandated under resolution 687 (1991),

Affirming that in order for the Special Commission to carry out its mandate under paragraph 9 (b) (i), (ii) and (iii) of resolution 687 (1991) to inspect Iraq's chemical and biological weapons and ballistic missile capabilities and to take possession of them for destruction, removal or rendering harmless, full disclosure on the part of Iraq as required in paragraph 9 (a) of resolution 687 (1991) is essential,

Affirming that in order for the IAEA with the assistance and cooperation of the Special Commission, to determine what nuclear-weapons-usable material or any subsystems or components or any research, development, support or manufacturing facilities related to them need, in accordance with paragraph 13 of resolution 687 (1991), to be destroyed, removed or rendered harmless, Iraq is required to make a declaration of all its nuclear programmes including any which it claims are for purposes not related to nuclear-weapons-usable material,

Affirming that the aforementioned failures of Iraq to act in strict conformity with its obligations under resolution 687 (1991) constitutes a material breach of its acceptance of the relevant provisions

or [of] resolution 687 (1991) which established a cease-fire and provided the conditions essential to the restoration of peace and security in the region,

Affirming further that Iraq's failure to comply with its safeguards agreement with the International Atomic Energy Agency, concluded pursuant to the Treaty on the Non-Proliferation of Nuclear Weapons of 1 July 1968, as established by the resolution of the Board of Governors of the IAEA of 18 July 1991 (GOV/2531), constitutes a breach of its international obligations,

Determined to ensure full compliance with resolution 687 (1991) and in particular its section C,

Acting under Chapter VII of the Charter,

1. Condemns Iraq's serious violation of a number of its obligations under section C of resolution 687 (1991) and of its undertakings to cooperate with the Special Commission and the IAEA, which constitutes a material breach of the relevant provisions of resolution 687 which established a cease-fire and provided the conditions essential to the restoration of peace and security in the region,

2. Further condemns non-compliance by the Government of Iraq with its obligations under its safeguards agreement with the International Atomic Energy Agency, as established by the resolution of the Board of Governors of 18 July, which constitutes a violation of its commitments as a party to the Treaty on the Non-Proliferation of Nuclear Weapons of 1 July 1968,

3. Demands that Iraq

(i) provide full, final and complete disclosure, as required by resolution 687 (1991), of all aspects of its programmes to develop weapons of mass destruction and ballistic missiles with a range greater than 150 kilometres, and of all holdings of such weapons, their components and production facilities and locations, as well as all other nuclear programmes, including any which it claims are for purposes not related to nuclear-weapons-usable material, without further delay,

(ii) allow the Special Commission, the IAEA and their Inspection Teams immediate, unconditional and unrestricted access to any and all areas, facilities, equipment, records and means of transportation which they wish to inspect,

(iii) cease immediately any attempt to conceal, or any movement or destruction of any material or equipment relating to its nuclear, chemical or biological weapons or ballistic missile programmes, or material or equipment relating to its other nuclear activities without notification to and prior consent of the Special Commission,

(iv) make available immediately to the Special Commission, the IAEA and their Inspection Teams any items to which they were previously denied access,

(v) allow the Special Commission, the IAEA and their Inspection Teams to conduct both fixed wing and helicopter flights throughout Iraq for all relevant purposes including inspection, surveillance, aerial surveys, transportation and logistics without interference of any kind and upon such terms and conditions as may be determined by the Special Commission, and to make full use of their own aircraft and such airfields in Iraq as they may determine are most appropriate for the work of the Commission,

(vi) halt all nuclear activities of any kind, except for use of isotopes for medical, agricultural or industrial purposes until the Security Council determines that Iraq is in full compliance with this resolution and paragraphs 12 and 13 of resolution 687 (1991), and the IAEA determines that Iraq is in full compliance with its safeguards agreement with that Agency,

(vii) ensure the complete implementation of the privileges, immunities and facilities of the representatives of the Special Commission and the IAEA in accordance with its previous undertakings and their complete safety and freedom of movement,

(viii) immediately provide or facilitate the provision of any transportation, medical or logistical support requested by the Special Commission, the IAEA and their Inspection Teams,

(ix) respond fully, completely and promptly to any questions or requests from the Special Commission, the IAEA and their Inspection Teams,

4. Determines that Iraq retains no ownership interest in items to be destroyed, removed or rendered harmless pursuant to paragraph 12 of resolution 687 (1991),

5. Requires that the Government of Iraq forthwith comply fully and without delay with all its international obligations, including those set out in the present resolution, in resolution 687 (1991), in the Treaty on the Non-Proliferation of Nuclear Weapons of 1 July 1968 and its safeguards agreement with the IAEA.

6. Decides to remain seized of this matter.

Source: United Nations Security Council Resolutions, http://www.un.org/Docs/scres/1991/scres91.htm.

83. Iraqi Letter to the United Nations, September 25, 1991, and the Security Council's Official Reply, September 27, 1991

Introduction

Under the terms of United Nations (UN) Security Council Resolution 687, passed on April 2, 1991, Iraq was obliged to permit UN inspectors unimpeded access to the country and all appropriate facilities to ensure its compliance with demands for the destruction of its stockpiles of and ability to manufacture chemical, biological, and nuclear weapons. The resolution also established the United Nations Special Commission (UNSCOM) to supervise and inspect the Iraqi weapons program. By August 1991, it was clear that Iraqi officials were making every possible effort to conceal their stocks of nuclear materials and were seeking to debar representatives of the UN and the International Atomic Energy Authority (IAEA) from entering related facilities within Iraq. Security Council Resolution 707 of August 15, 1991, reaffirmed the determination of the UN to ensure that Iraq was not equipping itself with such weapons and once again demanded that Iran grant all inspection teams unimpeded access to all its arsenals, stockpiles, manufacturing plants, and other appropriate venues. The following month, on September 24, 1991, Iraqi officials placed 44 nuclear inspectors whom the UN had dispatched to Baghdad under detention and forbade them to make copies of documents relating to nuclear weapons that they had unearthed. The incident quickly developed into a major international crisis. On September 25, 1991, Iraq's ambassador to the UN, Abdul Amir al-Anbari, wrote to the president of the Security Council, Jean-Bernard Mérimée, demanding that Rolf Ekéus, UNSCOM's director, visit Baghdad within 48 hours to resolve the situation. Anbari announced that Iraq would not permit inspectors to enter into the record submitted to the UN documents that were unacceptable to Iraq. He also claimed that UNSCOM was dominated by Americans, who were simply seeking to implement their own government's policies in disregard of UN Security Council resolutions. In response, the Security Council deplored Iraq's repeated breaches of Resolutions 687 and 707 and expressed its confidence in UNSCOM. It did, however, state that it had no objection in principle to a joint Iraqi-UNSCOM inventory of documents and weapons-related materials. For more than a decade, the issue of Iraq's continuing efforts to develop weapons of mass destruction would further bedevil its relations with the UN and the United States. Between 1991 and 1995, UNSCOM personnel discovered evidence of a massive Iraqi effort to develop biological and nuclear weapons and confiscated large quantities of weapons-related materials. In 1996 UNSCOM blew up a germ warfare center in al-Hakam. Some UNSCOM employees believed that by the late 1990s their efforts had seriously crippled Iraq's ability to develop weapons of mass destruction, while others were more skeptical. Iraq's persistent interest in acquiring such weapons was, however, a major factor in the continued imposition of UN economic sanctions well into the 21st century, until President Saddam Hussein and his government were finally overthrown.

Primary Source

Mr. President,

On instructions from my Government, I have the honor to inform you as follows:

1. With a view to solving the problem [of the detainment of the inspectors] satisfactorily and avoiding any difficulties, Iraq wishes Mr. Rolf Ekeus to go to Baghdad so that we may discuss with him ways of remedying the current situation and so that the modalities for the use of German helicopters may be considered.

2. Should Mr. Ekeus not go to Baghdad within 48 hours, the Iraqi authorities insist that the Iraqi side and the inspection team jointly draw up a record of all the documents and photographs taken by the team before the team is authorized to remove anything whatsoever from the site.

3. The Iraqi authorities do not and will not acknowledge any document or photograph that has not been entered in the record jointly drawn up by the two parties. Any allegation based on documents or photographs that have not been entered in the joint record will be indicative of a premeditated intention to prejudice Iraq's interests.

Iraq once again strongly protests at the inspection team's actions, particularly those of the leader of the team, Mr. David Kay. Moreover, we reiterate what we have already indicated to Mr. Rolf Ekeus, namely, that the main source of the difficulties being encountered is the fact that inspection missions are entrusted to a large number of United States nationals. These United States nationals simply implement the policies of their Government, which persists in violating both the letter and the spirit of the resolutions of the Security Council and imposes its hostile policies on the Iraqi leadership.

Thank you,

Abdul Amir al-Anbari,

Iraqi Ambassador to the United Nations

Mr. Abdul Amir al-Anbari,

In reply to your letter dated 25 September 1991, I have the honor to inform you on behalf of the Security Council of the following:

1. The Council deplores Iraq's repeated violations of its obligations under resolutions 687 and 707 and reiterates its demand that the inspectors of the Special Commission and the International Atomic Energy Agency be released immediately with all the material they hold. The Council has no objection to the immediate establishment in this particular case of a joint inventory, in the presence of Iraqi officials, enabling the inspection team to fulfill the responsibility entrusted to it by the Security Council.

2. Mr. Ekeus has already contacted your mission on the modalities and scheduling of the next inspection missions, which will use helicopters of the Special Commission.

3. The Council reaffirms its strong support for the items of the Special Commission and the International Atomic Energy Agency, whose members are highly conscious of their responsibilities as international civil servants and are performing difficult tasks with the full authority of the Security Council in accordance with the Charter of the United Nations.

Thank you,

Jean-Bernard Mérimée,

President, United Nations Security Council

> **Source:** "Texts of Iraqi Letter to U.N. and the Council President's Reply," *New York Times,* http://www.nytimes.com/1991/09/27/world/texts-of-iraqi-letter-to-un-and-the-council-president-s-reply.html?pagewanted=1.

84. President Bill Clinton, Address to the Nation on the Strike on Iraqi Intelligence Headquarters, June 26, 1993, and Letter to Congressional Leaders on the Strike on Iraqi Intelligence Headquarters, June 28, 1993 [Excerpts]

Introduction

President Saddam Hussein of Iraq may well have regarded his country's defeat in the 1991 Persian Gulf War as almost a personal insult on the part of President George H. W. Bush, justifying Hussein in launching a vendetta. In April 1993, three months after leaving office, Bush visited Kuwait City, a trip intended to celebrate his role in winning the war. That month Kuwaiti authorities arrested 16 individuals, including 2 Iraqis, whom they claimed were the leaders in a plot sponsored by the Iraqi government to mount a car bomb assassination attack against Bush during his time in Kuwait. By May, reports of the alleged assassination conspiracy had surfaced in the U.S. press, generating growing pressure for appropriate retaliation from Congress, State Department officials, and allied Arab governments, particularly that of Saudi Arabia. In late June 1993 Democratic president Bill Clinton, facing steadily increasing demands that he respond forcefully to the international affront to the U.S. government that such a plot represented, authorized American air strikes on Iraqi intelligence headquarters in Baghdad, where the scheme to kill Bush had allegedly originated. In a televised address to the nation, Clinton defended his decision to order American naval vessels in the Persian Gulf to fire 23 Tomahawk cruise missiles, each carrying 1,000 pounds of high explosives, against this target. Eight civilians died in the operation, a collateral death toll that its architects considered acceptable. Clinton argued that this demonstration was needed to convince Hussein that the United States would respond strongly to all provocations and would not tolerate revenge attacks on its leaders. In a letter to the U.S. Congress two days later informing that body of an operation whose notification to Congress was required under the 1973 War Powers Act, Clinton justified his action as a necessary, "limited and proportionate action" undertaken by the United States in self-defense. The air strikes were dramatic proof that the new presidential administration would take a hard line against any Iraqi provocations. In the early 21st century, journalists and others continued to debate whether Hussein or his intelligence service had indeed been involved in the plot against Bush. No conclusive evidence either proving or disproving such allegations has yet emerged.

Primary Source

June 26, 1993

My fellow Americans, this evening I want to speak with you about an attack by the Government of Iraq against the United States and the actions we have just taken to respond.

This past April, the Kuwaiti Government uncovered what they suspected was a car bombing plot to assassinate former President George Bush while he was visiting Kuwait City. The Kuwaiti authorities arrested 16 suspects, including 2 Iraqi nationals. Following those arrests, I ordered our own intelligence and law enforcement agencies to conduct a thorough and independent investigation. Over the past several weeks, officials from those agencies reviewed a range of intelligence information, traveled to Kuwait and elsewhere, extensively interviewed the suspects, and thoroughly examined the forensic evidence.

This Thursday, Attorney General Reno and Director of Central Intelligence Woolsey gave me their findings. Based on their investigation there is compelling evidence that there was, in fact, a plot to assassinate former President Bush and that this plot, which included the use of a powerful bomb made in Iraq, was directed and pursued by the Iraqi intelligence service.

We should not be surprised by such deeds, coming as they do from a regime like Saddam Hussein's, which is ruled by atrocity, slaughtered its own people, invaded two neighbors, attacked others, and engaged in chemical and environmental warfare. Saddam has repeatedly violated the will and conscience of the international community. But this attempt at revenge by a tyrant against the leader of the world coalition that defeated him in war is particularly loathsome and cowardly. We thank God it was unsuccessful. The authorities who foiled it have the appreciation of all Americans.

It is clear that this was no impulsive or random act. It was an elaborate plan devised by the Iraqi Government and directed against a former President of the United States because of actions he took as President. As such, the Iraqi attack against President Bush was an attack against our country and against all Americans. We could not and have not let such action against our Nation go unanswered.

From the first days of our Revolution, America's security has depended on the clarity of this message: Don't tread on us. A firm and commensurate response was essential to protect our sovereignty, to send a message to those who engage in state-sponsored terrorism, to deter further violence against our people, and to affirm the expectation of civilized behavior among nations.

Therefore, on Friday I ordered our forces to launch a cruise missile attack on the Iraqi intelligence service's principal command-and-control facility in Baghdad. Those missiles were launched this afternoon at 4:22 eastern daylight time. They landed approximately an hour ago. I have discussed this action with the congressional leadership and with our allies and friends in the region. And I have called for an emergency meeting of the United Nations Security Council to expose Iraq's crime.

These actions were directed against the Iraqi Government, which was responsible for the assassination plot. Saddam Hussein has demonstrated repeatedly that he will resort to terrorism or aggression if left unchecked. Our intent was to target Iraq's capacity to support violence against the United States and other nations and to deter Saddam Hussein from supporting such outlaw behavior in the future. Therefore, we directed our action against the facility associated with Iraq's support of terrorism, while making every effort to minimize the loss of innocent life.

There should be no mistake about the message we intend these actions to convey to Saddam Hussein, to the rest of the Iraqi leadership, and to any nation, group, or person who would harm our leaders or our citizens. We will combat terrorism. We will deter aggression. We will protect our people.

The world has repeatedly made clear what Iraq must do to return to the community of nations. And Iraq has repeatedly refused. If Saddam and his regime contemplate further illegal provocative actions, they can be certain of our response.

[...]

Finally, I want to say this to all the American people: While the cold war has ended, the world is not free of danger. And I am determined to take the steps necessary to keep our Nation secure. We will keep our forces ready to fight. We will work to head off emerging threats, and we will take action when action is required. That is precisely what we have done today.

Letter to Congressional Leaders on the Strike on Iraqi Intelligence Headquarters June 28, 1993

Commencing at approximately 4:22 p.m. (EST) on June 26, 1993, at my direction, U.S. naval forces launched a Tomahawk cruise missile strike on the Iraqi Intelligence Service's (IIS) principal command and control complex in Baghdad. This facility is the headquarters for the IIS, which planned the failed attempt to assassinate former President Bush during his visit to Kuwait in April of this year. This U.S. military action was completed upon impact of the missiles on target at approximately 6 p.m. (EST).

Operating under the United States Central Command, two U.S. Navy surface ships launched a total of 23 precision-guided Tomahawk missiles in this coordinated strike upon the key facilities in the IIS compound. The USS PETERSON (DD 969) launched 14 missiles from its position in the Red Sea, while the USS CHANCEL-LORSVILLE (CG 62) in the Arabian Gulf launched nine missiles. The timing of this operation, with missiles striking at approximately 2:00 a.m. local Iraqi time, was chosen carefully so as to minimize risks to innocent civilians. Initial reports indicate that heavy damage was inflicted on the complex. Regrettably, there were some collateral civilian casualties.

I ordered this military response only after I considered the results of a thorough and independent investigation by U.S. intelligence and law enforcement agencies. The reports by Attorney General Reno and Director of Central Intelligence Woolsey provided compelling evidence that the operation that threatened the life of President Bush in Kuwait City in April was directed and pursued by the Iraqi Intelligence Service and that the Government of Iraq bore direct responsibility for this effort. The Government of Iraq acted unlawfully in attempting to carry out Saddam Hussein's threats against former President Bush because of actions he took as President. The evidence of the Government of Iraq's violence and terrorism demonstrates that Iraq poses a continuing threat to United States nationals and shows utter disregard for the will of the international community as expressed in Security Council Resolutions

and the United Nations Charter. Based on the Government of Iraq's pattern of disregard for international law, I concluded that there was no reasonable prospect that new diplomatic initiatives or economic measures could influence the current Government of Iraq to cease planning future attacks against the United States.

Consequently, in the exercise of our inherent right of self-defense as recognized in Article 51 of the United Nations Charter and pursuant to my constitutional authority with respect to the conduct of foreign relations and as Commander in Chief, I ordered a military strike that directly targeted a facility Iraqi intelligence implicated in the plot against the former Chief Executive. In accordance with Article 51 of the United Nations Charter, this action was reported immediately to the Security Council on June 26. On June 27, Ambassador Albright provided evidence of Iraq's assassination attempts to the United Nations Security Council, which had been convened in emergency session at our request.

I am certain that you share my sincere hope that the limited and proportionate action taken by the United States Government will frustrate and help deter and preempt future unlawful actions on the part of the Government of Iraq. Nonetheless, in the event that Iraqi violence, aggression, or state-sponsored terrorism against the United States continues, I will direct such additional measures in our exercise of the right of self-defense as may be necessary and appropriate to protect United States citizens.

[...]

Source: William J. Clinton, *Public Papers of the Presidents of the United States: William J. Clinton, 1993*, Book 1 (Washington, DC: U.S. Government Printing Office, 1994), 938–941.

85. Richard Shelby, Speech and Report on the Persian Gulf War Syndrome, March 17, 1994 [Excerpt]

Introduction

Numerous soldiers who served in the 1990–1991 Persian Gulf War, up to 30 percent of the 700,000 American servicemen in the theater and a substantial number of the British contingent, reported suffering a wide range of often baffling health problems in the aftermath of that conflict. These included fatigue, headaches, memory problems, muscle and joint pains, digestive difficulties, impaired vision, hair loss, skin problems, and shortness of breath and respiratory problems. It was also suggested that veterans of the war were more susceptible to immune system disorders, brain and other cancers, amyotrophic lateral sclerosis, fibromyalgia, and infertility and that their children were more likely to suffer from birth defects. Some specialists believed that these problems were related to Persian Gulf War military personnel's exposure, probably at relatively low levels, to a variety of toxins, including an antianthrax vaccine commonly used to protect soldiers from exposure to potential biological weapons; chemical weapons using nerve gas and mustard gas covertly employed by Saddam Hussein's forces against coalition units; chemicals released due to coalition bombing attacks on Iraqi industrial plants and arsenals of chemical weapons; pesticides and insect repellents; drugs used to provide coalition soldiers with protection against nerve gases; and by-products of combustion by depleted uranium antitank ammunition. Three years after the war, Senator Richard Shelby of Alabama, a Democrat who later switched to the Republican Party, submitted a lengthy report to Congress on the possibility that chemical and biological weapons used in the Persian Gulf War theater were responsible for the inexplicable and sometimes devastatingly debilitating illnesses that many veterans reported suffering. Although the Department of Defense remained reluctant to admit the links, there appeared to be at least a strong possibility that some troops in the war had been exposed to chemical or biological agents, permanently affecting their health. Shelby's report presented considerable evidence that on numerous occasions during the conflict and the buildup preceding it military authorities had detected the presence of chemical agents and had sought further detailed information from the Defense Department on the subject. By the mid-2000s, official studies in both the United States and Great Britain suggested that Persian Gulf War veterans in both countries did show higher rates of assorted health difficulties than was the case among control groups who had not served there.

Primary Source

Mr. SHELBY. Mr. President, I am here today to issue a report following my investigation into the possible presence of chemical and biological weapons agents in the theater of operations during the Persian Gulf war. Additionally, I will discuss the possible connection between service in the Persian Gulf and the unexplained illness affecting thousands of veterans and their families.

When Iraqi forces, at the direction of Saddam Hussein, crossed into Kuwait on August 2, 1990, they set off a chain reaction of events that resulted in the assembling of the largest coalition of forces since the Second World War. Countries that had been on opposite sides of the cold war were now joined with the expressed goal of driving Saddam Hussein's troops out of Kuwait.

The United States led this effort with over 600,000 members of our armed services, including over 200,000 reservists.

At the time of the Iraqi invasion, there was a strong belief among the coalition forces that chemical and even biological agents would be used as weapons by Iraq.

Within a year after the highly successful Desert Storm operation, reports surfaced of a mystery illness affecting many veterans, primarily members of the National Guard and Reserve, who served in Saudi Arabia.

This group is experiencing symptoms commonplace to many known illnesses. However, in the case of the Gulf War veterans, we have not been able to diagnose the causes of the illnesses and the illnesses themselves have not responded to any known treatments.

I have seen firsthand the devastating, frustrating, and debilitating effects that this illness has had on many of these veterans. Citizens who were once healthy and able bodied can no longer hold jobs or participate as active members of society.

Little progress has been made even though Congress mandated the establishment of a Desert Shield–Desert Storm registry, and treatment centers were created for the Gulf war syndrome. Veterans, increasingly frustrated by the inability of the Department of Veterans Affairs to treat their illness, began to seek treatment outside of the Department of Defense and Department of Veterans Affairs medical community.

My involvement in this issue has spanned 2 years.

Early on, I met with a group of veterans after a town meeting that I held and pledged that I would do everything in my power to get them proper treatment and to find the causes of their ailments.

The anxiety and fear experienced by our ill veterans was intensified throughout this period by constant reports in foreign and domestic media about the presence of chemical weapons agents during the Gulf war.

I cannot imagine a greater fear than that experienced by someone who suffers from a mysterious illness and believes it may have been caused by exposure to chemical weapons.

As chairman of the Subcommittee on Force Requirements and Personnel of the Senate Armed Services Committee, I heard from afflicted veterans and saw first-hand the symptoms of these ailments.

Following this hearing, Dr. Charles Jackson of the Tuskegee Alabama Veterans Medical Center diagnosed a patient as suffering from Gulf war syndrome and chemical-biological warfare exposure. In response to this announcement and pressure from Congress, the Department of Veterans Affairs established a pilot program to test Persian Gulf veterans for possible exposure to chemical weapons agents.

As a result of these events, Senator Sam Nunn, chairman of the Committee on Armed Services, sent me, along with people on our staff and the people from DOD, to Europe and then to the Middle East to investigate the possible presence of chemical and biological weapon agents during Operation Desert Storm, as well as the possible connection between service in the Persian Gulf and the unexplained illness affecting thousands of veterans.

Mr. President, I went to Europe to determine the validity of the two then reported detections of chemical warfare agents by Czech soldiers.

Instead, there were not only two, but five separate detections of chemical weapons agents in the Persian Gulf.

No one with whom I spoke could provide a solution to the mysterious illness; however, they could not rule out a possible link between the presence of chemical agents and the gulf war syndrome. Only the U.S. Department of Defense and the British Government have denied that chemical agents could have caused the illness.

In light of my involvement, I have come to five major conclusions which I would like to share with you today.

First, I have no doubt that chemical agents, accurately verified by the Czech chemical detection units, were present in the theater of operations during the Persian Gulf war.

Both Czech and French forces detected and verified the presence of nerve and mustard agents at low levels during Desert Storm.

Second, we may never be able to determine the origin of these chemical agents. While, I believe that we can rule out Iraqi Scud or Frog missiles, and Iraqi artillery, there still exists several possibilities. For example, the low-level chemical presence could have resulted from United States or coalition forces bombing Iraqi chemical weapons facilities or caches of Iraqi weapons on the Saudi border.

It is also feasible that a cloud of nerve agent, dissipating in intensity, could have traveled under the correct climate conditions.

There is also the possibility of a training accident involving chemical agents among coalition forces. Finally, it is possible that the detections were the result of Saudi officials attempting to test the abilities of the Czechs whom they had engaged to assist in chemical detections.

Third, although a direct connection between the existence of low-levels of chemical agents in the theater of operations and the Persian Gulf syndrome cannot be established at this time, such a connection cannot and should not be discounted. Little information is available on exposure to low levels of chemical agents, but I believe that the work being done at Walter Reed Army Medical Center is on the right track in this area. We must give it our full support.

Fourth, the Department of Defense has proven reluctant to pursue or, in certain instances, to provide the information necessary to prove or disapprove allegations about the presence of chemical agents in the theater of operations. After my contact with our allies, we found that various chemical detections were reported to central command headquarters and were included in operational logs. Only then, and after traveling half-way around the world, did Department of Defense officials admit that they had been aware of these same instances.

While I have not yet determined the reason for this apparent aversion to full disclosure by DOD, the staff working on this issue from our committee has been constantly challenged by the Department's evasiveness, inconsistency, and reluctance to work toward a common goal here.

Finally, Mr. President, and I believe alarmingly, the Persian Gulf medical records of members of the 24th Naval Reserve Battalion are inexplicably missing from their files.

Mr. President, despite the Czech and French detections and numerous reports, the Department of Defense is still reluctant to admit that there were chemical weapons agents present in the Persian Gulf. I cannot understand why they have taken this stand since we fully expected to be confronted with chemical weapons when we went there.

I can only conclude, Mr. President, that when dealing with the Department of Defense on this issue, you have to ask the right question to receive the right answer. I do not believe they understand that we are only seeking the truth in a way to help our veterans. Therefore, I am going to continue to ask question after question until we find the right answer from DOD.

[...]

Source: U.S. Congress, "Senator Shelby's Conclusions on the Persian Gulf Syndrome," U.S. Government Printing Office, http://www.gpo.gov/fdsys/pkg/CREC-1994-03-17/html/CREC-1994-03-17-pt1-PgS7.htm.

86. United Nations Secretary-General Kofi Annan, Report on the Situation in Afghanistan and Its Implications for International Peace, November 14, 1997 [Excerpts]

Introduction

By 1997, the persistent civil war in Afghanistan seemed an almost intractable problem. Even after the Islamic fundamentalist Taliban mujahideen took power in late 1996, fighting between them and their rivals continued unabated. Appeals from the international community and from the United Nations (UN) Special Mission to Afghanistan urging all sides to negotiate a cease-fire proved unavailing. In November 1997 UN secretary-general Kofi Annan issued a report on Afghanistan in which he made his frustration over the Afghan situation extremely clear. Afghanistan, he charged, was "a place where even responsible local political authorities, let alone a central government, have virtually ceased to exist." Warring factions had been unable to compromise with each other. "Even today," he complained, "the Afghan parties seem determined to go on fighting, while outside Powers continue to provide material, financial and other support to their respective clients inside Afghanistan." While some of the "major Powers" had begun to demonstrate interest in resolving the Afghan morass, they "had yet to demonstrate the necessary degree of determination to move the situation forward." The secretary-general laid the blame for continuing conflict impartially on "the Afghan factions," who were doing the actual fighting, and their various international supporters, who "all enthusiastically proclaim their support to the United Nations peacemaking efforts but at the same time continue to fan the conflict by pouring in arms, money and other supplies to their preferred Afghan factions." He believed that if the conflict was to be ended, all outside suppliers would have to impose and observe a complete arms embargo on Afghanistan. Should this occur, he hoped that it might prove the first step in negotiating a cease-fire and then a permanent settlement. The secretary-general believed that foreign governments could, if they wished, encourage these developments, and he discerned some faint signs that they might be prepared to do so. Otherwise, in his frank if undiplomatic opinion, "the role of the United Nations in Afghanistan is little more than that of an alibi to provide cover for the inaction—or worse—of the international community at large." Forceful and bluntly uncompromising in its portrayal of a deteriorating Afghan situation and in its allocation of blame among the parties concerned, the report suggested a depressing level of Afghan and international collusion in the continuation of brutal civil conflict in that country.

Primary Source

The Situation in Afghanistan and Its Implications for International Peace and Security

[...]

II. Recent Developments in Afghanistan

A. Military situation

4. The military balance between the Afghan warring factions see-sawed wildly in 1997. The factions fought hard for control of northern Afghanistan and the northern approaches to Kabul. However, despite the expenditure of large quantities of externally supplied ammunition and equipment, and the loss of many lives and the displacement of civilian populations, neither side succeeded in recording sizeable gains of territory or significant political advantage. By early November 1997, the predominantly Pushtun Taliban continued to hold approximately two thirds of the country but had not been able to capture the territories in the north, which are largely populated by the Tajik, Uzbek and Hazara ethnic groups.

5. The Afghan antagonists were the Taliban and the five-party Northern Alliance which is formally known as the Islamic and National Front for the Salvation of Afghanistan. The Taliban continued to control most provinces in the south, south-west and south-east, including Kabul and the cities of Kandahar, Herat and Jalalabad. The Northern Alliance, which operated from the provincial capitals of Mazar-i-Sharif, Bamyan, Taloqan and Maimana, was in control of the provinces in northern and central Afghanistan....

[...]

9. Severe fighting broke out again in September when the Taliban, supported by defections of local Pushtun commanders, renewed their attempt to take Mazar-i-Sharif. However, like their first attempt in May, the Taliban's initial gains were wiped out by counter-attacks and defections from the Taliban side.

Both military and civilian casualties were high, with an estimated 2,000 Taliban troops either killed or captured since May. In the fighting east of Mazar, both sides overran a refugee camp of some 7,000 displaced Tajik nationals, causing several deaths and injuries and creating a situation of near panic among the refugees. Fighting continued for control of the northern city of Kunduz, which has been in the hands of the Taliban or pro-Taliban independent commanders since May 1997.

10. In the central region, sporadic fighting continued between the Taliban and Hezb-i-Wahdat faction. Taliban aircraft attacked Bamyan several times in July and August. In this connection, I should like to draw the special attention of the international community to the fact that the continued fighting in Afghanistan has had devastating effects not only on its people but also on its vast reservoir of rich cultural heritage. A case in point was the recent incident in which a bomb blast near the larger of the two great Buddha statues in Bamyan caused some damage to the head of the statue.

11. In the west, fighting occurred in the Morghab river area in Badghis province but with little change in frontline positions. The Herat, Kandahar and Jalalabad regions were generally calm.

B. Political situation

12. As the fighting continued, the political situation in Afghanistan remained deadlocked. The deepening division of the country along ethnic lines, reinforced by external military and political support, continued to inhibit efforts to engender political dialogue among the factions. Throughout 1997, neither the Taliban nor its rivals appear to have given serious consideration to a political, as opposed to a military, solution to the conflict.

13. An unsettled leadership problem within the Northern Alliance also affected the political environment. Infighting was most pronounced in the predominantly Uzbek Jumbish movement, whose leader, General Dostum, was forced into exile in Turkey for four months by his rival, General Malik, after the latter's short-lived defection to the Taliban in May. While General Malik subsequently turned against the Taliban and helped to drive its forces out of Mazar, the return of General Dostum to Afghanistan on 12 September led to further political uncertainty in the north. Adding to the complex leadership problem was the death of newly designated Prime Minister Abdul Rahim Ghafoorzai in an aircraft accident at Bamyan airport in August.

14. The humanitarian and political activities of the United Nations in the Mazar-i-Sharif area were seriously disrupted by the renewed fighting and subsequent chaos, including explicit threats to United Nations personnel and the repeated looting of United Nations offices and equipment. At one point, some Afghan officials in Mazar falsely accused United Nations personnel of collaborating with the Taliban in directing its aerial attacks on the city and threatened them with retribution. Looted (and repainted) United Nations vehicles are brazenly used by local factions. I am extremely concerned by all of this, as well as by the refusal of General Malik to allow the International Committee of the Red Cross to visit the Taliban prisoners captured in May, a state of affairs that, as he has been informed on many occasions, is completely unacceptable to the United Nations and the international community at large.

15. Of similar concern is the Taliban's refusal to start negotiations with the Northern Alliance as a whole without preconditions, as well as its social and administrative practices. The mistreatment of girls and women, such as the denial of their rights to employment, health care and education, is especially worrying. Furthermore, Afghanistan has become the world's largest producer of heroin, with the vast majority of the poppies used for that purpose cultivated in areas controlled by the Taliban. The United Nations International Drug Control Programme recently announced that the Taliban had agreed to work out ways and means to eliminate poppy cultivation. I sincerely hope that the Taliban will ensure that the agreement is implemented faithfully and effectively.

16. The Taliban have made new efforts during 1997 to gain international recognition and support. Taliban representatives undertook a series of missions abroad, in particular to East Asia, the Gulf region and the United States of America. While the Governments of Pakistan, Saudi Arabia and the United Arab Emirates recognized the Taliban as the legitimate government of Afghanistan in May, other Governments have withheld their decision to extend de jure recognition.

17. Member States, in particular the countries surrounding Afghanistan, continue to express concern and frustration about the continuing civil war. Of particular concern to them are the negative implications of prolonged warfare and the imposition of an ultra-orthodox Islamic State on their borders.

[...]

18. Foreign military support to the two sides continued unabated throughout 1997. Reliable eyewitnesses reported many sorties of military deliveries in unmarked aircraft to bases of the Northern Alliance, as well as numerous deliveries by truck caravans of arms, ammunition and fuel to Taliban-controlled territory. United Nations employees also reported an encounter with an unidentified foreign military training unit of several hundred persons near Kabul. Such blatant violations of General Assembly and Security Council resolutions which call for a halt to foreign military intervention seriously undermine United Nations peacemaking efforts and serve to prolong the Afghan conflict. They also raised suspicions and worsened relations among the countries in the region.

[...]

V. Observations and Conclusions

36. Afghanistan, which was once a flashpoint of super-Power rivalry, has since become a typical post–cold war regional and ethnic conflict, where the major Powers no longer see a strategic incentive to get involved. It has also become a place where even responsible local political authorities, let alone a central government, have virtually ceased to exist. Herein lies much of the explanation why repeated international attempts to bring peace to the country have not borne fruit.

37. Since the early 1990s, the Afghan factions and warlords have failed to show the will to rise above their narrow factional interests and to start working together for national reconciliation. The United Nations successfully mediated the withdrawal of foreign forces from Afghanistan in the late 1980s. But, although the Najibullah regime was ready to hand over power to a broad-based transition mechanism, the Mujahideen parties were unable to agree among themselves on how to form such a mechanism. Their disagreements escalated to the point where Kabul was plunged into chaos and bloodshed once the Najibullah regime collapsed in April 1992. Since that time, the situation has only become worse.

38. Even today, the Afghan parties seem determined to go on fighting, while outside Powers continue to provide material, financial and other support to their respective clients inside Afghanistan. Meanwhile, although those major Powers that have potential influence in Afghanistan have recently started to show interest, they have yet to demonstrate the necessary degree of determination to move the situation forward.

39. In these circumstances, it is illusory to think that peace can be achieved. How can peace be imposed on faction leaders who are determined to fight it out to the finish and who receive seemingly unlimited supplies of arms from outside sponsors? It is this continued support from some outside Powers—combined with the apathy of the others who are not directly involved—which has strengthened the belief among the warlords and parties in Afghanistan that they can achieve their political, religious and social goals by force.

Responsibility of the Afghans

40. The Afghans, perhaps, understandably, are reluctant to accept responsibility for the repeated failures to put an end to their conflict. Nevertheless, the Afghan people cannot just simply shift all responsibilities for the tragedy that has befallen their country onto others. Even if they receive help from outside, it is the Afghans themselves who are fighting one another. Peace will become possible when—and only when—they truly desire it and start to work seriously for it.

41. Much to my regret, the Afghan factions have so far failed to prove that they are willing to lay down their arms and cooperate with the United Nations for peace. To be sure, every side proclaims its readiness to work with the United Nations and accuses the other party or parties of bearing alone the responsibility for the continued fighting. However, at any given time there has always been at least one party that has thought it could achieve military victory over its opponents and that, consequently, has rebuffed efforts to negotiate a ceasefire and only shown a willingness to compromise once the military situation has been reversed and it feels under threat. At the same time, there always exist spoilers inside and outside the country who are much better off with the continuation of the problem than they would be with the solution, a classic situation in failed States where warlords, smugglers, terrorists, drug dealers and others thrive amid the conflict and would only lose out with the return of peace, law and order.

Foreign interference

42. A similar situation prevails with the main foreign providers of support to the Afghan warring parties. They all enthusiastically proclaim their support to the United Nations peacemaking efforts but at the same time continue to fan the conflict by pouring in arms, money and other supplies to their preferred Afghan factions. These countries unanimously denounce "foreign interference," but are quick to add that arms are delivered only to "the other side."

43. These external players may have their own reasons for continuing to support their respective Afghan clients, but they must be held responsible for exacerbating the bloody conflict in Afghanistan. They must also be held accountable for building a fire which, they should be aware, is unlikely to remain indefinitely confined to Afghanistan. Indeed, that fire is already spreading beyond the borders of Afghanistan, posing a serious threat to the region and beyond in the shape of terrorism, banditry, narcotics trafficking, refugee flows, and increasing ethnic and sectarian tension.

44. The supply of arms and other materials from outside provides the essential wherewithal for the continued fighting in Afghanistan. It is apparent, in the light of the evidence collected so far, that large quantities of war-making materials are entering Afghanistan. It is hard to accept the argument that the Afghan warring factions are able to sustain the current level of fighting using only "those weapons and ammunition left by the Soviet troops." Neither is it credible that, with their limited financial capacity, those Afghan factions could afford to procure massive amounts of weapons on the black market and smuggle them into Afghanistan on their own.

International framework for settlement of the conflict

45. The unabated supply of arms, and the divergence of ways in which the countries concerned seem to be dealing with the conflict, lead me to believe that a solid international framework must be established in order to address the external aspects of the Afghan question. Such a framework would provide the neighbours of Afghanistan and other countries with an opportunity to discuss the question of foreign interference in a coherent manner. The main objective would be to debate how those countries could help the United Nations bring the Afghan parties to the negotiating table, including effective and fair ways to curb the flow of arms and other war-making materials into Afghanistan. Such countries should also find a way to speak unanimously by coordinating their individual peace initiatives through the United Nations. Only in this way would they send a message to the Afghans that the international community meant to achieve peace in Afghanistan and that the warring factions could no longer count on outside support.

46. One of the ways to curb the flow of arms into Afghanistan would be the imposition of an effective arms embargo. Although such an embargo should not become an end in itself, it is necessary for the United Nations and Member States to undertake preliminary studies on how a mandatory arms embargo could be implemented in a fair and verifiable manner. If the cost estimates for

such an embargo proved to be too high, other ways would need to be found to end, or at least significantly reduce, the supply of arms and other materials to the warring factions. One possibility would be for the countries concerned to take voluntary, unilateral but concerted actions by themselves to stop, to the degree possible, the supply of a designated list of goods to Afghanistan. This, of course, would also need to be done in a manner that did not provide advantage to any group.

[...]

Intra-Afghan talks

49. Parallel to this, I intend to maintain through UNSMA and at United Nations Headquarters close contact with the warring parties, as well as with other influential Afghan individuals and organizations, with a view to preparing the ground for an intra-Afghan dialogue. Such a dialogue, if realized, should focus at first on a ceasefire, to be followed by political negotiations leading to the establishment of a broad-based representative government. It goes without saying that, for such a government to be acceptable, it should reflect the interests of all the major social, political and religious segments of the country. I take note in this context that several Member States have offered to host such a dialogue.

50. It is hoped that a ceasefire and the beginning of a dialogue—or even the mere prospects for one—would serve to create its own momentum and, after some time, make it difficult for anyone to resume fighting. It is also hoped that the ceasefire and talks would give a boost to the efforts of some Afghan groups and individuals to mobilize Afghan public opinion in favour of peace.

[...]

Conclusions

53. As described in the preceding sections of the present report, a peaceful settlement in Afghanistan remains elusive notwithstanding the untiring efforts of the United Nations to broker peace among the country's warring factions. In the meantime, Afghanistan's civil war has continued to exact a staggering toll in terms of human lives and suffering as well as material destruction. What we are witnessing is a seemingly endless tragedy of epic proportions in which the Afghan people's yearning for peace is being systematically and continually betrayed by leaders and warlords driven by selfish ambitions and thirst for power.

54. In earlier reports I have observed that the Afghan parties and their external supporters, while continuing to pursue military solutions, often also profess support for resolutions of the General Assembly and the Security Council calling for a peaceful settlement. Regrettably, their actions seldom seem to be motivated, however, by a desire to contribute to the implementation of those resolutions. Similarly, it is discouraging that with few exceptions, the international community as a whole has shown only limited interest in adopting tangible measures to discourage the Afghan parties and their outside supporters from pursuing their bellicose aims and objectives.

55. There is no doubt that a number of Governments both inside and outside the region would be in a favourable position, should they so decide, to encourage the Afghan parties to overcome their differences and seek a peaceful settlement.

It is also clear, however, that as long as those Governments choose not to exercise their influence with the parties in a positive and constructive manner, the efforts made by my representatives, however dedicated and skilled, will not suffice to bring peace to Afghanistan. Sadly, it could be argued that in these circumstances the role of the United Nations in Afghanistan is little more than that of an alibi to provide cover for the inaction—or worse—of the international community at large.

[...]

Source: United Nations General Assembly Official Records, A/52/682, November 14, 1997.

87. Project for the New American Century, "Remove Saddam Hussein from Power," Open Letter to President Bill Clinton, January 26, 1998

Introduction

By the late 1990s, members of the increasingly influential neoconservative think tanks in the United States were ever more eager to demonstrate American power by removing President Saddam Hussein of Iraq from power. In January 1998 the Washington-based think tank Project for the New American Century, established in the spring of 1997, issued an open letter to President Bill Clinton urging that he use his impending State of the Union address to announce "the removal of Saddam Hussein's regime from power" as a major U.S. strategic policy objective. The letter stated that "containment" of Hussein was no longer effective and that he was evading the regime of United Nations (UN) inspections intended to prevent Iraq from obtaining or manufacturing weapons of mass destruction. So long as Iraq was governed by

Hussein, the signatories argued, it would be a destabilizing factor in the Middle East, threatening "our friends and allies like Israel and the moderate Arab states" and jeopardizing "a significant portion of the world's supply of oil." Existing UN resolutions, the letter urged, gave the United States adequate authority to take forceful action to overthrow Hussein. Clinton confined his response to relatively limited air strikes against Iraq and the continuation of sanctions. Those signing the letter included R. James Woolsey, a past Central Intelligence Agency (CIA) director under Clinton, and former secretary of defense Donald Rumsfeld as well as several well-known neoconservative pundits, notably William J. Bennett, Jeffrey Bergner, Francis Fukuyama, Robert Kagan, and William Kristol. Of its 17 signatories, 11 individuals subsequently held high National Security Council or State Department, Defense Department, or Commerce Department positions after Republican president George W. Bush took office in January 2001. The most influential among these appointees were Rumsfeld, secretary of defense from January 2001 until January 2007; Paul Wolfowitz, deputy secretary of defense throughout Bush's first term; and Richard Armitage, deputy secretary of state from 2001 to 2005.

Primary Source

We are writing you because we are convinced that current American policy toward Iraq is not succeeding, and that we may soon face a threat in the Middle East more serious than any we have known since the end of the Cold War. In your upcoming State of the Union Address, you have an opportunity to chart a clear and determined course for meeting this threat. We urge you to seize that opportunity, and to enunciate a new strategy that would secure the interests of the U.S. and our friends and allies around the world. That strategy should aim, above all, at the removal of Saddam Hussein's regime from power. We stand ready to offer our full support in this difficult but necessary endeavor.

The policy of "containment" of Saddam Hussein has been steadily eroding over the past several months. As recent events have demonstrated, we can no longer depend on our partners in the Gulf War coalition to continue to uphold the sanctions or to punish Saddam when he blocks or evades UN inspections. Our ability to ensure that Saddam Hussein is not producing weapons of mass destruction, therefore, has substantially diminished. Even if full inspections were eventually to resume, which now seems highly unlikely, experience has shown that it is difficult if not impossible to monitor Iraq's chemical and biological weapons production. The lengthy period during which the inspectors will have been unable to enter many Iraqi facilities has made it even less likely that they will be able to uncover all of Saddam's secrets. As a result, in the not-too-distant future we will be unable to determine with any reasonable level of confidence whether Iraq does or does not possess such weapons.

Such uncertainty will, by itself, have a seriously destabilizing effect on the entire Middle East. It hardly needs to be added that if Saddam does acquire the capability to deliver weapons of mass destruction, as he is almost certain to do if we continue along the present course, the safety of American troops in the region, of our friends and allies like Israel and the moderate Arab states, and a significant portion of the world's supply of oil will all be put at hazard. As you have rightly declared, Mr. President, the security of the world in the first part of the 21st century will be determined largely by how we handle this threat.

Given the magnitude of the threat, the current policy, which depends for its success upon the steadfastness of our coalition partners and upon the cooperation of Saddam Hussein, is dangerously inadequate. The only acceptable strategy is one that eliminates the possibility that Iraq will be able to use or threaten to use weapons of mass destruction. In the near term, this means a willingness to undertake military action as diplomacy is clearly failing. In the long term, it means removing Saddam Hussein and his regime from power. That now needs to become the aim of American foreign policy.

We urge you to articulate this aim, and to turn your Administration's attention to implementing a strategy for removing Saddam's regime from power. This will require a full complement of diplomatic, political and military efforts. Although we are fully aware of the dangers and difficulties in implementing this policy, we believe the dangers of failing to do so are far greater. We believe the U.S. has the authority under existing UN resolutions to take the necessary steps, including military steps, to protect our vital interests in the Gulf. In any case, American policy cannot continue to be crippled by a misguided insistence on unanimity in the UN Security Council.

We urge you to act decisively. If you act now to end the threat of weapons of mass destruction against the U.S. or its allies, you will be acting in the most fundamental national security interests of the country. If we accept a course of weakness and drift, we put our interests and our future at risk.

Sincerely,

Elliott Abrams	Richard L. Armitage	William J. Bennett
Jeffrey Bergner	John Bolton	Paula Dobriansky
Francis Fukuyama	Robert Kagan	Zalmay Khalilzad
William Kristol	Richard Perle	Peter W. Rodman
Donald Rumsfeld	William Schneider, Jr.	Vin Weber
Paul Wolfowitz	R. James Woolsey	Robert B. Zoellick

Source: "Letter to President Clinton," Project for the New American Century, http://www.newamericancentury.org/iraqclintonletter.htm.

88. World Islamic Front, "Jihad against Jews and Crusaders" Statement, February 23, 1998 [Excerpt]

Introduction

In August 1996 Osama bin Laden, leader of the militant Islamic group Al Qaeda, issued a fatwa, or declaration of religious warfare, that focused primarily upon driving the United States out of Saudi Arabia, the state of which he was a citizen. Eighteen months later, he was the moving spirit when an organization calling itself the World Islamic Front issued a second such statement. The signatories of this declaration included not just bin Laden but also Ayman al-Zawahiri, head of the Egypt-based Jihad Group; Abu-Yasir Rifa-I Ahmad Taha of the Egyptian Islamic Group; the Pakistani sheikh Mir Hamzah, secretary of the organization Jamiat-ul-Ulema-e-Pakistan; and Fazlul Rahman, head of the Bangladesh Jihad Movement. The four Egyptian, Pakistani, and Bangladeshi groups were all relatively small, and the well-financed Al Qaeda constituted the backbone of the World Islamic Front. The new fatwa expanded the emphasis of the earlier pronouncement, condemning the policies of the United States toward Saudi Arabia and also U.S. support for Israel and the continuing American economic and military sanctions on Iraq. The World Islamic Front called on All Muslims "to kill the Americans and their allies—civilians and military"—wherever possible. The following August, Al Qaeda personnel simultaneously detonated car bombs close to the American embassies in two African capitals, Dar es Salaam, Tanzania, and Nairobi, Kenya. Some American diplomats and embassy employees died, but the majority of the victims were African passers-by in the neighboring streets. In Nairobi, 213 people died and around 4,000 people were injured, while in Dar es Salaam at least 12 people died and another 85 were wounded. Two weeks later, on August 20, 1998, U.S. president Bill Clinton responded by ordering Operation INFINITE REACH in which cruise missiles struck alleged Al Qaeda bases in Sudan and Afghanistan. Unfortunately, the outcome was somewhat anticlimactic. The hope was to kill bin Laden and some of his top lieutenants, but this objective failed. It also later transpired that one Sudanese target the missiles did destroy and the U.S. government initially described as a chemical weapons factory was instead a pharmaceutical plant producing medicines for civilian consumption.

Primary Source

Shaykh Usamah Bin-Muhammad Bin-Ladin

Ayman al-Zawahiri, amir of the Jihad Group in Egypt

Abu-Yasir Rifa'i Ahmad Taha, Egyptian Islamic Group

Shaykh Mir Hamzah, secretary of the Jamiat-ul-Ulema-e-Pakistan

Fazlur Rahman, amir of the Jihad Movement in Bangladesh

Praise be to Allah, who revealed the Book, controls the clouds, defeats factionalism, and says in His Book: "But when the forbidden months are past, then fight and slay the pagans wherever ye find them, seize them, beleaguer them, and lie in wait for them in every stratagem (of war)"; and peace be upon our Prophet, Muhammad Bin-'Abdallah, who said: "I have been sent with the sword between my hands to ensure that no one but Allah is worshipped, Allah who put my livelihood under the shadow of my spear and who inflicts humiliation and scorn on those who disobey my orders."

The Arabian Peninsula has never—since Allah made it flat, created its desert, and encircled it with seas—been stormed by any forces like the crusader armies spreading in it like locusts, eating its riches and wiping out its plantations. All this is happening at a time in which nations are attacking Muslims like people fighting over a plate of food. In the light of the grave situation and the lack of support, we and you are obliged to discuss current events, and we should all agree on how to settle the matter.

No one argues today about three facts that are known to everyone; we will list them, in order to remind everyone:

First, for over seven years the United States has been occupying the lands of Islam in the holiest of places, the Arabian Peninsula, plundering its riches, dictating to its rulers, humiliating its people, terrorizing its neighbors, and turning its bases in the Peninsula into a spearhead through which to fight the neighboring Muslim peoples.

If some people have in the past argued about the fact of the occupation, all the people of the Peninsula have now acknowledged it. The best proof of this is the Americans' continuing aggression against the Iraqi people using the Peninsula as a staging post, even though all its rulers are against their territories being used to that end, but they are helpless.

Second, despite the great devastation inflicted on the Iraqi people by the crusader-Zionist alliance, and despite the huge number of those killed, which has exceeded 1 million . . . despite all this, the Americans are once again trying to repeat the horrific massacres, as though they are not content with the protracted blockade imposed after the ferocious war or the fragmentation and devastation.

So here they come to annihilate what is left of this people and to humiliate their Muslim neighbors.

Third, if the Americans' aims behind these wars are religious and economic, the aim is also to serve the Jews' petty state and divert attention from its occupation of Jerusalem and murder of Muslims there. The best proof of this is their eagerness to destroy Iraq, the strongest neighboring Arab state, and their endeavor to fragment all the states of the region such as Iraq, Saudi Arabia, Egypt, and Sudan into paper statelets and through their disunion and weakness to guarantee Israel's survival and the continuation of the brutal crusade occupation of the Peninsula.

All these crimes and sins committed by the Americans are a clear declaration of war on Allah, his messenger, and Muslims. And ulema have throughout Islamic history unanimously agreed that the jihad is an individual duty if the enemy destroys the Muslim countries. . . .

On that basis, and in compliance with Allah's order, we issue the following fatwa to all Muslims:

The ruling to kill the Americans and their allies—civilians and military—is an individual duty for every Muslim who can do it in any country in which it is possible to do it, in order to liberate the al-Aqsa Mosque and the holy mosque [Mecca] from their grip, and in order for their armies to move out of all the lands of Islam, defeated and unable to threaten any Muslim. This is in accordance with the words of Almighty Allah, "and fight the pagans all together as they fight you all together," and "fight them until there is no more tumult or oppression, and there prevail justice and faith in Allah."

This is in addition to the words of Almighty Allah: "And why should ye not fight in the cause of Allah and of those who, being weak, are ill-treated (and oppressed)?—women and children, whose cry is: 'Our Lord, rescue us from this town, whose people are oppressors; and raise for us from thee one who will help!'"

We—with Allah's help—call on every Muslim who believes in Allah and wishes to be rewarded to comply with Allah's order to kill the Americans and plunder their money wherever and whenever they find it. We also call on Muslim ulema, leaders, youths, and soldiers to launch the raid on Satan's U.S. troops and the devil's supporters allying with them, and to displace those who are behind them so that they may learn a lesson.

[. . .]

Source: "Jihad against Jews and Crusaders. World Islamic Front Statement," Federation of American Scientists, http://www.fas.org/irp/world/para/docs/980223-fatwa.htm.

89. U.S. Congress, Iraq Liberation Act, October 31, 1998

Introduction

In the wake of President Saddam Hussein's expulsion of United Nations Special Commission (UNSCOM) and International Atomic Energy Authority (IAEA) inspectors from Iraq, the U.S. Congress passed an act finding that Iraq was in breach of both the obligations

it had accepted following the Persian Gulf War of United Nations (UN) Security Council resolutions. The Iraq Liberation Act (P.L. 105-338) detailed human rights abuses and repression by President Saddam Hussein against both foreign nationals and his own people. The preamble to the act also noted that on May 1, 1998, President Bill Clinton had signed Public Law 105-174, making US$5 million available to support Iraqi "democratic opposition" groups. Section 3 of the new act went further than this, stating forthrightly that "It should be the policy of the United States to support efforts to remove the regime headed by Saddam Hussein from power in Iraq and to promote the emergence of a democratic government to replace that regime." The new act authorized the president to designate appropriate "Iraqi democratic opposition organizations" to receive humanitarian, military, and broadcasting assistance, setting an upper limit of $97 million on such aid. Humanitarian assistance could be provided to areas of Iraq controlled by such organizations, and the act specifically envisaged providing such groups with military equipment and training. The act made the implementation of "regime change" the open and official policy of the U.S. government and also envisaged establishing a potential future international war crimes tribunal in Iraq "for the purpose of indicting, prosecuting, and imprisoning Saddam Hussein and other Iraqi officials who are responsible for crimes against humanity, genocide, and other criminal violations of international law." The House passed this act by 360 votes to 38, and it received unanimous support in the Senate. On February 4, 1999, President Clinton designated seven Iraqi opposition groups as qualifying for aid under the Iraq Liberation Act: the Iraqi National Accord, the Iraqi National Congress, the Islamic Movement of Iraqi Kurdistan, the Kurdistan Democratic Party, the Movement for Constitutional Monarchy, the Patriotic Union of Kurdistan, and the Supreme Council for the Islamic Revolution in Iraq.

Primary Source

SECTION 1. SHORT TITLE.

This Act may be cited as the 'Iraq Liberation Act of 1998'.

SEC. 2. FINDINGS.

The Congress makes the following findings:

(1) On September 22, 1980, Iraq invaded Iran, starting an 8 year war in which Iraq employed chemical weapons against Iranian troops and ballistic missiles against Iranian cities.

(2) In February 1988, Iraq forcibly relocated Kurdish civilians from their home villages in the Anfal campaign, killing an estimated 50,000 to 180,000 Kurds.

(3) On March 16, 1988, Iraq used chemical weapons against Iraqi Kurdish civilian opponents in the town of Halabja, killing an

estimated 5,000 Kurds and causing numerous birth defects that affect the town today.

(4) On August 2, 1990, Iraq invaded and began a 7 month occupation of Kuwait, killing and committing numerous abuses against Kuwaiti civilians, and setting Kuwait's oil wells ablaze upon retreat.

(5) Hostilities in Operation Desert Storm ended on February 28, 1991, and Iraq subsequently accepted the ceasefire conditions specified in United Nations Security Council Resolution 687 (April 3, 1991) requiring Iraq, among other things, to disclose fully and permit the dismantlement of its weapons of mass destruction programs and submit to long-term monitoring and verification of such dismantlement.

(6) In April 1993, Iraq orchestrated a failed plot to assassinate former President George Bush during his April 14–16, 1993, visit to Kuwait.

(7) In October 1994, Iraq moved 80,000 troops to areas near the border with Kuwait, posing an imminent threat of a renewed invasion of or attack against Kuwait.

(8) On August 31, 1996, Iraq suppressed many of its opponents by helping one Kurdish faction capture Irbil, the seat of the Kurdish regional government.

(9) Since March 1996, Iraq has systematically sought to deny weapons inspectors from the United Nations Special Commission on Iraq (UNSCOM) access to key facilities and documents, has on several occasions endangered the safe operation of UNSCOM helicopters transporting UNSCOM personnel in Iraq, and has persisted in a pattern of deception and concealment regarding the history of its weapons of mass destruction programs.

(10) On August 5, 1998, Iraq ceased all cooperation with UNSCOM, and subsequently threatened to end long-term monitoring activities by the International Atomic Energy Agency and UNSCOM.

(11) On August 14, 1998, President Clinton signed Public Law 105-235, which declared that 'the Government of Iraq is in material and unacceptable breach of its international obligations' and urged the President 'to take appropriate action, in accordance with the Constitution and relevant laws of the United States, to bring Iraq into compliance with its international obligations'.

(12) On May 1, 1998, President Clinton signed Public Law 105-174, which made $5,000,000 available for assistance to the Iraqi democratic opposition for such activities as organization, training, communication and dissemination of information, developing and implementing agreements among opposition groups,

compiling information to support the indictment of Iraqi officials for war crimes, and for related purposes.

SEC. 3. SENSE OF THE CONGRESS REGARDING UNITED STATES POLICY TOWARD IRAQ.

It should be the policy of the United States to support efforts to remove the regime headed by Saddam Hussein from power in Iraq and to promote the emergence of a democratic government to replace that regime.

SEC. 4. ASSISTANCE TO SUPPORT A TRANSITION TO DEMOCRACY IN IRAQ.

(a) AUTHORITY TO PROVIDE ASSISTANCE—The President may provide to the Iraqi democratic opposition organizations designated in accordance with section 5 the following assistance:

(1) BROADCASTING ASSISTANCE—(A) Grant assistance to such organizations for radio and television broadcasting by such organizations to Iraq.

(B) There is authorized to be appropriated to the United States Information Agency $2,000,000 for fiscal year 1999 to carry out this paragraph.

(2) MILITARY ASSISTANCE—(A) The President is authorized to direct the drawdown of defense articles from the stocks of the Department of Defense, defense services of the Department of Defense, and military education and training for such organizations.

(B) The aggregate value (as defined in section 644(m) of the Foreign Assistance Act of 1961) of assistance provided under this paragraph may not exceed $97,000,000.

(b) HUMANITARIAN ASSISTANCE—The Congress urges the President to use existing authorities under the Foreign Assistance Act of 1961 to provide humanitarian assistance to individuals living in areas of Iraq controlled by organizations designated in accordance with section 5, with emphasis on addressing the needs of individuals who have fled to such areas from areas under the control of the Saddam Hussein regime.

(c) RESTRICTION ON ASSISTANCE—No assistance under this section shall be provided to any group within an organization designated in accordance with section 5 which group is, at the time the assistance is to be provided, engaged in military cooperation with the Saddam Hussein regime.

(d) NOTIFICATION REQUIREMENT—The President shall notify the congressional committees specified in section 634A of the Foreign

Assistance Act of 1961 at least 15 days in advance of each obligation of assistance under this section in accordance with the procedures applicable to reprogramming notifications under section 634A.

(e) REIMBURSEMENT RELATING TO MILITARY ASSISTANCE—

(1) IN GENERAL—Defense articles, defense services, and military education and training provided under subsection (a)(2) shall be made available without reimbursement to the Department of Defense except to the extent that funds are appropriated pursuant to paragraph (2).

(2) AUTHORIZATION OF APPROPRIATIONS—There are authorized to be appropriated to the President for each of the fiscal years 1998 and 1999 such sums as may be necessary to reimburse the applicable appropriation, fund, or account for the value (as defined in section 644(m) of the Foreign Assistance Act of 1961) of defense articles, defense services, or military education and training provided under subsection (a)(2).

(f) AVAILABILITY OF FUNDS—(1) Amounts authorized to be appropriated under this section are authorized to remain available until expended.

(2) Amounts authorized to be appropriated under this section are in addition to amounts otherwise available for the purposes described in this section.

(g) AUTHORITY TO PROVIDE ASSISTANCE—Activities under this section (including activities of the nature described in subsection (b)) may be undertaken notwithstanding any other provision of law.

SEC. 5. DESIGNATION OF IRAQI DEMOCRATIC OPPOSITION ORGANIZATION.

(a) INITIAL DESIGNATION—Not later than 90 days after the date of the enactment of this Act, the President shall designate one or more Iraqi democratic opposition organizations that the President determines satisfy the criteria set forth in subsection (c) as eligible to receive assistance under section 4.

(b) DESIGNATION OF ADDITIONAL ORGANIZATIONS—At any time subsequent to the initial designation pursuant to subsection (a), the President may designate one or more additional Iraqi democratic opposition organizations that the President determines satisfy the criteria set forth in subsection (c) as eligible to receive assistance under section 4.

(c) CRITERIA FOR DESIGNATION—In designating an organization pursuant to this section, the President shall consider only organizations that—

(1) include a broad spectrum of Iraqi individuals, groups, or both, opposed to the Saddam Hussein regime; and

(2) are committed to democratic values, to respect for human rights, to peaceful relations with Iraq's neighbors, to maintaining Iraq's territorial integrity, and to fostering cooperation among democratic opponents of the Saddam Hussein regime.

(d) NOTIFICATION REQUIREMENT—At least 15 days in advance of designating an Iraqi democratic opposition organization pursuant to this section, the President shall notify the congressional committees specified in section 634A of the Foreign Assistance Act of 1961 of his proposed designation in accordance with the procedures applicable to reprogramming notifications under section 634A.

SEC. 6. WAR CRIMES TRIBUNAL FOR IRAQ.

Consistent with section 301 of the Foreign Relations Authorization Act, Fiscal Years 1992 and 1993 (Public Law 102-138), House Concurrent Resolution 137, 105th Congress (approved by the House of Representatives on November 13, 1997), and Senate Concurrent Resolution 78, 105th Congress (approved by the Senate on March 13, 1998), the Congress urges the President to call upon the United Nations to establish an international criminal tribunal for the purpose of indicting, prosecuting, and imprisoning Saddam Hussein and other Iraqi officials who are responsible for crimes against humanity, genocide, and other criminal violations of international law.

SEC. 7. ASSISTANCE FOR IRAQ UPON REPLACEMENT OF SADDAM HUSSEIN REGIME.

It is the sense of the Congress that once the Saddam Hussein regime is removed from power in Iraq, the United States should support Iraq's transition to democracy by providing immediate and substantial humanitarian assistance to the Iraqi people, by providing democracy transition assistance to Iraqi parties and movements with democratic goals, and by convening Iraq's foreign creditors to develop a multilateral response to Iraq's foreign debt incurred by Saddam Hussein's regime.

SEC. 8. RULE OF CONSTRUCTION.

Nothing in this Act shall be construed to authorize or otherwise speak to the use of United States Armed Forces (except as provided in section 4(a)(2)) in carrying out this Act.

Source: *Iraq Liberation Act of 1998*, Public Law 105-338, *U.S. Statutes at Large* 112 (1998): 3178.

90. President Bill Clinton, Televised Address to the Nation on Operation DESERT FOX, December 16, 1998 [Excerpt]

Introduction

After the Persian Gulf War, throughout the 1990s U.S. and United Nations (UN) relations with Iraq remained fraught. Under the cease-fire agreement, UN inspectors were entitled to enter Iraq and examine all potential weapons production facilities to ensure that President Saddam Hussein was not engaged in manufacturing chemical, biological, or nuclear weapons of mass destruction. In August 1998 Hussein proclaimed that Iraq would refuse to permit any further inspections. UN inspectors returned in November but were denied full access to Iraqi weapons facilities, and the following month the UN withdrew its inspectors from Baghdad. On December 16, 1998, in an address to the American people, U.S. president Bill Clinton announced a major U.S. and British program of aerial bombings and cruise missile strikes against suspected Iraqi weapons production and storage facilities, intended to degrade that country's capability to produce chemical, biological, or nuclear weapons. Also targeted were the headquarters and barracks of the Republican Guard, Hussein's elite forces; presidential palaces; and air defense systems. Clinton emphasized that Hussein had failed to comply with UN requirements and that during the previous three weeks the United States and Great Britain had given the Iraqi president repeated opportunities to cooperate with UN inspectors, virtually all of which he had subverted. Clinton warned that force was the only language that Iraq understood and that unless the United States took military action at this time, Hussein would proceed to develop destructive weapons, which he would not hesitate to use to dominate the entire region around Iraq. Clinton presented the four-day DESERT FOX bombing program as a prudent deterrent measure essential to preventing Hussein from threatening his neighbors at a later date. Clinton also defended the continuing economic sanctions program against Iraq—under whose terms that country could only sell limited quantities of oil on the international market, with the proceeds of such sales supposedly earmarked purely for humanitarian purposes within Iraq—on the grounds that if these restrictions were lifted, Hussein would use oil sales to finance the acquisition of military armaments. After the bombings, which American military officers believed had largely accomplished their objectives within four days, Iraq refused to permit the return of UN inspection teams. An undeclared air war between Iraq and British and American forces in the region continued for more than four years, with Anglo-American air and naval units regularly launching extensive missile attacks and bombing raids against Iraqi facilities. Aerial hostilities escalated dramatically in the months prior to the official beginning of the 2003 military campaign against Iraq.

Primary Source

THE PRESIDENT: Good evening. Earlier today, I ordered America's Armed Forces to strike military and security targets in Iraq. They are joined by British forces. Their mission is to attack Iraq's nuclear, chemical, and biological programs, and its military capacity to threaten its neighbors. Their purpose is to protect the national interest of the United States and, indeed, the interest of people throughout the Middle East and around the world. Saddam Hussein must not be allowed to threaten his neighbors or the world with nuclear arms, poison gas, or biological weapons.

I want to explain why I have decided, with the unanimous recommendation of my national security team, to use force in Iraq, why we have acted now and what we aim to accomplish.

Six weeks ago, Saddam Hussein announced that he would no longer cooperate with the United Nations weapons inspectors, called UNSCOM. They are highly professional experts from dozens of countries. Their job is to oversee the elimination of Iraq's capability to retain, create and use weapons of mass destruction, and to verify that Iraq does not attempt to rebuild that capability. The inspectors undertook this mission, first, seven and a half years ago, at the end of the Gulf War, when Iraq agreed to declare and destroy its arsenal as a condition of the cease-fire.

The international community had good reason to set this requirement. Other countries possess weapons of mass destruction and ballistic missiles. With Saddam, there's one big difference: he has used them, not once but repeatedly—unleashing chemical weapons against Iranian troops during a decade-long war, not only against soldiers, but against civilians; firing Scud missiles at the citizens of Israel, Saudi Arabia, Bahrain, and Iran—not only against a foreign enemy, but even against his own people, gassing Kurdish civilians in Northern Iraq.

The international community had little doubt then, and I have no doubt today, that left unchecked, Saddam Hussein will use these terrible weapons again.

The United States has patiently worked to preserve UNSCOM, as Iraq has sought to avoid its obligation to cooperate with the inspectors. On occasion, we've had to threaten military force, and Saddam has backed down. Faced with Saddam's latest act of defiance in late October, we built intensive diplomatic pressure on Iraq, backed by overwhelming military force in the region. The U.N. Security Council voted 15 to zero to condemn Saddam's actions and to demand that he immediately come into compliance. Eight Arab nations—Egypt, Syria, Saudi Arabia, Kuwait, Bahrain, Qatar, United Arab Emirates, and Oman—warned that Iraq alone would bear responsibility for the consequences of defying the U.N.

When Saddam still failed to comply, we prepared to act militarily. It was only then, at the last possible moment, that Iraq backed down. It pledged to the U.N. that it had made—and I quote—"a clear and unconditional decision to resume cooperation with the weapons inspectors."

I decided then to call off the attack, with our airplanes already in the air, because Saddam had given in to our demands. I concluded then that the right thing to do was to use restraint and give Saddam one last chance to prove his willingness to cooperate.

I made it very clear at that time what "unconditional cooperation" meant, based on existing U.N. resolutions and Iraq's own commitments. And along with Prime Minister Blair of Great Britain, I made it equally clear that if Saddam failed to cooperate fully, we would be prepared to act without delay, diplomacy or warning.

Now, over the past three weeks, the U.N. weapons inspectors have carried out their plan for testing Iraq's cooperation. The testing period ended this weekend, and last night, UNSCOM's Chairman, Richard Butler, reported the results to U.N. Secretary General Annan. The conclusions are stark, sobering and profoundly disturbing.

In four out of the five categories set forth, Iraq has failed to cooperate. Indeed, it actually has placed new restrictions on the inspectors. Here are some of the particulars:

Iraq repeatedly blocked UNSCOM from inspecting suspect sites. For example, it shut off access to the headquarters of its ruling party, and said it will deny access to the party's other offices, even though U.N. resolutions make no exception for them and UNSCOM has inspected them in the past.

Iraq repeatedly restricted UNSCOM's ability to obtain necessary evidence. For example, Iraq obstructed UNSCOM's effort to photograph bombs related to its chemical weapons program. It tried to stop an UNSCOM biological weapons team from videotaping a site and photocopying documents, and prevented Iraqi personnel from answering UNSCOM's questions.

Prior to the inspection of another site, Iraq actually emptied out the building, removing not just documents, but even the furniture and the equipment. Iraq has failed to turn over virtually all the documents requested by the inspectors; indeed, we know that Iraq ordered the destruction of weapons related documents in anticipation of an UNSCOM inspection.

So Iraq has abused its final chance. As the UNSCOM report concludes—and again I quote—"Iraq's conduct ensured that no progress was able to be made in the fields of disarmament. In light of this experience, and in the absence of full cooperation by Iraq, it must, regrettably, be recorded again that the Commission is not able to conduct the work mandated to it by the Security Council with respect to Iraq's prohibited weapons program."

In short, the inspectors are saying that, even if they could stay in Iraq, their work would be a sham. Saddam's deception has defeated their effectiveness. Instead of the inspectors disarming Saddam, Saddam has disarmed the inspectors.

This situation presents a clear and present danger to the stability of the Persian Gulf and the safety of people everywhere. The international community gave Saddam one last chance to resume cooperation with the weapons inspectors. Saddam has failed to seize the chance.

And so we had to act, and act now. Let me explain why.

First, without a strong inspections system, Iraq would be free to retain and begin to rebuild its chemical, biological, and nuclear weapons programs in months, not years.

Second, if Saddam can cripple the weapons inspections system and get away with it, he would conclude that the international community, led by the United States, has simply lost its will. He will surmise that he has free rein to rebuild his arsenal of destruction. And some day, make no mistake, he will use it again, as he has in the past.

Third, in halting our air strikes in November, I gave Saddam a chance, not a license. If we turn our backs on his defiance, the credibility of U.S. power as a check against Saddam will be destroyed. We will not only have allowed Saddam to shatter the inspections system that controls his weapons of mass destruction program; we also will have fatally undercut the fear of force that stops Saddam from acting to gain domination in the region.

That is why, on the unanimous recommendation of my national security team, including the Vice President, Secretary of Defense, the Chairman of the Joint Chiefs of Staff, the Secretary of State, and the National Security Advisor, I have ordered a strong, sustained series of air strikes against Iraq. They are designed to degrade Saddam's capacity to develop and deliver weapons of mass destruction, and to degrade his ability to threaten his neighbors. At the same time, we are delivering a powerful message to Saddam: If you act recklessly, you will pay a heavy price.

We acted today because, in the judgment of my military advisors, a swift response would provide the most surprise and the least opportunity for Saddam to prepare. If we had delayed for even a matter of days from Chairman Butler's report, we would have given Saddam more time to disperse forces and protect his weapons.

Also, the Muslim holy month of Ramadan begins this weekend. For us to initiate military action during Ramadan would be profoundly offensive to the Muslim world, and therefore, would damage our relations with Arab countries and the progress we have made in the Middle East. That is something we wanted very much to avoid without giving Iraq a month's head start to prepare for potential action against it.

Finally, our allies, including Prime Minister Tony Blair of Great Britain, concurred that now is the time to strike. I hope Saddam will come into cooperation with the inspection system now and comply with the relevant U.N. Security Council resolutions. But we have to be prepared that he will not, and we must deal with the very real danger he poses. So we will pursue a long-term strategy to contain Iraq and its weapons of mass destruction, and work toward the day when Iraq has a government worthy of its people.

First, we must be prepared to use force again if Saddam takes threatening actions, such as trying to reconstitute his weapons of mass destruction or their delivery systems, threatening his neighbors, challenging allied aircraft over Iraq, or moving against his own Kurdish citizens. The credible threat to use force and, when necessary, the actual use of force, is the surest way to contain Saddam's weapons of mass destruction program, curtail his aggression and prevent another Gulf War.

Second, so long as Iraq remains out of compliance, we will work with the international community to maintain and enforce economic sanctions. Sanctions have caused Saddam more than $120 billion—resources that would have been used to rebuild his military. The sanctions system allows Iraq to sell oil for food, for medicine, for other humanitarian supplies for the Iraqi people. We have no quarrel with them. But without the sanctions, we would see the oil-for-food program become oil-for-tanks, resulting in a greater threat to Iraq's neighbors and less food for its people.

The hard fact is that so long as Saddam remains in power, he threatens the well-being of his people, the peace of his region, the security of the world. The best way to end that threat once and for all is with the new Iraqi government, a government ready to live in peace with its neighbors, a government that respects the rights of its people.

Bringing change in Baghdad will take time and effort. We will strengthen our engagement with the full range of Iraqi opposition forces and work with them effectively and prudently.

The decision to use force is never cost-free. Whenever American forces are placed in harm's way, we risk the loss of life. And while our strikes are focused on Iraq's military capabilities, there will be unintended Iraqi casualties. Indeed, in the past, Saddam has intentionally placed Iraqi civilians in harm's way in a cynical bid to sway international opinion. We must be prepared for these realities. At the same time, Saddam should have absolutely no doubt: If he lashes out at his neighbors, we will respond forcefully.

Heavy as they are, the costs of action must be weighed against the price of inaction. If Saddam defies the world and we fail to respond, we will face a far greater threat in the future. Saddam will strike again at his neighbors; he will make war on his own people. And mark my words, he will develop weapons of mass destruction. He will deploy them, and he will use them. Because we are acting today, it is less likely that we will face these dangers in the future.

[. . .]

Source: William J. Clinton, "President Clinton's Statement on Air Strike against Iraq," The White House, Office of the Press Secretary, http://clinton5.nara.gov/WH/New/html/19981216–3611.html.

91. United Nations Security Council Resolutions 712, 715, 773, 778, 806, 833, 949, 986, 1051, 1060, 1115, 1134, 1137, 1154, 1194, 1205, 1284, September 19, 1991–December 17, 1999 [Excerpts]

Introduction

Although Iraq repeatedly asked the United Nations (UN) to lift the international economic sanctions imposed on it after August 2, 1990, that banned most Iraqi oil sales and other commercial and financial contacts with the outside world, these remained in place until after the 2003 Iraq War. The major reason for the continued imposition of sanctions was Iraq's persistent failure to cooperate with UN-sponsored efforts to prevent its acquisition or manufacture of chemical, biological, or nuclear weapons of mass destruction, as mandated in 1991 by Security Council Resolutions 687 and 707. Resolution 706, passed in August 1991, authorized limited sales of Iraqi petroleum, to be used in part to cover the expenses of UN weapons inspection teams in Iraq; in part to compensate foreign governments, organizations, and individuals for losses suffered due to Iraq's invasion of Kuwait; and in part to provide food, medicines, and other humanitarian items needed by Iraq's population. Security Council Resolution 712, adopted on September 19, 1991, sought to utilize funds for these purposes, but the Iraqi government refused to cooperate in this enterprise. Resolution 778, passed by the Security Council in October 1992, sought to address the failure to establish any mechanism to deploy Iraqi oil revenues to finance humanitarian efforts in that country by ordering all UN member states to place all funds under their control derived from Iraqi oil sales in an escrow account under UN administration, a temporary solution that failed to ensure that Iraq would accept goods intended for humanitarian purposes. Fears that Iraq sought to block the operations of a boundary commission established to delineate the precise frontier between Kuwait and Iraq led the UN to pass several resolutions that sought to facilitate this body's work and endorse its decisions. From 1996 onward, the belief that Iraq was surreptitiously developing weapons of mass destruction (WMDs) led the UN to pass several resolutions demanding that the Iraqi government cease such efforts and permit UN inspectors unfettered access to potential production facilities throughout the country in order to verify whether or not Iraq was still developing such weapons. Various UN resolutions proclaimed that the ending of international economic sanctions against Iraq would be conditional on Iraq abandoning all undertakings to acquire WMDs.

Primary Source

Resolution 712 (September 18, 1991)

The Security Council,

Recalling its previous relevant resolutions and in particular resolutions 661 (1990), 686 (1991), 687 (1991), 688 (1991), 692 (1991), 699 (1991), 705 (1991) and 706 (1991),

Expressing its appreciation for the report (S/23006) dated 4 September 1991 submitted by the Secretary-General pursuant to paragraph 5 of resolution 706 (1991),

Reaffirming its concern about the nutritional and health situation of the Iraqi civilian population, and the risk of a further deterioration of this situation, and underlining the need in this context for fully up-to-date assessments of the situation in all parts of Iraq as a basis for the equitable distribution of humanitarian relief to all segments of the Iraqi civilian population,

Recalling that the activities to be carried out by or on behalf of the Secretary-General to meet the purposes referred to in resolution 706 (1991) and the present resolution enjoy the privileges and immunities of the United Nations,

Acting under Chapter VII of the Charter of the United Nations,

1. Confirms the figure mentioned in paragraph 1 of resolution 706 (1991) as the sum authorized for the purpose of that paragraph, and reaffirms its intention to review this sum on the basis of its ongoing assessment of the needs and requirements, in accordance with paragraph 1(d) of resolution 706 (1991);

2. Invites the Committee established by resolution 661 (1990) to authorize immediately pursuant to paragraph 1(d) of resolution 706 (1991), the release by the Secretary-General from the escrow account of the first one-third portion of the sum referred to in paragraph 1 above, such release to take place as required subject to the availability of funds in the account and, in the case of payments to finance the purchase of foodstuffs, medicines and materials and supplies for essential civilian needs which have been notified or approved in accordance with existing procedures, subject to compliance with the procedures laid down in the report of the Secretary-General as approved in paragraph 3 below;

3. Approves the recommendations in the Secretary-General report as contained in its paragraphs 57 (d) and 58;

4. Encourages the Secretary-General and the Committee established by resolution 661 (1990) to cooperate, in close consultation with the Government of Iraq, on a continuing basis to ensure the most effective implementation of the scheme approved in this resolution;

[...]

7. Reaffirms that the inspectors and other experts on mission for the United Nations, appointed for the purpose of this resolution, enjoy privileges and immunities in accordance with the Convention on the Privileges and Immunities of the United Nations, and demands that Iraq shall allow them full freedom of movement and all necessary facilities;

[...]

9. Urges that any provision to Iraq of foodstuffs, medicines or other items of a humanitarian character, in addition to those purchased with the funds referred to in paragraph 1 of this resolution, be undertaken through arrangements which assure their equitable distribution to meet humanitarian needs;

10. Requests the Secretary-General to take the actions necessary to implement the above decisions, and authorizes him to enter into any arrangements or agreements necessary to accomplish this;

11. Calls upon States to cooperate fully in the implementation of resolution 706 (1991) and the present resolution in particular with respect to any measures regarding the import of petroleum and petroleum products and the export of foodstuffs, medicines and materials and supplies for essential civilian needs as referred to in paragraph 20 of resolution 687 (1991), and also with respect to the privileges and immunities of the United Nations and its personnel implementing this resolution; and to ensure that there are no diversions from the purposes laid down in these resolutions;

12. Decides to remain seized of the matter.

Resolution 715 (1991)

Adopted by the Security Council at its 3012th meeting, on 11 October 1991

The Security Council,

Recalling its resolutions 687 (1991) of 3 April 1991 and 707 (1991) of 15 August 1991, and its other resolutions on this matter,

Recalling in particular that under resolution 687 (1991) the Secretary-General and the Director General of the International Atomic Energy Agency (IAEA) were requested to develop plans for future ongoing monitoring and verification, and to submit them to the Security Council for approval,

Taking note of the report and note of the Secretary-General (S/22871/Rev.1 and S/22872/Rev.1), transmitting the plans submitted by the Secretary-General and the Director General of the International Atomic Energy Agency,

Acting under Chapter VII of the Charter of the United Nations,

1. Approves, in accordance with the provisions of resolutions 687 (1991), 707 (1991) and the present resolution, the plans submitted by the Secretary-General and the Director General of the International Atomic Energy Agency (S/22871/Rev.1 and S/22872/Rev.1);

2. Decides that the Special Commission shall carry out the plan submitted by the Secretary-General (S/22871/Rev.1), as well as continuing to discharge its other responsibilities under resolutions 687 (1991), 699 (1991) and 707 (1991) and performing such other functions as are conferred upon it under the present resolution;

3. Requests the Director General of the International Atomic Energy Agency to carry out, with the assistance and cooperation of the Special Commission, the plan submitted by him (S/22872/Rev.1) and to continue to discharge his other responsibilities under resolutions 687 (1991), 699 (1991) and 707 (1991);

[...]

5. Demands that Iraq meet unconditionally all its obligations under the plans approved by the present resolution and cooperate fully with the Special Commission and the Director General of the International Atomic Energy Agency in carrying out the plans;

[...]

7. Requests the Committee established under resolution 661 (1990), the Special Commission and the Director General of the International Atomic Energy Agency to develop in cooperation a mechanism for monitoring any future sales or supplies by other countries to Iraq of items relevant to the implementation of section C of resolution 687 (1991) and other relevant resolutions, including the present resolution and the plans approved hereunder;

Resolution 773 (August 26, 1992)

The Security Council,

Reaffirming its resolution 687 (1991) of 3 April 1991, and in particular paragraphs 2, 3 and 4 thereof, and its resolution 689 (1991) of 9 April 1991,

Recalling the report of the Secretary-General dated 2 May 1991 concerning the establishment of the United Nations Iraq-Kuwait Boundary Demarcation Commission (the Commission) and the subsequent exchange of letters of 6 and 13 May 1991 (S/22558, S/22592 and S/22593),

Having considered the Secretary-General's letter of 12 August 1992 to the President of the Security Council transmitting the further report of the Commission,

Recalling in this connection that through the demarcation process the Commission is not reallocating territory between Kuwait and Iraq, but it is simply carrying out the technical task necessary to demarcate for the first time the precise coordinates of the boundary set out in the Agreed Minutes between the State of Kuwait and the Republic of Iraq regarding the restoration of Friendly Relations, Recognition and Related Matters signed by them on 4 October 1963, and that this task is being carried out in the special circumstances following Iraq's invasion of Kuwait and pursuant to resolution 687 (1991) and the Secretary-General's report for implementing paragraph 3 of that resolution (S/22558),

1. Welcomes the Secretary-General's letter of 12 August to the President of the Council and the further report of the Commission enclosed therewith;

2. Expresses its appreciation to the Commission for its work on the demarcation of the land boundary, and welcomes its demarcation decisions;

3. Welcomes also the decision of the Commission to consider the Eastern section of the boundary, which includes the offshore boundary, at its next session and urges the Commission to demarcate this part of the boundary as soon as possible and thus complete its work;

4. Underlines its guarantee of the inviolability of the above-mentioned international boundary and its decision to take as appropriate all necessary measures to that end in accordance with the Charter, as provided for in paragraph 4 of resolution 687 (1991);

5. Welcomes further the Secretary-General's intention to carry out at the earliest practicable time the realignment of the demilitarized zone referred to in paragraph 5 of resolution 687 (1991) to correspond to the international boundary demarcated by the Commission, with the consequent removal of the Iraqi police posts;

6. Urges the two States concerned to cooperate fully with the work of the Commission;

7. Decides to remain seized of the matter.

Resolution 778 (1992)

Adopted by the Security Council at its 3117th meeting, on 2 October 1992

The Security Council,

Recalling its previous relevant resolutions and in particular resolutions 706 (1991) and 712 (1991),

Taking note of the letter of 15 July 1992 from the Secretary-General to the President of the Security Council on Iraq's compliance with the obligations placed on it by resolution 687 (1991) and subsequent resolutions,

Condemning Iraq's continued failure to comply with its obligations under relevant resolutions,

Reaffirming its concern about the nutritional and health situation of the Iraqi civilian population, and the risk of a further deterioration of this situation, and recalling in this regard its resolutions 706 (1991) and 712 (1991), which provide a mechanism for providing humanitarian relief to the Iraqi population, and resolution 688 (1991), which provides a basis for humanitarian relief efforts in Iraq,

Having regard to the fact that the period of six months referred to in resolutions 706 (1991) and 712 (1991) expired on 18 March 1992,

Deploring Iraq's refusal to cooperate in the implementation of resolutions 706 (1991) and 712 (1991), which puts its civilian population at risk, and which results in the failure by Iraq to meet its obligations under relevant Security Council resolutions,

Recalling that the escrow account provided for in resolutions 706 (1991) and 712 (1991) will consist of Iraqi funds administered by the Secretary-General which will be used to pay contributions to the Compensation Fund, the full costs of carrying out the tasks authorized by section C of resolution 687 (1991), the full costs incurred by the United Nations in facilitating the return of all Kuwaiti property seized by Iraq, half the costs of the Boundary Commission, and the cost to the United Nations of implementing resolution 706 (1991) and of other necessary humanitarian activities in Iraq,

Recalling that Iraq, as stated in paragraph 16 of resolution 687 (1991), is liable for all direct damages resulting from its invasion and occupation of Kuwait, without prejudice to its debts and obligations arising prior to 2 August 1990, which will be addressed through the normal mechanisms,

Recalling its decision in resolution 692 (1991) that the requirement for Iraqi contributions to the Compensation Fund applies to certain Iraqi petroleum and petroleum products exported from Iraq after 2 April 1991,

Acting under Chapter VII of the Charter of the United Nations,

1. *Decides* that all States in which there are funds of the Government of Iraq, or its State bodies, corporations, or agencies, that represent the proceeds of sale of Iraqi petroleum or petroleum products, paid for by or on behalf of the purchaser on or after 6 August 1990, shall cause the transfer of those funds (or equivalent amounts) as soon as possible to the escrow account provided for in resolutions 706 (1991) and 712 (1991); provided that this paragraph shall not require any State to cause the transfer of such funds in excess of 200 million dollars or to cause the transfer of more than fifty per cent of the total funds transferred or contributed pursuant to paragraphs 1, 2 and 3 of this resolution; and further provided that States may exclude from the operation of this paragraph any funds which have already been released to a claimant or supplier prior to the adoption of this resolution, or any other funds subject to or required to satisfy the rights of third parties, at the time of the adoption of this resolution;

2. *Decides* that all States in which there are petroleum or petroleum products owned by the Government of Iraq, or its State bodies, corporations, or agencies, shall take all feasible steps to purchase or arrange for the sale of such petroleum or petroleum products at fair market value, and thereupon to transfer the proceeds as soon as possible to the escrow account provided for in resolution 706 (1991) and 712 (1991);

3. *Urges* all States to contribute funds from other sources to the escrow account as soon as possible;

4. *Decides* that all States shall provide the Secretary-General with any information needed for the effective implementation of this resolution and that they shall take the necessary measures to ensure that banks and other bodies and persons provide all relevant information necessary to identify the funds referred to in paragraphs 1 and 2 above and details of any transactions relating thereto, or the said petroleum or petroleum products, with a view to such information being utilized by all States and by the Secretary-General in the effective implementation of this resolution;

5. *Requests* the Secretary-General:

(a) To ascertain the whereabouts and amounts of the said petroleum products and the proceeds of sale referred to in paragraphs 1 and 2 of this resolution, drawing on the work already done under the auspices of the Compensation Commission, and report the results of the Security Council as soon as possible;

(b) To ascertain the costs of United Nations activities concerning the elimination of weapons of mass destruction, the provision of humanitarian relief in Iraq, and the other United Nations operations specified in paragraphs 2 and 3 of resolution 706 (1991); and

(c) to take the following actions:

(i) transfer to the Compensation Fund, from the funds referred to in paragraphs 1 and 2 of this resolution, the percentage referred to in paragraph 10 of this resolution; and

(ii) use of the remainder of funds referred to in paragraphs 1, 2 and 3 of this resolution for the costs of United Nations activities concerning the elimination of weapons of mass destruction, the provision of humanitarian relief in Iraq, and the other United Nations operations specified in paragraphs 2 and 3 of resolution 706 (1991), taking into account any preference expressed by States transferring or contributing funds as to the allocation of such funds among these purposes;

6. *Decides* that for so long as oil exports take place pursuant to the system provided in resolutions 706 (1991) and 712 (1991) or to the eventual lifting of sanctions pursuant to paragraph 22 of resolution 687 (1991), implementation of paragraphs 1 to 5 of this resolution shall be suspended and all proceeds of those oil exports shall immediately be transferred by the Secretary-General in the currency in which the transfer to the escrow account had been made, to the accounts or States from which funds had been provided under paragraphs 1, 2 and 3 of this resolution, to the extent required to replace in full the amounts so provided (together with applicable interest); and that, if necessary for this purpose, any other funds remaining in the escrow account shall similarly be transferred to those accounts or States; provided, however, that the Secretary-General may retain and use any funds urgently

needed for the purposes specified in paragraph 5 (c) (ii) of this resolution;

[...]

11. *Decides* that no further Iraqi assets shall be released for purposes set forth in paragraph 20 of resolution 687 (1991) except to the sub-account of the escrow account, established pursuant to paragraph 3 of resolution 712 (1991), or directly to the United Nations for humanitarian activities in Iraq;

[...]

13. *Calls upon* all States to cooperate fully in the implementation of this resolution;

14. *Decides* to remain seized of this matter.

Resolution 806 (1993)

Adopted by the Security Council at its 3171st meeting, on 5 February 1993

The Security Council,

Reaffirms its resolution 687 (1991) of 3 April 1991, and in particular paragraphs 2, 3, 4 and 5 thereof, and its resolutions 689 (1991) of 9 April 1991 and 773 (1992) of 26 August 1992, and its other resolutions on this matter,

Having considered the report of the Secretary-General of 18 January 1993 (S/25123),

Noting with approval that work is being completed on the realignment of the demilitarized zone referred to in paragraph 5 of resolution 687 (1991) to correspond to the international boundary demarcated by the United Nations Iraq-Kuwait Boundary Demarcation Commission,

Deeply concerned at recent actions by Iraq in violation of relevant Security Council resolutions, including the series of border incidents involving the United Nations Iraq-Kuwait Observation Mission (UNIKOM),

Recalling the statements made by the President on behalf of the Council on 8 January 1993 (S/25081) and on 11 January 1993 (S/25091),

Acting under Chapter VII of the Charter of the United Nations,

1. Underlines once again its guarantee of the inviolability of the international boundary between the State of Kuwait and the

Republic of Iraq and its decision to take as appropriate all necessary measures to that end in accordance with the Charter, as provided for in paragraph 4 of resolution 687 (1991);

2. Approves the report, and decides to extend the terms of reference of UNIKOM to include the functions contained in paragraph 5 of the report;

3. Requests the Secretary-General to plan and execute a phased deployment of the strengthening of UNIKOM taking into account the need for economy and other relevant factors and to report to the Council on any step he intends to take following an initial deployment;

[...]

Resolution 833 (1993)

Adopted by the Security Council at its 3224th meeting, on 27 May 1993

The Security Council,

Reaffirming its resolution 687 (1991) of 3 April 1991, and in particular paragraphs 2, 3 and 4 thereof, its resolution 689 (1991) of 9 April 1991, its resolution 773 (1992) of 26 August 1992, and its resolution 806 (1993) of 5 February 1993,

[...]

Recalling in this connection that through the demarcation process the Commission was not reallocating territory between Kuwait and Iraq, but it was simply carrying out the technical task necessary to demarcate for the first time the precise coordinates of the boundary set out in the "Agreed Minutes between the State of Kuwait and the Republic of Iraq regarding the Restoration of Friendly Relations, Recognition and Related Matters" signed by them on 4 October 1963, and that this task was carried out in the special circumstances following Iraq's invasion of Kuwait and pursuant to resolution 687 (1991) and the Secretary-General's report for implementing paragraph 3 of that resolution (S/22558),

Reminding Iraq of its obligations under resolution 687 (1991), and in particular paragraph 2 thereof, and under other relevant resolutions of the Council, and of its acceptance of the resolutions of the Council adopted pursuant to Chapter VII of the Charter of the United Nations, which forms the basis for the cease-fire,

Noting with approval the Secretary-General's instruction to the United Nations Iraq-Kuwait Observation Mission (UNIKOM) to finalize the realignment of the demilitarized zone with the entire

international boundary between Iraq and Kuwait demarcated by the Commission,

Welcoming the Secretary-General's decision to make the necessary arrangements for the maintenance of the physical representation of the boundary, as recommended by the Commission in Section X (c) of its report, until other technical arrangements are established between Iraq and Kuwait for this purpose,

Acting under Chapter VII of the Charter of the United Nations,

[...]

4. Reaffirms that the decisions of the Commission regarding the demarcation of the boundary are final;

5. Demands that Iraq and Kuwait in accordance with international law and relevant Security Council resolutions respect the inviolability of the international boundary, as demarcated by the Commission, and the right to navigational access;

6. Underlines and reaffirms its decision to guarantee the inviolability of the above-mentioned international boundary which has not been finally demarcated by the Commission and to take as appropriate all necessary measures to that end in accordance with the Charter, as provided for in paragraph 4 of resolution 687 (1991) and paragraph 4 of resolution 773 (1992);

7. Decides to remain seized of the matter.

Resolution 949 (1994)

Adopted by the Security Council at its 3438th meeting, on 15 October 1994

The Security Council,

Recalling all its previous relevant resolutions, and reaffirming resolutions 678 (1990) of 29 November 1990, 686 (1991) of 2 March 1991, 687 (1991) of 3 April 1991, 689 (1991) of 9 April 1991 and 833 (1993) of 27 May 1993, and in particular paragraph 2 of resolution 678 (1990),

Recalling that Iraq's acceptance of resolution 687 (1991) adopted pursuant to Chapter VII of the Charter of the United Nations forms the basis of the cease-fire,

Noting past Iraqi threats and instances of actual use of force against its neighbours,

Recognizing that any hostile or provocative action directed against its neighbours by the Government of Iraq constitutes a threat to peace and security in the region,

Welcoming all diplomatic and other efforts to resolve the crisis,

Determined to prevent Iraq from resorting to threats and intimidation of its neighbours and the United Nations,

Underlining that it will consider Iraq fully responsible for the serious consequences of any failure to fulfil the demands in the present resolution,

Noting that Iraq has affirmed its readiness to resolve in a positive manner the issue of recognizing Kuwait's sovereignty and its borders as endorsed by resolution 833 (1993), but underlining that Iraq must unequivocally commit itself by full and formal constitutional procedures to respect Kuwait's sovereignty, territorial integrity and borders, as required by resolutions 687 (1991) and 833 (1993),

Reaffirming the commitment of all Member States to the sovereignty, territorial integrity and political independence of Kuwait and Iraq,

Reaffirming its statement of 8 October 1994 (S/1994/PRST/58),

Taking note of the letter from the Permanent Representative of Kuwait of 6 October 1994 (S/1994/1137), regarding the statement by the Revolution Command Council of Iraq of 6 October 1994,

Taking note also of the letter from the Permanent Representative of Iraq of 10 October 1994 (S/1994/1149), announcing that the Government of Iraq had decided to withdraw the troops recently deployed in the direction of the border with Kuwait,

Acting under Chapter VII of the Charter of the United Nations,

1. Condemns recent military deployments by Iraq in the direction of the border with Kuwait;

2. Demands that Iraq immediately complete the withdrawal of all military units recently deployed to southern Iraq to their original positions;

3. Demands that Iraq not again utilize its military or any other forces in a hostile or provocative manner to threaten either its neighbours or United Nations operations in Iraq;

4. Demands therefore that Iraq not redeploy to the south the units referred to in paragraph 2 above or take any other action to enhance its military capacity in southern Iraq;

5. Demands that Iraq cooperate fully with the United Nations Special Commission;

6. Decides to remain actively seized of the matter.

Resolution 986 (1995)

Adopted by the Security Council at its 3519th meeting, on 14 April 1995

The Security Council,

Recalling its previous relevant resolutions,

Concerned by the serious nutritional and health situation of the Iraqi population, and by the risk of a further deterioration in this situation,

Convinced of the need as a temporary measure to provide for the humanitarian needs of the Iraqi people until the fulfilment by Iraq of the relevant Security Council resolutions, including notably resolution 687 (1991) of 3 April 1991, allows the Council to take further action with regard to the prohibitions referred to in resolution 661 (1990) of 6 August 1990, in accordance with the provisions of those resolutions,

Convinced also of the need for equitable distribution of humanitarian relief to all segments of the Iraqi population throughout the country,

Reaffirming the commitment of all Member States to the sovereignty and territorial integrity of Iraq,

Acting under Chapter VII of the Charter of the United Nations,

1. Authorizes States, notwithstanding the provisions of paragraphs 3 (a), 3 (b) and 4 of resolution 661 (1990) and subsequent relevant resolutions, to permit the import of petroleum and petroleum products originating in Iraq, including financial and other essential transactions directly relating thereto, sufficient to produce a sum not exceeding a total of one billion United States dollars every 90 days for the purposes set out in this resolution and subject to the following conditions:

(a) Approval by the Committee established by resolution 661 (1990), in order to ensure the transparency of each transaction and its conformity with the other provisions of this resolution, after submission of an application by the State concerned, endorsed by the Government of Iraq, for each proposed purchase of Iraqi petroleum and petroleum products, including details of the purchase price at fair market value, the export route, the opening of a letter of credit payable to the escrow account to be established by the Secretary-General for the purposes of this resolution, and of any other directly related financial or other essential transaction;

(b) Payment of the full amount of each purchase of Iraqi petroleum and petroleum products directly by the purchaser in the State concerned into the escrow account to be established by the Secretary-General for the purposes of this resolution;

2. Authorizes Turkey, notwithstanding the provisions of paragraphs 3 (a), 3 (b) and 4 of resolution 661 (1990) and the provisions of paragraph 1 above, to permit the import of petroleum and petroleum products originating in Iraq sufficient, after the deduction of the percentage referred to in paragraph 8 (c) below for the Compensation Fund, to meet the pipeline tariff charges, verified as reasonable by the independent inspection agents referred to in paragraph 6 below, for the transport of Iraqi petroleum and petroleum products through the Kirkuk-Yumurtalik pipeline in Turkey authorized by paragraph 1 above;

[. . .]

6. Directs the Committee established by resolution 661 (1990) to monitor the sale of petroleum and petroleum products to be exported by Iraq via the Kirkuk-Yumurtalik pipeline from Iraq to Turkey and from the Mina al-Bakr oil terminal, with the assistance of independent inspection agents appointed by the Secretary-General, who will keep the Committee informed of the amount of petroleum and petroleum products exported from Iraq after the date of entry into force of paragraph 1 of this resolution, and will verify that the purchase price of the petroleum and petroleum products is reasonable in the light of prevailing market conditions, and that, for the purposes of the arrangements set out in this resolution, the larger share of the petroleum and petroleum products is shipped via the Kirkuk-Yumurtalik pipeline and the remainder is exported from the Mina al-Bakr oil terminal;

7. Requests the Secretary-General to establish an escrow account for the purposes of this resolution, to appoint independent and certified public accountants to audit it, and to keep the Government of Iraq fully informed;

8. Decides that the funds in the escrow account shall be used to meet the humanitarian needs of the Iraqi population and for the following other purposes, and requests the Secretary-General to use the funds deposited in the escrow account:

(a) To finance the export to Iraq, in accordance with the procedures of the Committee established by resolution 661 (1990), of medicine, health supplies, foodstuffs, and materials and supplies for essential civilian needs, as referred to in paragraph 20 of resolution 687 (1991) provided that:

(i) Each export of goods is at the request of the Government of Iraq;

(ii) Iraq effectively guarantees their equitable distribution, on the basis of a plan submitted to and approved by the Secretary-General, including a description of the goods to be purchased;

(iii) The Secretary-General receives authenticated confirmation that the exported goods concerned have arrived in Iraq;

(b) To complement, in view of the exceptional circumstances prevailing in the three Governorates mentioned below, the distribution by the Government of Iraq of goods imported under this resolution, in order to ensure an equitable distribution of humanitarian relief to all segments of the Iraqi population throughout the country, by providing between 130 million and 150 million United States dollars every 90 days to the United Nations Inter-Agency Humanitarian Programme operating within the sovereign territory of Iraq in the three northern Governorates of Dihouk, Arbil and Suleimaniyeh, except that if less than one billion United States dollars worth of petroleum or petroleum products is sold during any 90 day period, the Secretary-General may provide a proportionately smaller amount for this purpose;

[. . .]

(g) To make available up to 10 million United States dollars every 90 days from the funds deposited in the escrow account for the payments envisaged under paragraph 6 of resolution 778 (1992) of 2 October 1992;

9. Authorizes States to permit, notwithstanding the provisions of paragraph 3 (c) of resolution 661 (1990):

(a) The export to Iraq of the parts and equipment which are essential for the safe operation of the Kirkuk-Yumurtalik pipeline system in Iraq, subject to the prior approval by the Committee established by resolution 661 (1990) of each export contract;

(b) Activities directly necessary for the exports authorized under subparagraph (a) above, including financial transactions related thereto;

10. Decides that, since the costs of the exports and activities authorized under paragraph 9 above are precluded by paragraph 4 of resolution 661 (1990) and by paragraph 11 of resolution 778 (1991) from being met from funds frozen in accordance with those provisions, the cost of such exports and activities may, until funds begin to be paid into the escrow account established for the purposes of this resolution, and following approval in each case by the Committee established by resolution 661 (1990), exceptionally be financed by letters of credit, drawn against future oil sales the proceeds of which are to be deposited in the escrow account;

11. Requests the Secretary-General to report to the Council 90 days after the date of entry into force of paragraph 1 above, and again prior to the end of the initial 180 day period, on the basis of observation by United Nations personnel in Iraq, and on the basis of consultations with the Government of Iraq, on whether Iraq has ensured the equitable distribution of medicine, health supplies, foodstuffs, and materials and supplies for essential civilian needs, financed in accordance with paragraph 8 (a) above, including in his reports any observations he may have on the adequacy of the revenues to meet Iraq's humanitarian needs, and on Iraq's capacity to export sufficient quantities of petroleum and petroleum products to produce the sum referred to in paragraph 1 above;

12. Requests the Committee established by resolution 661 (1990), in close coordination with the Secretary-General, to develop expedited procedures as necessary to implement the arrangements in paragraphs 1, 2, 6, 8, 9 and 10 of this resolution and to report to the Council 90 days after the date of entry into force of paragraph 1 above and again prior to the end of the initial 180 day period on the implementation of those arrangements;

13. Requests the Secretary-General to take the actions necessary to ensure the effective implementation of this resolution, authorizes him to enter into any necessary arrangements or agreements, and requests him to report to the Council when he has done so;

[...]

17. Affirms that nothing in this resolution affects Iraq's duty scrupulously to adhere to all of its obligations concerning servicing and repayment of its foreign debt, in accordance with the appropriate international mechanisms;

18. Also affirms that nothing in this resolution should be construed as infringing the sovereignty or territorial integrity of Iraq;

19. Decides to remain seized of the matter.

Resolution 1051 (1996)

Adopted by the Security Council at its 3644th meeting, on 27 March 1996

The Security Council,

Reaffirming its resolution 687 (1991) of 8 April 1991, and in particular section C thereof, its resolution 707 (1991) of 15 August 1991 and its resolution 715 (1991) of 11 October 1991 and the plans for ongoing monitoring and verification approved thereunder,

Recalling the request in paragraph 7 of its resolution 715 (1991) to the Committee established under resolution 661 (1990), the

Special Commission and the Director General of the International Atomic Energy Agency (IAEA) to develop in cooperation a mechanism for monitoring any future sales or supplies by other countries to Iraq of items relevant to the implementation of section C of resolution 687 (1991) and other relevant resolutions, including resolution 715 (1991) and the plans approved thereunder,

[...]

Acting under Chapter VII of the Charter of the United Nations,

1. Approves, pursuant to the relevant provisions of its resolutions 687 (1991) and 715 (1991), the provisions for the monitoring mechanism contained in annex I of the aforementioned letter of 7 December 1995 (S/1995/1017), subject to the terms of this resolution;

[...]

5. Decides, subject to paragraphs 4 and 7 of this resolution, that all States shall:

(a) Transmit to the joint unit constituted by the Special Commission and the Director General of the IAEA under paragraph 16 of the mechanism the notifications, with the data from potential exporters, and all other relevant information when available to the States, as requested in the mechanism on the intended sale or supply from their territories of any items or technologies which are subject to such notification in accordance with paragraphs 9, 11, 13, 24, 25, 27 and 28 of the mechanism;

(b) Report to the joint unit, in accordance with paragraphs 13, 24, 25, 27 and 28 of the mechanism, any information they may have at their disposal or may receive from suppliers in their territories of attempts to circumvent the mechanism or to supply Iraq with items prohibited to Iraq under the plans for ongoing monitoring and verification approved by resolution 715 (1991), or where the procedures for special exceptions laid down in paragraphs 24 and 25 of the mechanism have not been followed by Iraq;

6. Decides that the notifications required under paragraph 5 above shall be provided to the joint unit by Iraq, in respect of all items and technologies referred to in paragraph 12 of the mechanism, as from the date agreed upon between the Special Commission and the Director General of the IAEA and Iraq, and in any event not later than sixty days after the adoption of this resolution;

7. Decides that the notifications required under paragraph 5 above shall be provided to the joint unit by all other States as from the date the Secretary-General and the Director General of the IAEA, after their consultations with the members of the Council

and other interested States, report to the Council indicating that they are satisfied with the preparedness of States for the effective implementation of the mechanism;

[...]

12. Calls upon all States and international organizations to cooperate fully with the Committee established under resolution 661 (1990), the Special Commission and the Director General of the IAEA in the fulfilment of their tasks in connection with the mechanism, including supplying such information as may be sought by them in implementation of the mechanism;

13. Calls upon all States to adopt as soon as possible such measures as may be necessary under their national procedures to implement the mechanism;

14. Decides that all States shall, not later than 45 days after the adoption of this resolution, be provided by the Special Commission and the Director General of the IAEA with information necessary to make preparatory arrangements at the national level prior to the implementation of the provisions of the mechanism;

15. Demands that Iraq meet unconditionally all its obligations under the mechanism approved by this resolution and cooperate fully with the Special Commission and the Director General of the IAEA in the carrying out of their tasks under this resolution and the mechanism by such means as they may determine in accordance with their mandates from the Council;

Resolution 1060 (1996)

Adopted by the Security Council at its 3672nd meeting on 12 June 1996

The Security Council,

Recalling all its previous relevant resolutions, and in particular its resolutions 687 (1991) of 3 April 1991, 707 (1991) of 15 August 1991 and 715 (1991) of 11 October 1991,

[...]

Reiterating the commitment of all Member States to the sovereignty, territorial integrity and political independence of Kuwait and Iraq,

Recalling in this context the notes from the Secretary-General of 21 July 1993 (S/26127) and 1 December 1993 (S/26825),

Noting the progress made in the work of the Special Commission towards the elimination of Iraq's programmes of weapons of mass destruction, and outstanding problems, reported by the Chairman of the Special Commission,

Noting with concern the incidents on 11 and 12 June 1996, reported to members of the Council by the Executive Chairman of the Special Commission, when access by a Special Commission inspection team to sites in Iraq designated for inspection by the Commission was excluded by the Iraqi authorities,

Emphasizing the importance the Council attaches to full compliance by Iraq with its obligations under resolutions 687 (1991), 707 (1991) and 715 (1991) to permit immediate, unconditional and unrestricted access to the Special Commission to any site which the Commission wishes to inspect,

Emphasizing the unacceptability of any attempts by Iraq to deny access to any such site,

Acting under Chapter VII of the Charter of the United Nations,

1. Deplores the refusal of the Iraqi authorities to allow access to sites designated by the Special Commission, which constitutes a clear violation of the provisions of Security Council resolutions 687 (1991), 707 (1991) and 715 (1991);

2. Demands that Iraq cooperate fully with the Special Commission in accordance with the relevant resolutions; and that the Government of Iraq allow the Special Commission inspection teams immediate, unconditional and unrestricted access to any and all areas, facilities, equipment, records and means of transportation which they wish to inspect;

3. Expresses its full support to the Special Commission in its efforts to ensure implementation of its mandate under the relevant resolutions of the Council;

4. Decides to remain seized of the matter.

Resolution 1115 (1997)

Adopted by the Security Council at its 3792nd meeting, on 21 June 1997

The Security Council,

Recalling all its previous relevant resolutions, and in particular its resolutions 687 (1991) of 3 April 1991, 707 (1991) of 15 August 1991, 715 (1991) of 11 October 1991 and 1060 (1996) of 12 June 1996,

Recalling also the letter from the Executive Chairman of the Special Commission to the President of the Security Council of 12 June 1997

(S/1997/474), which reported to the Council the incidents on 10 and 12 June 1997 when access by a Special Commission inspection team to sites in Iraq designated for inspection by the Commission was excluded by the Iraqi authorities,

Determined to ensure full compliance by Iraq with its obligations under all previous resolutions, in particular resolutions 687 (1991), 707 (1991), 715 (1991) and 1060 (1996) to permit immediate, unconditional and unrestricted access to the Special Commission to any site which the Commission wishes to inspect,

Stressing the unacceptability of any attempts by Iraq to deny access to any such site,

Reiterating the commitment of all Member States to the sovereignty, territorial integrity and political independence of Kuwait and Iraq,

Acting under Chapter VII of the Charter of the United Nations,

1. Condemns the repeated refusal of the Iraqi authorities to allow access to sites designated by the Special Commission, which constitutes a clear and flagrant violation of the provisions of Security Council resolutions 687 (1991), 707 (1991), 715 (1991) and 1060 (1996);

2. Demands that Iraq cooperate fully with the Special Commission in accordance with the relevant resolutions; and that the Government of Iraq allow the Special Commission inspection teams immediate, unconditional and unrestricted access to any and all areas, facilities, equipment, records and means of transportation which they wish to inspect in accordance with the mandate of the Special Commission;

3. Demands further that the Government of Iraq give immediate, unconditional and unrestricted access to officials and other persons under the authority of the Iraqi Government whom the Special Commission wishes to interview, so that the Special Commission may fully discharge its mandate;

4. Requests the Chairman of the Special Commission to include in his consolidated progress reports under resolution 1051 (1996) an annex evaluating Iraq's compliance with paragraphs 2 and 3 of this resolution;

5. Decides not to conduct the reviews provided for in paragraphs 21 and 28 of resolution 687 (1991) until after the next consolidated progress report of the Special Commission, due on 11 October 1997, after which time those reviews will resume in accordance with resolution 687 (1991);

6. Expresses the firm intention, unless the Special Commission advises the Council in the report referred to in paragraphs 4 and 5

that Iraq is in substantial compliance with paragraphs 2 and 3 of this resolution, to impose additional measures on those categories of Iraqi officials responsible for the non-compliance;

7. Reaffirms its full support to the Special Commission in its efforts to ensure the implementation of its mandate under the relevant resolutions of the Council;

8. Decides to remain seized of the matter.

Resolution 1134 (1997)

Adopted by the Security Council at its 3826th meeting, on 23 October 1997

The Security Council,

Recalling all its previous relevant resolutions, and in particular its resolutions 687 (1991) of 3 April 1991, 707 (1991) of 15 August 1991, 715 (1991) of 11 October 1991, 1060 (1996) of 12 June 1996, and 1115 (1997) of 21 June 1997,

Having considered the report of the Executive Chairman of the Special Commission dated 6 October 1997 (S/1997/774),

Expressing grave concern at the report of additional incidents since the adoption of resolution 1115 (1997) in which access by the Special Commission inspection teams to sites in Iraq designated for inspection by the Commission was again denied by the Iraqi authorities,

Stressing the unacceptability of any attempts by Iraq to deny access to such sites,

Taking note of the progress nevertheless achieved by the Special Commission, as set out in the report of the Executive Chairman, towards the elimination of Iraq's programme of weapons of mass destruction,

Reaffirming its determination to ensure full compliance by Iraq with all its obligations under all previous relevant resolutions and reiterating its demand that Iraq allow immediate, unconditional and unrestricted access to the Special Commission to any site which the Commission wishes to inspect, and in particular allow the Special Commission and its inspection teams to conduct both fixed wing and helicopter flights throughout Iraq for all relevant purposes including inspection, surveillance, aerial surveys, transportation and logistics without interferences of any kind and upon such terms and conditions as may be determined by the Special Commission, and to make use of their own aircraft and such airfields in Iraq as they may determine are most appropriate for the work of the Commission,

Recalling that resolution 1115 (1997) expresses the Council's firm intention, unless the Special Commission has advised the Council that Iraq is in substantial compliance with paragraphs 2 and 3 of that resolution, to impose additional measures on those categories of Iraqi officials responsible for the non-compliance,

Reiterating the commitment of all Member States to the sovereignty, territorial integrity and political independence of Kuwait and Iraq,

Acting under Chapter VII of the Charter of the United Nations,

1. Condemns the repeated refusal of the Iraqi authorities, as detailed in the report of the Executive Chairman of the Special Commission, to allow access to sites designated by the Special Commission, and especially Iraqi actions endangering the safety of Special Commission personnel, the removal and destruction of documents of interest to the Special Commission and interference with the freedom of movement of Special Commission personnel;

2. Decides that such refusals to cooperate constitute a flagrant violation of Security Council resolutions 687 (1991), 707 (1991), 715 (1991) and 1060 (1996), and notes that the Special Commission in the report of the Executive Chairman was unable to advise that Iraq was in substantial compliance with paragraphs 2 and 3 of resolution 1115 (1997);

3. Demands that Iraq cooperate fully with the Special Commission in accordance with the relevant resolutions, which constitute the governing standard of Iraqi compliance;

4. Demands in particular that Iraq without delay allow the Special Commission inspection teams immediate, unconditional and unrestricted access to any and all areas, facilities, equipment, records and means of transportation which they wish to inspect in accordance with the mandate of the Special Commission, as well as to officials and other persons under the authority of the Iraqi Government whom the Special Commission wishes to interview so that the Special Commission may fully discharge its mandate;

5. Requests the Chairman of the Special Commission to include in all future consolidated progress reports prepared under resolution 1051 (1996) an annex evaluating Iraq's compliance with paragraphs 2 and 3 of resolution 1115 (1997);

6. Expresses the firm intention—if the Special Commission reports that Iraq is not in compliance with paragraphs 2 and 3 of resolution 1115 (1997) or if the Special Commission does not advise the Council in the report of the Executive Chairman due on 11 April 1998 that Iraq is in compliance with paragraphs 2 and 3 of resolution 1115 (1997)—to adopt measures which would oblige all States to prevent without delay the entry into or transit through

their territories of all Iraqi officials and members of the Iraqi armed forces who are responsible for or participate in instances of non-compliance with paragraphs 2 and 3 of resolution 1115 (1997), provided that the entry of a person into a particular State on a specified date may be authorized by the Committee established by resolution 661 (1990), and provided that nothing in this paragraph shall oblige a State to refuse entry into its own territory to its own nationals or persons carrying out bona fide diplomatic assignments or missions;

7. Decides further, on the basis of all incidents related to the implementation of paragraphs 2 and 3 of resolution 1115 (1997), to begin to designate, in consultation with the Special Commission, individuals whose entry or transit would be prevented upon implementation of the measures set out in paragraph 6 above;

8. Decides not to conduct the reviews provided for in paragraphs 21 and 28 of resolution 687 (1991) until after the next consolidated progress report of the Special Commission, due on 11 April 1998, after which those reviews will resume in accordance with resolution 687 (1991), beginning on 26 April 1998;

9. Reaffirms its full support for the authority of the Special Commission under its Executive Chairman to ensure the implementation of its mandate under the relevant resolutions of the Council;

10. Decides to remain seized of the matter.

Resolution 1137 (1997)

Adopted by the Security Council at its 3831st meeting, on 12 November 1997

The Security Council,

Recalling all its previous relevant resolutions, and in particular its resolutions 687 (1991) of 3 April 1991, 707 (1991) of 15 August 1991, 715 (1991) of 11 October 1991, 1060 (1996) of 12 June 1996, 1115 (1997) of 21 June 1997, and 1134 (1997) of 23 October 1997,

Taking note with grave concern of the letter of 29 October 1997 from the Deputy Prime Minister of Iraq to the President of the Security Council (S/1997/829) conveying the unacceptable decision of the Government of Iraq to seek to impose conditions on its cooperation with the Special Commission, of the letter of 2 November 1997 from the Permanent Representative of Iraq to the United Nations to the Executive Chairman of the Special Commission (S/1997/837, annex) which reiterated the unacceptable demand that the reconnaissance aircraft operating on behalf of the Special Commission be withdrawn from use and which implicitly threatened the safety of such aircraft, and of the letter of 6 November 1997 from the Minister of Foreign Affairs of Iraq to the

President of the Security Council (S/1997/855) admitting that Iraq has moved dual-capable equipment which is subject to monitoring by the Special Commission,

Also taking note with grave concern of the letters of 30 October 1997 (S/1997/830) and 2 November 1997 (S/1997/836) from the Executive Chairman of the Special Commission to the President of the Security Council advising that the Government of Iraq had denied entry to Iraq to two Special Commission officials on 30 October 1997 and 2 November 1997 on the grounds of their nationality, and of the letters of 3 November 1997 (S/1997/837), 4 November 1997 (S/1997/843), 5 November 1997 (S/1997/851) and 7 November 1997 (S/1997/864) from the Executive Chairman of the Special Commission to the President of the Security Council advising that the Government of Iraq had denied entry to sites designated for inspection by the Special Commission on 3, 4, 5, 6 and 7 November 1997 to Special Commission inspectors on the grounds of their nationality, and of the additional information in the Executive Chairman's letter of 5 November 1997 to the President of the Security Council (S/1997/851) that the Government of Iraq has moved significant pieces of dual-capable equipment subject to monitoring by the Special Commission, and that monitoring cameras appear to have been tampered with or covered,

Welcoming the diplomatic initiatives, including that of the high-level mission of the Secretary-General, which have taken place in an effort to ensure that Iraq complies unconditionally with its obligations under the relevant resolutions,

Deeply concerned at the report of the high-level mission of the Secretary-General on the results of its meetings with the highest levels of the Government of Iraq,

Recalling that its resolution 1115 (1997) expressed its firm intention, unless the Special Commission advised the Council that Iraq is in substantial compliance with paragraphs 2 and 3 of that resolution, to impose additional measures on those categories of Iraqi officials responsible for the non-compliance,

Recalling also that its resolution 1134 (1997) reaffirmed its firm intention, if inter alia the Special Commission reports that Iraq is not in compliance with paragraphs 2 and 3 of resolution 1115 (1997), to adopt measures which would oblige States to refuse the entry into or transit through their territories of all Iraqi officials and members of the Iraqi armed forces who are responsible for or participate in instances of non-compliance with paragraphs 2 and 3 of resolution 1115 (1997),

Recalling further the Statement of its President of 29 October 1997 (S/PRST/1997/49) in which the Council condemned the decision of the Government of Iraq to try to dictate the terms of its compliance with its obligation to cooperate with the Special Commission,

and warned of the serious consequences of Iraq's failure to comply immediately and fully and without conditions or restrictions with its obligations under the relevant resolutions,

Reiterating the commitment of all Member States to the sovereignty, territorial integrity and political independence of Kuwait and Iraq,

Determined to ensure immediate and full compliance without conditions or restrictions by Iraq with its obligations under the relevant resolutions,

Determining that this situation continues to constitute a threat to international peace and security,

Acting under Chapter VII of the Charter,

1. Condemns the continued violations by Iraq of its obligations under the relevant resolutions to cooperate fully and unconditionally with the Special Commission in the fulfilment of its mandate, including its unacceptable decision of 29 October 1997 to seek to impose conditions on cooperation with the Special Commission, its refusal on 30 October 1997 and 2 November 1997 to allow entry to Iraq to two Special Commission officials on the grounds of their nationality, its denial of entry on 3, 4, 5, 6 and 7 November 1997 to sites designated by the Special Commission for inspection to Special Commission inspectors on the grounds of their nationality, its implicit threat to the safety of the reconnaissance aircraft operating on behalf of the Special Commission, its removal of significant pieces of dual-use equipment from their previous sites, and its tampering with monitoring cameras of the Special Commission;

2. Demands that the Government of Iraq rescind immediately its decision of 29 October 1997;

3. Demands also that Iraq cooperate fully and immediately and without conditions or restrictions with the Special Commission in accordance with the relevant resolutions, which constitute the governing standard of Iraqi compliance;

4. Decides, in accordance with paragraph 6 of resolution 1134 (1997), that States shall without delay prevent the entry into or transit through their territories of all Iraqi officials and members of the Iraqi armed forces who were responsible for or participated in the instances of non-compliance detailed in paragraph 1 above, provided that the entry of a person into a particular State on a specified date may be authorized by the Committee established by resolution 661 (1990) of 6 August 1990, and provided that nothing in this paragraph shall oblige a State to refuse entry into its own territory to its own nationals, or to persons carrying out bona fide diplomatic assignments, or missions approved by the Committee established by resolution 661 (1990);

5. Decides also, in accordance with paragraph 7 of resolution 1134 (1997), to designate in consultation with the Special Commission a list of individuals whose entry or transit will be prevented under the provisions of paragraph 4 above, and requests the Committee established by resolution 661 (1990) to develop guidelines and procedures as appropriate for the implementation of the measures set out in paragraph 4 above, and to transmit copies of these guidelines and procedures, as well as a list of the individuals designated, to all Member States;

6. Decides that the provisions of paragraphs 4 and 5 above shall terminate one day after the Executive Chairman of the Special Commission reports to the Council that Iraq is allowing the Special Commission inspection teams immediate, unconditional and unrestricted access to any and all areas, facilities, equipment, records and means of transportation which they wish to inspect in accordance with the mandate of the Special Commission, as well as to officials and other persons under the authority of the Iraqi Government whom the Special Commission wishes to interview so that the Special Commission may fully discharge its mandate;

7. Decides that the reviews provided for in paragraphs 21 and 28 of resolution 687 (1991) shall resume in April 1998 in accordance with paragraph 8 of resolution 1134 (1997), provided that the Government of Iraq shall have complied with paragraph 2 above;

8. Expresses the firm intention to take further measures as may be required for the implementation of this resolution;

9. Reaffirms the responsibility of the Government of Iraq under the relevant resolutions to ensure the safety and security of the personnel and equipment of the Special Commission and its inspection teams;

10. Reaffirms also its full support for the authority of the Special Commission under its Executive Chairman to ensure the implementation of its mandate under the relevant resolutions of the Council;

11. Decides to remain seized of the matter.

Resolution 1154 (1998)

Adopted by the Security Council at its 3858th meeting, on 2 March 1998

The Security Council,

Recalling all its previous relevant resolutions, which constitute the governing standard of Iraqi compliance,

Determined to ensure immediate and full compliance by Iraq without conditions or restrictions with its obligations under resolution 687 (1991) and the other relevant resolutions,

Reaffirming the commitment of all Member States to the sovereignty, territorial integrity and political independence of Iraq, Kuwait and the neighbouring States,

Acting under Chapter VII of the Charter of the United Nations,

1. Commends the initiative by the Secretary-General to secure commitments from the Government of Iraq on compliance with its obligations under the relevant resolutions, and in this regard endorses the memorandum of understanding signed by the Deputy Prime Minister of Iraq and the Secretary-General on 23 February 1998 (S/1998/166) and looks forward to its early and full implementation;

2. Requests the Secretary-General to report to the Council as soon as possible with regard to the finalization of procedures for Presidential sites in consultation with the Executive Chairman of the United Nations Special Commission and the Director General of the International Atomic Energy Agency (IAEA);

3. Stresses that compliance by the Government of Iraq with its obligations, repeated again in the memorandum of understanding, to accord immediate, unconditional and unrestricted access to the Special Commission and the IAEA in conformity with the relevant resolutions is necessary for the implementation of resolution 687 (1991), but that any violation would have severest consequences for Iraq;

4. Reaffirms its intention to act in accordance with the relevant provisions of resolution 687 (1991) on the duration of the prohibitions referred to in that resolution and notes that by its failure so far to comply with its relevant obligations Iraq has delayed the moment when the Council can do so;

5. Decides, in accordance with its responsibility under the Charter, to remain actively seized of the matter, in order to ensure implementation of this resolution, and to secure peace and security in the area.

Resolution 1194 (1998)

Adopted by the Security Council at its 3924th meeting, on 9 September 1998

The Security Council,

Recalling all its previous relevant resolutions, and in particular its resolutions 687 (1991) of 3 April 1991, 707 (1991) of 15 August

1991, 715 (1991) of 11 October 1991, 1060 (1996) of 12 June 1996, 1115 (1997) of 21 June 1997 and 1154 (1998) of 2 March 1998,

Noting the announcement by Iraq on 5 August 1998 that it had decided to suspend cooperation with the United Nations Special Commission and the International Atomic Energy Agency (IAEA) on all disarmament activities and restrict ongoing monitoring and verification activities at declared sites, and/or actions implementing the above decision,

Stressing that the necessary conditions do not exist for the modification of the measures referred to in section F of resolution 687 (1991),

Recalling the letter from the Executive Chairman of the Special Commission to the President of the Security Council of 12 August 1998 (S/1998/767), which reported to the Council that Iraq had halted all disarmament activities of the Special Commission and placed limitations on the rights of the Commission to conduct its monitoring operations,

Recalling also the letter from the Director General of the IAEA to the President of the Security Council of 11 August 1998 (S/1998/766) which reported the refusal by Iraq to cooperate in any activity involving investigation of its clandestine nuclear programme and other restrictions of access placed by Iraq on the ongoing monitoring and verification programme of the IAEA,

Noting the letters of 18 August 1998 from the President of the Security Council to the Executive Chairman of the Special Commission and the Director General of the IAEA (S/1998/769, S/1998/768), which expressed the full support of the Security Council for those organizations in the implementation of the full range of their mandated activities, including inspections,

Recalling the Memorandum of Understanding signed by the Deputy Prime Minister of Iraq and the Secretary-General on 23 February 1998 (S/1998/166), in which Iraq reiterated its undertaking to cooperate fully with the Special Commission and the IAEA,

Noting that the announcement by Iraq of 5 August 1998 followed a period of increased cooperation and some tangible progress achieved since the signing of the Memorandum of Understanding,

Reiterating its intention to respond favourably to future progress made in the disarmament process and reaffirming its commitment to comprehensive implementation of its resolutions, in particular resolution 687 (1991),

Determined to ensure full compliance by Iraq with its obligations under all previous resolutions, in particular resolutions 687 (1991), 707 (1991), 715 (1991), 1060 (1996), 1115 (1997) and

1154 (1998), to permit immediate, unconditional and unrestricted access to the Special Commission and the IAEA to all sites which they wish to inspect, and to provide the Special Commission and the IAEA with all the cooperation necessary for them to fulfil their mandates under those resolutions,

Stressing the unacceptability of any attempts by Iraq to deny access to any sites or to refuse to provide the necessary cooperation,

Expressing its readiness to consider, in a comprehensive review, Iraq's compliance with its obligations under all relevant resolutions once Iraq has rescinded its above-mentioned decision and demonstrated that it is prepared to fulfil all its obligations, including, in particular on disarmament issues, by resuming full cooperation with the Special Commission and the IAEA consistent with the Memorandum of Understanding, as endorsed by the Council in resolution 1154 (1998), and to that end welcoming the proposal of the Secretary-General for such a comprehensive review and inviting the Secretary-General to provide his views in that regard,

Reiterating the commitment of all Member States to the sovereignty, territorial integrity and political independence of Kuwait and Iraq,

Acting under Chapter VII of the Charter of the United Nations,

1. Condemns the decision by Iraq of 5 August 1998 to suspend cooperation with the Special Commission and the IAEA, which constitutes a totally unacceptable contravention of its obligations under resolutions 687 (1991), 707 (1991), 715 (1991), 1060 (1996), 1115 (1997) and 1154 (1998), and the Memorandum of Understanding signed by the Deputy Prime Minister of Iraq and the Secretary-General on 23 February 1998;

2. Demands that Iraq rescind its above-mentioned decision and cooperate fully with the Special Commission and the IAEA in accordance with its obligations under the relevant resolutions and the Memorandum of Understanding as well as resume dialogue with the Special Commission and the IAEA immediately;

3. Decides not to conduct the review scheduled for October 1998 provided for in paragraphs 21 and 28 of resolution 687 (1991), and not to conduct any further such reviews until Iraq rescinds its above-mentioned decision of 5 August 1998 and the Special Commission and the IAEA report to the Council that they are satisfied that they have been able to exercise the full range of activities provided for in their mandates, including inspections;

4. Reaffirms its full support for the Special Commission and the IAEA in their efforts to ensure the implementation of their mandates under the relevant resolutions of the Council;

5. Reaffirms its full support for the Secretary-General in his efforts to urge Iraq to rescind its above-mentioned decision;

6. Reaffirms its intention to act in accordance with the relevant provisions of resolution 687 (1991) on the duration of the prohibitions referred to in that resolution and notes that by its failure so far to comply with its relevant obligations Iraq has delayed the moment when the Council can do so;

7. Decides to remain seized of the matter.

Resolution 1205 (1998)

Adopted by the Security Council at its 3939th meeting, on 5 November 1998

The Security Council,

Recalling all its previous relevant resolutions on the situation in Iraq, in particular its resolution 1154 (1998) of 2 March 1998 and 1194 (1998) of 9 September 1998,

Noting with alarm the decision of Iraq on 31 October 1998 to cease cooperation with the United Nations Special Commission, and its continued restrictions on the work of the International Atomic Energy Agency (IAEA),

Noting the letters from the Deputy Executive Chairman of the Special Commission of 31 October 1998 (S/1998/1023) and from the Executive Chairman of the Special Commission of 2 November 1998 (S/1998/1032) to the President of the Security Council, which reported to the Council the decision by Iraq and described the implications of that decision for the work of the Special Commission, and noting also the letter from the Director General of the IAEA of 3 November 1998 (S/1998/1033, annex) which described the implications of the decision for the work of the IAEA,

Determined to ensure immediate and full compliance by Iraq without conditions or restrictions with its obligations under resolution 687 (1991) of 3 April 1991 and the other relevant resolutions,

Recalling that the effective operation of the Special Commission and the IAEA is essential for the implementation of resolution 687 (1991),

Reaffirming its readiness to consider, in a comprehensive review, Iraq's compliance with its obligations under all relevant resolutions once Iraq has rescinded its above-mentioned decision and its decision of 5 August 1998 and demonstrated that it is prepared to fulfil all its obligations, including in particular on disarmament issues, by resuming full cooperation with the Special Commission and the IAEA consistent with the Memorandum of Understanding

signed by the Deputy Prime Minister of Iraq and the Secretary-General on 23 February 1998 (S/1998/166), endorsed by the Council in resolution 1154 (1998),

Reiterating the commitment of all Member States to the sovereignty, territorial integrity and political independence of Kuwait and Iraq,

Acting under Chapter VII of the Charter of the United Nations,

1. Condemns the decision by Iraq of 31 October 1998 to cease cooperation with the Special Commission as a flagrant violation of resolution 687 (1991) and other relevant resolutions;

2. Demands that Iraq rescind immediately and unconditionally the decision of 31 October 1998, as well as the decision of 5 August 1998, to suspend cooperation with the Special Commission and to maintain restrictions on the work of the IAEA, and that Iraq provide immediate, complete and unconditional cooperation with the Special Commission and the IAEA;

3. Reaffirms its full support for the Special Commission and the IAEA in their efforts to ensure the implementation of their mandates under the relevant resolutions of the Council;

4. Expresses its full support for the Secretary-General in his efforts to seek full implementation of the Memorandum of Understanding of 23 February 1998;

5. Reaffirms its intention to act in accordance with the relevant provisions of resolution 687 (1991) on the duration of the prohibitions referred to in that resolution, and notes that by its failure so far to comply with its relevant obligations Iraq has delayed the moment when the Council can do so;

6. Decides, in accordance with its primary responsibility under the Charter for the maintenance of international peace and security, to remain actively seized of the matter.

Resolution 1284 (1999)

Adopted by the Security Council at its 4084th meeting, on 17 December 1999

The Security Council,

Recalling its previous relevant resolutions....

Stressing the importance of a comprehensive approach to the full implementation of all relevant Security Council resolutions regarding Iraq and the need for Iraqi compliance with these resolutions,

Recalling the goal of establishing in the Middle East a zone free from weapons of mass destruction and all missiles for their delivery and the objective of a global ban on chemical weapons as referred to in paragraph 14 of resolution 687 (1991),

Concerned at the humanitarian situation in Iraq, and *determined* to improve that situation,

Recalling with concern that the repatriation and return of all Kuwaiti and third country nationals or their remains, present in Iraq on or after 2 August 1990, pursuant to paragraph 2 (c) of resolution 686 (1991) of 2 March 1991 and paragraph 30 of resolution 687 (1991), have not yet been fully carried out by Iraq,

Recalling that in its resolutions 686 (1991) and 687 (1991) the Council demanded that Iraq return in the shortest possible time all Kuwaiti property it had seized, and *noting* with regret that Iraq has still not complied fully with this demand,

Acknowledging the progress made by Iraq towards compliance with the provisions of resolution 687 (1991), but *noting* that, as a result of its failure to implement the relevant Council resolutions fully, the conditions do not exist which would enable the Council to take a decision pursuant to resolution 687 (1991) to lift the prohibitions referred to in that resolution,

Reiterating the commitment of all Member States to the sovereignty, territorial integrity and political independence of Kuwait, Iraq and the neighbouring States,

Acting under Chapter VII of the Charter of the United Nations, and *taking into account* that operative provisions of this resolution relate to previous resolutions adopted under Chapter VII of the Charter,

A.

1. *Decides* to establish, as a subsidiary body of the Council, the United Nations Monitoring, Verification and Inspection Commission (UNMOVIC) which replaces the Special Commission established pursuant to paragraph 9 (b) of resolution 687 (1991);

2. *Decides also* that UNMOVIC will undertake the responsibilities mandated to the Special Commission by the Council with regard to the verification of compliance by Iraq with its obligations under paragraphs 8, 9 and 10 of resolution 687 (1991) and other related resolutions, that UNMOVIC will establish and operate, as was recommended by the panel on disarmament and current and future ongoing monitoring and verification issues, a reinforced system of ongoing monitoring and verification, which will implement the plan approved by the Council in resolution 715 (1991) and address unresolved disarmament issues, and that UNMOVIC will identify, as necessary in accordance with its mandate, additional sites in

Iraq to be covered by the reinforced system of ongoing monitoring and verification;

3. *Reaffirms* the provisions of the relevant resolutions with regard to the role of the IAEA in addressing compliance by Iraq with paragraphs 12 and 13 of resolution 687 (1991) and other related resolutions, and *requests* the Director General of the IAEA to maintain this role with the assistance and cooperation of UNMOVIC;

4. *Reaffirms* its resolutions 687 (1991), 699 (1991), 707 (1991), 715 (1991), 1051 (1996), 1154 (1998) and all other relevant resolutions and statements of its President, which establish the criteria for Iraqi compliance, *affirms* that the obligations of Iraq referred to in those resolutions and statements with regard to cooperation with the Special Commission, unrestricted access and provision of information will apply in respect of UNMOVIC, and *decides* in particular that Iraq shall allow UNMOVIC teams immediate, unconditional and unrestricted access to any and all areas, facilities, equipment, records and means of transport which they wish to inspect in accordance with the mandate of UNMOVIC, as well as to all officials and other persons under the authority of the Iraqi Government whom UNMOVIC wishes to interview so that UNMOVIC may fully discharge its mandate;

[...]

7. *Decides* that UNMOVIC and the IAEA, not later than 60 days after they have both started work in Iraq, will each draw up, for approval by the Council, a work programme for the discharge of their mandates, which will include both the implementation of the reinforced system of ongoing monitoring and verification, and the key remaining disarmament tasks to be completed by Iraq pursuant to its obligations to comply with the disarmament requirements of resolution 687 (1991) and other related resolutions, which constitute the governing standard of Iraqi compliance, and *further decides* that what is required of Iraq for the implementation of each task shall be clearly defined and precise;

[...]

B.

13. *Reiterates* the obligation of Iraq, in furtherance of its commitment to facilitate the repatriation of all Kuwaiti and third country nationals referred to in paragraph 30 of resolution 687 (1991), to extend all necessary cooperation to the International Committee of the Red Cross, and *calls upon* the Government of Iraq to resume cooperation with the Tripartite Commission and Technical Subcommittee established to facilitate work on this issue;

14. *Requests* the Secretary-General to report to the Council every four months on compliance by Iraq with its obligations regarding

the repatriation or return of all Kuwaiti and third country nationals or their remains, to report every six months on the return of all Kuwaiti property, including archives, seized by Iraq, and to appoint a high-level coordinator for these issues;

C.

15. *Authorizes* States, notwithstanding the provisions of paragraphs 3 (a), 3 (b) and 4 of resolution 661 (1990) and subsequent relevant resolutions, to permit the import of any volume of petroleum and petroleum products originating in Iraq, including financial and other essential transactions directly relating thereto, as required for the purposes and on the conditions set out in paragraph 1 (a) and (b) and subsequent provisions of resolution 986 (1995) and related resolutions;

16. *Underlines,* in this context, its intention to take further action, including permitting the use of additional export routes for petroleum and petroleum products, under appropriate conditions otherwise consistent with the purpose and provisions of resolution 986 (1995) and related resolutions;

17. *Directs* the Committee established by resolution 661 (1990) to approve, on the basis of proposals from the Secretary-General, lists of humanitarian items, including foodstuffs, pharmaceutical and medical supplies, as well as basic or standard medical and agricultural equipment and basic or standard educational items, *decides,* notwithstanding paragraph 3 of resolution 661 (1990) and paragraph 20 of resolution 687 (1991), that supplies of these items will not be submitted for approval of that Committee, except for items subject to the provisions of resolution 1051 (1996), and will be notified to the Secretary-General and financed in accordance with the provisions of paragraph 8 (a) and 8 (b) of resolution 986 (1995), and *requests* the Secretary-General to inform the Committee in a timely manner of all such notifications received and actions taken;

18. *Requests* the Committee established by resolution 661 (1990) to appoint, in accordance with resolutions 1175 (1998) and 1210 (1998), a group of experts, including independent inspection agents appointed by the Secretary-General in accordance with paragraph 6 of resolution 986 (1995), *decides* that this group will be mandated to approve speedily contracts for the parts and the equipments necessary to enable Iraq to increase its exports of petroleum and petroleum products, according to lists of parts and equipments approved by that Committee for each individual project, and *requests* the Secretary-General to continue to provide for the monitoring of these parts and equipments inside Iraq;

19. *Encourages* Member States and international organizations to provide supplementary humanitarian assistance to Iraq and published material of an educational character to Iraq;

20. *Decides* to suspend, for an initial period of six months from the date of the adoption of this resolution and subject to review, the implementation of paragraph 8 (g) of resolution 986 (1995);

21. *Requests* the Secretary-General to take steps to maximize, drawing as necessary on the advice of specialists, including representatives of international humanitarian organizations, the effectiveness of the arrangements set out in resolution 986 (1995) and related resolutions including the humanitarian benefit to the Iraqi population in all areas of the country, and *further requests* the Secretary-General to continue to enhance as necessary the United Nations observation process in Iraq, ensuring that all supplies under the humanitarian programme are utilized as authorized, to bring to the attention of the Council any circumstances preventing or impeding effective and equitable distribution and to keep the Council informed of the steps taken towards the implementation of this paragraph;

[...]

27. *Calls upon* the Government of Iraq:

(i) to take all steps to ensure the timely and equitable distribution of all humanitarian goods, in particular medical supplies, and to remove and avoid delays at its warehouses;

(ii) to address effectively the needs of vulnerable groups, including children, pregnant women, the disabled, the elderly and the mentally ill among others, and to allow freer access, without any discrimination, including on the basis of religion or nationality, by United Nations agencies and humanitarian organizations to all areas and sections of the population for evaluation of their nutritional and humanitarian condition;

(iii) to prioritize applications for humanitarian goods under the arrangements set out in resolution 986 (1995) and related resolutions;

(iv) to ensure that those involuntarily displaced receive humanitarian assistance without the need to demonstrate that they have resided for six months in their places of temporary residence;

(v) to extend full cooperation to the United Nations Office for Project Services mine-clearance programme in the three northern Governorates of Iraq and to consider the initiation of the demining efforts in other Governorates;

28. *Requests* the Secretary-General to report on the progress made in meeting the humanitarian needs of the Iraqi people and on the revenues necessary to meet those needs, including recommendations on necessary additions to the current allocation for oil spare parts and equipment, on the basis of a comprehensive survey of

the condition of the Iraqi oil production sector, not later than 60 days from the date of the adoption of this resolution and updated thereafter as necessary;

29. *Expresses* its readiness to authorize additions to the current allocation for oil spare parts and equipment, on the basis of the report and recommendations requested in paragraph 28 above, in order to meet the humanitarian purposes set out in resolution 986 (1995) and related resolutions;

30. *Requests* the Secretary-General to establish a group of experts, including oil industry experts, to report within 100 days of the date of adoption of this resolution on Iraq's existing petroleum production and export capacity and to make recommendations, to be updated as necessary, on alternatives for increasing Iraq's petroleum production and export capacity in a manner consistent with the purposes of relevant resolutions, and on the options for involving foreign oil companies in Iraq's oil sector, including investments, subject to appropriate monitoring and controls;

[. . .]

D.

33. *Expresses its intention,* upon receipt of reports from the Executive Chairman of UNMOVIC and from the Director General of the IAEA that Iraq has cooperated in all respects with UNMOVIC and the IAEA in particular in fulfilling the work programmes in all the aspects referred to in paragraph 7 above, for a period of 120 days after the date on which the Council is in receipt of reports from both UNMOVIC and the IAEA that the reinforced system of ongoing monitoring and verification is fully operational, to suspend with the fundamental objective of improving the humanitarian situation in Iraq and securing the implementation of the Council's resolutions, for a period of 120 days renewable by the Council, and subject to the elaboration of effective financial and other operational measures to ensure that Iraq does not acquire prohibited items, prohibitions against the import of commodities and products originating in Iraq, and prohibitions against the sale, supply and delivery to Iraq of civilian commodities and products other than those referred to in paragraph 24 of resolution 687 (1991) or those to which the mechanism established by resolution 1051 (1996) applies;

34. *Decides* that in reporting to the Council for the purposes of paragraph 33 above, the Executive Chairman of UNMOVIC will include as a basis for his assessment the progress made in completing the tasks referred to in paragraph 7 above;

35. *Decides* that if at any time the Executive Chairman of UNMOVIC or the Director General of the IAEA reports that Iraq is not cooperating in all respects with UNMOVIC or the IAEA or if Iraq is in the process of acquiring any prohibited items, the suspension of the prohibitions referred to in paragraph 33 above shall terminate on the fifth working day following the report, unless the Council decides to the contrary;

36. *Expresses its intention* to approve arrangements for effective financial and other operational measures, including on the delivery of and payment for authorized civilian commodities and products to be sold or supplied to Iraq, in order to ensure that Iraq does not acquire prohibited items in the event of suspension of the prohibitions referred to in paragraph 33 above, to begin the elaboration of such measures not later than the date of the receipt of the initial reports referred to in paragraph 33 above, and to approve such arrangements before the Council decision in accordance with that paragraph;

37. *Further expresses its intention* to take steps, based on the report and recommendations requested in paragraph 30 above, and consistent with the purpose of resolution 986 (1995) and related resolutions, to enable Iraq to increase its petroleum production and export capacity, upon receipt of the reports relating to the cooperation in all respects with UNMOVIC and the IAEA referred to in paragraph 33 above;

38. *Reaffirms* its intention to act in accordance with the relevant provisions of resolution 687 (1991) on the termination of prohibitions referred to in that resolution;

39. *Decides* to remain actively seized of the matter and *expresses its intention* to consider action in accordance with paragraph 33 above no later than 12 months from the date of the adoption of this resolution provided the conditions set out in paragraph 33 above have been satisfied by Iraq.

Source: United Nations Security Council, "Resolutions," United Nations, http://www.un.org/documents/scres.htm.

92. National Commission on Terrorist Attacks Upon the United States, Final Report, July 22, 2004 [Excerpt]

Introduction

In November 2002, slightly more than a year after the September 11, 2001, terrorist attacks on targets in New York and Washington, D.C., Congress established a bipartisan commission to investigate all the circumstances surrounding these events. Congress was responding in part to public frustration, expressed in particular by the families of those killed on September 11, as to how the attacks could have taken place. The body was cochaired by Thomas Kean, the Republican former governor of New Jersey, and Lee Hamilton, the Democratic former congressman from Indiana, and included five Republicans and five Democrats appointed by President George W. Bush with input from Congress. In the course of its deliberations, the commission interviewed more than 1,200 individuals and scrutinized more than 2.5 million pages of documentation, some of it top secret. The president and vice president gave evidence before the commission, although no transcript was kept of their interviews. Some critics, including families of the September 11 victims, claimed that the commission's members were too close to the inner circles of power and in some cases had business links to the Arab world. The report, more than 560 pages in length, gave a detailed account of the events of September 11, 2001, and the previous growth during the 1990s of Al Qaeda and other Islamic extremist groups targeting the United States; identified weaknesses in U.S. security procedures, which if remedied might have prevented the attacks; stated that measures that the U.S. government had taken prior to September 2001 to address the dangers that Al Qaeda presented had been inadequate; highlighted failures to mobilize or pool intelligence resources; and warned that although the Al Qaeda headquarters in Afghanistan had been destroyed and many of the organization's top leaders had been killed, the United States was still not safe from terrorist threats. The report called for the appointment of a national intelligence director to coordinate the various overlapping and competing intelligence agencies. On the international front, the 9/11 report urged that the U.S. government should not merely attack terrorists but should also mount a major propaganda initiative to win over the Islamic world to American ideals, providing assistance for education and economic development and encouraging the growth of democratic regimes and respect for human rights. The report also called for long-term American and international commitments to the futures of both Pakistan and Afghanistan and suggested that the United States should encourage internal reforms in its ally, Saudi Arabia.

Primary Source

THE 9/11 COMMISSION REPORT

Final Report of the National Commission on Terrorist Attacks Upon the United States

EXECUTIVE SUMMARY

We present the narrative of this report and the recommendations that flow from it to the President of the United States, the United States Congress, and the American people for their consideration. Ten Commissioners—five Republicans and five Democrats chosen by elected leaders from our nation's capital at a time of great partisan division—have come together to present this report without dissent.

We have come together with a unity of purpose because our nation demands it. September 11, 2001, was a day of unprecedented shock and suffering in the history of the United States. The nation was unprepared.

A NATION TRANSFORMED

At 8:46 on the morning of September 11, 2001, the United States became a nation transformed.

An airliner traveling at hundreds of miles per hour and carrying some 10,000 gallons of jet fuel plowed into the North Tower of the World Trade Center in Lower Manhattan. At 9:03, a second airliner hit the South Tower. Fire and smoke billowed upward. Steel, glass, ash, and bodies fell below. The Twin Towers, where up to 50,000 people worked each day, both collapsed less than 90 minutes later.

At 9:37 that same morning, a third airliner slammed into the western face of the Pentagon. At 10:03, a fourth airliner crashed in a field in southern Pennsylvania. It had been aimed at the United States Capitol or the White House, and was forced down by heroic passengers armed with the knowledge that America was under attack.

More than 2,600 people died at the World Trade Center; 125 died at the Pentagon; 256 died on the four planes. The death toll surpassed that at Pearl Harbor in December 1941.

This immeasurable pain was inflicted by 19 young Arabs acting at the behest of Islamist extremists headquartered in distant Afghanistan. Some had been in the United States for more than a year, mixing with the rest of the population. Though four had training as pilots, most were not well-educated. Most spoke English poorly, some hardly at all. In groups of four or five, carrying with them only small knives, box cutters, and cans of Mace or pepper spray, they had hijacked the four planes and turned them into deadly guided missiles.

Why did they do this? How was the attack planned and conceived? How did the U.S. government fail to anticipate and prevent it? What can we do in the future to prevent similar acts of terrorism?

A Shock, Not a Surprise

The 9/11 attacks were a shock, but they should not have come as a surprise. Islamist extremists had given plenty of warning that they meant to kill Americans indiscriminately and in large numbers. Although Usama Bin Ladin himself would not emerge as a signal threat until the late 1990s, the threat of Islamist terrorism grew over the decade.

In February 1993, a group led by Ramzi Yousef tried to bring down the World Trade Center with a truck bomb. They killed six and wounded a thousand. Plans by Omar Abdel Rahman and others to blow up the Holland and Lincoln tunnels and other New York City landmarks were frustrated when the plotters were arrested. In October 1993, Somali tribesmen shot down U.S. helicopters, killing 18 and wounding 73 in an incident that came to be known as "Black Hawk down." Years later it would be learned that those Somali tribesmen had received help from al Qaeda.

In early 1995, police in Manila uncovered a plot by Ramzi Yousef to blow up a dozen U.S. airliners while they were flying over the Pacific. In November 1995, a car bomb exploded outside the office of the U.S. program manager for the Saudi National Guard in Riyadh, killing five Americans and two others. In June 1996, a truck bomb demolished the Khobar Towers apartment complex in Dhahran, Saudi Arabia, killing 19 U.S. servicemen and wounding hundreds. The attack was carried out primarily by Saudi Hezbollah, an organization that had received help from the government of Iran.

Until 1997, the U.S. intelligence community viewed Bin Ladin as a financier of terrorism, not as a terrorist leader. In February 1998, Usama Bin Ladin and four others issued a self-styled fatwa, publicly declaring that it was God's decree that every Muslim should try his utmost to kill any American, military or civilian, anywhere in the world, because of American "occupation" of Islam's holy places and aggression against Muslims.

In August 1998, Bin Ladin's group, al Qaeda, carried out near-simultaneous truck bomb attacks on the U.S. embassies in Nairobi, Kenya, and Dar es Salaam, Tanzania. The attacks killed 224 people, including 12 Americans, and wounded thousands more.

In December 1999, Jordanian police foiled a plot to bomb hotels and other sites frequented by American tourists, and a U.S. Customs agent arrested Ahmed Ressam at the U.S. Canadian border as he was smuggling in explosives intended for an attack on Los Angeles International Airport.

In October 2000, an al Qaeda team in Aden, Yemen, used a motorboat filled with explosives to blow a hole in the side of a destroyer, the USS Cole, almost sinking the vessel and killing 17 American sailors.

The 9/11 attacks on the World Trade Center and the Pentagon were far more elaborate, precise, and destructive than any of these earlier assaults. But by September 2001, the executive branch of the U.S. government, the Congress, the news media, and the American public had received clear warning that Islamist terrorists meant to kill Americans in high numbers.

Who Is the Enemy?

Who is this enemy that created an organization capable of inflicting such horrific damage on the United States? We now know

that these attacks were carried out by various groups of Islamist extremists. The 9/11 attack was driven by Usama Bin Ladin.

In the 1980s, young Muslims from around the world went to Afghanistan to join as volunteers in a jihad (or holy struggle) against the Soviet Union. A wealthy Saudi, Usama Bin Ladin, was one of them. Following the defeat of the Soviets in the late 1980s, Bin Ladin and others formed al Qaeda to mobilize jihads elsewhere.

The history, culture, and body of beliefs from which Bin Ladin shapes and spreads his message are largely unknown to many Americans. Seizing on symbols of Islam's past greatness, he promises to restore pride to people who consider themselves the victims of successive foreign masters. He uses cultural and religious allusions to the holy Qur'an and some of its interpreters. He appeals to people disoriented by cyclonic change as they confront modernity and globalization. His rhetoric selectively draws from multiple sources—Islam, history, and the region's political and economic malaise.

Bin Ladin also stresses grievances against the United States widely shared in the Muslim world. He inveighed against the presence of U.S. troops in Saudi Arabia, which is the home of Islam's holiest sites, and against other U.S. policies in the Middle East.

Upon this political and ideological foundation, Bin Ladin built over the course of a decade a dynamic and lethal organization. He built an infrastructure and organization in Afghanistan that could attract, train, and use recruits against ever more ambitious targets. He rallied new zealots and new money with each demonstration of al Qaeda's capability. He had forged a close alliance with the Taliban, a regime providing sanctuary for al Qaeda.

By September 11, 2001, al Qaeda possessed

- leaders able to evaluate, approve, and supervise the planning and direction of a major operation;
- a personnel system that could recruit candidates, indoctrinate them, vet them, and give them the necessary training;
- communications sufficient to enable planning and direction of operatives and those who would be helping them;
- an intelligence effort to gather required information and form assessments of enemy strengths and weaknesses;
- the ability to move people great distances; and
- the ability to raise and move the money necessary to finance an attack.

1998 to September 11, 2001

The August 1998 bombings of U.S. embassies in Kenya and Tanzania established al Qaeda as a potent adversary of the United States.

After launching cruise missile strikes against al Qaeda targets in Afghanistan and Sudan in retaliation for the embassy bombings, the Clinton administration applied diplomatic pressure to try to persuade the Taliban regime in Afghanistan to expel Bin Ladin. The administration also devised covert operations to use CIA-paid foreign agents to capture or kill Bin Ladin and his chief lieutenants. These actions did not stop Bin Ladin or dislodge al Qaeda from its sanctuary.

By late 1998 or early 1999, Bin Ladin and his advisers had agreed on an idea brought to them by Khalid Sheikh Mohammed (KSM) called the "planes operation." It would eventually culminate in the 9/11 attacks. Bin Ladin and his chief of operations, Mohammed Atef, occupied undisputed leadership positions atop al Qaeda. Within al Qaeda, they relied heavily on the ideas and enterprise of strong-willed field commanders, such as KSM, to carry out worldwide terrorist operations.

KSM claims that his original plot was even grander than those carried out on 9/11—ten planes would attack targets on both the East and West coasts of the United States. This plan was modified by Bin Ladin, KSM said, owing to its scale and complexity. Bin Ladin provided KSM with four initial operatives for suicide plane attacks within the United States, and in the fall of 1999 training for the attacks began. New recruits included four from a cell of expatriate Muslim extremists who had clustered together in Hamburg, Germany. One became the tactical commander of the operation in the United States: Mohamed Atta.

U.S. intelligence frequently picked up reports of attacks planned by al Qaeda. Working with foreign security services, the CIA broke up some al Qaeda cells. The core of Bin Ladin's organization nevertheless remained intact. In December 1999, news about the arrests of the terrorist cell in Jordan and the arrest of a terrorist at the U.S.-Canadian border became part of a "millennium alert." The government was galvanized, and the public was on alert for any possible attack.

In January 2000, the intense intelligence effort glimpsed and then lost sight of two operatives destined for the "planes operation." Spotted in Kuala Lumpur, the pair were lost passing through Bangkok. On January 15, 2000, they arrived in Los Angeles.

Because these two al Qaeda operatives had spent little time in the West and spoke little, if any, English, it is plausible that they or KSM would have tried to identify, in advance, a friendly contact in the United States. We explored suspicions about whether these two operatives had a support network of accomplices in the United States. The evidence is thin—simply not there for some cases, more worrisome in others.

We do know that soon after arriving in California, the two al Qaeda operatives sought out and found a group of ideologically like-minded Muslims with roots in Yemen and Saudi Arabia, individuals mainly associated with a young Yemeni and others who attended a mosque in San Diego. After a brief stay in Los Angeles about which we know little, the al Qaeda operatives lived openly in San Diego under their true names. They managed to avoid attracting much attention.

By the summer of 2000, three of the four Hamburg cell members had arrived on the East Coast of the United States and had begun pilot training. In early 2001, a fourth future hijacker pilot, Hani Hanjour, journeyed to Arizona with another operative, Nawaf al Hazmi, and conducted his refresher pilot training there. A number of al Qaeda operatives had spent time in Arizona during the 1980s and early 1990s.

During 2000, President Bill Clinton and his advisers renewed diplomatic efforts to get Bin Ladin expelled from Afghanistan. They also renewed secret efforts with some of the Taliban's opponents—the Northern Alliance—to get enough intelligence to attack Bin Ladin directly. Diplomatic efforts centered on the new military government in Pakistan, and they did not succeed. The efforts with the Northern Alliance revived an inconclusive and secret debate about whether the United States should take sides in Afghanistan's civil war and support the Taliban's enemies. The CIA also produced a plan to improve intelligence collection on al Qaeda, including the use of a small, unmanned airplane with a video camera, known as the Predator.

After the October 2000 attack on the USS Cole, evidence accumulated that it had been launched by al Qaeda operatives, but without confirmation that Bin Ladin had given the order. The Taliban had earlier been warned that it would be held responsible for another Bin Ladin attack on the United States. The CIA described its findings as a "preliminary judgment"; President Clinton and his chief advisers told us they were waiting for a conclusion before deciding whether to take military action. The military alternatives remained unappealing to them.

The transition to the new Bush administration in late 2000 and early 2001 took place with the Cole issue still pending. President George W. Bush and his chief advisers accepted that al Qaeda was responsible for the attack on the Cole, but did not like the options available for a response.

Bin Ladin's inference may well have been that attacks, at least at the level of the Cole, were risk free.

The Bush administration began developing a new strategy with the stated goal of eliminating the al Qaeda threat within three to five years.

During the spring and summer of 2001, U.S. intelligence agencies received a stream of warnings that al Qaeda planned, as one report put it, "something very, very, very big." Director of Central Intelligence George Tenet told us, "The system was blinking red."

Although Bin Ladin was determined to strike in the United States, as President Clinton had been told and President Bush was reminded in a Presidential Daily Brief article briefed to him in August 2001, the specific threat information pointed overseas. Numerous precautions were taken overseas. Domestic agencies were not effectively mobilized. The threat did not receive national media attention comparable to the millennium alert.

While the United States continued disruption efforts around the world, its emerging strategy to eliminate the al Qaeda threat was to include an enlarged covert action program in Afghanistan, as well as diplomatic strategies for Afghanistan and Pakistan. The process culminated during the summer of 2001 in a draft presidential directive and arguments about the Predator aircraft, which was soon to be deployed with a missile of its own, so that it might be used to attempt to kill Bin Ladin or his chief lieutenants. At a September 4 meeting, President Bush's chief advisers approved the draft directive of the strategy and endorsed the concept of arming the Predator. This directive on the al Qaeda strategy was awaiting President Bush's signature on September 11, 2001.

Though the "planes operation" was progressing, the plotters had problems of their own in 2001. Several possible participants dropped out; others could not gain entry into the United States (including one denial at a port of entry and visa denials not related to terrorism). One of the eventual pilots may have considered abandoning the planes operation. Zacarias Moussaoui, who showed up at a flight training school in Minnesota, may have been a candidate to replace him.

Some of the vulnerabilities of the plotters become clear in retrospect. Moussaoui aroused suspicion for seeking fast-track training on how to pilot large jet airliners. He was arrested on August 16, 2001, for violations of immigration regulations. In late August, officials in the intelligence community realized that the terrorists spotted in Southeast Asia in January 2000 had arrived in the United States.

These cases did not prompt urgent action. No one working on these late leads in the summer of 2001 connected them to the high level of threat reporting. In the words of one official, no analytic work foresaw the lightning that could connect the thundercloud to the ground.

As final preparations were under way during the summer of 2001, dissent emerged among al Qaeda leaders in Afghanistan over whether to proceed. The Taliban's chief, Mullah Omar, opposed attacking the United States. Although facing opposition from many of his senior lieutenants, Bin Ladin effectively overruled their objections, and the attacks went forward.

September 11, 2001

The day began with the 19 hijackers getting through a security checkpoint system that they had evidently analyzed and knew how to defeat. Their success rate in penetrating the system was 19 for 19. They took over the four flights, taking advantage of air crews and cockpits that were not prepared for the contingency of a suicide hijacking.

On 9/11, the defense of U.S. air space depended on close interaction between two federal agencies: the Federal Aviation Administration (FAA) and North American Aerospace Defense Command (NORAD). Existing protocols on 9/11 were unsuited in every respect for an attack in which hijacked planes were used as weapons.

What ensued was a hurried attempt to improvise a defense by civilians who had never handled a hijacked aircraft that attempted to disappear, and by a military unprepared for the transformation of commercial aircraft into weapons of mass destruction.

A shootdown authorization was not communicated to the NORAD air defense sector until 28 minutes after United 93 had crashed in Pennsylvania. Planes were scrambled, but ineffectively, as they did not know where to go or what targets they were to intercept. And once the shootdown order was given, it was not communicated to the pilots. In short, while leaders in Washington believed that the fighters circling above them had been instructed to "take out" hostile aircraft, the only orders actually conveyed to the pilots were to "ID type and tail."

Like the national defense, the emergency response on 9/11 was necessarily improvised.

In New York City, the Fire Department of New York, the New York Police Department, the Port Authority of New York and New Jersey, the building employees, and the occupants of the buildings did their best to cope with the effects of almost unimaginable events-unfolding furiously over 102 minutes. Casualties were nearly 100 percent at and above the impact zones and were very high among first responders who stayed in danger as they tried to save lives. Despite weaknesses in preparations for disaster, failure to achieve unified incident command, and inadequate communications among responding agencies, all but approximately one hundred of the thousands of civilians who worked below the impact zone escaped, often with help from the emergency responders.

At the Pentagon, while there were also problems of command and control, the emergency response was generally effective. The Incident Command System, a formalized management structure for emergency response in place in the National Capital Region, overcame the inherent complications of a response across local, state, and federal jurisdictions.

Operational Opportunities

We write with the benefit and handicap of hindsight. We are mindful of the danger of being unjust to men and women who made choices in conditions of uncertainty and in circumstances over which they often had little control.

Nonetheless, there were specific points of vulnerability in the plot and opportunities to disrupt it. Operational failures—opportunities that were not or could not be exploited by the organizations and systems of that time—included

- not watchlisting future hijackers Hazmi and Mihdhar, not trailing them after they traveled to Bangkok, and not informing the FBI about one future hijacker's U.S. visa or his companion's travel to the United States;
- not sharing information linking individuals in the Cole attack to Mihdhar;
- not taking adequate steps in time to find Mihdhar or Hazmi in the United States;
- not linking the arrest of Zacarias Moussaoui, described as interested in flight training for the purpose of using an airplane in a terrorist act, to the heightened indications of attack;
- not discovering false statements on visa applications;
- not recognizing passports manipulated in a fraudulent manner;
- not expanding no-fly lists to include names from terrorist watchlists;
- not searching airline passengers identified by the computer-based CAPPS screening system; and
- not hardening aircraft cockpit doors or taking other measures to prepare for the possibility of suicide hijackings.

GENERAL FINDINGS

Since the plotters were flexible and resourceful, we cannot know whether any single step or series of steps would have defeated them. What we can say with confidence is that none of the measures adopted by the U.S. government from 1998 to 2001 disturbed or even delayed the progress of the al Qaeda plot. Across the government, there were failures of imagination, policy, capabilities, and management.

Imagination

The most important failure was one of imagination. We do not believe leaders understood the gravity of the threat. The terrorist danger from Bin Ladin and al Qaeda was not a major topic for policy debate among the public, the media, or in the Congress. Indeed, it barely came up during the 2000 presidential campaign.

Al Qaeda's new brand of terrorism presented challenges to U.S. governmental institutions that they were not well-designed to meet. Though top officials all told us that they understood the danger, we believe there was uncertainty among them as to whether this was just a new and especially venomous version of the ordinary terrorist threat the United States had lived with for decades, or it was indeed radically new, posing a threat beyond any yet experienced.

As late as September 4, 2001, Richard Clarke, the White House staffer long responsible for counterterrorism policy coordination, asserted that the government had not yet made up its mind how to answer the question: "Is al Qida a big deal?"

A week later came the answer.

Policy

Terrorism was not the overriding national security concern for the U.S. government under either the Clinton or the pre-9/11 Bush administration.

The policy challenges were linked to this failure of imagination. Officials in both the Clinton and Bush administrations regarded a full U.S. invasion of Afghanistan as practically inconceivable before 9/11.

Capabilities

Before 9/11, the United States tried to solve the al Qaeda problem with the capabilities it had used in the last stages of the Cold War and its immediate aftermath. These capabilities were insufficient. Little was done to expand or reform them.

The CIA had minimal capacity to conduct paramilitary operations with its own personnel, and it did not seek a large-scale expansion of these capabilities before 9/11. The CIA also needed to improve its capability to collect intelligence from human agents.

At no point before 9/11 was the Department of Defense fully engaged in the mission of countering al Qaeda, even though this was perhaps the most dangerous foreign enemy threatening the United States.

America's homeland defenders faced outward. NORAD itself was barely able to retain any alert bases at all. Its planning scenarios occasionally considered the danger of hijacked aircraft being guided to American targets, but only aircraft that were coming from overseas.

The most serious weaknesses in agency capabilities were in the domestic arena. The FBI did not have the capability to link the collective knowledge of agents in the field to national priorities. Other domestic agencies deferred to the FBI.

FAA capabilities were weak. Any serious examination of the possibility of a suicide hijacking could have suggested changes to fix glaring vulnerabilities—expanding no-fly lists, searching passengers identified by the CAPPS screening system, deploying federal air marshals domestically, hardening cockpit doors, alerting air crews to a different kind of hijacking possibility than they had been trained to expect. Yet the FAA did not adjust either its own training or training with NORAD to take account of threats other than those experienced in the past.

Management

The missed opportunities to thwart the 9/11 plot were also symptoms of a broader inability to adapt the way government manages problems to the new challenges of the twenty-first century. Action officers should have been able to draw on all available knowledge about al Qaeda in the government. Management should have ensured that information was shared and duties were clearly assigned across agencies, and across the foreign-domestic divide.

There were also broader management issues with respect to how top leaders set priorities and allocated resources. For instance, on December 4, 1998, DCI Tenet issued a directive to several CIA officials and the DDCI for Community Management, stating: "We are at war. I want no resources or people spared in this effort, either inside CIA or the Community." The memorandum had little overall effect on mobilizing the CIA or the intelligence community. This episode indicates the limitations of the DCI's authority over the direction of the intelligence community, including agencies within the Department of Defense.

The U.S. government did not find a way of pooling intelligence and using it to guide the planning and assignment of responsibilities for joint operations involving entities as disparate as the CIA, the FBI, the State Department, the military, and the agencies involved in homeland security.

SPECIFIC FINDINGS

Unsuccessful Diplomacy

Beginning in February 1997, and through September 11, 2001, the U.S. government tried to use diplomatic pressure to persuade the Taliban regime in Afghanistan to stop being a sanctuary for al Qaeda, and to expel Bin Ladin to a country where he could face justice. These efforts included warnings and sanctions, but they all failed.

The U.S. government also pressed two successive Pakistani governments to demand that the Taliban cease providing a sanctuary for Bin Ladin and his organization and, failing that, to cut off their support for the Taliban. Before 9/11, the United States could not find a mix of incentives and pressure that would persuade Pakistan to reconsider its fundamental relationship with the Taliban.

From 1999 through early 2001, the United States pressed the United Arab Emirates, one of the Taliban's only travel and financial outlets to the outside world, to break off ties and enforce sanctions, especially those related to air travel to Afghanistan. These efforts achieved little before 9/11.

Saudi Arabia has been a problematic ally in combating Islamic extremism. Before 9/11, the Saudi and U.S. governments did not fully share intelligence information or develop an adequate joint effort to track and disrupt the finances of the al Qaeda organization. On the other hand, government officials of Saudi Arabia at the highest levels worked closely with top U.S. officials in major initiatives to solve the Bin Ladin problem with diplomacy.

Lack of Military Options

In response to the request of policymakers, the military prepared an array of limited strike options for attacking Bin Ladin and his organization from May 1998 onward. When they briefed policymakers, the military presented both the pros and cons of those strike options and the associated risks. Policymakers expressed frustration with the range of options presented.

Following the August 20, 1998, missile strikes on al Qaeda targets in Afghanistan and Sudan, both senior military officials and policymakers placed great emphasis on actionable intelligence as the key factor in recommending or deciding to launch military action against Bin Ladin and his organization. They did not want to risk significant collateral damage, and they did not want to miss Bin Ladin and thus make the United States look weak while making Bin Ladin look strong. On three specific occasions in 1998–1999, intelligence was deemed credible enough to warrant planning for possible strikes to kill Bin Ladin. But in each case the strikes did not go forward, because senior policymakers did not regard the intelligence as sufficiently actionable to offset their assessment of the risks.

The Director of Central Intelligence, policymakers, and military officials expressed frustration with the lack of actionable intelligence. Some officials inside the Pentagon, including those in the special forces and the counterterrorism policy office, also expressed frustration with the lack of military action. The Bush administration began to develop new policies toward al Qaeda in 2001, but military plans did not change until after 9/11.

Problems within the Intelligence Community

The intelligence community struggled throughout the 1990s and up to 9/11 to collect intelligence on and analyze the phenomenon of transnational terrorism. The combination of an overwhelming number of priorities, flat budgets, an outmoded structure, and bureaucratic rivalries resulted in an insufficient response to this new challenge.

Many dedicated officers worked day and night for years to piece together the growing body of evidence on al Qaeda and to understand the threats. Yet, while there were many reports on Bin Laden and his growing al Qaeda organization, there was no comprehensive review of what the intelligence community knew and what it did not know, and what that meant. There was no National Intelligence Estimate on terrorism between 1995 and 9/11.

Before 9/11, no agency did more to attack al Qaeda than the CIA. But there were limits to what the CIA was able to achieve by disrupting terrorist activities abroad and by using proxies to try to capture Bin Ladin and his lieutenants in Afghanistan. CIA officers were aware of those limitations.

To put it simply, covert action was not a silver bullet. It was important to engage proxies in Afghanistan and to build various capabilities so that if an opportunity presented itself, the CIA could act on it. But for more than three years, through both the late Clinton and early Bush administrations, the CIA relied on proxy forces, and there was growing frustration within the CIA's Counterterrorist Center and in the National Security Council staff with the lack of results. The development of the Predator and the push to aid the Northern Alliance were products of this frustration.

Problems in the FBI

From the time of the first World Trade Center attack in 1993, FBI and Department of Justice leadership in Washington and New York became increasingly concerned about the terrorist threat from Islamist extremists to U.S. interests, both at home and abroad. Throughout the 1990s, the FBI's counterterrorism efforts against international terrorist organizations included both intelligence and criminal investigations. The FBI's approach to investigations was case-specific, decentralized, and geared toward prosecution. Significant FBI resources were devoted to after-the-fact investigations of major terrorist attacks, resulting in several prosecutions.

The FBI attempted several reform efforts aimed at strengthening its ability to prevent such attacks, but these reform efforts failed to implement organization-wide institutional change. On September 11, 2001, the FBI was limited in several areas critical to an effective preventive counterterrorism strategy. Those working

counterterrorism matters did so despite limited intelligence collection and strategic analysis capabilities, a limited capacity to share information both internally and externally, insufficient training, perceived legal barriers to sharing information, and inadequate resources.

Permeable Borders and Immigration Controls

There were opportunities for intelligence and law enforcement to exploit al Qaeda's travel vulnerabilities. Considered collectively, the 9/11 hijackers

- included known al Qaeda operatives who could have been watchlisted;
- presented passports manipulated in a fraudulent manner;
- presented passports with suspicious indicators of extremism;
- made detectable false statements on visa applications;
- made false statements to border officials to gain entry into the United States; and
- violated immigration laws while in the United States.

Neither the State Department's consular officers nor the Immigration and Naturalization Service's inspectors and agents were ever considered full partners in a national counterterrorism effort. Protecting borders was not a national security issue before 9/11.

Permeable Aviation Security

Hijackers studied publicly available materials on the aviation security system and used items that had less metal content than a handgun and were most likely permissible. Though two of the hijackers were on the U.S. TIPOFF terrorist watchlist, the FAA did not use TIPOFF data. The hijackers had to beat only one layer of security—the security checkpoint process. Even though several hijackers were selected for extra screening by the CAPPS system, this led only to greater scrutiny of their checked baggage. Once on board, the hijackers were faced with aircraft personnel who were trained to be nonconfrontational in the event of a hijacking.

Financing

The 9/11 attacks cost somewhere between $400,000 and $500,000 to execute. The operatives spent more than $270,000 in the United States. Additional expenses included travel to obtain passports and visas, travel to the United States, expenses incurred by the plot leader and facilitators outside the United States, and expenses incurred by the people selected to be hijackers who ultimately did not participate.

The conspiracy made extensive use of banks in the United States. The hijackers opened accounts in their own names, using passports and other identification documents. Their transactions were unremarkable and essentially invisible amid the billions of dollars flowing around the world every day.

To date, we have not been able to determine the origin of the money used for the 9/11 attacks. Al Qaeda had many sources of funding and a pre-9/11 annual budget estimated at $30 million. If a particular source of funds had dried up, al Qaeda could easily have found enough money elsewhere to fund the attack.

An Improvised Homeland Defense

The civilian and military defenders of the nation's airspace—FAA and NORAD—were unprepared for the attacks launched against them. Given that lack of preparedness, they attempted and failed to improvise an effective homeland defense against an unprecedented challenge.

The events of that morning do not reflect discredit on operational personnel. NORAD's Northeast Air Defense Sector personnel reached out for information and made the best judgments they could based on the information they received. Individual FAA controllers, facility managers, and command center managers were creative and agile in recommending a nationwide alert, ground-stopping local traffic, ordering all aircraft nationwide to land, and executing that unprecedented order flawlessly.

At more senior levels, communication was poor. Senior military and FAA leaders had no effective communication with each other. The chain of command did not function well. The President could not reach some senior officials. The Secretary of Defense did not enter the chain of command until the morning's key events were over. Air National Guard units with different rules of engagement were scrambled without the knowledge of the President, NORAD, or the National Military Command Center.

Emergency Response

The civilians, firefighters, police officers, emergency medical technicians, and emergency management professionals exhibited steady determination and resolve under horrifying, overwhelming conditions on 9/11. Their actions saved lives and inspired a nation.

Effective decisionmaking in New York was hampered by problems in command and control and in internal communications. Within the Fire Department of New York, this was true for several reasons: the magnitude of the incident was unforeseen; commanders had difficulty communicating with their units; more units were actually dispatched than were ordered by the chiefs; some units self-dispatched; and once units arrived at the World Trade Center, they were neither comprehensively accounted for nor coordinated. The Port Authority's response was hampered

by the lack both of standard operating procedures and of radios capable of enabling multiple commands to respond to an incident in unified fashion. The New York Police Department, because of its history of mobilizing thousands of officers for major events requiring crowd control, had a technical radio capability and protocols more easily adapted to an incident of the magnitude of 9/11.

Congress

The Congress, like the executive branch, responded slowly to the rise of transnational terrorism as a threat to national security. The legislative branch adjusted little and did not restructure itself to address changing threats. Its attention to terrorism was episodic and splintered across several committees. The Congress gave little guidance to executive branch agencies on terrorism, did not reform them in any significant way to meet the threat, and did not systematically perform robust oversight to identify, address, and attempt to resolve the many problems in national security and domestic agencies that became apparent in the aftermath of 9/11.

So long as oversight is undermined by current congressional rules and resolutions, we believe the American people will not get the security they want and need. The United States needs a strong, stable, and capable congressional committee structure to give America's national intelligence agencies oversight, support, and leadership.

Are We Safer?

Since 9/11, the United States and its allies have killed or captured a majority of al Qaeda's leadership; toppled the Taliban, which gave al Qaeda sanctuary in Afghanistan; and severely damaged the organization. Yet terrorist attacks continue. Even as we have thwarted attacks, nearly everyone expects they will come. How can this be?

The problem is that al Qaeda represents an ideological movement, not a finite group of people. It initiates and inspires, even if it no longer directs. In this way it has transformed itself into a decentralized force. Bin Ladin may be limited in his ability to organize major attacks from his hideouts. Yet killing or capturing him, while extremely important, would not end terror. His message of inspiration to a new generation of terrorists would continue.

Because of offensive actions against al Qaeda since 9/11, and defensive actions to improve homeland security, we believe we are safer today. But we are not safe. We therefore make the following recommendations that we believe can make America safer and more secure.

RECOMMENDATIONS

Three years after 9/11, the national debate continues about how to protect our nation in this new era. We divide our recommendations into two basic parts: What to do, and how to do it.

WHAT TO DO? A GLOBAL STRATEGY

The enemy is not just "terrorism." It is the threat posed specifically by Islamist terrorism, by Bin Ladin and others who draw on a long tradition of extreme intolerance within a minority strain of Islam that does not distinguish politics from religion, and distorts both.

The enemy is not Islam, the great world faith, but a perversion of Islam. The enemy goes beyond al Qaeda to include the radical ideological movement, inspired in part by al Qaeda, that has spawned other terrorist groups and violence. Thus our strategy must match our means to two ends: dismantling the al Qaeda network and, in the long term, prevailing over the ideology that contributes to Islamist terrorism.

The first phase of our post-9/11 efforts rightly included military action to topple the Taliban and pursue al Qaeda. This work continues. But long-term success demands the use of all elements of national power: diplomacy, intelligence, covert action, law enforcement, economic policy, foreign aid, public diplomacy, and homeland defense. If we favor one tool while neglecting others, we leave ourselves vulnerable and weaken our national effort.

What should Americans expect from their government? The goal seems unlimited: Defeat terrorism anywhere in the world. But Americans have also been told to expect the worst: An attack is probably coming; it may be more devastating still.

Vague goals match an amorphous picture of the enemy. Al Qaeda and other groups are popularly described as being all over the world, adaptable, resilient, needing little higher-level organization, and capable of anything. It is an image of an omnipotent hydra of destruction. That image lowers expectations of government effectiveness.

It lowers them too far. Our report shows a determined and capable group of plotters. Yet the group was fragile and occasionally left vulnerable by the marginal, unstable people often attracted to such causes. The enemy made mistakes. The U.S. government was not able to capitalize on them.

No president can promise that a catastrophic attack like that of 9/11 will not happen again. But the American people are entitled to expect that officials will have realistic objectives, clear guidance, and effective organization. They are entitled to see standards for performance so they can judge, with the help of their elected representatives, whether the objectives are being met.

We propose a strategy with three dimensions: (1) attack terrorists and their organizations, (2) prevent the continued growth of Islamist terrorism, and (3) protect against and prepare for terrorist attacks.

Attack Terrorists and Their Organizations

- Root out sanctuaries. The U.S. government should identify and prioritize actual or potential terrorist sanctuaries and have realistic country or regional strategies for each, utilizing every element of national power and reaching out to countries that can help us.
- Strengthen long-term U.S. and international commitments to the future of Pakistan and Afghanistan.
- Confront problems with Saudi Arabia in the open and build a relationship beyond oil, a relationship that both sides can defend to their citizens and includes a shared commitment to reform.

Prevent the Continued Growth of Islamist Terrorism

In October 2003, Secretary of Defense Donald Rumsfeld asked if enough was being done "to fashion a broad integrated plan to stop the next generation of terrorists." As part of such a plan, the U.S. government should

- Define the message and stand as an example of moral leadership in the world. To Muslim parents, terrorists like Bin Ladin have nothing to offer their children but visions of violence and death. America and its friends have the advantage—our vision can offer a better future.
- Where Muslim governments, even those who are friends, do not offer opportunity, respect the rule of law, or tolerate differences, then the United States needs to stand for a better future.
- Communicate and defend American ideals in the Islamic world, through much stronger public diplomacy to reach more people, including students and leaders outside of government. Our efforts here should be as strong as they were in combating closed societies during the Cold War.
- Offer an agenda of opportunity that includes support for public education and economic openness.
- Develop a comprehensive coalition strategy against Islamist terrorism, using a flexible contact group of leading coalition governments and fashioning a common coalition approach on issues like the treatment of captured terrorists.
- Devote a maximum effort to the parallel task of countering the proliferation of weapons of mass destruction.

- Expect less from trying to dry up terrorist money and more from following the money for intelligence, as a tool to hunt terrorists, understand their networks, and disrupt their operations.

Protect against and Prepare for Terrorist Attacks

- Target terrorist travel, an intelligence and security strategy that the 9/11 story showed could be at least as powerful as the effort devoted to terrorist finance.
- Address problems of screening people with biometric identifiers across agencies and governments, including our border and transportation systems, by designing a comprehensive screening system that addresses common problems and sets common standards. As standards spread, this necessary and ambitious effort could dramatically strengthen the world's ability to intercept individuals who could pose catastrophic threats.
- Quickly complete a biometric entry-exit screening system, one that also speeds qualified travelers.
- Set standards for the issuance of birth certificates and sources of identification, such as driver's licenses.
- Develop strategies for neglected parts of our transportation security system. Since 9/11, about 90 percent of the nation's $5 billion annual investment in transportation security has gone to aviation, to fight the last war.
- In aviation, prevent arguments about a new computerized profiling system from delaying vital improvements in the "no-fly" and "automatic selectee" lists. Also, give priority to the improvement of checkpoint screening.
- Determine, with leadership from the President, guidelines for gathering and sharing information in the new security systems that are needed, guidelines that integrate safeguards for privacy and other essential liberties.
- Underscore that as government power necessarily expands in certain ways, the burden of retaining such powers remains on the executive to demonstrate the value of such powers and ensure adequate supervision of how they are used, including a new board to oversee the implementation of the guidelines needed for gathering and sharing information in these new security systems.
- Base federal funding for emergency preparedness solely on risks and vulnerabilities, putting New York City and Washington, D.C., at the top of the current list. Such assistance should not remain a program for general revenue sharing or pork-barrel spending.
- Make homeland security funding contingent on the adoption of an incident command system to strengthen teamwork in a crisis, including a regional approach. Allocate more radio spectrum and improve connectivity for public safety communications, and encourage widespread adoption of newly developed standards for private-sector

emergency preparedness—since the private sector controls 85 percent of the nation's critical infrastructure.

HOW TO DO IT? A DIFFERENT WAY OF ORGANIZING GOVERNMENT

The strategy we have recommended is elaborate, even as presented here very briefly. To implement it will require a government better organized than the one that exists today, with its national security institutions designed half a century ago to win the Cold War. Americans should not settle for incremental, ad hoc adjustments to a system created a generation ago for a world that no longer exists.

Our detailed recommendations are designed to fit together. Their purpose is clear: to build unity of effort across the U.S. government. As one official now serving on the front lines overseas put it to us: "One fight, one team."

We call for unity of effort in five areas, beginning with unity of effort on the challenge of counterterrorism itself:

- unifying strategic intelligence and operational planning against Islamist terrorists across the foreign-domestic divide with a National Counterterrorism Center;
- unifying the intelligence community with a new National Intelligence Director;
- unifying the many participants in the counterterrorism effort and their knowledge in a network-based information sharing system that transcends traditional governmental boundaries;
- unifying and strengthening congressional oversight to improve quality and accountability; and
- strengthening the FBI and homeland defenders.

Unity of Effort: A National Counterterrorism Center

The 9/11 story teaches the value of integrating strategic intelligence from all sources into joint operational planning—with both dimensions spanning the foreign-domestic divide.

- In some ways, since 9/11, joint work has gotten better. The effort of fighting terrorism has flooded over many of the usual agency boundaries because of its sheer quantity and energy. Attitudes have changed. But the problems of coordination have multiplied. The Defense Department alone has three unified commands (SOCOM, CENTCOM, and NORTHCOM) that deal with terrorism as one of their principal concerns.
- Much of the public commentary about the 9/11 attacks has focused on "lost opportunities." Though characterized as problems of "watchlisting," "information sharing," or

"connecting the dots," each of these labels is too narrow. They describe the symptoms, not the disease.

- Breaking the older mold of organization stovepiped purely in executive agencies, we propose a National Counterterrorism Center (NCTC) that would borrow the joint, unified command concept adopted in the 1980s by the American military in a civilian agency, combining the joint intelligence function alongside the operations work.
- The NCTC would build on the existing Terrorist Threat Integration Center and would replace it and other terrorism "fusion centers" within the government. The NCTC would become the authoritative knowledge bank, bringing information to bear on common plans. It should task collection requirements both inside and outside the United States.
- The NCTC should perform joint operational planning, assigning lead responsibilities to existing agencies and letting them direct the actual execution of the plans.
- Placed in the Executive Office of the President, headed by a Senate-confirmed official (with rank equal to the deputy head of a cabinet department) who reports to the National Intelligence Director, the NCTC would track implementation of plans. It would be able to influence the leadership and the budgets of the counterterrorism operating arms of the CIA, the FBI, and the departments of Defense and Homeland Security.
- The NCTC should not be a policymaking body. Its operations and planning should follow the policy direction of the president and the National Security Council.

Unity of Effort: A National Intelligence Director

Since long before 9/11—and continuing to this day—the intelligence community is not organized well for joint intelligence work. It does not employ common standards and practices in reporting intelligence or in training experts overseas and at home. The expensive national capabilities for collecting intelligence have divided management. The structures are too complex and too secret.

- The community's head—the Director of Central Intelligence—has at least three jobs: running the CIA, coordinating a 15-agency confederation, and being the intelligence analyst-in-chief to the president. No one person can do all these things.
- A new National Intelligence Director should be established with two main jobs: (1) to oversee national intelligence centers that combine experts from all the collection disciplines against common targets—like counterterrorism or nuclear proliferation; and (2) to oversee the agencies that contribute to the national intelligence program, a task that includes setting common standards for personnel and information technology.

- The national intelligence centers would be the unified commands of the intelligence world—a long-overdue reform for intelligence comparable to the 1986 Goldwater-Nichols law that reformed the organization of national defense. The home services—such as the CIA, DIA, NSA, and FBI—would organize, train, and equip the best intelligence professionals in the world, and would handle the execution of intelligence operations in the field.
- This National Intelligence Director (NID) should be located in the Executive Office of the President and report directly to the president, yet be confirmed by the Senate. In addition to overseeing the National Counterterrorism Center described above (which will include both the national intelligence center for terrorism and the joint operations planning effort), the NID should have three deputies:
  - For foreign intelligence (a deputy who also would be the head of the CIA)
  - For defense intelligence (also the under secretary of defense for intelligence)
  - For homeland intelligence (also the executive assistant director for intelligence at the FBI or the under secretary of homeland security for information analysis and infrastructure protection)
- The NID should receive a public appropriation for national intelligence, should have authority to hire and fire his or her intelligence deputies, and should be able to set common personnel and information technology policies across the intelligence community.
- The CIA should concentrate on strengthening the collection capabilities of its clandestine service and the talents of its analysts, building pride in its core expertise.
- Secrecy stifles oversight, accountability, and information sharing. Unfortunately, all the current organizational incentives encourage overclassification. This balance should change; and as a start, open information should be provided about the overall size of agency intelligence budgets.

Unity of Effort: Sharing Information

The U.S. government has access to a vast amount of information. But it has a weak system for processing and using what it has. The system of "need to know" should be replaced by a system of "need to share."

- The President should lead a government-wide effort to bring the major national security institutions into the information revolution, turning a mainframe system into a decentralized network. The obstacles are not technological. Official after official has urged us to call attention to problems with the unglamorous "back office" side of government operations.

- But no agency can solve the problems on its own—to build the network requires an effort that transcends old divides, solving common legal and policy issues in ways that can help officials know what they can and cannot do. Again, in tackling information issues, America needs unity of effort.

Unity of Effort: Congress

Congress took too little action to adjust itself or to restructure the executive branch to address the emerging terrorist threat. Congressional oversight for intelligence—and counterterrorism—is dysfunctional. Both Congress and the executive need to do more to minimize national security risks during transitions between administrations.

- For intelligence oversight, we propose two options: either a joint committee on the old model of the Joint Committee on Atomic Energy or a single committee in each house combining authorizing and appropriating committees. Our central message is the same: the intelligence committees cannot carry out their oversight function unless they are made stronger, and thereby have both clear responsibility and accountability for that oversight.
- Congress should create a single, principal point of oversight and review for homeland security. There should be one permanent standing committee for homeland security in each chamber.
- We propose reforms to speed up the nomination, financial reporting, security clearance, and confirmation process for national security officials at the start of an administration, and suggest steps to make sure that incoming administrations have the information they need.

Unity of Effort: Organizing America's Defenses in the United States

We have considered several proposals relating to the future of the domestic intelligence and counterterrorism mission. Adding a new domestic intelligence agency will not solve America's problems in collecting and analyzing intelligence within the United States. We do not recommend creating one.

- We propose the establishment of a specialized and integrated national security workforce at the FBI, consisting of agents, analysts, linguists, and surveillance specialists who are recruited, trained, rewarded, and retained to ensure the development of an institutional culture imbued with a deep expertise in intelligence and national security.
- At several points we asked: Who has the responsibility for defending us at home? Responsibility for America's national defense is shared by the Department of Defense, with its new Northern Command, and by the Department of

Homeland Security. They must have a clear delineation of roles, missions, and authority.
- The Department of Defense and its oversight committees should regularly assess the adequacy of Northern Command's strategies and planning to defend against military threats to the homeland.
- The Department of Homeland Security and its oversight committees should regularly assess the types of threats the country faces, in order to determine the adequacy of the government's plans and the readiness of the government to respond to those threats.

We call on the American people to remember how we all felt on 9/11, to remember not only the unspeakable horror but how we came together as a nation—one nation. Unity of purpose and unity of effort are the way we will defeat this enemy and make America safer for our children and grandchildren.

We look forward to a national debate on the merits of what we have recommended, and we will participate vigorously in that debate.

Source: National Commission on Terrorist Attacks Upon the United States, *The 9/11 Commission Report,* http://www.9-11commission .gov/report/index.htm.

93. President George W. Bush, Address to a Joint Session of Congress and the American People on the U.S. Response to the September 11 Terrorist Attacks, September 20, 2001 [Excerpts]

Introduction

Nine days after the airborne attacks that destroyed the World Trade Center in New York and damaged the Pentagon in Washington, D.C., President George W. Bush addressed a joint session of Congress. He first applauded the courage of those Americans who had helped to rescue the wounded and thanked Congress and foreign nations and citizens for their support. Bush then declared that the events of September 11, 2001, represented "an act of war against our country" and against "freedom itself." Al Qaeda, the group responsible for the attacks, was, he warned, only one of numerous Islamic terrorist organizations active in more than 60 countries. While stating his respect for the Muslim faith, Bush declared that the United States was declaring a "war on terror," not just against al Qaeda but against all other terrorist organizations, one that would "not end until every terrorist group of global reach has been found, stopped, and defeated." Bush called on the Taliban regime in Afghanistan, which was providing the well-funded Al Qaeda organization with an operational base and training facilities, to dissociate itself from Al Qaeda, hand over to American authorities all its leaders currently in Afghanistan, and close down the group's training camps. Otherwise, the Taliban regime would itself face U.S. military intervention. Moreover, Bush warned, this would be only the beginning of a lengthy American campaign against terrorism. In perhaps rather overblown rhetoric, Bush declared that what was at stake was "not just America's freedom. This is the world's fight. This is civilization's fight." The terrorists, he charged, "hate our freedoms—our freedom of religion, our freedom of speech, our freedom to vote and assemble and disagree with each other." He asked the entire "civilized world" to rally to the side of the United States and proclaimed that "Freedom and fear are at war. The advance of human freedom—the great achievement of our time, and the great hope of every time—now depends on us." Bush's grandiose language and his depiction of the effort to eradicate international terrorism as a Manichaean battle between good and evil, the forces of light and the forces of darkness, recalled the rhetoric of the Cold War that had dominated so much of the 20th century.

Primary Source

[…]

In the normal course of events, Presidents come to this Chamber to report on the state of the Union. Tonight, no such report is needed. It has already been delivered by the American people.

We have seen it in the courage of passengers, who rushed terrorists to save others on the ground….

We have seen the state of our Union in the endurance of rescuers, working past exhaustion. We have seen the unfurling of flags, the lighting of candles, the giving of blood, the saying of prayers in English, Hebrew, and Arabic. We have seen the decency of a loving and giving people who have made the grief of strangers their own.

My fellow citizens, for the last 9 days, the entire world has seen for itself the state of our Union, and it is strong.

Tonight we are a country awakened to danger and called to defend freedom. Our grief has turned to anger and anger to resolution. Whether we bring our enemies to justice or bring justice to our enemies, justice will be done.

[…]

And on behalf of the American people, I thank the world for its outpouring of support. America will never forget the sounds of our national anthem playing at Buckingham Palace, on the streets of Paris, and at Berlin's Brandenburg Gate. We will not forget South Korean children gathering to pray outside our Embassy in Seoul,

or the prayers of sympathy offered at a mosque in Cairo. We will not forget moments of silence and days of mourning in Australia and Africa and Latin America.

Nor will we forget the citizens of 80 other nations who died with our own: dozens of Pakistanis; more than 130 Israelis; more than 250 citizens of India; men and women from El Salvador, Iran, Mexico, and Japan; and hundreds of British citizens. America has no truer friend than Great Britain. Once again, we are joined together in a great cause—so honored the British Prime Minister [Tony Blair] has crossed an ocean to show his unity with America. Thank you for coming, friend.

On September 11th, enemies of freedom committed an act of war against our country. Americans have known wars, but for the past 136 years, they have been wars on foreign soil, except for one Sunday in 1941. Americans have known the casualties of war, but not at the center of a great city on a peaceful morning. Americans have known surprise attacks, but never before on thousands of civilians. All of this was brought upon us in a single day, and night fell on a different world, a world where freedom itself is under attack.

Americans have many questions tonight. Americans are asking, who attacked our country? The evidence we have gathered all points to a collection of loosely affiliated terrorist organizations known as Al Qaida.

They are some of the murderers indicted for bombing American Embassies in Tanzania and Kenya and responsible for bombing the U.S.S. *Cole*. Al Qaida is to terror what the Mafia is to crime. But its goal is not making money. Its goal is remaking the world and imposing its radical beliefs on people everywhere.

The terrorists practice a fringe form of Islamic extremism that has been rejected by Muslim scholars and the vast majority of Muslim clerics, a fringe movement that perverts the peaceful teachings of Islam. The terrorists' directive commands them to kill Christians and Jews, to kill all Americans, and make no distinctions among military and civilians, including women and children.

This group and its leader, a person named Usama bin Laden, are linked to many other organizations in different countries, including the Egyptian Islamic Jihad and the Islamic Movement of Uzbekistan. There are thousands of these terrorists in more than 60 countries. They are recruited from their own nations and neighborhoods and brought to camps in places like Afghanistan, where they are trained in the tactics of terror. They are sent back to their homes or sent to hide in countries around the world to plot evil and destruction.

The leadership of Al Qaida has great influence in Afghanistan and supports the Taliban regime in controlling most of that country. In

Afghanistan, we see Al Qaida's vision for the world. Afghanistan's people have been brutalized. Many are starving, and many have fled.

Women are not allowed to attend school. You can be jailed for owning a television. Religion can be practiced only as their leaders dictate. A man can be jailed in Afghanistan if his beard is not long enough.

The United States respects the people of Afghanistan—after all, we are currently its largest source of humanitarian aid—but we condemn the Taliban regime. It is not only repressing its own people; it is threatening people everywhere by sponsoring and sheltering and supplying terrorists. By aiding and abetting murder, the Taliban regime is committing murder.

And tonight the United States of America makes the following demands on the Taliban: Deliver to United States authorities all the leaders of Al Qaida who hide in your land. Release all foreign nationals, including American citizens, you have unjustly imprisoned. Protect foreign journalists, diplomats, and aid workers in your country. Close immediately and permanently every terrorist training camp in Afghanistan, and hand over every terrorist and every person in their support structure to appropriate authorities. Give the United States full access to terrorist training camps, so we can make sure they are no longer operating.

These demands are not open to negotiation or discussion. The Taliban must act and act immediately. They will hand over the terrorists, or they will share in their fate.

I also want to speak tonight directly to Muslims throughout the world. We respect your faith. It's practiced freely by many millions of Americans and by millions more in countries that America counts as friends. Its teachings are good and peaceful, and those who commit evil in the name of Allah blaspheme the name of Allah. The terrorists are traitors to their own faith, trying, in effect, to hijack Islam itself.

The enemy of America is not our many Muslim friends; it is not our many Arab friends. Our enemy is a radical network of terrorists and every government that supports them.

Our war on terror begins with Al Qaida, but it does not end there.

It will not end until every terrorist group of global reach has been found, stopped, and defeated.

Americans are asking, why do they hate us? They hate what we see right here in this Chamber, a democratically elected government. Their leaders are self-appointed. They hate our freedoms—our freedom of religion, our freedom of speech, our freedom to vote and assemble and disagree with each other.

They want to overthrow existing governments in many Muslim countries, such as Egypt, Saudi Arabia, and Jordan. They want to drive Israel out of the Middle East. They want to drive Christians and Jews out of vast regions of Asia and Africa.

These terrorists kill not merely to end lives but to disrupt and end a way of life. With every atrocity, they hope that America grows fearful, retreating from the world and forsaking our friends. They stand against us, because we stand in their way.

We are not deceived by their pretenses to piety. We have seen their kind before. They are the heirs of all the murderous ideologies of the 20th century. By sacrificing human life to serve their radical visions, by abandoning every value except the will to power, they follow in the path of fascism and Nazism and totalitarianism. And they will follow that path all the way, to where it ends, in history's unmarked grave of discarded lies.

Americans are asking, how will we fight and win this war? We will direct every resource at our command—every means of diplomacy, every tool of intelligence, every instrument of law enforcement, every financial influence, and every necessary weapon of war—to the disruption and to the defeat of the global terror network.

This war will not be like the war against Iraq a decade ago, with a decisive liberation of territory and a swift conclusion. It will not look like the air war above Kosovo 2 years ago, where no ground troops were used and not a single American was lost in combat.

Our response involves far more than instant retaliation and isolated strikes. Americans should not expect one battle but a lengthy campaign, unlike any other we have ever seen. It may include dramatic strikes, visible on TV, and covert operations, secret even in success. We will starve terrorists of funding, turn them one against another, drive them from place to place, until there is no refuge or no rest. And we will pursue nations that provide aid or safe haven to terrorism. Every nation, in every region, now has a decision to make: Either you are with us, or you are with the terrorists. From this day forward, any nation that continues to harbor or support terrorism will be regarded by the United States as a hostile regime.

Our Nation has been put on notice: We are not immune from attack. We will take defensive measures against terrorism to protect Americans.

Today dozens of Federal departments and agencies, as well as State and local governments, have responsibilities affecting homeland security.

These efforts must be coordinated at the highest level.

So tonight I announce the creation of a Cabinet-level position reporting directly to me, the Office of Homeland Security. And tonight I also announce a distinguished American to lead this effort to strengthen American security, a military veteran, an effective Governor, a true patriot, a trusted friend, Pennsylvania's Tom Ridge. He will lead, oversee, and coordinate a comprehensive national strategy to safeguard our country against terrorism and respond to any attacks that may come.

These measures are essential. But the only way to defeat terrorism as a threat to our way of life is to stop it, eliminate it, and destroy it where it grows. Many will be involved in this effort, from FBI agents to intelligence operatives to the reservists we have called to active duty. All deserve our thanks, and all have our prayers. And tonight, a few miles from the damaged Pentagon, I have a message for our military:

Be ready. I've called the Armed Forces to alert, and there is a reason.

The hour is coming when America will act, and you will make us proud.

This is not, however, just America's fight, and what is at stake is not just America's freedom. This is the world's fight. This is civilization's fight. This is the fight of all who believe in progress and pluralism, tolerance and freedom.

We ask every nation to join us. We will ask, and we will need, the help of police forces, intelligence services, and banking systems around the world. The United States is grateful that many nations and many international organizations have already responded with sympathy and with support, nations from Latin America to Asia, to Africa, to Europe, to the Islamic world. Perhaps the NATO Charter reflects best the attitude of the world: An attack on one is an attack on all.

The civilized world is rallying to America's side. They understand that if this terror goes unpunished, their own cities, their own citizens may be next. Terror, unanswered, cannot only bring down buildings, it can threaten the stability of legitimate governments. And you know what? We're not going to allow it.

Americans are asking, what is expected of us? I ask you to live your lives and hug your children. I know many citizens have fears tonight, and I ask you to be calm and resolute, even in the face of a continuing threat.

I ask you to uphold the values of America and remember why so many have come here. We are in a fight for our principles, and our first responsibility is to live by them. No one should be singled out for unfair treatment or unkind words because of their ethnic background or religious faith.

I ask you to continue to support the victims of this tragedy with your contributions. Those who want to give can go to a central source of information, libertyunites.org, to find the names of groups providing direct help in New York, Pennsylvania, and Virginia.

The thousands of FBI agents who are now at work in this investigation may need your cooperation, and I ask you to give it.

I ask for your patience with the delays and inconveniences that may accompany tighter security and for your patience in what will be a long struggle.

I ask your continued participation and confidence in the American economy. Terrorists attacked a symbol of American prosperity. They did not touch its source. America is successful because of the hard work and creativity and enterprise of our people. These were the true strengths of our economy before September 11th, and they are our strengths today.

And finally, please continue praying for the victims of terror and their families, for those in uniform, and for our great country. Prayer has comforted us in sorrow and will help strengthen us for the journey ahead.

Tonight I thank my fellow Americans for what you have already done and for what you will do. And ladies and gentlemen of the Congress, I thank you, their representatives, for what you have already done and for what we will do together.

Tonight we face new and sudden national challenges. We will come together to improve air safety, to dramatically expand the number of air marshals on domestic flights and take new measures to prevent hijacking.

We will come together to promote stability and keep our airlines flying, with direct assistance during this emergency.

We will come together to give law enforcement the additional tools it needs to track down terror here at home. We will come together to strengthen our intelligence capabilities, to know the plans of terrorists before they act and find them before they strike. We will come together to take active steps that strengthen America's economy and put our people back to work.

[. . .]

After all that has just passed, all the lives taken and all the possibilities and hopes that died with them, it is natural to wonder if America's future is one of fear. Some speak of an age of terror. I know there are struggles ahead and dangers to face. But this country will define our times, not be defined by them. As long as the

United States of America is determined and strong, this will not be an age of terror; this will be an age of liberty, here and across the world.

Great harm has been done to us. We have suffered great loss. And in our grief and anger, we have found our mission and our moment. Freedom and fear are at war. The advance of human freedom, the great achievement of our time and the great hope of every time, now depends on us. Our Nation—this generation—will lift a dark threat of violence from our people and our future. We will rally the world to this cause by our efforts, by our courage. We will not tire; we will not falter; and we will not fail.

It is my hope that in the months and years ahead, life will return almost to normal. We'll go back to our lives and routines, and that is good. Even grief recedes with time and grace. But our resolve must not pass. Each of us will remember what happened that day and to whom it happened. We'll remember the moment the news came, where we were, and what we were doing. Some will remember an image of a fire or a story of rescue. Some will carry memories of a face and a voice gone forever.

And I will carry this: It is the police shield of a man named George Howard, who died at the World Trade Center trying to save others. It was given to me by his mom, Arlene [Arlene Howard], as a proud memorial to her son. It is my reminder of lives that ended and a task that does not end. I will not forget this wound to our country and those who inflicted it. I will not yield; I will not rest; I will not relent in waging this struggle for freedom and security for the American people.

The course of this conflict is not known, yet its outcome is certain. Freedom and fear, justice and cruelty have always been at war, and we know that God is not neutral between them.

Fellow citizens, we'll meet violence with patient justice, assured of the rightness of our cause and confident of the victories to come. In all that lies before us, may God grant us wisdom, and may He watch over the United States of America.

Source: "Address to a Joint Session of Congress and the American People," U.S. Department of Homeland Security, http://www.dhs .gov/xnews/speeches/speech_0016.shtm.

94. Project for the New American Century, "Lead the World to Victory," Open Letter to President George W. Bush, September 20, 2001

Introduction

Ten days after Al Qaeda operatives destroyed the World Trade Center in New York and seriously damaged the Pentagon building in Washington, D.C., the neoconservative think tank Project for the New American Century addressed an open letter to President George W. Bush. This document not only endorsed calls by the president and Secretary of State Colin Powell for the United States and its citizens to wage all-out "war on terror" but also renewed the organization's earlier appeals to his Democratic predecessor, Bill Clinton, to overthrow the government of President Saddam Hussein of Iraq. Even if there were no direct links between Iraq and Al Qaeda's recent operation, the letter argued, Hussein was nonetheless a leading terrorist, and the United States should "provide full military and financial support to the Iraqi opposition" and "back up [this] commitment . . . by all necessary means." While not necessarily endorsing full-scale war against Iraq, this statement certainly did not preclude such action. Other policies that the Project for the New American Century supported included military action in Afghanistan to eliminate Al Qaeda forces and the Taliban government; efforts to destroy the radical Islamic group Hezbollah and to persuade Iran and Syria to cease their assistance to it; strong backing for Israel, including American insistence that the Palestinian National Authority (PNA) move decisively against terrorism in areas it controlled; and major increases in defense spending. Prominent members of Project for the New American Century who now held office within the Bush administration were precluded from signing this letter but were in positions that would facilitate their implementation of its prescriptions. They included Defense Secretary Donald Rumsfeld and his deputy, Paul Wolfowitz; Peter W. Rodman, assistance secretary of defense for international security affairs; Richard Perle, chairman of the Pentagon's Defense Policy Board; William Schneider Jr., chairman of the Pentagon's Defense Science Board; Elliott Abrams, National Security Council senior director for Near East, Southeast Asian, and North African affairs; Deputy Secretary of State Richard Armitage; John Bolton, undersecretary of state for arms control and international security; Paula Dobriansky, undersecretary of state for global affairs; Zalmay Khalilzad, special assistant to the president and senior director for Southwest Asia, Near East, and North African affairs at the National Security Council, who later successively became U.S. ambassador to Afghanistan, Iraq, and the United Nations (UN); and Robert B. Zoellick, U.S. trade representative.

Primary Source

The Honorable George W. Bush
President of the United States

Washington, DC

Dear Mr. President,

We write to endorse your admirable commitment to "lead the world to victory" in the war against terrorism. We fully support your call for "a broad and sustained campaign" against the "terrorist organizations and those who harbor and support them." We agree with Secretary of State Powell that the United States must find and punish the perpetrators of the horrific attack of September 11, and we must, as he said, "go after terrorism wherever we find it in the world" and "get it by its branch and root." We agree with the Secretary of State that U.S. policy must aim not only at finding the people responsible for this incident, but must also target those "other groups out there that mean us no good" and "that have conducted attacks previously against U.S. personnel, U.S. interests and our allies."

In order to carry out this "first war of the 21st century" successfully, and in order, as you have said, to do future "generations a favor by coming together and whipping terrorism," we believe the following steps are necessary parts of a comprehensive strategy.

Osama bin Laden

We agree that a key goal, but by no means the only goal, of the current war on terrorism should be to capture or kill Osama bin Laden, and to destroy his network of associates. To this end, we support the necessary military action in Afghanistan and the provision of substantial financial and military assistance to the anti-Taliban forces in that country.

Iraq

We agree with Secretary of State Powell's recent statement that Saddam Hussein "is one of the leading terrorists on the face of the Earth. . . ." It may be that the Iraqi government provided assistance in some form to the recent attack on the United States. But even if evidence does not link Iraq directly to the attack, any strategy aiming at the eradication of terrorism and its sponsors must include a determined effort to remove Saddam Hussein from power in Iraq. Failure to undertake such an effort will constitute an early and perhaps decisive surrender in the war on international terrorism. The United States must therefore provide full military and financial support to the Iraqi opposition. American military force should be used to provide a "safe zone" in Iraq from which the opposition can operate. And American forces must be prepared to back up our commitment to the Iraqi opposition by all necessary means.

Hezbollah

Hezbollah is one of the leading terrorist organizations in the world. It is suspected of having been involved in the 1998 bombings of the American embassies in Africa, and implicated in the bombing of the U.S. Marine barracks in Beirut in 1983. Hezbollah clearly falls in the category cited by Secretary Powell of groups "that mean us no good" and "that have conducted attacks previously against U.S. personnel, U.S. interests and our allies." Therefore, any war against terrorism must target Hezbollah. We believe the administration should demand that Iran and Syria immediately cease all military, financial, and political support for Hezbollah and its operations. Should Iran and Syria refuse to comply, the administration should consider appropriate measures of retaliation against these known state sponsors of terrorism.

Israel and the Palestinian Authority

Israel has been and remains America's staunchest ally against international terrorism, especially in the Middle East. The United States should fully support our fellow democracy in its fight against terrorism. We should insist that the Palestinian Authority put a stop to terrorism emanating from territories under its control and imprison those planning terrorist attacks against Israel. Until the Palestinian Authority moves against terror, the United States should provide it no further assistance.

U.S. Defense Budget

A serious and victorious war on terrorism will require a large increase in defense spending. Fighting this war may well require the United States to engage a well-armed foe, and will also require that we remain capable of defending our interests elsewhere in the world. We urge that there be no hesitation in requesting whatever funds for defense are needed to allow us to win this war.

There is, of course, much more that will have to be done. Diplomatic efforts will be required to enlist other nations' aid in this war on terrorism. Economic and financial tools at our disposal will have to be used. There are other actions of a military nature that may well be needed. However, in our judgement the steps outlined above constitute the minimum necessary if this war is to be fought effectively and brought to a successful conclusion. Our purpose in writing is to assure you of our support as you do what must be done to lead the nation to victory in this fight.

Sincerely,

William Kristol

Richard V. Allen	Gary Bauer	Jeffrey Bell
William J. Bennett	Rudy Boshwitz	Jeffrey Bergner
Eliot Cohen	Seth Cropsey	Midge Decter
Thomas Donnelly	Nicholas Eberstadt	Hillel Fradkin
Aaron Friedberg	Francis Fukuyama	Frank Gaffney
Jeffrey Gedmin	Reuel Marc Gerecht	Charles Hill
Bruce P. Jackson	Eli S. Jacobs	Michael Joyce
Donald Kagan	Robert Kagan	Jeane Kirkpatrick
Charles Krauthammer	John Lehman	Clifford May
Martin Peretz	Richard Perle	Norman Podhoretz
Stephen P. Rosen	Randy Scheunemann	Gary Schmitt
William Schneider, Jr.	Richard H. Shultz	Henry Sokolski
Stephen J. Solarz	Vin Weber	Leon Wieseltier
Marshall Wittmann		

Source: "Letter to President Bush on the War on Terrorism," Project for the New American Century, http://www.newamericancentury.org/Bushletter.htm.

95. Edward W. Said, "The Clash of Ignorance," October 2001 [Excerpts]

Introduction

To many observers, the attacks against symbolic American landmarks, including the World Trade Center in New York and the Pentagon building in Washington, D.C., that the Islamic terrorist organization Al Qaeda launched on September 11, 2001, seemed to validate the thesis put forward some years earlier by Harvard University professor Samuel Huntington that once the Cold War had ended, a "clash of civilizations" would dominate the international scene. The two "civilizations" that he believed were most likely to come into conflict were Islam and the Western Judeo-Christian culture. Writing in the intellectual journal of opinion *The Nation* in October 2001, another leading academic celebrity, the Palestinian-born Edward W. Said of Columbia University, dissented from this view. Said argued that depicting all Muslims as followers of Al Qaeda's leader Osama bin Laden and therefore adamantly opposed to the West was far too simplistic, and ignored the existence within Islam of strongly anti–Al Qaeda elements. Said drew attention to a long history of "exchange, cross-fertilization, and sharing" between the West and Islam, one as significant as that of "wars of religion and imperial conquest." Said took issue with the use of Manichaean rhetoric that divided the world into bad and good, "vast abstractions that may give momentary satisfaction but little self-knowledge or informed analysis." He also questioned the inclination by some right-wing American officials within the administration of U.S. president George W. Bush "to draw lines in the sand, to undertake crusades" against an abstract and near-omnipotent enemy that they tended to identify with Islam. Perceptive though it was, Said's analysis had far less impact than that of Huntington, and many in both the West and Islam continued to perceive world affairs in terms of an almost inevitable clash of civilizations.

Primary Source

"The Clash of Ignorance"

Edward W. Said

Samuel Huntington's article "The Clash of Civilizations?" appeared in the Summer 1993 issue of *Foreign Affairs,* where it immediately attracted a surprising amount of attention and reaction. Because the article was intended to supply Americans with an original thesis about "a new phase" in world politics after the end of the cold war, Huntington's terms of argument seemed compellingly large, bold, even visionary. He very clearly had his eye on rivals in the policy-making ranks, theorists such as Francis Fukuyama and his "end of history" ideas, as well as the legions who had celebrated the onset of globalism, tribalism and the dissipation of the state. But they, he allowed, had understood only some aspects of this new period. He was about to announce the "crucial, indeed a central, aspect" of what "global politics is likely to be in the coming years." Unhesitatingly he pressed on:

"It is my hypothesis that the fundamental source of conflict in this new world will not be primarily ideological or primarily economic. The great divisions among humankind and the dominating source of conflict will be cultural. *Nation* states will remain the most powerful actors in world affairs, but the principal conflicts of global politics will occur between nations and groups of different civilizations. The clash of civilizations will dominate global politics. The fault lines between civilizations will be the battle lines of the future."

Most of the argument in the pages that followed relied on a vague notion of something Huntington called "civilization identity" and "the interactions among seven or eight [*sic*] major civilizations," of which the conflict between two of them, Islam and the West, gets the lion's share of his attention. In this belligerent kind of thought, he relies heavily on a 1990 article by the veteran Orientalist Bernard Lewis, whose ideological colors are manifest in its title, "The Roots of Muslim Rage." In both articles, the personification of enormous entities called "the West" and "Islam" is recklessly affirmed, as if hugely complicated matters like identity and culture existed in a cartoonlike world where Popeye and Pluto bash each other mercilessly, with one always more virtuous pugilist getting the upper hand over his adversary. Certainly neither Huntington nor Lewis has much time to spare for the internal dynamics and plurality of every civilization, or for the fact that the major contest in most modern cultures concerns the definition or interpretation of each culture, or for the unattractive possibility that a great deal of demagogy and down-right ignorance is involved in presuming to speak for a whole religion or civilization. No, the West is the West, and Islam Islam.

The challenge for Western policy-makers, says Huntington, is to make sure that the West gets stronger and fends off all the others, Islam in particular. More troubling is Huntington's assumption that his perspective, which is to survey the entire world from a perch outside all ordinary attachments and hidden loyalties, is the correct one, as if everyone else were scurrying around looking for the answers that he has already found. In fact, Huntington is an ideologist, someone who wants to make "civilizations" and "identities" into what they are not: shut-down, sealed-off entities that have been purged of the myriad currents and countercurrents that animate human history, and that over centuries have made it possible for that history not only to contain wars of religion and imperial conquest but also to be one of exchange, cross-fertilization and sharing. This far less visible history is ignored in the rush to highlight the ludicrously compressed and constricted warfare that "the clash of civilizations" argues is the reality. When he published his book by the same title in 1996, Huntington tried to give his argument a little more subtlety and many, many more footnotes; all he did, however, was confuse himself and demonstrate what a clumsy writer and inelegant thinker he was.

The basic paradigm of West versus the rest (the cold war opposition reformulated) remained untouched, and this is what has persisted, often insidiously and implicitly, in discussion since the terrible events of September 11. The carefully planned and horrendous, pathologically motivated suicide attack and mass slaughter by a small group of deranged militants has been turned into proof of Huntington's thesis. Instead of seeing it for what it is— the capture of big ideas (I use the word loosely) by a tiny band of crazed fanatics for criminal purposes—international luminaries from former Pakistani Prime Minister Benazir Bhutto to Italian Prime Minister Silvio Berlusconi have pontificated about Islam's troubles, and in the latter's case have used Huntington's ideas to rant on about the West's superiority, how "we" have Mozart and Michelangelo and they don't. (Berlusconi has since made a half-hearted apology for his insult to "Islam.")

But why not instead see parallels, admittedly less spectacular in their destructiveness, for Osama bin Laden and his followers in cults like the Branch Davidians or the disciples of the Rev. Jim Jones at Guyana or the Japanese Aura Shinrikyo? Even the normally sober British weekly The *Economist,* in its issue of September 22–28, can't resist reaching for the vast generalization, praising Huntington extravagantly for his "cruel and sweeping, but nonetheless acute" observations about Islam. "Today," the journal says with unseemly solemnity, Huntington writes that "the world's billion or so Muslims are 'convinced of the superiority of their culture, and obsessed with the inferiority of their power.'" Did he canvas 100 Indonesians, 200 Moroccans, 500 Egyptians and fifty Bosnians? Even if he did, what sort of sample is that?

Uncountable are the editorials in every American and European newspaper and magazine of note adding to this vocabulary of gigantism and apocalypse, each use of which is plainly designed not to edify but to inflame the reader's indignant passion as a member of the "West" and what we need to do. Churchillian rhetoric is used inappropriately by self-appointed combatants in the West's, and especially America's, war against its haters, despoilers, destroyers, with scant attention to complex histories that defy such reductiveness and have seeped from one territory into another, in the process overriding the boundaries that are supposed to separate us all into divided armed camps.

This is the problem with unedifying labels like Islam and the West: They mislead and confuse the mind, which is trying to make sense of a disorderly reality that won't be pigeonholed or strapped down as easily as all that. I remember interrupting a man who, after a lecture I had given at a West Bank university in 1994, rose from the audience and started to attack my ideas as "Western," as opposed to the strict Islamic ones he espoused. "Why are you wearing a suit and tie?" was the first retort that came to mind. "They're Western too." He sat down with an embarrassed smile on his face, but I recalled the incident when information on the September 11 terrorists started to come in: how they had mastered all the technical details required to inflict their homicidal evil on the World Trade Center, the Pentagon and the aircraft they had commandeered. Where does one draw the line between "Western" technology and, as Berlusconi declared, "Islam's" inability to be a part of "modernity"?

One cannot easily do so, of course. How finally inadequate are the labels, generalizations and cultural assertions. At some level, for instance, primitive passions and sophisticated know-how converge in ways that give the lie to a fortified boundary not only between "West" and "Islam" but also between past and present, us and them, to say nothing of the very concepts of identity and nationality about which there is unending disagreement and debate. A unilateral decision made to draw lines in the sand, to undertake crusades, to oppose their evil with our good, to extirpate terrorism and, in Paul Wolfowitz's nihilistic vocabulary, to end nations entirely, doesn't make the supposed entities any easier to see; rather, it speaks to how much simpler it is to make bellicose statements for the purpose of mobilizing collective passions than to reflect, examine, sort out what it is we are dealing with in reality, the interconnectedness of innumerable lives, "ours" as well as "theirs."

[. . .]

For there are closer ties between apparently warring civilizations than most of us would like to believe; both Freud and Nietzsche showed how the traffic across carefully maintained, even policed boundaries moves with often terrifying ease. But then such fluid ideas, full of ambiguity and skepticism about notions that we hold on to, scarcely furnish us with suitable, practical guidelines for situations such as the one we face now. Hence the altogether more reassuring battle orders (a crusade, good versus evil, freedom against fear, etc.) drawn out of Huntington's alleged opposition between Islam and the West, from which official discourse drew its vocabulary in the first days after the September 11 attacks. There's since been a noticeable de-escalation in that discourse, but to judge from the steady amount of hate speech and actions, plus reports of law enforcement efforts directed against Arabs, Muslims and Indians all over the country, the paradigm stays on.

One further reason for its persistence is the increased presence of Muslims all over Europe and the United States. Think of the populations today of France, Italy, Germany, Spain, Britain, America, even Sweden, and you must concede that Islam is no longer on the fringes of the West but at its center. But what is so threatening about that presence? Buried in the collective culture are memories of the first great Arab-Islamic conquests, which began in the seventh century and which, as the celebrated Belgian historian Henri Pirenne wrote in his landmark book *Mohammed and Charlemagne* (1939), shattered once and for all the ancient unity of the Mediterranean, destroyed the Christian-Roman synthesis and gave rise to a new civilization dominated by northern powers (Germany and Carolingian France) whose mission, he seemed to be saying, is to resume defense of the "West" against its historical-cultural enemies. What Pirenne left out, alas, is that in the creation of this new line of defense the West drew on the humanism, science, philosophy, sociology and historiography of Islam, which had already interposed itself between Charlemagne's world and classical antiquity. Islam is inside from the start, as even Dante, great enemy of Mohammed, had to concede when he placed the Prophet at the very heart of his Inferno.

Then there is the persisting legacy of monotheism itself, the Abrahamic religions, as Louis Massignon aptly called them. Beginning with Judaism and Christianity, each is a successor haunted by what came before; for Muslims, Islam fulfills and ends the line of prophecy. There is still no decent history or demystification of the many-sided contest among these three followers—not one of them by any means a monolithic, unified camp—of the most jealous of all gods, even though the bloody modern convergence on Palestine furnishes a rich secular instance of what has been so tragically irreconcilable about them. Not surprisingly, then, Muslims and Christians speak readily of crusades and jihads, both of them eliding the Judaic presence with often sublime insouciance. Such an agenda, says Eqbal Ahmad, is "very reassuring to the men and women who are stranded in the middle of the ford, between the deep waters of tradition and modernity."

But we are all swimming in those waters, Westerners and Muslims and others alike. And since the waters are part of the ocean

of history, trying to plow or divide them with barriers is futile. These are tense times, but it is better to think in terms of powerful and powerless communities, the secular politics of reason and ignorance, and universal principles of justice and injustice, than to wander off in search of vast abstractions that may give momentary satisfaction but little self-knowledge or informed analysis. "The Clash of Civilizations" thesis is a gimmick like "The War of the Worlds," better for reinforcing defensive self-pride than for critical understanding of the bewildering inter-dependence of our time.

Labels like Islam and the West mislead and confuse the mind, which is trying to make sense of a disorderly reality.

The "Clash of Civilizations" thesis is better for reinforcing self-pride than for a critical understanding of the interdependence of our time.

Source: Edward W. Said, "The Clash of Ignorance," *Nation* 273(12) (2001): 11–13.

96. U.S. Congress, The USA Patriot Act (Summary), October 26, 2001 [Excerpts]

Introduction

Less than seven weeks after the September 11, 2001, attacks, Congress voted on the USA Patriot Act (P.L. 107-56), a major legislative package designed to enhance the ability of the United States to oppose terrorism at home and abroad. The Senate passed the bill by a 98 to 1 majority, and the House passed it by a massive though slightly less overwhelming vote of 357 to 66. The lengthy act, drafted at great speed and in stressful circumstances, dramatically expanded the authority of the government to gather data through wiretaps, electronic surveillance, and other means, often covertly, on individuals and organizations suspected of being threats to the security of the United States. The act also imposed strict financial controls on the international movement of funds and broadened the power of the U.S. government to monitor and investigate money laundering connected with the support of terrorism. In addition, the act tightened immigration controls on individuals entering the United States. Civil liberties organizations later successfully challenged in court various provisions of the act, including those making it an offense for recipients of subpoenas to disclose to the subjects of investigations the fact that government agencies were scrutinizing their records. In March 2006 Congress renewed and made permanent most of the Patriot Act's remaining surveillance provisions. As the initial impact of September 2001 receded, many Americans nonetheless feared that the legislation was too broad and—while rather ironically proclaiming itself vital to maintaining freedom—imposed needless and undesirable restrictions on the civil liberties of both Americans and foreigners.

Primary Source

Summary as of:

10/24/2001—Passed House without amendment.

Uniting and Strengthening America by Providing Appropriate Tools Required to Intercept and Obstruct Terrorism (USA PATRIOT ACT) Act of 2001—Title I: Enhancing Domestic Security Against Terrorism—Establishes in the Treasury the Counterterrorism Fund.

(Sec. 102) Expresses the sense of Congress that: (1) the civil rights and liberties of all Americans, including Arab Americans, must be protected, and that every effort must be taken to preserve their safety; (2) any acts of violence or discrimination against any Americans be condemned; and (3) the Nation is called upon to recognize the patriotism of fellow citizens from all ethnic, racial, and religious backgrounds.

(Sec. 103) Authorizes appropriations for the Federal Bureau of Investigation's (FBI) Technical Support Center.

(Sec. 104) Authorizes the Attorney General to request the Secretary of Defense to provide assistance in support of Department of Justice (DOJ) activities relating to the enforcement of Federal criminal code (code) provisions regarding the use of weapons of mass destruction during an emergency situation involving a weapon (currently, chemical weapon) of mass destruction.

(Sec. 105) Requires the Director of the U.S. Secret Service to take actions to develop a national network of electronic crime task forces throughout the United States to prevent, detect, and investigate various forms of electronic crimes, including potential terrorist attacks against critical infrastructure and financial payment systems.

(Sec. 106) Modifies provisions relating to presidential authority under the International Emergency Powers Act to: (1) authorize the President, when the United States is engaged in armed hostilities or has been attacked by a foreign country or foreign nationals, to confiscate any property subject to U.S. jurisdiction of a foreign person, organization, or country that he determines has planned, authorized, aided, or engaged in such hostilities or attacks (the rights to which shall vest in such agency or person as the President may designate); and (2) provide that, in any judicial review of a determination made under such provisions, if the determination was based on classified information such information may be submitted to the reviewing court ex parte and in camera.

Title II: Enhanced Surveillance Procedures—Amends the Federal criminal code to authorize the interception of wire, oral, and electronic communications for the production of evidence of: (1) specified chemical weapons or terrorism offenses; and (2) computer fraud and abuse.

(Sec. 203) Amends rule 6 of the Federal Rules of Criminal Procedure (FRCrP) to permit the sharing of grand jury information that involves foreign intelligence or counterintelligence with Federal law enforcement, intelligence, protective, immigration, national defense, or national security officials (such officials), subject to specified requirements.

Authorizes an investigative or law enforcement officer, or an attorney for the Government, who, by authorized means, has obtained knowledge of the contents of any wire, oral, or electronic communication or evidence derived therefrom to disclose such contents to such officials to the extent that such contents include foreign intelligence or counterintelligence.

Directs the Attorney General to establish procedures for the disclosure of information (pursuant to the code and the FRCrP) that identifies a United States person, as defined in the Foreign Intelligence Surveillance Act of 1978 (FISA).

Authorizes the disclosure of foreign intelligence or counterintelligence obtained as part of a criminal investigation to such officials.

(Sec. 204) Clarifies that nothing in code provisions regarding pen registers shall be deemed to affect the acquisition by the Government of specified foreign intelligence information, and that procedures under FISA shall be the exclusive means by which electronic surveillance and the interception of domestic wire and oral (current law) and electronic communications may be conducted.

(Sec. 205) Authorizes the Director of the FBI to expedite the employment of personnel as translators to support counter-terrorism investigations and operations without regard to applicable Federal personnel requirements. Requires: (1) the Director to establish such security requirements as necessary for such personnel; and (2) the Attorney General to report to the House and Senate Judiciary Committees regarding translators.

(Sec. 206) Grants roving surveillance authority under FISA after requiring a court order approving an electronic surveillance to direct any person to furnish necessary information, facilities, or technical assistance in circumstances where the Court finds that the actions of the surveillance target may have the effect of thwarting the identification of a specified person.

(Sec. 207) Increases the duration of FISA surveillance permitted for non-U.S. persons who are agents of a foreign power.

(Sec. 208) Increases (from seven to 11) the number of district court judges designated to hear applications for and grant orders approving electronic surveillance. Requires that no fewer than three reside within 20 miles of the District of Columbia.

(Sec. 209) Permits the seizure of voice-mail messages under a warrant.

(Sec. 210) Expands the scope of subpoenas for records of electronic communications to include the length and types of service utilized, temporarily assigned network addresses, and the means and source of payment (including any credit card or bank account number).

(Sec. 211) Amends the Communications Act of 1934 to permit specified disclosures to Government entities, except for records revealing cable subscriber selection of video programming from a cable operator.

(Sec. 212) Permits electronic communication and remote computing service providers to make emergency disclosures to a governmental entity of customer electronic communications to protect life and limb.

(Sec. 213) Authorizes Federal district courts to allow a delay of required notices of the execution of a warrant if immediate notice may have an adverse result and under other specified circumstances.

(Sec. 214) Prohibits use of a pen register or trap and trace devices in any investigation to protect against international terrorism or clandestine intelligence activities that is conducted solely on the basis of activities protected by the first amendment to the U.S. Constitution.

(Sec. 215) Authorizes the Director of the FBI (or designee) to apply for a court order requiring production of certain business records for foreign intelligence and international terrorism investigations. Requires the Attorney General to report to the House and Senate Intelligence and Judiciary Committees semi-annually.

(Sec. 216) Amends the code to: (1) require a trap and trace device to restrict recoding or decoding so as not to include the contents of a wire or electronic communication; (2) apply a court order for a pen register or trap and trace devices to any person or entity providing wire or electronic communication service in the United States whose assistance may facilitate execution of the order; (3) require specified records kept on any pen register or trap and trace device on a packet-switched data network of a provider of electronic communication service to the public; and (4) allow a trap and trace device to identify the source (but not the contents) of a wire or electronic communication.

(Sec. 217) Makes it lawful to intercept the wire or electronic communication of a computer trespasser in certain circumstances.

(Sec. 218) Amends FISA to require an application for an electronic surveillance order or search warrant to certify that a significant purpose (currently, the sole or main purpose) of the surveillance is to obtain foreign intelligence information.

(Sec. 219) Amends rule 41 of the FRCrP to permit Federal magistrate judges in any district in which terrorism-related activities may have occurred to issue search warrants for searches within or outside the district.

(Sec. 220) Provides for nationwide service of search warrants for electronic evidence.

(Sec. 221) Amends the Trade Sanctions Reform and Export Enhancement Act of 2000 to extend trade sanctions to the territory of Afghanistan controlled by the Taliban.

(Sec. 222) Specifies that: (1) nothing in this Act shall impose any additional technical obligation or requirement on a provider of a wire or electronic communication service or other person to furnish facilities or technical assistance; and (2) a provider of such service, and a landlord, custodian, or other person who furnishes such facilities or technical assistance, shall be reasonably compensated for such reasonable expenditures incurred in providing such facilities or assistance.

(Sec. 223) Amends the Federal criminal code to provide for administrative discipline of Federal officers or employees who violate prohibitions against unauthorized disclosures of information gathered under this Act. Provides for civil actions against the United States for damages by any person aggrieved by such violations.

(Sec. 224) Terminates this title on December 31, 2005, except with respect to any particular foreign intelligence investigation beginning before that date, or any particular offense or potential offense that began or occurred before it.

(Sec. 225) Amends the Foreign Intelligence Surveillance Act of 1978 to prohibit a cause of action in any court against a provider of a wire or electronic communication service, landlord, custodian, or any other person that furnishes any information, facilities, or technical assistance in accordance with a court order or request for emergency assistance under such Act (for example, with respect to a wiretap).

Title III: International Money Laundering Abatement and Anti-Terrorist Financing Act of 2001—International Money Laundering Abatement and Financial Anti-Terrorism Act of 2001—Sunsets this Act after the first day of FY 2005 if Congress enacts a specified joint resolution to that effect.

Subtitle A: International Counter Money Laundering and Related Measures—Amends Federal law governing monetary transactions to prescribe procedural guidelines under which the Secretary of the Treasury (the Secretary) may require domestic financial institutions and agencies to take specified measures if the Secretary finds that reasonable grounds exist for concluding that jurisdictions, financial institutions, types of accounts, or transactions operating outside or within the United States, are of primary money laundering concern. Includes mandatory disclosure of specified information relating to certain correspondent accounts.

(Sec. 312) Mandates establishment of due diligence mechanisms to detect and report money laundering transactions through private banking accounts and correspondent accounts.

(Sec. 313) Prohibits U.S. correspondent accounts with foreign shell banks.

(Sec. 314) Instructs the Secretary to adopt regulations to encourage further cooperation among financial institutions, their regulatory authorities, and law enforcement authorities, with the specific purpose of encouraging regulatory authorities and law enforcement authorities to share with financial institutions information regarding individuals, entities, and organizations engaged in or reasonably suspected (based on credible evidence) of engaging in terrorist acts or money laundering activities. Authorizes such regulations to create procedures for cooperation and information sharing on matters specifically related to the finances of terrorist groups as well as their relationships with international narcotics traffickers.

Requires the Secretary to distribute annually to financial institutions a detailed analysis identifying patterns of suspicious activity and other investigative insights derived from suspicious activity reports and investigations by Federal, State, and local law enforcement agencies.

(Sec. 315) Amends Federal criminal law to include foreign corruption offenses as money laundering crimes.

(Sec. 316) Establishes the right of property owners to contest confiscation of property under law relating to confiscation of assets of suspected terrorists.

(Sec. 317) Establishes Federal jurisdiction over: (1) foreign money launderers (including their assets held in the United States); and (2) money that is laundered through a foreign bank.

(Sec. 319) Authorizes the forfeiture of money laundering funds from interbank accounts. Requires a covered financial institution,

upon request of the appropriate Federal banking agency, to make available within 120 hours all pertinent information related to anti-money laundering compliance by the institution or its customer. Grants the Secretary summons and subpoena powers over foreign banks that maintain a correspondent bank in the United States. Requires a covered financial institution to terminate within ten business days any correspondent relationship with a foreign bank after receipt of written notice that the foreign bank has failed to comply with certain judicial proceedings. Sets forth civil penalties for failure to terminate such relationship.

(Sec. 321) Subjects to record and report requirements for monetary instrument transactions: (1) any credit union; and (2) any futures commission merchant, commodity trading advisor, and commodity pool operator registered, or required to register, under the Commodity Exchange Act.

(Sec. 323) Authorizes Federal application for restraining orders to preserve the availability of property subject to a foreign forfeiture or confiscation judgment.

(Sec. 325) Authorizes the Secretary to issue regulations to ensure that concentration accounts of financial institutions are not used to prevent association of the identity of an individual customer with the movement of funds of which the customer is the direct or beneficial owner.

(Sec. 326) Directs the Secretary to issue regulations prescribing minimum standards for financial institutions regarding customer identity in connection with the opening of accounts.

Requires the Secretary to report to Congress on: (1) the most timely and effective way to require foreign nationals to provide domestic financial institutions and agencies with appropriate and accurate information; (2) whether to require foreign nationals to obtain an identification number (similar to a Social Security or tax identification number) before opening an account with a domestic financial institution; and (3) a system for domestic financial institutions and agencies to review Government agency information to verify the identities of such foreign nationals.

(Sec. 327) Amends the Bank Holding Company Act of 1956 and the Federal Deposit Insurance Act to require consideration of the effectiveness of a company or companies in combating money laundering during reviews of proposed bank shares acquisitions or mergers.

(Sec. 328) Directs the Secretary take reasonable steps to encourage foreign governments to require the inclusion of the name of the originator in wire transfer instructions sent to the United States and other countries, with the information to remain with the transfer from its origination until the point of disbursement. Requires annual progress reports to specified congressional committees.

(Sec. 329) Prescribes criminal penalties for Federal officials or employees who seek or accept bribes in connection with administration of this title.

(Sec. 330) Urges U.S. negotiations for international cooperation in investigations of money laundering, financial crimes, and the finances of terrorist groups, including record sharing by foreign banks with U.S. law enforcement officials and domestic financial institution supervisors.

Subtitle B: Bank Secrecy Act Amendments and Related Improvements—Amends Federal law known as the Bank Secrecy Act to revise requirements for civil liability immunity for voluntary financial institution disclosure of suspicious activities. Authorizes the inclusion of suspicions of illegal activity in written employment references.

(Sec. 352) Authorizes the Secretary to exempt from minimum standards for anti-money laundering programs any financial institution not subject to certain regulations governing financial recordkeeping and reporting of currency and foreign transactions.

(Sec. 353) Establishes civil penalties for violations of geographic targeting orders and structuring transactions to evade certain recordkeeping requirements. Lengthens the effective period of geographic targeting orders from 60 to 180 days.

(Sec. 355) Amends the Federal Deposit Insurance Act to permit written employment references to contain suspicions of involvement in illegal activity.

(Sec. 356) Instructs the Secretary to: (1) promulgate regulations requiring registered securities brokers and dealers, futures commission merchants, commodity trading advisors, and commodity pool operators, to file reports of suspicious financial transactions; (2) report to Congress on the role of the Internal Revenue Service in the administration of the Bank Secrecy Act; and (3) share monetary instruments transactions records upon request of a U.S. intelligence agency for use in the conduct of intelligence or counterintelligence activities, including analysis, to protect against international terrorism.

(Sec. 358) Amends the Right to Financial Privacy Act to permit the transfer of financial records to other agencies or departments upon certification that the records are relevant to intelligence or counterintelligence activities related to international terrorism.

Amends the Fair Credit Reporting Act to require a consumer reporting agency to furnish all information in a consumer's file to a government agency upon certification that the records are relevant to intelligence or counterintelligence activities related to international terrorism.

(Sec. 359) Subjects to mandatory records and reports on monetary instruments transactions any licensed sender of money or any other person who engages as a business in the transmission of funds, including through an informal value transfer banking system or network (e.g., hawala) of people facilitating the transfer of money domestically or internationally outside of the conventional financial institutions system.

(Sec. 360) Authorizes the Secretary to instruct the United States Executive Director of each international financial institution to use his or her voice and vote to: (1) support the use of funds for a country (and its institutions) which contributes to U.S. efforts against international terrorism; and (2) require an auditing of disbursements to ensure that no funds are paid to persons who commit or support terrorism.

(Sec. 361) Makes the existing Financial Crimes Enforcement Network a bureau in the Department of the Treasury.

(Sec. 362) Directs the Secretary to establish a highly secure network in the Network that allows financial institutions to file certain reports and receive alerts and other information regarding suspicious activities warranting immediate and enhanced scrutiny.

(Sec. 363) Increases to $1 million the maximum civil penalties (currently $10,000) and criminal fines (currently $250,000) for money laundering. Sets a minimum civil penalty and criminal fine of double the amount of the illegal transaction.

(Sec. 364) Amends the Federal Reserve Act to provide for uniform protection authority for Federal Reserve facilities, including law enforcement officers authorized to carry firearms and make warrantless arrests.

(Sec. 365) Amends Federal law to require reports relating to coins and currency of more than $10,000 received in a nonfinancial trade or business.

(Sec. 366) Directs the Secretary to study and report to Congress on: (1) the possible expansion of the currency transaction reporting requirements exemption system; and (2) methods for improving financial institution utilization of the system as a way of reducing the submission of currency transaction reports that have little or no value for law enforcement purposes.

Subtitle C: Currency Crimes—Establishes as a bulk cash smuggling felony the knowing concealment and attempted transport (or transfer) across U.S. borders of currency and monetary instruments in excess of $10,000, with intent to evade specified currency reporting requirements.

(Sec. 372) Changes from discretionary to mandatory a court's authority to order, as part of a criminal sentence, forfeiture of all property involved in certain currency reporting offenses. Leaves a court discretion to order civil forfeitures in money laundering cases.

(Sec. 373) Amends the Federal criminal code to revise the prohibition of unlicensed (currently, illegal) money transmitting businesses.

(Sec. 374) Increases the criminal penalties for counterfeiting domestic and foreign currency and obligations.

(Sec. 376) Amends the Federal criminal code to extend the prohibition against the laundering of money instruments to specified proceeds of terrorism.

(Sec. 377) Grants the United States extraterritorial jurisdiction where: (1) an offense committed outside the United States involves an access device issued, owned, managed, or controlled by a financial institution, account issuer, credit card system member, or other entity within U.S. jurisdiction; and (2) the person committing the offense transports, delivers, conveys, transfers to or through, or otherwise stores, secrets, or holds within U.S. jurisdiction any article used to assist in the commission of the offense or the proceeds of such offense or property derived from it.

Title IV: Protecting the Border—Subtitle A: Protecting the Northern Border—Authorizes the Attorney General to waive certain Immigration and Naturalization Service (INS) personnel caps with respect to ensuring security needs on the Northern border.

(Sec. 402) Authorizes appropriations to: (1) triple the number of Border Patrol, Customs Service, and INS personnel (and support facilities) at points of entry and along the Northern border; and (2) INS and Customs for related border monitoring technology and equipment.

(Sec. 403) Amends the Immigration and Nationality Act to require the Attorney General and the Federal Bureau of Investigation (FBI) to provide the Department of State and INS with access to specified criminal history extracts in order to determine whether or not a visa or admissions applicant has a criminal history. Directs the FBI to provide periodic extract updates. Provides for confidentiality.

Directs the Attorney General and the Secretary of State to develop a technology standard to identify visa and admissions applicants, which shall be the basis for an electronic system of law enforcement and intelligence sharing system available to consular, law enforcement, intelligence, and Federal border inspection personnel.

(Sec. 404) Amends the Department of Justice Appropriations Act, 2001 to eliminate certain INS overtime restrictions.

(Sec. 405) Directs the Attorney General to report on the feasibility of enhancing the Integrated Automated Fingerprint Identification System and other identification systems to better identify foreign individuals in connection with U.S. or foreign criminal investigations before issuance of a visa to, or permitting such person's entry or exit from, the United States. Authorizes appropriations.

Subtitle B: Enhanced Immigration Provisions—Amends the Immigration and Nationality Act to broaden the scope of aliens ineligible for admission or deportable due to terrorist activities to include an alien who: (1) is a representative of a political, social, or similar group whose political endorsement of terrorist acts undermines U.S. antiterrorist efforts; (2) has used a position of prominence to endorse terrorist activity, or to persuade others to support such activity in a way that undermines U.S. antiterrorist efforts (or the child or spouse of such an alien under specified circumstances); or (3) has been associated with a terrorist organization and intends to engage in threatening activities while in the United States.

(Sec. 411) Includes within the definition of "terrorist activity" the use of any weapon or dangerous device.

Redefines "engage in terrorist activity" to mean, in an individual capacity or as a member of an organization, to: (1) commit or to incite to commit, under circumstances indicating an intention to cause death or serious bodily injury, a terrorist activity; (2) prepare or plan a terrorist activity; (3) gather information on potential targets for terrorist activity; (4) solicit funds or other things of value for a terrorist activity or a terrorist organization (with an exception for lack of knowledge); (5) solicit any individual to engage in prohibited conduct or for terrorist organization membership (with an exception for lack of knowledge); or (6) commit an act that the actor knows, or reasonably should know, affords material support, including a safe house, transportation, communications, funds, transfer of funds or other material financial benefit, false documentation or identification, weapons (including chemical, biological, or radiological weapons), explosives, or training for the commission of a terrorist activity; to any individual who the actor knows or reasonably should know has committed or plans to commit a terrorist activity; or to a terrorist organization (with an exception for lack of knowledge).

Defines "terrorist organization" as a group: (1) designated under the Immigration and Nationality Act or by the Secretary of State; or (2) a group of two or more individuals, whether related or not, which engages in terrorist-related activities.

Provides for the retroactive application of amendments under this Act. Stipulates that an alien shall not be considered inadmissible or deportable because of a relationship to an organization that was not designated as a terrorist organization prior to enactment of this Act. States that the amendments under this section shall apply to all aliens in exclusion or deportation proceedings on or after the date of enactment of this Act.

Directs the Secretary of State to notify specified congressional leaders seven days prior to designating an organization as a terrorist organization. Provides for organization redesignation or revocation.

(Sec. 412) Provides for mandatory detention until removal from the United States (regardless of any relief from removal) of an alien certified by the Attorney General as a suspected terrorist or threat to national security. Requires release of such alien after seven days if removal proceedings have not commenced, or the alien has not been charged with a criminal offense. Authorizes detention for additional periods of up to six months of an alien not likely to be deported in the reasonably foreseeable future only if release will threaten U.S. national security or the safety of the community or any person. Limits judicial review to habeas corpus proceedings in the U.S. Supreme Court, the U.S. Court of Appeals for the District of Columbia, or any district court with jurisdiction to entertain a habeas corpus petition. Restricts to the U.S. Court of Appeals for the District of Columbia the right of appeal of any final order by a circuit or district judge.

(Sec. 413) Authorizes the Secretary of State, on a reciprocal basis, to share criminal- and terrorist-related visa lookout information with foreign governments.

(Sec. 414) Declares the sense of Congress that the Attorney General should: (1) fully implement the integrated entry and exit data system for airports, seaports, and land border ports of entry with all deliberate speed; and (2) begin immediately establishing the Integrated Entry and Exit Data System Task Force. Authorizes appropriations.

Requires the Attorney General and the Secretary of State, in developing the integrated entry and exit data system, to focus on the use of biometric technology and the development of tamper-resistant documents readable at ports of entry.

(Sec. 415) Amends the Immigration and Naturalization Service Data Management Improvement Act of 2000 to include the Office of Homeland Security in the Integrated Entry and Exit Data System Task Force.

(Sec. 416) Directs the Attorney General to implement fully and expand the foreign student monitoring program to include other approved educational institutions like air flight, language training, or vocational schools.

(Sec. 417) Requires audits and reports on implementation of the mandate for machine readable passports.

(Sec. 418) Directs the Secretary of State to: (1) review how consular officers issue visas to determine if consular shopping is a problem; and (2) if it is a problem, take steps to address it, and report on them to Congress.

[. . .]

Title V: Removing Obstacles to Investigating Terrorism—Authorizes the Attorney General to pay rewards from available funds pursuant to public advertisements for assistance to DOJ to combat terrorism and defend the Nation against terrorist acts, in accordance with procedures and regulations established or issued by the Attorney General, subject to specified conditions, including a prohibition against any such reward of $250,000 or more from being made or offered without the personal approval of either the Attorney General or the President.

(Sec. 502) Amends the State Department Basic Authorities Act of 1956 to modify the Department of State rewards program to authorize rewards for information leading to: (1) the dismantling of a terrorist organization in whole or significant part; and (2) the identification or location of an individual who holds a key leadership position in a terrorist organization. Raises the limit on rewards if the Secretary State determines that a larger sum is necessary to combat terrorism or defend the Nation against terrorist acts.

(Sec. 503) Amends the DNA Analysis Backlog Elimination Act of 2000 to qualify a Federal terrorism offense for collection of DNA for identification.

(Sec. 504) Amends FISA to authorize consultation among Federal law enforcement officers regarding information acquired from an electronic surveillance or physical search in terrorism and related investigations or protective measures.

(Sec. 505) Allows the FBI to request telephone toll and transactional records, financial records, and consumer reports in any investigation to protect against international terrorism or clandestine intelligence activities only if the investigation is not conducted solely on the basis of activities protected by the first amendment to the U.S. Constitution.

(Sec. 506) Revises U.S. Secret Service jurisdiction with respect to fraud and related activity in connection with computers. Grants the FBI primary authority to investigate specified fraud and computer related activity for cases involving espionage, foreign counter-intelligence, information protected against unauthorized disclosure for reasons of national defense or foreign relations, or restricted data, except for offenses affecting Secret Service duties.

(Sec. 507) Amends the General Education Provisions Act and the National Education Statistics Act of 1994 to provide for disclosure of educational records to the Attorney General in a terrorism investigation or prosecution.

[...]

Title VII: Increased Information Sharing for Critical Infrastructure Protection—Amends the Omnibus Crime Control and Safe Streets Act of 1968 to extend Bureau of Justice Assistance regional information sharing system grants to systems that enhance the investigation and prosecution abilities of participating Federal, State, and local law enforcement agencies in addressing multi-jurisdictional terrorist conspiracies and activities. Authorizes appropriations.

Title VIII: Strengthening the Criminal Laws Against Terrorism—Amends the Federal criminal code to prohibit specific terrorist acts or otherwise destructive, disruptive, or violent acts against mass transportation vehicles, ferries, providers, employees, passengers, or operating systems.

(Sec. 802) Amends the Federal criminal code to: (1) revise the definition of "international terrorism" to include activities that appear to be intended to affect the conduct of government by mass destruction; and (2) define "domestic terrorism" as activities that occur primarily within U.S. jurisdiction, that involve criminal acts dangerous to human life, and that appear to be intended to intimidate or coerce a civilian population, to influence government policy by intimidation or coercion, or to affect government conduct by mass destruction, assassination, or kidnapping.

(Sec. 803) Prohibits harboring any person knowing or having reasonable grounds to believe that such person has committed or to be about to commit a terrorism offense.

(Sec. 804) Establishes Federal jurisdiction over crimes committed at U.S. facilities abroad.

(Sec. 805) Applies the prohibitions against providing material support for terrorism to offenses outside of the United States.

(Sec. 806) Subjects to civil forfeiture all assets, foreign or domestic, of terrorist organizations.

(Sec. 808) Expands: (1) the offenses over which the Attorney General shall have primary investigative jurisdiction under provisions governing acts of terrorism transcending national boundaries; and (2) the offenses included within the definition of the Federal crime of terrorism.

(Sec. 809) Provides that there shall be no statute of limitations for certain terrorism offenses if the commission of such an offense resulted in, or created a foreseeable risk of, death or serious bodily injury to another person.

(Sec. 810) Provides for alternative maximum penalties for specified terrorism crimes.

(Sec. 811) Makes: (1) the penalties for attempts and conspiracies the same as those for terrorism offenses; (2) the supervised release terms for offenses with terrorism predicates any term of years or life; and (3) specified terrorism crimes Racketeer Influenced and Corrupt Organizations statute predicates.

(Sec. 814) Revises prohibitions and penalties regarding fraud and related activity in connection with computers to include specified cyber-terrorism offenses.

(Sec. 816) Directs the Attorney General to establish regional computer forensic laboratories, and to support existing laboratories, to develop specified cyber-security capabilities.

(Sec. 817) Prescribes penalties for knowing possession in certain circumstances of biological agents, toxins, or delivery systems, especially by certain restricted persons.

Title IX: Improved Intelligence—Amends the National Security Act of 1947 to require the Director of Central Intelligence (DCI) to establish requirements and priorities for foreign intelligence collected under the Foreign Intelligence Surveillance Act of 1978 and to provide assistance to the Attorney General (AG) to ensure that information derived from electronic surveillance or physical searches is disseminated for efficient and effective foreign intelligence purposes. Requires the inclusion of international terrorist activities within the scope of foreign intelligence under such Act.

(Sec. 903) Expresses the sense of Congress that officers and employees of the intelligence community should establish and maintain intelligence relationships to acquire information on terrorists and terrorist organizations.

[...]

(Sec. 905) Requires the AG or the head of any other Federal department or agency with law enforcement responsibilities to expeditiously disclose to the DCI any foreign intelligence acquired in the course of a criminal investigation.

(Sec. 906) Requires the AG, DCI, and Secretary of the Treasury to jointly report to Congress on the feasibility and desirability of reconfiguring the Foreign Asset Tracking Center and the Office of Foreign Assets Control to provide for the analysis and dissemination of foreign intelligence relating to the financial capabilities and resources of international terrorist organizations.

(Sec. 907) Requires the DCI to report to the appropriate congressional committees on the establishment and maintenance of the National Virtual Translation Center for timely and accurate translation of foreign intelligence for elements of the intelligence community.

(Sec. 908) Requires the AG to provide a program of training to Government officials regarding the identification and use of foreign intelligence.

Title X: Miscellaneous—Directs the Inspector General of the Department of Justice to designate one official to review allegations of abuse of civil rights, civil liberties, and racial and ethnic profiling by government employees and officials.

(Sec. 1002) Expresses the sense of Congress condemning acts of violence or discrimination against any American, including Sikh-Americans. Calls upon local and Federal law enforcement authorities to prosecute to the fullest extent of the law all those who commit crimes.

(Sec. 1004) Amends the Federal criminal code with respect to venue in money laundering cases to allow a prosecution for such an offense to be brought in: (1) any district in which the financial or monetary transaction is conducted; or (2) any district where a prosecution for the underlying specified unlawful activity could be brought, if the defendant participated in the transfer of the proceeds of the specified unlawful activity from that district to the district where the financial or monetary transaction is conducted.

States that: (1) a transfer of funds from one place to another, by wire or any other means, shall constitute a single, continuing transaction; and (2) any person who conducts any portion of the transaction may be charged in any district in which the transaction takes place.

Allows a prosecution for an attempt or conspiracy offense to be brought in the district where venue would lie for the completed offense, or in any other district where an act in furtherance of the attempt or conspiracy took place.

(Sec. 1005) First Responders Assistance Act—Directs the Attorney General to make grants to State and local governments to improve the ability of State and local law enforcement, fire departments, and first responders to respond to and prevent acts of terrorism. Authorizes appropriations.

(Sec. 1006) Amends the Immigration and Nationality Act to make inadmissible into the United States any alien engaged in money laundering. Directs the Secretary of State to develop a money laundering watchlist which: (1) identifies individuals worldwide who are known or suspected of money laundering; and (2) is readily accessible to, and shall be checked by, a consular or other Federal official before the issuance of a visa or admission to the United States.

(Sec. 1007) Authorizes FY 2002 appropriations for regional anti-drug training in Turkey by the Drug Enforcement Administration for police, as well as increased precursor chemical control efforts in South and Central Asia.

(Sec. 1008) Directs the Attorney General to conduct a feasibility study and report to Congress on the use of a biometric identifier scanning system with access to the FBI integrated automated fingerprint identification system at overseas consular posts and points of entry to the United States.

(Sec. 1009) Directs the FBI to study and report to Congress on the feasibility of providing to airlines access via computer to the names of passengers who are suspected of terrorist activity by Federal officials. Authorizes appropriations.

(Sec. 1010) Authorizes the use of Department of Defense funds to contract with local and State governments, during the period of Operation Enduring Freedom, for the performance of security functions at U.S. military installations.

[...]

(Sec. 1012) Amends the Federal transportation code to prohibit States from licensing any individual to operate a motor vehicle transporting hazardous material unless the Secretary of Transportation determines that such individual does not pose a security risk warranting denial of the license. Requires background checks of such license applicants by the Attorney General upon State request.

(Sec. 1013) Expresses the sense of the Senate on substantial new U.S. investment in bioterrorism preparedness and response.

(Sec. 1014) Directs the Office for State and Local Domestic Preparedness Support of the Office of Justice Programs to make grants to enhance State and local capability to prepare for and respond to terrorist acts. Authorizes appropriations for FY 2002 through 2007.

(Sec. 1015) Amends the Crime Identification Technology Act of 1998 to extend it through FY 2007 and provide for antiterrorism grants to States and localities. Authorizes appropriations.

(Sec. 1016) Critical Infrastructures Protection Act of 2001—Declares it is U.S. policy: (1) that any physical or virtual disruption of the operation of the critical infrastructures of the United States be rare, brief, geographically limited in effect, manageable, and minimally detrimental to the economy, human and government services, and U.S. national security; (2) that actions necessary to achieve this policy be carried out in a public-private partnership involving corporate and non-governmental organizations; and

(3) to have in place a comprehensive and effective program to ensure the continuity of essential Federal Government functions under all circumstances.

Establishes the National Infrastructure Simulation and Analysis Center to serve as a source of national competence to address critical infrastructure protection and continuity through support for activities related to counterterrorism, threat assessment, and risk mitigation.

Defines critical infrastructure as systems and assets, whether physical or virtual, so vital to the United States that their incapacity or destruction would have a debilitating impact on security, national economic security, national public health or safety, or any combination of those matters.

Authorizes appropriations.

> **Source:** U.S. Congress, "USA PATRIOT Act, Summary," Library of Congress, THOMAS, http://thomas.loc.gov/cgi-bin/bdquery/z?d107:HR03162:@@@D&summ2=m&.

97. President George W. Bush, "The Axis of Evil," State of the Union Address, January 29, 2002 [Excerpts]

Introduction

By the time U.S. president George W. Bush delivered his first State of the Union address after September 11, 2001, coalition forces under U.S. leadership had invaded Afghanistan, removed that country's Taliban government, and driven the Al Qaeda elements there into the mountains. While acclaiming these successes, Bush sought to expand them dramatically. He warned that this was only the beginning of a long-term U.S. war against terror, one that would involve not just operations against terrorists themselves but also major campaigns "to prevent regimes that sponsor terror from threatening America or our friends and allies with weapons of mass destruction." Among these Bush highlighted three countries—North Korea, Iran, and Iraq—and claimed that such states "and their terrorist allies constitute an axis of evil, arming to threaten the peace of the world." Should such nations obtain weapons of mass destruction, they were likely to pass these on to terrorists. Bush warned that the United States would not permit such nations to menace its security and that of the world and that the war on terror had "only begun." Bush called on Congress to approve major increases in defense spending and also to fund massive internal "homeland security" initiatives to safeguard the United States. To facilitate American recovery from the current domestic recession, he sought the mandating of major tax cuts and an economic stimulus spending program that would at least temporarily mean "small and short-term" deficit budgets. He also announced the creation of the USA Freedom Corps, asking every American to commit a lifetime 4,000 hours to some form of community service, an initiative that he claimed would mark the beginning of a new era of good citizenship in the United States but one that ultimately sank almost without a trace. In addition, he announced a new Peace Corps "effort to encourage development and education and opportunity in the Islamic world." Overall, Bush sought to rally Americans in support of a campaign to bring about "freedom's victory." The expansive foreign policy objectives that he charted had the potential to become almost unlimited commitments on the part of the United States.

Primary Source

THE PRESIDENT: . . . As we gather tonight, our nation is at war, our economy is in recession, and the civilized world faces unprecedented dangers. Yet the state of our Union has never been stronger. [Applause.]

We last met in an hour of shock and suffering. In four short months, our nation has comforted the victims, begun to rebuild New York and the Pentagon, rallied a great coalition, captured, arrested, and rid the world of thousands of terrorists, destroyed Afghanistan's terrorist training camps, saved a people from starvation, and freed a country from brutal oppression. [Applause.]

The American flag flies again over our embassy in Kabul. Terrorists who once occupied Afghanistan now occupy cells at Guantanamo Bay. [Applause.] And terrorist leaders who urged followers to sacrifice their lives are running for their own. [Applause.]

America and Afghanistan are now allies against terror. We'll be partners in rebuilding that country. . . . And this evening we welcome the distinguished interim leader of a liberated Afghanistan: Chairman Hamid Karzai. [Applause.]

The last time we met in this chamber, the mothers and daughters of Afghanistan were captives in their own homes, forbidden from working or going to school. Today women are free, and are part of Afghanistan's new government. And we welcome the new Minister of Women's Affairs, Doctor Sima Samar. [Applause.]

Our progress is a tribute to the spirit of the Afghan people, to the resolve of our coalition, and to the might of the United States military. [Applause.] When I called our troops into action, I did so with complete confidence in their courage and skill. And tonight, thanks to them, we are winning the war on terror. [Applause.] The men and women of our Armed Forces have delivered a message now clear to every enemy of the United States: Even 7,000 miles away, across oceans and continents, on mountaintops and in caves—you will not escape the justice of this nation. [Applause.]

[...]

Our cause is just, and it continues. Our discoveries in Afghanistan confirmed our worst fears, and showed us the true scope of the task ahead. We have seen the depth of our enemies' hatred in videos, where they laugh about the loss of innocent life. And the depth of their hatred is equaled by the madness of the destruction they design. We have found diagrams of American nuclear power plants and public water facilities, detailed instructions for making chemical weapons, surveillance maps of American cities, and thorough descriptions of landmarks in America and throughout the world.

What we have found in Afghanistan confirms that, far from ending there, our war against terror is only beginning. Most of the 19 men who hijacked planes on September the 11th were trained in Afghanistan's camps, and so were tens of thousands of others. Thousands of dangerous killers, schooled in the methods of murder, often supported by outlaw regimes, are now spread throughout the world like ticking time bombs, set to go off without warning.

Thanks to the work of our law enforcement officials and coalition partners, hundreds of terrorists have been arrested. Yet, tens of thousands of trained terrorists are still at large. These enemies view the entire world as a battlefield, and we must pursue them wherever they are. [Applause.] So long as training camps operate, so long as nations harbor terrorists, freedom is at risk. And America and our allies must not, and will not, allow it. [Applause.]

Our nation will continue to be steadfast and patient and persistent in the pursuit of two great objectives. First, we will shut down terrorist camps, disrupt terrorist plans, and bring terrorists to justice. And, second, we must prevent the terrorists and regimes who seek chemical, biological or nuclear weapons from threatening the United States and the world. [Applause.]

Our military has put the terror training camps of Afghanistan out of business, yet camps still exist in at least a dozen countries. A terrorist underworld—including groups like Hamas, Hezbollah, Islamic Jihad, Jaish-i-Mohammed—operates in remote jungles and deserts, and hides in the centers of large cities.

While the most visible military action is in Afghanistan, America is acting elsewhere. We now have troops in the Philippines, helping to train that country's armed forces to go after terrorist cells that have executed an American, and still hold hostages. Our soldiers, working with the Bosnian government, seized terrorists who were plotting to bomb our embassy. Our Navy is patrolling the coast of Africa to block the shipment of weapons and the establishment of terrorist camps in Somalia.

My hope is that all nations will heed our call, and eliminate the terrorist parasites who threaten their countries and our own. Many nations are acting forcefully. Pakistan is now cracking down on terror, and I admire the strong leadership of President Musharraf. [Applause.]

But some governments will be timid in the face of terror. And make no mistake about it: If they do not act, America will. [Applause.]

Our second goal is to prevent regimes that sponsor terror from threatening America or our friends and allies with weapons of mass destruction. Some of these regimes have been pretty quiet since September the 11th. But we know their true nature. North Korea is a regime arming with missiles and weapons of mass destruction, while starving its citizens.

Iran aggressively pursues these weapons and exports terror, while an unelected few repress the Iranian people's hope for freedom.

Iraq continues to flaunt its hostility toward America and to support terror. The Iraqi regime has plotted to develop anthrax, and nerve gas, and nuclear weapons for over a decade. This is a regime that has already used poison gas to murder thousands of its own citizens—leaving the bodies of mothers huddled over their dead children. This is a regime that agreed to international inspections—then kicked out the inspectors. This is a regime that has something to hide from the civilized world.

States like these, and their terrorist allies, constitute an axis of evil, arming to threaten the peace of the world. By seeking weapons of mass destruction, these regimes pose a grave and growing danger. They could provide these arms to terrorists, giving them the means to match their hatred. They could attack our allies or attempt to blackmail the United States. In any of these cases, the price of indifference would be catastrophic.

We will work closely with our coalition to deny terrorists and their state sponsors the materials, technology, and expertise to make and deliver weapons of mass destruction. We will develop and deploy effective missile defenses to protect America and our allies from sudden attack. [Applause.] And all nations should know: America will do what is necessary to ensure our nation's security.

We'll be deliberate, yet time is not on our side. I will not wait on events, while dangers gather. I will not stand by, as peril draws closer and closer. The United States of America will not permit the world's most dangerous regimes to threaten us with the world's most destructive weapons. [Applause.]

Our war on terror is well begun, but it is only begun. This campaign may not be finished on our watch—yet it must be and it will be waged on our watch.

We can't stop short. If we stop now—leaving terror camps intact and terror states unchecked—our sense of security would be false and temporary. History has called America and our allies to action, and it is both our responsibility and our privilege to fight freedom's fight. [Applause.]

Our first priority must always be the security of our nation, and that will be reflected in the budget I send to Congress. My budget supports three great goals for America: We will win this war; we'll protect our homeland; and we will revive our economy.

September the 11th brought out the best in America, and the best in this Congress. And I join the American people in applauding your unity and resolve. [Applause.] Now Americans deserve to have this same spirit directed toward addressing problems here at home. I'm a proud member of my party—yet as we act to win the war, protect our people, and create jobs in America, we must act, first and foremost, not as Republicans, not as Democrats, but as Americans. [Applause.]

It costs a lot to fight this war. We have spent more than a billion dollars a month—over $30 million a day—and we must be prepared for future operations. Afghanistan proved that expensive precision weapons defeat the enemy and spare innocent lives, and we need more of them. We need to replace aging aircraft and make our military more agile, to put our troops anywhere in the world quickly and safely. Our men and women in uniform deserve the best weapons, the best equipment, the best training—and they also deserve another pay raise. [Applause.]

My budget includes the largest increase in defense spending in two decades—because while the price of freedom and security is high, it is never too high. Whatever it costs to defend our country, we will pay. [Applause.]

The next priority of my budget is to do everything possible to protect our citizens and strengthen our nation against the ongoing threat of another attack. Time and distance from the events of September the 11th will not make us safer unless we act on its lessons. America is no longer protected by vast oceans. We are protected from attack only by vigorous action abroad, and increased vigilance at home.

My budget nearly doubles funding for a sustained strategy of homeland security, focused on four key areas: bioterrorism, emergency response, airport and border security, and improved intelligence. We will develop vaccines to fight anthrax and other deadly diseases. We'll increase funding to help states and communities train and equip our heroic police and firefighters. [Applause.] We will improve intelligence collection and sharing, expand patrols at our borders, strengthen the security of air travel, and use technology to track the arrivals and departures of visitors to the United States. [Applause.]

Homeland security will make America not only stronger, but, in many ways, better. Knowledge gained from bioterrorism research will improve public health. Stronger police and fire departments will mean safer neighborhoods. Stricter border enforcement will help combat illegal drugs. [Applause.] And as government works to better secure our homeland, America will continue to depend on the eyes and ears of alert citizens.

[. . .]

Once we have funded our national security and our homeland security, the final great priority of my budget is economic security for the American people. [Applause.] To achieve these great national objectives—to win the war, protect the homeland, and revitalize our economy—our budget will run a deficit that will be small and short-term, so long as Congress restrains spending and acts in a fiscally responsible manner. [Applause.] We have clear priorities and we must act at home with the same purpose and resolve we have shown overseas: We'll prevail in the war, and we will defeat this recession. [Applause.]

[. . .]

Good jobs also depend on reliable and affordable energy. This Congress must act to encourage conservation, promote technology, build infrastructure, and it must act to increase energy production at home so America is less dependent on foreign oil. [Applause.]

Good jobs depend on expanded trade. Selling into new markets creates new jobs, so I ask Congress to finally approve trade promotion authority. [Applause.] On these two key issues, trade and energy, the House of Representatives has acted to create jobs, and I urge the Senate to pass this legislation. [Applause.]

Good jobs depend on sound tax policy. [Applause.] Last year, some in this hall thought my tax relief plan was too small; some thought it was too big. [Applause.] But when the checks arrived in the mail, most Americans thought tax relief was just about right. [Applause.] Congress listened to the people and responded by reducing tax rates, doubling the child credit, and ending the death tax. For the sake of long-term growth and to help Americans plan for the future, let's make these tax cuts permanent. [Applause.]

The way out of this recession, the way to create jobs, is to grow the economy by encouraging investment in factories and equipment, and by speeding up tax relief so people have more money to spend. For the sake of American workers, let's pass a stimulus package. [Applause.]

[. . .]

None of us would ever wish the evil that was done on September the 11th. Yet after America was attacked, it was as if our entire country looked into a mirror and saw our better selves. We were reminded that we are citizens, with obligations to each other, to our country, and to history. We began to think less of the goods we can accumulate, and more about the good we can do.

For too long our culture has said, "If it feels good, do it." Now America is embracing a new ethic and a new creed: "Let's roll." [Applause.] In the sacrifice of soldiers, the fierce brotherhood of firefighters, and the bravery and generosity of ordinary citizens, we have glimpsed what a new culture of responsibility could look like. We want to be a nation that serves goals larger than self. We've been offered a unique opportunity, and we must not let this moment pass. [Applause.]

My call tonight is for every American to commit at least two years—4,000 hours over the rest of your lifetime—to the service of your neighbors and your nation. [Applause.] Many are already serving, and I thank you. If you aren't sure how to help, I've got a good place to start. To sustain and extend the best that has emerged in America, I invite you to join the new USA Freedom Corps. The Freedom Corps will focus on three areas of need: responding in case of crisis at home; rebuilding our communities; and extending American compassion throughout the world.

One purpose of the USA Freedom Corps will be homeland security. America needs retired doctors and nurses who can be mobilized in major emergencies; volunteers to help police and fire departments; transportation and utility workers well-trained in spotting danger.

Our country also needs citizens working to rebuild our communities. We need mentors to love children, especially children whose parents are in prison. And we need more talented teachers in troubled schools. USA Freedom Corps will expand and improve the good efforts of AmeriCorps and Senior Corps to recruit more than 200,000 new volunteers.

And America needs citizens to extend the compassion of our country to every part of the world. So we will renew the promise of the Peace Corps, double its volunteers over the next five years—[applause]—and ask it to join a new effort to encourage development and education and opportunity in the Islamic world. [Applause.]

This time of adversity offers a unique moment of opportunity—a moment we must seize to change our culture. Through the gathering momentum of millions of acts of service and decency and kindness, I know we can overcome evil with greater good. [Applause.] And we have a great opportunity during this time of war to lead the world toward the values that will bring lasting peace.

All fathers and mothers, in all societies, want their children to be educated, and live free from poverty and violence. No people on Earth yearn to be oppressed, or aspire to servitude, or eagerly await the midnight knock of the secret police.

If anyone doubts this, let them look to Afghanistan, where the Islamic "street" greeted the fall of tyranny with song and celebration. Let the skeptics look to Islam's own rich history, with its centuries of learning, and tolerance and progress. America will lead by defending liberty and justice because they are right and true and unchanging for all people everywhere. [Applause.]

No nation owns these aspirations, and no nation is exempt from them. We have no intention of imposing our culture. But America will always stand firm for the non-negotiable demands of human dignity: the rule of law; limits on the power of the state; respect for women; private property; free speech; equal justice; and religious tolerance. [Applause.]

America will take the side of brave men and women who advocate these values around the world, including the Islamic world, because we have a greater objective than eliminating threats and containing resentment. We seek a just and peaceful world beyond the war on terror.

In this moment of opportunity, a common danger is erasing old rivalries. America is working with Russia and China and India, in ways we have never before, to achieve peace and prosperity. In every region, free markets and free trade and free societies are proving their power to lift lives. Together with friends and allies from Europe to Asia, and Africa to Latin America, we will demonstrate that the forces of terror cannot stop the momentum of freedom. [Applause.]

The last time I spoke here, I expressed the hope that life would return to normal. In some ways, it has. In others, it never will. Those of us who have lived through these challenging times have been changed by them. We've come to know truths that we will never question: evil is real, and it must be opposed. [Applause.] Beyond all differences of race or creed, we are one country, mourning together and facing danger together. Deep in the American character, there is honor, and it is stronger than cynicism. And many have discovered again that even in tragedy—especially in tragedy—God is near. [Applause.]

In a single instant, we realized that this will be a decisive decade in the history of liberty, that we've been called to a unique role in human events. Rarely has the world faced a choice more clear or consequential.

Our enemies send other people's children on missions of suicide and murder. They embrace tyranny and death as a cause and a creed. We stand for a different choice, made long ago, on the day of our founding. We affirm it again today. We choose freedom and the dignity of every life. [Applause.]

Steadfast in our purpose, we now press on. We have known freedom's price. We have shown freedom's power. And in this great conflict, my fellow Americans, we will see freedom's victory.

> **Source:** George W. Bush, *Public Papers of the Presidents of the United States: George W. Bush, 2002*, Book 1 (Washington, DC: U.S. Government Printing Office, 2002), 129–136.

98. President George W. Bush, "New Threats Require New Thinking," Remarks at the U.S. Military Academy, West Point, June 1, 2002 [Excerpts]

Introduction

Speaking to the graduating class of military officers of 2002 at the U.S. Military Academy, West Point, President George W. Bush described a new strategy involving preemptive strikes to eradicate threats from terrorists or from hostile powers before these could jeopardize American strategy. The Cold War policies of "deterrence and containment" could, he claimed, no longer always suffice to safeguard the security of the United States and its allies against "shadowy terrorist networks with no nation or citizens to defend" or "unbalanced dictators with weapons of mass destruction." The United States could not afford to put its "faith in the word of tyrants who solemnly sign nonproliferation treaties and then systematically break them." Instead, the United States needed to take action against such threats before they could "fully materialize." Americans needed to "be ready for preemptive action when necessary to defend our liberty and to defend our lives." To do so, the government would be ready to use all appropriate means, whether diplomatic or military. Increasingly, "civilized nations" were "united by common dangers of terrorist violence and chaos" and also by "common values." Bush proclaimed that the United States, whose military strength was already "beyond challenge," intended to maintain this position, making it pointless for other nations to try to match it. In words that might equally have been used by Bush's two presidential predecessors, Bill Clinton and George H. W. Bush, to support the "new world order" or "globalization," President Bush declared that his country would also seek to encourage and provide assistance to nations that supported American values and chose the path of "human progress, based on nonnegotiable demands of human dignity, the rule of law, limits on the power of the state, respect for women and private property and free speech and equal justice and religious tolerance." Bush's proclamation that the U.S. government reserved the right to take preemptive action against any group or country that it considered a potential threat to its own security or that of its allies proved highly controversial, particularly since it seemed that the U.S. government assigned to itself the responsibility of defining

unilaterally both what constituted a threat and what the appropriate response might be. This strategic doctrine also opened the way for the United States to move against Iraq and potentially against Iran and North Korea, the two other nations that Bush had specifically placed on the "axis of evil" described in his January 2002 State of the Union address.

Primary Source

[...]

History has also issued its call to your generation. In your last year, America was attacked by a ruthless and resourceful enemy. You graduate from this Academy in a time of war, taking your place in an American military that is powerful and is honorable. Our war on terror is only begun, but in Afghanistan it was begun well.

[...]

This war will take many turns we cannot predict. Yet, I am certain of this: Wherever we carry it, the American flag will stand not only for our power but for freedom. Our Nation's cause has always been larger than our Nation's defense. We fight, as we always fight, for a just peace, a peace that favors human liberty. We will defend the peace against threats from terrorists and tyrants. We will preserve the peace by building good relations among the great powers. And we will extend the peace by encouraging free and open societies on every continent.

Building this just peace is America's opportunity and America's duty. From this day forward, it is your challenge as well, and we will meet this challenge together. You will wear the uniform of a great and unique country. America has no empire to extend or utopia to establish. We wish for others only what we wish for ourselves, safety from violence, the rewards of liberty, and the hope for a better life.

In defending the peace, we face a threat with no precedent. Enemies in the past needed great armies and great industrial capabilities to endanger the American people and our Nation. The attacks of September the 11th required a few hundred thousand dollars in the hands of a few dozen evil and deluded men. All of the chaos and suffering they caused came at much less than the cost of a single tank. The dangers have not passed. This Government and the American people are on watch. We are ready, because we know the terrorists have more money and more men and more plans.

The gravest danger to freedom lies at the perilous crossroads of radicalism and technology. When the spread of chemical and biological and nuclear weapons, along with ballistic missile technology—when that occurs, even weak states and small groups could attain a catastrophic power to strike great nations. Our enemies have declared this very intention and have been caught seeking these terrible weapons. They want the capability to blackmail us or to harm us or to harm our friends, and we will oppose them with all our power.

For much of the last century, America's defense relied on the cold war doctrines of deterrence and containment. In some cases, those strategies still apply, but new threats also require new thinking. Deterrence—the promise of massive retaliation against nations—means nothing against shadowy terrorist networks with no nation or citizens to defend. Containment is not possible when unbalanced dictators with weapons of mass destruction can deliver those weapons on missiles or secretly provide them to terrorist allies. We cannot defend America and our friends by hoping for the best. We cannot put our faith in the word of tyrants who solemnly sign nonproliferation treaties and then systemically break them. If we wait for threats to fully materialize, we will have waited too long.

Homeland defense and missile defense are part of stronger security; they're essential priorities for America. Yet, the war on terror will not be won on the defensive. We must take the battle to the enemy, disrupt his plans, and confront the worst threats before they emerge. In the world we have entered, the only path to safety is the path of action, and this Nation will act.

Our security will require the best intelligence to reveal threats hidden in caves and growing in laboratories. Our security will require modernizing domestic agencies such as the FBI, so they're prepared to act and act quickly against danger. Our security will require transforming the military you will lead, a military that must be ready to strike at a moment's notice in any dark corner of the world. And our security will require all Americans to be forward-looking and resolute, to be ready for preemptive action when necessary to defend our liberty and to defend our lives.

The work ahead is difficult. The choices we will face are complex. We must uncover terror cells in 60 or more countries, using every tool of finance, intelligence, and law enforcement. Along with our friends and allies, we must oppose proliferation and confront regimes that sponsor terror, as each case requires. Some nations need military training to fight terror, and we'll provide it. Other nations oppose terror but tolerate the hatred that leads to terror, and that must change. We will send diplomats where they are needed, and we will send you, our soldiers, where you're needed.

All nations that decide for aggression and terror will pay a price. We will not leave the safety of America and the peace of the planet at the mercy of a few mad terrorists and tyrants. We will lift this dark threat from our country and from the world.

Because the war on terror will require resolve and patience, it will also require firm moral purpose. In this way our struggle is similar to the cold war. Now, as then, our enemies are totalitarians, holding a creed of power with no place for human dignity. Now, as then, they seek to impose a joyless conformity, to control every life and all of life.

America confronted imperial communism in many different ways, diplomatic, economic, and military. Yet, moral clarity was essential to our victory in the cold war. When leaders like John F. Kennedy and Ronald Reagan refused to gloss over the brutality of tyrants, they gave hope to prisoners and dissidents and exiles and rallied free nations to a great cause.

Some worry that it is somehow undiplomatic or impolite to speak the language of right and wrong. I disagree. Different circumstances require different methods but not different moralities. Moral truth is the same in every culture, in every time, and in every place. Targeting innocent civilians for murder is always and everywhere wrong. Brutality against women is always and everywhere wrong. There can be no neutrality between justice and cruelty, between the innocent and the guilty. We are in a conflict between good and evil, and America will call evil by its name. By confronting evil and lawless regimes, we do not create a problem; we reveal a problem. And we will lead the world in opposing it.

As we defend the peace, we also have an historic opportunity to preserve the peace. We have our best chance since the rise of the nation-state in the 17th century to build a world where the great powers compete in peace instead of prepare for war. The history of the last century, in particular, was dominated by a series of destructive national rivalries that left battlefields and graveyards across the Earth. Germany fought France, the Axis fought the Allies, and then the East fought the West, in proxy wars and tense standoffs, against a backdrop of nuclear Armageddon.

Competition between great nations is inevitable, but armed conflict in our world is not. More and more, civilized nations find ourselves on the same side, united by common dangers of terrorist violence and chaos. America has and intends to keep military strengths beyond challenge, thereby making the destabilizing arms races of other eras pointless and limiting rivalries to trade and other pursuits of peace.

Today, the great powers are also increasingly united by common values, instead of divided by conflicting ideologies. The United States, Japan, and our Pacific friends, and now all of Europe, share a deep commitment to human freedom, embodied in strong alliances such as NATO. And the tide of liberty is rising in many other nations.

Generations of West Point officers planned and practiced for battles with Soviet Russia. I've just returned from a new Russia, now a country reaching toward democracy and our partner in the war against terror. Even in China, leaders are discovering that economic freedom is the only lasting source of national wealth. In time, they will find that social and political freedom is the only true source of national greatness.

When the great powers share common values, we are better able to confront serious regional conflicts together, better able to cooperate in preventing the spread of violence or economic chaos. In the past, great power rivals took sides in difficult regional problems, making divisions deeper and more complicated. Today, from the Middle East to South Asia, we are gathering broad international coalitions to increase the pressure for peace. We must build strong and great power relations when times are good to help manage crisis when times are bad. America needs partners to preserve the peace, and we will work with every nation that shares this noble goal.

And finally, America stands for more than the absence of war. We have a great opportunity to extend a just peace by replacing poverty, repression, and resentment around the world with hope of a better day. Through most of history, poverty was persistent, inescapable, and almost universal. In the last few decades, we've seen nations from Chile to South Korea build modern economies and freer societies, lifting millions of people out of despair and want. And there's no mystery to this achievement.

The 20th century ended with a single surviving model of human progress, based on nonnegotiable demands of human dignity, the rule of law, limits on the power of the state, respect for women, and private property and free speech and equal justice and religious tolerance. America cannot impose this vision, yet we can support and reward governments that make the right choices for their own people. In our development aid, in our diplomatic efforts, in our international broadcasting, and in our educational assistance, the United States will promote moderation and tolerance and human rights. And we will defend the peace that makes all progress possible.

When it comes to the common rights and needs of men and women, there is no clash of civilizations. The requirements of freedom apply fully to Africa and Latin America and the entire Islamic world. The peoples of the Islamic nations want and deserve the same freedoms and opportunities as people in every nation. And their governments should listen to their hopes.

[. . .]

Source: George W. Bush, *Public Papers of the Presidents of the United States: George W. Bush, 2002*, Book 1 (Washington, DC: U.S. Government Printing Office, 2002), 917–922.

99. Assistant U.S. Attorney General Jay S. Bybee, Memorandum to Alberto R. Gonzales, Counsel to the President, Standards of Conduct for Interrogation under 18 U.S.C. 2340–2340A, August 1, 2002 [Excerpts]

Introduction

Under President George W. Bush, U.S. officials demonstrated what many critics considered a disturbing readiness to ignore and discard the Geneva Convention and other accepted international humanitarian guidelines on the treatment of prisoners and civilians. The U.S. government had in the past signed not just the

Geneva Convention but also the United Nations (UN) Convention Against Torture and Other Cruel, Inhuman and Degrading Treatment or Punishment. At the request of Alberto R. Gonzales, White House legal counsel to the president and later attorney general of the United States, in August 2002 the Justice Department submitted a memorandum purporting to define what constituted torture. The memorandum stated that "certain acts may be cruel, inhuman, or degrading, but still not produce pain and suffering of the requisite intensity" to classify them as torture. Torture must inflict "pain accompanying serious physical injury, such as organ failure, impairment of bodily function, or even death." With Gonzales' encouragement and approval, the Defense Department and other U.S. agencies, such as the Central Intelligence Agency (CIA), apparently adopted these guidelines for the treatment of prisoners, whether military or civilian. Several months earlier, in January 2002, Gonzales had already given a legal opinion purporting that captured Taliban and Al Qaeda personnel in Afghanistan fell outside the bounds of the Geneva Convention, and so could be held incommunicado and subjected to treatment forbidden under the Geneva Convention. The Bush administration's unilateral reluctance to observe internationally accepted standards of humanitarian behavior even as it claimed to be fighting wars to defend "freedom" did great damage to its moral standing around the world. The demonstrated eagerness of top American officials to disregard such standards was considered to be one reason for subsequent pervasive abuses of Iraqi detainees by U.S. soldiers at Abu Ghraib, misconduct that when it became known greatly discredited the United States throughout the Arab world and beyond.

Primary Source

Memorandum for Alberto R. Gonzales, Counsel to the President

Re: Standards of Conduct for Interrogation under 18 U.S.C. §§ 2340–2340A

You have asked for our Office's views regarding the standards of conduct under the Convention Against Torture and Other Cruel, Inhuman and Degrading Treatment or Punishment as implemented by Sections 2340–2340A of title 18 of the United States Code. As we understand it, this question has arisen in the context of the conduct of interrogations outside of the United States. We conclude below that Section 2340A proscribes acts inflicting, and that are specifically intended to inflict, severe pain or suffering, whether mental or physical. Those acts must be of an extreme nature to rise to the level of torture within the meaning of Section 2340A and the Convention. We further conclude that certain acts may be cruel, inhuman, or degrading, but still not produce pain and suffering of the requisite intensity to fall within Section 2340A's proscription against torture. We conclude by examining possible defenses that would negate any claim that certain interrogation methods violate the statute.

In Part I, we examine the criminal statute's text and history. We conclude that for an act to constitute torture as defined in Section 2340, it must inflict pain that is difficult to endure. Physical pain amounting to torture must be equivalent in intensity to the pain accompanying serious physical injury, such as organ failure, impairment of bodily function, or even death. For purely mental pain or suffering to amount to torture under Section 2340, it must result in significant psychological harm of significant duration, e.g., lasting for months or even years. We conclude that the mental harm also must result from one of the predicate acts listed in the statute, namely: threats of imminent death; threats of infliction of the kind of pain that would amount to physical torture; infliction of such physical pain as a means of psychological torture; use of drugs or other procedures designed to deeply disrupt the senses, or fundamentally alter an individual's personality; or threatening to do any of these things to a third party. The legislative history simply reveals that Congress intended for the statute's definition to track the Convention's definition of torture and the reservations, understandings, and declarations that the United States submitted with its ratification. We conclude that the statute, taken as a whole, makes plain that it prohibits only extreme acts.

In Part II, we examine the text, ratification history, and negotiating history of the Torture Convention. We conclude that the treaty's text prohibits only the most extreme acts by reserving criminal penalties solely for torture and declining to require such penalties for "cruel, inhuman, or degrading treatment or punishment." This confirms our view that the criminal statute penalizes only the most egregious conduct. Executive branch interpretations and representations to the Senate at the time of ratification further confirm that the treaty was intended to reach only the most extreme conduct.

In Part III, we analyze the jurisprudence of the Torture Victims Protection Act, 28 U.S.C. §§ 1350 note (2000), which provides civil remedies for torture victims, to predict the standards that courts might follow in determining what actions reach the threshold of torture in the criminal context. We conclude from these cases that courts are likely to take a totality-of-the-circumstances approach, and will look to an entire course of conduct, to determine whether certain acts will violate Section 2340A. Moreover, these cases demonstrate that most often torture involves cruel and extreme physical pain. In Part IV, we examine international decisions regarding the use of sensory deprivation techniques. These cases make clear that while many of these techniques may amount to cruel, inhuman and degrading treatment, they do not produce pain or suffering of the necessary intensity to meet the definition of torture. From these decisions, we conclude that there is a wide range of such techniques that will not rise to the level of torture.

In Part V, we discuss whether Section 2340A may be unconstitutional if applied to interrogations undertaken of enemy combatants pursuant to the President's Commander-in-Chief powers. We find that in the circumstances of the current war against al Qaeda and its allies, prosecution under Section 2340A may be barred because enforcement of the statute would represent an unconstitutional infringement of the President's authority to conduct war. In Part VI, we discuss defenses to an allegation that an interrogation method might violate the statute. We conclude that, under the current circumstances, necessity or self-defense may justify interrogation methods that might violate Section 2340A.

[...]

Conclusion

For the foregoing reasons, we conclude that torture as defined in and proscribed by Sections 2340–2340A, covers only extreme acts. Severe pain is generally of the kind difficult for the victim to endure. Where the pain is physical, it must be of an intensity akin to that which accompanies serious physical injury such as death or organ failure. Severe mental pain requires suffering not just at the moment of infliction but it also requires lasting psychological harm, such as seen in mental disorders like post-traumatic stress disorder. Additionally, such severe mental pain can arise only from the predicate acts listed in Section 2340. Because the acts inflicting torture are extreme, there is significant range of acts that though they might constitute cruel, inhuman, or degrading treatment or punishment fail to rise to the level of torture.

Further, we conclude that under the circumstances of the current war against al Qaeda and its allies, application, of Section 2340A to interrogations undertaken pursuant to the President's Commander-in-Chief powers may be unconstitutional. Finally, even if an interrogation method might violate Section 2340A, necessity or self-defense could provide justifications that would eliminate any criminal liability.

Please let us know if we can be of further assistance.

Jay S. Bybee, Assistant Attorney General

Source: "Memorandum for Alberto R. Gonzales, Counsel for the President," United States Department of Justice, http://www.justice.gov/olc/docs/memo-gonzales-aug2002.pdf.

100. Brent Scowcroft, "Don't Attack Saddam," August 15, 2002
Introduction

Republicans from the administration of President George H. W. Bush, who had chosen in late February 1991 not to invade Iraq in an effort to overthrow President Saddam Hussein, were often uncomfortable with the growing enthusiasm that his son's administration displayed for war against Iraq. In August 2002 Brent Scowcroft, the elder Bush's national security adviser who had coauthored a foreign policy memoir with the former president, published an article in the conservative *Wall Street Journal* urging caution. Scowcroft admitted that Hussein was a "thoroughly evil" and brutal dictator, enamored of military force, who had in the past made war on his neighbors, and Scowcroft bluntly stated that "We will all be better off when he is gone." In Scowcroft's opinion, however, Hussein did not seek to attack the United States directly, only to "dominate the Persian Gulf, to control oil from the region, or both." His differences with the United States derived from the fact that it blocked these ambitions. He was unlikely to supply weapons to terrorist organizations he could not control, especially since such action was likely to bring the wrath of the United States down upon him. Scowcroft argued that while it might at some stage be desirable to bring about Hussein's overthrow, this would "undoubtedly be very expensive," and for some time to come the war on terror ought to the first priority for the United States. Invading Iraq would be likely to prove a major diversion from this objective, one that would make other states less willing to cooperate in the war against terror and might well destabilize other Middle Eastern regimes. Many Arab states would also resent such action, perceiving it as a deliberate downgrading of attempts to resolve the Israeli-Palestinian conflict. Successes in prosecuting the war against terror and reaching an Israeli-Palestinian settlement would, by contrast, ultimately facilitate international support for efforts to drive Hussein from power. Scowcroft's warning received considerable publicity, but the very fact that he chose to make his case in the media, not behind closed doors as a trusted confidential adviser, was evidence that President George W. Bush and officials close to him did not wish to hear his message and proposed to ignore it.

Primary Source

"Don't Attack Saddam—It Would Undermine Our Anti-terror Efforts"

By Brent Scowcroft

Our nation is presently engaged in a debate about whether to launch a war against Iraq. Leaks of various strategies for an attack on Iraq appear with regularity. The Bush administration vows regime change, but states that no decision has been made whether, much less when, to launch an invasion.

It is beyond dispute that Saddam Hussein is a menace. He terrorizes and brutalizes his own people. He has launched war on two of his neighbors. He devotes enormous effort to rebuilding his military forces and equipping them with weapons of mass destruction. We will all be better off when he is gone.

That said, we need to think through this issue very carefully. We need to analyze the relationship between Iraq and our other pressing priorities—notably the war on terrorism—as well as the best strategy and tactics available were we to move to change the regime in Baghdad.

Saddam's strategic objective appears to be to dominate the Persian Gulf, to control oil from the region, or both. That clearly poses a real threat to key U.S. interests. But there is scant evidence to tie Saddam to terrorist organizations, and even less to the September 11 attacks. Indeed Saddam's goals have little in common with the terrorists who threaten us, and there is little incentive for him to make common cause with them.

He is unlikely to risk his investment in weapons of mass destruction, much less his country, by handing such weapons to terrorists who would use them for their own purposes and leave Baghdad as the return address. Threatening to use these weapons for blackmail—much less their actual use—would open him and his entire regime to a devastating response by the U.S. While Saddam is thoroughly evil, he is above all a power-hungry survivor.

Saddam is a familiar dictatorial aggressor, with traditional goals for his aggression. There is little evidence to indicate that the United States itself is an object of his aggression. Rather, Saddam's problem with the U.S. appears to be that we stand in the way of his ambitions. He seeks weapons of mass destruction not to arm terrorists, but to deter us from intervening to block his aggressive designs.

Given Saddam's aggressive regional ambitions, as well as his ruthlessness and unpredictability, it may at some point be wise to remove him from power. Whether and when that point should come ought to depend on overall U.S. national security priorities. Our pre-eminent security priority—underscored repeatedly by the president—is the war on terrorism. An attack on Iraq at this time would seriously jeopardize, if not destroy, the global counterterrorist campaign we have undertaken.

The United States could certainly defeat the Iraqi military and destroy Saddam's regime. But it would not be a cakewalk. On the contrary, it undoubtedly would be very expensive—with serious consequences for the U.S. and global economy—and could as well be bloody. In fact, Saddam would be likely to conclude he had nothing left to lose, leading him to unleash whatever weapons of mass destruction he possesses.

Israel would have to expect to be the first casualty, as in 1991 when Saddam sought to bring Israel into the Gulf conflict. This time, using weapons of mass destruction, he might succeed, provoking Israel to respond, perhaps with nuclear weapons, unleashing an Armageddon in the Middle East. Finally, if we are to achieve our strategic objectives in Iraq, a military campaign very likely would have to be followed by a large-scale, long-term military occupation.

But the central point is that any campaign against Iraq, whatever the strategy, cost and risks, is certain to divert us for some indefinite period from our war on terrorism. Worse, there is a virtual consensus in the world against an attack on Iraq at this time. So long as that sentiment persists, it would require the U.S. to pursue a virtual go-it-alone strategy against Iraq, making any military operations correspondingly more difficult and expensive. The most serious cost, however, would be to the war on terrorism. Ignoring that clear sentiment would result in a serious degradation in international cooperation with us against terrorism. And make no mistake, we simply cannot win that war without enthusiastic international cooperation, especially on intelligence.

Possibly the most dire consequences would be the effect in the region. The shared view in the region is that Iraq is principally an obsession of the U.S. The obsession of the region, however, is the Israeli-Palestinian conflict. If we were seen to be turning our backs on that bitter conflict—which the region, rightly or wrongly, perceives to be clearly within our power to resolve—in order to go after Iraq, there would be an explosion of outrage against us. We would be seen as ignoring a key interest of the Muslim world in order to satisfy what is seen to be a narrow American interest.

Even without Israeli involvement, the results could well destabilize Arab regimes in the region, ironically facilitating one of Saddam's strategic objectives. At a minimum, it would stifle any cooperation on terrorism, and could even swell the ranks of the terrorists. Conversely, the more progress we make in the war on terrorism, and the more we are seen to be committed to resolving the Israel-Palestinian issue, the greater will be the international support for going after Saddam.

If we are truly serious about the war on terrorism, it must remain our top priority. However, should Saddam Hussein be found to be clearly implicated in the events of September 11, that could make him a key counterterrorist target, rather than a competing priority, and significantly shift world opinion toward support for regime change.

In any event, we should be pressing the United Nations Security Council to insist on an effective no-notice inspection regime for Iraq—anytime, anywhere, no permission required. On this point, senior administration officials have opined that Saddam Hussein would never agree to such an inspection regime. But if he did, inspections would serve to keep him off balance and under close observation, even if all his weapons of mass destruction capabilities were not uncovered. And if he refused, his rejection could provide the persuasive casus belli which many claim we do not now have. Compelling evidence that Saddam had acquired nuclear-weapons capability could have a similar effect.

In sum, if we will act in full awareness of the intimate interrelationship of the key issues in the region, keeping counterterrorism as our foremost priority, there is much potential for success across the entire range of our security interests—including Iraq. If we reject a comprehensive perspective, however, we put at risk our campaign against terrorism as well as stability and security in a vital region of the world.

Source: U.S. Congress, *Congressional Record*, 107th Cong., 2nd sess., 2002, 7763–7764.

101. United Nations Secretary-General Kofi Annan, "I Stand before You Today a Multilateralist," Speech Delivered to the United Nations General Assembly, September 12, 2002

Introduction

The prospect of an invasion of Iraq spearheaded by the United States left many other nations unenthusiastic. Few welcomed President George W. Bush's strategic doctrine whereby the United States claimed the right to take preemptive action against nations that it believed might at some subsequent date pose a threat to its own security. One year and a day after the September 11, 2001, attacks on the United States, Bush made a speech before the United Nations (UN) General Assembly in New York. By this point, Bush administration officials were loudly proclaiming the right of the United States to take unilateral action in the international arena as and when it pleased. Welcoming the president to the General Assembly, UN secretary-general Kofi Annan himself addressed that gathering. Annan considered his speech so significant that he released it to the press in advance, hoping that this would give it additional impact. Annan spoke out forcefully in support of multilateral action as a means of resolving international problems, working through such institutions as the UN. He warned that governments "committed to the rule of law at home, must be committed also to the rule of law abroad" and that it was in the interest of every state "to uphold international law and maintain international order." The secretary-general highlighted several outstanding world problems whose resolution, he believed, required multilateral action through international organizations. They included the ongoing Israeli-Palestinian conflict, assistance to Afghanistan to strengthen its new government's authority in that country and implement postwar reconstruction policies, and the nuclear standoff between India and Pakistan. Second among the outstanding disputes listed by Annan was the situation in Iraq. He urged Iraq to comply with the UN Security Council resolutions and readmit weapons inspectors to that country, and he asked all nations that possessed any influence with Iraq to persuade its government to follow this course, which he hoped would finally lead to the end of UN sanctions on Iraq.

Primary Source

We cannot begin today without reflecting on yesterday's anniversary—and on the criminal challenge so brutally thrown in our faces on 11 September 2001.

The terrorist attacks of that day were not an isolated event. They were an extreme example of a global scourge, which requires a broad, sustained and global response.

Broad, because terrorism can be defeated only if all nations unite against it.

Sustained, because the battle against terrorism will not be won easily, or overnight. It requires patience and persistence.

And global, because terrorism is a widespread and complex phenomenon, with many deep roots and exacerbating factors.

Mr. President, I believe that such a response can only succeed if we make full use of multilateral institutions.

I stand before you today as a multilateralist—by precedent, by principle, by Charter and by duty.

I also believe that every government that is committed to the rule of law at home, must be committed also to the rule of law abroad. And all States have a clear interest, as well as clear responsibility, to uphold international law and maintain international order.

Our founding fathers, the statesmen of 1945, had learnt that lesson from the bitter experience of two world wars and a great depression.

They recognized that international security is not a zero-sum game. Peace, security and freedom are not finite commodities—like land, oil or gold—which one State can acquire at another's expense. On the contrary, the more peace, security and freedom any one State has, the more its neighbours are likely to have.

And they recognized that, by agreeing to exercise sovereignty together, they could gain a hold over problems that would defeat any one of them acting separately.

If those lessons were clear in 1945, should they not be much more so today, in the age of globalization?

On almost no item on our agenda does anyone seriously contend that each nation can fend for itself. Even the most powerful countries know that they need to work with others, in multilateral institutions, to achieve their aims.

Only by multilateral action can we ensure that open markets offer benefits and opportunities to all.

Only by multilateral action can we give people in the least developed countries the chance to escape the ugly misery of poverty, ignorance and disease.

Only by multilateral action can we protect ourselves from acid rain, or global warming; from the spread of HIV/AIDS, the illicit trade in drugs, or the odious traffic in human beings.

That applies even more to the prevention of terrorism. Individual States may defend themselves, by striking back at terrorist groups and at the countries that harbour or support them. But only concerted vigilance and cooperation among all States, with constant, systematic exchange of information, offers any real hope of denying the terrorists their opportunities.

On all these matters, for any one State—large or small—choosing to follow or reject the multilateral path must not be a simple matter of political convenience. It has consequences far beyond the immediate context.

When countries work together in multilateral institutions—developing, respecting, and when necessary enforcing international law—they also develop mutual trust, and more effective cooperation on other issues.

The more a country makes use of multilateral institutions—thereby respecting shared values, and accepting the obligations and restraints inherent in those values—the more others will trust and respect it, and the stronger its chance to exercise true leadership.

And among multilateral institutions, this universal Organization has a special place.

Any State, if attacked, retains the inherent right of self-defence under Article 51 of the Charter. But beyond that, when States decide to use force to deal with broader threats to international peace and security, there is no substitute for the unique legitimacy provided by the United Nations.

Member States attach importance, great importance in fact, to such legitimacy and to the international rule of law. They have shown—notably in the action to liberate Kuwait, 12 years ago—that they are willing to take actions under the authority of the Security Council, which they would not be willing to take without it.

The existence of an effective international security system depends on the Council's authority—and therefore on the Council having the political will to act, even in the most difficult cases, when agreement seems elusive at the outset. The primary criterion for putting an issue on the Council's agenda should not be the receptiveness of the parties, but the existence of a grave threat to world peace.

Let me now turn to four current threats to world peace, where true leadership and effective action are badly needed.

First, the Israeli-Palestinian conflict. Recently, many of us have been struggling to reconcile Israel's legitimate security concerns with Palestinian humanitarian needs.

But these limited objectives cannot be achieved in isolation from the wider political context. We must return to the search for a just and comprehensive solution, which alone can bring security and prosperity to both peoples, and indeed to the whole region.

The ultimate shape of a Middle East peace settlement is well known. It was defined long ago in Security Council Resolutions 242 and 338, and its Israeli-Palestinian components were spelt out even more clearly in Resolution 1397: land for peace; end to terror and to occupation; two States, Israel and Palestine, living side by side within secure and recognized borders.

Both parties accept this vision. But we can reach it only if we move rapidly and in parallel on all fronts. The so-called "sequential" approach has failed.

As we agreed at the Quartet meeting in Washington last May, an international peace conference is needed without delay, to set out a roadmap of parallel steps: steps to strengthen Israel's security, steps to strengthen Palestinian economic and political institutions, and steps to settle the details of the final peace agreement. Meanwhile, humanitarian steps to relieve Palestinian suffering must be intensified. The need is urgent.

Second, the leadership of Iraq continues to defy mandatory resolutions adopted by the Security Council under Chapter VII of the Charter.

I have engaged Iraq in an in-depth discussion on a range of issues, including the need for arms inspectors to return, in accordance with the relevant Security Council resolutions.

Efforts to obtain Iraq's compliance with the Council's resolutions must continue. I appeal to all those who have influence with Iraq's leaders to impress on them the vital importance of accepting the weapons inspections. This is the indispensable first step towards assuring the world that all Iraq's weapons of mass destruction have indeed been eliminated, and—let me stress—towards the suspension and eventual ending of the sanctions that are causing so many hardships for the Iraqi people.

I urge Iraq to comply with its obligations—for the sake of its own people, and for the sake of world order. If Iraq's defiance continues, the Security Council must face its responsibilities.

Third, permit me to press all of you, as leaders of the international community, to maintain your commitment to Afghanistan.

I know I speak for all in welcoming President Karzai to this Assembly, and congratulating him on his escape from last week's vicious assassination attempt—a graphic reminder of how hard it is to uproot the remnants of terrorism in any country where it has taken root. It was the international community's shameful neglect of Afghanistan in the 1990s that allowed the country to slide into chaos, providing a fertile breeding ground for Al Qaeda.

Today, Afghanistan urgently needs help in two areas. The Government must be helped to extend its authority throughout the country. Without this, all else may fail. And donors must follow through on their commitments to help with rehabilitation, reconstruction and development. Otherwise the Afghan people will lose hope—and desperation, we know, breeds violence.

And finally, in South Asia the world has recently come closer than for many years past to a direct conflict between two countries with nuclear capability. The situation may now have calmed a little, but it remains perilous. The underlying cause must be addressed. If a fresh crisis erupts, the international community might have a role to play; though I gladly acknowledge—and indeed, strongly welcome—the efforts made by well-placed Member States to help the two leaders find a solution.

Excellencies, let me conclude by reminding you of your pledge two years ago, at the Millennium Summit, "to make the United Nations a more effective instrument" in the service of the peoples of the world.

Today I ask all of you to honour that pledge.

Let us all recognize, from now on—in each capital, in every nation, large and small—that the global interest is our national interest.

Source: Kofi Annan, "When Force Is Considered, There Is No Substitute for Legitimacy Provided," Speech before the United Nations General Assembly, SG/SM/8378, September 12, 2002, http://www.un.org/News/Press/docs/2002/SGSM8378.doc.htm.

102. President George W. Bush, Address before the United Nations General Assembly, September 12, 2002 [Excerpts]

Introduction

Speaking before the United Nations (UN) General Assembly immediately after UN Secretary-General Kofi Annan acclaimed the value of multilateral action, U.S. president George W. Bush challenged that organization to meet what he considered to be its responsibilities and enforce earlier Security Council resolutions against Iraq. Bush listed those Security Council resolutions that Iraq had to date ignored. He detailed President Saddam Hussein's human rights abuses against his internal Iraqi political opponents and the regime's "all-pervasive" repression. Iraq, Bush charged, was still holding more than 600 prisoners from the 1991 war over Kuwait, including 1 American pilot. Bush charged Iraq with support for terrorist organizations that targeted Iran, Israel, and the West and claimed that it was sheltering Al Qaeda operatives who had escaped from Afghanistan. The final and, in the Bush administration's prewar rhetoric, the most serious breach of UN Security Council resolutions was Iraq's continued possession and manufacture of weapons of mass destruction, including biological and chemical weapons, missiles, and an ongoing nuclear program, whose existence Iraq's government had sought to conceal from UN and International Atomic Energy Authority (IAEA) inspection teams. Bush argued that the United States wished to ensure that all nations respected the authority of the UN, which would not be the case if nations felt free to blatantly ignore that body's resolutions. "If the Iraqi regime wishes peace," Bush proclaimed, it must immediately observe all provisions of the resolutions dealing with Iraq passed by the Security Council over the past decade. If Iraq did not do so, the United States would work with the UN Security Council to enforce respect for that organization's authority. He told the assembled delegates that if they failed to act, the people of Iraq would continue to live in fear under a brutally repressive regime that would destabilize the entire Middle East and promote terrorist attacks far worse than had occurred one year earlier. The United States would in any case, Bush declared, "stand up for our security and for the permanent rights and the hopes of mankind." He invited his audience to join his own country in taking that stand.

Primary Source

Mr. Secretary-General, Mr. President, distinguished delegates, and ladies and gentlemen: We meet one year and one day after a terrorist attack brought grief to my country and brought grief to many citizens of our world. Yesterday we remembered the innocent lives taken that terrible morning. Today we turn to the urgent duty of protecting other lives, without illusion and without fear.

We've accomplished much in the last year in Afghanistan and beyond. We have much yet to do in Afghanistan and beyond. Many nations represented here have joined in the fight against global terror, and the people of the United States are grateful.

The United Nations was born in the hope that survived a world war, the hope of a world moving toward justice, escaping old patterns of conflict and fear. The founding members resolved that the peace of the world must never again be destroyed by the will and wickedness of any man. We created a United Nations Security Council so that, unlike the League of Nations, our deliberations would be more than talk, our resolutions would be more than wishes. After generations of deceitful dictators and broken treaties and squandered lives, we dedicated ourselves to standards of human dignity shared by all and to a system of security defended by all.

[. . .]

Our common security is challenged by regional conflicts, ethnic and religious strife that is ancient but not inevitable. In the Middle East, there can be no peace for either side without freedom for both sides. America stands committed to an independent and democratic Palestine, living side by side with Israel in peace and security. Like all other people, Palestinians deserve a government that serves their interests and listens to their voices. My Nation will continue to encourage all parties to step up to their responsibilities as we seek a just and comprehensive settlement to the conflict.

Above all, our principles and our security are challenged today by outlaw groups and regimes that accept no law of morality and have no limit to their violent ambitions. In the attacks on America a year ago, we saw the destructive intentions of our enemies. This threat hides within many nations, including my own. In cells and camps, terrorists are plotting further destruction and building new bases for their war against civilization. And our greatest fear is that terrorists will find a shortcut to their mad ambitions when an outlaw regime supplies them with the technologies to kill on a massive scale.

In one place—in one regime—we find all these dangers in their most lethal and aggressive forms, exactly the kind of aggressive threat the United Nations was born to confront.

Twelve years ago, Iraq invaded Kuwait without provocation, and the regime's forces were poised to continue their march to seize other countries and their resources. Had Saddam Hussein been appeased instead of stopped, he would have endangered the peace and stability of the world. Yet this aggression was stopped by the might of coalition forces and the will of the United Nations.

To suspend hostilities, to spare himself, Iraq's dictator [Saddam Hussein] accepted a series of commitments. The terms were clear to him and to all, and he agreed to prove he is complying with every one of those obligations. He has proven instead only his contempt for the United Nations and for all his pledges. By breaking every pledge, by his deceptions, and by his cruelties, Saddam Hussein has made the case against himself.

In 1991, Security Council Resolution 688 demanded that the Iraqi regime cease at once the repression of its own people, including the systematic repression of minorities, which the Council said threatened international peace and security in the region. This demand goes ignored.

Last year, the U.N. Commission on Human Rights found that Iraq continues to commit extremely grave violations of human rights and that the regime's repression is all-pervasive. Tens of thousands of political opponents and ordinary citizens have been subjected to arbitrary arrest and imprisonment, summary execution, and torture by beating and burning, electric shock, starvation, mutilation, and rape. Wives are tortured in front of their husbands, children in the presence of their parents, and all of these horrors concealed from the world by the apparatus of a totalitarian state.

In 1991, the U.N. Security Council, through Resolutions 686 and 687, demanded that Iraq return all prisoners from Kuwait and other lands. Iraq's regime agreed. It broke this promise. Last year, the Secretary-General's high-level coordinator [Yuli Vorontsov] for this issue reported that Kuwaiti, Saudi, Indian, Syrian, Lebanese, Iranian, Egyptian, Bahraini, and Omani nationals remain unaccounted for—more than 600 people. One American pilot is among them.

In 1991, the U.N. Security Council, through Resolution 687, demanded that Iraq renounce all involvement with terrorism and permit no terrorist organizations to operate in Iraq. Iraq's regime agreed. It broke this promise. In violation of Security Council Resolution 1373, Iraq continues to shelter and support terrorist organizations that direct violence against Iran, Israel, and Western governments. Iraqi dissidents abroad are targeted for murder. In 1993, Iraq attempted to assassinate the Amir of Kuwait [Jabir al-Ahmad al-Jabir Al Sabah] and a former American President [George Bush]. Iraq's Government openly praised the attacks of September the 11th, and Al Qaida terrorists escaped from Afghanistan and are known to be in Iraq.

In 1991, the Iraqi regime agreed to destroy and stop developing all weapons of mass destruction and long-range missiles and to prove to the world it has done so by complying with rigorous inspections. Iraq has broken every aspect of this fundamental pledge.

From 1991 to 1995, the Iraqi regime said it had no biological weapons. After a senior official in its weapons program defected and exposed this lie, the regime admitted to producing tens of thousands of liters of anthrax and other deadly biological agents for use with Scud warheads, aerial bombs, and aircraft spray tanks. U.N. inspectors believe Iraq has produced 2 to 4 times the amount of biological agents it declared and has failed to account for more than 3 metric tons of material that could be used to produce biological weapons. Right now, Iraq is expanding and improving facilities that were used for the production of biological weapons. United Nations inspections also revealed that Iraq likely maintains stockpiles of VX, mustard, and other chemical agents and that the regime is rebuilding and expanding facilities capable of producing chemical weapons.

And in 1995, after 4 years of deception, Iraq finally admitted it had a crash nuclear weapons program prior to the Gulf war. We know now, were it not for that war, the regime in Iraq would likely have possessed a nuclear weapon no later than 1993.

Today, Iraq continues to withhold important information about its nuclear program, weapons design, procurement logs, experiment data, an accounting of nuclear materials, and documentation of foreign assistance. Iraq employs capable nuclear scientists and technicians. It retains physical infrastructure needed to build a nuclear weapon. Iraq has made several attempts to buy high-strength aluminum tubes used to enrich uranium for a nuclear weapon. Should Iraq acquire fissile material, it would be able to build a nuclear weapon within a year. And Iraq's state-controlled media has reported numerous meetings between Saddam Hussein and his nuclear scientists, leaving little doubt about his continued appetite for these weapons.

Iraq also possesses a force of Scud-type missiles with ranges beyond the 150 kilometers permitted by the U.N. Work at testing and production facilities shows that Iraq is building more long-range missiles, that it can inflict mass death throughout the region.

In 1990, after Iraq's invasion of Kuwait, the world imposed economic sanctions on Iraq. Those sanctions were maintained after the war to compel the regime's compliance with Security Council resolutions. In time, Iraq was allowed to use oil revenues to buy food. Saddam Hussein has subverted this program, working around the sanctions to buy missile technology and military materials. He blames the suffering of Iraq's people on the United Nations, even as he uses his oil wealth to build lavish palaces for himself and to buy arms for his country. By refusing to comply with his own agreements, he bears full guilt for the hunger and misery of innocent Iraqi citizens.

In 1991, Iraq promised U.N. inspectors immediate and unrestricted access to verify Iraq's commitment to rid itself of weapons of mass destruction and long-range missiles. Iraq broke this promise, spending 7 years deceiving, evading, and harassing U.N. inspectors before ceasing cooperation entirely. Just months after the 1991 ceasefire, the Security Council twice renewed its demand that the Iraqi regime cooperate fully with inspectors, condemning Iraq's serious violations of its obligations. The Security Council again renewed that demand in 1994 and twice more in 1996, deploring Iraq's clear violations of its obligations. The Security Council renewed its demand three more times in 1997, citing flagrant violations, and three more times in 1998, calling Iraq's behavior totally unacceptable. And in 1999, the demand was renewed yet again.

As we meet today, it's been almost 4 years since the last U.N. inspectors set foot in Iraq, 4 years for the Iraqi regime to plan and to build and to test behind the cloak of secrecy.

We know that Saddam Hussein pursued weapons of mass murder even when inspectors were in his country. Are we to assume that he stopped when they left? The history, the logic, and the facts lead to one conclusion: Saddam Hussein's regime is a grave and gathering danger. To suggest otherwise is to hope against the evidence. To assume this regime's good faith is to bet the lives of millions and the peace of the world in a reckless gamble. And this is a risk we must not take.

Delegates to the General Assembly, we have been more than patient. We've tried sanctions. We've tried the carrot of oil for food and the stick of coalition military strikes. But Saddam Hussein has defied all these efforts and continues to develop weapons of mass destruction. The first time we may be completely certain he has a—nuclear weapons is when, God forbids, he uses one. We owe it to all our citizens to do everything in our power to prevent that day from coming.

The conduct of the Iraqi regime is a threat to the authority of the United Nations and a threat to peace. Iraq has answered a decade of U.N. demands with a decade of defiance. All the world now faces a test and the United Nations a difficult and defining moment. Are

Security Council resolutions to be honored and enforced or cast aside without consequence? Will the United Nations serve the purpose of its founding, or will it be irrelevant?

The United States helped found the United Nations. We want the United Nations to be effective and respectful and successful. We want the resolutions of the world's most important multilateral body to be enforced. And right now those resolutions are being unilaterally subverted by the Iraqi regime. Our partnership of nations can meet the test before us by making clear what we now expect of the Iraqi regime.

If the Iraqi regime wishes peace, it will immediately and unconditionally forswear, disclose, and remove or destroy all weapons of mass destruction, long-range missiles, and all related material.

If the Iraqi regime wishes peace, it will immediately end all support for terrorism and act to suppress it, as all states are required to do by U.N. Security Council resolutions.

If the Iraqi regime wishes peace, it will cease persecution of its civilian population, including Shi'a, Sunnis, Kurds, Turkomans, and others, again as required by Security Council resolutions.

If the Iraqi regime wishes peace, it will release or account for all Gulf war personnel whose fate is still unknown. It will return the remains of any who are deceased, return stolen property, accept liability for losses resulting from the invasion of Kuwait, and fully cooperate with international efforts to resolve these issues, as required by Security Council resolutions.

If the Iraqi regime wishes peace, it will immediately end all illicit trade outside the oil-for-food program. It will accept U.N. administration of funds from that program, to ensure that the money is used fairly and promptly for the benefit of the Iraqi people.

If all these steps are taken, it will signal a new openness and accountability in Iraq. And it could open the prospect of the United Nations helping to build a government that represents all Iraqis, a government based on respect for human rights, economic liberty, and internationally supervised elections.

The United States has no quarrel with the Iraqi people. They've suffered too long in silent captivity. Liberty for the Iraqi people is a great moral cause and a great strategic goal. The people of Iraq deserve it; the security of all nations requires it. Free societies do not intimidate through cruelty and conquest, and open societies do not threaten the world with mass murder. The United States supports political and economic liberty in a unified Iraq.

We can harbor no illusions, and that's important today to remember. Saddam Hussein attacked Iran in 1980 and Kuwait in 1990. He's fired ballistic missiles at Iran and Saudi Arabia, Bahrain, and Israel. His regime once ordered the killing of every person between the ages of 15 and 70 in certain Kurdish villages in northern Iraq. He has gassed many Iranians and 40 Iraqi villages.

My Nation will work with the U.N. Security Council to meet our common challenge. If Iraq's regime defies us again, the world must move deliberately, decisively to hold Iraq to account. We will work with the U.N. Security Council for the necessary resolutions.

But the purposes of the United States should not be doubted. The Security Council resolutions will be enforced, the just demands of peace and security will be met, or action will be unavoidable. And a regime that has lost its legitimacy will also lose its power.

Events can turn in one of two ways. If we fail to act in the face of danger, the people of Iraq will continue to live in brutal submission. The regime will have new power to bully and dominate and conquer its neighbors, condemning the Middle East to more years of bloodshed and fear. The regime will remain unstable—the region will remain unstable, with little hope of freedom, and isolated from the progress of our times. With every step the Iraqi regime takes toward gaining and deploying the most terrible weapons, our own options to confront that regime will narrow. And if an emboldened regime were to supply these weapons to terrorist allies, then the attacks of September the 11th would be a prelude to far greater horrors.

If we meet our responsibilities, if we overcome this danger, we can arrive at a very different future. The people of Iraq can shake off their captivity. They can one day join a democratic Afghanistan and a democratic Palestine, inspiring reforms throughout the Muslim world. These nations can show by their example that honest government and respect for women and the great Islamic tradition of learning can triumph in the Middle East and beyond. And we will show that the promise of the United Nations can be fulfilled in our time.

Neither of these outcomes is certain. Both have been set before us. We must choose between a world of fear and a world of progress. We cannot stand by and do nothing while dangers gather. We must stand up for our security and for the permanent rights and the hopes of mankind. By heritage and by choice, the United States of America will make that stand. And delegates to the United Nations, you have the power to make that stand as well.

Source: George W. Bush, *Public Papers of the Presidents of the United States: George W. Bush, 2002,* Book 2 (Washington, DC: U.S. Government Printing Office, 2003), 1572–1567.

103. Central Intelligence Agency Director George Tenet, Letter to Senator Bob Graham, October 7, 2002

Introduction

The centerpiece of the case for war against Iraq made by officials of President George W. Bush's administration during 2002 and early 2003 was the allegation that President Saddam Hussein already possessed militarily significant stockpiles of weapons of biological, chemical, and nuclear mass destruction and was well on the way to purchasing or manufacturing even greater destructive capabilities. Democratic senator Bob Graham, chairman of the U.S. Senate's Select Committee on Intelligence, had scrutinized numerous classified intelligence reports on the subject and remained skeptical as to whether Hussein actually possessed such armaments and, even if he did, whether Iraq would be able to use these to attack the United States. In October 2002 Graham wrote to Central Intelligence Agency (CIA) director George Tenet requesting an assessment of how likely Hussein was to employ weapons of mass destruction (WMDs) against the United States. Tenet's reply cited classified CIA estimates that although Hussein was not currently authorizing the use of Iraqi weaponry for terrorist operations against the United States, if he believed he could not prevent "a U.S.-led attack" he might be willing to launch terrorist attacks with his own forces or to make WMDs available to anti-American terrorist groups. Tenet warned, however, that as Hussein's WMDs arsenal grew, he would be more likely to use such armaments for "blackmail" and "deterrence." Tenet claimed to have "solid evidence" of significant links between Iraq and Al Qaeda, including high-level contacts and discussions, and of the presence of Al Qaeda members and training camps within Iraq. Tenet also suggested that Hussein was becoming increasingly willing to support terrorists. Subsequent events revealed that at the time few if any consequential ties existed between Iraq and Al Qaeda and that Tenet had greatly exaggerated the potential threat of Iraqi-backed terrorist attacks on the United States.

Primary Source

In response to your letter of 4 October 2002, we have made unclassified material available to further the Senate's forthcoming open debate on a Joint Resolution concerning Iraq.

As always, our declassification efforts seek a balance between your need for unfettered debate and our need to protect sources and methods. We have also been mindful of a shared interest in not providing to Saddam a blueprint of our intelligence capabilities and shortcoming, or with insight into our expectation of how he will and will not act. The salience of such concerns is only heightened by the possibility for hostilities between the U.S. and Iraq.

These are some of the reasons why we did not include our classified judgments on Saddam's decision making regarding the use of weapons of mass destruction (WMD) in our recent unclassified paper on Iraq's Weapons of Mass Destruction. Viewing your request with those concerns in mind, however, we can declassify the following from the paragraphs you requested.

Baghdad for now appears to be drawing a line short of conducting terrorist attacks with conventional or CBW against the United States.

Should Saddam conclude that a US-led attack could no longer be deterred, he probably would become much less constrained in adopting terrorist actions. Such terrorism might involve conventional means, as with Iraq's unsuccessful attempt at a terrorist offensive in 1991, or CBW.

Saddam might decide that the extreme step of assisting Islamist terrorists in conducting a WMD attack against the United States would be his last chance to exact vengeance by taking a large number of victims with him.

Regarding the 2 October closed hearing, we can declassify the following dialogue.

Senator Levin: . . . If (Saddam) didn't feel threatened, did not feel threatened, is it likely that he would initiate an attack using a weapon of mass destruction?

Senior Intelligence Witness: . . . My judgment would be that the probability of him initiating an attack—let me put a time frame on it—in the foreseeable future, given the conditions we understand now, the likelihood I think would be low.

Senator Levin: Now if he did initiate an attack you've . . . indicated he would probably attempt clandestine attacks against us. . . . But what about his use of weapons of mass destruction? If we initiate an attack and he thought he was in extremis or otherwise, what's the likelihood in response to our attack that he would use chemical or biological weapons?

Senior Intelligence Witness: Pretty high, in my view.

In the above dialogue, the witness's qualifications—"in the foreseeable future, given the conditions we understand now"—were intended to underscore that the likelihood of Saddam using WMD for blackmail, deterrence, or otherwise grows as his arsenal builds. Moreover, if Saddam used WMD, it would disprove his repeated denials that he has such weapons.

Regarding Senator Bayh's question of Iraqi links to al-Qa'ida, Senators could draw from the following points for unclassified discussions:

Our understanding of the relationship between Iraq and al-Qa'ida is evolving and is based on sources of varying reliability. Some of the information we have received comes from detainees, including some of high rank.

We have solid reporting of senior level contacts between Iraq and al-Qa'ida going back a decade.

Credible information indicates that Iraq and al-Qa'ida have discussed safe haven and reciprocal non-aggression.

Since Operation Enduring Freedom, we have solid evidence of the presence in Iraq of al-Qa'ida members, including some that have been in Baghdad.

We have credible reporting that al-Qa'ida leaders sought contacts in Iraq who could help them acquire WMD capabilities. The reporting also stated that Iraq has provided training to al-Qa'ida members in the areas of poisons and gases and making conventional bombs.

Iraq's increasing support to extremist Palestinians, coupled with growing indications of a relationship with al-Qa'ida, suggest that Baghdad's links to terrorists will increase, even absent US military action.

Source: George Tenet, Letter to Senator Bob Graham, October 7, 2002, http://www.gwu.edu/~nsarchiv/NSAEBB/NSAEBB80/wmd17.pdf.

104. U.S. Congress, Joint Resolution Authorizing the Use of Military Force against Iraq, October 16, 2002 [Excerpts]

Introduction

In October 2002 both U.S. Houses of Congress passed a resolution authorizing the president to employ military force against Iraq in order to safeguard U.S. national security and force that country to honor outstanding United Nations (UN) Security Council resolutions. The preamble to this resolution cited numerous reasons in justification of American military intervention. First and foremost were Iraq's efforts to acquire and produce weapons of mass destruction, which the resolution stated that Iraq possessed, threatening American national security and "international peace and security in the Persian Gulf region." The resolution also cited Iraq's attacks on American and coalition armed forces personnel in and near Iraq, including an alleged 1993 attempt to assassinate former president George H. W. Bush. The resolution specifically stated that Iraq was assisting international terrorist organizations, including Al Qaeda, and providing a safe haven for their operatives. The resolution referred to past statements by Congress supporting "the use of all necessary means to achieve the goals of the United Nations Security Council." In addition, the resolution appealed to the Iraq Liberation Act passed by Congress in 1998, mandating U.S. support for efforts to promote regime change in Iraq and the emergence of a democratic government there. Finally, Congress mentioned President George W. Bush's commitment to the UN the previous month that his country would work with that organization to ensure that Iraq honored its obligations under UN Security Council resolutions. The resolution issued by the U.S. Congress stated that Congress favored efforts by Bush to do so and to "obtain prompt and decisive action by the Security Council to ensure that Iraq" complied fully with all its demands. The resolution also authorized the president to use his country's armed forces as appropriate to defend the United States against the continuing threat from Iraq and to "enforce all relevant United Nations Security Council resolutions regarding Iraq." While requiring reports from the president every 60 days, Congress gave the president broad latitude to define and implement what action he considered was needed. If not quite a blank check on Iraq for Bush, the resolution nonetheless came fairly close to being one. On October 10, 2002, the House passed the resolution by a vote of 296 to 133, and the following day the Senate, by a vote of 77 to 23, did likewise. The substantial majorities it received, despite massive antiwar demonstrations around the world and in the United States and Europe, indicated how strongly the American political momentum for war was building. On October 16, 2002, a triumphant Bush signed the resolution into law.

Primary Source

H.J. Res. 114. A joint resolution to authorize the use of United States Armed Forces against Iraq. October 16, 2002

AUTHORIZATION FOR USE OF MILITARY FORCE AGAINST IRAQ RESOLUTION OF 2002

Public Law 107-243

107th Congress

Joint Resolution

To authorize the use of United States Armed Forces against Iraq.

Whereas in 1990 in response to Iraq's war of aggression against and illegal occupation of Kuwait, the United States forged a coalition of nations to liberate Kuwait and its people in order to defend the national security of the United States and enforce United Nations Security Council resolutions relating to Iraq;

Whereas after the liberation of Kuwait in 1991, Iraq entered into a United Nations sponsored cease-fire agreement pursuant to which Iraq unequivocally agreed, among other things, to eliminate its nuclear, biological, and chemical weapons programs and the means to deliver and develop them, and to end its support for international terrorism;

Whereas the efforts of international weapons inspectors, United States intelligence agencies, and Iraqi defectors led to the discovery that Iraq had large stockpiles of chemical weapons and a large scale biological weapons program, and that Iraq had an advanced nuclear weapons development program that was much closer to producing a nuclear weapon than intelligence reporting had previously indicated;

Whereas Iraq, in direct and flagrant violation of the cease-fire, attempted to thwart the efforts of weapons inspectors to identify and destroy Iraq's weapons of mass destruction stockpiles and development capabilities, which finally resulted in the withdrawal of inspectors from Iraq on October 31, 1998;

Whereas in Public Law 105-235 (August 14, 1998), Congress concluded that Iraq's continuing weapons of mass destruction programs threatened vital United States interests and international peace and security, declared Iraq to be in "material and unacceptable breach of its international obligations" and urged the President "to take appropriate action, in accordance with the Constitution and relevant laws of the United States, to bring Iraq into compliance with its international obligations";

Whereas Iraq both poses a continuing threat to the national security of the United States and international peace and security in the Persian Gulf region and remains in material and unacceptable breach of its international obligations by, among other things, continuing to possess and develop a significant chemical and biological weapons capability, actively seeking a nuclear weapons capability, and supporting and harboring terrorist organizations;

Whereas Iraq persists in violating resolutions of the United Nations Security Council by continuing to engage in brutal repression of its civilian population thereby threatening international peace and security in the region, by refusing to release, repatriate, or account for non-Iraqi citizens wrongfully detained by Iraq, including an American serviceman, and by failing to return property wrongfully seized by Iraq from Kuwait;

Whereas the current Iraqi regime has demonstrated its capability and willingness to use weapons of mass destruction against other nations and its own people;

Whereas the current Iraqi regime has demonstrated its continuing hostility toward, and willingness to attack, the United States, including by attempting in 1993 to assassinate former President Bush and by firing on many thousands of occasions on United States and Coalition Armed Forces engaged in enforcing the resolutions of the United Nations Security Council;

Whereas members of al Qaida, an organization bearing responsibility for attacks on the United States, its citizens, and interests, including the attacks that occurred on September 11, 2001, are known to be in Iraq;

Whereas Iraq continues to aid and harbor other international terrorist organizations, including organizations that threaten the lives and safety of United States citizens;

Whereas the attacks on the United States of September 11, 2001, underscored the gravity of the threat posed by the acquisition of weapons of mass destruction by international terrorist organizations;

Whereas Iraq's demonstrated capability and willingness to use weapons of mass destruction, the risk that the current Iraqi regime will either employ those weapons to launch a surprise attack against the United States or its Armed Forces or provide them to international terrorists who would do so, and the extreme magnitude of harm that would result to the United States and its citizens from such an attack, combine to justify action by the United States to defend itself;

Whereas United Nations Security Council Resolution 678 (1990) authorizes the use of all necessary means to enforce United Nations Security Council Resolution 660 (1990) and subsequent relevant resolutions and to compel Iraq to cease certain activities that threaten international peace and security, including the development of weapons of mass destruction and refusal or obstruction of United Nations weapons inspections in violation of United Nations Security Council Resolution 687 (1991), repression of its civilian population in violation of United Nations Security Council Resolution 688 (1991), and threatening its neighbors or United Nations operations in Iraq in violation of United Nations Security Council Resolution 949 (1994);

Whereas in the Authorization for Use of Military Force Against Iraq Resolution (Public Law 102-1), Congress has authorized the President "to use United States Armed Forces pursuant to United Nations Security Council Resolution 678 (1990) in order to achieve implementation of Security Council Resolution 660, 661, 662, 664, 665, 666, 667, 669, 670, 674, and 677";

Whereas in December 1991, Congress expressed its sense that it "supports the use of all necessary means to achieve the goals of United Nations Security Council Resolution 687 as being consistent with the Authorization of Use of Military Force Against Iraq Resolution (Public Law 102-1)," that Iraq's repression of its civilian population violates United Nations Security Council Resolution 688 and "constitutes a continuing threat to the peace, security, and stability of the Persian Gulf region," and that Congress, "supports the use of all necessary means to achieve the goals of United Nations Security Council Resolution 688";

Whereas the Iraq Liberation Act of 1998 (Public Law 105-338) expressed the sense of Congress that it should be the policy of the United States to support efforts to remove from power the current Iraqi regime and promote the emergence of a democratic government to replace that regime;

Whereas on September 12, 2002, President Bush committed the United States to "work with the United Nations Security Council to meet our common challenge" posed by Iraq and to "work for the necessary resolutions," while also making clear that "the Security Council resolutions will be enforced, and the just demands of peace and security will be met, or action will be unavoidable";

Whereas the United States is determined to prosecute the war on terrorism and Iraq's ongoing support for international terrorist groups combined with its development of weapons of mass destruction in direct violation of its obligations under the 1991 cease-fire and other United Nations Security Council resolutions make clear that it is in the national security interests of the United States and in furtherance of the war on terrorism that all relevant United Nations Security Council resolutions be enforced, including through the use of force if necessary;

Whereas Congress has taken steps to pursue vigorously the war on terrorism through the provision of authorities and funding requested by the President to take the necessary actions against international terrorists and terrorist organizations, including those nations, organizations, or persons who planned, authorized, committed, or aided the terrorist attacks that occurred on September 11, 2001, or harbored such persons or organizations;

Whereas the President and Congress are determined to continue to take all appropriate actions against international terrorists and terrorist organizations, including those nations, organizations, or persons who planned, authorized, committed, or aided the terrorist attacks that occurred on September 11, 2001, or harbored such persons or organizations;

Whereas the President has authority under the Constitution to take action in order to deter and prevent acts of international terrorism against the United States, as Congress recognized in the joint resolution on Authorization for Use of Military Force (Public Law 107-40); and Whereas it is in the national security interests of the United States to restore international peace and security to the Persian Gulf region:

Now, therefore, be it

Resolved by the Senate and House of Representatives of the United States of America in Congress [NOTE: Authorization for Use of Military Force Against Iraq Resolution of 2002. 50 USC 1541 note] assembled,

[. . .]

SEC. 2. SUPPORT FOR UNITED STATES DIPLOMATIC EFFORTS.

The Congress of the United States supports the efforts by the President to—

(1) strictly enforce through the United Nations Security Council all relevant Security Council resolutions regarding Iraq and encourages him in those efforts; and

(2) obtain prompt and decisive action by the Security Council to ensure that Iraq abandons its strategy of delay, evasion and noncompliance and promptly and strictly complies with all relevant Security Council resolutions regarding Iraq.

SEC. 3. AUTHORIZATION FOR USE OF UNITED STATES ARMED FORCES.

(a) Authorization.—The President is authorized to use the Armed Forces of the United States as he determines to be necessary and appropriate in order to—

(1) defend the national security of the United States against the continuing threat posed by Iraq; and

(2) enforce all relevant United Nations Security Council resolutions regarding Iraq.

(b) Presidential Determination.—In connection with the exercise of the authority granted in subsection (a) to use force the President shall, prior to such exercise or as soon thereafter as may be feasible, but no later than 48 hours after exercising such authority, make available to the Speaker of the House of Representatives and the President pro tempore of the Senate his determination that—

(1) reliance by the United States on further diplomatic or other peaceful means alone either (A) will not adequately protect the national security of the United States against the continuing threat posed by Iraq or (B) is not likely to lead to enforcement of all relevant United Nations Security Council resolutions regarding Iraq; and

(2) acting pursuant to this joint resolution is consistent with the United States and other countries continuing to take the necessary actions against international terrorist and terrorist organizations, including those nations, organizations, or persons who planned, authorized, committed or aided the terrorist attacks that occurred on September 11, 2001.

(c) War Powers Resolution Requirements.—

(1) Specific statutory authorization.—Consistent with section 8(a)(1) of the War Powers Resolution, the Congress declares that this section is intended to constitute specific statutory authorization within the meaning of section 5(b) of the War Powers Resolution.

(2) Applicability of other requirements.—Nothing in this joint resolution supersedes any requirement of the War Powers Resolution.

[. . .]

Source: *Authorization for Use of Military Force against Iraq Resolution of 2002,* Public Law 107-243, *U.S. Statutes at Large* 116 (2002): 1498.

105. Osama bin Laden, "Letter to the American People," November 2002 [Excerpts]

Introduction

On September 11, 2001, 19 terrorists who belonged to the Al Qaeda network headed by the Islamic terrorist leader Osama bin Laden attacked the United States. Three hijacked civilian airliners flew into the two towers of the World Trade Center in New York City and the Pentagon building in Washington, D.C., headquarters of the U.S. Department of Defense, killing close to 3,000 people in all. Bin Laden, a fundamentalist Muslim militant from a wealthy Saudi family, had mounted several earlier attacks on American military installations and other facilities elsewhere and viewed the United States as the greatest enemy of Islam and was fanatically determined to wage a religious war, or jihad, against Americans and all allied with them. In several public statements, including the "Letter to the American People" published in Arabic on the Internet in 2002 and later translated into English, he enumerated what he viewed as American threats and enmity toward Islam. Bin Laden cited what he considered to be the immoral and irreligious character of American life, which was an affront to Muslim principles. Foremost among U.S. offenses, however, he placed American support for Israel, followed by its presence in the Persian Gulf and American opposition to various Muslim governments and groups around the world. After the September 11 attacks, U.S. president George W. Bush quickly declared that waging a global "war on terror" wherever it raised its head was now by far the most significant U.S. foreign policy priority. The links that bin Laden drew between his organization's attacks on American landmarks and other facilities and his adamant hostility to Israel meant that the U.S. government and the American people were likely to view Palestinian and other terrorist operations against that country and its citizens and Israeli measures designed to repress them in the context of worldwide international efforts to combat the threat of armed Islamic militancy.

Primary Source

[. . .]

Some American writers have published articles under the title 'On what basis are we fighting?' These articles have generated a number of responses, some of which adhered to the truth and were based on Islamic Law, and others which have not. Here we wanted to outline the truth—as an explanation and warning—hoping for Allah's reward, seeking success and support from Him.

While seeking Allah's help, we form our reply based on two questions directed at the Americans:

(Q1) Why are we fighting and opposing you?

(Q2) What are we calling you to, and what do we want from you?

As for the first question: Why are we fighting and opposing you? The answer is very simple:

(1) Because you attacked us and continue to attack us.

(a) You attacked us in Palestine:

(i) Palestine, which has sunk under military occupation for more than 80 years. The British handed over Palestine, with your help and your support, to the Jews, who have occupied it for more than 50 years; years overflowing with oppression, tyranny, crimes, killing, expulsion, destruction and devastation. The creation and continuation of Israel is one of the greatest crimes, and you are the leaders of its criminals. And of course there is no need to explain and prove the degree of American support for Israel. The creation of Israel is a crime which must be erased. Each and every person whose hands have become polluted in the contribution towards this crime must pay its price, and pay for it heavily.

(ii) It brings us both laughter and tears to see that you have not yet tired of repeating your fabricated lies that the Jews have a historical right to Palestine, as it was promised to them in the Torah. Anyone who disputes with them on this alleged fact is accused of anti-semitism. This is one of the most fallacious, widely-circulated fabrications in history. The people of Palestine are pure Arabs and original Semites. It is the Muslims who are the inheritors of Moses (peace be upon him) and the inheritors of the real Torah that has not been changed. Muslims believe in all of the Prophets, including Abraham, Moses, Jesus and Muhammad, peace and blessings of Allah be upon them all. If the followers of Moses have been promised a right to Palestine in the Torah, then the Muslims are the most worthy nation of this.

When the Muslims conquered Palestine and drove out the Romans, Palestine and Jerusalem returned to Islam, the religion of all the Prophets peace be upon them. Therefore, the call to a historical right to Palestine cannot be raised against the Islamic Ummah that believes in all the Prophets of Allah (peace and blessings be upon them)—and we make no distinction between them.

(iii) The blood pouring out of Palestine must be equally revenged. You must know that the Palestinians do not cry alone; their women are not widowed alone; their sons are not orphaned alone.

(b) You attacked us in Somalia; you supported the Russian atrocities against us in Chechnya, the Indian oppression against us in Kashmir, and the Jewish aggression against us in Lebanon.

(c) Under your supervision, consent and orders, the governments of our countries which act as your agents, attack us on a daily basis;

(i) These governments prevent our people from establishing the Islamic Shariah, using violence and lies to do so.

(ii) These governments give us a taste of humiliation, and places us in a large prison of fear and subdual.

(iii) These governments steal our Ummah's wealth and sell them to you at a paltry price.

(iv) These governments have surrendered to the Jews, and handed them most of Palestine, acknowledging the existence of their state over the dismembered limbs of their own people.

(v) The removal of these governments is an obligation upon us, and a necessary step to free the Ummah, to make the Shariah the supreme law and to regain Palestine. And our fight against these governments is not separate from our fight against you.

(d) You steal our wealth and oil at paltry prices because of you[r] international influence and military threats. This theft is indeed the biggest theft ever witnessed by mankind in the history of the world.

(e) Your forces occupy our countries; you spread your military bases throughout them; you corrupt our lands, and you besiege our sanctities, to protect the security of the Jews and to ensure the continuity of your pillage of our treasures.

(f) You have starved the Muslims of Iraq, where children die every day. It is a wonder that more than 1.5 million Iraqi children have died as a result of your sanctions, and you did not show concern. Yet when 3000 of your people died, the entire world rises and has not yet sat down.

(g) You have supported the Jews in their idea that Jerusalem is their eternal capital, and agreed to move your embassy there. With your help and under your protection, the Israelis are planning to destroy the Al-Aqsa mosque. Under the protection of your weapons, Sharon entered the Al-Aqsa mosque, to pollute it as a preparation to capture and destroy it.

(2) These tragedies and calamities are only a few examples of your oppression and aggression against us. It is commanded by our religion and intellect that the oppressed have a right to return the aggression. Do not await anything from us but Jihad, resistance and revenge. Is it in any way rational to expect that after America has attacked us for more than half a century, that we will then leave her to live in security and peace?!!

(3) You may then dispute that all the above does not justify aggression against civilians, for crimes they did not commit and offenses in which they did not partake:

(a) This argument contradicts your continuous repetition that America is the land of freedom, and its leaders in this world. Therefore, the American people are the ones who choose their government by way of their own free will; a choice which stems from their agreement to its policies. Thus the American people have chosen, consented to, and affirmed their support for the Israeli oppression of the Palestinians, the occupation and usurpation of their land, and its continuous killing, torture, punishment

and expulsion of the Palestinians. The American people have the ability and choice to refuse the policies of their Government and even to change it if they want.

(b) The American people are the ones who pay the taxes which fund the planes that bomb us in Afghanistan, the tanks that strike and destroy our homes in Palestine, the armies which occupy our lands in the Arabian Gulf, and the fleets which ensure the blockade of Iraq. These tax dollars are given to Israel for it to continue to attack us and penetrate our lands. So the American people are the ones who fund the attacks against us, and they are the ones who oversee the expenditure of these monies in the way they wish, through their elected candidates.

(c) Also the American army is part of the American people. It is this very same people who are shamelessly helping the Jews fight against us.

(d) The American people are the ones who employ both their men and their women in the American Forces which attack us.

(e) This is why the American people cannot be not innocent of all the crimes committed by the Americans and Jews against us.

(f) Allah, the Almighty, legislated the permission and the option to take revenge. Thus, if we are attacked, then we have the right to attack back. Whoever has destroyed our villages and towns, then we have the right to destroy their villages and towns. Whoever has stolen our wealth, then we have the right to destroy their economy. And whoever has killed our civilians, then we have the right to kill theirs.

The American Government and press still refuses to answer the question:

Why did they attack us in New York and Washington?

If [Israeli prime minister Ariel] Sharon is a man of peace in the eyes of Bush, then we are also men of peace!!! America does not understand the language of manners and principles, so we are addressing it using the language it understands.

(Q2) As for the second question that we want to answer: What are we calling you to, and what do we want from you?

(1) The first thing that we are calling you to is Islam.

(a) The religion of the Unification of God; of freedom from associating partners with Him, and rejection of this; of complete love of Him, the Exalted; of complete submission to His Laws; and of the discarding of all the opinions, orders, theories and religions which contradict with the religion He sent down to His Prophet

Muhammad (peace be upon him). Islam is the religion of all the prophets, and makes no distinction between them—peace be upon them all.

It is to this religion that we call you; the seal of all the previous religions. It is the religion of Unification of God, sincerity, the best of manners, righteousness, mercy, honour, purity, and piety. It is the religion of showing kindness to others, establishing justice between them, granting them their rights, and defending the oppressed and the persecuted. It is the religion of enjoining the good and forbidding the evil with the hand, tongue and heart. It is the religion of Jihad in the way of Allah so that Allah's Word and religion reign Supreme. And it is the religion of unity and agreement on the obedience to Allah, and total equality between all people, without regarding their colour, sex, or language.

(b) It is the religion whose book—the Quran—will remained [sic] preserved and unchanged, after the other Divine books and messages have been changed. The Quran is the miracle until the Day of Judgment. Allah has challenged anyone to bring a book like the Quran or even ten verses like it.

(2) The second thing we call you to, is to stop your oppression, lies, immorality and debauchery that has spread among you.

(a) We call you to be a people of manners, principles, honour, and purity; to reject the immoral acts of fornication, homosexuality, intoxicants, gambling, and trading with interest.

We call you to all of this that you may be freed from that which you have become caught up in; that you may be freed from the deceptive lies that you are a great nation, that your leaders spread amongst you to conceal from you the despicable state to which you have reached.

(b) It is saddening to tell you that you are the worst civilization witnessed by the history of mankind:

(i) You are the nation who, rather than ruling by the Shariah of Allah in its Constitution and Laws, choose to invent your own laws as you will and desire. You separate religion from your policies, contradicting the pure nature which affirms Absolute Authority to the Lord and your Creator. You flee from the embarrassing question posed to you: How is it possible for Allah the Almighty to create His creation, grant them power over all the creatures and land, grant them all the amenities of life, and then deny them that which they are most in need of: knowledge of the laws which govern their lives?

(ii) You are the nation that permits Usury, which has been forbidden by all the religions. Yet you build your economy and investments on Usury. As a result of this, in all its different forms and guises, the Jews have taken control of your economy, through

which they have then taken control of your media, and now control all aspects of your life making you their servants and achieving their aims at your expense; precisely what Benjamin Franklin warned you against.

(iii) You are a nation that permits the production, trading and usage of intoxicants. You also permit drugs, and only forbid the trade of them, even though your nation is the largest consumer of them.

(iv) You are a nation that permits acts of immorality, and you consider them to be pillars of personal freedom. You have continued to sink down this abyss from level to level until incest has spread amongst you, in the face of which neither your sense of honour nor your laws object.

Who can forget your President Clinton's immoral acts committed in the official Oval office? After that you did not even bring him to account, other than that he 'made a mistake', after which everything passed with no punishment. Is there a worse kind of event for which your name will go down in history and [be] remembered by nations?

(v) You are a nation that permits gambling in all its forms. The companies practice this as well, resulting in the investments becoming active and the criminals becoming rich.

(vi) You are a nation that exploits women like consumer products or advertising tools calling upon customers to purchase them. You use women to serve passengers, visitors, and strangers to increase your profit margins. You then rant that you support the liberation of women.

(vii) You are a nation that practices the trade of sex in all its forms, directly and indirectly. Giant corporations and establishments are established on this, under the name of art, entertainment, tourism and freedom, and other deceptive names you attribute to it.

(viii) And because of all this, you have been described in history as a nation that spreads diseases that were unknown to man in the past. Go ahead and boast to the nations of man, that you brought them AIDS as a Satanic American Invention.

(ix) You have destroyed nature with your industrial waste and gases more than any other nation in history. Despite this, you refuse to sign the Kyoto agreement so that you can secure the profit of your greedy companies and industries.

(x) Your law is the law of the rich and wealthy people, who hold sway in their political parties, and fund their election campaigns with their gifts. Behind them stand the Jews, who control your policies, media and economy.

(xi) That which you are singled out for in the history of mankind, is that you have used your force to destroy mankind more than any other nation in history; not to defend principles and values, but to hasten to secure your interests and profits. You who dropped a nuclear bomb on Japan, even though Japan was ready to negotiate an end to the war. How many acts of oppression, tyranny and injustice have you carried out, O callers to freedom?

(xii) Let us not forget one of your major characteristics: your duality in both manners and values; your hypocrisy in manners and principles. All manners, principles and values have two scales: one for you and one for the others.

(a) The freedom and democracy that you call to is for yourselves and for white race only; as for the rest of the world, you impose upon them your monstrous, destructive policies and Governments, which you call the 'American friends'. Yet you prevent them from establishing democracies. When the Islamic party in Algeria wanted to practice democracy and they won the election, you unleashed your agents in the Algerian army onto them, and to attack them with tanks and guns, to imprison them and torture them—a new lesson from the 'American book of democracy'!!!

(b) Your policy on prohibiting and forcibly removing weapons of mass destruction to ensure world peace: it only applies to those countries which you do not permit to possess such weapons. As for the countries you consent to, such as Israel, then they are allowed to keep and use such weapons to defend their security. Anyone else who you suspect might be manufacturing or keeping these kinds of weapons, you call them criminals and you take military action against them.

(c) You are the last ones to respect the resolutions and policies of International Law, yet you claim to want to selectively punish anyone else who does the same. Israel has for more than 50 years been pushing UN resolutions and rules against the wall with the full support of America.

(d) As for the war criminals which you censure and form criminal courts for—you shamelessly ask that your own are granted immunity!! However, history will not forget the war crimes that you committed against the Muslims and the rest of the world; those you have killed in Japan, Afghanistan, Somalia, Lebanon and Iraq will remain a shame that you will never be able to escape. It will suffice to remind you of your latest war crimes in Afghanistan, in which densely populated innocent civilian villages were destroyed, bombs were dropped on mosques causing the roof of the mosque to come crashing down on the heads of the Muslims praying inside. You are the ones who broke the agreement with the Mujahideen when they left Qunduz, bombing them in Jangi fort, and killing more than 1,000 of your prisoners through suffocation and thirst. Allah alone knows how many people have died by torture at the hands of you and your agents. Your planes remain in the Afghan skies, looking for anyone remotely suspicious.

(e) You have claimed to be the vanguards of Human Rights, and your Ministry of Foreign affairs issues annual reports containing statistics of those countries that violate any Human Rights. However, all these things vanished when the Mujahideen hit you, and you then implemented the methods of the same documented governments that you used to curse. In America, you captured thousands the Muslims and Arabs, took them into custody with neither reason, court trial, nor even disclosing their names. You issued newer, harsher laws.

What happens in Guantanamo is a historical embarrassment to America and its values, and it screams into your faces—you hypocrites, "What is the value of your signature on any agreement or treaty?"

(3) What we call you to thirdly is to take an honest stance with yourselves—and I doubt you will do so—to discover that you are a nation without principles or manners, and that the values and principles to you are something which you merely demand from others, not that which you yourself must adhere to.

(4) We also advise you to stop supporting Israel, and to end your support of the Indians in Kashmir, the Russians against the Chechens and to also cease supporting the Manila Government against the Muslims in Southern Philippines.

(5) We also advise you to pack your luggage and get out of our lands. We desire for you goodness, guidance, and righteousness, so do not force us to send you back as cargo in coffins.

(6) Sixthly, we call upon you to end your support of the corrupt leaders in our countries. Do not interfere in our politics and method of education. Leave us alone, or else expect us in New York and Washington.

(7) We also call you to deal with us and interact with us on the basis of mutual interests and benefits, rather than the policies of subdual, theft and occupation, and not to continue your policy of supporting the Jews because this will result in more disasters for you.

If you fail to respond to all these conditions, then prepare for fight with the Islamic Nation. The Nation of Monotheism, that puts complete trust on Allah and fears none other than Him....

[...]

The Nation of Martyrdom; the Nation that desires death more than you desire life.

[...]

The Islamic Nation that was able to dismiss and destroy the previous evil Empires like yourself; the Nation that rejects your attacks, wishes to remove your evils, and is prepared to fight you. You are well aware that the Islamic Nation, from the very core of its soul, despises your haughtiness and arrogance.

If the Americans refuse to listen to our advice and the goodness, guidance and righteousness that we call them to, then be aware that you will lose this Crusade Bush began, just like the other previous Crusades in which you were humiliated by the hands of the Mujahideen, fleeing to your home in great silence and disgrace. If the Americans do not respond, then their fate will be that of the Soviets who fled from Afghanistan to deal with their military defeat, political breakup, ideological downfall, and economic bankruptcy.

This is our message to the Americans, as an answer to theirs. Do they now know why we fight them and over which form of ignorance, by the permission of Allah, we shall be victorious?

> **Source:** Osama bin Laden, "Letter to the American People," GlobalSecurity.org, http://www.globalsecurity.org/security/library/report/2002/021120-ubl.htm.

106. United Nations Security Council Resolution 1441, November 8, 2002 [Excerpt]

Introduction

Under pressure from the United States and Great Britain, which were moving toward a war with Iraq that they seemed to welcome, in November 2002 the United Nations (UN) Security Council passed a resolution that most of its members hoped would resolve the situation without hostilities. At this stage, the primary justification that the U.S. and British governments cited in favor of military intervention was their belief that Iraq was amassing large quantities of biological, chemical, and nuclear weapons of mass destruction (WMDs). Earlier 1991 resolutions mandated that as a condition of the restoration of peace, Iraq allow UN inspectors free access to all its weapons manufacturing and storage facilities in order to verify that the country was neither producing nor stockpiling WMDs, but since 1998 all such cooperation by Iraq had been lacking. The UN therefore demanded that Iraq address its failure to comply with earlier resolutions and put in place practical arrangements to restore unfettered access and inspections by appropriate personnel of both the International Atomic Energy Authority (IAEA) and the UN. The resolution specifically declared that it represented "a final opportunity" to allow Iraq to comply with its "disarmament obligations." Security Council members passed

the resolution unanimously. Several members, notably Russia, China, and France, hoped that this would suffice to avert war. Even though Britain and the United States, which also voted for the resolution, undoubtedly believed that it would prove unavailing and ineffective, U.S. president George W. Bush and British prime minister Tony Blair felt it necessary to support the resolution, if only to demonstrate that before resorting to outright war, they had explored all other alternative avenues open to them. In December 2002 after the passage of this resolution, President Saddam Hussein of Iraq allowed personnel of the United Nations Monitoring, Verification and Inspection Commission (UNMOVIC), created in December 1999, to enter Iraq, where they remained until March 2003. During that time UNMOVIC inspectors failed to find any evidence that Iraq possessed significant WMDs.

Primary Source

The United Nations, International Law, and the War in Iraq S/RES/1441 (2002)

8 November 2002

UN Security Council Resolution 1441 (2002)

Adopted by the Security Council at its 4644th meeting, on 8 November 2002

The Security Council, Recalling all its previous relevant resolutions, in particular its resolutions 661 (1990) of 6 August 1990, 678 (1990) of 29 November 1990, 686 (1991) of 2 March 1991, 687 (1991) of 3 April 1991, 688 (1991) of 5 April 1991, 707 (1991) of 15 August 1991, 715 (1991) of 11 October 1991, 986 (1995) of 14 April 1995, and 1284 (1999) of 17 December 1999, and all the relevant statements of its President,

Recalling also its resolution 1382 (2001) of 29 November 2001 and its intention to implement it fully,

Recognizing the threat Iraq's non-compliance with Council resolutions and proliferation of weapons of mass destruction and long-range missiles poses to international peace and security,

Recalling that its resolution 678 (1990) authorized Member States to use all necessary means to uphold and implement its resolution 660 (1990) of 2 August 1990 and all relevant resolutions subsequent to resolution 660 (1990) and to restore international peace and security in the area,

Further recalling that its resolution 687 (1991) imposed obligations on Iraq as a necessary step for achievement of its stated objective of restoring international peace and security in the area,

Deploring the fact that Iraq has not provided an accurate, full, final, and complete disclosure, as required by resolution 687

(1991), of all aspects of its programmes to develop weapons of mass destruction and ballistic missiles with a range greater than one hundred and fifty kilometres, and of all holdings of such weapons, their components and production facilities and locations, as well as all other nuclear programmes, including any which it claims are for purposes not related to nuclear-weapons-usable material,

Deploring further that Iraq repeatedly obstructed immediate, unconditional, and unrestricted access to sites designated by the United Nations Special Commission (UNSCOM) and the International Atomic Energy Agency (IAEA), failed to cooperate fully and unconditionally with UNSCOM and IAEA weapons inspectors, as required by resolution 687 (1991), and ultimately ceased all cooperation with UNSCOM and the IAEA in 1998,

Deploring the absence, since December 1998, in Iraq of international monitoring, inspection, and verification, as required by relevant resolutions, of weapons of mass destruction and ballistic missiles, in spite of the Council's repeated demands that Iraq provide immediate, unconditional, and unrestricted access to the United Nations Monitoring, Verification and Inspection Commission (UNMOVIC), established in resolution 1284 (1999) as the successor organization to UNSCOM, and the IAEA, and regretting the consequent prolonging of the crisis in the region and the suffering of the Iraqi people,

Deploring also that the Government of Iraq has failed to comply with its commitments pursuant to resolution 687 (1991) with regard to terrorism, pursuant to resolution 688 (1991) to end repression of its civilian population and to provide access by international humanitarian organizations to all those in need of assistance in Iraq, and pursuant to resolutions 686 (1991), 687 (1991), and 1284 (1999) to return or cooperate in accounting for Kuwaiti and third country nationals wrongfully detained by Iraq, or to return Kuwaiti property wrongfully seized by Iraq,

Recalling that in its resolution 687 (1991) the Council declared that a ceasefire would be based on acceptance by Iraq of the provisions of that resolution, including the obligations on Iraq contained therein,

Determined to ensure full and immediate compliance by Iraq without conditions or restrictions with its obligations under resolution 687 (1991) and other relevant resolutions and recalling that the resolutions of the Council constitute the governing standard of Iraqi compliance,

Recalling that the effective operation of UNMOVIC, as the successor organization to the Special Commission, and the IAEA is essential for the implementation of resolution 687 (1991) and other relevant resolutions,

Noting that the letter dated 16 September 2002 from the Minister for Foreign Affairs of Iraq addressed to the Secretary-General is a necessary first step toward rectifying Iraq's continued failure to comply with relevant Council resolutions,

Noting further the letter dated 8 October 2002 from the Executive Chairman of UNMOVIC and the Director-General of the IAEA to General Al-Saadi of the Government of Iraq laying out the practical arrangements, as a follow-up to their meeting in Vienna, that are prerequisites for the resumption of inspections in Iraq by UNMOVIC and the IAEA, and expressing the gravest concern at the continued failure by the Government of Iraq to provide confirmation of the arrangements as laid out in that letter,

Reaffirming the commitment of all Member States to the sovereignty and territorial integrity of Iraq, Kuwait, and the neighbouring States,

Commending the Secretary-General and members of the League of Arab States and its Secretary-General for their efforts in this regard,

Determined to secure full compliance with its decisions, Acting under Chapter VII of the Charter of the United Nations,

1. Decides that Iraq has been and remains in material breach of its obligations under relevant resolutions, including resolution 687 (1991), in particular through Iraq's failure to cooperate with United Nations inspectors and the IAEA, and to complete the actions required under paragraphs 8 to 13 of resolution 687 (1991);

2. Decides, while acknowledging paragraph 1 above, to afford Iraq, by this resolution, a final opportunity to comply with its disarmament obligations under relevant resolutions of the Council; and accordingly decides to set up an enhanced inspection regime with the aim of bringing to full and verified completion the disarmament process established by resolution 687 (1991) and subsequent resolutions of the Council;

3. Decides that, in order to begin to comply with its disarmament obligations, in addition to submitting the required biannual declarations, the Government of Iraq shall provide to UNMOVIC, the IAEA, and the Council, not later than 30 days from the date of this resolution, a currently accurate, full, and complete declaration of all aspects of its programmes to develop chemical, biological, and nuclear weapons, ballistic missiles, and other delivery systems such as unmanned aerial vehicles and dispersal systems designed for use on aircraft, including any holdings and precise locations of such weapons, components, subcomponents, stocks of agents, and related material and equipment, the locations and work of its research, development and production facilities, as well as all other chemical, biological, and nuclear programmes, including

any which it claims are for purposes not related to weapon production or material;

4. Decides that false statements or omissions in the declarations submitted by Iraq pursuant to this resolution and failure by Iraq at any time to comply with, and cooperate fully in the implementation of, this resolution shall constitute a further material breach of Iraq's obligations and will be reported to the Council for assessment in accordance with paragraphs 11 and 12 below;

5. Decides that Iraq shall provide UNMOVIC and the IAEA immediate, unimpeded, unconditional, and unrestricted access to any and all, including underground, areas, facilities, buildings, equipment, records, and means of transport which they wish to inspect, as well as immediate, unimpeded, unrestricted, and private access to all officials and other persons whom UNMOVIC or the IAEA wish to interview in the mode or location of UNMOVIC's or the IAEA's choice pursuant to any aspect of their mandates; further decides that UNMOVIC and the IAEA may at their discretion conduct interviews inside or outside of Iraq, may facilitate the travel of those interviewed and family members outside of Iraq, and that, at the sole discretion of UNMOVIC and the IAEA, such interviews may occur without the presence of observers from the Iraqi Government; and instructs UNMOVIC and requests the IAEA to resume inspections no later than 45 days following adoption of this resolution and to update the Council 60 days thereafter;

6. Endorses the 8 October 2002 letter from the Executive Chairman of UNMOVIC and the Director-General of the IAEA to General Al-Saadi of the Government of Iraq, which is annexed hereto, and decides that the contents of the letter shall be binding upon Iraq;

7. Decides further that, in view of the prolonged interruption by Iraq of the presence of UNMOVIC and the IAEA and in order for them to accomplish the tasks set forth in this resolution and all previous relevant resolutions and notwithstanding prior understandings, the Council hereby establishes the following revised or additional authorities, which shall be binding upon Iraq, to facilitate their work in Iraq:

—UNMOVIC and the IAEA shall determine the composition of their inspection teams and ensure that these teams are composed of the most qualified and experienced experts available;

—All UNMOVIC and IAEA personnel shall enjoy the privileges and immunities, corresponding to those of experts on mission, provided in the Convention on Privileges and Immunities of the United Nations and the Agreement on the Privileges and Immunities of the IAEA;

—UNMOVIC and the IAEA shall have unrestricted rights of entry into and out of Iraq, the right to free, unrestricted, and immediate movement to and from inspection sites, and the right to inspect any sites and buildings, including immediate, unimpeded, unconditional, and unrestricted access to Presidential Sites equal to that at other sites, notwithstanding the provisions of resolution 1154 (1998) of 2 March 1998;

—UNMOVIC and the IAEA shall have the right to be provided by Iraq the names of all personnel currently and formerly associated with Iraq's chemical, biological, nuclear, and ballistic missile programmes and the associated research, development, and production facilities;

—Security of UNMOVIC and IAEA facilities shall be ensured by sufficient United Nations security guards;

—UNMOVIC and the IAEA shall have the right to declare, for the purposes of freezing a site to be inspected, exclusion zones, including surrounding areas and transit corridors, in which Iraq will suspend ground and aerial movement so that nothing is changed in or taken out of a site being inspected;

—UNMOVIC and the IAEA shall have the free and unrestricted use and landing of fixed- and rotary-winged aircraft, including manned and unmanned reconnaissance vehicles;

—UNMOVIC and the IAEA shall have the right at their sole discretion verifiably to remove, destroy, or render harmless all prohibited weapons, subsystems, components, records, materials, and other related items, and the right to impound or close any facilities or equipment for the production thereof; and

—UNMOVIC and the IAEA shall have the right to free import and use of equipment or materials for inspections and to seize and export any equipment, materials, or documents taken during inspections, without search of UNMOVIC or IAEA personnel or official or personal baggage;

8. Decides further that Iraq shall not take or threaten hostile acts directed against any representative or personnel of the United Nations or the IAEA or of any Member State taking action to uphold any Council resolution;

9. Requests the Secretary-General immediately to notify Iraq of this resolution, which is binding on Iraq; demands that Iraq confirm within seven days of that notification its intention to comply fully with this resolution; and demands further that Iraq cooperate immediately, unconditionally, and actively with UNMOVIC and the IAEA;

10. Requests all Member States to give full support to UNMOVIC and the IAEA in the discharge of their mandates, including by providing any information related to prohibited programmes or

other aspects of their mandates, including on Iraqi attempts since 1998 to acquire prohibited items, and by recommending sites to be inspected, persons to be interviewed, conditions of such interviews, and data to be collected, the results of which shall be reported to the Council by UNMOVIC and the IAEA;

11. Directs the Executive Chairman of UNMOVIC and the Director-General of the IAEA to report immediately to the Council any interference by Iraq with inspection activities, as well as any failure by Iraq to comply with its disarmament obligations, including its obligations regarding inspections under this resolution;

12. Decides to convene immediately upon receipt of a report in accordance with paragraphs 4 or 11 above, in order to consider the situation and the need for full compliance with all of the relevant Council resolutions in order to secure international peace and security;

13. Recalls, in that context, that the Council has repeatedly warned Iraq that it will face serious consequences as a result of its continued violations of its obligations;

14. Decides to remain seized of the matter.

[. . .]

> **Source:** United Nations Security Council, S/Res/1441 (2002), November 8, 2002, http://www.worldpress.org/specials/iraq/unscr1441.htm.

107. U.S. Congress, The Homeland Security Act (Summary), November 25, 2002 [Excerpts]

Introduction

The U.S. Homeland Security Act (Public Law No. 107-296), passed a little more than a year after the terrorist attacks of September 11, 2001, was a sweeping piece of antiterrorist legislation. The act established the Department of Homeland Security that was mandated to coordinate and facilitate all internal antiterrorist efforts and handle domestic emergencies within the United States. The new department, which by 2007 had around 184,000 employees, had overall responsibility for ensuring security in airports and other transportation facilities and for supervising immigration and customs controls, all of which became far more restrictive and cumbersome than in the past. Tighter security procedures in travel and the protection of public buildings that might be terrorist targets were the most visible aspect of the department's activities and were probably the area in which it most impinged on the lives of average Americans and visitors to the United States. The department

was also charged with safeguarding the United States against attacks by either conventional weapons or biological, chemical, or nuclear agents. To facilitate its efforts, the department was given broad authority to monitor and scrutinize the activities of American citizens and others physically present in the United States and to detain such individuals without trial or access to outside assistance for lengthy periods. Domestically and internationally, these provisions provoked considerable uneasiness among many critics on the grounds that they contravened constitutional guarantees of freedom of speech, religion, assembly, and privacy and the right to counsel and due process of law, values that American leaders claimed to be protecting at home and abroad. Conservatives, however, claimed that such curbs were essential to prevent further terrorist assaults on the United States and its citizens.

Primary Source

Summary as of:

11/19/2002—Passed Senate amended.

Homeland Security Act of 2002—**Title I: Department of Homeland Security**—(Sec. 101) Establishes a Department of Homeland Security (DHS) as an executive department of the United States, headed by a Secretary of Homeland Security (Secretary) appointed by the President, by and with the advice and consent of the Senate, to: (1) prevent terrorist attacks within the United States; (2) reduce the vulnerability of the United States to terrorism; (3) minimize the damage, and assist in the recovery, from terrorist attacks that occur within the United States; (4) carry out all functions of entities transferred to DHS; (5) ensure that the functions of the agencies and subdivisions within DHS that are not related directly to securing the homeland are not diminished or neglected except by a specific Act of Congress; (6) ensure that the overall economic security of the United States is not diminished by efforts, activities, and programs aimed at securing the homeland; and (7) monitor connections between illegal drug trafficking and terrorism, coordinate efforts to sever such connections, and otherwise contribute to efforts to interdict illegal drug trafficking. Vests primary responsibility for investigating and prosecuting acts of terrorism in Federal, State, and local law enforcement agencies with proper jurisdiction except as specifically provided by law with respect to entities transferred to DHS under this Act.

(Sec. 102) Directs the Secretary to appoint a Special Assistant to carry out specified homeland security liaison activities between DHS and the private sector.

(Sec. 103) Creates the following: (1) a Deputy Secretary of Homeland Security; (2) an Under Secretary for Information Analysis and Infrastructure Protection; (3) an Under Secretary for Science and Technology; (4) an Under Secretary for Border and Transportation Security; (5) an Under Secretary for Emergency Preparedness and Response; (6) a Director of the Bureau of Citizenship and Immigration Services; (7) an Under Secretary for Management; (8) not more than 12 Assistant Secretaries; and (9) a General Counsel. Establishes an Inspector General (to be appointed under the Inspector General Act of 1978). Requires the following individuals to assist the Secretary in the performance of the Secretary's functions: (1) the Commandant of the Coast Guard; (2) the Director of the Secret Service; (3) a Chief Information Officer; (4) a Chief Human Capital Officer; (5) a Chief Financial Officer; and (6) an Officer for Civil Rights and Civil Liberties.

Title II: Information Analysis and Infrastructure Protection—Subtitle A: Directorate for Information Analysis and Infrastructure Protection; Access to Information—(Sec. 201)

Establishes in the Department: (1) a Directorate for Information Analysis and Infrastructure Protection, headed by an Under Secretary for Information Analysis and Infrastructure Protection; (2) an Assistant Secretary for Information Analysis; and (3) an Assistant Secretary for Infrastructure Protection.

Requires the Under Secretary to: (1) access, receive, and analyze law enforcement and intelligence information from Federal, State, and local agencies and the private sector to identify the nature, scope, and identity of terrorist threats to the United States, as well as potential U.S. vulnerabilities; (2) carry out comprehensive assessments of vulnerabilities of key U.S. resources and critical infrastructures; (3) integrate relevant information, analyses, and vulnerability assessments to identify protection priorities; (4) ensure timely and efficient Department access to necessary information for discharging responsibilities; (5) develop a comprehensive national plan for securing key U.S. resources and critical infrastructures; (6) recommend necessary measures to protect such resources and infrastructure in coordination with other entities; (7) administer the Homeland Security Advisory System; (8) review, analyze, and make recommendations for improvements in policies and procedures governing the sharing of law enforcement, intelligence, and intelligence-related information and other information related to homeland security within the Federal Government and between the Federal Government and State and local government agencies and authorities; (9) disseminate Department homeland security information to other appropriate Federal, State, and local agencies; (10) consult with the Director of Central Intelligence (DCI) and other appropriate Federal intelligence, law enforcement, or other elements to establish collection priorities and strategies for information relating the terrorism threats; (11) consult with State and local governments and private entities to ensure appropriate exchanges of information relating to such threats; (12) ensure the protection from unauthorized disclosure of homeland security and intelligence information; (13) request additional information from appropriate entities relating to threats of terrorism in the United States; (14) establish and utilize a secure communications and information technology infrastructure for receiving and analyzing data; (15) ensure the compatibility and privacy protection of shared information databases and analytical tools; (16) coordinate training and other support to facilitate the identification and sharing of information; (17) coordinate activities with elements of the intelligence community, Federal, State, and local law enforcement agencies, and the private sector; and (18) provide intelligence and information analysis and support to other elements of the Department. Provides for: (1) staffing, including the use of private sector analysts; and (2) cooperative agreements for the detail of appropriate personnel.

Transfers to the Secretary the functions, personnel, assets, and liabilities of the following entities: (1) the National Infrastructure Protection Center of the Federal Bureau of Investigation (other than the Computer Investigations and Operations Section); (2) the National Communications System of the Department of Defense; (3) the Critical Infrastructure Assurance Offices of the Department of Commerce; (4) the National Infrastructure Simulation and Analysis Center of the Department of Energy and its energy security and assurance program; and (5) the Federal Computer Incident Response Center of the General Services Administration.

Amends the National Security Act of 1947 to include as elements of the intelligence community the Department elements concerned with analyses of foreign intelligence information.

(Sec. 202) Gives the Secretary access to all reports, assessments, analyses, and unevaluated intelligence relating to threats of terrorism against the United States, and to all information concerning infrastructure or other vulnerabilities to terrorism, whether or not such information has been analyzed. Requires all Federal agencies to promptly provide to the Secretary: (1) all reports, assessments, and analytical information relating to such threats and to other areas of responsibility assigned to the Secretary; (2) all information concerning the vulnerability of U.S. infrastructure or other U.S. vulnerabilities to terrorism, whether or not it has been analyzed; (3) all other information relating to significant and credible threats of terrorism, whether or not it has been analyzed; and (4) such other information or material as the President may direct. Requires the Secretary to be provided with certain terrorism-related information from law enforcement agencies that is currently required to be provided to the DCI.

Subtitle B: Critical Infrastructure Information—Critical Infrastructure Information Act of 2002—(Sec. 213) Allows a critical infrastructure protection program to be so designated by either the President or the Secretary.

(Sec. 214) Exempts from the Freedom of Information Act and other Federal and State disclosure requirements any critical infrastructure information that is voluntarily submitted to a covered Federal agency for use in the security of critical infrastructure and protected systems, analysis, warning, interdependency study, recovery, reconstitution, or other informational purpose when accompanied by an express statement that such information is being submitted voluntarily in expectation of such nondisclosure protection. Requires the Secretary to establish specified procedures for the receipt, care, and storage by Federal agencies of critical infrastructure information voluntarily submitted. Provides criminal penalties for the unauthorized disclosure of such information.

Authorizes the Federal Government to issue advisories, alerts, and warnings to relevant companies, targeted sectors, other governmental entities, or the general public regarding potential threats to critical infrastructure.

Subtitle C: Information Security—(Sec. 221) Requires the Secretary to establish procedures on the use of shared information that: (1) limit its re-dissemination to ensure it is not used for an unauthorized purpose; (2) ensure its security and confidentiality; (3) protect the constitutional and statutory rights of individuals who are subjects of such information; and (4) provide data integrity through the timely removal and destruction of obsolete or erroneous names and information.

(Sec. 222) Directs the Secretary to appoint a senior Department official to assume primary responsibility for information privacy policy.

(Sec. 223) Directs the Under Secretary to provide: (1) to State and local government entities and, upon request, to private entities that own or operate critical information systems, analysis and warnings related to threats to and vulnerabilities of such systems, as well as crisis management support in response to threats to or attacks upon such systems; and (2) technical assistance, upon request, to private sector and other government entities with respect to emergency recovery plans to respond to major failures of such systems.

(Sec. 224) Authorizes the Under Secretary to establish a national technology guard (known as NET Guard) to assist local communities to respond to and recover from attacks on information systems and communications networks.

(Sec. 225) Cyber Security Enhancement Act of 2002—Directs the U.S. Sentencing Commission to review and amend Federal sentencing guidelines and otherwise address crimes involving fraud in connection with computers and access to protected information, protected computers, or restricted data in interstate or foreign commerce or involving a computer used by or for the Federal Government. Requires a Commission report to Congress on actions taken and recommendations regarding statutory penalties for violations. Exempts from criminal penalties any disclosure

made by an electronic communication service to a Federal, State, or local governmental entity if made in the good faith belief that an emergency involving danger of death or serious physical injury to any person requires disclosure without delay. Requires any government entity receiving such a disclosure to report it to the Attorney General.

Amends the Federal criminal code to: (1) prohibit the dissemination by electronic means of any such protected information; (2) increase criminal penalties for violations which cause death or serious bodily injury; (3) authorize the use by appropriate officials of emergency pen register and trap and trace devices in the case of either an immediate threat to a national security interest or an ongoing attack on a protected computer that constitutes a crime punishable by a prison term of greater than one year; (4) repeal provisions which provide a shorter term of imprisonment for certain offenses involving protection from the unauthorized interception and disclosure of wire, oral, or electronic communications; and (5) increase penalties for repeat offenses in connection with unlawful access to stored communications.

Subtitle D: Office of Science and Technology—(Sec. 231) Establishes within the Department of Justice (DOJ) an Office of Science and Technology whose mission is to: (1) serve as the national focal point for work on law enforcement technology (investigative and forensic technologies, corrections technologies, and technologies that support the judicial process); and (2) carry out programs that improve the safety and effectiveness of such technology and improve technology access by Federal, State, and local law enforcement agencies. Sets forth Office duties, including: (1) establishing and maintaining technology advisory groups and performance standards; (2) carrying out research, development, testing, evaluation, and cost-benefit analyses for improving the safety, effectiveness, and efficiency of technologies used by Federal, State, and local law enforcement agencies; and (3) operating the regional National Law Enforcement and Corrections Technology Centers (established under this Subtitle) and establishing additional centers. Requires the Office Director to report annually on Office activities.

(Sec. 234) Authorizes the Attorney General to transfer to the Office any other DOJ program or activity determined to be consistent with its mission. Requires a report from the Attorney General to the congressional judiciary committees on the implementation of this Subtitle.

(Sec. 235) Requires the Office Director to operate and support National Law Enforcement and Corrections Technology Centers and, to the extent necessary, establish new centers through a merit-based, competitive process. Requires such Centers to: (1) support research and development of law enforcement technology; (2) support the transfer and implementation of such technology; (3) assist in the development and dissemination of guidelines and technological standards; and (4) provide technology assistance, information, and support for law enforcement, corrections, and criminal justice purposes. Requires the Director to: (1) convene an annual meeting of such Centers; and (2) report to Congress assessing the effectiveness of the Centers and identifying the number of Centers necessary to meet the technology needs of Federal, State, and local law enforcement in the United States.

(Sec. 237) Amends the Omnibus Crime Control and Safe Streets Act of 1968 to require the National Institute of Justice to: (1) research and develop tools and technologies relating to prevention, detection, investigation, and prosecution of crime; and (2) support research, development, testing, training, and evaluation of tools and technology for Federal, State, and local law enforcement agencies.

Title III: Science and Technology in Support of Homeland Security—(Sec. 301) Establishes in DHS a Directorate of Science and Technology, headed by an Under Secretary for Science and Technology, to be responsible for: (1) advising the Secretary regarding research and development (R&D) efforts and priorities in support of DHS missions; (2) developing a national policy and strategic plan for identifying priorities, goals, objectives and policies for, and coordinating the Federal Government's civilian efforts to identify and develop countermeasures to chemical, biological, radiological, nuclear, and other emerging terrorist threats; (3) supporting the Under Secretary for Information Analysis and Infrastructure Protection by assessing and testing homeland security vulnerabilities and possible threats; (4) conducting basic and applied R&D activities relevant to DHS elements, provided that such responsibility does not extend to human health-related R&D activities; (5) establishing priorities for directing, funding, and conducting national R&D and procurement of technology systems for preventing the importation of chemical, biological, radiological, nuclear, and related weapons and material and for detecting, preventing, protecting against, and responding to terrorist attacks; (6) establishing a system for transferring homeland security developments or technologies to Federal, State, and local government and private sector entities; (7) entering into agreements with the Department of Energy (DOE) regarding the use of the national laboratories or sites and support of the science and technology base at those facilities; (8) collaborating with the Secretary of Agriculture and the Attorney General in the regulation of certain biological agents and toxins as provided in the Agricultural Bioterrorism Protection Act of 2002; (9) collaborating with the Secretary of Health and Human Services and the Attorney General in determining new biological agents and toxins that shall be listed as select agents in the Code of Federal Regulations; (10) supporting U.S. leadership in science and technology; (11) establishing and administering the primary R&D activities of DHS; (12) coordinating and integrating all DHS R&D activities; (13) coordinating

with other appropriate executive agencies in developing and carrying out the science and technology agenda of DHS to reduce duplication and identify unmet needs; and (14) developing and overseeing the administration of guidelines for merit review of R&D projects throughout DHS and for the dissemination of DHS research.

(Sec. 303) Transfers to the Secretary: (1) specified DOE functions, including functions related to chemical and biological national security programs, nuclear smuggling programs and activities within the proliferation detection program, the nuclear assessment program, designated life sciences activities of the biological and environmental research program related to microbial pathogens, the Environmental Measurements Laboratory, and the advanced scientific computing research program at Lawrence Livermore National Laboratory; and (2) the National Bio-Weapons Defense Analysis Center of DOD.

(Sec. 304) Requires the HHS Secretary, with respect to civilian human health-related R&D activities relating to HHS countermeasures for chemical, biological, radiological, and nuclear and other emerging terrorist threats, to: (1) set priorities, goals, objectives, and policies and develop a coordinated strategy for such activities in collaboration with the Secretary to ensure consistency with the national policy and strategic plan; and (2) collaborate with the Secretary in developing specific benchmarks and outcome measurements for evaluating progress toward achieving such priorities and goals.

[...]

(Sec. 305) Authorizes the Secretary, acting through the Under Secretary, to establish or contract with one or more federally funded R&D centers to provide independent analysis of homeland security issues or to carry out other responsibilities under this Act.

[...]

(Sec. 307) Establishes the Homeland Security Advanced Research Projects Agency to be headed by a Director who shall be appointed by the Secretary and who shall report to the Under Secretary. Requires the Director to administer the Acceleration Fund for Research and Development of Homeland Security Technologies (established by this Act) to award competitive, merit-reviewed grants, cooperative agreements, or contracts to public or private entities to: (1) support basic and applied homeland security research to promote revolutionary changes in technologies that would promote homeland security; (2) advance the development, testing and evaluation, and deployment of critical homeland security technologies; and (3) accelerate the prototyping and deployment of technologies that would address homeland security vulnerabilities. Allows the Director to solicit proposals to address specific vulnerabilities. Requires the Director to periodically hold homeland security technology demonstrations to improve contact among technology developers, vendors, and acquisition personnel.

Authorizes appropriations to the Fund. Earmarks ten percent of such funds for each fiscal year through FY 2005 for the Under Secretary, through joint agreement with the Commandant of the Coast Guard, to carry out R&D of improved ports, waterways, and coastal security surveillance and perimeter protection capabilities to minimize the possibility that Coast Guard cutters, aircraft, helicopters, and personnel will be diverted from non-homeland security missions to the ports, waterways, and coastal security mission.

(Sec. 308) Requires the Secretary, acting through the Under Secretary, to: (1) operate extramural R&D programs to ensure that colleges, universities, private research institutes, and companies (and consortia thereof) from as many areas of the United States as practicable participate; and (2) establish a university-based center or centers for homeland security which shall establish a coordinated, university-based system to enhance the Nation's homeland security. Authorizes the Secretary, through the Under Secretary, to: (1) draw upon the expertise of any Government laboratory; and (2) establish a headquarters laboratory for DHS and additional laboratory units.

[. . .]

Establishes within the Directorate of Science and Technology an Office for National Laboratories which shall be responsible for the coordination and utilization of DOE national laboratories and sites in a manner to create a networked laboratory system to support DHS missions.

(Sec. 310) Directs the Secretary of Agriculture to transfer to the Secretary the Plum Island Animal Disease Center of the Department of Agriculture and provides for continued Department of Agriculture access to such Center.

(Sec. 311) Establishes within DHS a Homeland Security Science and Technology Advisory Committee to make recommendations with respect to the activities of the Under Secretary.

(Sec. 312) Directs the Secretary to establish the Homeland Security Institute, a federally funded R&D center. Includes among authorized duties for the Institute: (1) determination of the vulnerabilities of the Nation's critical infrastructures; (2) assessment of the costs and benefits of alternative approaches to enhancing security; and (3) evaluation of the effectiveness of measures deployed to enhance the security of institutions, facilities, and infrastructure that may be terrorist targets.

(Sec. 313) Requires the Secretary to establish and promote a program to encourage technological innovation in facilitating the mission of DHS, to include establishment of: (1) a centralized Federal clearinghouse to further the dissemination of information on technologies; and (2) a technical assistance team to assist in screening submitted proposals.

Title IV: Directorate of Border and Transportation Security— Subtitle A: Under Secretary for Border and Transportation Security—(Sec. 401) Establishes in DHS a Directorate of Border and Transportation Security to be headed by an Under Secretary for Border and Transportation Security. Makes the Secretary, acting through the Under Secretary for Border and Transportation Security, responsible for: (1) preventing the entry of terrorists and the instruments of terrorism into the United States; (2) securing the borders, territorial waters, ports, terminals, waterways, and air, land, and sea transportation systems of the United States; (3) carrying out the immigration enforcement functions vested by statute in, or performed by, the Commissioner of Immigration and Naturalization immediately before their transfer to the Under Secretary; (4) establishing and administering rules governing the granting of visas or other forms of permission to enter the United States to individuals who are not citizens or aliens lawfully admitted for permanent residence in the United States; (5) establishing national immigration enforcement policies and priorities; (6) administering the customs laws of the United States (with certain exceptions); (7) conducting the inspection and related administrative functions of the Department of Agriculture transferred to the Secretary; and (8) ensuring the speedy, orderly, and efficient flow of lawful traffic and commerce in carrying out the foregoing responsibilities.

(Sec. 403) Transfers to the Secretary the functions, personnel, assets, and liabilities of: (1) the U.S. Customs Service; (2) the Transportation Security Administration; (3) the Federal Protective Service of the General Services Administration (GSA); (4) the Federal Law Enforcement Training Center of the Department of the Treasury; and (5) the Office for Domestic Preparedness of the Office of Justice Programs of the Department of Justice (DOJ).

[. . .]

Subtitle C: Miscellaneous Provisions

[. . .]

(Sec. 425) Amends Federal aviation law to require the Under Secretary of Transportation for Security to take certain action, if, in his discretion or at the request of an airport, he determines that the Transportation Security Administration is not able to deploy explosive detection systems at all airports required to have them by December 31, 2002. Requires the Under Secretary, in such circumstances, to: (1) submit to specified congressional committees a detailed plan for the deployment of explosive detection systems at such airport by December 31, 2003; and (2) take all necessary action to ensure that alternative means of screening all checked baggage is implemented.

(Sec. 426) Replaces the Secretary of Transportation with the Secretary of Homeland Security as chair of the Transportation Security Oversight Board. Requires the Secretary of Transportation to consult with the Secretary before approving airport development project grants relating to security equipment or the installation of bulk explosive detection systems.

(Sec. 427) Directs the Secretary, in coordination with the Secretary of Agriculture, the Secretary of Health and Human Services, and the head of each other department or agency determined to be appropriate by the Secretary, to ensure that appropriate information concerning inspections of articles that are imported or entered into the United States, and are inspected or regulated by one or more affected agencies, is timely and efficiently exchanged between the affected agencies. Requires the Secretary to report to Congress on the progress made in implementing this section.

(Sec. 428) Grants the Secretary exclusive authority to issue regulations with respect to, administer, and enforce the Immigration and Nationality Act (INA) and all other immigration and nationality laws relating to the functions of U.S. diplomatic and consular officers in connection with the granting or refusal of visas, and authority to refuse visas in accordance with law and to develop programs of homeland security training for consular officers, which authorities shall be exercised through the Secretary of State. Denies the Secretary authority, however, to alter or reverse the decision of a consular officer to refuse a visa to an alien.

Grants the Secretary authority also to confer or impose upon any U.S. officer or employee, with the consent of the head of the executive agency under whose jurisdiction such officer or employee is serving, any of these specified functions.

Authorizes the Secretary of State to direct a consular officer to refuse a visa to an alien if the Secretary of State deems such refusal necessary or advisable in the foreign policy or security interests of the United States.

Authorizes the Secretary to assign employees of DHS to any diplomatic and consular posts abroad to review individual visa applications and provide expert advice and training to consular officers regarding specific security threats relating to such applications and to conduct investigations with respect to matters under the Secretary's jurisdiction.

Directs the Secretary to study and report to Congress on the role of foreign nationals in the granting or refusal of visas and other documents authorizing entry of aliens into the United States.

Requires the Director of the Office of Science and Technology Policy to report to Congress on how the provisions of this section will affect procedures for the issuance of student visas.

Terminates after enactment of this Act all third party screening visa issuance programs in Saudi Arabia. Requires on-site personnel of DHS to review all visa applications prior to adjudication.

(Sec. 429) Requires visa denial information to be entered into the electronic data system as provided for in the Enhanced Border Security and Visa Entry Reform Act of 2002. Prohibits an alien denied a visa from being issued a subsequent visa unless the reviewing consular officer makes specified findings concerning waiver of ineligibility.

(Sec. 430) Establishes within the Directorate of Border and Transportation Security the Office for Domestic Preparedness to: (1) coordinate Federal preparedness for acts of terrorism, working with all State, local, tribal, county, parish, and private sector emergency response providers; (2) coordinate or consolidate systems of communications relating to homeland security at all levels of government; (3) direct and supervise Federal terrorism preparedness grant programs for all emergency response providers; and (4) perform specified other related duties.

Subtitle D: Immigration Enforcement Functions—(Sec. 441) Transfers from the Commissioner of Immigration and Naturalization to the Under Secretary for Border and Transportation Security all functions performed under the following programs, and all personnel, assets, and liabilities pertaining to such programs, immediately before such transfer occurs: (1) the Border Patrol program; (2) the detention and removal program; (3) the intelligence program; (4) the investigations program; and (5) the inspections program.

(Sec. 442) Establishes in the Department of Homeland Security (DHS) the Bureau of Border Security, headed by the Assistant Secretary of the Bureau of Border Security who shall: (1) report directly to the Under Secretary; (2) establish and oversee the policies for performing functions transferred to the Under Secretary and delegated to the Assistant Secretary by the Under Secretary; and (3) advise the Under Secretary with respect to any policy or operation of the Bureau that may affect the Bureau of Citizenship and Immigration Services.

Directs the Assistant Secretary to: (1) administer the program to collect information relating to nonimmigrant foreign students and other exchange program participants; and (2) implement a managerial rotation program.

Establishes the position of Chief of Policy and Strategy for the Bureau of Border Security, who shall: (1) make immigration enforcement policy recommendations; and (2) coordinate immigration policy issues with the Chief of Policy and Strategy for the Bureau of Citizenship and Immigration Services.

[...]

will enforce relevant INA provisions.

(Sec. 446) Expresses the sense of Congress that completing the 14-mile border fence project near San Diego, California, mandated by the Illegal Immigration Reform and Immigrant Responsibility Act of 1996 should be a priority for the Secretary.

Subtitle E: Citizenship and Immigration Services—(Sec. 451) Establishes in DHS a Bureau of Citizenship and Immigration Services, headed by the Director of the Bureau of Citizenship and Immigration Services, who shall: (1) establish the policies for performing and administering transferred functions; (2) establish national immigration services policies and priorities; and (3) implement a managerial rotation program.

Authorizes the Director to implement pilot initiatives to eliminate the backlog of immigration benefit applications.

Transfers all Immigration and Naturalization Service (INS) adjudications and related personnel and funding to the Director.

[...]

Subtitle F: General Immigration Provisions—(Sec. 471) Abolishes INS upon completion of all transfers from it as provided for by this Act.

[...]

Title V: Emergency Preparedness and Response—(Sec. 501) Establishes in DHS a Directorate of Emergency Preparedness and Response, headed by an Under Secretary.

(Sec. 502) Requires the responsibilities of the Secretary, acting through the Under Secretary, to include: (1) helping to ensure the effectiveness of emergency response providers to terrorist attacks, major disasters, and other emergencies; (2) with respect to the Nuclear Incident Response Team, establishing and certifying compliance with standards, conducting joint and other exercises and training, and providing funds to the Department of Energy and the Environmental Protection Agency for homeland security planning, training, and equipment; (3) providing the Federal Government's response to terrorist attacks and major disasters; (4) aiding recovery from terrorist attacks and major disasters; (5) building a comprehensive national incident management system with Federal, State, and local governments to respond to such attacks and

disasters; (6) consolidating existing Federal Government emergency response plans into a single, coordinated national response plan; and (7) developing comprehensive programs for developing interoperative communications technology and helping to ensure that emergency response providers acquire such technology.

(Sec. 503) Transfers to the Secretary the functions, personnel, assets, and liabilities of: (1) the Federal Emergency Management Agency (FEMA); (2) the Integrated Hazard Information System of the National Oceanic and Atmospheric Administration, which shall be renamed FIRESAT; (3) the National Domestic Preparedness Office of the FBI; (4) the Domestic Emergency Support Teams of DOJ; (5) the Office of Emergency Preparedness, the National Disaster Medical System, and the Metropolitan Medical Response System of HHS; and (6) the Strategic National Stockpile of HHS.

(Sec. 504) Requires the Nuclear Incident Response Team, at the direction of the Secretary (in connection with an actual or threatened terrorist attack, major disaster, or other emergency in the United States), to operate as an organizational unit of DHS under the Secretary's authority and control.

(Sec. 505) Provides that, with respect to all public health-related activities to improve State, local, and hospital preparedness and response to chemical, biological, radiological, and nuclear and other emerging terrorist threats carried out by HHS (including the Public Health Service), the Secretary of HHS shall set priorities and preparedness goals and further develop a coordinated strategy for such activities in collaboration with the Secretary.

[...]

Title VIII: Coordination With Non-Federal Entities; Inspector General; United States Secret Service; Coast Guard; General Provisions—Subtitle A: Coordination with Non-Federal Entities—(Sec. 801) Establishes within the Office of the Secretary the Office for State and Local Government Coordination to oversee and coordinate Department homeland security programs for and relationships with State and local governments.

[...]

Subtitle C: United States Secret Service—(Sec. 821) Transfers to the Secretary the functions of the United States Secret Service, which shall be maintained as a distinct entity within DHS.

Subtitle D: Acquisitions—(Sec. 831) Authorizes the Secretary to carry out a five-year pilot program under which the Secretary may exercise specified authorities in carrying out: (1) basic, applied, and advanced research and development projects for response to existing or emerging terrorist threats; and (2) defense prototype projects....

[...]

(Sec. 878) Directs the Secretary to appoint a senior DHS official to assume primary responsibility for coordinating policy and operations within DHS and between DHS and other Federal departments and agencies with respect to interdicting the entry of illegal drugs into the United States and tracking and severing connections between illegal drug trafficking and terrorism.

(Sec. 879) Establishes within the Office of the Secretary an Office of International Affairs, headed by a Director, to: (1) promote information and education exchange on homeland security best practices and technologies with friendly nations; (2) identify areas for homeland security information and training exchange where the United States has a demonstrated weakness and another friendly nation has a demonstrated expertise; (3) plan and undertake international conferences, exchange programs, and training activities; and (4) manage international activities within DHS in coordination with other Federal officials with responsibility for counter-terrorism matters.

[...]

(Sec. 885) Authorizes the Secretary to establish a permanent Joint Interagency Homeland Security Task Force, composed of representatives from military and civilian agencies, for the purpose of anticipating terrorist threats and taking actions to prevent harm to the United States.

[...]

(Sec. 895) Amends the Federal Rules of Criminal Procedure to treat as contempt of court any knowing violation of guidelines jointly issued by the Attorney General and DCI with respect to disclosure of grand jury matters otherwise prohibited. Allows disclosure to appropriate Federal, State, local, or foreign government officials of grand jury matters involving a threat of grave hostile acts of a foreign power, domestic or international sabotage or terrorism, or clandestine intelligence gathering activities by an intelligence service or network of a foreign power (threat), within the United States or elsewhere. Permits disclosure to appropriate foreign government officials of grand jury matters that may disclose a violation of the law of such government. Requires State, local, and foreign officials to use disclosed information only in conformity with guidelines jointly issued by the Attorney General and the DCI.

(Sec. 896) Amends the Federal criminal code to authorize Federal investigative and law enforcement officers conducting communications interception activities, who have obtained knowledge of the contents of any intercepted communication or derivative evidence, to disclose such contents or evidence to: (1) a foreign investigative or law enforcement officer if the disclosure is appropriate

to the performance of the official duties of the officer making or receiving the disclosure; and (2) any appropriate Federal, State, local, or foreign government official if the contents or evidence reveals such a threat, for the purpose of preventing or responding to such threat. Provides guidelines for the use and disclosure of the information.

(Sec. 897) Amends the Uniting and Strengthening America by Providing Appropriate Tools Required to Intercept and Obstruct Terrorism Act (USA PATRIOT ACT) of 2001 to make lawful the disclosure to appropriate Federal, State, local, or foreign government officials of information obtained as part of a criminal investigation that reveals such a threat.

(Sec. 898) Amends the Foreign Intelligence Surveillance Act of 1978 to allow Federal officers who conduct electronic surveillance and physical searches in order to acquire foreign intelligence information to consult with State and local law enforcement personnel to coordinate efforts to investigate or protect against such a threat.

Title IX: National Homeland Security Council—(Sec. 901) Establishes within the Executive Office of the President the Homeland Security Council to advise the President on homeland security matters.

(Sec. 903) Includes as members of the Council: (1) the President; (2) the Vice President; (3) the Secretary; (4) the Attorney General; and (5) the Secretary of Defense.

(Sec. 904) Requires the Council to: (1) assess the objectives, commitments, and risks of the United States in the interest of homeland security and make recommendations to the President; and (2) oversee and review Federal homeland security policies and make policy recommendations to the President.

(Sec. 906) Authorizes the President to convene joint meetings of the Homeland Security Council and the National Security Council.

[...]

Title XIV: Arming Pilots Against Terrorism—Arming Pilots Against Terrorism Act—(Sec. 1402) Amends Federal law to direct the Under Secretary of Transportation for Security (in the Transportation Security Administration) to establish a two-year pilot program to: (1) deputize volunteer pilots of air carriers as Federal law enforcement officers to defend the flight decks of aircraft against acts of criminal violence or air piracy (Federal flight deck officers); and (2) provide training, supervision, and equipment for such officers.

Requires the Under Secretary to begin the process of training and deputizing qualified pilots to be Federal flight deck officers under the program. Allows the Under Secretary to request another Federal agency to deputize such officers.

Directs the Under Secretary to authorize flight deck officers to carry firearms and to use force, including lethal force, according to standards and circumstances the Under Secretary prescribes. Shields air carriers from liability for damages in Federal or State court arising out of a Federal flight deck officer's use of or failure to use a firearm. Shields flight deck officers from liability for acts or omissions in defending the flight deck of an aircraft against acts of criminal violence or air piracy, except in cases of gross negligence or willful misconduct.

[...]

Declares the sense of Congress that the Federal air marshal program is critical to aviation security, and that nothing in this Act shall be construed as preventing the Under Secretary from implementing and training Federal air marshals.

(Sec. 1403) Directs the Under Secretary, in updating the guidance for training flight and cabin crews, to issue a rule to: (1) require both classroom and effective hands-on situational training in specified elements of self-defense; (2) require training in the proper conduct of a cabin search, including the duty time required to conduct it; (3) establish the required number of hours of training and the qualifications for training instructors; (4) establish the intervals, number of hours, and elements of recurrent training; (5) ensure that air carriers provide the initial training within 24 months of the enactment of this Act. Directs the Under Secretary to designate an official in the Transportation Security Administration to be responsible for overseeing the implementation of the training program; and (6) ensure that no person is required to participate in any hands-on training activity that such person believes will have an adverse impact on his or her health or safety.

Amends the Aviation and Transportation Security Act to authorize the Under Secretary to take certain enhanced security measures, including to require that air carriers provide flight attendants with a discreet, hands-free, wireless method of communicating with the pilot of an aircraft.

Directs the Under Secretary to study and report to Congress on the benefits and risks of providing flight attendants with nonlethal weapons to aide in combating air piracy and criminal violence on commercial airlines.

(Sec. 1404) Directs the Secretary of Transportation to study and report within six months to Congress on: (1) the number of armed Federal law enforcement officers (other than Federal air marshals) who travel on commercial airliners annually, and the frequency of their travel; (2) the cost and resources necessary to provide such

officers with supplemental aircraft anti-terrorism training comparable to the training that Federal air marshals receive; (3) the cost of establishing a program at a Federal law enforcement training center for the purpose of providing new Federal law enforcement recruits with standardized training comparable to Federal air marshal training; (4) the feasibility of implementing a certification program designed to ensure that Federal law enforcement officers have completed aircraft anti-terrorism training, and track their travel over a six-month period; and (5) the feasibility of staggering the flights of such officers to ensure the maximum amount of flights have a certified trained Federal officer on board.

(Sec. 1405) Amends Federal aviation law to require the Under Secretary to respond within 90 days of receiving a request from an air carrier for authorization to allow pilots of the air carrier to carry less-than-lethal weapons.

[...]

(Sec. 1514) Provides that nothing in this Act shall be construed to authorize the development of a national identification system or card.

[...]

Title XVI: Corrections to Existing Law Relating to Airline Transportation Security—(Sec. 1601) Amends Federal aviation law to require the Administrator of the Federal Aviation Administration (FAA), along with the Under Secretary of Transportation for Security, to each conduct research (including behavioral research) and development activities to develop, modify, test, and evaluate a system, procedure, facility, or device to protect passengers and property against acts of criminal violence, aircraft piracy, and terrorism and to ensure security.

[...]

Title XVII: Conforming and Technical Amendments....

(Sec. 1706) Transfers from the Administrator of General Services to the Secretary of Homeland Security law enforcement authority for the protection of Federal property.

(Sec. 1708) Establishes in DOD a National Bio-Weapons Defense Analysis Center to develop countermeasures to potential attacks by terrorists using weapons of mass destruction.

[...]

Source: U.S. Congress, "Homeland Security Act of 2002," Library of Congress, THOMAS, http://thomas.loc.gov/cgi-bin/bdquery/z?d107:HR05005:@@@D&summ2=m&.

108. U.S. Secretary of Defense Donald Rumsfeld, "Old Europe," Press Conference Briefing at the Foreign Press Center, January 22, 2003 [Excerpts]

Introduction

In late 2002 and early 2003 major European nations, most notably France and Germany, did not share the obvious eagerness for war with Iraq of several top American and British leaders, including President George W. Bush and Prime Minister Tony Blair, together with U.S. defense secretary Donald Rumsfeld. To American officials' chagrin as the probability of war increased, France and Germany refused to contribute troops to "the coalition of the willing" nations assembled to undertake any such venture. Several formerly communist East European, Baltic, and Balkan states, including Poland, the Czech Republic, Slovakia, Latvia, Lithuania, Estonia, Croatia, Slovenia, Albania, Macedonia, Romania, and Bulgaria, were by contrast enthusiastic supporters and contributed troops, in part because they wished to burnish their credentials for membership in the North Atlantic Treaty Organization (NATO) and the European Union (EU). Rumsfeld stirred up considerable controversy when, in a January 2003 press conference, he contrasted what he implied were the effete and tired states of "old Europe" with the more dynamic and vigorous "new Europe" that had just escaped from communist rule. He compounded the offense by stating that "Germany has been a problem, and France has been a problem," while suggesting that within Europe the "center of gravity is shifting to the east." French and German leaders responded with outrage. When France condemned the eventual U.S. invasion of Iraq two months later, Franco-American relations plummeted to an even lower ebb as American politicians and pundits called for boycotts of French wines and suggested that french fries be renamed "freedom fries."

Primary Source

[...]

Q: Mr. Secretary, Carl Hanlon, Global Television, Canada. Sir, Canada's foreign minister stated again today that the United States must get United Nations approval to go to war with Iraq. Are you still hoping that Canada would support President Bush's so-called "coalition of the willing" if you end up going to war with Iraq without the U.N.?

Rumsfeld: You know, the United States and Canada are close friends and allies and neighbors, and we've participated together in so many activities across the globe, [we] currently are with respect to the global war on terror, allies in NATO. It's up to Canada to decide what it wishes to do. Each country has a somewhat

different circumstance, a somewhat different history, a somewhat different perspective, and I think each country is inevitably going to do that which they feel is appropriate to them.

I can say this: that there are a very large number of countries who have said, regardless of whether there is a second resolution in the United Nations, that they are anxious and willing and ready to join a coalition of the willing. There is a very large number of countries also that are prepared in the event there is a second resolution regardless—almost regardless of what it says. It might simply say that in fact the Iraqis have not been cooperative, or it might go the extra step and say that they haven't been cooperative and therefore the United Nations recommends the use of all appropriate force. I don't know what—how that will play out; it's not knowable.

But it seems to me it's asking a lot for other countries to step forward publicly and say where they are on this until and unless the case has been fully made, and the president has indicated that he's concluded that force must be used. And at that moment, people then will be making their judgments and participating or not, as they and their people feel is appropriate. And as far as I'm concerned, I think that's the way it ought to work. Every country is a sovereign nation.

[...]

Q: Thank you. This is Hasan Hazar, *Turkey Daily*. . . . Although the United States does very intensive public diplomacy campaigns to the Islamic world, anti-Americanism is growing all over the world. What is the reason, what is the reaction of that?

Rumsfeld: Well, I would have to say that the United States is not very effective in public diplomacy. We have wonderful people working on it, and they work hard on it, and they're talented and they do a good job. But what they're up against is a flow of information that's coming out of these extremists that are trying to hijack that religion, and feeding people in the madrassas schools a line that the West and other religions are against them and that, therefore, they should engage in terrorist acts.

And it seems to me that we have a task, not just the United States, but the world. I would think—you cast it as though it's the United States and the Moslem world, or the United States and people who are anti–United States. I think that's a bit of an oversimplification. I think there's a real struggle taking place in the Moslem faith. There are an awful lot of people who are unhappy that extremists and small groups of clerics are teaching young people things that aren't true; teaching people that the best thing they can do is not learn a language, not learn mathematics, not learn how they can provide for themselves in the world, instead, filling their heads with hate against the West and against progress, and encouraging them to conduct suicide campaigns.

Now, that religion needs to take back its religion from people who are teaching that. The whole world is part of this process; it's not just the United States.

Let me just say something that I feel very deeply. It's the year 2003. Here we are, we're all sitting here and we're safe and sound. And there isn't anybody when they walk out of this place who is afraid they're going to get shot, or blown up, or face a biological attack, or a chemical attack or a nuclear attack. What's taking place in the world today in—with the proliferation of weapons of mass destruction, biological weapons, nuclear weapons, is so pervasive that as you look out over the horizon—you guess—five years? ten years?—there are going to be three, four, five more nuclear powers, and they're not going to be countries like the United Kingdom or France or the United States; they're going to be countries like North Korea; they're going to be terrorist states; and they're going to be states that have relationships with terrorist organizations. The ease of transporting and developing biologicals that can kill hundreds of thousands of human beings is easy; it does not take a genius to do that. They're easy to make, they're easy to transport and they're easy to deliver. And that's the kind of a world we're living in.

Now, that is not a problem for the United States only. It's a problem for the whole world. And at some point, the people of the world are going to be so shocked and jarred by events like 9/11 that they're going to make a judgment that they need to do something differently; that they can't sit back and say, "Oh, what about all this anti-Americanism? Or what about all this stuff? Or why doesn't the United States do this or that?"

They're going to be deeply concerned because they're going to have every right in the world to be deeply concerned. And the time to get ahead of that is now, before it all happens, not after. Let there be no doubt.

[. . .]

Q: Sir, a question about the mood among European allies. You were talking about the Islamic world a second ago. But now the European allies. If you look at, for example, France, Germany, also a lot of people in my own country—I'm from Dutch public TV, by the way—it seems that a lot of Europeans rather give the benefit of the doubt to Saddam Hussein than President George Bush. These are U.S. allies. What do you make of that?

Rumsfeld: Well, it's—what do I make of it?

Q: They have no clerics. They have no Muslim clerics there.

Rumsfeld: . . . What do I think about it? Well, there isn't anyone alive who wouldn't prefer unanimity. I mean, you just always would like everyone to stand up and say, Way to go! That's the right to do, United States.

Now, we rarely find unanimity in the world. I was ambassador to NATO, and I—when we would go in and make a proposal, there wouldn't be unanimity. There wouldn't even be understanding. And we'd have to be persuasive. We'd have to show reasons. We'd have to—have to give rationales. We'd have to show facts. And, by golly, I found that Europe on any major issue is given—if there's leadership and if you're right, and if your facts are persuasive, Europe responds. And they always have.

Now, you're thinking of Europe as Germany and France. I don't. I think that's old Europe. If you look at the entire NATO Europe today, the center of gravity is shifting to the east. And there are a lot of new members. And if you just take the list of all the members of NATO and all of those who have been invited in recently—what is it? Twenty-six, something like that?—you're right. Germany has been a problem, and France has been a problem.

Q: But opinion polls—

Rumsfeld: But—just a minute. Just a minute. But you look at vast numbers of other countries in Europe. They're not with France and Germany on this, they're with the United States.

Now, you cite public opinion polls. Fair enough. Political leaders have to interest themselves in where the public is, and talk to them, and think about that, and then—and provide leadership to them. . . .

And that's—that's what political leaders are supposed to do, is to lead. And they—they're responsible for engaging facts and making assessments and then going out before their people and telling them their honest conviction as to what their country ought to do. And if a country doesn't agree with us, heck, that's happened lots of times in history.

[. . .]

Source: Donald Rumsfeld, "Secretary Rumsfeld Briefs at the Foreign Press Center," U.S. Department of Defense, http://www.defense.gov/Transcripts/Transcript.aspx?TranscriptID=1330.

109. Hans Blix, Report to United Nations Security Council, February 14, 2003 [Excerpts]

Introduction

In November 2002 Saddam Hussein, alarmed by the passage of United Nations (UN) Security Council Resolution 1441 and by the obvious eagerness with which American and British leaders contemplated invading Iraq, allowed weapons inspectors from the United Nations Monitoring, Verification and Inspection Commission (UNMOVIC) and the International Atomic Energy Authority (IAEA) to reenter Iraq after a four-year hiatus. Reporting to the UN in February 2003, UNMOVIC chairman Hans Blix described his organization's efforts to inspect weapons facilities in Iraq. He stated that 250 UNMOVIC and IAEA inspectors and support staff drawn from 60 countries were at that time present in Iraq. Iraqi officials had proved cooperative in allowing inspectors access to more than 300 sites, most of them "performed without notice." Blix stated that to date UNMOVIC had not located any "weapons of mass destruction and related proscribed items and programs." Blix did warn that open questions remained over large quantities of chemical agents that Iraq's government had not yet accounted for and stated that Iraq itself, whose officials claimed that many such materials had been "poured into the ground years ago," must "squarely tackle" the task of providing evidence of what had happened to these materials. Iraq still possessed missiles capable of being configured to a range of more than 150 miles, which were proscribed under UN Security Council resolutions, and Blix intended to take this matter up with Iraq's government. UNMOVIC had begun to interview Iraqi officials in private, with no government minders present. UNMOVIC was also improving its surveillance capabilities and was planning to use U-2 long-range reconnaissance aircraft to monitor the movement of Iraqi weapons and changes in known weapon sites. Though condemning Iraq's past efforts to evade cooperation with weapons inspection teams for most of the 1990s, Blix's tone was one of guarded optimism, stating that although ongoing open-ended monitoring of the cessation of weapons programs would probably be required, the time needed to complete disarmament inspections and ascertain Iraq's compliance with Security Resolution 1441 of November 2002 could be relatively short if Iraq gave "active and unconditional cooperation."

Primary Source

Since I reported to the Security Council on 27 January, UNMOVIC has had two further weeks of operational and analytical work in New York and active inspections in Iraq. This brings the total period of inspections so far to 11 weeks. Since then, we have also listened on 5 February to the presentation to the Council by the US Secretary of State and the discussion that followed. Lastly, Dr. ElBaradei and I have held another round of talks in Baghdad with our counterparts and with Vice President Ramadan on 8 and 9 February.

Let me begin today's briefing with a short account of the work being performed by UNMOVIC in Iraq.

[...]

Since we arrived in Iraq, we have conducted more than 400 inspections covering more than 300 sites. All inspections were performed

without notice, and access was almost always provided promptly. In no case have we seen convincing evidence that the Iraqi side knew in advance that the inspectors were coming.

The inspections have taken place throughout Iraq at industrial sites, ammunition depots, research centres, universities, presidential sites, mobile laboratories, private houses, missile production facilities, military camps and agricultural sites. At all sites which had been inspected before 1998, re-baselining activities were performed. This included the identification of the function and contents of each building, new or old, at a site. It also included verification of previously tagged equipment, application of seals and tags, taking samples and discussions with the site personnel regarding past and present activities. At certain sites, ground-penetrating radar was used to look for underground structures or buried equipment.

Through the inspections conducted so far, we have obtained a good knowledge of the industrial and scientific landscape of Iraq, as well as of its missile capability but, as before, we do not know every cave and corner. Inspections are effectively helping to bridge the gap in knowledge that arose due to the absence of inspections between December 1998 and November 2002.

More than 200 chemical and more than 100 biological samples have been collected at different sites. Three-quarters of these have been screened using our own analytical laboratory capabilities at the Baghdad Centre (BOMVIC). The results to date have been consistent with Iraq's declarations.

We have now commenced the process of destroying approximately 50 litres of mustard gas declared by Iraq that was being kept under UNMOVIC seal at the Muthanna site. One-third of the quantity has already been destroyed. The laboratory quantity of thiodiglycol, a mustard gas precursor, which we found at another site, has also been destroyed.

[...]

In my 27 January update to the Council, I said that it seemed from our experience that Iraq had decided in principle to provide cooperation on process, most importantly prompt access to all sites and assistance to UNMOVIC in the establishment of the necessary infrastructure. This impression remains, and we note that access to sites has so far been without problems, including those that had never been declared or inspected, as well as to Presidential sites and private residences.

In my last updating, I also said that a decision to cooperate on substance was indispensable in order to bring, through inspection, the disarmament task to completion and to set the monitoring system on a firm course. Such cooperation, as I have noted, requires more than the opening of doors. In the words of resolution 1441 (2002)—it requires immediate, unconditional and active efforts by Iraq to resolve existing questions of disarmament—either by presenting remaining proscribed items and programmes for elimination or by presenting convincing evidence that they have been eliminated. In the current situation, one would expect Iraq to be eager to comply. . . .

How much, if any, is left of Iraq's weapons of mass destruction and related proscribed items and programmes? So far, UNMOVIC has not found any such weapons, only a small number of empty chemical munitions, which should have been declared and destroyed. Another matter—and one of great significance—is that many proscribed weapons and items are not accounted for. To take an example, a document, which Iraq provided, suggested to us that some 1,000 tonnes of chemical agent were "unaccounted for." One must not jump to the conclusion that they exist. However, that possibility is also not excluded. If they exist, they should be presented for destruction. If they do not exist, credible evidence to that effect should be presented.

We are fully aware that many governmental intelligence organizations are convinced and assert that proscribed weapons, items and programmes continue to exist. The US Secretary of State presented material in support of this conclusion. Governments have many sources of information that are not available to inspectors. Inspectors, for their part, must base their reports only on evidence, which they can, themselves, examine and present publicly. Without evidence, confidence cannot arise.

In my earlier briefings, I have noted that significant outstanding issues of substance were listed in two Security Council documents from early 1999 (S/1999/94 and S/1999/356) and should be well known to Iraq. I referred, as examples, to the issues of anthrax, the nerve agent VX and long-range missiles, and said that such issues "deserve to be taken seriously by Iraq rather than being brushed aside." . . . The declaration submitted by Iraq on 7 December last year, despite its large volume, missed the opportunity to provide the fresh material and evidence needed to respond to the open questions. This is perhaps the most important problem we are facing. Although I can understand that it may not be easy for Iraq in all cases to provide the evidence needed, it is not the task of the inspectors to find it. Iraq itself must squarely tackle this task and avoid belittling the questions.

[. . .]

At the meeting in Baghdad on 8 and 9 February, the Iraqi side addressed some of the important outstanding disarmament issues and gave us a number of papers, e.g., regarding anthrax and growth material, the nerve agent VX and missile production. Experts who were present from our side studied the papers during the evening of 8 February and met with Iraqi experts in the morning of 9 February for further clarifications. Although no new evidence was provided in the papers and no open issues were closed through them or the expert discussions, the presentation of the papers could be indicative of a more active attitude focusing on important open issues.

The Iraqi side suggested that the problem of verifying the quantities of anthrax and two VX-precursors, which had been declared unilaterally destroyed, might be tackled through certain technical and analytical methods. Although our experts are still assessing the suggestions, they are not very hopeful that it could prove possible to assess the quantities of material poured into the ground years ago. Documentary evidence and testimony by staff that dealt with the items still appears to be needed.

Not least against this background, a letter of 12 February from Iraq's National Monitoring Directorate may be of relevance. It presents a list of 83 names of participants "in the unilateral destruction in the chemical field, which took place in the summer of 1991." As the absence of adequate evidence of that destruction has been and remains an important reason why quantities of chemicals have been deemed "unaccounted for," the presentation of a list of persons who can be interviewed about the actions appears useful and pertains to cooperation on substance. I trust that the Iraqi side will put together a similar list of names of persons who participated in the unilateral destruction of other proscribed items, notably in the biological field.

The Iraqi side also informed us that the commission, which had been appointed in the wake of our finding 12 empty chemical weapons warheads, had had its mandate expanded to look for any still existing proscribed items. This was welcomed.

A second commission, we learnt, has now been appointed with the task of searching all over Iraq for more documents relevant to the elimination of proscribed items and programmes. It is headed by the former Minister of Oil, General Amer Rashid, and is to have very extensive powers of search in industry, administration and even private houses.

The two commissions could be useful tools to come up with proscribed items to be destroyed and with new documentary evidence. They evidently need to work fast and effectively to convince us, and the world, that it is a serious effort.

The matter of private interviews was discussed at length during our meeting in Baghdad. The Iraqi side confirmed the commitment, which it made to us on 20 January, to encourage persons asked to accept such interviews, whether in or out of Iraq. So far, we have only had interviews in Baghdad. A number of persons have declined to be interviewed, unless they were allowed to have an official present or were allowed to tape the interview. Three persons that had previously refused interviews on UNMOVIC's terms, subsequently accepted such interviews just prior to our talks in Baghdad on 8 and 9 February. These interviews proved informative. No further interviews have since been accepted on our terms. I hope this will change. We feel that interviews conducted without any third party present and without tape recording would provide the greatest credibility.

At the recent meeting in Baghdad, as on several earlier occasions, my colleague Dr. ElBaradei and I have urged the Iraqi side to enact legislation implementing the UN prohibitions regarding weapons of mass destruction. This morning we had a message that a Presidential decree has now been issued containing prohibitions with regard to importation and production of biological, chemical and nuclear weapons. We have not yet had time to study the details of the text of the decree.

Intelligence

Mr. President, I should like to make some comments on the role of intelligence in connection with inspections in Iraq.

A credible inspection regime requires that Iraq provide full cooperation on "process"—granting immediate access everywhere to inspectors—and on substance, providing full declarations supported by relevant information and material and evidence. However, with the closed society in Iraq of today and the history of inspections there, other sources of information, such as defectors and government intelligence agencies are required to aid the inspection process.

I remember myself how, in 1991, several inspections in Iraq, which were based on information received from a Government, helped to disclose important parts of the nuclear weapons programme. It was realized that an international organization authorized to perform inspections anywhere on the ground could make good use of information obtained from governments with eyes in the sky, ears in the ether, access to defectors, and both eyes and ears on the market for weapons-related material. It was understood that the information residing in the intelligence services of governments could come to very active use in the international effort to prevent proliferation of weapons of mass destruction. This remains true and we have by now a good deal of experience in the matter.

International organizations need to analyse such information critically and especially benefit when it comes from more than one source. The intelligence agencies, for their part, must protect their sources and methods. Those who provide such information must know that it will be kept in strict confidence and be known to very few people. UNMOVIC has achieved good working relations with intelligence agencies and the amount of information provided has

been gradually increasing. However, we must recognize that there are limitations and that misinterpretations can occur.

Intelligence information has been useful for UNMOVIC. In one case, it led us to a private home where documents mainly relating to laser enrichment of uranium were found. In other cases, intelligence has led to sites where no proscribed items were found. Even in such cases, however, inspection of these sites were useful in proving the absence of such items and in some cases the presence of other items—conventional munitions. It showed that conventional arms are being moved around the country and that movements are not necessarily related to weapons of mass destruction.

The presentation of intelligence information by the US Secretary of State suggested that Iraq had prepared for inspections by cleaning up sites and removing evidence of proscribed weapons programmes. I would like to comment only on one case, which we are familiar with, namely, the trucks identified by analysts as being for chemical decontamination at a munitions depot. This was a declared site, and it was certainly one of the sites Iraq would have expected us to inspect. We have noted that the two satellite images of the site were taken several weeks apart. The reported movement of munitions at the site could just as easily have been a routine activity as a movement of proscribed munitions in anticipation of imminent inspection. Our reservation on this point does not detract from our appreciation of the briefing.

Plans for the immediate future

Yesterday, UNMOVIC informed the Iraqi authorities of its intention to start using the U-2 surveillance aircraft early next week under arrangements similar to those UNSCOM had followed. We are also in the process of working out modalities for the use of the French Mirage aircraft starting late next week and for the drones supplied by the German Government. The offer from Russia of an Antonov aircraft, with night vision capabilities, is a welcome one and is next on our agenda for further improving UNMOVIC's and IAEA's technical capabilities. These developments are in line with suggestions made in a non-paper recently circulated by France, suggesting a further strengthening of the inspection capabilities.

It is our intention to examine the possibilities for surveying ground movements, notably by trucks. In the face of persistent intelligence reports for instance about mobile biological weapons production units, such measures could well increase the effectiveness of inspections.

[. . .]

UNMOVIC is not infrequently asked how much more time it needs to complete its task in Iraq. The answer depends upon which task one has in mind—the elimination of weapons of mass destruction and related items and programmes, which were prohibited in 1991—the disarmament task—or the monitoring that no new proscribed activities occur. The latter task, though not often focused upon, is highly significant—and not controversial. It will require monitoring, which is "ongoing," that is, open-ended until the Council decides otherwise.

By contrast, the task of "disarmament" foreseen in resolution 687 (1991) and the progress on "key remaining disarmament tasks" foreseen in resolution 1284 (1999) as well as the "disarmament obligations," which Iraq was given a "final opportunity to comply with" under resolution 1441 (2002), were always required to be fulfilled in a shorter time span. Regrettably, the high degree of cooperation required of Iraq for disarmament through inspection was not forthcoming in 1991. Despite the elimination, under UNSCOM and IAEA supervision, of large amounts of weapons, weapons-related items and installations over the years, the task remained incomplete, when inspectors were withdrawn almost 8 years later at the end of 1998.

If Iraq had provided the necessary cooperation in 1991, the phase of disarmament—under resolution 687 (1991)—could have been short and a decade of sanctions could have been avoided. Today, three months after the adoption of resolution 1441 (2002), the period of disarmament through inspection could still be short, if "immediate, active and unconditional cooperation" with UNMOVIC and the IAEA were to be forthcoming.

> **Source:** Hans Blix, "Briefing of the Security Council, 14 February 2003: An Update on Inspections," United Nations, http://www.un.org/Depts/unmovic/new/pages/security_council_briefings.asp#6.

110. France, Germany, and Russia, Memorandum on Iraqi Sanctions, Submitted to the United Nations Security Council, March 5, 2003

Introduction

The governments of France, Germany, and Russia were all unenthusiastic over the Anglo-American drive toward war with Iraq and refused to join the coalition for that purpose. In late February 2003 Britain, the United States, and Spain submitted a draft resolution to the United Nations (UN) Security Council declaring that Iraq had failed to comply with Resolution 1441 of November 2003 and thus had forfeited its "final opportunity" to avoid action by the Security Council. France and Russia were both permanent Security Council members, entitled to veto any resolution with which they disagreed, and at that time Germany was

also a nonpermanent Security Council member. Responding to the Anglo-American draft resolution, the foreign ministers of these three countries—Dominique de Villepin of France, Ivan S. Ivanov of Russia, and Joschka Fischer of Germany—released a joint statement, which they also submitted to the Security Council. This declared that the new inspection measures in Iraq undertaken by the United Nations Monitoring, Verification and Inspection Commission (UNMOVIC) and the International Atomic Energy Authority (IAEA) were producing encouraging results and should continue. The statement called on Iraq's government to provide fuller cooperation with UNMOVIC and the IAEA and to speed up the timetable for inspections. In addition, the statement called for a definite and detailed time schedule for inspections of each program. In conclusion, Russia and France uncompromisingly stated that since there was now a good chance of reaching a peaceful settlement on Iraq and other Middle Eastern issues, they would "not let a proposed resolution pass that would authorize the use of force." Both stated that if necessary they would veto such a resolution. Their stance meant that the Security Council was deadlocked on the use of force in Iraq, making it impossible for the United States and Great Britain to obtain a resolution specifically authorizing their invasion of Iraq. Anglo-American efforts in the first half of March to craft a compromise failed. The war that began on March 20, 2003, therefore lacked outright UN endorsement.

Primary Source

Joint statement by Mr. de Villepin, Mr. Ivanov and Mr. Fischer

(Paris, 5 March 2003)

Our common objective remains the full and effective disarmament of Iraq, in compliance with resolution 1441 (2002).

We consider that this objective can be achieved by the peaceful means of the inspections.

We moreover observe that these inspections are producing increasing encouraging results:

- The destruction of the Al-Samoud missiles has started and is making progress;
- Iraqis are providing biological and chemical information;
- The interviews with Iraqi scientists are continuing.

Russia, Germany and France resolutely support Messrs. Blix and ElBaradei and consider the meeting of the Security Council on 7 March to be an important step in the process put in place.

We firmly call for the Iraqi authorities to cooperate more actively with the inspectors to fully disarm their country. These inspections cannot continue indefinitely.

We consequently ask that the inspections now be speeded up, in keeping with the proposals put forward in the memorandum submitted to the Security Council by our three countries. We must:

- Specify and prioritize the remaining issues, programme by programme;
- Establish, for each point, detailed timelines.

Using this method, the inspectors have to present without any delay their work programme accompanied by regular progress reports to the Security Council. This programme could provide for a meeting clause to enable the Council to evaluate the overall results of this process.

In these circumstances, we will not let a proposed resolution pass that would authorize the use of force.

Russia and France, as permanent members of the Security Council, will assume all their responsibilities on this point.

We are at a turning point. Since our goal is the peaceful and full disarmament of Iraq, we have today the chance to obtain through peaceful means a comprehensive settlement for the Middle East, starting with a move forward in the peace process, by:

- Publishing and implementing the roadmap;
- Putting together a general framework for the Middle East, based on stability and security, renunciation of force, arms control and trust-building measures.

Source: United Nations Security Council, S/2003/253, March 5, 2003, http://www.un.int/france/documents_anglais/030305_mae_france_irak.htm.

111. Spain, the United Kingdom, and the United States, Draft Resolution on Iraq, March 7, 2003

Introduction

Before embarking on outright war against Iraq, the United States and British governments hoped to obtain a United Nations (UN) Security Council Resolution specifically authorizing them to do so. British prime minister Tony Blair was particularly eager for such a resolution because such a mandate would significantly enhance his position within his own ruling Labour Party, whose members were badly divided over the desirability of invading Iraq. In late February 2003 the United States, Britain, and Spain,

another member of the "coalition of the willing" that were preparing to invade Iraq, submitted a draft resolution to the Security Council. This document stated that the declaration that Iraq had submitted to the Security Council detailing its progress toward disarmament contained "false statements and omissions" and that Iraq had therefore declined to comply with Resolution 1441 of November 2002. This, in turn, meant that Iraq had "failed to take the final opportunity afforded it in Resolution 1441." While the resolution did not specifically call for military intervention against Iraq, it represented the strongest endorsement that the three powers thought they were likely to win from the Security Council. As events transpired, they failed to obtain even this level of support. France, a permanent Security Council member, expressed its readiness to veto any such resolution and, together with Russia and Germany, submitted a statement affirming confidence in the weapons inspection process then under way in Iraq and seeking its acceleration. Britain then proposed a resolution offering six conditions that Hussein would have to meet expeditiously in order to avoid war but could not obtain even 9 of 15 Security Council votes favoring such action. Permanent members Russia and China were particularly unenthusiastic, fearing that an authorization for preemptive action against Iraq might set an undesirable precedent whereby, at some future date, the United States or other powers might move against themselves. Eventually, the United States, Britain, and other coalition members decided to make war on Iraq without the mandate of a further UN Security Council resolution specifically countenancing such action.

Primary Source

Recalling all its previous relevant resolutions, in particular its resolutions 661 (1990) of 6 August 1990, 678 (1990) of 29 November 1990, 686 (1991) of 2 March 1991, 687 (1991) of 3 April 1991, 688 (1991) of 5 April 1991, 707 (1991) of 15 August 1991, 715 (1991) of 11 October 1991, 986 (1995) of 14 April 1995, and 1284 (1999) of 17 December 1999, and 1441 (2002) of 8 November all the relevant statements of its president,

Recalling that in its resolution 687 (1991) the council declared that a cease-fire would be based on acceptance by Iraq of the provisions of that resolution, including the obligations on Iraq contained therein,

Recalling that its resolution 1441 (2002), while acknowledging that Iraq has been and remains in material breach of its obligations, afforded Iraq a final opportunity to comply with its disarmament obligations under relevant resolutions,

Recalling that in its resolution 1441 (2002) the council decided that false statements or omissions in the declaration submitted by Iraq pursuant to that resolution and failure by Iraq at any time to comply with and cooperate fully in the implementation of, that resolution, would constitute a further material breach,

Noting, that in that context, that in its resolution 1441 (2002), the council recalled that it has repeatedly warned Iraq that it will face serious consequences as a result of its continued violations of its obligations,

Noting that Iraq has submitted a declaration pursuant to its resolution 1441 (2002) containing false statements and omissions and has failed to comply with, and cooperate fully in the implementation of, that resolution,

Reaffirming the commitment of all member states to the sovereignty and territorial integrity of Iraq, Kuwait, and the neighboring states,

Mindful of its primary responsibility under the charter of the United Nations for the maintenance of international peace and security,

Recognizing the threat Iraq's noncompliance with council resolutions and proliferation of weapons of mass destruction and long-range missiles poses to international peace and security,

Determined to secure full compliance with its decisions and to restore international peace and security in the area,

Acting under Chapter VII of the charter of the United Nations,

Decides that Iraq has failed to take the final opportunity afforded to it in resolution 1441 (2002).

Decides to remain seized of the matter.

Source: United Nations Security Council, S/2003/215, March 7, 2003, http://www.nuclearinfo.org/documents/singh.pdf.

112. President George W. Bush, Remarks at the American Enterprise Institute Annual Dinner, February 26, 2003 [Excerpt]

Introduction

By early 2003, many officials in the administration of U.S. president George W. Bush saw war against Iraq not just as a means of removing an unpleasant Middle Eastern dictator who was antagonistic to the United States but also as a catalyst for bringing about radical change throughout the entire Persian Gulf region. In a speech to the American Enterprise Institute, a leading Washington-based neoconservative think tank that had provided much

of the personnel and intellectual underpinning for his foreign policy initiatives, Bush laid out the rationale for this perspective toward regime change in Iraq. Once again Bush stressed the dangers that, in his view, President Saddam Hussein's government in Iraq posed to the United States and its allies. Bush also highlighted the repressive nature of Hussein's rule. The U.S. president then argued that establishing a democratic, stable, and free government in Iraq "would serve as a dramatic and inspiring example of freedom for other nations in the region," encouraging their governments and populations to implement similar reforms. This, in turn, would bring a new era of peace and economic development. The overthrow of Hussein would, in addition, demonstrate that the international community would not tolerate the existence of governments that supported and encouraged terrorist movements, which the president hoped would persuade those currently guilty of providing such assistance to cease doing so. The removal of external support for terrorism would, he believed, enhance the position of moderate Palestinians, facilitating a lasting settlement of the Israeli-Palestinian dispute. Bush was speaking to a sympathetic audience, which included a number of individuals who had been instrumental in developing the Middle Eastern strategy that he himself was laying out before them.

Primary Source

[...]

We meet here during a crucial period in the history of our Nation and of the civilized world. Part of that history was written by others; the rest will be written by us. On a September morning, threats that had gathered for years, in secret and far away, led to murder in our country on a massive scale. As a result, we must look at security in a new way, because our country is a battlefield in the first war of the 21st century.

We learned a lesson: The dangers of our time must be confronted actively and forcefully, before we see them again in our skies and in our cities. And we set a goal: We will not allow the triumph of hatred and violence in the affairs of men.

Our coalition of more than 90 countries is pursuing the networks of terror with every tool of law enforcement and with military power. We have arrested or otherwise dealt with many key commanders of Al Qaida. Across the world, we are hunting down the killers one by one. We are winning. And we're showing them the definition of American justice. And we are opposing the greatest danger in the war on terror, outlaw regimes arming with weapons of mass destruction.

In Iraq, a dictator is building and hiding weapons that could enable him to dominate the Middle East and intimidate the civilized world, and we will not allow it. This same tyrant has close ties to terrorist organizations and could supply them with the terrible means to strike this country, and America will not permit it. The danger posed by Saddam Hussein and his weapons cannot be ignored or wished away. The danger must be confronted. We hope that the Iraqi regime will meet the demands of the United Nations and disarm, fully and peacefully. If it does not, we are prepared to disarm Iraq by force. Either way, this danger will be removed.

The safety of the American people depends on ending this direct and growing threat. Acting against the danger will also contribute greatly to the long-term safety and stability of our world. The current Iraqi regime has shown the power of tyranny to spread discord and violence in the Middle East. A liberated Iraq can show the power of freedom to transform that vital region, by bringing hope and progress into the lives of millions. America's interests in security and America's belief in liberty both lead in the same direction, to a free and peaceful Iraq.

The first to benefit from a free Iraq would be the Iraqi people themselves. Today they live in scarcity and fear under a dictator who has brought them nothing but war and misery and torture. Their lives and their freedom matter little to Saddam Hussein, but Iraqi lives and freedom matter greatly to us.

Bringing stability and unity to a free Iraq will not be easy. Yet that is no excuse to leave the Iraqi regime's torture chambers and poison labs in operation. Any future the Iraqi people choose for themselves will be better than the nightmare world that Saddam Hussein has chosen for them.

If we must use force, the United States and our coalition stand ready to help the citizens of a liberated Iraq. We will deliver medicine to the sick, and we are now moving into place nearly 3 million emergency rations to feed the hungry. We'll make sure that Iraq's 55,000 food distribution sites, operating under the oil-for-food program, are stocked and open as soon as possible. The United States and Great Britain are providing tens of millions of dollars to the U.N. High Commission on Refugees and to such groups as the World Food Program and UNICEF to provide emergency aid to the Iraqi people.

We will also lead in carrying out the urgent and dangerous work of destroying chemical and biological weapons. We will provide security against those who try to spread chaos or settle scores or threaten the territorial integrity of Iraq. We will seek to protect Iraq's natural resources from sabotage by a dying regime and ensure those resources are used for the benefit of the owners, the Iraqi people.

The United States has no intention of determining the precise form of Iraq's new Government. That choice belongs to the Iraqi people. Yet, we will ensure that one brutal dictator is not replaced by another. All Iraqis must have a voice in the new Government, and all citizens must have their rights protected.

Rebuilding Iraq will require a sustained commitment from many nations, including our own. We will remain in Iraq as long as necessary and not a day more. America has made and kept this kind of commitment before, in the peace that followed a World War. After defeating enemies, we did not leave behind occupying armies; we left constitutions and parliaments. We established an atmosphere of safety, in which responsible, reform-minded local leaders could build lasting institutions of freedom. In

societies that once bred fascism and militarism, liberty found a permanent home.

There was a time when many said that the cultures of Japan and Germany were incapable of sustaining democratic values. Well, they were wrong. Some say the same of Iraq today. They are mistaken. The nation of Iraq, with its proud heritage, abundant resources, and skilled and educated people, is fully capable of moving toward democracy and living in freedom.

The world has a clear interest in the spread of democratic values, because stable and free nations do not breed the ideologies of murder. They encourage the peaceful pursuit of a better life. And there are hopeful signs of a desire for freedom in the Middle East. Arab intellectuals have called on Arab governments to address the "freedom gap" so their peoples can fully share in the progress of our times. Leaders in the region speak of a new Arab charter that champions internal reform, greater political participation, economic openness, and free trade. And from Morocco to Bahrain and beyond, nations are taking genuine steps toward political reform. A new regime in Iraq would serve as a dramatic and inspiring example of freedom for other nations in the region.

It is presumptuous and insulting to suggest that a whole region of the world, or the one-fifth of humanity that is Muslim, is somehow untouched by the most basic aspirations of life. Human cultures can be vastly different, yet the human heart desires the same good things everywhere on Earth. In our desire to be safe from brutal and bullying oppression, human beings are the same. In our desire to care for our children and give them a better life, we are the same. For these fundamental reasons, freedom and democracy will always and everywhere have greater appeal than the slogans of hatred and the tactics of terror.

Success in Iraq could also begin a new stage for Middle Eastern peace and set in motion progress towards a truly democratic Palestinian state. The passing of Saddam Hussein's regime will deprive terrorist networks of a wealthy patron that pays for terrorist training and offers rewards to families of suicide bombers. And other regimes will be given a clear warning that support for terror will not be tolerated.

Without this outside support for terrorism, Palestinians who are working for reform and long for democracy will be in a better position to choose new leaders, true leaders who strive for peace, true leaders who faithfully serve the people. A Palestinian state must be a reformed and peaceful state that abandons forever the use of terror.

For its part, the new Government of Israel, as the terror threat is removed and security improves, will be expected to support the creation of a viable Palestinian state and to work as quickly as possible toward a final status agreement. As progress is made toward peace, settlement activity in the occupied territories must end. And the Arab states will be expected to meet their responsibilities to oppose terrorism, to support the emergence of a peaceful and democratic Palestine, and state clearly they will live in peace with Israel.

The United States and other nations are working on a roadmap for peace. We are setting out the necessary conditions for progress toward the goal of two states, Israel and Palestine, living side by side in peace and security. It is the commitment of our Government and my personal commitment to implement the roadmap and to reach that goal. Old patterns of conflict in the Middle East can be broken, if all concerned will let go of bitterness and hatred and violence and get on with the serious work of economic development and political reform and reconciliation. America will seize every opportunity in pursuit of peace. And the end of the present regime in Iraq would create such an opportunity.

In confronting Iraq, the United States is also showing our commitment to effective international institutions. We are a permanent member of the United Nations Security Council. We helped to create the Security Council. We believe in the Security Council so much that we want its words to have meaning.

The global threat of proliferation of weapons of mass destruction cannot be confronted by one nation alone. The world needs today and will need tomorrow international bodies with the authority and the will to stop the spread of terror and chemical and biological and nuclear weapons. A threat to all must be answered by all. High-minded pronouncements against proliferation mean little unless the strongest nations are willing to stand behind them and use force if necessary. After all, the United Nations was created, as Winston Churchill said, to "make sure that the force of right will, in the ultimate issue, be protected by the right of force."

Another resolution is now before the Security Council. If the Council responds to Iraq's defiance with more excuses and delays, if all its authority proves to be empty, the United Nations will be severely weakened as a source of stability and order. If the members rise to this moment, then the Council will fulfill its founding purpose.

I've listened carefully as people and leaders around the world have made known their desire for peace. All of us want peace. The threat to peace does not come from those who seek to enforce the just demands of the civilized world. The threat to peace comes from those who flout those demands. If we have to act, we will act to restrain the violent and defend the cause of peace. And by acting, we will signal to outlaw regimes that in this new century, the boundaries of civilized behavior will be respected.

Protecting those boundaries carries a cost. If war is forced upon us by Iraq's refusal to disarm, we will meet an enemy [Saddam Hussein] who hides his military forces behind civilians, who has terrible weapons, who is capable of any crime. The dangers are real, as our soldiers and sailors, airmen and marines fully understand. Yet, no military has ever been better prepared to meet these challenges.

Members of our Armed Forces also understand why they may be called to fight. They know that retreat before a dictator guarantees even greater sacrifices in the future. They know that America's cause is right and just, liberty for an oppressed people and security for the American people. And I know something about these men

and women who wear our uniform: They will complete every mission they are given with skill and honor and courage.

Much is asked of America in this year 2003. The work ahead is demanding. It will be difficult to help freedom take hold in a country that has known three decades of dictatorship, secret police, internal divisions, and war. It will be difficult to cultivate liberty and peace in the Middle East, after so many generations of strife. Yet the security of our Nation and the hope of millions depend on us, and Americans do not turn away from duties because they are hard. We have met great tests in other times, and we will meet the tests of our time.

We go forward with confidence, because we trust in the power of human freedom to change lives and nations. By the resolve and purpose of America and of our friends and allies, we will make this an age of progress and liberty. Free people will set the course of history, and free people will keep the peace of the world.

Source: George W. Bush, *Public Papers of the Presidents of the United States: George Bush, 2003,* Book 1 (Washington, DC: U.S. Government Printing Office, 2003), 216–220.

113. President George W. Bush, Address to the Nation on Iraq, March 17, 2003

Introduction

With Anglo-American efforts to obtain a United Nations (UN) Security Council mandate for war against Iraq deadlocked, on March 17, 2003, U.S. president George W. Bush announced to the American people his administration's decision to use force against Iraq. Once more he stated that Iraq possessed biological and chemical weapons of mass destruction and was developing a nuclear capability, which made it a threat already to the United States, one that would only grow in the future and that within a few years would be far more menacing. Bush also claimed that Iraq provided sanctuary, funding, and safe haven to terrorist organizations, including Al Qaeda. The UN, Bush rather provocatively claimed, had failed to meet its responsibility to deal with President Saddam Hussein of Iraq, but the United States and its coalition of allies would do so. Bush told Hussein that only if he and his sons left Iraq within 48 hours could war be avoided. Bush appealed to the Iraqi military to abandon Hussein and offer no resistance to invading coalition forces. Bush also warned Iraqi officials against destroying the country's oil industry, "a source of wealth that belongs to the Iraqi people," and to disobey any orders instructing them to utilize weapons of mass destruction against the invaders or their own people. The U.S. president promised the Iraqi people that once Hussein and his followers had been ousted, they themselves would enjoy the benefits of democracy and "set an example to all the Middle East of a vital and peaceful and self-governing nation." Although Bush claimed that his country had no feasible alternative except war, his administration had clearly sought this conflict despite much international opposition. Major demonstrations in protest took place around the world, although in the United States early polls showed public support for Bush's policies on Iraq peaking at more than 70 percent in the war's early days, and even former critics of the intervention tended to mute their misgivings and rally around their country's armed forces.

Primary Source

My fellow citizens, events in Iraq have now reached the final days of decision. For more than a decade, the United States and other nations have pursued patient and honorable efforts to disarm the Iraqi regime without war. That regime pledged to reveal and destroy all its weapons of mass destruction as a condition for ending the Persian Gulf war in 1991.

Since then, the world has engaged in 12 years of diplomacy. We have passed more than a dozen resolutions in the United Nations Security Council. We have sent hundreds of weapons inspectors to oversee the disarmament of Iraq. Our good faith has not been returned.

The Iraqi regime has used diplomacy as a ploy to gain time and advantage. It has uniformly defied Security Council resolutions demanding full disarmament. Over the years, U.N. weapon inspectors have been threatened by Iraqi officials, electronically bugged, and systematically deceived. Peaceful efforts to disarm the Iraqi regime have failed again and again because we are not dealing with peaceful men.

Intelligence gathered by this and other governments leaves no doubt that the Iraq regime continues to possess and conceal some of the most lethal weapons ever devised. This regime has already used weapons of mass destruction against Iraq's neighbors and against Iraq's people.

The regime has a history of reckless aggression in the Middle East. It has a deep hatred of America and our friends. And it has aided, trained, and harbored terrorists, including operatives of Al Qaida.

The danger is clear: Using chemical, biological or, one day, nuclear weapons obtained with the help of Iraq, the terrorists could fulfill their stated ambitions and kill thousands or hundreds of thousands of innocent people in our country or any other.

The United States and other nations did nothing to deserve or invite this threat. But we will do everything to defeat it. Instead of drifting along toward tragedy, we will set a course toward safety. Before the day of horror can come, before it is too late to act, this danger will be removed.

The United States of America has the sovereign authority to use force in assuring its own national security. That duty falls to me as Commander in Chief, by the oath I have sworn, by the oath I will keep.

Recognizing the threat to our country, the United States Congress voted overwhelmingly last year to support the use of force against Iraq. America tried to work with the United Nations to address this threat because we wanted to resolve the issue peacefully. We believe in the mission of the United Nations. One reason the U.N. was founded after the Second World War was to confront aggressive dictators actively and early, before they can attack the innocent and destroy the peace.

In the case of Iraq, the Security Council did act in the early 1990s. Under Resolutions 678 and 687, both still in effect, the United States and our allies are authorized to use force in ridding Iraq of weapons of mass destruction. This is not a question of authority. It is a question of will.

Last September, I went to the U.N. General Assembly and urged the nations of the world to unite and bring an end to this danger. On November 8th, the Security Council unanimously passed Resolution 1441, finding Iraq in material breach of its obligations and vowing serious consequences if Iraq did not fully and immediately disarm.

Today, no nation can possibly claim that Iraq has disarmed, and it will not disarm so long as Saddam Hussein holds power. For the last 4 1/2 months, the United States and our allies have worked within the Security Council to enforce that Council's longstanding demands. Yet, some permanent members of the Security Council have publicly announced they will veto any resolution that compels the disarmament of Iraq. These governments share our assessment of the danger but not our resolve to meet it.

Many nations, however, do have the resolve and fortitude to act against this threat to peace, and a broad coalition is now gathering to enforce the just demands of the world. The United Nations Security Council has not lived up to its responsibilities, so we will rise to ours.

In recent days, some governments in the Middle East have been doing their part. They have delivered public and private messages urging the dictator to leave Iraq, so that disarmament can proceed peacefully. He has thus far refused.

All the decades of deceit and cruelty have now reached an end. Saddam Hussein and his sons must leave Iraq within 48 hours. Their refusal to do so will result in military conflict, commenced at a time of our choosing. For their own safety, all foreign nationals, including journalists and inspectors, should leave Iraq immediately.

Many Iraqis can hear me tonight in a translated radio broadcast, and I have a message for them: If we must begin a military campaign, it will be directed against the lawless men who rule your country and not against you. As our coalition takes away their power, we will deliver the food and medicine you need. We will tear down the apparatus of terror, and we will help you to build a new Iraq that is prosperous and free. In a free Iraq, there will be no more wars of aggression against your neighbors, no more poison factories, no more executions of dissidents, no more torture chambers and rape rooms. The tyrant will soon be gone. The day of your liberation is near.

It is too late for Saddam Hussein to remain in power. It is not too late for the Iraqi military to act with honor and protect your country by permitting the peaceful entry of coalition forces to eliminate weapons of mass destruction. Our forces will give Iraqi military units clear instructions on actions they can take to avoid being attacked and destroyed. I urge every member of the Iraqi military and intelligence services: If war comes, do not fight for a dying regime that is not worth your own life.

And all Iraqi military and civilian personnel should listen carefully to this warning: In any conflict, your fate will depend on your actions. Do not destroy oil wells, a source of wealth that belongs to the Iraqi people. Do not obey any command to use weapons of mass destruction against anyone, including the Iraqi people. War crimes will be prosecuted. War criminals will be punished. And it will be no defense to say, "I was just following orders."

Should Saddam Hussein choose confrontation, the American people can know that every measure has been taken to avoid war and every measure will be taken to win it. Americans understand the costs of conflict because we have paid them in the past. War has no certainty, except the certainty of sacrifice. Yet, the only way to reduce the harm and duration of war is to apply the full force and might of our military, and we are prepared to do so.

If Saddam Hussein attempts to cling to power, he will remain a deadly foe until the end. In desperation, he and terrorist groups might try to conduct terrorist operations against the American people and our friends. These attacks are not inevitable. They are, however, possible. And this very fact underscores the reason we cannot live under the threat of blackmail. The terrorist threat to America and the world will be diminished the moment that Saddam Hussein is disarmed.

Our Government is on heightened watch against these dangers. Just as we are preparing to ensure victory in Iraq, we are taking further actions to protect our homeland. In recent days, American authorities have expelled from the country certain individuals with ties to Iraqi intelligence services. Among other measures, I have directed additional security of our airports and increased Coast Guard patrols of major seaports. The Department of Homeland Security is working closely with the Nation's Governors to increase armed security at critical facilities across America.

Should enemies strike our country, they would be attempting to shift our attention with panic and weaken our morale with fear. In this, they would fail. No act of theirs can alter the course or shake the resolve of this country. We are a peaceful people. Yet we're not a fragile people, and we will not be intimidated by thugs and killers. If our enemies dare to strike us, they and all who have aided them will face fearful consequences.

We are now acting because the risks of inaction would be far greater. In 1 year, or 5 years, the power of Iraq to inflict harm on all free nations would be multiplied many times over. With these capabilities, Saddam Hussein and his terrorist allies could choose the moment of deadly conflict when they are strongest. We choose to meet that threat now, where it arises, before it can appear suddenly in our skies and cities.

The cause of peace requires all free nations to recognize new and undeniable realities. In the 20th century, some chose to appease murderous dictators, whose threats were allowed to grow into genocide and global war. In this century, when evil men plot chemical, biological, and nuclear terror, a policy of appeasement could bring destruction of a kind never before seen on this Earth.

Terrorists and terror states do not reveal these threats with fair notice, in formal declarations. And responding to such enemies only after they have struck first is not self-defense; it is suicide. The security of the world requires disarming Saddam Hussein now.

As we enforce the just demands of the world, we will also honor the deepest commitments of our country. Unlike Saddam Hussein, we believe the Iraqi people are deserving and capable of human liberty. And when the dictator has departed, they can set an example to all the Middle East of a vital and peaceful and self-governing nation.

The United States, with other countries, will work to advance liberty and peace in that region. Our goal will not be achieved overnight, but it can come over time. The power and appeal of human liberty is felt in every life and every land. And the greatest power of freedom is to overcome hatred and violence and turn the creative gifts of men and women to the pursuits of peace.

That is the future we choose. Free nations have a duty to defend our people by uniting against the violent. And tonight, as we have done before, America and our allies accept that responsibility.

Source: George W. Bush, *Public Papers of the Presidents of the United States: George Bush, 2003*, Book 1 (Washington, DC: U.S. Government Printing Office, 2003), 277–280.

114. President Hamid Karzai of Afghanistan, State of the Nation Speech, Radio Afghanistan, Kabul, Afghanistan, April 8, 2003 [Excerpts]

Introduction

Transitional president Hamid Karzai of Afghanistan, the internationally well-regarded Pashtun tribal aristocrat who headed Afghanistan's government from late 2001 onward, displayed some apprehension that the new American war against Iraq would divert U.S. attention and resources from Afghanistan's continuing problems. In a remarkably frank State of the Union address that he delivered to his people in April 2003, 10 months after he was chosen provisional president, Karzai showed himself very much aware that while progress had been made, Afghanistan's many difficult issues still remained unresolved. His address celebrated progress that had been made in reconstructing the country's economy, infrastructure, educational, and health care systems as well as in international relations and facilitating the return of refugees but also mentioned some major "shortcomings and flaws." Creation and training of a national army and police force had gone slowly, and these institutions were still inadequate, while many nongovernment militias around the country still possessed arms, and "[t]he rule of the gun has not been wiped out in all parts of the country." Bribery and corruption remained rife in government departments, and officials often expropriated private property. Provincial administrations frequently declined to transfer revenues to the capital in Kabul. Government officials were still selected and promoted largely on the basis of personal connections, and there was little transparency in administration. Three hundred thousand Afghans were still living in camps for displaced persons. Karzai announced that in the coming year he hoped to take "[t]ough measures" to remedy these situations and enforce law and order throughout the country while training young men who would be able to provide the nucleus of new army and police forces. If successful, these initiatives would enable Karzai's government to strengthen its authority over all Afghanistan.

Primary Source

[...]

I promised you my compatriots during my speech of congratulations on Nowruz that I would shortly inform you about the activities of the Transitional Islamic State of Afghanistan over the last year and I would tell you what we have done and what we have not done. Now I am keeping my promise by presenting the government's report.

Security and defence

Peace, stability and security:

The conflicts ended generally across the country in the solar year 1381 (2002–2003), and it was because the establishment of the new regime put an end to the reasons for the conflicts. Fighting was eliminated across the country. However, there can be no doubt that occasionally clashes have taken place among some groups and commanders, or the remnants of Taleban and Al-Qa'idah have had clashes with the counter-terrorism coalition in some areas of the country. But generally, the rule and influence of the terrorists of Al-Qa'idah and other monsters are diminishing day by day. It is because the public at large in Afghanistan and the vast sections of the people hate war. They want to live in peace, in security, within their country. They want their fields and gardens to flourish and to shape their lives that have been shattered for 23 years. They are seeking to settle in their houses, villages and cities honourably and respectably.

It is noteworthy that the memories of the sacrifices rendered by our people and countrymen of Afghanistan in their struggle to safeguard security in the country and in securing the country's frontiers and fighting against Al-Qa'idah and other anti-Afghan militant evils. Our people have rendered similar services in history, which could be compared with their struggle against the terrorists and Al-Qa'idah at the present time. All we Afghans are determined that from now on, no one should play with our lives and fate. We would not let them disrupt the peace in our country and force us to leave our country and take refuge in other countries.

We witnessed the convention of the Emergency Loya Jerga last year in the month of Saratan (June–July), comprising Afghans of every class and tribe, including representatives of the refugee Afghans. The discussion lasted for seven days. They carried out the duties assigned to them in an independent, peaceful and brotherly environment. The council concluded with unity and accord.

The convening of the Loya Jerga in the country, after the years of unrest, war and destitution, is a manifestation of the existence of political stability. The government ministries and the institutions that are responsible for safeguarding peace and security have also made progress in the formation of the National Army, the police force, and in security affairs last year....

[...]

Law and order

Various aspects of reconstruction work:

Afghanistan needs general reconstruction in the economic, social, political, administrative and cultural fields. Businessmen, investors, governmental and non-governmental organizations (NGOs), the United Nations and other international organizations commenced this reconstruction work on a different level last year. But it is impossible to rehabilitate all of the devastation in Afghanistan in one or two years. Thus we should be patient, as we do not have the resources and the opportunities. Every project we undertake is dependent on assistance.

Our most important work in the reconstruction process was that we activated the deadlocked administration in Afghanistan. However it still has flaws and shortcomings. The good point is that the doors of the government departments opened to people across the country....

[...]

What's happening in the economy

Economic performance:

Out of the aid given to Afghanistan by donor countries last year, 25.5 billion afghani currency have been given to the UN, 21.6 billion Afghani to international and Afghani NGOs and some has been given to emigrants abroad and international organizations, and only 13.3 billion afghani have been given to the Afghan government. The ordinary budget of Afghanistan for last year was 460 million dollars, which is equal to 20.7 billion new afghani currency. A very small amount of this budget, approximately 60 million dollars have been obtained from state revenues, and the rest of it was dependent on foreign aid. The customs revenues of some provinces have been transferred to the central account, but complete revenues have not reached the capital. However, the state has done some important work in other economic sectors, the important ones of which are the following:

Banking and monetary reforms:

One of the prominent achievements of the Transitional Islamic State of Afghanistan last year was printing new afghani banknotes, including reforms in the banking system. The new afghani banknotes have strong backup and it is evident that this currency is competing with foreign currencies on the market. With the printing of the new afghani banknotes, inflation and a currency crisis was prevented in the country. A single currency unit was established all over the country and our people, who were facing the problem of foreign currencies and different afghani currencies, were freed of these problems. Some problems that still exist in some provinces will be eliminated, God willing, after reforms in the banking system this year.

Commerce:

Last year, Afghanistan's trade at home and abroad was gradually improving. Afghan exports to foreign countries started again. The sanctions that had been imposed on the export of Afghan commodities to foreign markets under the Taleban have been lifted now. Afghan commodities such as rugs and carpets, dried and fresh fruit, herbal remedies, Astrakhan fur hats and other animal skins, different handicrafts, light industry and other products, have made their way to the markets of America, Europe and Asia. The United States of America and the European Union countries have eased their custom duties on Afghan exports and the Indian government has taken a similar step and some Afghan export commodities have been exempted from customs duties.

To develop trade even further, joint chambers of commerce have been set up by Afghan businessmen and some foreign countries such as America, Britain, Iran, India and Japan. Inside and outside the country, Afghans have expressed their interest in setting up trading companies. Last year, 2,602 trade companies and 97 individuals were given business permits.

[. . .]

Preservation of human rights

Preservation of the rights of masses and the rights of women:

The government sent high-ranking government authorities to all of the provinces in the country last year to prevent the injustice, cruelty, and lawlessness caused by gunmen and some other officials in the country's provinces. The delegations observed closely the affairs in every province and its districts and examined the security of the highways. They presented detailed reports to the government. And the council of the ministers removed some of the corrupt people from their posts, based on the reports and they took measures to remove all of the factors that caused trouble to people.

In addition to that, the members of the judiciary and justice departments of the government and the law-enforcement and human rights agencies were sent to examine the conditions of the prisoners and all of the minor and major, visible and hidden, male and female jails in the country. Some of them are still engaged in examining the jails.

[. . .]

Foreign relations

The country's foreign relations:

Thanks be to God Almighty that after many years of political isolation, Afghanistan once again joined the international community as a solid and respectable member last year and established relations with the countries of the world. At the present time, more than 65 countries and international institutions have political agencies in our country. The political agencies of Afghanistan are active in some countries. Seven embassies and four consulates have been added to the structure of the Foreign Ministry of Afghanistan. During the Year 1381 (solar year 2002–2003), 94 senior delegations and heads of different countries visited Afghanistan. Similarly, senior delegations of the Afghan government made visits to different countries. The national and international prestige of Afghanistan has been regained and the nations of the world respect our country and people today and now the Afghan passport is valued all over the world.

The country's foreign policy is based on mutual respect, non-interference in others' affairs, respecting the stability, territorial integrity, political sovereignty, national recognition and maintaining friendly relations with all the countries of the world. Afghanistan desires strong and transparent friendly relations with all the countries of the world, particularly the neighbouring countries and the Islamic countries.

We have established friendly relations with many countries of the world for reconstruction, development and bolstering the country's economic, political, social and cultural institutions of the country and for attraction of aid and cooperation and we give great priority to establishment of relations in every sector with our neighbours. We assure all our neighbours that Afghanistan will observe peaceful norms of coexistence and good neighbourliness and would always remain a genuine friend to its neighbours. We expect our neighbours to behave in a similar manner. The Kabul declaration, which was passed at the conference of foreign ministers of the neighbours of Afghanistan in the month of Jadi (December–January) last year, was a positive and effective step towards bolstering friendly relations with our neighbours. We believe that our neighbours will respect the declaration.

Government shortcomings

Dear countrymen,

I am putting the achievements of the Transitional Islamic State of Afghanistan in words very briefly and precisely and making you aware about everything in general. All the ministries and independent departments have prepared their progress reports in detail and will be publishing them in the Annual Publication of Afghanistan, which has resumed its publication after an interval of 10-years pause, to further inform our countrymen. Similarly, the ministers would give their own progress reports to the nation. The report that I presented to you dear countrymen was a report on the work done by government bodies. I should mention that last year the government performance also had shortcomings and flaws. It is my responsibility to inform my countrymen about the shortcomings.

The process of forming the National Army proceeded slowly last year. As you know, the training of the young recruits to the National Army started during the interim administration, but it had not produced results that could meet the expectations of people.

Our work to reform the police system and establish a national police force had many flaws. We could not put together a single skilled and professional police battalion to prevent demonstrations and in the past year two tragic incidents involving harsh police behaviour with regard to students have occurred. One occurred at the Polytechnic institute and the other with students of Kabul University during Ramadan the Islamic month of fasting, which still troubles my soul.

The collection of arms from irresponsible forces has continued in many parts of the count[r]y, but this procedure has not been satisfactory.

The government has not managed to do anything to reform the civil administration! Bribery has continued in all government departments, municipalities and security agencies and several customs institutions with full effect, and the law-enforcement and public rights agencies have failed to stop bribery.

The rule of the gun has not been wiped out in all parts of the country. We witnessed that robbers and thieves used uniforms and security posts and had established checkpoints on the public highways and extorted money from passengers and tradesman. They have caused people trouble and appropriated state revenues. Despite all the many efforts made by the state, still state revenues from across Afghanistan are not being transferred to the capital.

Commissions have been set up to improve the affairs of different sections of the departments and the government institutions, but they have failed to achieve anything.

There has not been any significant progress made within the government when it comes to cadres either. Personal relations still count for more than rules and regulation when selecting cadres, appointing and transferring them. And the assessment of performance at government institutions has been critically weak with respect to government cadres and it still is.

Still some of the persecutors have illegally snatched the shops, flats, residences, and land of a number of our compatriots. Departments of preserving the rights of the masses could not return the properties to their original owners.

Cutting down the woodland continued last year, and effective measures were not taken to prevent this action. Lawlessness, violation of the rules and regulations continued in the provinces and the capital city. And all those unfair activities, harmful to the nation, have marred the process of promoting the governance and dominance of the government departments. A number of NGOs, that work in different walks of life and are supported by donor countries and international organizations, which allows them to render services in the country, have worked on useful projects. But we still have no clear way of and solution for coordinating and improving their performance, and having transparent statistics for the Afghan nation.

Regrettably, for various reasons 300,000 of our destitute compatriots are living a miserable life in displaced persons' camps inside the country, especially in the western and southwestern regions. However, the government and our international coordinators provided them with urgent humanitarian assistance last year, including food, clothing, fuel and medical services. They still have not yet been returned to their homes.

In conclusion

Dear sisters and brothers, as you know, we had achievements, but also some aspects of our affairs were flawed and defective last year. Despite the difficulties that are hindering us, our vision for the construction of an independent, prosperous, honoured, respected and affluent country is still firm. Tough measures will be taken this year to achieve this target. Our major target is to enforce the law and order situation, peace and stability, and the dominance of the democratic system on a national level. The lack of absolute security and peace has been the factor holding back reconstruction in the country. The government has taken measures to enforce countrywide security and liberate people from evil warlords.

The enforcement of disarmament, demilitarization and the participation of militant personnel in the affairs of society, will be announced this year. Their financial resources, which are over 125 million dollars, are also to be determined. It is planned that before 15 Sowr (5 May) their relevant offices will be ready. From the 15 Sowr (5 May) till the end of Jawza (May), the equipment and their accessories will be ready and the foundation work on the programme would start on the 1st Saratan (22 June). The programme that is supported by Japan and the United Nations will be implemented countrywide in several stages. It will shortly be started in two or three provinces, and arms will be collected by 100,000 armed people, including all of the armed forces and the existing government forces.

The implementation of this programme would play a key role in ensuring the peace process. The course of training the youngsters in the National Army, which will be supported by the United States of America, will be stepped up. Most of the donor countries have expressed complete support in this respect. The proposals on the reform of the police and frontier forces would be implemented with the assistance of Germany according to a decree that was signed this week.

The police training centre with a capacity of 7,000 police personnel has been taken into account, which will gradually provide to capital city and other provinces with professional and experienced forces.

A well equipped radio communications system between the capital city and all of the other provinces will be established this year, which will enable the capital to learn about the events happening in every corner of the country as soon as possible.

The comprehensive modification and equipping of the national security forces are included in the country's foundation programmes this year. Subordinated to the security issue, another of the government's basic priorities is the rehabilitation of the war-ravaged government institutions. The government has received only 30 percent of the pledged assistance last year. It is planned that most of the assistance would be transferred directly to the government this year, and that would be spent on reconstruction in the country with due consent.

The reconstruction of the highways in Kabul will be seriously undertaken this year. Attention to the reconstruction of the irrigation system and the dams, restoring the major irrigation projects and hydropower generation are among our priorities.

The government is to pay particular attention to the special sector for improving the standard of living of the masses, and the provision of employment. The government will remain committed to all of its pledges to attract internal and foreign investments, will provide the opportunity for work and activities across the country for the special investors and internal and foreign capitalists. I am hopeful that those who have obtained commercial and manufacturing license would start their work this year.

By the grace of the Almighty, the abundance of snowfall and rain has reduced the various problems of the farmers and gardeners all over the country. The government will support farmers and market gardeners who practice mechanized agriculture, clear the dams, canals and brooks, campaign against the animal illnesses and the plant pests.

The programme of national unanimity is one of the government's major programmes. This programme was started in five provinces in the country to ensure the rights of every Afghan village in the reconstruction and expansion. I hope that the programme will start in the next three to four months. The point is that within the next three to four years something like 1 million afghanis will be allocated, so that people will be able to propose and implement small reconstruction and expansion programmes based on common consent. For the improvement of the lives of government personnel, the government will reshuffle the civil departments. The first stage of the survey in the country will be completed by the end of this year to obtain the required information and to improve the economic, social and political development in the country.

The ordinary budget of the government this year has been estimated at 24.7 billion afghanis. We are hopeful that 9 billion afghanis will be generated from the internal sources, and the rest, 15.7 billion afghanis, will be transferred from foreign assistance. The government is striving to get the internal revenues transferred to the capital city from across the country this year, so that the money that has been expected from the internal sources will be obtained in full in this way.

Government enterprises are in the worst conditions, and in most of the cases they are a burden on the government. The government will take some effective measures to enhance and reshuffle the system of the enterprises.

The government has appropriated a notable amount for education, to improve the state of education this year.

The government is planning to enhance the ability of the Ministry of Health and other health departments to expand medical services and improve public health and the campaign against the fatal and epidemic diseases, so that in emergencies they will be able to assist our compatriots. The number of clinics will be expanded, and our hospitals will be equipped with machinery and medicines and it has also been planned to set up mobile clinics for nomads. The government, with the assistance of friendly countries especially England, has taken tough measures to prevent poppy cultivation and the production of narcotics, and will implement practical programmes to safeguard the environment.

[...]

Source: Hamid Karzai, "State-of-the-Nation Speech," Radio Afghanistan (Dari and Pashto), Kabul, Afghanistan, April 8, 2003.

115. Secretary of Defense Donald Rumsfeld and General Richard B. Myers, "Stuff Happens," Department of Defense News Briefing, April 11, 2003 [Excerpts]

Introduction

The quick victory in April 2003 of the U.S.-led coalition against Iraq sparked a brief period of near-euphoria among American officials. As American forces entered Baghdad, Secretary of Defense Donald Rumsfeld confidently expected the reestablishment of order in Iraq to be swift and relatively unproblematic. In a press conference at the Defense Department's Pentagon headquarters, he jubilantly highlighted photographs of cheering Iraqis waving American flags and welcoming the coalition forces "not as invaders or occupiers, but as liberators." This would, he exulted, convince Arabs that "America is a friend of Arab people." Rumsfeld declared that the process of establishing an interim Iraqi government "chosen by the Iraqi people, not by anyone else, and based on democratic principles" would shortly begin. He clearly expected the transition to be easy and painless. Quizzed by journalists as to whether law and order had broken down in Iraq and whether accounts that widespread "looting" of museums, archives, government offices,

and private homes had occurred were symptoms of "anarchy" and "lawlessness," Rumsfeld and General Richard B. Myers, chairman of the U.S. Joint Chiefs of Staff (JCS), minimized the significance of such episodes. In words that soon became notorious, Rumsfeld proclaimed: "Stuff happens! . . . . And it's untidy, and freedom's untidy, and free people are free to make mistakes and commit crimes and do bad things. They're also free to live their lives and do wonderful things, and that's what's going to happen here." Rumsfeld's optimism soon seemed misplaced and shortsighted. The subsequent protracted inability of either the occupying forces or the coalition-sponsored Iraqi government to restore order and stability in the country and reconcile competing political forces there was a major factor behind the abrasive Rumsfeld's resignation in December 2006 as secretary of defense.

Primary Source

Rumsfeld: . . . The scenes we've witnessed in Baghdad and other free Iraqi cities belie the widespread early commentary suggesting that Iraqis were ambivalent or even opposed to the coalition's arrival in their country. I think it's fair to say that they were not ambivalent or opposed, but they were understandably frightened of the regime of Saddam Hussein and the retaliation or retribution that they could have suffered. And now, as their fear of the former Iraqi dictator lessens, the true sentiments of a large majority, I believe, of the Iraqi people are surfacing. And I think it's increasingly clear that most welcome coalition forces and see them not as invaders or occupiers, but as liberators.

The images of thousands of cheering Iraqis, celebrating and embracing coalition forces, are being broadcast throughout the world, including the Arab world. And possibly for the first time, Arab people are seeing the people of Iraq waving American flags and thanking the men and women in uniform for risking their lives to free them from tyranny. I think it's important that that message be seen, for America is a friend of Arab people. And now, finally, Arab people are hearing the same message, not from U.S. officials, but from their fellow Arabs, the liberated people of Iraq.

Meanwhile, we're working to expand the flow of free information to the Iraqi people. We're moving a ground station to Baghdad to expand the coverage area for radio and television broadcasts. We've begun broadcasting a one-hour news program and are moving to restore Iraqi radio and television networks. We're doing this because access to free information is critical to building a free society.

At the same time, we're working with free Iraqis, those in liberated areas, and those who have returned from abroad, to establish— begin the process of establishing—an interim authority which will help pave the way for a new Iraqi government, a government that will be chosen by the Iraqi people, not by anyone else, and based on democratic principles and peaceful coexistence with its neighbors and with the world. The makeup of this interim authority and the government that emerges from it will be decided by the free Iraqi people.

In areas where the war is winding down, coalition forces are bringing humanitarian aid and are working with a number of international organizations in other countries to deliver food, water, medicine and other necessities.

[...]

Q: Mr. Secretary, you spoke of the television pictures that went around the world earlier of Iraqis welcoming U.S. forces with open arms. But now television pictures are showing looting and other signs of lawlessness. Are you, sir, concerned that what's being reported from the region as anarchy in Baghdad and other cities might wash away the goodwill the United States has built? And, are U.S. troops capable of or inclined to be police forces in Iraq?

Rumsfeld: Well, I think the way to think about that is that if you go from a repressive regime that has—it's a police state, where people are murdered and imprisoned by the tens of thousands—and then you go to something other than that—a liberated Iraq—that you go through a transition period. And in every country, in my adult lifetime, that's had the wonderful opportunity to do that, to move from a repressed dictatorial regime to something that's freer, we've seen in that transition period there is untidiness, and there's no question but that that's not anyone's choice.

On the other hand, if you think of those pictures, very often the pictures are pictures of people going into the symbols of the regime—into the palaces, into the boats, and into the Ba'ath Party headquarters, and into the places that have been part of that repression. And, while no one condones looting, on the other hand, one can understand the pent-up feelings that may result from decades of repression and people who have had members of their family killed by that regime, for them to be taking their feelings out on that regime.

With respect to the second part of your question, we do feel an obligation to assist in providing security, and the coalition forces are doing that. They're patrolling in various cities. Where they see looting, they're stopping it, and they will be doing so. The second step, of course, is to not do that on a permanent basis but, rather, to find Iraqis who can assist in providing police support in those cities and various types of stabilizing and security assistance, and we're in the process of doing that.

Q: How quickly do you hope to do that? Isn't that a pressing problem?

Rumsfeld: Wait. Wait. But in answer to your—direct answer to your question—are we concerned that this would offset it, the feeling of liberation—suggests that, "Gee, maybe they were better off repressed." And I don't think there's anyone in any of those pictures, or any human being who's not free, who wouldn't prefer to be free, and recognize that you pass through a transition period like this and accept it as part of the price of getting from a repressed regime to freedom.

[...]

Rumsfeld: Let me say one other thing. The images you are seeing on television you are seeing over, and over, and over, and it's the same picture of some person walking out of some building with a vase, and you see it 20 times, and you think, "My goodness, were there that many vases?" [Laughter.] "Is it possible that there were that many vases in the whole country?"

Q: Do you think that the words "anarchy" and "lawlessness" are ill-chosen—

Rumsfeld: Absolutely. I picked up a newspaper today and I couldn't believe it. I read eight headlines that talked about chaos, violence, unrest. And it just was Henny Penny—"The sky is falling." I've never seen anything like it! And here is a country that's being liberated, here are people who are going from being repressed and held under the thumb of a vicious dictator, and they're free. And all this newspaper could do, with eight or 10 headlines, they showed a man bleeding, a civilian, who they claimed we had shot—one thing after another. It's just unbelievable how people can take that away from what is happening in that country!

Do I think those words are unrepresentative? Yes.

Q: Mr. Secretary, could I follow that up?

[...]

Q: I think the question is, if you—if a foreign military force came into your neighborhood and did away with the police, and left you at the mercy of criminals, how long would you feel liberated?

Rumsfeld: Well, that's a fair question. First of all, the foreign military force came into their neighborhood and did not do away with any police. There may have been some police who fled, because the people didn't like them, and because they'd been doing things to the people in the local community that the people wanted to have a word with them about. But we haven't gone in and done away with any police. In fact, we're looking for police in those villages and towns who can, in fact, assist in providing order, to the extent there are people who can do it in a manner that's consistent with our values.

[. . .]

Q: Given how predictable the lack of law and order was, as you said, from past conflicts, was there part of General Franks' plan to deal with it? And—

Rumsfeld: Of course.

Q: Well, what is it?

Rumsfeld: This is fascinating. This is just fascinating. From the very beginning, we were convinced that we would succeed, and that means that that regime would end. And we were convinced that as we went from the end of that regime to something other than that regime, there would be a period of transition. And, you cannot do everything instantaneously; it's never been done, everything instantaneously. We did, however, recognize that there was at least a chance of catastrophic success, if you will, to reverse the phrase, that you could in a given place or places have a victory that occurred well before reasonable people might have expected it, and that we needed to be ready for that; we needed to be ready with medicine, with food, with water. And, we have been.

And, you say, "Well, what was it in the plan?" The plan is a complex set of conclusions or ideas that then have a whole series of alternative excursions that one can do, depending on what happens. And, they have been doing that as they've been going along. And, they've been doing a darn good job.

Q: Yes, but Mr. Secretary, I'm asking about what plan was there to restore law and order?

Rumsfeld: Well, let's just take a city. Take the port city, Umm Qasr—what the plan was. Well, the British went in, they built a pipeline bringing water in from Kuwait; they cleared the mine of ports [sic]; they brought ships in with food; they've been providing security. In fact, they've done such a lousy job, that the city has gone from 15,000 to 40,000. Now think of that. Why would people vote with their feet and go into this place that's so bad? The reason they're going in is because there's food, there's water, there's medicine and there's jobs. That's why. The British have done a fantastic job. They've done an excellent job.

And, does that mean you couldn't go in there and take a television camera or get a still photographer and take a picture of something that was imperfect, untidy? I could do that in any city in America. Think what's happened in our cities when we've had riots, and problems, and looting. Stuff happens! But in terms of what's going on in that country, it is a fundamental misunderstanding to see those images over, and over, and over again of some boy walking out with a vase and say, "Oh, my goodness, you didn't have

a plan." That's nonsense. They know what they're doing, and they're doing a terrific job. And it's untidy, and freedom's untidy, and free people are free to make mistakes and commit crimes and do bad things. They're also free to live their lives and do wonderful things, and that's what's going to happen here.

[. . .]

Q: There's some additional specificity here. While you have just expressed yet again your dismay at the international news media, in fact, the reporting does factually show there are some certain number of Iraqi citizens that have spoken on-camera quite directly about their own concerns about the safety and security in Baghdad and that situation. There have also been absolutely verified reports that it is not just regime targets but indeed hospitals, banks, other facilities essential to society. The ICRC has been on TV today saying that hospitals are being looted, not regime targets you're speaking of, and that they can't even get there to resupply these essential hospitals.

Now, my question is, General Brooks said this morning that the military—U.S. military—did not want to reconstruct the Iraqi police force in Baghdad because the feeling of the U.S. military is that that the Iraqi police force has been operating against the U.S. military. He didn't feel that was a secure solution. So with some specificity, what type of Iraqi force can you bring to bear in Baghdad to have Iraqis help restore security? And, what types of specific tasks are you now going to assign the U.S. military to do to help restore the situation, which the people of Baghdad appear to be concerned about?

[. . .]

Rumsfeld: Well, hospitals. No, let's go back to what you said about people.

You could take a camera and a microphone, and stick it in front of a thousand people in Iraq today, and you could find someone saying every single thing you've said and every single thing I've said. You're going to find it all across the spectrum. You know, it's the facts on the ground where a person is that determines how they feel about it. And, there are some very dangerous places in that country and some very difficult situations.

And, there is no question but there is a hospital that was looted. There also is this fact. The Saddam Hussein regime and the Ba'ath Party put their headquarters in hospitals all over that country. They have been doing it systematically. Have we been complaining about that? Have we been photographing that? Have we been bemoaning that? No! Why? Because there wasn't a free press. You couldn't get in to do it; you'd get thrown out. You'd get thrown in jail if you were an Iraqi and you tried to do it.

A hundred and twenty-three schools were Ba'ath Party headquarters. Is that a good thing to do to a school? Is that a good thing to do to a hospital? No. But was there any complaint about it? No, there was no complaint. Is it true that a hospital was looted? Yes. Is that unfortunate? Yes. Do we have medicines and medical supplies coming in behind to help the people in those situations? You bet we do.

Q: But I guess what I'm not hearing here is, either one of you gentlemen, what tasks, with some specificity if you can, what U.S. military forces in Baghdad will now be doing to help calm the situation, or do you just—

Rumsfeld: They're already doing it. They're already going to hospitals that are being looted and stopping it. If you look carefully, you'll see images of people being arrested for looting, and they're walking out with those little white things on their wrists and said "Don't do that." And, they take them out of there and they tell them to go someplace else. And, that's happening all over the place.

[...]

Rumsfeld: Our folks are operating to the extent they can in Baghdad in creating a presence and dissuading people from looting. And, for suddenly the biggest problem in the world to be looting is really notable.

[...]

Q: If I may, Secretary Rumsfeld—Terry Call from the [inaudible word] Newspaper Group—let me ask a question that is relevant to your duties as Secretary of Defense, of—and General Myers, as the chairman, for a very successful military operation. And, that relevant question is, could both of you address how consistent with your optimistic and most hopeful results has the military operation been to date? And correspondingly, do you and General Myers have the same confidence, in a straightforward way, that the rebuilding of Iraq as a successful society, with American assistance, will be consistent, as you've tried to describe to the group here? Are we—[off mike]—militarily, sir, as you expect in six months we may be regarding the civil affairs matters?

[Pause.]

Rumsfeld: I had a list, a long list, of three or four, five, six pages of things that could go wrong, because I tend to be conservative and cautious. And I looked it over this morning, and a number, a large number, haven't happened bad.

[...]

Some of them are still open—that could still go bad. There's no question about that. There's still some tough stuff ahead, and—but

one has to say that the speed that was used and the care that was used in the targeting, and the tactical surprise that was achieved by starting the ground war before the air war, undoubtedly contributed to the fact that a number of those things didn't happen bad. The oil wells weren't all blown up, and there's not a major humanitarian crisis, despite the fact that someone's looting someplace. There were not large refugee numbers. There were not large internally displaced people numbers. So we feel good about that.

The task we've got ahead of us now is an awkward one, because you have to go from a transition—from a repressed regime to an unrepressed regime that is free to do good things and also do bad things, and we're going to see both. And, we expect that, and we also expect people to report both. That's fine.

But as we go through this, I feel that we've got a group of wonderful people who have thought this through, that are engaged in the process, that have done the planning that will see that the kinds of food, and medicine, and water, and assistance that are needed will happen. Will it be perfect? No. Will it be bumpy? Sure. How do you go from—take a—look at every other country that's done this. Look at East Germany, and Romania, and the Soviet Union, pieces of that—it isn't an easy thing to do. And, we can't do it for them; the Iraqi people are going to have to do this, in the last analysis. We can help, and we want to create an environment that is as secure as possible, and that is as stable as possible, so that they can find their sea legs, if you will, and get themselves on a path to the future.

[...]

Q: Mr. Secretary, why don't you just update us a little bit on what progress you're making, if any, on some of the unfinished missions you outlined the other day, specifically accounting for senior regime leadership, such as the ones on these playing cards that were distributed today, the search for weapons of mass destruction, and what about the American prisoners of war? Can you tell us you're making any progress on any of those three fronts?

Rumsfeld: I think, I hope when I spoke those words that I prefaced it by saying the first task is to prevail in this conflict and to stop the forces of Saddam Hussein in the areas that they continue to operate in, and to reduce the violence. That is the principal assignment. And, then to point out how much work was still ahead of us, I listed all of these six, eight, 10 things that are on our priority list. They will, of necessity, follow along behind, although, as I said, when there happens to be a weapon of mass destruction suspect site in an area that we occupy, and if people have time, they'll look at it. And, then they'll send things out to be examined and looked at. We clearly have people dedicated to trying to find the prisoners of war, ours and others from the '91 war. And as we are successful in any of those things, we'll report them. Undoubtedly, there will be embedded reporters there when they happen and will report them.

But I don't have anything particular to note, except that there are documentations that have been retrieved and they are being looked at. We are looking for people. We continue to look for people who can help us find the people we want to find, and people who can help us find the weapon sites of interest and people who can help us find records, for example, of Ba'ath Party members and the like. But I don't have anything of note to report.

[. . .]

Q: Sir, I had a follow-up on the weapons of mass destruction issue. We keep hearing "results are pending, results are pending" of these early finds. What can—

Rumsfeld: Of which one of this—

Q: Well, the finding weapons of mass destruction. Here's my question: What can you guarantee the U.S. public and a skeptical world that U.S. soldiers will eventually find, without any shadow of a doubt in your mind, by way of raw agents, weapons facilities? And how long should they wait before they start making conclusions that maybe the U.S. didn't have the evidence in the first place?

[. . .]

Rumsfeld: You said how long should they wait, how should they— before they lose—I've got a lot of confidence in the American people. . . .

Secretary Powell presented a presentation to the United Nations and the world. He laid out intelligence community estimates from the Central Intelligence Agency, and there is not a doubt but that we will, over a period of time, find people who can tell us where to go look for those things. We are not going to find them, in my view, just as I never believed the inspectors would, by running around seeing if they can open a door and surprise somebody and find something, because these people have learned that they can live in an inspection environment—the Iraqis did; they functioned in that environment, they designed their workplaces to do that. Things were mobile, things were underground, things were in tunnels, things were hidden, things were dispersed. Now, are we going to find that? No. It's a big country. What we're going to do is we're going to find the people who will tell us that, and we're going to find ways to encourage them to tell us that.

[. . .]

Source: "DoD News Briefing—Secretary Rumsfeld and Gen. Myers," United States Department of Defense, http://www.defense.gov/Transcripts/Transcript.aspx?TranscriptID=2367.

116. Summary of Letter Purportedly Sent by Iran to the U.S. Government, Spring 2003

Introduction

The administration of U.S. president George W. Bush was hostile to Iran. In his January 2002 State of the Union speech, Bush went so far as to proclaim Iran part of an "axis of evil" of rogue states, its other members being North Korea and Iraq, that sponsored terrorism, sought to develop weapons of mass destruction, and had the potential to destabilize the peace of the world. As U.S. pressure on Iran to renounce plans to develop nuclear weapons and refrain from assisting Shiite insurgents with Iraq intensified during 2006 and 2007, old rumors that Iranian policy had not always been so decidedly intransigent as American officials suggested resurfaced. Several former U.S. diplomats claimed that in the spring of 2003 Iran made overtures to the United States through Mohammad Javad Zarif, Iranian ambassador to the United Nations (UN) in New York. In late April or early May 2003 the Swiss ambassador to Tehran, Tim Guldimann, then allegedly handed American officials in Washington a letter making concrete proposals for the improvement of relations. Allegedly, this letter reached Guldimann through Sadegh Kharazi, Iranian ambassador to France and the nephew of Kamal Kharazi, Iran's foreign minister. Reports further suggested that it had the blessing of all major Iranian leaders, including Ayatollah Ali Khameini, the regime's supreme leader. Alarm at the swift American overthrow of Saddam Hussein and military conquest of Iraq and the apprehensions that Iran might be next were believed to be major reasons impelling Iranian officials to make these overtures to the United States. American recipients in the Bush administration, however, reportedly rejected the proposals and even complained to the Swiss government that those diplomats who had forwarded it to Washington had exceeded their authority. In late 2006 the Western media reproduced what purported to be the gist of these proposals, a memorandum that may have originally been attached to a cover letter. The document suggested that Iran and the United States open a dialogue based on "mutual respect." Iranian objectives in this dialogue would include the restoration of normal diplomatic relations with the United States, the ending of American and international sanctions on Iran, the establishment of a democratic government in Iraq that would accept Iranian interests in that nation and claims for compensation, access to advanced technology for peaceful purposes, recognition of Iranian regional security interests, and the ending of foreign support for the anti-Iranian People's Mujahedin of Iran terrorist group, which sought to overthrow the existing Iranian government. In return Iran would renounce all efforts to develop weapons of mass destruction; act decisively against terrorists, especially Al Qaeda, within its borders; support Iraq's political stabilization under a nonreligious government; and acquiesce in the Arab-Israeli peace process while ending its support both for

Palestinian opposition groups committed to violent methods and for radical anti-Israeli Hezbollah guerrillas in Lebanon. The memorandum suggested a schedule of steps and stages in which this program might be achieved. Although over the next three years the Bush administration moved to normalize relations with Libya, a longtime Middle Eastern opponent of the United States that had for many years supported terrorist organizations and operations, including some that targeted Americans, the administration was less accommodating toward Iran. Critics later charged that in light of the major problems and tensions that by 2006 had soured relations between Iran and the United States to the point that they were almost unworkable, the Iranian initiative of 2003 represented a major lost opportunity to reach a workable understanding with a former enemy.

Primary Source

Iran has communicated to the US its readiness to open direct talks about its nuclear programme as a first step towards tackling other issues, such as terrorism and the Israeli-Palestinian conflict, but US officials say the Bush administration is keeping the door closed.

Iranian aims:

(The US accepts a dialogue **"in mutual respect"** and agrees that Iran puts the following aims on the agenda)

- **Halt in US hostile behavior and rectification of status of Iran in the US:** (interference in internal or external relations, "axis of evil", terrorism list.)
- Abolishment of all sanctions: commercial sanctions, frozen assets, judgments (FSIA), impediments in international trade and financial institutions
- Iraq: democratic and fully representative government in Iraq, support of Iranian claims for Iraqi reparations, respect for Iranian national interests in Iraq and religious links to Najaf/Karbal.
- **Full access to peaceful nuclear technology, biotechnology and chemical technology**
- Recognition of **Iran's legitimate security interests in the region** with according defense capacity.
- Terrorism: pursuit of anti-Iranian terrorists, above all MKO and support for repatriation of their members in Iraq, decisive action against anti Iranian terrorists, above all MKO and affiliated organizations in the US

US aims: (Iran accepts a dialogue **"in mutual respect"** and agrees that the US puts the following aims on the agenda)

1. **WMD:** full transparency for security that there are no Iranian endeavors to develop or possess WMD, full cooperation with IAEA based on Iranian adoption of all relevant instruments (93+2 and all further IAEA protocols)

2. **Terrorism:** decisive action against any terrorists (above all Al Qaida) on Iranian territory, full cooperation and exchange of all relevant information.

3. **Iraq:** coordination of Iranian influence for activity supporting political stabilization and the establishment of democratic institutions and a non-religious government.

4. **Middle East:**
   1) stop of any material support to Palestinian opposition groups (Hamas, Jihad etc.) from Iranian territory, pressure on these organizations to stop violent action against civilians within borders of 1967.
   2) action on Hizbollah to become a mere political organization within Lebanon
   3) acceptance of the Arab League Beirut declaration (Saudi initiative, two-states-approach)

Steps:

I. Communication of mutual agreement on the following procedure

II. Mutual simultaneous statements "We have always been ready for direct and authoritative talks with the US/with Iran in good faith and with the aim of discussing—in mutual respect—our common interests and our mutual concerns based on merits and objective realities, but we have always made it clear that, such talks can only be held, if genuine progress for a solution of our own concerns can be achieved."

III. A first direct meeting on the appropriate level (for instance in Paris) will be held with the previously agreed aims
   a. of a **decision on the first mutual steps**
      - **Iraq:** establishment of a common group, active Iranian support for Iraq stabilization, US-commitment to actively support Iranian reparation claims within the discussions on Iraq foreign debts.
      - **Terorrism:** US-commitment to disarm and remove MKO from Iraq and take action in accordance with SCR1373 against its leadership, Iranian commitment for enhanced action against Al Qaida members in Iran, agreement on cooperation and information exchange
      - Iranian general statement "to support a peaceful solution in the Middle East involving the parties concerned"
      - US general statement that "Iran did not belong to 'the axis of evil'"
      - US-acceptance to halt its impediments against Iran in international financial and trade institutions
   b. of the establishment **of the parallel working groups** on disarmament, regional security and economic cooperation. Their **aim is an agreement on three**

parallel road maps, for the discussions of these working groups, each side accepts that the other side's aims (see above) are put on the agenda:

1) **Disarmament:** road map, which combines the mutual aims of, on the one side, full transparency by international commitments and guarantees to abstain from WMD with, on the other side, full access to western technology (in the three areas),

2) **Terrorism and regional security:** road map for above mentioned aims on the Middle east and terrorism

3) **Economic cooperation:** road map for the abolishment of the sanctions, rescinding of judgments, and un-freezing of assets

c. of agreement on a time-table for implementation

d. and of **a public statement after this first meeting on the achieved agreements**

Source: "Purported Iranian Letter of 2003 Proposing Cooperation with USA," MidEast Web, http://www.mideastweb.org/iranian_letter_of_2003.htm.

117. President George W. Bush, "Major Combat Operations in Iraq Have Ended," Address to the Nation on Iraq from USS *Abraham Lincoln*, May 1, 2003 [Excerpt]

Introduction

On March 20, 2003, the invasion of Iraq by allied forces from a "coalition of the willing" led by the United States began. Six weeks later, an ebullient U.S. president George W. Bush was in the copilot's seat when a S-3B Viking plane landed on the deck of the nuclear-powered aircraft carrier USS *Abraham Lincoln*, then cruising off the California coast. Speaking under a huge banner that declared "Mission Accomplished," words that would later come back to haunt him, the euphoric president declared that "Major combat operations in Iraq have ended." Bush exulted in well-publicized incidents, quickly broadcast around the world, in which Iraqis had welcomed allied forces with celebrations and toppled massive statues of former Iraqi president Saddam Hussein. The American military, he proclaimed, radiated "strength and kindness and good will" and were "the best of our country." Bush happily declared that the nature of war had changed and that "new tactics and precision weapons" made it possible "to free a nation" from "a dangerous and aggressive regime" and do so "without directing violence against civilians." He announced that coalition forces would remain in Iraq until order had been

restored and the "transition from dictatorship to democracy" had been accomplished but would then leave. Victory in Iraq was, the triumphant president stated, just one success in an ongoing war on terror that had not yet been completed but nonetheless represented the "turning of the tide" in that conflict. He told his audience of servicemen and women that after a battle, American troops "want nothing more than to return home." As his presidency ended several years later, with more American military personnel dead in Iraq since the supposed ending of major hostilities than before that date, prospects for the withdrawal of U.S. forces from that country had come to seem decidedly elusive.

Primary Source

Thank you all very much. Admiral Kelly, Captain Card, officers and sailors of the U.S.S. *Abraham Lincoln,* my fellow Americans: Major combat operations in Iraq have ended. In the battle of Iraq, the United States and our allies have prevailed. And now our coalition is engaged in securing and reconstructing that country.

In this battle, we have fought for the cause of liberty and for the peace of the world. Our Nation and our coalition are proud of this accomplishment; yet it is you, the members of the United States military, who achieved it. Your courage, your willingness to face danger for your country and for each other, made this day possible. Because of you, our Nation is more secure. Because of you, the tyrant [Saddam Hussein] has fallen, and Iraq is free.

Operation Iraqi Freedom was carried out with a combination of precision and speed and boldness the enemy did not expect and the world had not seen before. From distant bases or ships at sea, we sent planes and missiles that could destroy an enemy division or strike a single bunker. Marines and soldiers charged to Baghdad across 350 miles of hostile ground, in one of the swiftest advances of heavy arms in history. You have shown the world the skill and the might of the American Armed Forces.

This Nation thanks all the members of our coalition who joined in a noble cause. We thank the Armed Forces of the United Kingdom, Australia, and Poland, who shared in the hardships of war. We thank all the citizens of Iraq who welcomed our troops and joined in the liberation of their own country. And tonight I have a special word for Secretary Rumsfeld [Donald H. Rumsfeld] for General Franks [Tommy R. Franks] and for all the men and women who wear the uniform of the United States: America is grateful for a job well done.

The character of our military through history—the daring of Normandy, the fierce courage of Iwo Jima, the decency and idealism that turned enemies into allies—is fully present in this generation. When Iraqi civilians looked into the faces of our service men and women, they saw strength and kindness and good will. When I look at the members of the United States military, I see the best of our country, and I'm honored to be your Commander in Chief.

In the images of fallen statues, we have witnessed the arrival of a new era. For a hundred years of war, culminating in the nuclear age, military technology was designed and deployed to inflict casualties on an ever-growing scale. In defeating Nazi Germany and Imperial Japan, Allied forces destroyed entire cities, while enemy leaders who started the conflict were safe until the final days. Military power was used to end a regime by breaking a nation.

Today, we have the greater power to free a nation by breaking a dangerous and aggressive regime. With new tactics and precision weapons, we can achieve military objectives without directing violence against civilians. No device of man can remove the tragedy from war; yet it is a great advance when the guilty have far more to fear from war than the innocent.

In the images of celebrating Iraqis, we have also seen the ageless appeal of human freedom. Decades of lies and intimidation could not make the Iraqi people love their oppressors or desire their own enslavement. Men and women in every culture need liberty like they need food and water and air. Everywhere that freedom arrives, humanity rejoices, and everywhere that freedom stirs, let tyrants fear.

We have difficult work to do in Iraq. We're bringing order to parts of that country that remain dangerous. We're pursuing and finding leaders of the old regime, who will be held to account for their crimes. We've begun the search for hidden chemical and biological weapons and already know of hundreds of sites that will be investigated. We're helping to rebuild Iraq, where the dictator [Saddam Hussein] built palaces for himself instead of hospitals and schools. And we will stand with the new leaders of Iraq as they establish a Government of, by, and for the Iraqi people.

The transition from dictatorship to democracy will take time, but it is worth every effort. Our coalition will stay until our work is done. And then we will leave, and we will leave behind a free Iraq.

The battle of Iraq is one victory in a war on terror that began on September the 11th, 2001, and still goes on. That terrible morning, 19 evil men, the shock troops of a hateful ideology, gave America and the civilized world a glimpse of their ambitions. They imagined, in the words of one terrorist, that September the 11th would be the "beginning of the end of America." By seeking to turn our cities into killing fields, terrorists and their allies believed that they could destroy this Nation's resolve and force our retreat from the world. They have failed.

In the battle of Afghanistan, we destroyed the Taliban, many terrorists, and the camps where they trained. We continue to help the Afghan people lay roads, restore hospitals, and educate all of their children. Yet we also have dangerous work to complete. As I speak, a Special Operations task force, led by the 82d Airborne, is on the trail of the terrorists and those who seek to undermine the free Government of Afghanistan. America and our coalition will finish what we have begun.

From Pakistan to the Philippines to the Horn of Africa, we are hunting down Al Qaida killers. Nineteen months ago, I pledged that the terrorists would not escape the patient justice of the United States. And as of tonight, nearly one-half of Al Qaida's senior operatives have been captured or killed.

The liberation of Iraq is a crucial advance in the campaign against terror. We've removed an ally of Al Qaida and cut off a source of terrorist funding. And this much is certain: No terrorist network will gain weapons of mass destruction from the Iraqi regime, because the regime is no more.

In these 19 months that changed the world, our actions have been focused and deliberate and proportionate to the offense. We have not forgotten the victims of September the 11th—the last phone calls, the cold murder of children, the searches in the rubble. With those attacks, the terrorists and their supporters declared war on the United States, and war is what they got.

Our war against terror is proceeding according to the principles that I have made clear to all: Any person involved in committing or planning terrorist attacks against the American people becomes an enemy of this country and a target of American justice; any person, organization, or government that supports, protects, or harbors terrorists is complicit in the murder of the innocent and equally guilty of terrorist crimes; any outlaw regime that has ties to terrorist groups and seeks or possesses weapons of mass destruction is a grave danger to the civilized world and will be confronted; and anyone in the world, including the Arab world, who works and sacrifices for freedom has a loyal friend in the United States of America.

Our commitment to liberty is America's tradition, declared at our founding, affirmed in Franklin Roosevelt's Four Freedoms, asserted in the Truman Doctrine and in Ronald Reagan's challenge to an evil empire. We are committed to freedom in Afghanistan, in Iraq, and in a peaceful Palestine. The advance of freedom is the surest strategy to undermine the appeal of terror in the world. Where freedom takes hold, hatred gives way to hope. When freedom takes hold, men and women turn to the peaceful pursuit of a better life. American values and American interests lead in the same direction: We stand for human liberty.

The United States upholds these principles of security and freedom in many ways, with all the tools of diplomacy, law enforcement, intelligence, and finance. We're working with a broad coalition of nations that understand the threat and our shared responsibility to meet it. The use of force has been and remains our last resort. Yet all can know, friend and foe alike, that our Nation has a mission: We will answer threats to our security, and we will defend the peace.

Our mission continues. Al Qaida is wounded, not destroyed. The scattered cells of the terrorist network still operate in many nations, and we know from daily intelligence that they continue to plot against free people. The proliferation of deadly weapons remains a serious danger. The enemies of freedom are not idle, and neither are we. Our Government has taken unprecedented measures to defend the homeland, and we will continue to hunt down the enemy before he can strike.

The war on terror is not over, yet it is not endless. We do not know the day of final victory, but we have seen the turning of the tide. No act of the terrorists will change our purpose or weaken our resolve or alter their fate. Their cause is lost. Free nations will press on to victory.

[...]

Source: George W. Bush, *Public Papers of the Presidents of the United States: George Bush, 2003,* Book 1 (Washington, DC: U.S. Government Printing Office, 2003), 410–413.

118. United Nations Security Council Resolutions 1483, 1490, 1500, 1511, May 22–October 16, 2003

Introduction

With the 2003 Iraq War officially declared to have ended, the United Nations (UN) sought to reaffirm its authority over Iraq and provide for that country's political and economic reconstruction and its reintegration into the international community. The UN finally lifted nonmilitary sanctions on Iraq. In addition, the UN recognized the United States and Great Britain, the key nations in the military coalition that had defeated Iraq, as "Occupying Powers," jointly termed "the Authority," and urged them to work "towards the restoration of conditions of security and stability and the creation of conditions in which the Iraqi people can freely determine their own future." All parties involved were urged to respect the Geneva Conventions regarding the treatment of prisoners of war and civilian populations in occupied territories. The UN secretary-general was urged to appoint a special representative for Iraq who would direct and coordinate UN activities and agencies in that country, with the objective of assisting the people of Iraq by providing humanitarian assistance, facilitating the restoration and establishment of effective governmental and legal institutions and reforms, encouraging economic reconstruction, and protecting human rights. An interim Iraqi administration was to be established as soon as possible as a transitional step on the road to the establishment of a representative government that would take over the responsibilities of the Authority. A Development Fund for Iraq was also to be established, and all monies remaining in escrow from the Oil-for-Food Program would be transferred to this fund. In July 2003 Security Council Resolution 1490 disbanded the United Nations Iraq-Kuwait Observation Mission (UNIKOM) and ended the 15-kilometer demilitarized zone separating Kuwait and Iraq. In August 2003 Resolution 1500 welcomed the establishment of "the broadly representative Governing Council of Iraq" as an important transitional step toward full Iraqi self-government and established the UN Assistance Mission for Iraq. The more comprehensive Resolution 1511, cosponsored by the United States, Great Britain, Spain, and Cameroon, four of the nations that had been members of the coalition that fought the 2003 war, offered a more extensive roadmap for the restoration of

civilian government in Iraq. This resolution was presented in the aftermath of several terrorist attacks within Iraq since August 2003 against such targets as the Jordanian and Turkish embassies in Baghdad, the Imam Ali Mosque in Najaf, and the UN Mission in Baghdad. In the latter truck bombing, 22 people, including the popular UN envoy Sergio Vieira de Mello, had died, and the hold of the occupying powers on Iraq was already beginning to seem tenuous. Resolution 1511 welcomed the decision of Iraq's new Governing Council to take speedy steps to draft a new constitution and recognized that body as the interim government of Iraq. The Authority was directed to return responsibility for Iraq's government to the Iraqi people "as soon as practicable." The Governing Council was invited to formulate a timetable and program to draft a new Iraqi constitution and hold national democratic elections no later than mid-December 2003. The UN requested all member states to provide Iraq with further humanitarian assistance. The resolution promised the good offices of the UN in promoting "national dialogue and consensus-building" in Iraq. The resolution also authorized the creation of a multinational security force to help maintain order in Iraq until that country's own police and security forces were trained and equipped to do so themselves. All UN member states were directed to prevent the entry of terrorist operatives or armaments into Iraq. In hindsight, within three years, much of the program envisaged in this resolution, especially the anticipated speedy progress toward the restoration of peace and order within Iraq, would come to seem unduly optimistic and unrealistic.

Primary Source

Security Council Resolution 1483 (2003) [On Lifting the Economic Sanctions on Iraq Imposed by Resolution 661 (1990)]. May 22, 2003.

Resolution 1483 (2003)

Adopted by the Security Council at its 4761st meeting, on 22 May 2003

The Security Council,
    Recalling all its previous relevant resolutions,
    Reaffirming the sovereignty and territorial integrity of Iraq,
    Reaffirming also the importance of the disarmament of Iraqi weapons of mass destruction and of eventual confirmation of the disarmament of Iraq,
    Stressing the right of the Iraqi people freely to determine their own political future and control their own natural resources, welcoming the commitment of all parties concerned to support the creation of an environment in which they may do so as soon as possible, and expressing resolve that the day when Iraqis govern themselves must come quickly,
    Encouraging efforts by the people of Iraq to form a representative government based on the rule of law that affords equal rights and justice to all Iraqi citizens without regard to ethnicity, religion,

or gender, and, in this connection, recalls resolution 1325 (2000) of 31 October 2000,

Welcoming the first steps of the Iraqi people in this regard, and noting in this connection the 15 April 2003 Nasiriyah statement and the 28 April 2003 Baghdad statement,

Resolved that the United Nations should play a vital role in humanitarian relief, the reconstruction of Iraq, and the restoration and establishment of national and local institutions for representative governance,

Noting the statement of 12 April 2003 by the Ministers of Finance and Central Bank Governors of the Group of Seven Industrialized Nations in which the members recognized the need for a multilateral effort to help rebuild and develop Iraq and for the need for assistance from the International Monetary Fund and the World Bank in these efforts,

Welcoming also the resumption of humanitarian assistance and the continuing efforts of the Secretary-General and the specialized agencies to provide food and medicine to the people of Iraq,

Welcoming the appointment by the Secretary-General of his Special Adviser on Iraq,

Affirming the need for accountability for crimes and atrocities committed by the previous Iraqi regime,

Stressing the need for respect for the archaeological, historical, cultural, and religious heritage of Iraq, and for the continued protection of archaeological, historical, cultural, and religious sites, museums, libraries, and monuments,

Noting the letter of 8 May 2003 from the Permanent Representatives of the United States of America and the United Kingdom of Great Britain and Northern Ireland to the President of the Security Council (S/2003/538) and recognizing the specific authorities, responsibilities, and obligations under applicable international law of these states as occupying powers under unified command (the "Authority"),

Noting further that other States that are not occupying powers are working now or in the future may work under the Authority,

Welcoming further the willingness of Member States to contribute to stability and security in Iraq by contributing personnel, equipment, and other resources under the Authority,

Concerned that many Kuwaitis and Third-State Nationals still are not accounted for since 2 August 1990,

Determining that the situation in Iraq, although improved, continues to constitute a threat to international peace and security,

Acting under Chapter VII of the Charter of the United Nations,

1. Appeals to Member States and concerned organizations to assist the people of Iraq in their efforts to reform their institutions and rebuild their country, and to contribute to conditions of stability and security in Iraq in accordance with this resolution;

2. Calls upon all Member States in a position to do so to respond immediately to the humanitarian appeals of the United Nations and other international organizations for Iraq and to help meet the humanitarian and other needs of the Iraqi people by providing food, medical supplies, and resources necessary for reconstruction and rehabilitation of Iraq's economic infrastructure;

3. Appeals to Member States to deny safe haven to those members of the previous Iraqi regime who are alleged to be responsible for crimes and atrocities and to support actions to bring them to justice;

4. Calls upon the Authority, consistent with the Charter of the United Nations and other relevant international law, to promote the welfare of the Iraqi people through the effective administration of the territory, including in particular working towards the restoration of conditions of security and stability and the creation of conditions in which the Iraqi people can freely determine their own political future;

5. Calls upon all concerned to comply fully with their obligations under international law including in particular the Geneva Conventions of 1949 and the Hague Regulations of 1907;

6. Calls upon the Authority and relevant organizations and individuals to continue efforts to locate, identify, and repatriate all Kuwaiti and Third-State Nationals or the remains of those present in Iraq on or after 2 August 1990, as well as the Kuwaiti archives, that the previous Iraqi regime failed to undertake, and, in this regard, directs the High-Level Coordinator, in consultation with the International Committee of the Red Cross and the Tripartite Commission and with the appropriate support of the people of Iraq and in coordination with the Authority, to take steps to fulfil his mandate with respect to the fate of Kuwaiti and Third-State National missing persons and property;

7. Decides that all Member States shall take appropriate steps to facilitate the safe return to Iraqi institutions of Iraqi cultural property and other items of archaeological, historical, cultural, rare scientific, and religious importance illegally removed from the Iraq National Museum, the National Library, and other locations in Iraq since the adoption of resolution 661 (1990) of 6 August 1990, including by establishing a prohibition on trade in or transfer of such items and items with respect to which reasonable suspicion exists that they have been illegally removed, and calls upon the United Nations Educational, Scientific, and Cultural Organization, Interpol, and other international organizations, as appropriate, to assist in the implementation of this paragraph;

8. Requests the Secretary-General to appoint a Special Representative for Iraq whose independent responsibilities shall involve reporting regularly to the Council on his activities under this resolution, coordinating activities of the United Nations in post-conflict processes in Iraq, coordinating

among United Nations and international agencies engaged in humanitarian assistance and reconstruction activities in Iraq, and, in coordination with the Authority, assisting the people of Iraq through:

(a) coordinating humanitarian and reconstruction assistance by United Nations agencies and between United Nations agencies and non-governmental organizations;

(b) promoting the safe, orderly, and voluntary return of refugees and displaced persons;

(c) working intensively with the Authority, the people of Iraq, and others concerned to advance efforts to restore and establish national and local institutions for representative governance, including by working together to facilitate a process leading to an internationally recognized, representative government of Iraq;

(d) facilitating the reconstruction of key infrastructure, in cooperation with other international organizations;

(e) promoting economic reconstruction and the conditions for sustainable development, including through coordination with national and regional organizations, as appropriate, civil society, donors, and the international financial institutions;

(f) encouraging international efforts to contribute to basic civilian administration functions;

(g) promoting the protection of human rights;

(h) encouraging international efforts to rebuild the capacity of the Iraqi civilian police force; and

(i) encouraging international efforts to promote legal and judicial reform;

9. Supports the formation, by the people of Iraq with the help of the Authority and working with the Special Representative, of an Iraqi interim administration as a transitional administration run by Iraqis, until an internationally recognized, representative government is established by the people of Iraq and assumes the responsibilities of the Authority;

10. Decides that, with the exception of prohibitions related to the sale or supply to Iraq of arms and related materiel other than those arms and related materiel required by the Authority to serve the purposes of this and other related resolutions, all prohibitions related to trade with Iraq and the provision of financial or economic resources to Iraq established by resolution 661 (1990) and subsequent relevant resolutions, including resolution 778 (1992) of 2 October 1992, shall no longer apply;

11. Reaffirms that Iraq must meet its disarmament obligations, encourages the United Kingdom of Great Britain and Northern Ireland and the United States of America to keep the Council informed of their activities in this regard, and underlines the intention of the Council to revisit the mandates of the United Nations Monitoring, Verification, and Inspection Commission and the International Atomic Energy Agency as set forth in resolutions 687 (1991) of 3 April 1991, 1284 (1999) of 17 December 1999, and 1441 (2002) of 8 November 2002;

12. Notes the establishment of a Development Fund for Iraq to be held by the Central Bank of Iraq and to be audited by independent public accountants approved by the International Advisory and Monitoring Board of the Development Fund for Iraq and looks forward to the early meeting of that International Advisory and Monitoring Board, whose members shall include duly qualified representatives of the Secretary-General, of the Managing Director of the International Monetary Fund, of the Director-General of the Arab Fund for Social and Economic Development, and of the President of the World Bank;

13. Notes further that the funds in the Development Fund for Iraq shall be disbursed at the direction of the Authority, in consultation with the Iraqi interim administration, for the purposes set out in paragraph 14 below;

14. Underlines that the Development Fund for Iraq shall be used in a transparent manner to meet the humanitarian needs of the Iraqi people, for the economic reconstruction and repair of Iraq's infrastructure, for the continued disarmament of Iraq, and for the costs of Iraqi civilian administration, and for other purposes benefiting the people of Iraq;

15. Calls upon the international financial institutions to assist the people of Iraq in the reconstruction and development of their economy and to facilitate assistance by the broader donor community, and welcomes the readiness of creditors, including those of the Paris Club, to seek a solution to Iraq's sovereign debt problems;

16. Requests also that the Secretary-General, in coordination with the Authority, continue the exercise of his responsibilities under Security Council resolution 1472 (2003) of 28 March 2003 and 1476 (2003) of 24 April 2003, for a period of six months following the adoption of this resolution, and terminate within this time period, in the most cost effective manner, the ongoing operations of the "Oil-for-Food" Programme (the "Programme"), both at headquarters level and in the field, transferring responsibility for the administration of any remaining activity under the Programme to the Authority, including by taking the following necessary measures:

(a) to facilitate as soon as possible the shipment and authenticated delivery of priority civilian goods as identified by the Secretary-General and representatives designated by him, in coordination with the Authority and the Iraqi interim administration, under approved and funded contracts previously concluded by the previous Government of Iraq, for the humanitarian relief of the people of Iraq, including, as necessary, negotiating adjustments in the terms or conditions of these contracts and respective letters of credit as set forth in paragraph 4 (d) of resolution 1472 (2003);

(b) to review, in light of changed circumstances, in coordination with the Authority and the Iraqi interim administration, the relative utility of each approved and funded contract with a view to determining whether such contracts contain items required to meet the needs of the people of Iraq both now and during reconstruction, and to postpone action on those contracts determined to be of questionable utility and the respective letters of credit until an internationally recognized, representative government of Iraq is in a position to make its own determination as to whether such contracts shall be fulfilled;

(c) to provide the Security Council within 21 days following the adoption of this resolution, for the Security Council's review and consideration, an estimated operating budget based on funds already set aside in the account established pursuant to paragraph 8 (d) of resolution 986 (1995) of 14 April 1995, identifying:

(i) all known and projected costs to the United Nations required to ensure the continued functioning of the activities associated with implementation of the present resolution, including operating and administrative expenses associated with the relevant United Nations agencies and programmes responsible for the implementation of the Programme both at Headquarters and in the field;

(ii) all known and projected costs associated with termination of the Programme;

(iii) all known and projected costs associated with restoring Government of Iraq funds that were provided by Member States to the Secretary-General as requested in paragraph 1 of resolution 778 (1992); and

(iv) all known and projected costs associated with the Special Representative and the qualified representative of the Secretary-General identified to serve on the International Advisory and Monitoring Board, for the six month time period defined above, following which these costs shall be borne by the United Nations;

(d) to consolidate into a single fund the accounts established pursuant to paragraphs 8 (a) and 8 (b) of resolution 986 (1995);

(e) to fulfil all remaining obligations related to the termination of the Programme, including negotiating, in the most cost effective manner, any necessary settlement payments, which shall be made from the escrow accounts established pursuant to paragraphs 8 (a) and 8 (b) of resolution 986 (1995), with those parties that previously have entered into contractual obligations with the Secretary-General under the Programme, and to determine, in coordination with the Authority and the Iraqi interim administration, the future status of contracts undertaken by the United Nations and related United Nations agencies under the accounts established pursuant to paragraphs 8 (b) and 8 (d) of resolution 986 (1995);

(f) to provide the Security Council, 30 days prior to the termination of the Programme, with a comprehensive strategy developed in close coordination with the Authority and the Iraqi interim administration that would lead to the delivery of all relevant documentation and the transfer of all operational responsibility of the Programme to the Authority;

17. Requests further that the Secretary-General transfer as soon as possible to the Development Fund for Iraq 1 billion United States dollars from unencumbered funds in the accounts established pursuant to paragraphs 8 (a) and 8 (b) of resolution 986 (1995), restore Government of Iraq funds that were provided by Member States to the Secretary-General as requested in paragraph 1 of resolution 778 (1992), and decides that, after deducting all relevant United Nations expenses associated with the shipment of authorized contracts and costs to the Programme outlined in paragraph 16 (c) above, including residual obligations, all surplus funds in the escrow accounts established pursuant to paragraphs 8 (a), 8 (b), 8 (d), and 8 (f) of resolution 986 (1995) shall be transferred at the earliest possible time to the Development Fund for Iraq;

18. Decides to terminate effective on the adoption of this resolution the functions related to the observation and monitoring activities undertaken by the Secretary-General under the Programme, including the monitoring of the export of petroleum and petroleum products from Iraq;

19. Decides to terminate the Committee established pursuant to paragraph 6 of resolution 661 (1990) at the conclusion of the six month period called for in paragraph 16 above and further decides that the Committee shall identify individuals and entities referred to in paragraph 23 below;

20. Decides that all export sales of petroleum, petroleum products, and natural gas from Iraq following the date of the adoption of this resolution shall be made consistent with prevailing international market best practices, to be audited by independent public accountants reporting to the International Advisory and Monitoring Board referred to in paragraph 12 above in order to ensure transparency, and decides further that, except as provided in paragraph 21 below, all proceeds from such sales shall be deposited into the Development Fund for Iraq until such time as an

internationally recognized, representative government of Iraq is properly constituted;

21. Decides further that 5 percent of the proceeds referred to in paragraph 20 above shall be deposited into the Compensation Fund established in accordance with resolution 687 (1991) and subsequent relevant resolutions and that, unless an internationally recognized, representative government of Iraq and the Governing Council of the United Nations Compensation Commission, in the exercise of its authority over methods of ensuring that payments are made into the Compensation Fund, decide otherwise, this requirement shall be binding on a properly constituted, internationally recognized, representative government of Iraq and any successor thereto;

22. Noting the relevance of the establishment of an internationally recognized, representative government of Iraq and the desirability of prompt completion of the restructuring of Iraq's debt as referred to in paragraph 15 above, further decides that, until December 31, 2007, unless the Council decides otherwise, petroleum, petroleum products, and natural gas originating in Iraq shall be immune, until title passes to the initial purchaser from legal proceedings against them and not be subject to any form of attachment, garnishment, or execution, and that all States shall take any steps that may be necessary under their respective domestic legal systems to assure this protection, and that proceeds and obligations arising from sales thereof, as well as the Development Fund for Iraq, shall enjoy privileges and immunities equivalent to those enjoyed by the United Nations except that the above-mentioned privileges and immunities will not apply with respect to any legal proceeding in which recourse to such proceeds or obligations is necessary to satisfy liability for damages assessed in connection with an ecological accident, including an oil spill, that occurs after the date of adoption of this resolution;

23. Decides that all Member States in which there are:

(a) funds or other financial assets or economic resources of the previous Government of Iraq or its state bodies, corporations, or agencies, located outside Iraq as of the date of this resolution, or

(b) funds or other financial assets or economic resources that have been removed from Iraq, or acquired, by Saddam Hussein or other senior officials of the former Iraqi regime and their immediate family members, including entities owned or controlled, directly or indirectly, by them or by persons acting on their behalf or at their direction, shall freeze without delay those funds or other financial assets or economic resources and, unless these funds or other financial assets or economic resources are themselves the subject of a prior judicial, administrative, or arbitral lien or judgement, immediately shall cause their transfer to the Development Fund for Iraq, it being understood that, unless otherwise addressed, claims made by private individuals or non-government entities on those transferred funds or other financial assets may be presented to the internationally recognized, representative government of Iraq; and decides further that all such funds or other financial assets or economic resources shall enjoy the same privileges, immunities, and protections as provided under paragraph 22;

24. Requests the Secretary-General to report to the Council at regular intervals on the work of the Special Representative with respect to the implementation of this resolution and on the work of the International Advisory and Monitoring Board and encourages the United Kingdom of Great Britain and Northern Ireland and the United States of America to inform the Council at regular intervals of their efforts under this resolution;

25. Decides to review the implementation of this resolution within twelve months of adoption and to consider further steps that might be necessary;

26. Calls upon Member States and international and regional organizations to contribute to the implementation of this resolution;

27. Decides to remain seized of this matter.

Security Council Resolution 1490 (2003) [On Extension of the Mandate of the UN Iraq-Kuwait Observation Mission (UNIKOM)]. July 3, 2003.

Resolution 1490 (2003)

Adopted by the Security Council at its 4783rd meeting, on 3 July 2003

The Security Council,

Recalling all its previous relevant resolutions, including resolutions 687 (1991) of 3 April 1991, 689 (1991) of 9 April 1991, 806 (1993) of 5 February 1993, 833 (1993) of 27 May 1993 and 1483 (2003) of 22 May 2003,

Taking note of the Secretary-General's report of 17 June 2003 (S/2003/656) on the United Nations Iraq-Kuwait Observation Mission (UNIKOM),

Reaffirming the commitment of all Member States to the sovereignty and territorial integrity of Iraq and Kuwait,

Recognizing that the continued operation of UNIKOM and a demilitarized zone established under resolution 687 (1991) are no longer necessary to protect against threats to international security posed by Iraqi actions against Kuwait,

Expressing its appreciation for the substantial voluntary contributions made to the Observation Mission by the Government of Kuwait,

Commending the superior role played by UNIKOM and Department of Peacekeeping Operations (DPKO) personnel, and noting also that UNIKOM successfully fulfilled its mandate from 1991 to 2003,

Acting under Chapter VII of the Charter of the United Nations,

1. Decides to continue the mandate of UNIKOM for a final period until 6 October 2003;

2. Directs the Secretary-General to negotiate the transfer of UNIKOM's non-removable property and of those assets that cannot be disposed otherwise to the States of Kuwait and Iraq, as appropriate;

3. Decides to end the demilitarized zone extending 10 kilometres into Iraq and 5 kilometres into Kuwait from the Iraq-Kuwait border at the end of UNIKOM's mandate on 6 October 2003;

4. Requests the Secretary-General to report to the Council on the completion of UNIKOM's mandate;

5. Expresses its appreciation of the decision of the Government of Kuwait to defray since 1 November 1993 two thirds of the cost of the Observation Mission;

6. Decides to remain seized of the matter.

Security Council Resolution 1500 (2003) [On Establishment of the UN Assistance Mission for Iraq]. August 14, 2003.

Resolution 1500 (2003)

Adopted by the Security Council at its 4808th meeting, on 14 August 2003

The Security Council,

Recalling all its previous relevant resolutions, in particular resolution 1483 (2003) of 22 May 2003,

Reaffirming the sovereignty and territorial integrity of Iraq,

Reaffirming also the vital role for the United Nations in Iraq which was set out in relevant paragraphs of resolution 1483 (2003),

Having considered the report of the Secretary-General of 15 July 2003 (S/2003/715),

1. Welcomes the establishment of the broadly representative Governing Council of Iraq on 13 July 2003, as an important step towards the formation by the people of Iraq of an internationally recognized, representative government that will exercise the sovereignty of Iraq;

2. Decides to establish the United Nations Assistance Mission for Iraq to support the Secretary-General in the fulfilment of his mandate under resolution 1483 in accordance with the structure and responsibilities set out in his report of 15 July 2003, for an initial period of twelve months;

3. Decides to remain seized of this matter.

Security Council Resolution 1511 (2003) [On Authorizing a Multinational Force under Unified Command to Take All Necessary Measures to Contribute to the Maintenance of Security and Stability in Iraq]. October 16, 2003.

Resolution 1511 (2003)

Adopted by the Security Council at its 4844th meeting, on 16 October 2003

The Security Council,

Reaffirming its previous resolutions on Iraq, including resolution 1483 (2003) of 22 May 2003 and 1500 (2003) of 14 August 2003, and on threats to peace and security caused by terrorist acts, including resolution 1373 (2001) of 28 September 2001, and other relevant resolutions,

Underscoring that the sovereignty of Iraq resides in the State of Iraq, reaffirming the right of the Iraqi people freely to determine their own political future and control their own natural resources, reiterating its resolve that the day when Iraqis govern themselves must come quickly, and recognizing the importance of international support, particularly that of countries in the region, Iraq's neighbours, and regional organizations, in taking forward this process expeditiously,

Recognizing that international support for restoration of conditions of stability and security is essential to the well-being of the people of Iraq as well as to the ability of all concerned to carry out their work on behalf of the people of Iraq, and welcoming Member State contributions in this regard under resolution 1483 (2003),

Welcoming the decision of the Governing Council of Iraq to form a preparatory constitutional committee to prepare for a constitutional conference that will draft a constitution to embody the aspirations of the Iraqi people, and urging it to complete this process quickly,

Affirming that the terrorist bombings of the Embassy of Jordan on 7 August 2003, of the United Nations headquarters in Baghdad on 19 August 2003, of the Imam Ali Mosque in Najaf on 29 August 2003, and of the Embassy of Turkey on 14 October 2003, and the murder of a Spanish diplomat on 9 October 2003 are attacks on the people of Iraq, the United Nations, and the international community, and deploring the assassination of Dr. Akila al-Hashimi, who died on 25 September 2003, as an attack directed against the future of Iraq,

In that context, recalling and reaffirming the statement of its President of 20 August 2003 (S/PRST/2003/13) and resolution 1502 (2003) of 26 August 2003,

Determining that the situation in Iraq, although improved, continues to constitute a threat to international peace and security,

Acting under Chapter VII of the Charter of the United Nations,

1. Reaffirms the sovereignty and territorial integrity of Iraq, and underscores, in that context, the temporary nature

of the exercise by the Coalition Provisional Authority (Authority) of the specific responsibilities, authorities, and obligations under applicable international law recognized and set forth in resolution 1483 (2003), which will cease when an internationally recognized, representative government established by the people of Iraq is sworn in and assumes the responsibilities of the Authority, inter alia through steps envisaged in paragraphs 4 through 7 and 10 below;

2. Welcomes the positive response of the international community, in fora such as the Arab League, the Organization of the Islamic Conference, the United Nations General Assembly, and the United Nations Educational, Scientific and Cultural Organization, to the establishment of the broadly representative Governing Council as an important step towards an internationally recognized, representative government;

3. Supports the Governing Council's efforts to mobilize the people of Iraq, including by the appointment of a cabinet of ministers and a preparatory constitutional committee to lead a process in which the Iraqi people will progressively take control of their own affairs;

4. Determines that the Governing Council and its ministers are the principal bodies of the Iraqi interim administration, which, without prejudice to its further evolution, embodies the sovereignty of the State of Iraq during the transitional period until an internationally recognized, representative government is established and assumes the responsibilities of the Authority;

5. Affirms that the administration of Iraq will be progressively undertaken by the evolving structures of the Iraqi interim administration;

6. Calls upon the Authority, in this context, to return governing responsibilities and authorities to the people of Iraq as soon as practicable and requests the Authority, in cooperation as appropriate with the Governing Council and the Secretary-General, to report to the Council on the progress being made;

7. Invites the Governing Council to provide to the Security Council, for its review, no later than 15 December 2003, in cooperation with the Authority and, as circumstances permit, the Special Representative of the Secretary-General, a timetable and a programme for the drafting of a new constitution for Iraq and for the holding of democratic elections under that constitution;

8. Resolves that the United Nations, acting through the Secretary-General, his Special Representative, and the United Nations Assistance Mission in Iraq, should strengthen its vital role in Iraq, including by providing humanitarian relief, promoting the economic reconstruction of and conditions for sustainable development in Iraq, and

advancing efforts to restore and establish national and local institutions for representative government;

9. Requests that, as circumstances permit, the Secretary-General pursue the course of action outlined in paragraphs 98 and 99 of the report of the Secretary-General of 17 July 2003 (S/2003/715);

10. Takes note of the intention of the Governing Council to hold a constitutional conference and, recognizing that the convening of the conference will be a milestone in the movement to the full exercise of sovereignty, calls for its preparation through national dialogue and consensus-building as soon as practicable and requests the Special Representative of the Secretary-General, at the time of the convening of the conference or, as circumstances permit, to lend the unique expertise of the United Nations to the Iraqi people in this process of political transition, including the establishment of electoral processes;

11. Requests the Secretary-General to ensure that the resources of the United Nations and associated organizations are available, if requested by the Iraqi Governing Council and, as circumstances permit, to assist in furtherance of the programme provided by the Governing Council in paragraph 7 above, and encourages other organizations with expertise in this area to support the Iraqi Governing Council, if requested;

12. Requests the Secretary-General to report to the Security Council on his responsibilities under this resolution and the development and implementation of a timetable and programme under paragraph 7 above;

13. Determines that the provision of security and stability is essential to the successful completion of the political process as outlined in paragraph 7 above and to the ability of the United Nations to contribute effectively to that process and the implementation of resolution 1483 (2003), and authorizes a multinational force under unified command to take all necessary measures to contribute to the maintenance of security and stability in Iraq, including for the purpose of ensuring necessary conditions for the implementation of the timetable and programme as well as to contribute to the security of the United Nations Assistance Mission for Iraq, the Governing Council of Iraq and other institutions of the Iraqi interim administration, and key humanitarian and economic infrastructure;

14. Urges Member States to contribute assistance under this United Nations mandate, including military forces, to the multinational force referred to in paragraph 13 above;

15. Decides that the Council shall review the requirements and mission of the multinational force referred to in paragraph 13 above not later than one year from the date of this resolution, and that in any case the mandate of the force shall expire upon the completion of the political process

as described in paragraphs 4 through 7 and 10 above, and expresses readiness to consider on that occasion any future need for the continuation of the multinational force, taking into account the views of an internationally recognized, representative government of Iraq;

16. Emphasizes the importance of establishing effective Iraqi police and security forces in maintaining law, order, and security and combating terrorism consistent with paragraph 4 of resolution 1483 (2003), and calls upon Member States and international and regional organizations to contribute to the training and equipping of Iraqi police and security forces;

17. Expresses deep sympathy and condolences for the personal losses suffered by the Iraqi people and by the United Nations and the families of those United Nations personnel and other innocent victims who were killed or injured in these tragic attacks;

18. Unequivocally condemns the terrorist bombings of the Embassy of Jordan on 7 August 2003, of the United Nations headquarters in Baghdad on 19 August 2003, and of the Imam Ali Mosque in Najaf on 29 August 2003, and of the Embassy of Turkey on 14 October 2003, the murder of a Spanish diplomat on 9 October 2003, and the assassination of Dr. Akila al-Hashimi, who died on 25 September 2003, and emphasizes that those responsible must be brought to justice;

19. Calls upon Member States to prevent the transit of terrorists to Iraq, arms for terrorists, and financing that would support terrorists, and emphasizes the importance of strengthening the cooperation of the countries of the region, particularly neighbours of Iraq, in this regard;

20. Appeals to Member States and the international financial institutions to strengthen their efforts to assist the people of Iraq in the reconstruction and development of their economy, and urges those institutions to take immediate steps to provide their full range of loans and other financial assistance to Iraq, working with the Governing Council and appropriate Iraqi ministries;

21. Urges Member States and international and regional organizations to support the Iraq reconstruction effort initiated at the 24 June 2003 United Nations Technical Consultations, including through substantial pledges at the 23–24 October 2003 International Donors Conference in Madrid;

22. Calls upon Member States and concerned organizations to help meet the needs of the Iraqi people by providing resources necessary for the rehabilitation and reconstruction of Iraq's economic infrastructure;

23. Emphasizes that the International Advisory and Monitoring Board (IAMB) referred to in paragraph 12 of resolution 1483 (2003) should be established as a priority, and reiterates that the Development Fund for Iraq shall be used in a transparent manner as set out in paragraph 14 of resolution 1483 (2003);

24. Reminds all Member States of their obligations under paragraphs 19 and 23 of resolution 1483 (2003) in particular the obligation to immediately cause the transfer of funds, other financial assets and economic resources to the Development Fund for Iraq for the benefit of the Iraqi people;

25. Requests that the United States, on behalf of the multinational force as outlined in paragraph 13 above, report to the Security Council on the efforts and progress of this force as appropriate and not less than every six months;

26. Decides to remain seized of the matter.

Source: United Nations Security Council, S/Res/1483(2003), May 22, 2003; S/Res/1490(2003), July 3, 2003; S/Res/1500(2003), August 14, 2003; and S/Res/1511(2003), October 16, 2003.

119. "A Strike at Europe's Heart," Madrid, Spain, *Time*, Sunday, March 14, 2004 [Excerpts]

Introduction

Al Qaeda and related Muslim militant organizations sometimes succeeded in carrying through on threats to retaliate against those nations that participated in military intervention against Afghanistan and Iraq. On March 11, 2004, 10 explosions took place within four minutes on four commuter trains traveling into Madrid, the Spanish capital, killing 191 people and seriously injuring another 2,000 people. The Spanish government initially blamed the bombings on the Basque separatist movement, but that organization denied all responsibility. Eventually 29 individuals, Algerian, Syrian, and Moroccan Islamic extremists from the Moroccan Islamic Combatant Group (MICG) and some Spanish sympathizers, were charged with the bombings; another 5 to 8 suspects were believed to have evaded capture. The MICG was a North African–based organization loosely linked to Al Qaeda, an indication of the difficulties that antiterrorist governments faced in tracking down a highly fragmented militant movement with numerous different groups and factions that often acted independently of each other. In national elections held a few days after the Madrid bombings, the Spanish people responded by voting their existing Conservative government out of power. Despite pleas from American and British officials to stand firm, its Socialist successor quickly withdrew all the 1,300 Spanish military personnel then in Iraq. Critics charged that by demonstrating that terrorist tactics could provoke dramatic reverses in policy, this decision only encouraged further such attacks on civilians.

Primary Source

A Strike at Europe's Heart

He was one of hundreds of rescue workers who combed through the wreckage Thursday, looking for survivors in the scorched and twisted compartments of a commuter train at Madrid's El Pozo del Tío Raimundo station. When he came across an unremarkable sports bag, he assumed it belonged to one of the victims and put it aside; at some point amid the grim triage the bag was taken to a local police station, where it was added to a mountain of unclaimed personal possessions—purses, briefcases, shoes, coats, laptop computers. In the chaotic aftermath of the Madrid bomb attacks, no one thought to open the bag.

And then it rang. At 7:40 p.m., exactly 12 hours after a series of bombs had gone off on four trains, a mobile phone in the sports bag sounded an alarm, according to the Madrid daily *El País*. When investigators looked inside for the phone, they found it attached to two copper detonators, which were connected to 10 kg of a gelatinous dynamite. The bag was stuffed with nails and screws to heighten the bomb's power. For some reason, the device did not detonate. Instead, it became the biggest break yet in the hunt for those responsible for the massacre.

A mobile-phone bomb is a simple but effective way to commit mass murder from a distance. The tactic worked 10 times during the Thursday-morning rush hour in Madrid, as powerful explosives ripped open carriages, killing at least 200 commuters and wounding more than 1,500 others. Two similar devices were destroyed by police in controlled explosions. But thanks to a terrorist's mistake and a rescue worker's accidental discovery, the final bomb survived. It proved to be lucky 13 for the investigators: the Motorola handset and its SIM card supplied the vital clues that led to the arrests on Saturday afternoon of five suspects—three Moroccans and two Indian nationals. The five were held in connection with illegal manipulation of the phone and its SIM card.

Two Spanish citizens of Indian origin were also questioned by the police. According to a Spanish government official, at least two and possibly all four of the Indians ran a shop in Madrid where they sold—not always legally—prepaid SIM cards. Spanish defense analyst Rafael L. Bardají suggests they may have been unwitting collaborators in the train bombings. "Perhaps the poor guys were only the people who prepared the illegal phones," he says. "The question is: To whom did they sell the phones?"

In announcing the detentions, Interior Minister Angel Acebes said, "We're continuing to work on all fronts," referring to the possibility that the Basque terrorist group ETA may have been behind the attacks, "although these arrests open an important new avenue of investigation." It was a far cry from even earlier that day when the Minister still considered ETA the prime suspect.

Spanish and French authorities say the Moroccans may be linked to the synchronized suicide bombings that killed 33 innocent people in Casablanca last May. Government sources in Morocco are more emphatic, telling *TIME* that there was evidence that all three had connections to the extremist groups believed to have directed those attacks, Salafia Jihadia and its offshoot cell, Assirat al Moustaqim (Straight Path). These groups, Moroccan sources say, are associated with Osama bin Laden's al-Qaeda network. The Casablanca operation loosely resembled the Madrid massacre: there were well-orchestrated blasts in five locations, and in each instance the explosives were carried in bags or rucksacks. One important difference: the Casablanca attacks were all suicide bombings. So far, Spanish investigators have found no evidence that suicide bombers were at work in Madrid. "They were in Spain for a reason," says independent terrorism expert Roland Jacquard. "The thesis now is . . . they've been continuing work there to replicate the Casablanca strike in even bolder form."

The Islamic connection got another boost late on Saturday night when Acebes announced that the Spanish government had retrieved a videotaped message from a man purporting to be al-Qaeda's military spokesman in Europe. The local Madrid television station TeleMadrid received a call from a man with an Arab accent saying a tape had been placed in a wastebasket near the city's main mosque and the municipal morgue. Police secured the area, picked up the tape and translated it. According to Acebes, a man speaking Arabic with a Moroccan accent identifies himself as Abu Dujan al-Afghani, the al-Qaeda military spokesman, and says: "We declare our responsibility for what happened in Madrid . . . It is a response to your collaboration with the criminals Bush and his allies . . . There will be more if God wills it. You love life and we love death . . . if you don't put an end to your injustices more and more blood will run." Spanish law-enforcement officials are checking the tape's authenticity.

This was, in fact, the second claim of responsibility from a group related to al-Qaeda. On Thursday night, the London-based al-Quds al-Arabi received an e-mail from the Abu Hafs al-Masri Brigades, named for an al-Qaeda leader killed in a U.S. missile attack in Afghanistan. The message said one of its "death squads" had planted the bombs to settle "old accounts with Spain . . . America's ally in its war against Islam." The statement went on: "The death squad succeeded in penetrating the crusader European depths and striking one of the pillars of the crusader alliance" and warned that another attack against the U.S. is "90% ready—and coming soon." The New York City Police Department sent—and Morocco planned to send—teams of investigators to Madrid, and the FBI also offered assistance; all hoped to gather intelligence they might need at home.

The Brigades had made bogus claims before, including authorship of last summer's power outage in the northeastern U.S. But the

Brigades also claimed to have carried out November's bombings of synagogues and British targets in Istanbul, in which 61 died, and the August bombing of the U.N. headquarters in Baghdad, in which 22 died. Some intelligence experts take the Brigades seriously—they could be "the new military wing of al-Qaeda in charge of external jihad," says Mustafa Alani, Middle East security expert at the London-based Royal United Services Institute for Defense and Security Studies—but no one has yet verified its role in these attacks. Even so, there is no question that the November bombings of the British consulate and a British-based bank in Istanbul had shown that bin Laden's disciples were able to target Western interests at Europe's doorstep. If Madrid turns out to be the Islamic extremist's handiwork, it means al-Qaeda has blasted open the door and stormed inside.

The arrests seemed finally to clear the confusion that had descended on Madrid in the aftermath of the attacks. Before anyone knew what was in the sports bag, most Spaniards instinctively fingered the Basque terror group ETA, which has killed more than 800 people in a campaign of terror against the Spanish state spanning four decades. Just hours after the attacks, Acebes was adamant that there was "no cause for doubt" that ETA was to blame. Government officials and members of the ruling Popular Party (PP) pointed to what they said were hallmarks of ETA involvement: the bombings took place just three days before Sunday's general election, which ETA had vowed to disrupt; ETA had targeted the railway system before; and only last month Spanish police had foiled ETA attempts to transport large quantities of explosives into Madrid.

But the train blasts also differed from the Basque group's traditional modus operandi in important ways: the absence of a warning, which ETA usually gives, the deliberate targeting of civilians and the sheer scale of the operation. Despite the government's professed certainty of ETA's guilt, doubts began to creep in. Then, on Thursday evening, Acebes announced that in Alcalá de Henares, a town 30 km northeast of Madrid where three of the ill-fated trains originated and the fourth passed through, police had found an abandoned white Renault Kangoo van containing seven copper detonators and a tape of Koranic verses recited in Arabic. The discovery harked back to the hours after the attacks in New York City and Washington on Sept. 11, 2001, when a rental car was found in the parking lot of Boston's Logan airport, containing flight manuals in Arabic. That vehicle was the start of the trail that led American investigators to al-Qaeda. The van in Alcalá de Henares was another piece of evidence that pointed to Islamic radicals rather than Basque terrorists.

If there had been no warning from ETA, there had certainly been a declaration of intent from al-Qaeda. A tape aired in October— the voice purported to be bin Laden's—had singled out Spain for retribution because of its government's staunch support for the war in Iraq. And documents on an Arabic website studied by Norwegian defense researchers in recent months indicated that al-Qaeda was considering attacks on Madrid ahead of the election. The 42-page document, titled "Jihad's Iraq," had been submitted to the discussion forum of a politically oriented website that no longer exists, according to Brynjar Lia of the Norwegian Defense Research Establishment. The section of the report devoted to Spain read in part: "We must exploit to the maximum the proximity of the election in Spain . . . We believe that the Spanish government cannot tolerate more than two or three attacks before it will be forced to pull out" of Iraq. According to Lia, the document seems authentic, though he emphasizes that it contains no specific attack orders: "It's an overall guideline for strategies that the jihadis should pursue in the future." If that was all speculation, the van and the sports bag now provided Spanish investigators with real, physical evidence.

And it didn't take them long to connect the dots. Nearly 24 hours before Acebes announced the arrests, Spanish authorities were warning French security services that the Madrid blasts could indeed be the work of an Islamic group. Sources tell *Time* that this was one of the reasons the French government boosted its security status to red, the second-highest state of alert. Paris was already concerned about the possibility of an attack by an Islamic terror group. In a recent taped message bin Laden's deputy, Ayman al-Zawahiri, explicitly warned of retribution against France's ban on Muslim head scarves in public schools. The Spanish intelligence forced France to consider itself in the crosshairs, according to a French security official. "We know if we're not next, we're after the ones who are next," he said. "And that's what everyone in Europe is thinking to themselves today."

Back in Madrid, news of the arrests brought about a shift in the political mood just hours ahead of the general election. Until then, analysts had believed that widespread anger at ETA would favor the Popular Party of departing Prime Minister José María Aznar, which has advocated a hard line against the Basque group. Some opponents charged the government with exaggerating the evidence against ETA and downplaying the al-Qaeda theory for political gain. On Thursday, Foreign Minister Ana Palacio had sent out a dispatch to all Spanish ambassadors requesting that they "take advantage of any occasions that present themselves to confirm ETA's responsibility for these brutal attacks." Analysts suggested that if voters believed al-Qaeda was responsible, they might take their anger out on the PP, which had put Spain on bin Laden's hit list by signing up for the war in Iraq.

There certainly was anger in the air outside the PP headquarters in Madrid as Acebes announced the arrests. The spontaneous antigovernment demonstrations that started at 6 p.m. in front of PP headquarters in Madrid grew substantially. By the early hours of Sunday morning, there were an estimated 5,000 people gathering close to Atocha station. Angry over what they see as government manipulation, many demonstrators blamed Aznar for provoking the attacks. "Yesterday, we were marching in mourning. Tonight it's out of revulsion at the politics that produced this terrorism," said Francisco Rodríguez, a middle-aged insurance-firm employee. "I hold the government responsible for the deaths on Thursday because we went out to support an unjust war."

[. . .]

Even before al-Qaeda's claims of responsibility, intelligence experts in Washington saw bin Laden's fingerprints in the wreckage. "There's no doubt in my mind it's al-Qaeda," said one senior counterterror veteran at the FBI. Wherever this investigation leads, the war on terror has taken yet another deadly new turn. As one U.S. intelligence official notes, the absence of suicide bombers in Madrid is a sobering development. "You don't have to kill yourself to blow something up," this official says. Since suicide bombers are a finite resource, terrorists could be more inspired than ever to mount devastating attacks by remote control. In other words, Madrid rolled out an innovation that other terrorists will surely copy, says Tarine Fairman, who retired last month as a top international counterterrorism agent at the FBI. "They've introduced a technique that we knew about and were concerned about," he warns, "but are not prepared to deal with."

Source: "A Strike at Europe's Heart," Time Europe Online, March 14, 2004, http://www.time.com/time/europe/html/040322/story.html.

120. Lieutenant General Anthony Jones and Major General George R. Fay, Executive Summary of Report, Investigation of Intelligence Activities at Abu Ghraib, August 23, 2004

Introduction

In the spring of 2004 repeated reports of widespread abuse and torture of civilian detainees in the Iraqi prison camp of Abu Ghraib began circulating in the international media. Abu Ghraib held between 6,000 and 7,000 Iraqi prisoners, most of whom had been arrested on suspicion of insurgent activities. Brigadier General Janis Karpinski, who commanded the prison at this time, later stated that around 90 percent of such prisoners were innocent of any wrongdoing. Credible reports, buttressed by graphic photographs, appeared on television and in the *New Yorker* magazine in late April and early May 2004. U.S. Defense Department officials were already aware of these allegations and in early 2004 had instructed Lieutenant General Ricardo S. Sanchez to investigate

them. The task ultimately fell to Major General Antonio M. Taguba, whose report appeared in early May. Although the report was marked "Secret/No Foreign Dissemination," large portions of it appeared almost immediately on the Internet and in the media. The Taguba Report drew on the testimony of numerous witnesses to describe pervasive physical, psychological, and sexual abuse of prisoners at the prison camp in October and November 2003, mistreatment that amounted to torture and contravened the Geneva Conventions governing behavior toward prisoners. The report also depicted an understaffed prison camp manned by poorly trained and ignorant American military personnel, whom the military police and intelligence officers deliberately encouraged to abuse prisoners as a means of softening up such captives for subsequent interrogation. The Sanchez Report recommended the suspension from duty of Karpinski, who commanded the camp at this time, and she was later demoted to colonel. Sixteen other soldiers were also suspended from duty, and 7 low-ranking soldiers directly responsible for abuses were subsequently court-martialed. The incidents seriously damaged the international image of the United States, undercutting its claims that it represented the cause of human rights and freedom in Iraq and around the world and bringing condemnation from the United Nations (UN). Photographs of the torture, terrorization, humiliation, and sexual abuse of naked and terrified prisoners were shown repeatedly on Arab television and posted on the Internet. In May 2004 President George W. Bush and Secretary of Defense Donald Rumsfeld publicly apologized for these events. Critics nonetheless claimed that the incidents at Abu Ghraib were symptomatic of a broader readiness by senior Bush administration officials to discard and ignore the Geneva Conventions and sanction the illegal detention and torture of prisoners as and when it suited their own convenience.

Public criticism of the Taguba Report on abuses against Iraqi detainees held at the Abu Ghraib prison facility by American troops centered on suggestions that the document had been too narrowly focused in terms of ascribing blame only to low-level personnel and had concentrated too exclusively on the army while ignoring the role of military intelligence. Many who condemned the mistreatment of prisoners at Abu Ghraib felt that the court-martials and censure of relatively low-ranking military personnel allowed higher-level officials, such as Bush and Rumsfeld, to evade responsibility for crimes whose root cause lay in policies that top Bush administration figures had enthusiastically initiated and encouraged. In June 2004 two senior officers, Lieutenant General Anthony Jones and Major General George R. Fay, began a further investigation into the role that efforts to obtain intelligence information from detainees had played in provoking abuses. Their report stated that military forces at Abu Ghraib had found themselves "severely under-resourced," lacking "adequate personnel and equipment," and operating in a hostile environment they had not anticipated. When President George W. Bush declared the end of major hostilities in Iraq, American forces were only holding

600 Iraqi prisoners, but in the autumn of 2003 "the number of detainees rose exponentially" as the result of tactical counterinsurgency operations. The report found that although the majority of incidents of abuse had not been related to interrogations, 27 military intelligence personnel also repeatedly encouraged or participated in the abuse of detainees. Senior-level officers were faulted for poor leadership in failing to issue clear and consistent guidelines on interrogation and the treatment of prisoners and for being slow in responding to reports on abuses submitted to them by the International Committee of the Red Cross. The report claimed, however, that had Defense Department and U.S. Army doctrine been properly followed abuses would not have occurred and suggested that many of the problems encountered arose from the fact that military personnel had been "[w]orking alongside non-DoD organizations/agencies in detention facilities." To many critics, it seemed that the military still sought to protect its own and was unwilling to address the issue of whether official U.S. policies on the treatment of prisoners now contravened internationally accepted standards and conventions.

Primary Source

Executive Summary

Investigation of Intelligence Activities At Abu Ghraib. August 23, 2004.

Background

This investigation was ordered initially by LTG Ricardo S. Sanchez, Commander, Combined Joint Task Force Seven (CJTF-7). LTG Sanchez appointed MG George R. Fay as investigating officer under the provisions of Army Regulation 381-10, Procedure 15. MG Fay was appointed to investigate allegations that members of the 205th Military Intelligence Brigade (205 MI BDE) were involved in detainee abuse at the Abu Ghraib Detention Facility. Specifically, MG Fay was to determine whether 205 MI BDE personnel requested, encouraged, condoned, or solicited Military Police (MP) personnel to abuse detainees and whether MI personnel comported with established interrogation procedures and applicable laws and regulations.

On 16 June 2004, Acting Secretary of the Army R. L. Brownlee appointed General Paul J. Kern, Commander, US Army Materiel Command (AMC), as the new Procedure 15 appointing authority. On 25 June 2004, GEN Kern appointed LTG Anthony R. Jones, Deputy Commanding General, US Army Training and Doctrine Command, as an additional Procedure 15 investigating officer. MG Fay was retained as an investigating officer.

Without reinvestigating areas reviewed by MG Fay, LTG Jones was specifically directed to focus on whether organizations or personnel higher than the 205th MI BDE chain of command, or events

and circumstances outside of the 205th MI Brigade, were involved, directly or indirectly, in the questionable activities regarding alleged detainee abuse at Abu Ghraib prison.

The investigative teams conducted a comprehensive review of all available background documents and statements pertaining to Abu Ghraib from a wide variety of sources. These sources included the reports written by MG Geoffrey Miller, MG Donald Ryder, MG Antonio Taguba and the Department of Army Inspector General. LTG Jones interviewed LTG Sanchez and MG Barbara Fast, the CJTF-7 Senior Intelligence Staff Officer. MG Fay's team conducted over 170 interviews concerning the interviewees' knowledge of interrogation and detention operations at Abu Ghraib and/or their knowledge of and involvement in detainee abuse. MG Fay's interviews included interviews with MG Fast, MG Walter Wojdakowski, MG Geoffrey Miller, MG Thomas Miller, and BG Janis Karpinski.

Operational Environment

The events at Abu Ghraib cannot be understood in a vacuum. Three interrelated aspects of the operational environment played important roles in the abuses that occurred at Abu Ghraib. First, from the time V Corps transitioned to become CJTF-7, and throughout the period under investigation, it was not resourced adequately to accomplish the missions of the CJTF: stability and support operations (SASO) and support to the Coalition Provisional Authority (CPA). The CJTF-7 headquarters lacked adequate personnel and equipment. In addition, the military police and military intelligence units at Abu Ghraib were severely under-resourced. Second, providing support to the Coalition Provisional Authority (CPA) required greater resources than envisioned in operational plans. Third, operational plans envisioned that CJTF-7 would execute SASO and provide support to the CPA in a relatively non-hostile environment. In fact, opposition was robust and hostilities continued throughout the period under investigation. Therefore, CJTF-7 had to conduct tactical counter-insurgency operations, while also executing its planned missions.

These three circumstances delayed establishment of an intelligence architecture and degraded the ability of the CJTF-7 staff to execute its assigned tasks, including oversight of interrogation and detention operations at Abu Ghraib.

When hostilities were declared over, US forces had control of only 600 Enemy Prisoners of War (EPW) and Iraqi criminals. In the fall of 2003, the number of detainees rose exponentially due to tactical operations to capture counter-insurgents dangerous to U.S. forces and Iraqi civilians. At that time, the CJTF-7 commander believed he had no choice but to use Abu Ghraib as the central detention facility.

Command and staff actions and inaction must be understood in the context of the operational environment discussed above.

In light of the operational environment, and CJTF-7 staff and subordinate unit's under-resourcing and increased missions, the CJTF-7 Commander had to prioritize efforts. CJTF-7 devoted its resources to fighting the counter-insurgency and supporting the CPA, thereby saving Coalition and civilian Iraqi lives and assisting in the transition to Iraqi self-rule. In the over-all scheme of OIF, the CJTF-7 Commander and staff performed above expectations.

Abuse

Clearly abuses occurred at the prison at Abu Ghraib. There is no single, simple explanation for why this abuse at Abu Ghraib happened. The primary causes are misconduct (ranging from inhumane to sadistic) by a small group of morally corrupt soldiers and civilians, a lack of discipline on the part of the leaders and Soldiers of the 205th MI BDE and a failure or lack of leadership by multiple echelons within CJTF-7.

Contributing factors can be traced to issues affecting Command and Control, Doctrine, Training, and the experience of the Soldiers we asked to perform this vital mission.

For purposes of this report, abuse is defined as treatment of detainees that violated U.S. criminal law or international law or treatment that was inhumane or coercive without lawful justification. Whether the Soldier or contractor knew, at the time of the acts, that the conduct violated any law or standard, is not an element of the definition.

The abuses at Abu Ghraib primarily fall into two categories: a) intentional violent or sexual abuse and, b) abusive actions taken based on misinterpretations or confusion regarding law or policy.

LTG Jones found that while senior level officers did not commit the abuse at Abu Ghraib they did bear responsibility for lack of oversight of the facility, failing to respond in a timely manner to the reports from the International Committee of the Red Cross and for issuing policy memos that failed to provide clear, consistent guidance for execution at the tactical level.

MG Fay has found that from 25 July 2003 to 6 February 2004, twenty-seven 205 MI BDE Personnel allegedly requested, encouraged, condoned or solicited Military Police (MP) personnel to abuse detainees and/or participated in detainee abuse and/or violated established interrogation procedures and applicable laws and regulations during interrogation operations at Abu Ghraib.

Most, though not all, of the violent or sexual abuses occurred separately from scheduled interrogations and did not focus on persons held for intelligence purposes. No policy, directive or doctrine directly or indirectly caused violent or sexual abuse. In these cases, Soldiers knew they were violating the approved techniques and procedures.

Confusion about what interrogation techniques were authorized resulted from the proliferation of guidance and information from other theaters of operation; individual interrogator experiences in other theaters; and, the failure to distinguish between interrogation operations in other theaters and Iraq. This confusion contributed to the occurrence of some of the non-violent and non-sexual abuses.

MG Taguba and MG Fay reviewed the same photographs as supplied by the US Army Criminal Investigation Command (CID). MG Fay identified one additional photograph depicting abuse by MI personnel that had not been previously identified by MG Taguba. MG Fay also identified other abuse that had not been photographed.

Alleged incidents of abuse by military personnel have been referred to the CID for criminal investigation and the chain of command for disciplinary action. Alleged incidents of abuse by civilian contractors have been referred through the Department of Defense to the Department of Justice.

Discipline and Leadership

Military Intelligence and Military Police units had missions throughout the Iraqi Theater of Operations (ITO), however, 205th MI Brigade and 800th Military Police Brigade leaders at Abu Ghraib failed to execute their assigned responsibilities. The leaders from units located at Abu Ghraib or with supervision over Soldiers and units at Abu Ghraib, failed to supervise subordinates or provide direct oversight of this important mission. These leaders failed to properly discipline their Soldiers. These leaders failed to learn from prior mistakes and failed to provide continued mission-specific training. The 205th MI Brigade Commander did not assign a specific subordinate unit to be responsible for interrogations at Abu Ghraib and did not ensure that a Military Intelligence chain of command at Abu Ghraib was established. The absence of effective leadership was a factor in not sooner discovering and taking actions to prevent both the violent/sexual abuse incidents and the misinterpretation/confusion incidents.

Neither Department of Defense nor Army doctrine caused any abuses. Abuses would not have occurred had doctrine been followed and mission training conducted.

Nonetheless, certain facets of interrogation and detention operations doctrine need to be updated, refined or expanded, including, the concept, organization, and operations of a Joint Interrogation and Debriefing Center (JIDC); guidance for interrogation techniques at both tactical and strategic levels; the roles, responsibilities and relationships between Military Police and Military

Intelligence personnel at detention facilities; and, the establishment and organization of a Joint Task Force structure and, in particular, its intelligence architecture.

Other Contributing Factors

Demands on the Human Intelligence (HUMINT) capabilities in a counterinsurgency and in the future joint operational environment will continue to tax tactical and strategic assets. The Army needs trained and experienced tactical HUMINT personnel.

Working alongside non-DOD organizations/agencies in detention facilities proved complex and demanding. The perception that non-DOD agencies had different rules regarding interrogation and detention operations was evident. Interrogation and detention policies and limits of authority should apply equally to all agencies in the Iraqi Theater of Operations.

"Ghost Detainees"

The appointing authority and investigating officers made a specific finding regarding the issue of "ghost detainees" within Abu Ghraib. It is clear that the interrogation practices of other government agencies led to a loss of accountability at Abu Ghraib. DoD must document and enforce adherence by other government agencies with established DoD practices and procedures while conducting detainee interrogation operations at DoD facilities. This matter requires further investigation and, in accordance with the provisions of AR 381-10, Part 15, is being referred to the DoD Inspector General, as the DoD liaison with other government agencies for appropriate investigation and evaluation. Soldiers/Sailors/Airmen/Marines should never be put in a position that potentially puts them at risk for noncompliance with the Geneva Convention or Laws of Land Warfare.

Conclusion

Leaders and Soldiers throughout Operation Iraqi Freedom were confronted with a complex and dangerous operational environment. Although a clear breakdown in discipline and leadership, the events at Abu Ghraib should not blind us from the noble conduct of the vast majority of our Soldiers. We are a values based profession in which the clear majority of our Soldiers and leaders take great pride.

A clear vote of confidence should be extended by the senior leadership to the leaders and Soldiers who continue to perform extraordinarily in supporting our Nation's wartime mission. Many of our Soldiers have paid the ultimate sacrifice to preserve the freedoms and liberties that America and our Army represent throughout the world.

23 August 2004

Source: "Executive Summary: Investigation of Intelligence Activities at Abu Ghraib," United States Department of Defense, http://www .defense.gov/news/aug2004/d20040825fay.pdf.

121. White House Press Statement on Lifting of Sanctions on Libya, September 20, 2004

Introduction

American military success in invading Iraq and removing President Saddam Hussein from power made other longtime opponents of the United States exceptionally nervous. For more than 30 years since taking power in Libya in 1969 as head of a radical Islamic regime, Colonel Muammar Qaddafi had headed an Arab regime militantly hostile toward the United States. He had been a dedicated supporter of extremist elements within the Palestine Liberation Organization (PLO), which took refuge in Tripoli, Libya's capital, after its 1982 expulsion from Beirut, and had financed and provided asylum to other terrorist groups, especially the Abu Nidal organization that launched spectacular assaults on Israel and the West. The United States broke diplomatic relations with Libya in 1980, and in 1981 and again in 1986 U.S. president Ronald Reagan ordered heavy airstrikes against Libya in retaliation for specific terrorist operations. For decades, the two states remained on deeply antagonistic terms. In late 2003, however, Qaddafi responded to Saddam Hussein's downfall by moving to improve Libya's relationship with the United States. Libya agreed to end its program to develop weapons of mass destruction, including measures to enrich uranium to fuel nuclear armaments; to open all its weapons facilities to international inspection; and to destroy all suspect materials or hand them over to the United Nations (UN). Qaddafi also agreed not to facilitate efforts to acquire weapons of mass destruction in countries whose proliferation efforts were the subject of international concern. In addition, Qaddafi agreed to renounce his support for terrorist activities and to pay compensation to the families of victims of Pan Am Flight 103, which exploded over Lockerbie, Scotland, in December 1988, killing 270 people, an episode for which Libya accepted responsibility. President George W. Bush's administration rewarded Qaddafi in September 2004 by ending the state of U.S. national emergency against Libya in place since 1986 and removing a wide range of economic sanctions on that country. U.S. trade with Libya was now permitted, as were direct air flights, and U.S. commerce with Libya was now eligible for funding from U.S. government programs to finance foreign trade. The Bush administration hinted that if Libya made more progress on such issues as human rights, further concessions might follow. As the icy atmosphere of U.S.-Libyan dealings slowly thawed, in May 2006 the United States and Libya resumed full diplomatic relations. It was no secret that by this juncture the Bush administration hoped that this demonstration of the potential for even a longtime enemy to normalize its relations with the United States by renouncing efforts to develop weapons of mass destruction might induce Iran to cease its program to enrich uranium and acquire nuclear armaments.

Primary Source

THE WHITE HOUSE
Office of the Press Secretary

September 20, 2004

STATEMENT BY THE PRESS SECRETARY

Today, the United States has reached another milestone in the President's effort to combat the proliferation of weapons of mass destruction and the means of their delivery. Over the last nine months, Libya has worked with international organizations and the United States and United Kingdom to eliminate its WMD and longer-range missile programs in a transparent and verifiable manner. Libya's efforts open the path to better relations with the United States and other free nations.

These accomplishments are significant. Libya facilitated the removal of all significant elements of its declared nuclear weapons program, signed the IAEA Additional Protocol, began a process of converting the Rabta facility to a pharmaceutical plant, destroyed chemical munitions and secured chemical agent for destruction under international supervision, declared its chemical agents to the Organization for the Prevention of Chemical Weapons, eliminated its Scud-C missile force, and agreed to eliminate its Scud-B missiles. Libya turned over nuclear weapons documentation, removed highly enriched uranium for its research reactor and equipment for uranium enrichment, allowed international personnel site access, and pledged to halt all military trade with countries of proliferation concern. Revelations by Libya greatly aided the international community's effort to understand and cripple the global black market in the world's most dangerous technologies.

Libya has also agreed to an ongoing trilateral arrangement in which the United States, the United Kingdom and Libya will address any other WMD-related issues as well as to further projects for mutual cooperation such as redirection of Libyan WMD personnel. The progress in US-Libyan relations reflects the cooperation and support exhibited by Libyan officials and experts over the last nine months. As a result, concerns over weapons of mass destruction no longer pose a barrier to the normalization of US-Libyan relations.

At the beginning of this process, the President committed to respond to concrete Libyan actions in good faith, noting that Libya "can regain a secure and respected place among the nations and,

over time, better relations with the United States." In recognition of these achievements and our assessment that Libya has continued to meet the standard it set on December 19 to eliminate WMD and MTCR-class missiles and other developments, the President has:

—Terminated the national emergency declared in 1986 under the International Emergency Economic Powers Act (IEEPA), and revoked related Executive Orders. This rescinds the remaining economic sanctions under IEEPA and ends the need for Treasury Department licences for trade with Libya. It also permits direct air service and regular charter flights, subject to standard safety and other regulatory requirements. This action also unblocks assets belonging to Libyan and non-Libyan entities that were frozen when the national emergency was imposed.

—Adopted, as a general policy, the strategy of providing a level playing field for US business in Libya through the use of U.S. Government programs such as those administered by the Departments of Agriculture and Commerce, the Export-Import Bank, Overseas Private Insurance Corporation, and Trade Development Agency, as well as to waive the prohibitions on the availability of foreign tax credits. This policy will be furthered through the use of statutory waiver authorities where necessary and in some cases through proposed legislative relief from sanctions that would otherwise stand in the way.

As a result, we expect the families of the victims of Pan Am 103 to receive over $1 billion in additional compensation from Libya. The determination and courage of the Pan Am 103 families, in almost sixteen years of efforts to hold Libya accountable before the world, contributed greatly to efforts to secure an agreement under which Libya agreed to end all its WMD programs and pledged to end all connections with terrorism.

In conjunction with U.S. action to unblock frozen assets, with respect to the remaining cases brought against it by U.S. victims of terrorism Libya has reaffirmed to us that it has a policy and practice of carrying out agreed settlements and responding in good faith to legal cases brought against it, including court judgments and arbitral awards. We expect Libya to honor this commitment.

The US will continue its dialogue with Libya on human rights, political and economic modernization, and regional political developments. We welcome Libya's engagement with Amnesty International. We also share the European Community's concern over the plight of the Bulgarian medics. Diplomatic engagement and cooperation in education, health care, and scientific training can build the foundation for stronger relations. The United States supports Libya's efforts to reap the benefits of engagement, including prosperity and security for its citizens. As the President stated in December, 2003, "Should Libya pursue internal reform, America will be ready to help its people to build a more free and prosperous country." None of today's actions change Libya's status as a State Sponsor of Terrorism. We remain seriously concerned by the allegations of Libyan involvement in an assassination plot against Crown Prince Abdullah of Saudi Arabia and we have raised our concerns with the Libyan government. These concerns must be addressed. We welcome Libya's formal renunciation of terrorism and Libyan support in the global war against terrorism, but we must establish confidence that Libya has made a strategic decision that is being carried out in practice by all Libyan agencies and officials.

Source: "Bush Lifts Trade, Transportation Sanctions on Libya," U.S. Department of State, http://www.america.gov/st/washfile-english/2004/September/20040920184448ndyblehs0.3003351.html.

122. United Nations Security Council Resolution 1566 Condemning the Use of Terror, October 8, 2004

Introduction

In 2004 the United Nations (UN) Security Council for the first time passed a resolution uncompromisingly condemning the use of terror against civilians, whatever the circumstances. Russia, which in the past had declined to endorse such blanket denunciations of terrorist tactics, introduced this resolution, impelled by the massacre by Chechnyan gunmen in September 2004 of several hundred children and adults held hostage at a school in Beslan, Ossetia. Terrorist operations had also recently killed hundreds in Baghdad, Iraq, including the head of the UN mission there, and Israelis, Russians, and Egyptians had died in attacks in the Sinai. China, France, Germany, Romania, Spain (where Islamic terrorists had placed bombs on trains in Madrid in retaliation for Spanish participation in the Iraq war), the United Kingdom, and the United States all cosponsored the resolution. States were urged to cooperate with each other and with regional and international organizations, including the UN Counter-Terrorism Committee and the "'Al Qaida/Taliban Sanctions Committee,'" in combating terror by all means possible. The resolution also emphasized the need to "enhanc[e] dialogue" and broaden "understanding among civilizations" and to address "unresolved regional conflicts" and "global issues, including development issues," provisions to which Pakistan drew particular attention. As with most UN resolutions, there were no provisions for enforcement, but the fact that the Security Council had passed this declaration was evidence that even states that had once endorsed or at least turned a blind eye to the use of terrorist tactics now considered these unacceptable.

Primary Source

The Security Council,

Reaffirming its resolutions 1267 (1999) of 15 October 1999 and 1373 (2001) of 28 September 2001 as well as its other resolutions concerning threats to international peace and security caused by terrorism,

Recalling in this regard its resolution 1540 (2004) of 28 April 2004,

Reaffirming also the imperative to combat terrorism in all its forms and manifestations by all means, in accordance with the Charter of the United Nations and international law,

Deeply concerned by the increasing number of victims, including children, caused by acts of terrorism motivated by intolerance or extremism in various regions of the world,

Calling upon States to cooperate fully with the Counter-Terrorism Committee (CTC) established pursuant to resolution 1373 (2001), including the recently established Counter-Terrorism Committee Executive Directorate (CTED), the "Al-Qaida/Taliban Sanctions Committee" established pursuant to resolution 1267 (1999) and its Analytical Support and Sanctions Monitoring Team, and the Committee established pursuant to resolution 1540 (2004), and *further calling* upon such bodies to enhance cooperation with each other,

Reminding States that they must ensure that any measures taken to combat terrorism comply with all their obligations under international law, and should adopt such measures in accordance with international law, in particular international human rights, refugee, and humanitarian law,

Reaffirming that terrorism in all its forms and manifestations constitutes one of the most serious threats to peace and security,

Considering that acts of terrorism seriously impair the enjoyment of human rights and threaten the social and economic development of all States and undermine global stability and prosperity,

Emphasizing that enhancing dialogue and broadening the understanding among civilizations, in an effort to prevent the indiscriminate targeting of different religions and cultures, and addressing unresolved regional conflicts and the full range of global issues, including development issues, will contribute to international cooperation, which by itself is necessary to sustain the broadest possible fight against terrorism,

Reaffirming its profound solidarity with victims of terrorism and their families,

Acting under Chapter VII of the Charter of the United Nations,

1. *Condemns* in the strongest terms all acts of terrorism irrespective of their motivation, whenever and by whomsoever committed, as one of the most serious threats to peace and security;

2. Calls upon States to cooperate fully in the fight against terrorism, especially with those States where or against whose citizens terrorist acts are committed, in accordance with their obligations under international law, in order to find, deny safe haven and bring to justice, on the basis of the principle to extradite or prosecute, any person who supports, facilitates, participates or attempts to participate in the financing, planning, preparation or commission of terrorist acts or provides safe havens;

3. Recalls that criminal acts, including against civilians, committed with the intent to cause death or serious bodily injury, or taking of hostages, with the purpose to provoke a state of terror in the general public or in a group of persons or particular persons, intimidate a population or compel a government or an international organization to do or to abstain from doing any act, which constitute offences within the scope of and as defined in the international conventions and protocols relating to terrorism, are under no circumstances justifiable by considerations of a political, philosophical, ideological, racial, ethnic, religious or other similar nature, and *calls upon* all States to prevent such acts and, if not prevented, to ensure that such acts are punished by penalties consistent with their grave nature;

4. Calls upon all States to become party, as a matter of urgency, to the relevant international conventions and protocols whether or not they are a party to regional conventions on the matter;

5. Calls upon Member States to cooperate fully on an expedited basis in resolving all outstanding issues with a view to adopting by consensus the draft comprehensive convention on international terrorism and the draft international convention for the suppression of acts of nuclear terrorism;

6. Calls upon relevant international, regional and subregional organizations to strengthen international cooperation in the fight against terrorism and to intensify their interaction with the United Nations and, in particular, the CTC with a view to facilitating full and timely implementation of resolution 1373 (2001);

7. Requests the CTC in consultation with relevant international, regional and subregional organizations and the United Nations bodies to develop a set of best practices to assist States in implementing the provisions of resolution 1373 (2001) related to the financing of terrorism;

8. Directs the CTC, as a matter of priority and, when appropriate, in close cooperation with relevant international, regional and subregional organizations to start visits to States, with the consent of the States concerned, in order to enhance the monitoring of the implementation of resolution 1373 (2001) and facilitate the provision of technical and other assistance for such implementation;

9. Decides to establish a working group consisting of all members of the Security Council to consider and submit recommendations to the Council on practical measures to be imposed upon individuals, groups or entities involved in or associated with terrorist activities, other than those designated by the Al-Qaida/Taliban Sanctions Committee, including more effective procedures considered to be appropriate for bringing them to justice through prosecution or extradition, freezing of their financial assets, preventing their movement through the territories of Member States, preventing supply to them of all types of arms and related material, and on the procedures for implementing these measures;

10. Requests further the working group, established under paragraph 9 to consider the possibility of establishing an international fund to compensate victims of terrorist acts and their families, which might be financed through voluntary contributions, which could consist in part of assets seized from terrorist organizations, their members and sponsors, and submit its recommendations to the Council;

11. Requests the Secretary-General to take, as a matter of urgency, appropriate steps to make the CTED fully operational and to inform the Council by 15 November 2004;

12. Decides to remain actively seized of the matter.

Source: United Nations Security Council Official Records, S/RES/1566, October 8, 2004.

123. President George W. Bush, Address to the American People on the Iraqi Elections, January 30, 2005

Introduction

In January 2005 national elections for a 275-member transitional Iraqi National Assembly were held in Iraq, the first occasion in Iraq's history in which open polling to decide on its government had taken place. The assembly was expected to draft a new constitution, under which further elections would then be held to decide on a long-term Iraqi government. Most parties representing Iraq's minority Arab Sunni Muslim community boycotted the elections, and on the election day itself at least 44 people died in 9 incidents around Iraq as opponents of the polls sought to intimidate other Iraqis from voting by mounting more than 100 attacks on polling places. Even so, about 58 percent of Iraqis, 8.4 million altogether, went to the polls. Representatives of the Shiite Muslim community won a majority of seats, with the United Iraqi Alliance, effectively supported by Grand Ayatollah Ali al-Sistani, Iraq's highest

Shiite Muslim cleric, in first place, with 48 percent of the votes, followed by the Democratic Patriotic Alliance of Kurdistan, which received 26 percent. The boycott by Arab Sunni parties, groups associated in the past with deposed Iraqi president Saddam Hussein, who argued that the safety of those voting for them could not be guaranteed, meant that those organizations had extremely limited representation in the assembly, but they were nonetheless assured that their views on the new constitution would be taken into account. International observers who monitored the polls felt that the elections had on the whole been fair and free. The holding of the elections brought a brief burst of international optimism over the future of Iraq. An exultant U.S. president George W. Bush acclaimed them as the first step on the road to a free and democratic Iraq capable of governing itself and maintaining domestic peace, stability, and order. In December 2005 the president greeted the result of national elections for a permanent Iraqi National Assembly based on proportional representation with similar enthusiasm and welcomed the eventual establishment in May 2006 of a coalition government headed by Shia politician Nouri al-Maliki. Over the next year, the resurgence of bitter and increasingly violent sectarian conflict within Iraq and the inability of successive Iraqi leaders to resolve internal divisions would make such short-lived hopes seem increasingly illusory and unrealistic.

Primary Source

The President: Today the people of Iraq have spoken to the world, and the world is hearing the voice of freedom from the center of the Middle East.

In great numbers, and under great risk, Iraqis have shown their commitment to democracy. By participating in free elections, the Iraqi people have firmly rejected the anti-democratic ideology of the terrorists. They have refused to be intimidated by thugs and assassins. And they have demonstrated the kind of courage that is always the foundation of self-government.

Some Iraqis were killed while exercising their rights as citizens. We also mourn the American and British military personnel who lost their lives today. Their sacrifices were made in a vital cause of freedom, peace in a troubled region, and a more secure future for us all.

The Iraqi people, themselves, made this election a resounding success. Brave patriots stepped forward as candidates. Many citizens volunteered as poll workers. More than 100,000 Iraqi security force personnel guarded polling places and conducted operations against terrorist groups. One news account told of a voter who had lost a leg in a terror attack last year, and went to the polls today, despite threats of violence. He said, "I would have crawled here if I had to. I don't want terrorists to kill other Iraqis like they tried to kill me. Today I am voting for peace."

Across Iraq today, men and women have taken rightful control of their country's destiny, and they have chosen a future of freedom and peace. In this process, Iraqis have had many friends at their side. The European Union and the United Nations gave important assistance in the election process. The American military and our diplomats, working with our coalition partners, have been skilled and relentless, and their sacrifices have helped to bring Iraqis to this day. The people of the United States have been patient and resolute, even in difficult days.

The commitment to a free Iraq now goes forward. This historic election begins the process of drafting and ratifying a new constitution, which will be the basis of a fully democratic Iraqi government. Terrorists and insurgents will continue to wage their war against democracy, and we will support the Iraqi people in their fight against them. We will continue training Iraqi security forces so this rising democracy can eventually take responsibility for its own security.

There's more distance to travel on the road to democracy. Yet Iraqis are proving they're equal to the challenge. On behalf of the American people, I congratulate the people of Iraq on this great and historic achievement.

Source: "President Congratulates Iraqis on Election," The White House, President George W. Bush, http://georgewbush-whitehouse .archives.gov/news/releases/2005/01/20050130-2.html.

124. Commission on the Intelligence Capabilities of the United States Regarding Weapons of Mass Destruction, Report to the President, March 31, 2005

Introduction

The primary rationale that U.S. and British leaders put forth in advance of hostilities to justify their determination to go to war against Saddam Hussein was that under his leadership, Iraq was developing formidable stockpiles of biological, chemical, and nuclear weapons of mass destruction that posed a major threat to regional stability and were also likely to be made available to terrorists for operations against Western powers. American officials also alleged that close links existed between Saddam Hussein and the Al Qaeda terrorist organization that had masterminded the September 11, 2001, attacks on the United States and several other assaults on U.S. military and diplomatic targets abroad during the 1990s. In September 2002 the British government published a dossier, which later was demonstrated to have been based on inaccurate information, claiming that Iraq already had substantial arsenals of such weapons and was in the process of producing more. In a February 2003 presentation to the United Nations (UN), the initially skeptical U.S. secretary of state Colin Powell cited the existence of major quantities of weapons of mass destruction in Iraq as a fact. To the considerable embarrassment of both British and American leaders, the invasion coalition forces failed to locate any appreciable amounts of weapons of mass destruction, and it was determined that Hussein's nuclear program had been rudimentary and unlikely to pose any threat for the foreseeable future. Under pressure from Congress, in February 2004 U.S. president George W. Bush established a public commission to investigate how and why his country's intelligence agencies had provided top officials with such misleading information on Hussein's preinvasion weapons program. The commission was cochaired by former Virginia governor and senator Charles Robb, a Democrat, and the Republican judge Laurence Silberman, and its members included Senator John McCain of Arizona, a staunch supporter of the war in Iraq and potential Republican presidential candidate who later won his party's 2008 nomination, plus several well-connected former officials from the defense and intelligence apparatus. The report concluded that a major intelligence failure had indeed occurred in this case and that the intelligence community was not only fragmented and poorly coordinated but also had based its assessments of the Iraq weapons situation on inadequate and unreliable data. The report's authors also identified another problem: the fact that at some point intelligence analysts realized that the government officials who were the ultimate recipients of their estimates would not welcome skeptical views, a climate of opinion that at least subconsciously helped to shape their own conclusions.

Primary Source

Mr. President:

With this letter, we transmit the report of the Commission on the Intelligence Capabilities of the United States Regarding Weapons of Mass Destruction. Our unanimous report is based on a lengthy investigation, during which we interviewed hundreds of experts from inside and outside the Intelligence Community and reviewed thousands of documents. Our report offers 74 recommendations for improving the U.S. Intelligence Community (all but a handful of which we believe can be implemented without statutory change). But among these recommendations a few points merit special emphasis.

We conclude that the Intelligence Community was dead wrong in almost all of its pre-war judgments about Iraq's weapons of mass destruction. This was a major intelligence failure. Its principal causes were the Intelligence Community's inability to collect good information about Iraq's WMD programs, serious errors in analyzing what information it could gather, and a failure to make clear just how much of its analysis was based on assumptions, rather than good evidence. On a matter of this importance, we simply cannot afford failures of this magnitude.

After a thorough review, the Commission found no indication that the Intelligence Community distorted the evidence regarding Iraq's weapons of mass destruction. What the intelligence professionals told you about Saddam Hussein's programs was what they believed. They were simply wrong.

As you asked, we looked as well beyond Iraq in our review of the Intelligence Community's capabilities. We conducted case studies of our intelligence agencies' recent performance assessing the risk of WMD in Libya and Afghanistan, and our current capabilities with respect to several of the world's most dangerous state and non-state proliferation threats. Out of this more comprehensive review, we report both bad news and good news. The bad news is that we still know disturbingly little about the weapons programs and even less about the intentions of many of our most dangerous adversaries.

The good news is that we have had some solid intelligence successes—thanks largely to innovative and multi-agency collection techniques.

Our review has convinced us that the best hope for preventing future failures is dramatic change. We need an Intelligence Community that is truly integrated, far more imaginative and willing to run risks, open to a new generation of Americans, and receptive to new technologies.

We have summarized our principal recommendations for the entire Intelligence Community in the Overview of the report. Here, we focus on recommendations that we believe only you can effect if you choose to implement them:

Give the DNI powers—and backing—to match his responsibilities.

In your public statement accompanying the announcement of Ambassador Negroponte's nomination as Director of National Intelligence (DNI), you have already moved in this direction. The new intelligence law makes the DNI responsible for integrating the 15 independent members of the Intelligence Community. But it gives him powers that are only relatively broader than before. The DNI cannot make this work unless he takes his legal authorities over budget, programs, personnel, and priorities to the limit. It won't be easy to provide this leadership to the intelligence components of the Defense Department, or to the CIA. They are some of the government's most headstrong agencies. Sooner or later, they will try to run around—or over—the DNI. Then, only your determined backing will convince them that we cannot return to the old ways.

Bring the FBI all the way into the Intelligence Community.

The FBI is one of the proudest and most independent agencies in the United States Government. It is on its way to becoming an effective intelligence agency, but it will never arrive if it insists on using only its own map. We recommend that you order an organizational reform of the Bureau that pulls all of its intelligence capabilities into one place and subjects them to the coordinating authority of the DNI—the same authority that the DNI exercises over Defense Department intelligence agencies. Under this recommendation, the counterterrorism and counterintelligence resources of the Bureau would become a single National Security Service inside the FBI. It would of course still be subject to the Attorney General's oversight and to current legal rules. The intelligence reform act almost accomplishes this task, but at crucial points it retreats into ambiguity.

Without leadership from the DNI, the FBI is likely to continue escaping effective integration into the Intelligence Community.

Demand more of the Intelligence Community.

The Intelligence Community needs to be pushed. It will not do its best unless it is pressed by policymakers—sometimes to the point of discomfort. Analysts must be pressed to explain how much they don't know; the collection agencies must be pressed to explain why they don't have better information on key topics. While policymakers must be prepared to credit intelligence that doesn't fit their preferences, no important intelligence assessment should be accepted without sharp questioning that forces the community to explain exactly how it came to that assessment and what alternatives might also be true. This is not "politicization"; it is a necessary part of the intelligence process.

And in the end, it is the key to getting the best from an Intelligence Community that, at its best, knows how to do astonishing things.

Rethink the President's daily brief.

The daily intelligence briefings given to you before the Iraq war were flawed.

Through attention-grabbing headlines and repetition of questionable data, these briefings overstated the case that Iraq was rebuilding its WMD programs. There are many other aspects of the daily brief that deserve to be reconsidered as well, but we are reluctant to make categorical recommendations on a process that in the end must meet your needs, not our theories. On one point, however, we want to be specific: while the DNI must be ultimately responsible for the content of your daily briefing, we do not believe that the DNI ought to prepare, deliver, or even attend every briefing. For if the DNI is consumed by current intelligence, the long-term needs of the Intelligence Community will suffer.

There is no more important intelligence mission than understanding the worst weapons that our enemies possess, and how they intend to use them against us. These are their deepest secrets, and unlocking them must be our highest priority. So far, despite some successes, our Intelligence Community has not been agile and innovative enough to provide the information that the nation needs. Other commissions and observers have said the same. We should not wait for another commission or another Administration to force widespread change in the Intelligence Community.

Very respectfully,

Laurence H. Silberman
    Co-Chairman

Charles S. Robb
    Co-Chairman

Richard C. Levin

John McCain

Henry S. Rowen

Walter B. Slocombe

William O. Studeman

Patricia M. Wald

Charles M. Vest

Lloyd Cutler

> **Source:** "Unclassified Version of the Report of the Commission on the Intelligence Capabilities of the United States Regarding Weapons of Mass Destruction," GPO Access, http://www.gpoaccess.gov/wmd/index.html.

125. British Prime Minister Tony Blair, Speech on the London Bombings, July 16, 2005

Introduction

On July 7, 2005, 4 British Muslim suicide bombers detonated bombs, three on the London underground and one on a bus, killing 52 people and seriously injuring 500 others. It was believed that the explosions in the British capital were undertaken by several Muslim terrorist sympathizers from towns in West Yorkshire in retribution for the country's involvement in military operations against Iraq and Afghanistan. Speaking to the Labour Party political conference 10 days later, British prime minister Tony Blair, who against the wishes of his own party had strongly supported both military interventions, emphasized that Britain, unlike Spain, would not reduce its commitments in either Iraq or Afghanistan in response to attacks that randomly targeted its own civilians. Blair remained resolute in his determination to stay the course against what he termed "an evil ideology" spearheaded by Al Qaeda, which demanded the establishment of fundamentalist Muslim states ruled by Sharia law throughout the Arab world, the "elimination of Israel," and the withdrawal of all Westerners from the Middle East. Such "fanaticism," Blair warned, "can't be moderated" and "has to be stood up to." Blair explicitly stated that such "barbaric ideas" were repulsive to most Muslims and were a perversion of Muslim ideology. He stated his intention of working with prominent British Muslim figures in efforts to "confront" such "extremists" and to encourage mutual understanding between different faiths. Blair's reaction to terrorist attacks on his country's capital differed from that of Spain the previous year, which also experienced bombings of commuter railway lines in Madrid, its own capital, shortly before a general election and soon responded by withdrawing its military forces from Iraq. Further terrorist attacks took place in Britain two years later, in the summer of 2007, shortly after Gordon Brown replaced Blair as prime minister, with several failed attempts to explode car bombs in London and a car bombing attack on Glasgow Airport in Scotland.

Primary Source

The greatest danger is that we fail to face up to the nature of the threat we are dealing with. What we witnessed in London last Thursday week was not an aberrant act.

It was not random. It was not a product of particular local circumstances in West Yorkshire.

Senseless though any such horrible murder is, it was not without sense for its organizers. It had a purpose. It was done according to a plan. It was meant.

What we are confronting here is an evil ideology.

It is not a clash of civilizations—all civilized people, Muslim or other, feel revulsion at it. But it is a global struggle and it is a battle of ideas, hearts and minds, both within Islam and outside it.

This is the battle that must be won, a battle not just about the terrorist methods but their views. Not just their barbaric acts, but their barbaric ideas. Not only what they do but what they think and the thinking they would impose on others.

This ideology and the violence that is inherent in it did not start a few years ago in response to a particular policy. Over the past 12 years, Al-Qaeda and its associates have attacked 26 countries, killed thousands of people, many of them Muslims.

They have networks in virtually every major country and thousands of fellow travelers. They are well-financed. Look at their websites.

They aren't unsophisticated in their propaganda. They recruit however and whoever they can and with success.

Neither is it true that they have no demands. They do. It is just that no sane person would negotiate on them.

They demand the elimination of Israel; the withdrawal of all Westerners from Muslim countries, irrespective of the wishes of people and government; the establishment of effectively Taliban states and Sharia law in the Arab world en route to one caliphate of all Muslim nations.

We don't have to wonder what type of country those states would be. Afghanistan was such a state. Girls put out of school.

Women denied even rudimentary rights. People living in abject poverty and oppression. All of it justified by reference to religious faith.

The 20th century showed how powerful political ideologies could be. This is a religious ideology, a strain within the world-wide religion of Islam, as far removed from its essential decency and truth as Protestant gunmen who kill Catholics, or vice versa, are from Christianity. But do not let us underestimate it or dismiss it.

Those who kill in its name believe genuinely that in doing it, they do God's work; they go to paradise.

From the mid-1990s onwards, statements from Al-Qaeda gave very clear expression to this ideology: "Every Muslim, the minute he can start differentiating, carries hatred towards the Americans, Jews and Christians. This is part of our ideology. The creation of Israel is a crime and it has to be erased."

"You should know that targeting Americans and Jews and killing them anywhere you find them on the earth is one of the greatest duties and one of the best acts of piety you can offer to God Almighty." Just as great is their hatred for so-called apostate governments in Muslim countries. This is why mainstream Muslims are also regarded as legitimate targets.

At last year's (Labour) party conference, I talked about this ideology in these terms.

Its roots are not superficial, but deep, in the madrassas of Pakistan, in the extreme forms of Wahabi doctrine in Saudi Arabia, in the former training camps of Al-Qaeda in Afghanistan; in the cauldron of Chechnya; in parts of the politics of most countries of the Middle East and many in Asia; in the extremist minority that now in every European city preach hatred of the West and our way of life.

This is what we are up against. It cannot be beaten except by confronting it, symptoms and causes, head-on. Without compromise and without delusion.

The extremist propaganda is cleverly aimed at their target audience. It plays on our tolerance and good nature.

It exploits the tendency to guilt of the developed world, as if it is our behaviour that should change, that if we only tried to work out and act on their grievances, we could lift this evil, that if we changed our behaviour, they would change theirs. This is a misunderstanding of a catastrophic order.

Their cause is not founded on an injustice. It is founded on a belief, one whose fanaticism is such it can't be moderated. It can't be remedied. It has to be stood up to.

And, of course, they will use any issue that is a matter of dissent within our democracy. But we should lay bare the almost-devilish logic behind such manipulation.

If it is the plight of the Palestinians that drives them, why, every time it looks as if Israel and Palestine are making progress, does the same ideology perpetrate an outrage that turns hope back into despair?

If it is Afghanistan that motivates them, why blow up innocent Afghans on their way to their first ever election? If it is Iraq that motivates them, why is the same ideology killing Iraqis by terror in defiance of an elected Iraqi government?

What was September 11, 2001 the reprisal for? Why even after the first Madrid bomb and the election of a new Spanish government, were they planning another atrocity when caught?

Why if it is the cause of Muslims that concerns them, do they kill so many with such callous indifference?

We must pull this up by its roots. Within Britain, we must join up with our Muslim community to take on the extremists. Worldwide, we should confront it everywhere it exists.

Next week I and other party leaders will meet key members of the Muslim community. Out of it I hope we can get agreed action to take this common fight forward. I want also to work with other nations to promote the true face of Islam worldwide.

Round the world, there are conferences already being held, numerous inter-faith dialogues in place, but we need to bring all of these activities together and give them focus.

We must be clear about how we win this struggle. We should take what security measures we can. But let us not kid ourselves.

In the end, it is by the power of argument, debate, true religious faith and true legitimate politics that we will defeat this threat.

That means not just arguing against their terrorism, but their politics and their perversion of religious faith. It means exposing as the rubbish it is, the propaganda about America and its allies wanting to punish Muslims or eradicate Islam.

It means championing our values of freedom, tolerance and respect for others. It means explaining why the suppression of women and the disdain for democracy are wrong.

The idea that elected governments are the preserve of those of any other faith or culture is insulting and wrong. Muslims believe in democracy just as much as any other faith and, given the chance, show it.

We must step up the urgency of our efforts. Here and abroad, the times the terrorists have succeeded are all too well known.

Less known are the times they have been foiled. The human life destroyed we can see. The billions of dollars every nation now spends is huge and growing. And they kill without limit.

They murdered over 50 innocent people (in London) last week. But it could have been over 500. And had it been, they would have rejoiced.

The spirit of our age is one in which the prejudices of the past are put behind us, where our diversity is our strength. It is this which is under attack. Moderates are not moderate through weakness but through strength. Now is the time to show it in defense of our common values.

Source: Tony Blair, Speech, Labour Party National Conference, London, July 16, 2005, http://news.bbc.co.uk/2/hi/uk_news/4689363.stm.

126. Iranian President Mahmood Ahmadinejad to U.S. President George W. Bush, May 8, 2006 [Excerpts]

Introduction

In response to repeated U.S. demands that Iran cease all efforts to enrich uranium and develop nuclear weapons and that it end support for insurgent groups in Iraq, Iranian president Mahmood Ahmadinejad, who took office in August 2005, sent a lengthy letter to U.S. president George W. Bush. Ahmadinejad, who had a doctorate in civil engineering and was known for his modest lifestyle, undiplomatically took Bush to task for betraying the ideals not just of Islam but also of Christianity. Ahmadinejad accused Bush of hypocrisy for waging war against Iraq and occupying that country at an enormous cost in both lives and money. The Iranian president assailed the human rights record of the United States, especially its extralegal detention of terrorist suspects at Guantánamo Bay and in secret prisons in Europe. He also attacked U.S. support for Israel and the Bush administration's efforts to pressure the new Hamas-dominated Palestinian government into accepting Israel's existence. Such policies, Ahmadinejad claimed, were damaging the popularity of the United States throughout the Middle East. He proclaimed Iran's right to utilize whatever scientific and technological knowledge was available to it, whether for military or peaceful purposes. He also attacked the record of the United States in supporting nondemocratic governments in Latin America and exploiting African material resources before turning to the lengthy U.S. history of intervention in Iran's affairs, which he considered equally reprehensible. He reminded Bush that after September 11, 2001, Iran had "declared its disgust with the perpetrators." Even so, Ahmadinejad suggested that the success of these massive attacks on American lives and property suggested that rogue elements within the U.S. intelligence and security services must have been implicated. Slightly paradoxically, Ahmadinejad then warned that the U.S. government's role in emphasizing the war on terror had encouraged unnecessary fear, panic, and insecurity among its citizens. He questioned the stated justification for the wars against both Afghanistan and Iraq. Bringing up the issue of social justice, Ahmadinejad also attacked Bush for spending vast amounts on war and armaments and violating human rights while millions of people in his own country and others lived in abject poverty. Ahmadinejad charged that the money devoted to military policies could and should have been spent on health, education, disaster relief, conflict mediation, and peaceful development. As it was, "global hatred of the American government" was increasing, and "[l]iberalism and Western Style democracy" had "failed." Ahmadinejad's letter was reminiscent of the missives and speeches of left-wing Third World leaders of the 1950s and 1960s. Its apocalyptic tone, theological references, and use of broad and sweeping concepts to depict the international arena also bore some resemblances to President Bush's own rhetorical style.

Primary Source

For some time now I have been thinking, how one can justify the undeniable contradictions that exist in the international arena— which are being constantly debated, especially in political forums and amongst university students. Many questions remain unanswered. These have prompted me to discuss some of the contradictions and questions, in the hopes that it might bring about an opportunity to redress them.

Can one be a follower of Jesus Christ (PBUH [Peace Be Upon Him]), the great Messenger of God,

Feel obliged to respect human rights,

Present liberalism as a civilization model,

Announce one's opposition to the proliferation of nuclear weapons and WMDs,

Make "War on Terror" his slogan, and finally,

Work towards the establishment of a unified international community—a community which Christ and the virtuous of the Earth will one day govern,

But at the same time,

Have countries attacked; The lives, reputations and possessions of people destroyed and on the slight chance of the presence of a few criminals in a village, city, or convoy for example, the entire village, city or convoy set ablaze.

Or because of the possibility of the existence of WMDs in one country, it is occupied, around one hundred thousand people killed, its water sources, agriculture and industry destroyed, close to 180,000 foreign troops put on the ground, sanctity of private homes of citizens broken, and the country pushed back perhaps fifty years. At what price? Hundreds of billions of dollars spent from the treasury of one country and certain other countries and tens of thousands of young men and women—as occupation troops—put in harm's way, taken away from family and loved ones, their hands stained with the blood of others, subjected to so much psychological pressure that everyday some commit suicide and those returning home suffer depression, become sickly and grapple with all sorts of ailments; while some are killed and their bodies handed to their families.

On the pretext of the existence of WMDs, this great tragedy came to engulf both the peoples of the occupied and the occupying country. Later it was revealed that no WMDs existed to begin with.

Of course Saddam was a murderous dictator. But the war was not waged to topple him; the announced goal of the war was to find and destroy weapons of mass destruction. He was toppled along the way towards another goal; nevertheless the people of the region are happy about it. I point out that throughout the many years of the imposed war on Iran Saddam was supported by the West.

Mr. President,

You might know that I am a teacher. My students ask me how can these actions be reconciled with the values outlined at the beginning of this letter and duty to the tradition of Jesus Christ (PBUH), the Messenger of peace and forgiveness?

There are prisoners in Guantanamo Bay that have not been tried, have no legal representation, their families cannot see them and are obviously kept in a strange land outside their own country. There is no international monitoring of their conditions and fate. No one knows whether they are prisoners, POWs, accused or criminals.

European investigators have confirmed the existence of secret prisons in Europe too. I could not correlate the abduction of a person, and him or her being kept in secret prisons, with the provisions of any judicial system. For that matter, I fail to understand how such actions correspond to the values outlined in the beginning of this letter, i.e., the teachings of Jesus Christ (PBUH), human rights and liberal values.

Young people, university students, and ordinary people have many questions about the phenomenon of Israel. I am sure you are familiar with some of them.

Throughout history many countries have been occupied, but I think the establishment of a new country with a new people, is a new phenomenon that is exclusive to our times.

Students are saying that sixty years ago such a country did not exist. They show old documents and globes and say try as we have, we have not been able to find a country named Israel.

I tell them to study the history of WWI and II. One of my students told me that during WWII, which more than tens of millions of people perished in, news about the war was quickly disseminated by the warring parties. Each touted their victories and the most recent battlefront defeat of the other party. After the war they claimed that six million Jews had been killed. Six million people that were surely related to at least two million families.

Again let us assume that these events are true. Does that logically translate into the establishment of the state of Israel in the Middle East or support for such a state? How can this phenomenon be rationalized or explained?

Mr. President,

I am sure you know how—and at what cost—Israel was established:

—Many thousands were killed in the process.

—Millions of indigenous people were made refugees.

—Hundreds of thousands of hectares of farmland, olive plantations, towns and villages were destroyed.

This tragedy is not exclusive to the time of establishment; unfortunately it has been ongoing for sixty years now.

A regime has been established which does not show mercy even to kids, destroys houses while the occupants are still in them, announces beforehand its list and plans to assassinate Palestinian figures, and keeps thousands of Palestinians in prison. Such a phenomenon is unique—or at the very least extremely rare—in recent memory.

Another big question asked by the people is "why is this regime being supported?"

Is support for this regime in line with the teachings of Jesus Christ (PBUH) or Moses (PBUH) or liberal values?

Or are we to understand that allowing the original inhabitants of these lands—inside and outside Palestine—whether they are Christian, Moslem or Jew, to determine their fate, runs contrary to principles of democracy, human rights and the teachings of prophets? If not, why is there so much opposition to a referendum?

The newly elected Palestinian administration recently took office. All independent observers have confirmed that this government represents the electorate. Incredibly, they have put the elected government under pressure and have advised it to recognize the Israeli regime, abandon the struggle and follow the programs of the previous government.

If the current Palestinian government had run on the above platform, would the Palestinian people have voted for it? Again, can such position taken in opposition to the Palestinian government be reconciled with the values outlined earlier? The people are also asking "why are all UNSC resolutions in condemnation of Israel vetoed?"

Mr. President,

As you are well aware, I live amongst the people and am in constant contact with them—many people from around the Middle East manage to contact me as well. They do not have faith in these dubious policies either. There is evidence that the people of the region are becoming increasingly angry with such policies.

It is not my intention to pose too many questions, but I need to refer to other points as well.

Why is it that any technological and scientific achievement reached in the Middle East region is translated into and portrayed as a threat to the Zionist regime? Is not scientific Research & Development one of the basic rights of nations?

You are familiar with history. Aside from the Middle Ages, in what other point in history has scientific and technical progress been a crime? Can the possibility of scientific achievements being utilized for military purposes be reason enough to oppose science and technology altogether? If such a supposition is true, then all scientific disciplines, including physics, chemistry, mathematics, medicine, engineering, etc. must be opposed.

Lies were told in the Iraqi matter. What was the result? I have no doubt that telling lies is reprehensible in any culture, and you do not like to be lied to.

Mr. President,

Don't Latin Americans have the right to ask why their elected governments are being opposed and coup leaders supported? Or, why must they constantly be threatened and live in fear?

The people of Africa are hardworking, creative and talented. They can play an important and valuable role in providing for the needs of humanity and contribute to its material and spiritual progress. Poverty and hardship in large parts of Africa are preventing this from happening. Don't they have the right to ask why their enormous wealth—including minerals—is being looted, despite the fact that they need it more than others?

Again, do such actions correspond to the teachings of Christ and the tenets of human rights?

The brave and faithful people of Iran too have many questions and grievances, including: the coup d'etat of 1953 and the subsequent toppling of the legal government of the day, opposition to the Islamic revolution, transformation of an Embassy into a headquarters supporting the activities of those opposing the Islamic Republic (many thousands of pages of documents corroborate this claim), support for Saddam in the war waged against Iran, the shooting down of the Iranian passenger plane, freezing the assets of the Iranian nation, increasing threats, anger and displeasure vis-à-vis the scientific and nuclear progress of the Iranian nation (just when all Iranians are jubilant and celebrating their country's progress), and many other grievances that I will not refer to in this letter.

Mr. President,

September Eleven was a horrendous incident. The killing of innocents is deplorable and appalling in any part of the world. Our government immediately declared its disgust with the perpetrators and offered its condolences to the bereaved and expressed its sympathies.

All governments have a duty to protect the lives, property and good standing of their citizens. Reportedly your government employs extensive security, protection and intelligence systems—and even hunts its opponents abroad. September Eleven was not a simple operation. Could it be planned and executed without coordination with intelligence and security services—or their extensive infiltration? Of course this is just an educated guess. Why have the various aspects of the attacks been kept secret? Why are we not told who botched their responsibilities? And, why aren't those responsible and the guilty parties identified and put on trial?

All governments have a duty to provide security and peace of mind for their citizens. For some years now, the people of your country and neighbors of world trouble spots do not have peace of mind. After 9/11, instead of healing and tending to the emotional wounds of the survivors and the American people—who had been immensely traumatized by the attacks—some Western media only intensified the climate of fear and insecurity—some constantly talked about the possibility of new terror attacks and kept the people in fear. Is that service to the American people? Is it possible to calculate the damages incurred from fear and panic?

American citizens lived in constant fear of fresh attacks that could come at any moment and in any place. They felt insecure in the streets, in their place of work and at home. Who would be happy with this situation? Why was the media, instead of conveying a feeling of security and providing peace of mind, giving rise to a feeling of insecurity?

Some believe that the hype paved the way—and was the justification—for an attack on Afghanistan. Again I need to refer to the role of media.

In media charters, correct dissemination of information and honest reporting of a story are established tenets. I express my deep regret about the disregard shown by certain Western media for these principles. The main pretext for an attack on Iraq was the existence of WMDs. This was repeated incessantly—for the public to finally believe—and the ground set for an attack on Iraq.

Will the truth not be lost in a contrived and deceptive climate?

Again, if the truth is allowed to be lost, how can that be reconciled with the earlier mentioned values?

Is the truth known to the Almighty lost as well?

Mr. President,

In countries around the world, citizens provide for the expenses of governments so that their governments in turn are able to serve them.

The question here is "what has the hundreds of billions of dollars, spent every year to pay for the Iraqi campaign, produced for the citizens?"

As Your Excellency is aware, in some states of your country, people are living in poverty. Many thousands are homeless and unemployment is a huge problem. Of course these problems exist—to a larger or lesser extent—in other countries as well. With these conditions in mind, can the gargantuan expenses of the campaign—paid from the public treasury—be explained and be consistent with the aforementioned principles?

What has been said, are some of the grievances of the people around the world, in our region and in your country. But my main contention—which I am hoping you will agree to some of it—is:

Those in power have a specific time in office and do not rule indefinitely, but their names will be recorded in history and will be constantly judged in the immediate and distant futures.

The people will scrutinize our presidencies.

Did we manage to bring peace, security and prosperity for the people or insecurity and unemployment?

Did we intend to establish justice or just support especial interest groups, and by forcing many people to live in poverty and hardship, made a few people rich and powerful—thus trading the approval of the people and the Almighty with theirs?

Did we defend the rights of the underprivileged or ignore them?

Did we defend the rights of all people around the world or imposed wars on them, interfered illegally in their affairs, established hellish prisons and incarcerated some of them?

Did we bring the world peace and security or raised the specter of intimidation and threats?

Did we tell the truth to our nation and others around the world or presented an inverted version of it?

Were we on the side of people or the occupiers and oppressors?

Did our administrations set out to promote rational behavior, logic, ethics, peace, fulfilling obligations, justice, service to the people, prosperity, progress and respect for human dignity or the force of guns, intimidation, insecurity, disregard for the people,

delaying the progress and excellence of other nations, and trample on people's rights?

And finally, they will judge us on whether we remained true to our oath of office—to serve the people, which is our main task, and the traditions of the prophets—or not?

Mr. President,

How much longer can the world tolerate this situation?

Where will this trend lead the world to?

How long must the people of the world pay for the incorrect decisions of some rulers?

How much longer will the specter of insecurity—raised from the stockpiles of weapons of mass destruction—haunt the people of the world?

How much longer will the blood of innocent men, women and children be spilled on the streets, and people's houses destroyed over their heads?

Are you pleased with the current condition of the world?

Do you think present policies can continue?

If billions of dollars spent on security, military campaigns and troop movement were instead spent on investment and assistance for poor countries, promotion of health, combating different diseases, education and improvement of mental and physical fitness, assistance to the victims of natural disasters, creation of employment opportunities and production, development projects and poverty alleviation, establishment of peace, mediation between disputing states, and extinguishing the flames of racial, ethnic and other conflicts, where would the world be today? Would not your government and people be justifiably proud?

Would not your administration's political and economic standing have been stronger?

And I am most sorry to say, would there have been an ever increasing global hatred of the American government?

Mr. President, it is not my intention to distress anyone.

If Prophet Abraham, Isaac, Jacob, Ishmael, Joseph, or Jesus Christ (PBUH) were with us today, how would they have judged such behavior? Will we be given a role to play in the promised world, where justice will become universal and Jesus Christ (PBUH) will be present? Will they even accept us?

My basic question is this: Is there no better way to interact with the rest of the world? Today there are hundreds of millions of Christians, hundreds of millions of Moslems and millions of people who follow the teachings of Moses (PBUH). All divine religions share and respect one word and that is "monotheism" or belief in a single God and no other in the world.

[...]

Mr. President,

According to divine verses, we have all been called upon to worship one God and follow the teachings of divine Prophets.

[...]

We believe a return to the teachings of the divine prophets is the only road leading to salvation. I have been told that Your Excellency follows the teachings of Jesus (PBUH) and believes in the divine promise of the rule of the righteous on Earth.

We also believe that Jesus Christ (PBUH) was one of the great prophets of the Almighty. He has been repeatedly praised in the Koran....

[...]

Divine prophets have promised:

The day will come when all humans will congregate before the court of the Almighty, so that their deeds are examined. The good will be directed towards Heaven and evildoers will meet divine retribution. I trust both of us believe in such a day, but it will not be easy to calculate the actions of rulers, because we must be answerable to our nations and all others whose lives have been directly or indirectly affected by our actions.

All prophets, speak of peace and tranquility for man—based on monotheism, justice and respect for human dignity.

Do you not think that if all of us come to believe in and abide by these principles, that is, monotheism, worship of God, justice, respect for the dignity of man, belief in the Last Day, we can overcome the present problems of the world—that are the result of disobedience to the Almighty and the teachings of prophets—and improve our performance?

Do you not think that belief in these principles promotes and guarantees peace, friendship and justice?

Do you not think that the aforementioned written or unwritten principles are universally respected?

Will you not accept this invitation? That is, a genuine return to the teachings of prophets, to monotheism and justice, to preserve human dignity and obedience to the Almighty and His prophets?

Mr. President,

History tells us that repressive and cruel governments do not survive. God has entrusted the fate of men to them. The Almighty has not left the universe and humanity to their own devices. Many things have happened contrary to the wishes and plans of governments. These tell us that there is a higher power at work and all events are determined by Him.

Can one deny the signs of change in the world today?

Is the situation of the world today comparable to that of ten years ago? Changes happen fast and come at a furious pace.

The people of the world are not happy with the status quo and pay little heed to the promises and comments made by a number of influential world leaders. Many people around the world feel insecure and oppose the spreading of insecurity and war and do not approve of and accept dubious policies.

The people are protesting the increasing gap between the haves and the have-nots and the rich and poor countries.

The people are disgusted with increasing corruption.

The people of many countries are angry about the attacks on their cultural foundations and the disintegration of families. They are equally dismayed with the fading of care and compassion. The people of the world have no faith in international organizations, because their rights are not advocated by these organizations.

Liberalism and Western style democracy have not been able to help realize the ideals of humanity. Today these two concepts have failed. Those with insight can already hear the sounds of the shattering and fall of the ideology and thoughts of the Liberal democratic systems.

We increasingly see that people around the world are flocking towards a main focal point—that is the Almighty God. Undoubtedly through faith in God and the teachings of the prophets, the people will conquer their problems. My question for you is: "Do you not want to join them?"

[...]

Source: "Full Text Letter of Islamic Republic of Iran President to American President," MidEastWeb, http://www.mideastweb.org/ahmadinejad_letter_to_bush.htm.

127. United Nations Security Council Resolution 1696, July 31, 2006

Introduction

Iran's continuing efforts to develop nuclear weapons were a subject of persistent international concern, as were those of North Korea. In both cases, major powers feared that should a regime whose leaders they considered erratic possess such weapons, this might destabilize the entire surrounding region. In July 2006 the United Nations (UN) Security Council passed Resolution 1696, proposed by China, France, Germany, Russia, Britain, and the United States, demanding that Iran halt its program of nuclear enrichment of uranium no later than August 31, 2006. Iran had previously announced its intention of resuming such activities after two years, during which they had been suspended while negotiations were in progress. The resolution passed by 14 votes to 1, with only the small Arab emirate of Qatar, which may have feared retribution from Iran, opposed, on the grounds that the situation in the region was "inflamed" and it would do no harm to wait a few days, until Iran had given an answer to earlier proposals by the six sponsoring powers. The Iranian representative to the UN deplored the resolution, stating that Iran had the right to enrich uranium for peaceful purposes and intended to exercise this right. The United States, on the other hand, publicly welcomed the resolution as a strong signal by the Security Council that the international community would not tolerate Iran's continued attempts to obtain nuclear weapons. Privately, however, at least some top officials in the administration of President George W. Bush believed that only military force would in the end prevent Iran from acquiring such armaments.

Primary Source

Resolution 1696 (2006)

Adopted by the Security Council at its 5500th meeting, on 31 July 2006

The Security Council,

Recalling the Statement of its President, S/PRST/2006/15, of 29 March 2006,

Reaffirming its commitment to the Treaty on the Non-proliferation of Nuclear Weapons, and recalling the right of States Party, in conformity with Articles I and II of that Treaty, to develop research, production and use of nuclear energy for peaceful purposes without discrimination,

Noting with serious concern the many reports of the IAEA Director General and resolutions of the IAEA Board of Governors related to Iran's nuclear programme, reported to it by the IAEA Director General, including IAEA Board resolution GOV/2006/14,

Noting with serious concern that the IAEA Director General's report of 27 February 2006 (GOV/2006/15) lists a number of outstanding issues and concerns on Iran's nuclear programme, including topics which could have a military nuclear dimension, and that the IAEA is unable to conclude that there are no undeclared nuclear materials or activities in Iran,

Noting with serious concern the IAEA Director General's report of 28 April 2006 (GOV/2006/27) and its findings, including that, after more than three years of Agency efforts to seek clarity about all aspects of Iran's nuclear programme, the existing gaps in knowledge continue to be a matter of concern, and that the IAEA is unable to make progress in its efforts to provide assurances about the absence of undeclared nuclear material and activities in Iran,

Noting with serious concern that, as confirmed by the IAEA Director General's report of 8 June 2006 (GOV/2006/38) Iran has not taken the steps required of it by the IAEA Board of Governors, reiterated by the Council in its statement of 29 March and which are essential to build confidence, and in particular Iran's decision to resume enrichment-related activities, including research and development, its recent expansion of and announcements about such activities, and its continued suspension of cooperation with the IAEA under the Additional Protocol,

Emphasizing the importance of political and diplomatic efforts to find a negotiated solution guaranteeing that Iran's nuclear programme is exclusively for peaceful purposes, and *noting* that such a solution would benefit nuclear non-proliferation elsewhere,

Welcoming the statement by the Foreign Minister of France, Philippe Douste-Blazy, on behalf of the Foreign Ministers of China, France, Germany, the Russian Federation, the United Kingdom, the United States and the High Representative of the European Union, in Paris on 12 July 2006 (S/2006/573),

Concerned by the proliferation risks presented by the Iranian nuclear programme, *mindful* of its primary responsibility under the Charter of the United Nations for the maintenance of international peace and security, and *being determined* to prevent an aggravation of the situation,

Acting under Article 40 of Chapter VII of the Charter of the United Nations in order to make mandatory the suspension required by the IAEA,

1. *Calls upon* Iran without further delay to take the steps required by the IAEA Board of Governors in its resolution GOV/2006/14, which are essential to build confidence in the exclusively peaceful purpose of its nuclear programme and to resolve outstanding questions;

2. *Demands*, in this context, that Iran shall suspend all enrichment-related and reprocessing activities, including research and development, to be verified by the IAEA;

3. *Expresses* the conviction that such suspension as well as full, verified Iranian compliance with the requirements set out by the IAEA Board of Governors, would contribute to a diplomatic, negotiated solution that guarantees Iran's nuclear programme is for exclusively peaceful purposes, *underlines* the willingness of the international community to work positively for such a solution, *encourages* Iran, in conforming to the above provisions, to re-engage with the international community and with the IAEA, and *stresses* that such engagement will be beneficial to Iran;

4. *Endorses*, in this regard, the proposals of China, France, Germany, the Russian Federation, the United Kingdom and the United States, with the support of the European Union's High Representative, for a long-term comprehensive arrangement which would allow for the development of relations and cooperation with Iran based on mutual respect and the establishment of international confidence in the exclusively peaceful nature of Iran's nuclear programme (S/2006/521);

5. *Calls upon* all States, in accordance with their national legal authorities and legislation and consistent with international law, to exercise vigilance and prevent the transfer of any items, materials, goods and technology that could contribute to Iran's enrichment-related and reprocessing activities and ballistic missile programmes;

6. *Expresses* its determination to reinforce the authority of the IAEA process, strongly supports the role of the IAEA Board of Governors, *commends and encourages* the Director General of the IAEA and its secretariat for their ongoing professional and impartial efforts to resolve all remaining outstanding issues in Iran within the framework of the Agency, *underlines* the necessity of the IAEA continuing its work to clarify all outstanding issues relating to Iran's nuclear programme, and *calls upon* Iran to act in accordance with the provisions of the Additional Protocol and to implement without delay all transparency measures as the IAEA may request in support of its ongoing investigations;

7. *Requests* by 31 August a report from the Director General of the IAEA primarily on whether Iran has established full and sustained suspension of all activities mentioned in this resolution, as well as on the process of Iranian compliance with all the steps required by the IAEA Board and with the above provisions of this resolution, to the IAEA Board of Governors and in parallel to the Security Council for its consideration;

8. *Expresses* its intention, in the event that Iran has not by that date complied with this resolution, then to adopt appropriate measures under Article 41 of Chapter VII of the Charter of the United Nations to persuade Iran to comply with this resolution and the requirements of the IAEA, and *underlines* that further decisions will be required should such additional measures be necessary;

9. *Confirms* that such additional measures will not be necessary in the event that Iran complies with this resolution;

10. *Decides* to remain seized of the matter.

> **Source:** United Nations Security Council Official Records, S/RES/1696, July 31, 2006.

128. President George W. Bush, "The War on Terror," Speech to the Military Officers Association of America, Capital Hilton Hotel, Washington, D.C., September 5, 2006 [Excerpts]

Introduction

Almost five years after the attacks of September 11, 2001, U.S. president George W. Bush addressed an audience of military officers, setting forth at length what he perceived was the nature of the war on terror in which the United States was still engaged. He affirmed that the United States would "accept nothing less than complete victory" in this battle. Bush depicted a world in which Al Qaeda and its supporters sought to reestablish an Islamic Sunni "Caliphate . . . encompassing all current and former Muslim lands, stretching from Europe to North Africa, the Middle East, and Southeast Asia," one that would reject peaceful coexistence with the non-Muslim world. The United States was, according to Bush, the "main obstacle" that prevented Osama bin Laden and his followers from accomplishing this goal, and they would use every means available to them to force the United States to withdraw. This made it essential for the United States to stand firm in both Afghanistan and Iraq. Shiite Muslims, such as the Lebanon-based Hezbollah group, who could count on support from Iran's Shiite leaders, who sought to equip their country with nuclear weapons, were equally hostile to the United States. Representing "different faces of the same threat," the Sunni and Shiite extremists intended to overthrow moderate Islamic governments and "impose a dark vision of violent radicalism across the Middle East." If they accomplished this, they would use their oil resources and nuclear weapons to "blackmail the free world." Describing how the United States would combat these threats, Bush summarized the official document, the "National Strategy for Combating Terrorism," released that day. First, the U.S. government was moving aggressively against terrorist groups and individuals at home and abroad. Second, it would "deny weapons of mass destruction to outlaw regimes and terrorists." Third, it would prevent terrorists from receiving support from "outlaw regimes." Fourth, the U.S. government was "determined to deny terrorist networks control of any nation, or territory within a nation." Finally, the United States would combat the ideological appeal of terrorists to new recruits by encouraging the spread of democracy and liberty throughout the Middle East. In the president's view, this was a global struggle between the forces of light and those of darkness, just as World War II and the Cold War had been, one in which "freedom is once again contending with the forces of darkness and tyranny." His speech gave a striking portrayal of a world where the United States was locked in an unavoidable but vital Manichaean contest, one in which "[a]ll civilized nations are bound together in this struggle between moderation and extremism."

Primary Source

THE PRESIDENT: . . . I'm proud to be here with active members of the United States military. Thank you for your service. I'm proud to be your Commander-in-Chief. [Applause.]

I am pleased also to stand with members of the diplomatic corps, including many representing nations that have been attacked by al Qaeda and its terrorist allies since September the 11th, 2001. [Applause.] Your presence here reminds us that we're engaged in a global war against an enemy that threatens all civilized nations. And today the civilized world stands together to defend our freedom; we stand together to defeat the terrorists; and were working to secure the peace for generations to come.

[. . .]

Next week, America will mark the fifth anniversary of September the 11th, 2001 terrorist attacks. As this day approaches, it brings with it a flood of painful memories. We remember the horror of watching planes fly into the World Trade Center, and seeing the towers collapse before our eyes. We remember the sight of the Pentagon, broken and in flames. We remember the rescue workers who rushed into burning buildings to save lives, knowing they might never emerge again. We remember the brave passengers who charged the cockpit of their hijacked plane, and stopped the terrorists from reaching their target and killing more innocent civilians. We remember the cold brutality of the enemy who inflicted this harm on our country—an enemy whose leader, Osama bin Laden, declared the massacre of nearly 3,000 people that day—I quote—"an unparalleled and magnificent feat of valor, unmatched by any in humankind before them."

In five years since our nation was attacked, al Qaeda and terrorists it has inspired have continued to attack across the world. They've killed the innocent in Europe and Africa and the Middle East, in Central Asia and the Far East, and beyond. Most recently, they attempted to strike again in the most ambitious plot since the attacks of September the 11th—a plan to blow up passenger planes headed for America over the Atlantic Ocean.

Five years after our nation was attacked, the terrorist danger remains. We're a nation at war—and America and her allies are fighting this war with relentless determination across the world. Together with our coalition partners, we've removed terrorist sanctuaries, disrupted their finances, killed and captured key operatives, broken up terrorist cells in America and other nations, and stopped new attacks before they're carried out. We're on the offense against the terrorists on every battlefront—and we'll accept nothing less than complete victory. [Applause.]

In the five years since our nation was attacked, we've also learned a great deal about the enemy we face in this war. We've learned about them through videos and audio recordings, and letters and statements they've posted on websites. We've learned about them from captured enemy documents that the terrorists have never meant for us to see. Together, these documents and statements have given us clear insight into the mind of our enemies—their ideology, their ambitions, and their strategy to defeat us.

We know what the terrorists intend to do because they've told us—and we need to take their words seriously. So today I'm going to describe—in the terrorists' own words, what they believe . . . what they hope to accomplish, and how they intend to accomplish it. I'll discuss how the enemy has adapted in the wake of our sustained offensive against them, and the threat posed by different strains of violent Islamic radicalism. I'll explain the strategy we're pursuing to protect America, by defeating the terrorists on the battlefield, and defeating their hateful ideology in the battle of ideas.

The terrorists who attacked us on September the 11th, 2001, are men without conscience—but they're not madmen. They kill in the name of a clear and focused ideology, a set of beliefs that are evil, but not insane. These al Qaeda terrorists and those who share their ideology are violent Sunni extremists. They're driven by a radical and perverted vision of Islam that rejects tolerance, crushes all dissent, and justifies the murder of innocent men, women and children in the pursuit of political power. They hope to establish a violent political utopia across the Middle East, which they call a "Caliphate"—where all would be ruled according to their hateful ideology. Osama bin Laden has called the 9/11 attacks—in his words—"a great step towards the unity of Muslims and establishing the Righteous . . . [Caliphate]."

This caliphate would be a totalitarian Islamic empire encompassing all current and former Muslim lands, stretching from Europe to North Africa, the Middle East, and Southeast Asia. We know this because al Qaeda has told us. About two months ago, the terrorist Zawahiri—he's al Qaeda's second in command—declared that al Qaeda intends to impose its rule in "every land that was a home for Islam, from [Spain] to Iraq. He went on to say, "The whole world is an open field for us."

We know what this radical empire would look like in practice, because we saw how the radicals imposed their ideology on the people of Afghanistan. Under the rule of the Taliban and al Qaeda, Afghanistan was a totalitarian nightmare—a land where women were imprisoned in their homes, men were beaten for missing prayer meetings, girls could not go to school, and children were forbidden the smallest pleasures like flying kites. Religious police roamed the streets, beating and detaining civilians for perceived offenses. Women were publicly whipped. Summary executions were held in Kabul's soccer stadium in front of cheering mobs. And Afghanistan was turned into a launching pad for horrific attacks against America and other parts of the civilized world—including many Muslim nations.

The goal of these Sunni extremists is to remake the entire Muslim world in their radical image. In pursuit of their imperial aims, these extremists say there can be no compromise or dialogue with those they call "infidels"—a category that includes America, the world's free nations, Jews, and all Muslims who reject their extreme vision of Islam. They reject the possibility of peaceful coexistence with the free world. Again, hear the words of Osama bin Laden earlier this year: "Death is better than living on this Earth with the unbelievers among us."

These radicals have declared their uncompromising hostility to freedom. It is foolish to think that you can negotiate with them. [Applause.] We see the uncompromising nature of the enemy in many captured terrorist documents. Here are just two examples: After the liberation of Afghanistan, coalition forces searching through a terrorist safe house in that country found a copy of the al Qaeda charter. This charter states that "there will be continuing enmity until everyone believes in Allah. We will not meet [the enemy] halfway. There will be no room for dialogue with them." Another document was found in 2000 by British police during an anti-terrorist raid in London—a grisly al Qaeda manual that includes chapters with titles such as "Guidelines for Beating and Killing Hostages." This manual declares that their vision of Islam "does not . . . make a truce with unbelief, but rather confronts it. The confrontation . . . calls for . . . the dialogue of bullets, the ideals of assassination, bombing, and destruction, and the diplomacy of the cannon and machine gun."

Still other captured documents show al Qaeda's strategy for infiltrating Muslim nations, establishing terrorist enclaves, overthrowing governments, and building their totalitarian empire. We see this strategy laid out in a captured al Qaeda document found during a recent raid in Iraq, which describes their plans to infiltrate and take over Iraq's western Anbar Province.

The document lays out an elaborate al Qaeda governing structure for the region that includes an Education Department, a Social Services Department, a Justice Department, and an "Execution Unit" responsible for "Sorting out, Arrest, Murder, and Destruction."

According to their public statements, countries that have—they have targeted stretch from the Middle East to Africa, to Southeast Asia. Through this strategy, al Qaeda and its allies intend to create numerous, decentralized operating bases across the world, from which they can plan new attacks, and advance their vision of a unified, totalitarian Islamic state that can confront and eventually destroy the free world.

These violent extremists know that to realize this vision, they must first drive out the main obstacle that stands in their way—the United States of America. According to al Qaeda, their strategy to defeat America has two parts: First, they're waging a campaign of terror across the world. They're targeting our forces abroad, hoping that the American people will grow tired of casualties and give up the fight. And they're targeting America's financial centers and economic infrastructure at home, hoping to terrorize us and cause our economy to collapse.

Bin Laden calls this his "bleed-until-bankruptcy plan." And he cited the attacks of 9/11 as evidence that such a plan can succeed. With the 9/11 attacks, Osama bin Laden says, "al Qaeda spent $500,000 on the event, while America . . . lost—according to the lowest estimate—$500 billion. . . . Meaning that every dollar of al Qaeda defeated a million dollars" of America. Bin Laden concludes from this experience that "America is definitely a great power, with . . . unbelievable military strength and a vibrant economy, but all of these have been built on a very weak and hollow foundation." He went on to say, "Therefore, it is very easy to target the flimsy base and concentrate on their weak points, and even if we're able to target one-tenth of these weak points, we will be able [to] crush and destroy them."

Secondly, along with this campaign of terror, the enemy has a propaganda strategy. Osama bin Laden laid out this strategy in a letter to the Taliban leader, Mullah Omar, that coalition forces uncovered in Afghanistan in 2002. In it, bin Laden says that al Qaeda intends to "[launch]," in his words, "a media campaign . . . to create a wedge between the American people and their government." This media campaign, bin Laden says, will send the American people a number of messages, including "that their government [will] bring them more losses, in finances and casualties." And he goes on to say that "they are being sacrificed . . . to serve . . . the big investors, especially the Jews." Bin Laden says that by delivering these messages, al Qaeda "aims at creating pressure from the American people on the American government to stop their campaign against Afghanistan."

Bin Laden and his allies are absolutely convinced they can succeed in forcing America to retreat and causing our economic collapse. They believe our nation is weak and decadent, and lacking in patience and resolve. And they're wrong. . . . [Applause.]

These terrorists hope to drive America and our coalition out of Afghanistan, so they can restore the safe haven they lost when coalition forces drove them out five years ago. But they've made clear that the most important front in their struggle against America is Iraq—the nation bin Laden has declared the "capital of the Caliphate." Hear the words of bin Laden: "I now address . . . the whole . . . Islamic nation: Listen and understand. . . . The most . . . serious issue today for the whole world is this Third World War . . . [that] is raging in [Iraq]." He calls it "a war of destiny between infidelity and Islam." He says, "The whole world is watching this war," and that it will end in "victory and glory or misery and humiliation." For al Qaeda, Iraq is not a distraction from their war on America—it is the central battlefield where the outcome of this struggle will be decided.

Here is what al Qaeda says they will do if they succeed in driving us out of Iraq: The terrorist Zawahiri has said that al Qaeda will proceed with "several incremental goals. The first stage: Expel the Americans from Iraq. The second stage: Establish an Islamic authority or amirate, then develop it and support it until it achieves the level of Caliphate. . . . The third stage: Extend the jihad wave to the secular countries neighboring Iraq. And the fourth stage: . . . the clash with Israel."

These evil men know that a fundamental threat to their aspirations is a democratic Iraq that can govern itself, sustain itself, and defend itself. They know that given a choice, the Iraqi people will never choose to live in the totalitarian state the extremists hope to establish. And that is why we must not, and we will not, give the enemy victory in Iraq by deserting the Iraqi people. [Applause.]

Last year, the terrorist Zarqawi declared in a message posted on the Internet that democracy "is the essence of infidelity and deviation from the right path." The Iraqi people disagree. Last December, nearly 12 million Iraqis from every ethnic and religious community turned out to vote in their country's third free election in less than a year. Iraq now has a unity government that represents Iraq's diverse population—and al Qaeda's top commander in Iraq breathed his last breath. [Applause.]

Despite these strategic setbacks, the enemy will continue to fight freedom's advance in Iraq, because they understand the stakes in this war. Again, hear the words of bin Laden, in a message to the American people earlier this year. He says: "The war is for you or for us to win. If we win it, it means your defeat and disgrace forever."

Now, I know some of our country hear the terrorists' words, and hope that they will not, or cannot, do what they say. History teaches that underestimating the words of evil and ambitious men is a terrible mistake. In the early 1900s, an exiled lawyer in Europe published a pamphlet called "What Is To Be Done?"—in which he laid out his plan to launch a communist revolution in Russia. The world did not heed Lenin's words, and paid a terrible price. The Soviet Empire he established killed tens of millions, and brought the world to the brink of thermonuclear war. In the 1920s, a failed Austrian painter published a book in which he explained his intention to build an Aryan super-state in Germany and take revenge on Europe and eradicate the Jews. The world ignored Hitler's words, and paid a terrible price. His Nazi regime killed millions in the gas chambers, and set the world aflame in war, before it was finally defeated at a terrible cost in lives.

Bin Laden and his terrorist allies have made their intentions as clear as Lenin and Hitler before them. The question is: Will we listen? Will we pay attention to what these evil men say? America and our coalition partners have made our choice. We're taking the words of the enemy seriously. We're on the offensive, and we will not rest, we will not retreat, and we will not withdraw from the fight, until this threat to civilization has been removed. [Applause.]

Five years into this struggle, it's important to take stock of what's been accomplished—and the difficult work that remains. Al Qaeda has been weakened by our sustained offensive against them, and today it is harder for al Qaeda's leaders to operate freely, to move money, or to communicate with their operatives and facilitators. Yet al Qaeda remains dangerous and determined. Bin Laden and Zawahiri remain in hiding in remote regions of this world. Al Qaeda continues to adapt in the face of our global campaign against them. Increasingly, al Qaeda is taking advantage of the Internet to disseminate propaganda, and to conduct "virtual recruitment" and "virtual training" of new terrorists. Al Qaeda's leaders no longer need to meet face-to-face with their operatives. They can find new suicide bombers, and facilitate new terrorist attacks, without ever laying eyes on those they're training, financing, or sending to strike us.

As al Qaeda changes, the broader terrorist movement is also changing, becoming more dispersed and self-directed. More and more, we're facing threats from locally established terrorist cells that are inspired by al Qaeda's ideology and goals, but do not necessarily have direct links to al Qaeda, such as training and funding. Some of these groups are made up of "homegrown" terrorists, militant extremists who were born and educated in Western nations, were indoctrinated by radical Islamists or attracted to their ideology, and joined the violent extremist cause. These locally established cells appear to be responsible for a number of attacks and plots, including those in Madrid, and Canada, and other countries across the world.

As we continue to fight al Qaeda and these Sunni extremists inspired by their radical ideology, we also face the threat posed by

Shia extremists, who are learning from al Qaeda, increasing their assertiveness, and stepping up their threats. Like the vast majority of Sunnis, the vast majority of Shia across the world reject the vision of extremists—and in Iraq, millions of Shia have defied terrorist threats to vote in free elections, and have shown their desire to live in freedom. The Shia extremists want to deny them this right. This Shia strain of Islamic radicalism is just as dangerous, and just as hostile to America, and just as determined to establish its brand of hegemony across the broader Middle East. And the Shia extremists have achieved something that al Qaeda has so far failed to do: In 1979, they took control of a major power, the nation of Iran, subjugating its proud people to a regime of tyranny, and using that nation's resources to fund the spread of terror and pursue their radical agenda.

Like al Qaeda and the Sunni extremists, the Iranian regime has clear aims: They want to drive America out of the region, to destroy Israel, and to dominate the broader Middle East. To achieve these aims, they are funding and arming terrorist groups like Hezbollah, which allow them to attack Israel and America by proxy. Hezbollah, the source of the current instability in Lebanon, has killed more Americans than any terrorist organization except al Qaeda. Unlike al Qaeda, they've not yet attacked the American homeland. Yet they're directly responsible for the murder of hundreds of Americans abroad. It was Hezbollah that was behind the 1983 bombing of the U.S. Marine barracks in Beirut that killed 241 Americans. And Saudi Hezbollah was behind the 1996 bombing of Khobar Towers in Saudi Arabia that killed 19 Americans, an attack conducted by terrorists who we believe were working with Iranian officials.

Just as we must take the words of the Sunni extremists seriously, we must take the words of the Shia extremists seriously. Listen to the words of Hezbollah's leader, the terrorist Nasrallah, who has declared his hatred of America. He says, "Let the entire world hear me. Our hostility to the Great Satan [America] is absolute. . . . Regardless of how the world has changed after 11 September, Death to America will remain our reverberating and powerful slogan: Death to America."

Iran's leaders, who back Hezbollah, have also declared their absolute hostility to America. Last October, Iran's President declared in a speech that some people ask—in his words—"whether a world without the United States and Zionism can be achieved. . . . I say that this . . . goal is achievable." Less than three months ago, Iran's President declared to America and other Western powers: "open your eyes and see the fate of pharaoh . . . if you do not abandon the path of falsehood . . . your doomed destiny will be annihilation." Less than two months ago, he warned: "The anger of Muslims may reach an explosion point soon. If such a day comes . . . [America and the West] should know that the waves of the blast will not remain within the boundaries of our region." He also delivered this message to the American people: "If you would like to have good relations with the Iranian nation in the future . . . bow down before the greatness of the Iranian nation and surrender. If you don't accept [to do this], the Iranian nation will . . . force you to surrender and bow down."

America will not bow down to tyrants. [Applause.]

The Iranian regime and its terrorist proxies have demonstrated their willingness to kill Americans—and now the Iranian regime is pursuing nuclear weapons. The world is working together to prevent Iran's regime from acquiring the tools of mass murder. The international community has made a reasonable proposal to Iran's leaders, and given them the opportunity to set their nation on a better course. So far, Iran's leaders have rejected this offer. Their choice is increasingly isolating the great Iranian nation from the international community, and denying the Iranian people an opportunity for greater economic prosperity. It's time for Iran's leaders to make a different choice. And we've made our choice. We'll continue to work closely with our allies to find a diplomatic solution. The world's free nations will not allow Iran to develop a nuclear weapon. [Applause.]

The Shia and Sunni extremists represent different faces of the same threat. They draw inspiration from different sources, but both seek to impose a dark vision of violent Islamic radicalism across the Middle East. They oppose the advance of freedom, and they want to gain control of weapons of mass destruction. If they succeed in undermining fragile democracies, like Iraq, and drive the forces of freedom out of the region, they will have an open field to pursue their dangerous goals. Each strain of violent Islamic radicalism would be emboldened in their efforts to topple moderate governments and establish terrorist safe havens.

Imagine a world in which they were able to control governments, a world awash with oil and they would use oil resources to punish industrialized nations. And they would use those resources to fuel their radical agenda, and pursue and purchase weapons of mass murder. And armed with nuclear weapons, they would blackmail the free world, and spread their ideologies of hate, and raise a mortal threat to the American people. If we allow them to do this, if we retreat from Iraq, if we don't uphold our duty to support those who are desirous to live in liberty, 50 years from now history will look back on our time with unforgiving clarity, and demand to know why we did not act.

I'm not going to allow this to happen—and no future American President can allow it either. America did not seek this global struggle, but we're answering history's call with confidence and a clear strategy. Today we're releasing a document called the "National Strategy for Combating Terrorism." This is an unclassified version of the strategy we've been pursuing since September the 11th, 2001. This strategy was first released in February 2003; it's been updated to take into account the changing nature of this enemy. This strategy document is posted on the White House website—whitehouse.gov. And I urge all Americans to read it.

Our strategy for combating terrorism has five basic elements:

First, we're determined to prevent terrorist attacks before they occur. So we're taking the fight to the enemy. The best way to protect America is to stay on the offense. Since 9/11, our coalition has captured or killed al Qaeda managers and operatives, and scores of other terrorists across the world. The enemy is living under constant pressure, and we intend to keep it that way—and this adds to our security. When terrorists spend their days working to avoid death or capture, it's harder for them to plan and execute new attacks.

We're also fighting the enemy here at home. We've given our law enforcement and intelligence professionals the tools they need to stop the terrorists in our midst. We passed the Patriot Act to break down the wall that prevented law enforcement and intelligence from sharing vital information. We created the Terrorist Surveillance Program to monitor the communications between al Qaeda commanders abroad and terrorist operatives within our borders. If al Qaeda is calling somebody in America, we need to know why, in order to stop attacks. [Applause.]

... And over the last five years, federal, state, and local law enforcement have used those tools to break up terrorist cells, and to prosecute terrorist operatives and supporters in New York, and Oregon, and Virginia, and Texas, and New Jersey, and Illinois, Ohio, and other states. By taking the battle to the terrorists and their supporters on our own soil and across the world, we've stopped a number of al Qaeda plots.

Second, we're determined to deny weapons of mass destruction to outlaw regimes and terrorists who would use them without hesitation. Working with Great Britain and Pakistan and other nations, the United States shut down the world's most dangerous nuclear trading cartel, the AQ Khan network. This network had supplied Iran and Libya and North Korea with equipment and know-how that advanced their efforts to obtain nuclear weapons. And we launched the Proliferation Security Initiative, a coalition of more than 70 nations that is working together to stop shipments related to weapons of mass destruction on land, at sea, and in the air. The greatest threat this world faces is the danger of extremists and terrorists armed with weapons of mass destruction—and this is a threat America cannot defeat on her own. We applaud the determined efforts of many nations around the world to stop the spread of these dangerous weapons. Together, we pledge we'll continue to work together to stop the world's most dangerous men from getting their hands on the world's most dangerous weapons. [Applause.]

Third, we're determined to deny terrorists the support of outlaw regimes. After September the 11th, I laid out a clear doctrine: America makes no distinction between those who commit acts of terror, and those that harbor and support them, because they're equally guilty of murder. Thanks to our efforts, there are now three fewer state sponsors of terror in the world than there were on September the 11th, 2001. Afghanistan and Iraq have been transformed from terrorist states into allies in the war on terror. And the nation of Libya has renounced terrorism, and given up its weapons of mass destruction programs, and its nuclear materials and equipment. Over the past five years, we've acted to disrupt the flow of weapons and support from terrorist states to terrorist networks. And we have made clear that any government that chooses to be an ally of terror has also chosen to be an enemy of civilization. [Applause.]

Fourth, we're determined to deny terrorist networks control of any nation, or territory within a nation. So, along with our coalition and the Iraqi government, we'll stop the terrorists from taking control of Iraq, and establishing a new safe haven from which to attack America and the free world. And we're working with friends and allies to deny the terrorists the enclaves they seek to establish in ungoverned areas across the world. By helping governments reclaim full sovereign control over their territory, we make ourselves more secure.

Fifth, we're working to deny terrorists new recruits, by defeating their hateful ideology and spreading the hope of freedom— by spreading the hope of freedom across the Middle East. For decades, American policy sought to achieve peace in the Middle East by pursuing stability at the expense of liberty. The lack of freedom in that region helped create conditions where anger and resentment grew, and radicalism thrived, and terrorists found willing recruits. And we saw the consequences on September the 11th, when the terrorists brought death and destruction to our country. The policy wasn't working.

The experience of September the 11th made clear, in the long run, the only way to secure our nation is to change the course of the Middle East. So America has committed its influence in the world to advancing freedom and liberty and democracy as the great alternatives to repression and radicalism. [Applause.] We're taking the side of democratic leaders and moderates and reformers across the Middle East. We strongly support the voices of tolerance and moderation in the Muslim world. We're standing with Afghanistan's elected government against al Qaeda and the Taliban remnants that are trying to restore tyranny in that country. We're standing with Lebanon's young democracy against the foreign forces that are seeking to undermine the country's sovereignty and independence. And we're standing with the leaders of Iraq's unity government as they work to defeat the enemies of freedom, and chart a more hopeful course for their people. This is why victory is so important in Iraq. By helping freedom succeed in Iraq, we will help America, and the Middle East, and the world become more secure.

During the last five years we've learned a lot about this enemy. We've learned that they're cunning and sophisticated. We've witnessed their ability to change their methods and their tactics with deadly speed—even as their murderous obsessions remain unchanging. We've seen that it's the terrorists who have declared war on Muslims, slaughtering huge numbers of innocent Muslim men and women around the world.

We know what the terrorists believe, we know what they have done, and we know what they intend to do. And now the world's free nations must summon the will to meet this great challenge. The road ahead is going to be difficult, and it will require more sacrifice. Yet we can have confidence in the outcome, because we've seen freedom conquer tyranny and terror before. In the 20th century, free nations confronted and defeated Nazi Germany. During the Cold War, we confronted Soviet communism, and today Europe is whole, free and at peace.

And now, freedom is once again contending with the forces of darkness and tyranny. This time, the battle is unfolding in a new region—the broader Middle East. This time, we're not waiting for our enemies to gather in strength. This time, we're confronting them before they gain the capacity to inflict unspeakable damage on the world, and we're confronting their hateful ideology before it fully takes root.

We see a day when people across the Middle East have governments that honor their dignity, and unleash their creativity, and count their votes. We see a day when across this region citizens are allowed to express themselves freely, women have full rights, and children are educated and given the tools necessary to succeed in life. And we see a day when all the nations of the Middle East are allies in the cause of peace.

We fight for this day, because the security of our own citizens depends on it. This is the great ideological struggle of the 21st century—and it is the calling of our generation. All civilized nations are bound together in this struggle between moderation and extremism. By coming together, we will roll back this grave threat to our way of life. We will help the people of the Middle East claim their freedom, and we will leave a safer and more hopeful world for our children and grandchildren.

Source: George W. Bush, "President Discusses Global War on Terror," The White House, President George W. Bush, http://georgewbush-whitehouse.archives.gov/news/releases/2006/09/20060905-4.html.

129. The Iraq Study Group Report, Executive Summary, December 6, 2006

Introduction

By early 2006, both Republicans and Democrats in the U.S. Congress were concerned that the situation in Iraq was apparently deteriorating, while the administration of President George W. Bush apparently had no definite exit strategy. With bipartisan support, in March 2006 Congress therefore established a blue-ribbon independent study group, cochaired by former Republican secretary of state James A. Baker III and former Democratic congressman Lee Hamilton, two widely respected political figures. Ten individuals, 5 Republicans and 5 Democrats, served on the Iraq Study Group. Congress appropriated $1 million to fund the panel's expenses. The study group established four expert working groups, focusing on economy and reconstruction, military and security, political development, and strategic environment, plus a panel of senior military advisers. Study group members visited Iraq in August and September and consulted with 170 people in all before preparing its report, interviewing top U.S. and Iraqi government officials, including President George W. Bush, Secretary of State Condoleezza Rice, and Secretary of Defense Donald H. Rumsfeld. The appearance of what became known as the Baker Report in December 2006 created something of a public sensation. The authors began by bluntly warning that "The situation in Iraq is grave and deteriorating." While frankly admitting that there was no guarantee of success, they recommended that the United States launch enhanced political and diplomatic efforts to stabilize Iraq, especially by working with neighboring states including Iran and Syria, countries with which American relations were problematic, and the broader international community, especially the European states, Russia, and the United Nations (UN). The Baker Report also called for a new and lasting American commitment to negotiating a permanent Arab-Israeli peace settlement, which the authors regarded as the key to peace in the Middle East. Within Iraq, the Baker Report called for a stronger Iraqi commitment to national reconciliation. The report considered but rejected a massive increase of 100,000 to 200,000 American troops in Iraq but endorsed a possible smaller short-term surge in U.S. armed forces there, with the objective of stabilizing the situation in Baghdad, Iraq's capital, or accelerating the emergence of a strong and credible Iraqi military that could control the situation. The Baker Report envisaged the withdrawal of all American troops from Iraq by the spring of 2008. The Bush administration treated the Baker Report and its authors with ostensible respect but, except for the surge in military personnel, which Bush endorsed in his January 2007 State of the Union speech, showed little enthusiasm for implementing most of the document's recommendations.

Primary Source

The situation in Iraq is grave and deteriorating. There is no path that can guarantee success, but the prospects can be improved.

In this report, we make a number of recommendations for actions to be taken in Iraq, the United States, and the region. Our most important recommendations call for new and enhanced diplomatic and political efforts in Iraq and the region, and a change in the primary mission of U.S. forces in Iraq that will enable the United States to begin to move its combat forces out of Iraq responsibly. We believe that these two recommendations are equally important and reinforce one another. If they are effectively implemented, and if the Iraqi government moves forward with national reconciliation, Iraqis will have an opportunity for a better future, terrorism will be dealt a blow, stability will be enhanced in an important part of the world, and America's credibility, interests, and values will be protected.

The challenges in Iraq are complex. Violence is increasing in scope and lethality. It is fed by a Sunni Arab insurgency, Shiite militias and death squads, al Qaeda, and widespread criminality. Sectarian conflict is the principal challenge to stability.

The Iraqi people have a democratically elected government, yet it is not adequately advancing national reconciliation, providing basic security, or delivering essential services. Pessimism is pervasive.

If the situation continues to deteriorate, the consequences could be severe. A slide toward chaos could trigger the collapse of Iraq's government and a humanitarian catastrophe. Neighboring countries could intervene. Sunni-Shia clashes could spread. Al Qaeda could win a propaganda victory and expand its base of operations. The global standing of the United States could be diminished. Americans could become more polarized.

During the past nine months we have considered a full range of approaches for moving forward. All have flaws. Our recommended course has shortcomings, but we firmly believe that it includes the best strategies and tactics to positively influence the outcome in Iraq and the region.

External Approach

The policies and actions of Iraq's neighbors greatly affect its stability and prosperity. No country in the region will benefit in the long term from a chaotic Iraq. Yet Iraq's neighbors are not doing enough to help Iraq achieve stability. Some are undercutting stability.

The United States should immediately launch a new diplomatic offensive to build an international consensus for stability in Iraq and the region. This diplomatic effort should include every country that has an interest in avoiding a chaotic Iraq, including all of Iraq's neighbors. Iraq's neighbors and key states in and outside the region should form a support group to reinforce security and national reconciliation within Iraq, neither of which Iraq can achieve on its own.

Given the ability of Iran and Syria to influence events within Iraq and their interest in avoiding chaos in Iraq, the United States should try to engage them constructively. In seeking to influence the behavior of both countries, the United States has disincentives and incentives available. Iran should stem the flow of arms and training to Iraq, respect Iraq's sovereignty and territorial integrity, and use its influence over Iraqi Shia groups to encourage national reconciliation. The issue of Iran's nuclear programs should continue to be dealt with by the five permanent members of the United Nations Security Council plus Germany. Syria should control its border with Iraq to stem the flow of funding, insurgents, and terrorists in and out of Iraq.

The United States cannot achieve its goals in the Middle East unless it deals directly with the Arab-Israeli conflict and regional instability. There must be a renewed and sustained commitment by the United States to a comprehensive Arab-Israeli peace on all fronts: Lebanon, Syria, and President Bush's June 2002 commitment to a two-state solution for Israel and Palestine. This commitment must include direct talks with, by, and between Israel, Lebanon, Palestinians (those who accept Israel's right to exist), and Syria.

As the United States develops its approach toward Iraq and the Middle East, the United States should provide additional political, economic, and military support for Afghanistan, including resources that might become available as combat forces are moved out of Iraq.

Internal Approach

The most important questions about Iraq's future are now the responsibility of Iraqis. The United States must adjust its role in Iraq to encourage the Iraqi people to take control of their own destiny.

The Iraqi government should accelerate assuming responsibility for Iraqi security by increasing the number and quality of Iraqi Army brigades. While this process is under way, and to facilitate it, the United States should significantly increase the number of U.S. military personnel, including combat troops, imbedded in and supporting Iraqi Army units. As these actions proceed, U.S. combat forces could begin to move out of Iraq.

The primary mission of U.S. forces in Iraq should evolve to one of supporting the Iraqi army, which would take over primary responsibility for combat operations. By the first quarter of 2008, subject to unexpected developments in the security situation on the ground, all combat brigades not necessary for force protection could be out of Iraq. At that time, U.S. combat forces in Iraq could be deployed only in units embedded with Iraqi forces, in rapid-reaction and special operations teams, and in training, equipping, advising, force protection, and search and rescue. Intelligence and support efforts would continue. A vital mission of those rapid reaction and special operations forces would be to undertake strikes against al Qaeda in Iraq.

It is clear that the Iraqi government will need assistance from the United States for some time to come, especially in carrying out security responsibilities. Yet the United States must make it clear to the Iraqi government that the United States could carry out its plans, including planned redeployments, even if the Iraqi government did not implement their planned changes. The United States must not make an open-ended commitment to keep large numbers of American troops deployed in Iraq.

As redeployment proceeds, military leaders should emphasize training and education of forces that have returned to the United States in order to restore the force to full combat capability. As equipment returns to the United States, Congress should appropriate sufficient funds to restore the equipment over the next five years.

The United States should work closely with Iraq's leaders to support the achievement of specific objectives—or milestones—on national reconciliation, security, and governance. Miracles cannot be expected, but the people of Iraq have the right to expect action and progress. The Iraqi government needs to show its own citizens—and the citizens of the United States and other countries—that it deserves continued support.

Prime Minister Nouri al-Maliki, in consultation with the United States, has put forward a set of milestones critical for Iraq. His list is a good start, but it must be expanded to include milestones that can strengthen the government and benefit the Iraqi people. President Bush and his national security team should remain in close and frequent contact with the Iraqi leadership to convey a clear message: there must be prompt action by the Iraqi government to make substantial progress toward the achievement of these milestones.

If the Iraqi government demonstrates political will and makes substantial progress toward the achievement of milestones on national reconciliation, security, and governance, the United States should make clear its willingness to continue training, assistance, and support for Iraq's security forces and to continue political, military, and economic support. If the Iraqi government does not make substantial progress toward the achievement of milestones on national reconciliation, security, and governance,

the United States should reduce its political, military, or economic support for the Iraqi government.

Our report makes recommendations in several other areas. They include improvements to the Iraqi criminal justice system, the Iraqi oil sector, the U.S. reconstruction efforts in Iraq, the U.S. budget process, the training of U.S. government personnel, and U.S. intelligence capabilities.

Conclusion

It is the unanimous view of the Iraq Study Group that these recommendations offer a new way forward for the United States in Iraq and the region. They are comprehensive and need to be implemented in a coordinated fashion. They should not be separated or carried out in isolation. The dynamics of the region are as important to Iraq as events within Iraq.

The challenges are daunting. There will be difficult days ahead. But by pursuing this new way forward, Iraq, the region, and the United States of America can emerge stronger.

Source: James Baker et al., "Iraq Study Group: The Report," United States Institute of Peace, http://www.usip.org/isg/iraq_study_group_report/report/1206/index.html.

130. United Nations Security Council Resolution 1737 Imposing Sanctions on Iran, December 23, 2006 [Excerpts]
Introduction

In July 2006 the United Nations (UN) Security Council passed Resolution 1696, proposed by China, France, Germany, Russia, Britain, and the United States, demanding that Iran halt its program of nuclear enrichment of uranium by August 31, 2006. Five months later, after Iran failed to comply with Resolution 1696 and rejected economic incentives offered by the UN should it do so, the Security Council passed Resolution 1737, sponsored by France, Germany, and the United Kingdom, subjecting Iran to sanctions. All UN members were forbidden to provide Iran with materials, equipment, or other assistance that might facilitate this program. All overseas assets of Iranian organizations and individuals involved in the nuclear program were frozen. Iran was also directed to grant representatives of the International Atomic Energy Authority (IAEA) access to all its nuclear facilities in order to verify whether it had complied with this resolution. China and Russia initially objected to this resolution, considering it too strong, but finally voted for it, though Russia continued to supply Iran with surface-to-air missiles after its passage. Iran's defiance of the UN continued, and on March 24, 2007, the Security Council unanimously passed Resolution 1747, submitted by France, Germany, and Britain, tightening sanctions on Iran. The British government was particularly incensed by Iran's seizure in the Shatt al-Arab waterway a few days earlier and continuing detention of 15 British naval personnel, whom Iranian officials claimed had entered Iranian territorial waters without permission. Sales and transfers of Iranian arms to all other countries were prohibited, a measure targeting Iran's suspected role in supplying weaponry to Shiite insurgents in Iraq and Hezbollah militants in Lebanon. Resolution 1747 urged all states to "exercise vigilance and restraint" in providing Iran with any major armaments or financing for these and to refuse to make any new grants or loans to Iran. The list of individuals and organizations involved in the Iranian nuclear program whose assets were to be frozen was expanded. Sanctions on Iran would be suspended should Iran suspend its own nuclear program. Critics immediately charged that as with previous resolutions, enforcement of the new sanctions depended almost entirely on the goodwill of UN member states.

Primary Source

Adopted by the Security Council at its 5612th meeting, on 23 December 2006

The Security Council,

Recalling the Statement of its President, S/PRST/2006/15, of 29 March 2006, and its resolution 1696 (2006) of 31 July 2006,

Reaffirming its commitment to the Treaty on the Non-Proliferation of Nuclear Weapons, and recalling the right of States Party, in conformity with Articles I and II of that Treaty, to develop research, production and use of nuclear energy for peaceful purposes without discrimination,

Reiterating its serious concern over the many reports of the IAEA Director General and resolutions of the IAEA Board of Governors related to Iran's nuclear programme, reported to it by the IAEA Director General, including IAEA Board resolution GOV/2006/14,

Reiterating its serious concern that the IAEA Director General's report of 27 February 2006 (GOV/2006/15) lists a number of outstanding issues and concerns on Iran's nuclear programme, including topics which could have a military nuclear dimension, and that the IAEA is unable to conclude that there are no undeclared nuclear materials or activities in Iran,

Reiterating its serious concern over the IAEA Director General's report of 28 April 2006 (GOV/2006/27) and its findings, including that, after more than three years of Agency efforts to seek clarity about all aspects of Iran's nuclear programme, the existing gaps in knowledge continue to be a matter of concern, and that the IAEA is

unable to make progress in its efforts to provide assurances about the absence of undeclared nuclear material and activities in Iran,

Noting with serious concern that, as confirmed by the IAEA Director General's reports of 8 June 2006 (GOV/2006/38), 31 August 2006 (GOV/2006/53) and 14 November 2006 (GOV/2006/64), Iran has not established full and sustained suspension of all enrichment-related and reprocessing activities as set out in resolution 1696 (2006), nor resumed its cooperation with the IAEA under the Additional Protocol, nor taken the other steps required of it by the IAEA Board of Governors, nor complied with the provisions of Security Council resolution 1696 (2006) and which are essential to build confidence, and *deploring* Iran's refusal to take these steps,

Emphasizing the importance of political and diplomatic efforts to find a negotiated solution guaranteeing that Iran's nuclear programme is exclusively for peaceful purposes, and *noting* that such a solution would benefit nuclear nonproliferation elsewhere, and *welcoming* the continuing commitment of China, France, Germany, the Russian Federation, the United Kingdom and the United States, with the support of the European Union's High Representative to seek a negotiated solution,

Determined to give effect to its decisions by adopting appropriate measures to persuade Iran to comply with resolution 1696 (2006) and with the requirements of the IAEA, and also to constrain Iran's development of sensitive technologies in support of its nuclear and missile programmes, until such time as the Security Council determines that the objectives of this resolution have been met,

Concerned by the proliferation risks presented by the Iranian nuclear programme and, in this context, by Iran's continuing failure to meet the requirements of the IAEA Board of Governors and to comply with the provisions of Security Council resolution 1696 (2006), *mindful* of its primary responsibility under the Charter of the United Nations for the maintenance of international peace and security,

Acting under Article 41 of Chapter VII of the Charter of the United Nations,

1. *Affirms* that Iran shall without further delay take the steps required by the IAEA Board of Governors in its resolution GOV/2006/14, which are essential to build confidence in the exclusively peaceful purpose of its nuclear programme and to resolve outstanding questions;

2. *Decides,* in this context, that Iran shall without further delay suspend the following proliferation sensitive nuclear activities:

(a) all enrichment-related and reprocessing activities, including research and development, to be verified by the IAEA; and

(b) work on all heavy water–related projects, including the construction of a research reactor moderated by heavy water, also to be verified by the IAEA;

3. *Decides* that all States shall take the necessary measures to prevent the supply, sale or transfer directly or indirectly from their territories, or by their nationals or using their flag vessels or aircraft to, or for the use in or benefit of, Iran, and whether or not originating in their territories, of all items, materials, equipment, goods and technology which could contribute to Iran's enrichment-related, reprocessing or heavy water-related activities, or to the development of nuclear weapon delivery systems, namely:

(a) those set out in sections B.2, B.3, B.4, B.5, B.6 and B.7 of INFCIRC/254/Rev.8/Part 1 in document S/2006/814;

(b) those set out in sections A.1 and B.1 of INFCIRC/254/Rev.8/Part 1 in document S/2006/814, except the supply, sale or transfer of:

(i) equipment covered by B.1 when such equipment is for light water reactors; (ii) low-enriched uranium covered by A.1.2 when it is incorporated in assembled nuclear fuel elements for such reactors;

(c) those set out in document S/2006/815, except the supply, sale or transfer of items covered by 19.A.3 of Category II;

(d) any additional items, materials, equipment, goods and technology, determined as necessary by the Security Council or the Committee established by paragraph 18 below (herein "the Committee"), which could contribute to enrichment-related, or reprocessing, or heavy water–related activities, or to the development of nuclear weapon delivery systems;

4. *Decides* that all States shall take the necessary measures to prevent the supply, sale or transfer directly or indirectly from their territories, or by their nationals or using their flag vessels or aircraft to, or for the use in or benefit of, Iran, and whether or not originating in their territories, of the following items, materials, equipment, goods and technology:

(a) those set out in INFCIRC/254/Rev.7/Part2 of document S/2006/814 if the State determines that they would contribute to enrichment-related, reprocessing or heavy water–related activities;

(b) any other items not listed in documents S/2006/814 or S/2006/815 if the State determines that they would contribute to enrichment-related, reprocessing or heavy water–related activities, or to the development of nuclear weapon delivery systems;

(c) any further items if the State determines that they would contribute to the pursuit of activities related to other topics about which the IAEA has expressed concerns or identified as outstanding;

5. *Decides* that, for the supply, sale or transfer of all items, materials, equipment, goods and technology covered by documents S/2006/814 and S/2006/815 the export of which to Iran is not prohibited by subparagraphs 3 (b), 3 (c) or 4 (a) above, States shall ensure that:

(a) the requirements, as appropriate, of the Guidelines as set out in documents S/2006/814 and S/2006/985 have been met; and

(b) they have obtained and are in a position to exercise effectively a right to verify the end-use and end-use location of any supplied item; and

(c) they notify the Committee within ten days of the supply, sale or transfer; and

(d) in the case of items, materials, equipment, goods and technology contained in document S/2006/814, they also notify the IAEA within ten days of the supply, sale or transfer;

6. *Decides* that all States shall also take the necessary measures to prevent the provision to Iran of any technical assistance or training, financial assistance, investment, brokering or other services, and the transfer of financial resources or services, related to the supply, sale, transfer, manufacture or use of the prohibited items, materials, equipment, goods and technology specified in paragraphs 3 and 4 above;

7. *Decides* that Iran shall not export any of the items in documents S/2006/814 and S/2006/815 and that all Member States shall prohibit the procurement of such items from Iran by their nationals, or using their flag vessels or aircraft, and whether or not originating in the territory of Iran;

8. *Decides* that Iran shall provide such access and cooperation as the IAEA requests to be able to verify the suspension outlined in paragraph 2 and to resolve all outstanding issues, as identified in IAEA reports, and *calls upon* Iran to ratify promptly the Additional Protocol;

9. *Decides* that the measures imposed by paragraphs 3, 4 and 6 above shall not apply where the Committee determines in advance and on a case-by-case basis that such supply, sale, transfer or provision of such items or assistance would clearly not contribute to the development of Iran's technologies in support of its proliferation sensitive nuclear activities and of development of nuclear weapon delivery systems, including where such items or assistance are for food, agricultural, medical or other humanitarian purposes, provided that:

(a) contracts for delivery of such items or assistance include appropriate end-user guarantees; and

(b) Iran has committed not to use such items in proliferation sensitive nuclear activities or for development of nuclear weapon delivery systems;

10. *Calls upon* all States to exercise vigilance regarding the entry into or transit through their territories of individuals who are engaged in, directly associated with or providing support for Iran's proliferation sensitive nuclear activities or for the development of nuclear weapon delivery systems, and *decides* in this regard that all States shall notify the Committee of the entry into or transit through their territories of the persons designated in the Annex to this resolution (herein "the Annex"), as well as of additional persons designated by the Security Council or the Committee as being engaged in, directly associated with or providing support for Iran's proliferation sensitive nuclear activities and for the development of nuclear weapon delivery systems, including through the involvement in procurement of the prohibited items, goods, equipment, materials and technology specified by and under the measures in paragraphs 3 and 4 above, except where such travel is for activities directly related to the items in subparagraphs 3 (b) (i) and (ii) above;

11. *Underlines* that nothing in the above paragraph requires a State to refuse its own nationals entry into its territory, and that all States shall, in the implementation of the above paragraph, take into account humanitarian considerations as well as the necessity to meet the objectives of this resolution, including where Article XV of the IAEA Statute is engaged;

12. *Decides* that all States shall freeze the funds, other financial assets and economic resources which are on their territories at the date of adoption of this resolution or at any time thereafter, that are owned or controlled by the persons or entities designated in the Annex, as well as those of additional persons or entities designated by the Security Council or by the Committee as being engaged in, directly associated with or providing support for Iran's proliferation sensitive nuclear activities or the development of nuclear weapon delivery systems, or by persons or entities acting on their behalf or at their direction, or by entities owned or controlled by them, including through illicit means, and that the measures in this paragraph shall cease to apply in respect of such persons or entities if, and at such time as, the Security Council or the Committee removes them from the Annex, and *decides further* that all States shall ensure that any funds, financial assets or economic resources are prevented from being made available by their nationals or by any persons or entities within their territories, to or for the benefit of these persons and entities;

[...]

16. *Decides* that technical cooperation provided to Iran by the IAEA or under its auspices shall only be for food, agricultural, medical, safety or other humanitarian purposes, or where it is necessary for projects directly related to the items specified in subparagraphs 3 (b) (i) and (ii) above, but that no such technical cooperation shall be provided that relates to the proliferation sensitive nuclear activities set out in paragraph 2 above;

17. *Calls upon* all States to exercise vigilance and prevent specialized teaching or training of Iranian nationals, within their territories or by their nationals, of disciplines which would contribute to Iran's proliferation sensitive nuclear activities and development of nuclear weapon delivery systems;

18. *Decides* to establish, in accordance with rule 28 of its provisional rules of procedure, a Committee of the Security Council consisting of all the members of the Council, to undertake the following tasks:

(a) to seek from all States, in particular those in the region and those producing the items, materials, equipment, goods and technology referred to in paragraphs 3 and 4 above, information regarding the actions taken by them to implement effectively the measures imposed by paragraphs 3, 4, 5, 6, 7, 8, 10 and 12 of this resolution and whatever further information it may consider useful in this regard;

(b) to seek from the secretariat of the IAEA information regarding the actions taken by the IAEA to implement effectively the measures imposed by paragraph 16 of this resolution and whatever further information it may consider useful in this regard;

(c) to examine and take appropriate action on information regarding alleged violations of measures imposed by paragraphs 3, 4, 5, 6, 7, 8, 10 and 12 of this resolution;

(d) to consider and decide upon requests for exemptions set out in paragraphs 9, 13 and 15 above;

(e) to determine as may be necessary additional items, materials, equipment, goods and technology to be specified for the purpose of paragraph 3 above;

(f) to designate as may be necessary additional individuals and entities subject to the measures imposed by paragraphs 10 and 12 above;

(g) to promulgate guidelines as may be necessary to facilitate the implementation of the measures imposed by this resolution and include in such guidelines a requirement on States to provide information where possible as to why any individuals and/or entities meet the criteria set out in paragraphs 10 and 12 and any relevant identifying information;

(h) to report at least every 90 days to the Security Council on its work and on the implementation of this resolution, with its observations and recommendations, in particular on ways to strengthen the effectiveness of the measures imposed by paragraphs 3, 4, 5, 6, 7, 8, 10 and 12 above;

19. *Decides* that all States shall report to the Committee within 60 days of the adoption of this resolution on the steps they have taken with a view to implementing effectively paragraphs 3, 4, 5, 6, 7, 8, 10, 12 and 17 above;

20. *Expresses* the conviction that the suspension set out in paragraph 2 above as well as full, verified Iranian compliance with the requirements set out by the IAEA Board of Governors, would contribute to a diplomatic, negotiated solution that guarantees Iran's nuclear programme is for exclusively peaceful purposes, *underlines* the willingness of the international community to work positively for such a solution, *encourages* Iran, in conforming to the above provisions, to re-engage with the international community and with the IAEA, and *stresses* that such engagement will be beneficial to Iran;

21. *Welcomes* the commitment of China, France, Germany, the Russian Federation, the United Kingdom and the United States, with the support of the European Union's High Representative, to a negotiated solution to this issue and encourages Iran to engage with their June 2006 proposals (S/2006/521), which were endorsed by the Security Council in resolution 1696 (2006), for a long-term comprehensive agreement which would allow for the development of relations and cooperation with Iran based on mutual respect and the establishment of international confidence in the exclusively peaceful nature of Iran's nuclear programme;

22. *Reiterates* its determination to reinforce the authority of the IAEA, strongly supports the role of the IAEA Board of Governors, *commends* and *encourages* the Director General of the IAEA and its secretariat for their ongoing professional and impartial efforts to resolve all remaining outstanding issues in Iran within the framework of the IAEA, *underlines* the necessity of the IAEA continuing its work to clarify all outstanding issues relating to Iran's nuclear programme;

23. *Requests* within 60 days a report from the Director General of the IAEA on whether Iran has established full and sustained suspension of all activities mentioned in this resolution, as well as on the process of Iranian compliance with all the steps required by the IAEA Board and with the other provisions of this resolution, to the IAEA Board of Governors and in parallel to the Security Council for its consideration;

24. *Affirms* that it shall review Iran's actions in the light of the report referred to in paragraph 23 above, to be submitted within 60 days, and:

(a) that it shall suspend the implementation of measures if and for so long as Iran suspends all enrichment-related and reprocessing activities, including research and development, as verified by the IAEA, to allow for negotiations;

(b) that it shall terminate the measures specified in paragraphs 3, 4, 5, 6, 7, 10 and 12 of this resolution as soon as it determines that Iran has fully complied with its obligations under the relevant resolutions of the Security Council and met the requirements of the IAEA Board of Governors, as confirmed by the IAEA Board;

(c) that it shall, in the event that the report in paragraph 23 above shows that Iran has not complied with this resolution, adopt further appropriate measures under Article 41 of Chapter VII of the Charter of the United Nations to persuade Iran to comply with this resolution and the requirements of the IAEA, and underlines that further decisions will be required should such additional measures be necessary;

25. *Decides* to remain seized of the matter.

Source: United Nations Security Council Official Records, S/RES/1737, December 23, 2006.

131. Human Rights Watch, Press Release on Saddam Hussein's Execution, December 30, 2006

Introduction

The trial and eventual execution in late 2006 of former Iraqi president Saddam Hussein sparked real international unease over the state of that country. Few doubted that Hussein had been responsible for numerous atrocities, including many others besides the killings of tens of thousands of Kurds in 1988 for which he was tried and hanged. Human rights organizations, including Human Rights Watch, nonetheless expressed concern over serious procedural flaws in his trial and appeal. The manner of Hussein's execution also enhanced the former dictator's reputation while tarnishing that of his enemies. The Iraqi government, which had custody of Hussein, insisted that he be put to death before the end of 2006 and was responsible for the arrangements for his execution. The hanging took place in private, witnessed by assorted Iraqi and international officials. Some of those attending secretly filmed it on cell phones, and the videos were quickly circulated in the world's media. They revealed that while Hussein faced his death with dignity and courage, some of the Iraqi guards and officials taunted and insulted him immediately before his execution. While those responsible or their families had probably suffered severely during Hussein's rule, the failure of the Iraqi authorities to prevent such disorderly behavior attracted heavy and embarrassing international criticism. So too did the botched execution a few days later of two other Hussein-era Iraqi officials, one of whom, a half brother of Hussein, was decapitated during his hanging. Iraq's Sunni population hailed Hussein as a martyr, and the manner of the once-hated dictator's death won him grudging posthumous respect from many of his foreign opponents. U.S. president George W. Bush, British prime minister Tony Blair, and other leading international figures publicly deplored the way in which Hussein's execution had been staged and appealed to the Iraqi government to insist that any future such events should be organized according to internationally accepted standards of human rights.

Primary Source

Iraq: Saddam Hussein Put to Death

Hanging after Flawed Trial Undermines Rule of Law

(New York, December 30, 2006)—The execution of former Iraqi President Saddam Hussein following a deeply flawed trial for crimes against humanity marks a significant step away from respect for human rights and the rule of law in Iraq, Human Rights Watch said today.

Human Rights Watch has for more than 15 years documented the human rights crimes committed by Hussein's former government, and has campaigned to bring the perpetrators to justice. These crimes include the killing of more than 100,000 Iraqi Kurds in Northern Iraq as part of the 1988 Anfal campaign.

"Saddam Hussein was responsible for massive human rights violations, but that can't justify giving him the death penalty, which is a cruel and inhuman punishment," said Richard Dicker, director of Human Rights Watch's International Justice Program.

The Iraqi High Tribunal sentenced Saddam Hussein and two others to death in November for the killing of 148 men and boys from the town of Dujail in 1982. The tribunal's statute prohibits, contrary to international law, the possibility of commuting a death sentence. It also requires that the execution take place within 30 days of the final appeal.

Human Rights Watch opposes the death penalty in all circumstances. Increasingly, governments are abolishing the death penalty in domestic law.

"The test of a government's commitment to human rights is measured by the way it treats its worst offenders," said Dicker. "History will judge these actions harshly."

A report issued in November 2006 by Human Rights Watch identified numerous serious flaws in the trial of Hussein for the Dujail executions. The 97-page report, "Judging Dujail: The First Trial Before the Iraqi High Tribunal," was based on 10 months of observation and dozens of interviews with judges, prosecutors and defense lawyers.

The report found, among other defects, that the Iraqi High Tribunal was undermined from the outset by Iraqi government actions that threatened the independence and perceived impartiality of the court. It outlined serious flaws in the trial, including failures to disclose key evidence to the defense, violations of the defendants' right to question prosecution witnesses, and the presiding judge's demonstrations of bias.

Hussein's defense lawyers had 30 days to file an appeal from the November 5 verdict. However, the trial judgment was only made available to them on November 22, leaving just two weeks to respond. The Appeals Chamber announced its confirmation of the verdict and the death sentence on December 26.

"It defies imagination that the Appeals Chamber could have thoroughly reviewed the 300-page judgment and the defense's written arguments in less than three weeks' time," said Dicker. "The appeals process appears even more flawed than the trial."

At the time of his hanging, Saddam Hussein and others were on trial for genocide for the 1988 Anfal campaign. The victims, including women, children and the elderly, were selected because they were Kurds who remained on their traditional lands in zones outside of areas controlled by Baghdad. Hussein's execution will therefore jeopardize the trial of these most serious crimes.

Source: "Iraq: Saddam Hussein Put to Death," Human Rights Watch, http://www.hrw.org/legacy/english/docs/2006/12/30/iraq14950_txt .htm.

132. White House Fact Sheet, "The New Way Forward in Iraq," January 10, 2007

Introduction

The administration of U.S. president George W. Bush responded promptly to the bipartisan December 2006 Iraq Study Group report, which called for a major new international and Iraqi effort to stabilize the country and prevent its breakdown into civil war. The National Security Council immediately began a review of U.S. policies toward Iraq, completed in early January 2007. When completed, the new review, a summary of which the White House issued as a press release, called for a major initiative to strengthen the Iraqi leadership and political, military, security, and economic institutions and forces so that the country's government would have the authority and power to win and maintain control of the nation. The strategy review openly acknowledged that the situation in Iraq "could not be graver" and that the position of the United States throughout the entire Middle East was in jeopardy. To facilitate efforts to regain control and restore order and stability, the United States promised Iraq additional troops and economic resources while building up Iraqi capabilities to handle the situation. All moderate Iraqi political forces were expected to work together in a coalition to combat extremism. While the new blueprint mentioned "efforts to counter Iranian and Syrian influence inside Iraq," conspicuously absent from the new strategy were the Iraq Study Group report's recommendations that the United States should "try to engage [Iran and Syria] constructively" and win their cooperation in stabilizing Iraq, through a "diplomatic effort . . . [aimed at] every country that has an interest in avoiding a chaotic Iraq, including all of Iraq's neighbors." The Bush administration clearly preferred to downplay such diplomatic initiatives in favor of concentrating on "strengthen[ing] defense ties with partner states in the region" and increasing the coalition's regional military presence and Middle Eastern support for the Global War on Terror. The same evening that this press release appeared, Bush addressed the nation, setting out the new strategy. The most controversial aspect of his speech was his pledge to dispatch an additional 20,000 American troops to Iraq, a surge that would, he claimed, enable coalition and Iraqi forces to regain control of Baghdad and surrounding areas. Bush stated that Iraq's prime minister, Nouri al-Maliki, had pledged that they would have a free hand in tackling all insurgents of every political or sectarian affiliation, something that had not been the case before. American troops would serve as military advisers, embedded in all units of the Iraqi security and military forces to train them and enhance their effectiveness. Bush told Americans that the Iraqi government would also institute major economic reforms and reintegrate former supporters of Saddam Hussein's regime into the political community. U.S. forces intended to move aggressively against Al Qaeda elements active in Iraq and also against their Iranian and Syrian sponsors. Bush intended to deploy an additional naval carrier strike group to the Middle East. In addition, the United States would launch diplomatic initiatives, in collaboration with Saudi Arabia, Egypt, Jordan, and the Gulf states, to bring peace to Iraq and also to resolve the decades-old Palestinian-Israeli dispute. Bush's new strategy incorporated a few elements from the Iraq Study Group's report but largely ignored its emphasis on collective international action involving all Iraq's neighbors and such institutions as the United Nations (UN) and the European Union (EU). Many observers, including leading generals who had served in Iraq, remained skeptical that the new surge in American troop strength would suffice to restore order in the country and permit the Maliki government to regain control.

Primary Source

The President's New Iraq Strategy Is Rooted In Six Fundamental Elements:

1. Let the Iraqis lead;
2. Help Iraqis protect the population;
3. Isolate extremists;
4. Create space for political progress;
5. Diversify political and economic efforts; and
6. Situate the strategy in a regional approach.
   - **Iraq Could Not Be Graver—The War On Terror Cannot Be Won If We Fail In Iraq.** Our enemies throughout the Middle East are trying to defeat us in Iraq. If we step back now, the problems in Iraq will become more lethal, and make our troops fight an uglier battle than we are seeing today.

Key Elements Of The New Approach: Security

Iraqi:

- Publicly acknowledge all parties are responsible for quelling sectarian violence.
- Work with additional Coalition help to regain control of the capital and protect the Iraqi population.
- Deliver necessary Iraqi forces for Baghdad and protect those forces from political interference.
- Commit to intensify efforts to build balanced security forces throughout the nation that provide security even-handedly for all Iraqis.
- Plan and fund eventual demobilization program for militias.

Coalition:

- Agree that helping Iraqis to provide population security is necessary to enable accelerated transition and political progress.
- Provide additional military and civilian resources to accomplish this mission.
- Increase efforts to support tribes willing to help Iraqis fight Al Qaeda in Anbar.
- Accelerate and expand the embed program while minimizing risk to participants.

Both Coalition And Iraqi:

- Continue counter-terror operations against Al Qaeda and insurgent organizations.
- Take more vigorous action against death squad networks.
- Accelerate transition to Iraqi responsibility and increase Iraqi ownership.

- Increase Iraqi security force capacity—both size and effectiveness—from 10 to 13 Army divisions, 36 to 41 Army Brigades, and 112 to 132 Army Battalions.
  - Establish a National Operations Center, National Counterterrorism Force, and National Strike Force.
  - Reform the Ministry of Interior to increase transparency and accountability and transform the National Police.

Key Elements Of The New Approach: Political

Iraqi:

- The Government of Iraq commits to:
  - Reform its cabinet to provide even-handed service delivery.
  - Act on promised reconciliation initiatives (oil law, de-Baathification law, Provincial elections).
  - Give Coalition and ISF authority to pursue ALL extremists.
- All Iraqi leaders support reconciliation.
- Moderate coalition emerges as strong base of support for unity government.

Coalition:

- Support political moderates so they can take on the extremists.
  - Build and sustain strategic partnerships with moderate Shi'a, Sunnis, and Kurds.
- Support the national compact and key elements of reconciliation with Iraqis in the lead.
- Diversify U.S. efforts to foster political accommodation outside Baghdad (more flexibility for local commanders and civilian leaders).
  - Expand and increase the flexibility of the Provincial Reconstruction Team (PRT) footprint.
  - Focus U.S. political, security, and economic resources at local level to open space for moderates, with initial priority to Baghdad and Anbar.

Both Coalition And Iraqi:

- Partnership between Prime Minister Maliki, Iraqi moderates, and the United States where all parties are clear on expectations and responsibilities.
- Strengthen the rule of law and combat corruption.
- Build on security gains to foster local and national political accommodations.
- Make Iraqi institutions even-handed, serving all of Iraq's communities on an impartial basis.

Key Elements Of The New Approach: Economic

Iraqi:

- Deliver economic resources and provide essential services to all areas and communities.
- Enact hydrocarbons law to promote investment, national unity, and reconciliation.
- Capitalize and execute jobs-producing programs.
- Match U.S. efforts to create jobs with longer term sustainable Iraqi programs.
- Focus more economic effort on relatively secure areas as a magnet for employment and growth.

Coalition:

- Refocus efforts to help Iraqis build capacity in areas vital to success of the government (e.g. budget execution, key ministries).
- Decentralize efforts to build Iraqi capacities outside the Green Zone.
  - Double the number of PRTs and civilians serving outside the Green Zone.
  - Establish PRT-capability within maneuver Brigade Combat Teams (BCTs).
- Greater integration of economic strategy with military effort.
  - Joint civil-military plans devised by PRT and BCT.
  - Remove legal and bureaucratic barriers to maximize cooperation and flexibility.

Key Elements Of The New Approach: Regional

Iraqi:

- Vigorously engage Arab states.
- Take the lead in establishing a regional forum to give support and help from the neighborhood.
- Counter negative foreign activity in Iraq.
- Increase efforts to counter PKK (Kurdistan Workers' Party).

Coalition:

- Intensify efforts to counter Iranian and Syrian influence inside Iraq.
- Increase military presence in the region.
- Strengthen defense ties with partner states in the region.
- Encourage Arab state support to Government of Iraq.
- Continue efforts to help manage relations between Iraq and Turkey.

- Continue to seek the region's full support in the War on Terror.

Both Coalition And Iraqi:

- Focus on the International Compact.
- Retain active U.N. engagement in Iraq—particularly for election support and constitutional review.

Source: "Fact Sheet: The New Way Forward in Iraq," The White House, President George W. Bush, http://georgewbush-whitehouse .archives.gov/news/releases/2007/01/20070110-3.html.

133. President George W. Bush, State of the Union Address, January 23, 2007 [Excerpts]

Introduction

The month after he received the Baker Report from the Iraq Study Group recommending major changes of strategy on Iraq, President George W. Bush gave his annual State of the Union address to Congress. For the first time in his presidency, the Democrats had won back control of Congress, where they now had a small majority in each House, meaning that the Republican Bush would now have to work with a Congress that would probably be less cooperative than in the past. Bush began his address with a plea for bipartisan support. Although he asked for a major domestic program to overhaul the expensive and increasingly strained Social Security, Medicare, and Medicaid entitlement programs, improve education and access to health care, and reform the immigration system, foreign policy, particularly the situation in Iraq, was the major focus of Bush's address. He presented America's battle with terrorist extremists, both Sunni and Shia Muslims, as "a decisive ideological struggle," which could only be won by "help[ing] men and women in the Middle East to build free societies and share in the rights of all humanity," thereby destroying the appeal to others of such groups as Al Qaeda and Hezbollah. Such groups, he argued, sought to "force our country to retreat from the world and abandon the cause of liberty." Should the United States withdraw prematurely from Iraq, this would mean that terrorists had won and would embolden them to seek further victories. Since the Iraqi government was not yet itself strong enough to "stop the sectarian violence in its capital" of Baghdad and elsewhere in the country, a temporary increase in American troop levels was necessary while Iraq's government built up and trained its own security forces to the point where they could maintain order themselves. Should the United States at this point choose to draw down its forces, civil war between Sunni and Shia extremists was likely, and the contagion

of this "chaos" was likely to spread throughout the Middle East, ultimately encouraging further terrorist attacks on American citizens and territory. Bush called for increases in the size of the U.S. military. He also sought to reduce American dependence on foreign oil by encouraging the development and use of alternative energy sources and increasing domestic oil production. Despite Bush's efforts to depict continuing and enhanced American military involvement in Iraq as vital to his country's own security, Congress remained skeptical. The following months would see repeated though unsuccessful attempts by legislators to begin the process of reducing U.S. troop commitments in Iraq.

Primary Source

The President: . . . The rite of custom brings us together at a defining hour—when decisions are hard and courage is needed. We enter the year 2007 with large endeavors underway, and others that are ours to begin. In all of this, much is asked of us. We must have the will to face difficult challenges and determined enemies—and the wisdom to face them together.

[. . .]

Extending hope and opportunity depends on a stable supply of energy that keeps America's economy running and America's environment clean. For too long our nation has been dependent on foreign oil. And this dependence leaves us more vulnerable to hostile regimes, and to terrorists—who could cause huge disruptions of oil shipments, and raise the price of oil, and do great harm to our economy.

It's in our vital interest to diversify America's energy supply—the way forward is through technology. We must continue changing the way America generates electric power, by even greater use of clean coal technology, solar and wind energy, and clean, safe nuclear power. [Applause.] We need to press on with battery research for plug-in and hybrid vehicles, and expand the use of clean diesel vehicles and biodiesel fuel. [Applause.] We must continue investing in new methods of producing ethanol— [applause]—using everything from wood chips to grasses, to agricultural wastes.

We made a lot of progress, thanks to good policies here in Washington and the strong response of the market. And now even more dramatic advances are within reach. Tonight, I ask Congress to join me in pursuing a great goal. Let us build on the work we've done and reduce gasoline usage in the United States by 20 percent in the next 10 years. [Applause.] When we do that we will have cut our total imports by the equivalent of three-quarters of all the oil we now import from the Middle East.

To reach this goal, we must increase the supply of alternative fuels, by setting a mandatory fuels standard to require 35 billion gallons of renewable and alternative fuels in 2017—and that is nearly five times the current target. [Applause.] At the same time, we need to reform and modernize fuel economy standards for cars the way we did for light trucks—and conserve up to 8.5 billion more gallons of gasoline by 2017.

Achieving these ambitious goals will dramatically reduce our dependence on foreign oil, but it's not going to eliminate it. And so as we continue to diversify our fuel supply, we must step up domestic oil production in environmentally sensitive ways. [Applause.] And to further protect America against severe disruptions to our oil supply, I ask Congress to double the current capacity of the Strategic Petroleum Reserve. [Applause.]

America is on the verge of technological breakthroughs that will enable us to live our lives less dependent on oil. And these technologies will help us be better stewards of the environment, and they will help us to confront the serious challenge of global climate change. [Applause.]

[. . .]

For all of us in this room, there is no higher responsibility than to protect the people of this country from danger. Five years have come and gone since we saw the scenes and felt the sorrow that the terrorists can cause. We've had time to take stock of our situation. We've added many critical protections to guard the homeland. We know with certainty that the horrors of that September morning were just a glimpse of what the terrorists intend for us—unless we stop them.

With the distance of time, we find ourselves debating the causes of conflict and the course we have followed. Such debates are essential when a great democracy faces great questions. Yet one question has surely been settled: that to win the war on terror we must take the fight to the enemy. [Applause.]

From the start, America and our allies have protected our people by staying on the offense. The enemy knows that the days of comfortable sanctuary, easy movement, steady financing, and free flowing communications are long over. For the terrorists, life since 9/11 has never been the same.

Our success in this war is often measured by the things that did not happen. We cannot know the full extent of the attacks that we and our allies have prevented, but here is some of what we do know: We stopped an al Qaeda plot to fly a hijacked airplane into the tallest building on the West Coast. We broke up a Southeast Asian terror cell grooming operatives for attacks inside the United States. We uncovered an al Qaeda cell developing anthrax to be used in attacks against America. And just last August, British authorities uncovered a plot to blow up passenger planes bound for America over the Atlantic Ocean. For each life saved, we owe a debt of gratitude to the brave public servants who devote their lives to finding the terrorists and stopping them. [Applause.]

Every success against the terrorists is a reminder of the shoreless ambitions of this enemy. The evil that inspired and rejoiced in 9/11 is still at work in the world. And so long as that's the case, America is still a nation at war.

In the mind of the terrorist, this war began well before September the 11th, and will not end until their radical vision is fulfilled. And these past five years have given us a much clearer view of the nature of this enemy. Al Qaeda and its followers are Sunni extremists, possessed by hatred and commanded by a harsh and narrow ideology. Take almost any principle of civilization, and their goal is the opposite. They preach with threats, instruct with bullets and bombs, and promise paradise for the murder of the innocent.

Our enemies are quite explicit about their intentions. They want to overthrow moderate governments, and establish safe havens from which to plan and carry out new attacks on our country. By killing and terrorizing Americans, they want to force our country to retreat from the world and abandon the cause of liberty. They would then be free to impose their will and spread their totalitarian ideology. Listen to this warning from the late terrorist Zarqawi: "We will sacrifice our blood and bodies to put an end to your dreams, and what is coming is even worse." Osama bin Laden declared: "Death is better than living on this Earth with the unbelievers among us."

These men are not given to idle words, and they are just one camp in the Islamist radical movement. In recent times, it has also become clear that we face an escalating danger from Shia extremists who are just as hostile to America, and are also determined to dominate the Middle East. Many are known to take direction from the regime in Iran, which is funding and arming terrorists like Hezbollah—a group second only to al Qaeda in the American lives it has taken.

The Shia and Sunni extremists are different faces of the same totalitarian threat. Whatever slogans they chant, when they slaughter the innocent they have the same wicked purposes. They want to kill Americans, kill democracy in the Middle East, and gain the weapons to kill on an even more horrific scale.

In the sixth year since our nation was attacked, I wish I could report to you that the dangers had ended. They have not. And so it remains the policy of this government to use every lawful and proper tool of intelligence, diplomacy, law enforcement, and military action to do our duty, to find these enemies, and to protect the American people. [Applause.]

This war is more than a clash of arms—it is a decisive ideological struggle, and the security of our nation is in the balance. To prevail, we must remove the conditions that inspire blind hatred, and drove 19 men to get onto airplanes and to come and kill us. What every terrorist fears most is human freedom—societies where men and women make their own choices, answer to their own conscience, and live by their hopes instead of their resentments. Free people are not drawn to violent and malignant ideologies—and most will choose a better way when they're given a chance. So we advance our own security interests by helping moderates and reformers and brave voices for democracy. The great question of our day is whether America will help men and women in the Middle East to build free societies and share in the rights of all humanity. And I say, for the sake of our own security, we must. [Applause.]

In the last two years, we've seen the desire for liberty in the broader Middle East—and we have been sobered by the enemy's fierce reaction. In 2005, the world watched as the citizens of Lebanon raised the banner of the Cedar Revolution; they drove out the Syrian occupiers and chose new leaders in free elections. In 2005, the people of Afghanistan defied the terrorists and elected a democratic legislature. And in 2005, the Iraqi people held three national elections, choosing a transitional government, adopting the most progressive, democratic constitution in the Arab world, and then electing a government under that constitution. Despite endless threats from the killers in their midst, nearly 12 million Iraqi citizens came out to vote in a show of hope and solidarity that we should never forget. [Applause.]

A thinking enemy watched all of these scenes, adjusted their tactics, and in 2006 they struck back. In Lebanon, assassins took the life of Pierre Gemayel, a prominent participant in the Cedar Revolution. Hezbollah terrorists, with support from Syria and Iran, sowed conflict in the region and are seeking to undermine Lebanon's legitimately elected government. In Afghanistan, Taliban and al Qaeda fighters tried to regain power by regrouping and engaging Afghan and NATO forces. In Iraq, al Qaeda and other Sunni extremists blew up one of the most sacred places in Shia Islam—the Golden Mosque of Samarra. This atrocity, directed at a Muslim house of prayer, was designed to provoke retaliation from Iraqi Shia—and it succeeded. Radical Shia elements, some of whom receive support from Iran, formed death squads. The result was a tragic escalation of sectarian rage and reprisal that continues to this day.

This is not the fight we entered in Iraq, but it is the fight we're in. Every one of us wishes this war were over and won. Yet it would not be like us to leave our promises unkept, our friends abandoned, and our own security at risk. [Applause.] Ladies and gentlemen: On this day, at this hour, it is still within our power to shape the outcome of this battle. Let us find our resolve, and turn events toward victory. [Applause.]

We're carrying out a new strategy in Iraq—a plan that demands more from Iraq's elected government, and gives our forces in Iraq the reinforcements they need to complete their mission. Our goal is a democratic Iraq that upholds the rule of law, respects the rights of its people, provides them security, and is an ally in the war on terror.

In order to make progress toward this goal, the Iraqi government must stop the sectarian violence in its capital. But the Iraqis are not yet ready to do this on their own. So we're deploying reinforcements of more than 20,000 additional soldiers and Marines to Iraq. The vast majority will go to Baghdad, where they will help Iraqi forces to clear and secure neighborhoods, and serve as advisers embedded in Iraqi Army units. With Iraqis in the lead, our forces will help secure the city by chasing down the terrorists, insurgents, and the roaming death squads. And in Anbar Province, where al Qaeda terrorists have gathered and local forces have begun showing a willingness to fight them, we're sending an additional 4,000 United States Marines, with orders to find the terrorists and clear them out. [Applause.] We didn't drive al Qaeda out of their safe haven in Afghanistan only to let them set up a new safe haven in a free Iraq.

The people of Iraq want to live in peace, and now it's time for their government to act. Iraq's leaders know that our commitment is not open-ended. They have promised to deploy more of their own troops to secure Baghdad—and they must do so. They pledged that they will confront violent radicals of any faction or political party—and they need to follow through, and lift needless restrictions on Iraqi and coalition forces, so these troops can achieve their mission of bringing security to all of the people of Baghdad. Iraq's leaders have committed themselves to a series of benchmarks—to achieve reconciliation, to share oil revenues among all of Iraq's citizens, to put the wealth of Iraq into the rebuilding of Iraq, to allow more Iraqis to re-enter their nation's civic life, to hold local elections, and to take responsibility for security in every Iraqi province. But for all of this to happen, Baghdad must be secure. And our plan will help the Iraqi government take back its capital and make good on its commitments.

My fellow citizens, our military commanders and I have carefully weighed the options. We discussed every possible approach. In the end, I chose this course of action because it provides the best chance for success. Many in this chamber understand that America must not fail in Iraq, because you understand that the consequences of failure would be grievous and far-reaching.

If American forces step back before Baghdad is secure, the Iraqi government would be overrun by extremists on all sides. We could expect an epic battle between Shia extremists backed by Iran, and Sunni extremists aided by al Qaeda and supporters of the old regime. A contagion of violence could spill out across the country—and in time, the entire region could be drawn into the conflict.

For America, this is a nightmare scenario. For the enemy, this is the objective. Chaos is the greatest ally—their greatest ally in this struggle. And out of chaos in Iraq would emerge an emboldened enemy with new safe havens, new recruits, new resources, and an even greater determination to harm America. To allow this to happen would be to ignore the lessons of September the 11th and invite tragedy. Ladies and gentlemen, nothing is more important at this moment in our history than for America to succeed in the Middle East, to succeed in Iraq and to spare the American people from this danger. [Applause.]

This is where matters stand tonight, in the here and now. I have spoken with many of you in person. I respect you and the arguments you've made. We went into this largely united, in our assumptions and in our convictions. And whatever you voted for, you did not vote for failure. Our country is pursuing a new strategy in Iraq, and I ask you to give it a chance to work. And I ask you to support our troops in the field, and those on their way. [Applause.]

The war on terror we fight today is a generational struggle that will continue long after you and I have turned our duties over to others. And that's why it's important to work together so our nation can see this great effort through. Both parties and both branches should work in close consultation. It's why I propose to establish a special advisory council on the war on terror, made up of leaders in Congress from both political parties. We will share ideas for how to position America to meet every challenge that confronts us. We'll show our enemies abroad that we are united in the goal of victory.

And one of the first steps we can take together is to add to the ranks of our military so that the American Armed Forces are ready for all the challenges ahead. [Applause.] Tonight I ask the Congress to authorize an increase in the size of our active Army and Marine Corps by 92,000 in the next five years. [Applause.] A second task we can take on together is to design and establish a volunteer Civilian Reserve Corps. Such a corps would function much like our military reserve. It would ease the burden on the Armed Forces by allowing us to hire civilians with critical skills to serve on missions abroad when America needs them. It would give people across America who do not wear the uniform a chance to serve in the defining struggle of our time.

Americans can have confidence in the outcome of this struggle because we're not in this struggle alone. We have a diplomatic strategy that is rallying the world to join in the fight against extremism. In Iraq, multinational forces are operating under a mandate from the United Nations. We're working with Jordan and Saudi Arabia and Egypt and the Gulf States to increase support for Iraq's government.

The United Nations has imposed sanctions on Iran, and made it clear that the world will not allow the regime in Tehran to acquire nuclear weapons. [Applause.] With the other members of the Quartet—the U.N., the European Union, and Russia—we're pursuing diplomacy to help bring peace to the Holy Land, and pursuing the establishment of a democratic Palestinian state living side-by-side with Israel in peace and security. [Applause.] In Afghanistan, NATO has taken the lead in turning back the Taliban and al Qaeda offensive—the first time the Alliance has deployed forces outside the North Atlantic area. Together with our partners in China, Japan, Russia, and South Korea, we're pursuing intensive diplomacy to achieve a Korean Peninsula free of nuclear weapons. [Applause.]

We will continue to speak out for the cause of freedom in places like Cuba, Belarus, and Burma—and continue to awaken the conscience of the world to save the people of Darfur.

[...]

Source: George W. Bush, "President Bush Delivers State of the Union Address," The White House, George W. Bush, http://georgewbush-whitehouse.archives.gov/news/releases/2007/01/20070123-2.html.

134. Lorenzo Cremonesi, Interview with Iraqi Prime Minister Nouri al-Maliki, January 18, 2007, Published in *Corriere della Sera*, January 23, 2007

Introduction

In early January 2007 U.S. president George W. Bush, responding in part to pressures arising from publication the previous month of the report of the Iraq Study Group, a high-level panel sponsored by the U.S. Congress, announced increases in American troop levels in Iraq and the implementation of a new strategy, which would require greater initiative and effectiveness on the part of Iraq's own government in encouraging national reconciliation through political, social, and economic reform and winning back control of the country from sectarian militia groups. Despite public commitments by the American president to Iraqi prime minister Nouri al-Maliki, influential officials within the Bush administration, including Secretary of State Condoleezza Rice, openly doubted whether Maliki had the ability or strength to handle the complicated and demanding Iraqi situation. The Bush administration and much international public opinion also deplored the Maliki government's conduct of the execution of deposed president Saddam Hussein in a hanging at which the condemned former dictator displayed dignity while subjected to taunts and harassment by bitter enemies who now held high positions in the new administration. Speaking to an Italian journalist, Maliki showed annoyance at such criticisms and suggested that Bush, whose Republican Party had lost control of Congress in the recent American midterm elections, was "caving in to internal pressures." Maliki complained that he himself had become the target of an unfair U.S. media campaign and that American officials rather than Iraq's government were the ones who were now "moribund." He also complained that in equipping the new Iraqi security forces, the United States had given too little too late and that had the Americans provided far more weapons and equipment at an earlier juncture to Iraqi personnel, far fewer civilians and U.S. troops would have died in Iraq. Maliki rejected claims that he was personally too close to Shiite Iraqi militia leader Moqtada al-Sadr and affirmed that the country's government would "rein in all the militias" and "must have a monopoly on force." In a sign that even American clients might resent overly mighty patrons, the prime minister also reminded his interviewer that Iraq's "foreign policy is independent from that of the United States." Maliki's interview might well have been designed to reassure critics within Iraq who considered him too close to the United States and sought to characterize him as an American puppet. The interview also demonstrated that despite earlier affirmations to the contrary, the ties linking the U.S. and Iraqi governments were becoming somewhat frayed.

Primary Source

Q. Mr. Prime Minister, once again, in the last few hours, President Bush has repeated that the way in which the execution of Saddam Hussein was conducted was a sectarian vendetta. And in Italy and elsewhere, calls to abolish the death penalty have increased. Wouldn't it have been better to have spared the life of Saddam Hussein?

The world forgets that we were victims of the pitiless regime of Saddam Hussein for decades. Tens of thousands of innocents were sent to their death after unmentionable torture. The elderly, women, and children died from chemical weapons. The world has forgotten the terror and brutality of the Ba'athist dictatorship. More than 160 members of my clan lost their lives, not to mention thousands in my political party (Da'wa). All were innocent and killed for their political ideas. But regardless, I want to repeat that the trial of Saddam and his accomplices was conducted correctly. The law was observed to the letter. It had nothing to do with sectarian vendetta. Following the execution I personally ordered the washing of the remains according to Muslim ritual and had them placed in a dignified wooden coffin. No victim of Saddam ever received such treatment. Of course, I am well aware that errors were committed during the hanging of Saddam and I've ordered the arrest and prosecution of the officer who shouted abuse and slogans.

But George Bush is criticizing you and Romano Prodi has asked the United Nations to launch a campaign against the death penalty.

It seems to me that Bush is caving in to internal pressures and is overwhelmed by the media and politicians. Perhaps he has lost control of the situation. And I'm sorry to see that because, in general, George Bush has a strong character. As to Prodi, I need only to remind you how Italy treated Mussolini. Before being executed, there was no trial. His executioners told him only to state his name and admit to his identity. I'm saying that the world should respect our laws, our history and our culture. The death penalty is allowed by our Constitution. Moreover, the Koran permits the death sentence and there's a verse that says that with death one creates life. Islamic religious law affirms that putting criminals to death protects human society.

Recently the US Secretary of State, Condoleezza Rice, stated publicly that your government is moribund. She suggested that you will not finish serving your term. Are you going to resign?

There is a media campaign deployed against me. And I certainly understand that the current US Administration is in great difficulty after its defeat at the polls a few weeks ago. And I've mentioned the weakness of George Bush. It seems to me it is the people in Washington who are moribund, not here in Baghdad. Our government functions better than many others. And I would advise Condoleezza Rice to avoid statements that only help the terrorists. These statements only encourage them. I would like to add that the terrorists may have delivered a defeat to America, but our government has not.

What is your opinion of the new US plan of intervention? And when do you think that Washington can begin to withdraw its troops from Iraq?

I will always be grateful to the Americans for having liberated Iraq from tyranny. It is thanks to the United States that we live in a climate of freedom and democracy, even if it is a work in progress. And our relationship will continue over the long term on economic, political and military issues. Having said this, I believe that the situation would have been far better had the United States immediately given our law enforcement authorities the weapons and equipment they need. If they had done this sooner, we would have had far fewer civilian and US troop casualties. We'll have to wait and see. I would not exclude a drastically improved situation that, within three to six months, would permit most US troops to leave.

You've promised a crackdown on the militias over the next few days. But you are suspected of connivance with Iran

and of being a staunch ally of Moqtada al-Sadr and the Mahdi Army.

We will rein in all the militias. We will display no discrimination or preference. All armed groups will be reined in, whether Sunni, Shi'ite or Kurdish. We will hit them everywhere, every base and every group. The law will be equally applied to all. The State must have a monopoly on force and this is the sole possible premise on which a functioning state can be built. We wish to have normal and good relations with our neighbors. Our foreign policy is independent from that of the United States. I personally met with Moqtada al-Sadr twice in the last four years. And in the last few days, the police have rounded up more than 400 members of the Mahdi Army. I think that is sufficient proof to show that I don't have a special relationship with any militia or political faction.

Do you agree that the violence in Iraq has degenerated into ethnic cleansing?

There are violent elements within the former Iraqi intelligence apparatus and groups that are led by ignorant people that are pursuing ethnic cleansing. This has been taking place among Shi'ites as well as Sunnis. But I don't believe that we will lapse into civil war. Peaceful coexistence triumphed in the past and I am confident that we will defeat the extremists. This is our plan: to wage war against terrorism. Forever—no matter how long it takes and without exception. If we fail the first time then we will try again.

Source: "Interview with Iraqi Prime Minister al-Maliki," Nur al-Cubicle, http://nuralcubicle.blogspot.com/2007/01/interview-with-iraqi-prime-minister-al_23.html.

135. Benazir Bhutto, Speech to the Council on Foreign Relations, New York, August 15, 2007

Introduction

Since September 2001, Pakistan had been a key U.S. ally in the war against Al Qaeda and Taliban forces in neighboring Afghanistan. By late 2007, however, the government of President Pervez Musharraf, a military man who had seized power in a coup in 1999, found it increasingly difficult to restrain radical Islamist elements within Pakistan. Taliban and Al Qaeda personnel had been able to regroup within Pakistan, in the mountainous provinces bordering Afghanistan, and used these as a safe haven for ever-fiercer efforts to destabilize and win control of Afghanistan. Many ordinary Pakistanis disliked their own government's pro-Western stance. There were also strong suspicions that at least some

members of Pakistan's powerful military, security, and intelligence services had strong sympathies for fundamentalist Muslim perspectives and therefore acquiesced in and perhaps even assisted in these ventures. Given these problematic circumstances, officials in President George W. Bush's administration began to cast around for a political leader who might be willing to move more decisively to check the growing power of radical Islam within Pakistan. Increasingly, they turned to former Pakistani prime minister Benazir Bhutto, the Oxford-educated daughter of a politically prominent family, who had twice been removed from office on charges of corruption and had been living in exile for several years. In such influential forums for policy makers as the Council on Foreign Relations in New York, Bhutto publicly affirmed her determination to oppose extremist Muslim forces within Pakistan and Afghanistan and sought to link the restoration of democracy in Pakistan with the country's ability to combat terrorism. With support from top American officials, in late 2007 Bhutto reached an understanding with Musharraf, who granted her amnesty from all the charges against her, allowing her to return to Pakistan without facing arrest and to campaign once again for the premiership in impending general elections. On December 27, 2007, she was assassinated while speaking at a political rally in Rawalpindi. Al Qaeda claimed responsibility for her murder, in which many suspected that the Pakistani security services were implicated. The following September, President Musharraf resigned from office as a means of avoiding charges of impeachment, and Bhutto's widower, Asif Ali Zardari, who had by then been cleared of numerous outstanding corruption charges against him, was elected president of Pakistan. Zardari had already announced his intention of combating fundamentalist Islamic forces within Pakistan and assisting the United States in the Global War on Terror and had also requested substantial economic and military aid for Pakistan from the United States and other Western countries. While Zardari appeared willing to serve as a pliable ally in the American-led campaign against Al Qaeda and the Taliban, it was less clear whether he possessed sufficient authority or political clout to deliver on his commitments to Western powers.

Primary Source

Ladies and gentlemen, it's a privilege for me to be here this afternoon as the guest of the Council on Foreign Relations. Thank you for inviting me.

And as I come here to have a conversation with you, I find that my country, Pakistan, is once again in a crisis, and it's a crisis that threatens not only my nation and region, but possibly could have repercussions on the entire world.

It's a crisis that has its roots almost half a century ago, when the military in my country first seized power, in 1958. Four military dictatorships—and most recently those of General Zia ul-Haq in the '80s and now General Musharraf—have ruled my nation for the last 30 years, except for a few years of civilian government. And so I believe that democracy has never really been given a chance to grow or nurture in my homeland.

As an example, I was only allowed to govern for five of the 10 years that my people elected me to govern. And now Pakistan has changed dramatically from the days when I left office, in 1996, for now, from areas previously controlled by my government, pro-Taliban forces linked to al Qaeda launch regular attacks on NATO troops across the border in Afghanistan.

In the view of my party, military dictatorship, first in the '80s and now again, under General Musharraf, has fueled the forces of extremism, and military dictatorship puts into place a government that is unaccountable, that is unrepresentative, undemocratic, and disconnected from the ordinary people in the country, disconnected from the aspirations of the people who make up Pakistan. Moreover, military dictatorship is born from the power of the gun, and so it undermines the concept of the rule of law and gives birth to a culture of might, a culture of weapons, violence and intolerance.

The suppression of democracy in my homeland has had profound institutional consequences. The major infrastructure building blocks of democracy have been weakened, political parties have been marginalized, NGOs are dismantled, judges sacked and civil society undermined. And by undermining the infrastructure of democracy, the regime that is in place to date was a regime put into place by the intelligence agencies after the flawed elections of 2002. This regime has not allowed the freedom of association, the freedom of movement, the freedom of speech for moderate political forces, and so by default, the mosques and the madrassas have become the only outlet of permitted political expression in the country.

And so just as the—we've seen the emergence of the religious parties, we've seen the emergence of the extremist groups, and just as the military dictatorship of the '80s used the so-called Islamic card to promote a military dictatorship while demonizing political parties, so too the present military establishment of this century has used the so-called Islamist card to pressurize the international community into supporting military dictatorship once again.

But I am here this afternoon to tell you that as far as we, the Pakistan People's Party, is concerned, the choice in Pakistan is not really between military dictatorship and religious parties; the choice for Pakistan is indeed between dictatorship and democracy. And I feel that the real choice that the world also faces today is the choice between dictatorship and democracy, and in the choice that we make between dictatorship and democracy lies the outcome of the battle between extremism and moderation in Pakistan.

The U.S. intelligence recent threat assessment stated that, and I quote, "Al Qaeda and the Taliban seem to be fairly well-settled into the safe haven spaces of Pakistan. We see more training, we see more money, we see more communications, we see that activity rising." That's the most recent U.S. national intelligence threat assessment. And so it's often surprising to those of us in Pakistan who see the international community back the present regime. But this backing continues, despite the regime's failure to stop the Taliban and al Qaeda reorganizing after they were defeated, demoralized and dispersed following the events of 9/11.

This is a regime under which the religious parties have risen, for the first time, to power, and they run two of Pakistan's four federating units—two most critical states of Pakistan, those that border Afghanistan. And even while the military dictatorship has allowed the religious parties to govern two of Pakistan's most critical four provinces, it has exiled the moderate leadership of the country, it has weakened internal law enforcement and allowed for a very bloody suppression of people's human rights.

The military operation in Baluchistan is an example of the brutality of the suppression. The killings that took place in Karachi on May 12th, where 48 peaceful political activists were gunned down in the streets of Karachi, and not one person has been arrested for those murders that were actually televised, shows the level to which the regime permits the suppression of the political opposition. And most recently, 17 members of my party were killed in Islamabad on July 17 at the hands of a suicide bomber.

The weakness of law enforcement has led to a series of suicide bombings, roadside bombings. To give you an example, since last July, 300 people have fallen victim to suicide bombers within Pakistan. Disappearances, too, which were unheard of in our country's history, have become the order of the day. And even as I speak to you, a Pak[istani] -origin American, Dr. Sarki, has disappeared, not because he supports extremists, but because he's a nationalist, and the level of intolerance for differing views is so high that people can disappear simply for supporting nationalism.

The West's close association with a military dictatorship, in my humble view, is alienating Pakistan's people and is playing into the hands of those hardliners who blame the West for the ills of the region. And it need not be this way. A people inspired by democracy, human rights and economic opportunity will turn their back decisively against extremism.

There is a silver lining on the clouds. The recent restoration of the chief justice of Pakistan to the Supreme Court has given hope to people of Pakistan that the unchecked power of the military will now finally come under a degree of scrutiny by the highest judicial institutions in the country. We in the PPP have kept the doors of dialogue open with the military regime to facilitate the transfer of democracy. This hasn't been a popular move, but we've done it because we think the stability of Pakistan is important to our own security as well as to regional security.

However, without progress on the issue of fair elections, this dialogue could founder. And now, as we approach the autumn, time is running out.

Ladies and gentlemen, I plan to return later this year to Pakistan to lead a democratic movement for the restoration of democracy. I seek to lead a democratic Pakistan which is free from the yoke of military dictatorship and that will cease to be a haven, the very petri dish of international terrorism. A democratic Pakistan that would help stabilize Afghanistan, relieving pressure on NATO troops. A democratic Pakistan that would pursue the drug barons and bust up the drug cartel that today is funding terrorism. A Pakistan where the rule of law is established so that no one has the permission to establish, recruit, train and run private armies and private militias. A democratic Pakistan that puts the welfare of its people as the centerpiece of its national policy.

And as I plan to return to Pakistan, I put my faith in the people of my country who have stood by my party and by myself through this long decade—more than a decade, 11 years since the PPP government was ousted—because they believe that the PPP can eliminate terrorism and give them security, and security will bring in the economic investment that can help us reverse the tide of rising poverty in the country, and by so doing, it will certainly undermine the forces of militancy and extremism.

Source: Benazir Bhutto, "A Conversation with Benazir Bhutto," August 15, 2007, http://www.cfr.org/publication/14041/.

136. General David H. Petraeus, Report to Congress on the Situation in Iraq, September 10–11, 2007 [Excerpt]

Introduction

In January 2007, President George W. Bush picked General David H. Petraeus as commander of the Multi-National Force in Iraq, with the mission to implement the policies of winning control of Iraq and handing over responsibility for the country's security and administration to Iraqi forces. Petraeus, a military intellectual, was one of the foremost experts on counterinsurgency, with a wide experience of nation-building operations in Bosnia and Haiti, who had previously commanded occupation forces in the Iraqi city of Mosul and headed the Multi-National Security Transition Command–Iraq. By early 2007 many members of the once-acquiescent U.S. Congress had become increasingly disillusioned

with the war. Resolutions to cut off funding for the war and set a timetable for the withdrawal of U.S. forces won strong support in Congress, although the president eventually vetoed them, meaning that the anticipated rate of progress toward greater security in Iraq would attract fierce congressional monitoring and scrutiny. In September 2007 Petraeus delivered a detailed report to Congress on the situation in Iraq. He summarized his findings in personal testimony before Congress, describing a country where the Multi-National Force and the Iraq government's own security personnel were gradually eliminating Al Qaeda and independent militia elements, reducing violence, and regaining control of ever-growing areas of Iraq. Petraeus expected to begin withdrawing American troops from Iraq by mid-2008. He was widely respected in Congress, and his report and recommendations were broadly accepted. As Petraeus came to the end of this assignment one year later in September 2008, levels of violence had fallen dramatically from the peak of early 2007. By that time Petraeus himself was modestly optimistic about the future prospects for Iraq, although he readily admitted that the situation was still fragile and that many tough challenges remained to be met.

Primary Source

[. . .]

At the outset, I would like to note that this is my testimony. Although I have briefed my assessment and recommendations to my chain of command, I wrote this testimony myself. It has not been cleared by, nor shared with, anyone in the Pentagon, the White House, or Congress.

As a bottom line up front, the military objectives of the surge are, in large measure, being met. In recent months, in the face of tough enemies and the brutal summer heat of Iraq, Coalition and Iraqi Security Forces have achieved progress in the security arena. Though the improvements have been uneven across Iraq, the overall number of security incidents in Iraq has declined in 8 of the past 12 weeks, with the numbers of incidents in the last two weeks at the lowest levels seen since June 2006.

One reason for the decline in incidents is that Coalition and Iraqi forces have dealt significant blows to Al Qaeda-Iraq. Though Al Qaeda and its affiliates in Iraq remain dangerous, we have taken away a number of their sanctuaries and gained the initiative in many areas.

We have also disrupted Shia militia extremists, capturing the head and numerous other leaders of the Iranian-supported Special Groups, along with a senior Lebanese Hezbollah operative supporting Iran's activities in Iraq.

Coalition and Iraqi operations have helped reduce ethno-sectarian violence, as well, bringing down the number of ethno-sectarian deaths substantially in Baghdad and across Iraq since the height of the sectarian violence last December. The number of overall civilian deaths has also declined during this period, although the numbers in each area are still at troubling levels.

Iraqi Security Forces have also continued to grow and to shoulder more of the load, albeit slowly and amid continuing concerns about the sectarian tendencies of some elements in their ranks. In general, however, Iraqi elements have been standing and fighting and sustaining tough losses, and they have taken the lead in operations in many areas.

Additionally, in what may be the most significant development of the past 8 months, the tribal rejection of Al Qaeda that started in Anbar Province and helped produce such significant change there has now spread to a number of other locations as well.

Based on all this and on the further progress we believe we can achieve over the next few months, I believe that we will be able to reduce our forces to the pre-surge level of brigade combat teams by next summer without jeopardizing the security gains that we have fought so hard to achieve.

Beyond that, while noting that the situation in Iraq remains complex, difficult, and sometimes downright frustrating, I also believe that it is possible to achieve our objectives in Iraq over time, though doing so will be neither quick nor easy.

Having provided that summary, I would like to review the nature of the conflict in Iraq, recall the situation before the surge, describe the current situation, and explain the recommendations I have provided to my chain of command for the way ahead in Iraq.

The Nature of the Conflict

The fundamental source of the conflict in Iraq is competition among ethnic and sectarian communities for power and resources. This competition *will* take place, and its resolution is key to producing long-term stability in the new Iraq. The question is whether the competition takes place more—or less—violently. This chart shows the security challenges in Iraq. Foreign and home-grown terrorists, insurgents, militia extremists, and criminals all push the ethno-sectarian competition toward violence. Malign actions by Syria and, especially, by Iran fuel that violence. Lack of adequate governmental capacity, lingering sectarian mistrust, and various forms of corruption add to Iraq's challenges.

The Situation in December 2006 and the Surge

In our recent efforts to look to the future, we found it useful to revisit the past. In December 2006, during the height of the ethno-sectarian violence that escalated in the wake of the bombing of the Golden Dome Mosque in Samarra, the leaders in Iraq at that time—General George Casey and Ambassador Zalmay Khalil-zad—concluded that the coalition was failing to achieve its objectives. Their review underscored the need to protect the population and reduce sectarian violence, especially in Baghdad. As a result, General Casey requested additional forces to enable the Coalition to accomplish these tasks, and those forces began to flow in January.

In the ensuing months, our forces and our Iraqi counterparts have focused on improving security, especially in Baghdad and the areas around it, wresting sanctuaries from Al Qaeda control, and disrupting the efforts of the Iranian-supported militia extremists. We have employed counterinsurgency practices that underscore the importance of units living among the people they are securing, and accordingly, our forces have established dozens of joint security stations and patrol bases manned by Coalition and Iraqi forces in Baghdad and in other areas across Iraq.

In mid-June, with all the surge brigades in place, we launched a series of offensive operations focused on: expanding the gains achieved in the preceding months in Anbar Province; clearing Baqubah, several key Baghdad neighborhoods, the remaining sanctuaries in Anbar Province, and important areas in the so-called "belts" around Baghdad; and pursuing Al Qaeda in the Diyala River Valley and several other areas.

Throughout this period, as well, we engaged in dialogue with insurgent groups and tribes, and this led to additional elements standing up to oppose Al Qaeda and other extremists. We also continued to emphasize the development of the Iraqi Security Forces and we employed non-kinetic means to exploit the opportunities provided by the conduct of our kinetic operations—aided in this effort by the arrival of additional Provincial Reconstruction Teams.

Current Situation and Trends

The progress our forces have achieved with our Iraqi counterparts has, as I noted at the outset, been substantial. While there have been setbacks as well as successes and tough losses along the way, overall, our tactical commanders and I see improvements in the security environment. We do not, however, just rely on gut feel or personal observations; we also conduct considerable data collection and analysis to gauge progress and determine trends. We do this by gathering and refining data from coalition *and* Iraqi operations centers, using a methodology that has been in place for well over a year and that has benefited over the past seven months from the increased presence of our forces living among the Iraqi people. We endeavor to ensure our analysis of that data is conducted with rigor and consistency, as our ability to achieve a nuanced understanding of the security environment is dependent on collecting and analyzing data in a consistent way over time. Two US intelligence agencies recently reviewed our methodology, and they concluded that the data we produce is the most accurate and authoritative in Iraq.

As I mentioned up front, and as the chart before you reflects, the level of security incidents has decreased significantly since the start of the surge of offensive operations in mid-June, declining in 8 of the past 12 weeks, with the level of incidents in the past two weeks the lowest since June 2006 and with the number of *attacks* this past week the lowest since April 2006.

Civilian deaths of *all* categories, less natural causes, have also declined considerably, by over 45% Iraq-wide since the height of the sectarian violence in December. This is shown by the top line on this chart, and the decline by some 70% in Baghdad is shown by the bottom line. Periodic mass casualty attacks by Al Qaeda have tragically added to the numbers outside Baghdad, in particular. Even without the sensational attacks, however, the level of civilian deaths is clearly still too high and continues to be of serious concern.

As the next chart shows, the number of *ethno-sectarian* deaths, an important subset of the overall civilian casualty figures, has also declined significantly since the height of the sectarian violence in December. Iraq-wide, as shown by the top line on this chart, the number of ethno-sectarian deaths has come down by over 55%, and it would have come down much further were it not for the casualties inflicted by barbaric Al Qaeda bombings attempting to reignite sectarian violence. In Baghdad, as the bottom line shows, the number of ethno-sectarian deaths has come down by some 80% since December. This chart also displays the density of sectarian incidents in various Baghdad neighborhoods and it both reflects the progress made in reducing ethno-sectarian violence in the Iraqi capital and identifies the areas that remain the most challenging.

As we have gone on the offensive in former Al Qaeda and insurgent sanctuaries, and as locals have increasingly supported our efforts, we have found a substantially increased number of arms, ammunition, and explosives caches. As this chart shows, we have, so far this year, already found and cleared over 4,400 caches, nearly 1,700 more than we discovered in all of last year. This may be a factor in the reduction in the number of overall improvised explosive device attacks in recent months, which as this chart shows, has declined sharply, by about one-third, since June.

The change in the security situation in Anbar Province has, of course, been particularly dramatic. As this chart shows, monthly attack levels in Anbar have declined from some 1,350 in October 2006 to a bit over 200 in August of this year. This dramatic decrease reflects the significance of the local rejection of Al Qaeda and the newfound willingness of local Anbaris to volunteer to serve in the

Iraqi Army and Iraqi Police Service. As I noted earlier, we are seeing similar actions in other locations, as well.

To be sure, trends have not been uniformly positive across Iraq, as is shown by this chart depicting violence levels in several key Iraqi provinces. The trend in Ninevah Province, for example, has been much more up and down, until a recent decline, and the same is true in Sala ad Din Province, though recent trends there and in Baghdad have been in the right direction. In any event, the overall trajectory in Iraq—a steady decline of incidents in the past three months—*is* still quite significant.

The number of car bombings and suicide attacks has also declined in each of the past 5 months, from a high of some 175 in March, as this chart shows, to about 90 this past month. While this trend in recent months has been heartening, the number of high profile attacks is still too high, and we continue to work hard to destroy the networks that carry out these barbaric attacks.

Our operations have, in fact, produced substantial progress against Al Qaeda and its affiliates in Iraq. As this chart shows, in the past 8 months, we have considerably reduced the areas in which Al Qaeda enjoyed sanctuary. We have also neutralized 5 media cells, detained the senior Iraqi leader of Al Qaeda-Iraq, and killed or captured nearly 100 other key leaders and some 2,500 rank-and-file fighters. Al Qaeda is certainly not defeated; however, it is off balance and we are pursuing its leaders and operators aggressively. Of note, as the recent National Intelligence Estimate on Iraq explained, these gains against Al Qaeda are a result of the synergy of actions by: conventional forces to deny the terrorists sanctuary; intelligence, surveillance, and reconnaissance assets to find the enemy; and special operations elements to conduct targeted raids. A combination of these assets is necessary to prevent the creation of a terrorist safe haven in Iraq.

In the past six months we have also targeted Shia militia extremists, capturing a number of senior leaders and fighters, as well as the deputy commander of Lebanese Hezbollah Department 2800, the organization created to support the training, arming, funding, and, in some cases, direction of the militia extremists by the Iranian Republican Guard Corps' Qods Force. These elements have assassinated and kidnapped Iraqi governmental leaders, killed and wounded our soldiers with advanced explosive devices provided by Iran, and indiscriminately rocketed civilians in the International Zone and elsewhere. It is increasingly apparent to both Coalition and Iraqi leaders that Iran, through the use of the Qods Force, seeks to turn the Iraqi Special Groups into a Hezbollah-like force to serve its interests and fight a proxy war against the Iraqi state and coalition forces in Iraq.

The most significant development in the past six months likely has been the increasing emergence of tribes and local citizens rejecting Al Qaeda and other extremists. This has, of course, been most visible in Anbar Province. A year ago the province was assessed as "lost" politically. Today, it is a model of what happens when local leaders and citizens decide to oppose Al Qaeda and reject its Taliban-like ideology. While Anbar is unique and the model it provides cannot be replicated everywhere in Iraq, it does demonstrate the dramatic change in security that is possible with the support and participation of local citizens. As this chart shows, other tribes have been inspired by the actions of those in Anbar and have volunteered to fight extremists as well. We have, in coordination with the Iraqi government's National Reconciliation Committee, been engaging these tribes and groups of local citizens who want to oppose extremists and to contribute to local security. Some 20,000 such individuals are already being hired for the Iraqi Police, thousands of others are being assimilated into the Iraqi Army, and thousands more are vying for a spot in Iraq's Security Forces.

Iraqi Security Forces

As I noted earlier, Iraqi Security Forces have continued to grow, to develop their capabilities, and to shoulder more of the burden of providing security for their country. Despite concerns about sectarian influence, inadequate logistics and supporting institutions, and an insufficient number of qualified commissioned and non-commissioned officers, Iraqi units are engaged around the country.

As this chart shows, there are now nearly 140 Iraqi Army, National Police, and Special Operations Forces Battalions in the fight, with about 95 of those capable of taking the lead in operations, albeit with some coalition support. Beyond that, all of Iraq's battalions have been heavily involved in combat operations that often result in the loss of leaders, soldiers, and equipment. These losses are among the shortcomings identified by operational readiness assessments, but we should not take from these assessments the impression that Iraqi forces are not in the fight and contributing. Indeed, despite their shortages, many Iraqi units across Iraq now operate with minimal coalition assistance.

As counterinsurgency operations require substantial numbers of boots on the ground, we are helping the Iraqis expand the size of their security forces. Currently, there are some 445,000 individuals on the payrolls of Iraq's Interior and Defense Ministries. Based on recent decisions by Prime Minister Maliki, the number of Iraq's security forces will grow further by the end of this year, possibly by as much as 40,000. Given the security challenges Iraq faces, we support this decision, and we will work with the two security ministries as they continue their efforts to expand their basic training capacity, leader development programs, logistical structures and elements, and various other institutional capabilities to support the substantial growth in Iraqi forces.

Significantly, in 2007, Iraq will, as in 2006, spend more on its security forces than it will receive in security assistance from the United States. In fact, Iraq is becoming one of the United States' larger foreign military sales customers, committing some $1.6 billion to FMS already, with the possibility of up to $1.8 billion more being committed before the end of this year. And I appreciate the attention that some members of Congress have recently given to speeding up the FMS process for Iraq.

To summarize, the security situation in Iraq is improving, and Iraqi elements are slowly taking on more of the responsibility for protecting their citizens. Innumerable challenges lie ahead; however, Coalition and Iraqi Security Forces have made progress toward achieving sustainable security. As a result, the United States will be in a position to reduce its forces in Iraq in the months ahead.

Recommendations

Two weeks ago I provided recommendations for the way ahead in Iraq to the members of my chain of command and the Joint Chiefs of Staff. The essence of the approach I recommended is captured in its title: "Security While Transitioning: From Leading to Partnering to Overwatch." This approach seeks to build on the security improvements our troopers and our Iraqi counterparts have fought so hard to achieve in recent months. It reflects recognition of the importance of securing the population *and* the imperative of transitioning responsibilities to Iraqi institutions and Iraqi forces as quickly as possible, but without rushing to failure. It includes substantial support for the continuing development of Iraqi Security Forces. It also stresses the need to continue the counterinsurgency strategy that we have been employing, but with Iraqis gradually shouldering more of the load. And it highlights the importance of regional and global diplomatic approaches. Finally, in recognition of the fact that this war is not only being fought on the ground in Iraq but also in cyberspace, it also notes the need to contest the enemy's growing use of that important medium to spread extremism.

The recommendations I provided were informed by operational and strategic considerations. The *operational* considerations include recognition that:

- military aspects of the surge have achieved progress and generated momentum;
- Iraqi Security Forces have continued to grow and have slowly been shouldering more of the security burden in Iraq;
- a mission focus on either population security or transition alone will not be adequate to achieve our objectives;
- success against Al Qaeda–Iraq and Iranian-supported militia extremists requires conventional forces as well as special operations forces; and

- the security and local political situations will enable us to draw down the surge forces.

My recommendations also took into account a number of *strategic* considerations:

- political progress will take place only if sufficient security exists;
- long-term US ground force viability will benefit from force reductions as the surge runs its course;
- regional, global, and cyberspace initiatives are critical to success; and
- Iraqi leaders understandably want to assume greater sovereignty in their country, although, as they recently announced, they do desire continued presence of coalition forces in Iraq in 2008 under a new UN Security Council Resolution and, following that, they want to negotiate a long term security agreement with the United States and other nations.

Based on these considerations, and having worked the battlefield geometry with Lieutenant General Ray Odierno to ensure that we retain and build on the gains for which our troopers have fought, I have recommended a drawdown of the surge forces from Iraq. In fact, later this month, the Marine Expeditionary Unit deployed as part of the surge will depart Iraq. Beyond that, if my recommendations are approved, that unit's departure will be followed by the withdrawal of a brigade combat team without replacement in mid-December and the further redeployment without replacement of four other brigade combat teams and the two surge Marine battalions in the first 7 months of 2008, until we reach the pre-surge level of 15 brigade combat teams by mid-July 2008.

I would also like to discuss the period beyond next summer. Force reductions *will* continue beyond the pre-surge levels of brigade combat teams that we will reach by mid-July 2008; however, in my professional judgment, it would be premature to make recommendations on the pace of such reductions at this time. In fact, our experience in Iraq has repeatedly shown that projecting too far into the future is not just difficult, it can be misleading and even hazardous. The events of the past six months underscore that point. When I testified in January, for example, no one would have dared to forecast that Anbar Province would have been transformed the way it has in the past 6 months. Nor would anyone have predicted that volunteers in one-time Al Qaeda strongholds like Ghazaliyah in western Baghdad or in Adamiya in eastern Baghdad would seek to join the fight against Al Qaeda. Nor would we have anticipated that a Shia-led government would accept significant numbers of Sunni volunteers into the ranks of the local police force in Abu Ghraib. Beyond that, on a less encouraging note, none of us earlier this year appreciated the extent of Iranian involvement in Iraq, something about which we and Iraq's leaders all now have greater concern.

In view of this, I do not believe it is reasonable to have an adequate appreciation for the pace of further reductions and mission adjustments beyond the summer of 2008 until about mid-March of next year. We will, no later than that time, consider factors similar to those on which I based the current recommendations, having by then, of course, a better feel for the security situation, the improvements in the capabilities of our Iraqi counterparts, and the enemy situation. I will then, as I did in developing the recommendations I have explained here today, also take into consideration the demands on our Nation's ground forces, although I believe that that consideration should once again inform, not drive, the recommendations I make.

This chart captures the recommendations I have described, showing the recommended reduction of brigade combat teams as the surge runs its course and illustrating the concept of our units adjusting their missions and transitioning responsibilities to Iraqis, as the situation and Iraqi capabilities permit. It also reflects the no-later-than date for recommendations on force adjustments beyond next summer and provides a possible approach we have considered for the future force structure and mission set in Iraq.

One may argue that the best way to speed the process in Iraq is to change the MNF-I mission from one that emphasizes population security, counter-terrorism, and transition, to one that is strictly focused on transition and counter-terrorism. Making that change now would, in our view, be premature. We have learned before that there is a real danger in handing over tasks to the Iraqi Security Forces before their capacity and local conditions warrant. In fact, the drafters of the recently released National Intelligence Estimate on Iraq recognized this danger when they wrote, and I quote, "We assess that changing the mission of Coalition forces from a primarily counterinsurgency and stabilization role to a primary combat support role for Iraqi forces and counterterrorist operations to prevent AQI from establishing a safe haven would erode security gains achieved thus far."

In describing the recommendations I have made, I should note again that, like Ambassador Crocker, I believe Iraq's problems will require a long-term effort. There are no easy answers or quick solutions. And though we both believe this effort can succeed, it will take time. Our assessments underscore, in fact, the importance of recognizing that a premature drawdown of our forces would likely have devastating consequences.

That assessment is supported by the findings of a 16 August Defense Intelligence Agency report on the implications of a rapid withdrawal of US forces from Iraq. Summarizing it in an unclassified fashion, it concludes that a rapid withdrawal would result in the further release of the strong centrifugal forces in Iraq and produce a number of dangerous results, including a high risk of disintegration of the Iraqi Security Forces; rapid deterioration of local security initiatives; Al Qaeda–Iraq regaining lost ground and freedom of maneuver; a marked increase in violence and further ethno-sectarian displacement and refugee flows; alliances of convenience by Iraqi groups with internal and external forces to gain advantages over their rivals; and exacerbation of already challenging regional dynamics, especially with respect to Iran.

Lieutenant General Odierno and I share this assessment and believe that the best way to secure our national interests and avoid an unfavorable outcome in Iraq is to continue to focus our operations on securing the Iraqi people while targeting terrorist groups and militia extremists and, as quickly as conditions are met, transitioning security tasks to Iraqi elements.

[...]

> **Source:** General David H. Petraeus, "Report to Congress on the Situation in Iraq," U.S. Department of Defense, http://www.defense.gov/pubs/pdfs/Petraeus-Testimony20070910.pdf.

137. Gordon Brown, Statement on Iraq, October 7, 2007 [Excerpts]

Introduction

Since 2001, Britain had steadily backed U.S.-led interventions in both Afghanistan and Iraq, contributing more troops than any other U.S. ally to the coalition forces in each war. In June 2007 the Labour politician Gordon Brown replaced Tony Blair as British prime minister. While Blair had been enthusiastic in pushing for war with Iraq, it was widely believed that Brown, despite publicly supporting Blair's policies during 10 years as chancellor of the exchequer, privately doubted the wisdom of British involvement in Iraq. The ongoing conflict was widely unpopular in Britain, and opinion polls showed that majorities of the general public favored withdrawal from Iraq and Afghanistan as the casualty figures among British forces in both theaters of war crept steadily upward. The new prime minister affirmed his country's commitment to securing a lasting settlement in both Iraq and Afghanistan. He also began a policy of reducing the number of British troops in Iraq and handing over responsibility for security to Iraqi forces. Since 2003 British forces had occupied the city of Basra, controlling the surrounding area. In September 2007 they withdrew from the city to barracks elsewhere. Despite U.S. objections, Brown began reducing the number of British troops in Iraq, announcing in October 2007 that he planned to withdraw about 2,500 of the 5,000 British soldiers there. An outbreak of violence in Basra aborted these plans, and in mid-2008 there were still 4,000 British troops in Iraq and 8,000 in Afghanistan. While accepting that they would probably keep some forces in Afghanistan for several years, in July 2008 top British military officials announced their intention of bringing

these numbers down to "sustainable" levels. By early 2009 media speculation was rife that Brown might refuse anticipated requests from Barack Obama, the newly installed U.S. president, to send additional British troops to Afghanistan. Brown's attitude and his determination to devise an exit strategy were symptomatic of a growing weariness among U.S. allies with the protracted, wearing, and costly military interventions.

Primary Source

Mr. Speaker, the statement I wish to make today is to set out detailed proposals for political reconciliation and economic reconstruction in Iraq, for the security of the Iraqi people, the future configuration, equipment for and security of our own armed forces, and about the obligations we owe to the local Iraqi staff who have supported us in our efforts.

[...]

Mr. Speaker, our strategy as a Government has been:

- first, to work to bring together the political groupings in Basra and across Iraq;
- second, to ensure that the security of the Iraqi people and the new Iraqi democracy is properly safeguarded, as well as the security of our own armed forces;
- and third, to work for an economy in Iraq where people have a stake in the future.

Our strategy is founded on the UN mandate renewed last November in UN Security Council Resolution 1723. Whatever disagreements there have been about our decision to go to war, there can be little disagreement about the unanimous UN position affirming the right of the Iraqi people freely to determine their own political future, calling upon "the International Community, particularly countries in the region and Iraq's neighbours, to support the Iraqi people in their pursuit of peace, stability, security, democracy and prosperity."

And so let me affirm: as I told Prime Minister Maliki last week—and as I have agreed with President Bush and our other allies—we will meet our obligations, honour our commitments and discharge our duties to the international community and to the people of Iraq.

The future depends first of all upon sustained progress on political reconciliation. That is why when I met Prime Minister Maliki and Vice President Hashemi in Baghdad last week, I said it was vital—and they agreed—that the 3 plus 1 leadership group of the Prime Minister and Presidency Council meet to take the political process forward; that key legislation be passed on sharing oil revenues, deba'athification, the constitutional review and provincial elections; that the government must reach out to disaffected groups, as well as decide on next steps on detainees; and that local elections go ahead in early 2008 making Provincial Councils more representative. And our message to the Government of Iraq—and to the leaders of all Iraq's communities and parties—is that they must make the long-term decisions needed to achieve reconciliation.

Mr. Speaker, the support of Iraq's neighbours—including a commitment to prevent financing and support for militias and insurgent groups—is also critical to ensuring security and political reconciliation.

I urge all nations to implement the International Compact to renew Iraq's economy, to participate in the Neighbours Conferences to boost cooperation and surmount divisions in the region, and to support the enhanced mission of the United Nations in Iraq. I renew our call that Iran and Syria play a more constructive role by halting their support for terrorists and armed groups operating in Iraq, by continuing to improve border security and by arresting and detaining foreign fighters trying to reach Iraq.

And we must all act against the presence of Al Qaeda in Iraq. When the people and security forces stand up to Al Qaeda as in Anbar province, which they had declared to be their base, they can be driven out.

[...]

As the Petraeus-Crocker report set out, the security gains made by the multinational forces this year have been significant. And as important as improving current security is building the capacity of the Iraqi forces so they can achieve our aim: that Iraqis step up and progressively take over security themselves.

In 2004 it was agreed with the Iraqi Government that in each of the country's 18 provinces security responsibility would progressively be returned to the Iraqi authorities as and when the conditions were right. Now we are in a position to announce further progress.

Over the past four years the UK has helped train over 13,000 Iraqi Army troops, including 10,000 now serving with the 10th Division which has been conducting operations in Basra and across the south of the country without the requirement for Coalition ground support. As we tackle corruption, 15,000 police officers are also now trained and equipped in Southern Iraq. And the Iraqi Army 14th Division—with around 11,000 men—are in the process of joining them and have already taken on responsibility for Basra City—bringing security forces in the south to almost 30,000 now and over 35,000 by June next year.

Since we handed over our base in Basra City in early September the present security situation has been calmer. Indeed in the last month there have been five indirect fire attacks on Basra Air Station compared with 87 in July. And while the four southern

provinces have around 20 percent of the Iraqi people they still account for less than 5 percent of the overall violence in Iraq.

Mr. Speaker, during our engagement in Iraq we have always made clear that all our decisions must be made on the basis of the assessments of our military commanders and actual conditions on the ground. As a result of the progress made in Southern Iraq, US, UK and Iraqi commanders judged over the last 15 months that three out of the four provinces in the UK's area of control in Southern Iraq were suitable for transition back to the Iraqis—and these have subsequently been transferred to Iraqi control.

As part of the process of putting the Iraqi forces in the lead in Basra, we have just gone through a demanding operation which involved consolidating our forces at Basra airport. This was successfully completed, as planned, early last month.

The next important stage in delivering our strategy to hand over security to the Iraqis is to move from a combat role in the rest of Basra province to "overwatch" which will itself have two distinct stages. In the first, the British forces that remain in Iraq will have the following tasks:

- training and mentoring the Iraqi army and police force;
- securing supply routes and policing the Iran-Iraq border;
- and the ability to come to the assistance of the Iraqi security forces when called upon.

Then, in the spring of next year—and guided as always by the advice of our military commanders—we plan to move to a second stage of "overwatch" where the Coalition would maintain a more limited re-intervention capacity and where the main focus will be on training and mentoring.

And I want now to explain how—after detailed discussions with our military commanders, a meeting of the National Security Committee, discussions with the Iraqi Government and our allies, and subject to conditions on the ground—we plan, from next spring, to reduce force numbers in southern Iraq to a figure of 2,500.

The first stage begins now. With the Iraqis already assuming greater security responsibility, we expect to:

- establish Provincial Iraqi Control in Basra province in the next two months as announced by the Prime Minister of Iraq,
- move to the first stage of "overwatch,"
- reduce numbers in southern Iraq from the 5,500 at the start of September to 4,500 immediately after Provincial Iraqi Control and then to 4,000,
- and then in the second stage of "overwatch," from the spring—and guided as always by the advice of our military

commanders—reduce to around 2,500 troops, with a further decision about the next phase made then. In both stages of "overwatch" around 500 logistics and support personnel will be based outside Iraq elsewhere in the region.

At all times achieving our long term aim of handing over security to the Iraqi armed forces and police, honouring our obligations to the Iraqi people and to their security, and ensuring the safety of our forces.

[...]

The purpose of economic reconstruction is to ensure ordinary Iraqis have an economic stake in the future. And so as a result of the work I launched with Prime Minister Maliki in July, the Provincial Council have created the Basra Investment Promotion Agency to stimulate private sector development and is forming a Basra Development Fund—financed by $30 million dollars from the Iraqi Finance Ministry—to help small businesses access finance and kick start economic growth.

And as announced this morning by the Government of Iraq, we have agreed on the need for a new Basra Development Commission which will bring national, regional and international business knowledge together to provide advice on how to increase investment and economic growth. The Commission will host a business leadership conference to strengthen the engagement of the UK private sector in Iraq and enhance regional investment networks. And it will help the Provincial authorities coordinate projects to strengthen Basra's position as an economic hub, including the development of Basra International Airport and the renovation of Umm Quasr Port.

And I can tell the House that in addition to our support for humanitarian assistance being announced by the Department for International Development today, Deputy Iraqi Prime Minster Barham Saleh has announced over $300 million dollars for investment in Basra from the 2007 Iraqi national budget, and this will be increased again in 2008, ensuring economic reconstruction can make real progress.

[...]

Mr. Speaker, I am convinced after my visit to the region that progress cannot be fully achieved without progress on Israeli-Palestinian issues. A few days ago this Government published its proposals for an economic road map to underpin the peace process, a programme for economic and social support for the rebuilding of the Palestinian economy and the reduction of the high levels of unemployment and poverty amongst the Palestinian people.

My Rt Hon. Friend the Foreign Secretary and I believe—as does the whole international community including the US, the EU and

the Arab League—that current dialogue between President Abbas and Prime Minister Olmert offers the best chance of final status negotiations since 2000. The next step is a meeting with the parties and key international players, hosted by the Americans, in November at which we would like to see an agreement that puts the Israelis and Palestinians on a path to real negotiations in 2008 leading to a final settlement of two states living side by side in peace and security.

There will also be a donors' conference in December, through which the international community will work with Prime Minister Fayyad to strengthen the economy and institutions of a future Palestinian state. And I welcome Tony Blair's work as Quartet Envoy on this. The UK will continue to support the political process and to provide support for humanitarian assistance and economic development. And I assure the House of my personal commitment to doing all we can to ensure progress.

Mr. Speaker, working for a successful conclusion to the Middle East Peace Process, taking on Al Qaeda terrorism and ensuring a more secure Iraq are all key to the future stability of the region.

As I have made clear, we have made commitments to the Iraqi people, through the United Nations, and we will honour these obligations.

We will continue to be actively engaged in Iraq's political and economic development.

We will continue to assist the Iraqi Government and its security forces to help build their capabilities—military, civilian and economic—so that they can take full responsibility for the security of their own country.

And we will never shirk from but continue to discharge our duties to them and to the international community.

[...]

Source: Gordon Brown, "Statement on Iraq," Number10.gov.uk, http://www.number10.gov.uk/Page13450.

138. Barack Obama, Plan for Ending the War in Iraq, Obama/Biden Campaign Website, 2008
Introduction

Senator Barack Obama of Illinois, the eventual Democratic presidential nominee in 2008, took a position on the war in Iraq very different from that of his rival for the presidency, Republican senator John W. McCain of Arizona, and incumbent president George W. Bush. Although McCain, a former naval aviator who had been a prisoner of war in Vietnam, differed from Bush on many issues, he was at one with the president in supporting the war against Iraq. Obama, by contrast, voted against U.S. intervention in Iraq in 2003 and argued that American forces should be withdrawn from that country as soon as possible. In early 2007 he introduced legislation in the U.S. Senate calling for an end to American military intervention in Iraq within the next year to 18 months. The real challenge to U.S. national security, Obama argued, was in Afghanistan, where the Bush administration's preoccupation with Iraq had starved occupying allied forces of the men and resources they needed to consolidate the initial victory of late 2001 against the Taliban and Al Qaeda. Obama therefore pledged that if elected, he would remove all American troops from Iraq as soon as possible while boosting U.S. forces in Afghanistan and pressuring other countries contributing to the anti-Taliban coalition in Afghanistan to increase their commitments too. Ironically, his proposals were not that far removed from the policies that Bush administration officials followed in practice during the last two years of Bush's presidency, as the troop surge of 2007 and associated political moves brought a new, unaccustomed, and still fragile stability to Iraq, allowing for the redeployment of some American forces to Afghanistan. In the first half of 2008 the number of U.S. military personnel in Afghanistan rose dramatically, numbering 26,607 in January and 48,250 in June, an increase of more than 80 percent. In September 2008 Bush announced that he intended to deploy a further 4,500 American soldiers in Afghanistan. In December, Bush signed a Status of Forces Agreement with Iraq, which anticipated the withdrawal of all American troops from that country by the end of 2011. Once he took office as president, Obama himself announced that he planned to continue the new Bush policies, with further increases to U.S. forces deployed in Afghanistan.

Primary Source

Plan for Ending the War in Iraq

The Problem

Inadequate Security and Political Progress in Iraq: Since the surge began, more than 1,000 American troops have died, and despite the improved security situation, the Iraqi government has not stepped forward to lead the Iraqi people and to reach the genuine political accommodation that was the stated purpose of the surge. Our troops have heroically helped reduce civilian casualties in Iraq to early 2006 levels. This is a testament to our military's hard work, improved counterinsurgency tactics, and enormous sacrifice by our troops and military families. It is also a consequence of the decision of many Sunnis to turn against al Qaeda in Iraq, and a lull in Shia militia activity. But the absence of genuine political accommodation in Iraq is a direct result of President Bush's failure to hold the Iraqi government accountable.

Strains on the Military: More than 1.75 million servicemen and women have served in Iraq or Afghanistan; more than 620,000 troops have completed multiple deployments. Military members have endured multiple deployments taxing both them and their families. Additionally, military equipment is wearing out at nine times the normal rate after years of constant use in Iraq's harsh environment. As Army Chief of Staff General George Casey said in March, "Today's Army is out of balance. The current demand for our forces in Iraq and Afghanistan exceeds the sustainable supply and limits our ability to provide ready forces for other contingencies."

Resurgent Al Qaeda in Afghanistan: The decision to invade Iraq diverted resources from the war in Afghanistan, making it harder for us to kill or capture Osama Bin Laden and others involved in the 9/11 attacks. Nearly seven years later, the Taliban has reemerged in southern Afghanistan while Al Qaeda has used the space provided by the Iraq war to regroup, train and plan for another attack on the United States. 2007 was the most violent year in Afghanistan since the invasion in 2001. The scale of our deployments in Iraq continues to set back our ability to finish the fight in Afghanistan, producing unacceptable strategic risks.

A New Strategy Needed: The Iraq war has lasted longer than World War I, World War II, and the Civil War. More than 4,000 Americans have died. More than 60,000 have been injured and wounded. The United States may spend $2.7 trillion on this war and its aftermath, yet we are less safe around the globe and more divided at home. With determined ingenuity and at great personal cost, American troops have found the right tactics to contain the violence in Iraq, but we still have the wrong strategy to press Iraqis to take responsibility at home, and restore America's security and standing in the world.

Barack Obama and Joe Biden's Plan

Judgment You Can Trust

In 2002, as the conventional thinking in Washington lined up with President Bush for war, Obama had the judgment and courage to speak out against going to war, and to warn of "an occupation of undetermined length, with undetermined costs, and undetermined consequences." He and Joe Biden are fully committed to ending the war in Iraq as president.

A Responsible, Phased Withdrawal

Barack Obama and Joe Biden believe we must be as careful getting out of Iraq as we were careless getting in. Immediately upon taking office, Obama will give his Secretary of Defense and military commanders a new mission in Iraq: ending the war. The removal of our troops will be responsible and phased, directed by military commanders on the ground and done in consultation with the Iraqi government. Military experts believe we can safely redeploy combat brigades from Iraq at a pace of 1 to 2 brigades a month that would remove them in 16 months. That would be the summer of 2010—more than 7 years after the war began.

Under the Obama-Biden plan, a residual force will remain in Iraq and in the region to conduct targeted counter-terrorism missions against al Qaeda in Iraq and to protect American diplomatic and civilian personnel. They will not build permanent bases in Iraq, but will continue efforts to train and support the Iraqi security forces as long as Iraqi leaders move toward political reconciliation and away from sectarianism.

Encouraging Political Accommodation

Barack Obama and Joe Biden believe that the U.S. must apply pressure on the Iraqi government to work toward real political accommodation. There is no military solution to Iraq's political differences, but the Bush Administration's blank check approach has failed to press Iraq's leaders to take responsibility for their future or to substantially spend their oil revenues on their own reconstruction.

Obama and Biden's plan offers the best prospect for lasting stability in Iraq. A phased withdrawal will encourage Iraqis to take the lead in securing their own country and making political compromises, while the responsible pace of redeployment called for by the Obama-Biden plan offers more than enough time for Iraqi leaders to get their own house in order. As our forces redeploy, Obama and Biden will make sure we engage representatives from all levels of Iraqi society—in and out of government—to forge compromises on oil revenue sharing, the equitable provision of services, federalism, the status of disputed territories, new elections, aid to displaced Iraqis, and the reform of Iraqi security forces.

Surging Diplomacy

Barack Obama and Joe Biden will launch an aggressive diplomatic effort to reach a comprehensive compact on the stability of Iraq and the region. This effort will include all of Iraq's neighbors—including Iran and Syria, as suggested by the bi-partisan Iraq Study Group Report. This compact will aim to secure Iraq's borders; keep neighboring countries from meddling inside Iraq; isolate al Qaeda; support reconciliation among Iraq's sectarian groups; and provide financial support for Iraq's reconstruction and development.

Preventing Humanitarian Crisis

Barack Obama and Joe Biden believe that America has both a moral obligation and a responsibility for security that demands we confront Iraq's humanitarian crisis—more than five million Iraqis are refugees or are displaced inside their own country. Obama and Biden will form an international working group to address this crisis. They will provide at least $2 billion to expand services to Iraqi refugees in neighboring countries, and ensure that Iraqis inside their own country can find sanctuary. Obama and Biden will also work with Iraqi authorities and the international community to hold the perpetrators of potential war crimes, crimes against humanity, and genocide accountable. They will reserve the right to intervene militarily, with our international partners, to suppress potential genocidal violence within Iraq.

The Status of Forces Agreement

Obama and Biden believe any Status of Forces Agreement, or any strategic framework agreement, should be negotiated in the context of a broader commitment by the U.S. to begin withdrawing its troops and forswearing permanent bases. Obama and Biden also believe that any security accord must be subject to Congressional approval. It is unacceptable that the Iraqi government will present the agreement to the Iraqi parliament for approval—yet the Bush administration will not do the same with the U.S. Congress. The Bush administration must submit the agreement to Congress or allow the next administration to negotiate an agreement that has bipartisan support here at home and makes absolutely clear that the U.S. will not maintain permanent bases in Iraq.

> **Source:** "Plan for Ending the War in Iraq," Organizing for America, http://www.barackobama.com/issues/iraq/index_campaign.php.

139. Agreement between the United States of America and the Republic of Iraq on the Withdrawal of United States Forces from Iraq and the Organization of Their Activities during Their Temporary Presence in Iraq, November 17, 2008 [Excerpts]

Introduction

United Nations (UN) Security Council Resolution 1790 of December 18, 2007, extended the mandate of coalition security forces in Iraq until the end of December 2008. As political pressure for withdrawal from Iraq mounted in the United States and a level of stability gradually came to prevail within Iraq following the U.S. troop surge of early 2007, American and Iraqi officials negotiated a formal agreement for the eventual withdrawal of all U.S. military forces. It was anticipated that this would take place at the end of 2011. Iraq's cabinet approved the agreement in November 2008, and the Iraqi parliament ratified it later that month. Under the agreement, it was expected that coalition troops would have withdrawn from Iraqi cities and into their bases by the end of June 2009. Coalition military personnel were subject to Iraqi jurisdiction if they committed serious crimes outside their own bases but not for offenses committed on base or in the course of their military duties, a provision that many Iraqis resented. It was expected that Iraqis would hold a referendum on the new agreement in mid-June 2009, which might lead to the withdrawal of forces as early as the middle of June 2010. There were also provisions for the extension of their period of stay should the Iraqi government request this on the grounds that domestic political instability required it. Some Iraqis, including the influential cleric Grand Ayatollah Sayyid Ali al-Sistani, argued that the pact placed Iraq in a position of neocolonial dependence, since for its duration the Iraqi government could not control the entry or exit of foreign forces and military equipment into Iraq. When Bush visited Baghdad in mid-December 2008 to sign the agreement and held a press conference with his hosts to mark the occasion, one Iraqi journalist made his displeasure with its terms clear by throwing his shoes at Bush, an action that made him an immediate hero throughout the Muslim world. Most Americans welcomed the agreement as tangible evidence that the situation in Iraq had improved and that all their country's troops would eventually be withdrawn. Eventually, a deadline of August 31, 2010, was set for the withdrawal of U.S. combat forces, though it was expected that a "transitional force" of 35,000 to 50,000 would still remain in place after that date, its mission restricted to training and assisting Iraqi units.

Primary Source

Preamble

The United States of America and the Republic of Iraq, referred to hereafter as "the Parties":

Recognizing the importance of: strengthening their joint security, contributing to world peace and stability, combating terrorism in Iraq, and cooperating in the security and defense spheres, thereby deterring aggression and threats against the sovereignty, security, and territorial integrity of Iraq and against its democratic, federal, and constitutional system;

Affirming that such cooperation is based on full respect for the sovereignty of each of them in accordance with the purposes and principles of the United Nations Charter;

Out of a desire to reach a common understanding that strengthens cooperation between them;

Without prejudice to Iraqi sovereignty over its territory, waters, and airspace; and

Pursuant to joint undertakings as two sovereign, independent, and coequal countries;

Have agreed to the following:

Article 1

Scope and Purpose

This Agreement shall determine the principal provisions and requirements that regulate the temporary presence, activities, and withdrawal of the United States Forces from Iraq.

[. . .]

Article 3

Laws

1. While conducting military operations pursuant to this Agreement, it is the duty of members of the United States Forces and of the civilian component to respect Iraqi laws, customs, traditions, and conventions and to refrain from any activities that are inconsistent with the letter and spirit of this Agreement. It is the duty of the United States to take all necessary measures for this purpose.

[. . .]

Article 4

Missions

1. The Government of Iraq requests the temporary assistance of the United States Forces for the purposes of supporting Iraq in its efforts to maintain security and stability in Iraq, including cooperation in the conduct of operations against al-Qaeda and other terrorist groups, outlaw groups, and remnants of the former regime.

2. All such military operations that are carried out pursuant to this Agreement shall be conducted with the agreement of the Government of Iraq. Such operations shall be fully coordinated with Iraqi authorities. The coordination of all such military operations shall be overseen by a Joint Military Operations Coordination Committee (JMOCC) to be established pursuant to this Agreement. Issues

regarding proposed military operations that cannot be resolved by the JMOCC shall be forwarded to the Joint Ministerial Committee.

3. All such operations shall be conducted with full respect for the Iraqi Constitution and the laws of Iraq. Execution of such operations shall not infringe upon the sovereignty of Iraq and its national interests, as defined by the Government of Iraq. It is the duty of the United States Forces to respect the laws, customs, and traditions of Iraq and applicable international law.

4. The Parties shall continue their efforts to cooperate to strengthen Iraq's security capabilities including, as may be mutually agreed, on training, equipping, supporting, supplying, and establishing and upgrading logistical systems, including transportation, housing, and supplies for Iraqi Security Forces.

5. The Parties retain the right to legitimate self defense within Iraq, as defined in applicable international law.

Article 5

Property Ownership

1. Iraq owns all buildings, non-relocatable structures, and assemblies connected to the soil that exist on agreed facilities and areas, including those that are used, constructed, altered, or improved by the United States Forces.

2. Upon their withdrawal, the United States Forces shall return to the Government of Iraq all the facilities and areas provided for the use of the combat forces of the United States, based on two lists. The first list of agreed facilities and areas shall take effect upon the entry into force of the Agreement. The second list shall take effect no later than June 30, 2009, the date for the withdrawal of combat forces from the cities, villages, and localities. The Government of Iraq may agree to allow the United States Forces the use of some necessary facilities for the purposes of this Agreement on withdrawal.

[...]

5. Upon the discovery of any historical or cultural site or finding any strategic resource in agreed facilities and areas, all works of construction, upgrading, or modification shall cease immediately and the Iraqi representatives at the Joint Committee shall be notified to determine appropriate steps in that regard.

6. The United States shall return agreed facilities and areas and any non-relocatable structures and assemblies on them that it had built, installed, or established during the term of this Agreement, according to mechanisms and priorities set forth by the Joint Committee. Such facilities and areas shall be handed over to the Government of Iraq free of any debts and financial burdens.

7. The United States Forces shall return to the Government of Iraq the agreed facilities and areas that have heritage, moral, and political significance and any non-relocatable structures and assemblies on them that it had built, installed, or established, according to mechanisms, priorities, and a time period as mutually agreed by the Joint Committee, free of any debts or financial burdens.

8. The United States Forces shall return the agreed facilities and areas to the Government of Iraq upon the expiration or termination of this Agreement, or earlier as mutually agreed by the Parties, or when such facilities are no longer required as determined by the JMOCC, free of any debts or financial burdens.

9. The United States Forces and United States contractors shall retain title to all equipment, materials, supplies, relocatable structures, and other movable property that was legitimately imported into or legitimately acquired within the territory of Iraq in connection with this Agreement.

Article 6

Use of Agreed Facilities and Areas

1. With full respect for the sovereignty of Iraq, and as part of exchanging views between the Parties pursuant to this Agreement, Iraq grants access and use of agreed facilities and areas to the United States Forces, United States contractors, United States contractor employees, and other individuals or entities as agreed upon by the Parties.

2. In accordance with this Agreement, Iraq authorizes the United States Forces to exercise within the agreed facilities and areas all rights and powers that may be necessary to establish, use, maintain, and secure such agreed facilities and areas. The Parties shall coordinate and cooperate regarding exercising these rights and powers in the agreed facilities and areas of joint use.

3. The United States Forces shall assume control of entry to agreed facilities and areas that have been provided for its exclusive use. The Parties shall coordinate the control of entry into agreed facilities and areas for joint use and in accordance with mechanisms set forth by the JMOCC. The Parties shall coordinate guard duties in areas adjacent to agreed facilities and areas through the JMOCC.

[...]

Article 9

Movement of Vehicles, Vessels, and Aircraft

1. With full respect for the relevant rules of land and maritime safety and movement, vessels and vehicles operated by or at the

time exclusively for the United States Forces may enter, exit, and move within the territory of Iraq for the purposes of implementing this Agreement. The JMOCC shall develop appropriate procedures and rules to facilitate and regulate the movement of vehicles.

2. With full respect for relevant rules of safety in aviation and air navigation, United States Government aircraft and civil aircraft that are at the time operating exclusively under a contract with the United States Department of Defense are authorized to over-fly, conduct airborne refueling exclusively for the purposes of implementing this Agreement over, and land and take off within, the territory of Iraq for the purposes of implementing this Agreement. The Iraqi authorities shall grant the aforementioned aircraft permission every year to land in and take off from Iraqi territory exclusively for the purposes of implementing this Agreement. United States Government aircraft and civil aircraft that are at the time operating exclusively under a contract with the United States Department of Defense, vessels, and vehicles shall not have any party boarding them without the consent of the authorities of the United States Forces. The Joint Sub-Committee concerned with this matter shall take appropriate action to facilitate the regulation of such traffic.

3. Surveillance and control over Iraqi airspace shall transfer to Iraqi authority immediately upon entry into force of this Agreement.

4. Iraq may request from the United States Forces temporary support for the Iraqi authorities in the mission of surveillance and control of Iraqi air space.

5. United States Government aircraft and civil aircraft that are at the time operating exclusively under contract to the United States Department of Defense shall not be subject to payment of any taxes, duties, fees, or similar charges, including overflight or navigation fees, landing, and parking fees at government airfields. Vehicles and vessels owned or operated by or at the time exclusively for the United States Forces shall not be subject to payment of any taxes, duties, fees, or similar charges, including for vessels at government ports. Such vehicles, vessels, and aircraft shall be free from registration requirements within Iraq.

6. The United States Forces shall pay fees for services requested and received.

[. . .]

Article 12

Jurisdiction

Recognizing Iraq's sovereign right to determine and enforce the rules of criminal and civil law in its territory, in light of Iraq's

request for temporary assistance from the United States Forces set forth in Article 4, and consistent with the duty of the members of the United States Forces and the civilian component to respect Iraqi laws, customs, traditions, and conventions, the Parties have agreed as follows:

Iraq shall have the primary right to exercise jurisdiction over members of the United States Forces and of the civilian component for the grave premeditated felonies enumerated pursuant to paragraph 8, when such crimes are committed outside agreed facilities and areas and outside duty status.

Iraq shall have the primary right to exercise jurisdiction over United States contractors and United States contractor employees.

The United States shall have the primary right to exercise jurisdiction over members of the United States Forces and of the civilian component for matters arising inside agreed facilities and areas; during duty status outside agreed facilities and areas; and in circumstances not covered by paragraph 1.

At the request of either Party, the Parties shall assist each other in the investigation of incidents and the collection and exchange of evidence to ensure the due course of justice.

Members of the United States Forces and of the civilian component arrested or detained by Iraqi authorities shall be notified immediately to United States Forces authorities and handed over to them within 24 hours from the time of detention or arrest. Where Iraq exercises jurisdiction pursuant to paragraph 1 of this Article, custody of an accused member of the United States Forces or of the civilian component shall reside with United States Forces authorities. United States Forces authorities shall make such accused persons available to the Iraqi authorities for purposes of investigation and trial.

The authorities of either Party may request the authorities of the other Party to waive its primary right to jurisdiction in a particular case. The Government of Iraq agrees to exercise jurisdiction under paragraph 1 above, only after it has determined and notifies the United States in writing within 21 days of the discovery of an alleged offense, that it is of particular importance that such jurisdiction be exercised.

7. Where the United States exercises jurisdiction pursuant to paragraph 3 of this Article, members of the United States Forces and of the civilian component shall be entitled to due process standards and protections pursuant to the Constitution and laws of the United States. Where the offense arising under paragraph 3 of this Article may involve a victim who is not a member of the United States Forces or of the civilian component, the Parties shall establish procedures through the Joint Committee to keep such persons

informed as appropriate of: the status of the investigation of the crime; the bringing of charges against a suspected offender; the scheduling of court proceedings and the results of plea negotiations; opportunity to be heard at public sentencing proceedings, and to confer with the attorney for the prosecution in the case; and, assistance with filing a claim under Article 21 of this Agreement. As mutually agreed by the Parties, United States Forces authorities shall seek to hold the trials of such cases inside Iraq. If the trial of such cases is to be conducted in the United States, efforts will be undertaken to facilitate the personal attendance of the victim at the trial.

8. Where Iraq exercises jurisdiction pursuant to paragraph 1 of this Article, members of the United States Forces and of the civilian component shall be entitled to due process standards and protections consistent with those available under United States and Iraqi law. The Joint Committee shall establish procedures and mechanisms for implementing this Article, including an enumeration of the grave premeditated felonies that are subject to paragraph 1 and procedures that meet such due process standards and protections. Any exercise of jurisdiction pursuant to paragraph 1 of this Article may proceed only in accordance with these procedures and mechanisms.

9. Pursuant to paragraphs 1 and 3 of this Article, United States Forces authorities shall certify whether an alleged offense arose during duty status. In those cases where Iraqi authorities believe the circumstances require a review of this determination, the Parties shall consult immediately through the Joint Committee, and United States Forces authorities shall take full account of the facts and circumstances and any information Iraqi authorities may present bearing on the determination by United States Forces authorities.

10. The Parties shall review the provisions of this Article every 6 months including by considering any proposed amendments to this Article taking into account the security situation in Iraq, the extent to which the United States Forces in Iraq are engaged in military operations, the growth and development of the Iraqi judicial system, and changes in United States and Iraqi law.

Article 13

Carrying Weapons and Apparel

Members of the United States Forces and of the civilian component may possess and carry weapons that are owned by the United States while in Iraq according to the authority granted to them under orders and according to their requirements and duties.

Members of the United States Forces may also wear uniforms during duty in Iraq.

[...]

Article 24

Withdrawal of the United States Forces from Iraq

Recognizing the performance and increasing capacity of the Iraqi Security Forces, the assumption of full security responsibility by those Forces, and based upon the strong relationship between the Parties, an agreement on the following has been reached:

1. All the United States Forces shall withdraw from all Iraqi territory no later than December 31, 2011.

2. All United States combat forces shall withdraw from Iraqi cities, villages, and localities no later than the time at which Iraqi Security Forces assume full responsibility for security in an Iraqi province, provided that such withdrawal is completed no later than June 30, 2009.

3. United States combat forces withdrawn pursuant to paragraph 2 above shall be stationed in the agreed facilities and areas outside cities, villages, and localities to be designated by the JMOCC before the date established in paragraph 2 above.

4. The United States recognizes the sovereign right of the Government of Iraq to request the departure of the United States Forces from Iraq at any time. The Government of Iraq recognizes the sovereign right of the United States to withdraw the United States Forces from Iraq at any time.

5. The Parties agree to establish mechanisms and arrangements to reduce the number of the United States Forces during the periods of time that have been determined, and they shall agree on the locations where the United States Forces will be present.

Article 25

Measures to Terminate the Application of Chapter VII to Iraq

Acknowledging the right of the Government of Iraq not to request renewal of the Chapter VII authorization for and mandate of the multinational forces contained in United Nations Security Council Resolution 1790 (2007) that ends on December 31, 2008;

Taking note of the letters to the UN Security Council from the Prime Minister of Iraq and the Secretary of State of the United States dated December 7 and December 10, 2007, respectively, which are annexed to Resolution 1790;

Taking note of section 3 of the Declaration of Principles for a Long-Term Relationship of Cooperation and Friendship, signed by the President of the United States and the Prime Minister of Iraq on November 26, 2007, which memorialized Iraq's call for extension of the above-mentioned mandate for a final period, to end not later than December 31, 2008:

Recognizing also the dramatic and positive developments in Iraq, and noting that the situation in Iraq is fundamentally different than that which existed when the UN Security Council adopted Resolution 661 in 1990, and in particular that the threat to international peace and security posed by the Government of Iraq no longer exists, the Parties affirm in this regard that with the termination on December 31, 2008 of the Chapter VII mandate and authorization for the multinational force contained in Resolution 1790, Iraq should return to the legal and international standing that it enjoyed prior to the adoption of UN Security Council Resolution 661 (1990), and that the United States shall use its best efforts to help Iraq take the steps necessary to achieve this by December 31, 2008.

Article 26

Iraqi Assets

1. To enable Iraq to continue to develop its national economy through the rehabilitation of its economic infrastructure, as well as providing necessary essential services to the Iraqi people, and to continue to safeguard Iraq's revenues from oil and gas and other Iraqi resources and its financial and economic assets located abroad, including the Development Fund for Iraq, the United States shall ensure maximum efforts to:

a. Support Iraq to obtain forgiveness of international debt resulting from the policies of the former regime.

b. Support Iraq to achieve a comprehensive and final resolution of outstanding reparation claims inherited from the previous regime, including compensation requirements imposed by the UN Security Council on Iraq.

2. Recognizing and understanding Iraq's concern with claims based on actions perpetrated by the former regime, the President of the United States has exercised his authority to protect from United States judicial process the Development Fund for Iraq and certain other property in which Iraq has an interest. The United States shall remain fully and actively engaged with the Government of Iraq with respect to continuation of such protections and with respect to such claims.

3. Consistent with a letter from the President of the United States to be sent to the Prime Minister of Iraq, the United States remains committed to assist Iraq in connection with its request that the UN Security Council extend the protections and other arrangements established in Resolution 1483 (2003) and Resolution 1546 (2003)

for petroleum, petroleum products, and natural gas originating in Iraq, proceeds and obligations from sale thereof, and the Development Fund for Iraq.

Article 27

Deterrence of Security Threats

In order to strengthen security and stability in Iraq and to contribute to the maintenance of international peace and stability, the Parties shall work actively to strengthen the political and military capabilities of the Republic of Iraq to deter threats against its sovereignty, political independence, territorial integrity, and its constitutional federal democratic system. To that end, the Parties agree as follows:

In the event of any external or internal threat or aggression against Iraq that would violate its sovereignty, political independence, or territorial integrity, waters, airspace, its democratic system or its elected institutions, and upon request by the Government of Iraq, the Parties shall immediately initiate strategic deliberations and, as may be mutually agreed, the United States shall take appropriate measures, including diplomatic, economic, or military measures, or any other measure, to deter such a threat.

The Parties agree to continue close cooperation in strengthening and maintaining military and security institutions and democratic political institutions in Iraq, including, as may be mutually agreed, cooperation in training, equipping, and arming the Iraqi Security Forces, in order to combat domestic and international terrorism and outlaw groups, upon request by the Government of Iraq.

Iraqi land, sea, and air shall not be used as a launching or transit point for attacks against other countries.

Article 28

The Green Zone

Upon entry into force of this Agreement the Government of Iraq shall have full responsibility for the Green Zone. The Government of Iraq may request from the United States Forces limited and temporary support for the Iraqi authorities in the mission of security for the Green Zone. Upon such request, relevant Iraqi authorities shall work jointly with the United States Forces authorities on security for the Green Zone during the period determined by the Government of Iraq.

Article 29

Implementing Mechanisms

Whenever the need arises, the Parties shall establish appropriate mechanisms for implementation of Articles of this Agreement, including those that do not contain specific implementation mechanisms.

Article 30

The Period for which the Agreement is Effective

1. This Agreement shall be effective for a period of three years, unless terminated sooner by either Party pursuant to paragraph 3 of this Article.

[...]

Source: "Agreement between the United States of America and the Republic of Iraq on the Withdrawal of United States Forces from Iraq and the Organization of Their Activities during Their Temporary Presence in Iraq," The White House, President George W. Bush, http://georgewbush-whitehouse.archives.gov/infocus/iraq/SE_SOFA.pdf.

140. President Barack Obama, Remarks at the State Department, January 22, 2009 [Excerpts]

Introduction

To liberals in the United States and around the world, Barack Obama's election as president seemed to promise a new era of American foreign policies that would be less unilateral, brash, and inhumane than those of former president George W. Bush's administration and more sensitive to concerns over human rights and internationally accepted standards of behavior. Two days after taking office, Obama switched his attention from the almost overwhelming domestic and global economic problems preoccupying him to focus on other international issues. In a visit to the State Department, he announced that from then on the United States would refrain from torturing suspects and close the infamous detention center at Guantánamo Bay in Cuba. Even though Obama did not renounce the extralegal rendition of terrorist suspects from other nations by U.S. operatives to third countries, where such individuals might be held indefinitely without trial and subjected to torture by non-Americans, Obama's new orders were a symbolic break with the Bush administration's readiness to sanction almost any extralegal activity in the name of antiterrorism. Obama stated his intention of moving forcefully to seek a solution of the perennial Israeli-Palestinian crisis, exacerbated in previous weeks as violence erupted between Israel and Hamas forces over Gaza. Moving from this immediate crisis, Obama expressed his determination to support efforts to eradicate the threat from fundamentalist Islamic forces in Afghanistan and also in neighboring Pakistan, which Taliban and Al Qaeda elements were using as a

base for military attacks on Afghanistan, destabilizing the fragile hold of civil authorities on the country. Shortly afterward, the White House announced that the administration was embarking on a full-scale strategy review for Afghanistan. Even before this was completed, in mid-February 2009 Obama decided to boost American forces in Afghanistan, already more than 50,000 strong, by dispatching an additional 12,000 combat troops and 5,000 support troops to Afghanistan by the early summer of 2009. This went some way toward meeting a request several months earlier by General David Kiernan, commander of U.S. forces in Afghanistan, for four more brigade combat teams and an additional aviation combat brigade. It was also evidence that Obama had been in earnest when making campaign pledges to devote more resources to Afghanistan if he was elected.

Primary Source

[...]

The inheritance of our young century demands a new era of American leadership. We must recognize that America's strength comes not just from the might of our arms or the scale of our wealth, but from our enduring values. And for the sake of our national security and the common aspirations of people around the globe, this era has to begin now.

This morning I signed three Executive orders. First, I can say without exception or equivocation that the United States will not torture. Second, we will close the Guantanamo Bay detention camp and determine how to deal with those who have been held there. And third, we will immediately undertake a comprehensive review to determine how to hold and try terrorism suspects to best protect our nation and the rule of law.

The world needs to understand that America will be unyielding in its defense of its security and relentless in its pursuit of those who would carry out terrorism or threaten the United States. And that's why, in this twilight struggle, we need a durable framework. The orders that I signed today should send an unmistakable signal that our actions in defense of liberty will be just as our cause, and that we the people will uphold our fundamental values as vigilantly as we protect our security. Once again, America's moral example must be the bedrock and the beacon of our global leadership.

We are confronted by extraordinary, complex, and interconnected global challenges: the war on terror, sectarian division, and the spread of deadly technology. We did not ask for the burden that history has asked us to bear, but Americans will bear it. We must bear it. Progress will not come quickly or easily, nor can we promise to right every single wrong around the world.

But we can pledge to use all elements of American power to protect our people and to promote our interests and ideals, starting with principled, focused, and sustained American diplomacy. . . .

It will be the policy of my administration to actively and aggressively seek a lasting peace between Israel and the Palestinians, as well as Israel and its Arab neighbors. To help us pursue these goals, Secretary Clinton and I have asked George Mitchell to serve as Special Envoy for Middle East Peace.

[. . .]

No one doubts the difficulty of the road ahead, and George outlined some of those difficulties. The tragic violence in Gaza and southern Israel offers a sobering reminder of the challenges at hand and the setbacks that will inevitably come.

It must also instill in us, though, a sense of urgency, as history shows us that strong and sustained American engagement can bridge divides and build the capacity that supports progress. And that is why we will be sending George to the region as soon as possible to help the parties ensure that the cease-fire that has been achieved is made durable and sustainable.

Let me be clear: America is committed to Israel's security, and we will always support Israel's right to defend itself against legitimate threats. For years, Hamas has launched thousands of rockets at innocent Israeli citizens. No democracy can tolerate such danger to its people, nor should the international community. And neither should the Palestinian people themselves, whose interests are only set back by acts of terror.

To be a genuine party to peace, the Quartet has made it clear that Hamas must meet clear conditions: recognize Israel's right to exist, renounce violence, and abide by past agreements.

Going forward, the outline for a durable cease-fire is clear. Hamas must end its rocket fire. Israel will complete the withdrawal of its forces from Gaza. The United States and our partners will support a credible anti-smuggling and interdiction regime so that Hamas cannot rearm.

Yesterday I spoke to President Mubarak and expressed my appreciation for the important role that Egypt played in achieving a cease-fire, and we look forward to Egypt's continued leadership and partnership in laying a foundation for a broader peace through a commitment to end smuggling from within its borders.

Now, just as the terror of rocket fire aimed at innocent Israelis is intolerable, so too is a future without hope for the Palestinians.

I was deeply concerned by the loss of Palestinian and Israeli life in recent days and by the substantial suffering and humanitarian needs in Gaza. Our hearts go out to Palestinian civilians who are in need of immediate food, clean water, and basic medical care, and who have faced suffocating poverty for far too long.

Now we must extend a hand of opportunity to those who seek peace. As part of a lasting cease-fire, Gaza's border crossings should be opened to allow the flow of aid and commerce, with an appropriate monitoring regime with the international and Palestinian Authority participating.

Relief efforts must be able to reach innocent Palestinians who depend on them. The United States will fully support an international donors conference to seek short-term humanitarian assistance and long-term reconstruction for the Palestinian economy. This assistance will be provided to, and guided by, the Palestinian Authority.

Lasting peace requires more than a long cease-fire. And that's why I will sustain an active commitment to seek two states living side by side in peace and security. Senator Mitchell will carry forward this commitment, as well as the effort to help Israel reach a broader peace with the Arab world that recognizes its rightful place in the community of nations.

I should add that the Arab Peace Initiative contains constructive elements that could help advance these efforts. Now is the time for Arab states to act on the initiatives promised by supporting the Palestinian Government under President Abbas and Prime Minister Fayyad, taking steps towards normalizing relations with Israel, and by standing up to extremism that threatens us all.

Jordan's constructive role in training Palestinian security forces and nurturing its relations with Israel provide a model for these efforts. And going forward, we must make it clear to all countries in the region that external support for terrorist organizations must stop.

Another urgent threat to global security is the deteriorating situation in Afghanistan and Pakistan. This is the central front in our enduring struggle against terrorism and extremism. There, as in the Middle East, we must understand that we cannot deal with our problems in isolation. There is no answer in Afghanistan that does not confront the Al Qaida and Taliban bases along the border, and there will be no lasting peace unless we expand spheres of opportunity for the people of Afghanistan and Pakistan. This is truly an international challenge of the highest order.

That's why Secretary Clinton and I are naming Ambassador Richard Holbrooke to be Special Representative for Afghanistan and

Pakistan. Ambassador Holbrooke is one of the most talented diplomats of his generation. Over several decades, he served on different continents and as an outstanding Ambassador to the United Nations. He has strengthened ties with our allies, tackled the toughest negotiations, and helped deliver a hard-earned peace as an architect of the Dayton Accords. He will help lead our effort to forge and implement a strategic and sustainable approach to this critical region.

The American people and the international community must understand that the situation is perilous and progress will take time. Violence is up dramatically in Afghanistan. A deadly insurgency has taken deep root. The opium trade is far and away the largest in the world. The Afghan Government has been unable to deliver basic services. Al Qaida and the Taliban strike from bases embedded in rugged, tribal terrain along the Pakistani border. And while we have yet to see another attack on our soil since 9/11, Al Qaida terrorists remain at large and remain plotting.

Going forward, we must set clear priorities in pursuit of achievable goals that contribute to our collective security. My administration is committed to refocusing attention and resources on Afghanistan and Pakistan and to spending those resources wisely. And that's why we are pursuing a careful review of our policy. We will seek stronger partnerships with the governments of the region, sustained cooperation with our NATO allies, deeper engagement with the Afghan and Pakistani people, and a comprehensive strategy to combat terror and extremism. We will provide the strategic guidance to meet our objectives. And we pledge to support the extraordinary Americans serving in Afghanistan, both military and civilian, with the resources that they need.

These appointments add to a team that will work with energy and purpose to meet the challenges of our time and to define a future of expanding security and opportunity. Difficult days lie ahead. As we ask more of ourselves, we will seek new partnerships and ask more of our friends, and more of people around the globe, because security in the 21st century is shared. But let there be no doubt about America's commitment to lead. We can no longer afford drift, and we can no long afford delay. Nor can we cede ground to those who seek destruction. A new era of American leadership is at hand, and the hard work has just begun.

[...]

Source: Barack Obama, "Remarks at the State Department, January 22, 2009," GPO Access, http://www.gpoaccess.gov/presdocs/2009/DCPD200900014.htm.

141. General David H. Petraeus, "The Future of the Alliance and the Mission in Afghanistan," Remarks for Panel Discussion, 45th Munich Security Conference, February 8, 2009 [Excerpts]

Introduction

As President Barack Obama settled into the Oval Office, he sought to implement the strategy, laid out during his campaign, of steadily withdrawing U.S. forces from Iraq while boosting the U.S. commitment to Afghanistan, where the military and political situation was widely considered precarious. In doing so, he turned for advice to General David H. Petraeus, regarded by most as the architect of the policies in Iraq that since the troop surge of early 2007 had brought greater stability to that country. In September 2008 Petraeus had become commander in chief of U.S. Central Command (CENTCOM), covering 20 countries and extending from Egypt to Pakistan. Policy makers hoped that Petraeus could repeat this accomplishment in Afghanistan. In a speech in Munich, Germany, in February 2009 Petraeus laid out his prescriptions for establishing comparable order in Afghanistan so that credible elections could be held in that country in August 2009. To do so would, in his view, demand an increased short-term military commitment by the United States and its allies to provide the improved security umbrella that he considered the necessary precondition for the implementation of internal political and economic reforms, including the elimination of corruption, designed to enhance the legitimacy of the existing Afghan government. Widely publicized and apparently well-founded allegations that the government of Hamid Karzai had practiced electoral fraud in the 2009 presidential contest and that close relatives of the president were implicated in narcotics trading and financial corruption did little to enhance its standing or credibility. In the first half of 2010 President Barack Obama deployed an additional 34,000 American troops in Afghanistan, in addition to close to 60,000 already in the country, to counter a growing Taliban threat. In late June 2010, with the military situation in Afghanistan nonetheless increasingly critical, well-authenticated media reports of complaints against Obama by General Stanley McChrystal, the U.S. commander in Afghanistan, caused the president to fire McChrystal and replace him with Petraeus. The hope was that Petraeus would prove as successful in winning over or eradicating Taliban opponents in Afghanistan as he had proved in waging counterinsurgency operations in Iraq.

Primary Source

[...]

This morning's topic is Afghanistan, which Secretary of Defense Gates recently described to the US Congress as posing "our greatest military challenge right now." As he noted, our fundamental objective in Afghanistan is to ensure that transnational terrorists are not able to reestablish the sanctuaries they enjoyed prior to 9/11. It was to eliminate such sanctuaries that we took action in Afghanistan in 2001. And preventing their reestablishment remains an imperative today—noting, to be sure, that achievement of that objective inevitably requires accomplishment of other interrelated tasks as well. . . .

Afghanistan has been a very tough endeavor. Certainly, there have been important achievements there over the past seven years—agreement on a constitution, elections, and establishment of a government; increased access to education, health care, media, and telecommunications; construction of a significant number of infrastructure projects; development of the Afghan National Army; and others.

But in recent years the resurgence of the Taliban and Al Qaeda has led to an increase in violence, especially in the southern and eastern parts of the country. Numerous other challenges have emerged as well, among them: difficulties in the development of governmental institutions that achieve legitimacy in the eyes of the Afghan people; corruption; expansion—until last year—of poppy production and the illegal narcotics industry; and difficulties in the establishment of the Afghan police.

In fact, there has been nothing easy about Afghanistan. And, as Senator Lieberman observed in a recent speech to the Brookings Institution, "Reversing Afghanistan's slide into insecurity will not come quickly, easily, or cheaply." Similarly, Secretary Gates told Congress, "This will undoubtedly be a long and difficult fight." I agree. In fact, I think it is important to be clear eyed about the challenges that lie ahead, while also remembering the importance of our objectives in Afghanistan and the importance of the opportunity that exists if we all intensify our efforts and work together to achieve those objectives.

Many observers have noted that there are no purely military solutions in Afghanistan. That is correct. Nonetheless, military action, while not sufficient by itself, is absolutely necessary, for security provides the essential foundation for the achievement of progress in all the other so-called lines of operation—recognizing, of course, that progress in other areas made possible by security improvements typically contributes to further progress in the security arena—creating an upward spiral in which improvements in one area reinforce progress in another.

Arresting and then reversing the downward spiral in security in Afghanistan thus will require not just additional military forces, but also more civilian contributions, greater unity of effort between civilian and military elements and with our Afghan partners, and a comprehensive approach, as well as sustained commitment and a strategy that addresses the situations in neighboring countries.

This morning, I'd like to describe in very general terms the resource requirements that are under discussion in Washington and various other national capitals. Then I'll describe briefly a few of the ideas that helped us in Iraq and that, properly adapted for Afghanistan, can help guide GEN McKiernan and ISAF.

THE NEED FOR MORE FORCES, ENABLERS, AND TRAINERS

In recent months, our President and many others have highlighted the need for additional forces in Afghanistan to reverse the downward spiral in security, help Afghan forces provide security for the elections on August 20th, and enable progress in the tasks essential to achievement of our objectives. Indeed, as has been announced in recent months, more US forces are entering operations as part of ISAF in Afghanistan now, more have been ordered to deploy, and the deployment of others is under consideration. Beyond that, the number of Afghan soldiers to be trained and equipped has been increased, and many of the other troop contributing nations will deploy additional forces, as well, with a number of commitments under discussion. And I would be remiss if I did not ask individual countries to examine what forces and other contributions they can provide as ISAF intensifies its efforts in preparation for the elections in August.

It is, of course not just additional combat forces that are required. ISAF also needs more so-called enablers to support the effort in Afghanistan—more intelligence, surveillance, and reconnaissance platforms and the connectivity to exploit the capabilities they bring; more military police, engineers, and logistics elements; additional special operations forces and civil affairs units; more lift and attack helicopters and fixed wing aircraft; additional air medevac assets; increases in information operations capabilities; and so on. Also required are more Embedded Training Teams, Operational Mentoring and Liaison Teams, and Police Mentoring Teams, all elements that are essential to building capable Afghan National Security Forces. . . .

As Senator Lieberman highlighted in his Brookings speech, a surge in civilian capacity is needed to match the increase in military forces in order to field adequate numbers of provincial reconstruction teams and other civilian elements—teams and personnel that are essential to help our Afghan partners expand their capabilities in key governmental areas, to support basic economic development, and to assist in the development of various important aspects of the rule of law, including initiatives to support the development of police and various judicial initiatives.

It is also essential, of course, that sufficient financial resources be provided for the effort in Afghanistan. It is hugely important that nations deliver on pledges of economic development assistance, that the Afghan National Army and Law and Order Trust Funds be fully financed, that support be maintained for the Afghan Reconstruction Trust Fund, and that resources continue to be provided for the projects conducted by our military units and PRTs at local levels. . . .

Of course, just more troops, civilians, dollars and Euros won't be enough. As students of history, we're keenly aware that Afghanistan has, over the years, been known as the graveyard of empires. It is, after all, a country that has never taken kindly to outsiders bent on conquering it. We cannot take that history lightly. And our awareness of it should caution us to recognize that, while additional forces are essential, their effectiveness will depend on how they are employed, as that, in turn, will determine how they are seen by the Afghan population.

COUNTERINSURGENCY FOR AFGHANISTAN

What I'd like to discuss next, then, are some of the concepts that our commanders have in mind as plans are refined to employ additional forces. . . . So here are some of those ideas:

First and foremost, our forces and those of our Afghan partners have to strive to secure and serve the population. We have to recognize that the Afghan people are the decisive "terrain." And together with our Afghan partners, we have to work to provide the people security, to give them respect, to gain their support, and to facilitate the provision of basic services, the development of the Afghan Security Forces in the area, the promotion of local economic development, and the establishment of governance that includes links to the traditional leaders in society and is viewed as legitimate in the eyes of the people.

Securing and serving the people requires that our forces be good neighbors. While it may be less culturally acceptable to live among the people in certain parts of Afghanistan than it was in Iraq, it is necessary to locate Afghan and ISAF forces where they can establish a persistent security presence. You can't commute to work in the conduct of counterinsurgency operations. Positioning outposts and patrol bases, then, requires careful thought, consultation with local leaders, and the establishment of good local relationships to be effective.

Positioning near those we and our Afghan partners are helping to secure also enables us to understand the neighborhood. A nuanced appreciation of the local situation is essential. Leaders and troopers have to understand the tribal structures, the power brokers, the good guys and the bad guys, local cultures and history, and how systems are supposed to work and do work. This

requires listening and being respectful of local elders and mullahs, and farmers and shopkeepers—and it also requires, of course, many cups of tea.

It is also essential that we achieve unity of effort, that we coordinate and synchronize the actions of all ISAF and Afghan forces—and those of our Pakistani partners across the border—and that we do the same with the actions of our embassy and international partners, our Afghan counterparts, local governmental leaders, and international and non-governmental organizations. Working to a common purpose is essential in the conduct of counterinsurgency operations.

We also, in support of and in coordination with our Afghan partners, need to help promote local reconciliation, although this has to be done very carefully and in accordance with the principles established in the Afghan Constitution. In concert with and in support of our Afghan partners, we need to identify and separate the "irreconcilables" from the "reconcilables," striving to create the conditions that can make the reconcilables part of the solution, even as we kill, capture, or drive out the irreconcilables. In fact, programs already exist in this area and careful application of them will be essential in the effort to fracture and break off elements of the insurgency in order to get various groups to put down their weapons and support the legitimate constitution of Afghanistan.

Having said that, we must pursue the enemy relentlessly and tenaciously. True irreconcilables, again, must be killed, captured, or driven out of the area. And we cannot shrink from that any more than we can shrink from being willing to support Afghan reconciliation with those elements that show a willingness to reject the insurgents and help Afghan and ISAF forces.

To ensure that the gains achieved endure, ISAF and Afghan forces have to hold areas that have been cleared. Once we fight to clear and secure an area, we must ensure that it is retained. The people—and local security forces—need to know that we will not abandon them. Additionally, we should look for ways to give local citizens a stake in the success of the local security effort and in the success of the new Afghanistan more broadly as well. To this end, a reformed, capable Afghan National Police force—with the necessary support from the international community and the alliance—is imperative to ensuring the ability to protect the population. And the new Afghan Population Protection Program announced by MOI Atmar holds considerable promise and deserves our support as well.

On a related note, to help increase the legitimacy of the Afghan government, we need to help our Afghan partners give the people a reason to support the government and their local authorities. This includes helping enable Afghan solutions to Afghan problems. And on a related note, given the importance of Afghan solutions and governance being viewed as legitimate by the people and in view of allegations of corruption, such efforts likely should feature support for what might be called an "Afghan accountability offensive" as well. That will be an important effort.

In all that we do as we perform various missions, we need to live our values. While our forces should not hesitate to engage and destroy an enemy, our troopers must also stay true to the values we hold dear. This is, after all, an important element that distinguishes us from the enemy, and it manifests itself in many ways, including making determined efforts to reduce to the absolute minimum civilian casualties—an effort furthered significantly by the tactical direction and partnering initiatives developed by GEN McKiernan with our Afghan counterparts.

We also must strive to be first with the truth. We need to beat the insurgents and extremists to the headlines and to pre-empt rumors. We can do that by getting accurate information to the chain of command, to our Afghan partners, and to the press as soon as is possible. Integrity is critical to this fight. Thus, when situations are bad, we should freely acknowledge that fact and avoid temptations to spin. Rather, we should describe the setbacks and failures we suffer and then state what we've learned from them and how we'll adjust to reduce the chances of similar events in the future.

Finally, we always must strive to learn and adapt. The situation in Afghanistan has changed significantly in the past several years and it continues to evolve. This makes it incumbent on us to assess the situation continually and to adjust our plans, operations, and tactics as required. We should share good ideas and best practices, but we also should never forget that what works in an area today may not work there tomorrow, and that what works in one area may not work in another.

IT WILL GET HARDER BEFORE IT GETS EASIER

In conclusion, allow me to reiterate the key points I've sought to make. We have a hugely important interest in ensuring that Afghanistan does not once again become a sanctuary for transnational terrorists. Achieving that core objective, in turn, requires the accomplishment of several other significant tasks. Although there have been impressive achievements in Afghanistan since 2001, the security situation has deteriorated markedly in certain areas in the past two years. Reversing that trend is necessary to improve security for the population, to permit the conduct of free and fair elections in August, and to enable progress in other important areas. Achieving security improvements will require more ISAF and Afghan security forces of all types—combat, combat support, logistics, trainers and advisors, special operations, and so on. Some additional forces are already deploying, further increases have been ordered or pledged, and more are under discussion. To be effective, the additional military forces

will need to be employed in accordance with counterinsurgency concepts applied by leaders who have a nuanced understanding of their areas of operation. And to complement and capitalize on the increased military resources, more civilian assets, adequate financial resources, close civil-military cooperation, and a comprehensive approach that encompasses regional states will be necessary. None of this will be easy. Indeed, as Vice President Biden observed recently, Afghanistan likely will get harder before it gets easier. And sustained progress will require sustained commitment. But, again, our objectives are of enormous importance, a significant opportunity is at hand, and we all need to summon the will and the resources necessary to make the most of it....

Source: Gen. David H. Petraeus, "The Future of the Alliance and the Mission in Afghanistan," United States Central Command, http://www.centcom.mil/from-the-commander/commanders-remarks-at-45th-munich-security-conference.

142. President Barack Obama, Address at Cairo University, June 4, 2009 [Excerpts]

Introduction

During his presidential campaign, Barack Obama stated his intention, if he was elected, of reaching out to the Muslim world in a spirit of conciliation and partnership. In his early months in office the new president was preoccupied with immediate problems. In early June 2009 at Cairo University in Egypt, Obama finally delivered a major and much-anticipated comprehensive address on relations between the United States and the Muslim world.

Primary Source

Remarks by the President on a New Beginning

Cairo University
Cairo, Egypt

PRESIDENT OBAMA: . . . I am honored to be in the timeless city of Cairo, and to be hosted by two remarkable institutions. For over a thousand years, Al-Azhar has stood as a beacon of Islamic learning; and for over a century, Cairo University has been a source of Egypt's advancement. And together, you represent the harmony between tradition and progress. . . .

We meet at a time of great tension between the United States and Muslims around the world—tension rooted in historical forces that go beyond any current policy debate. The relationship between Islam and the West includes centuries of coexistence and cooperation, but also conflict and religious wars. More recently, tension has been fed by colonialism that denied rights and opportunities to many Muslims, and a Cold War in which Muslim-majority countries were too often treated as proxies without regard to their own aspirations. Moreover, the sweeping change brought by modernity and globalization led many Muslims to view the West as hostile to the traditions of Islam.

Violent extremists have exploited these tensions in a small but potent minority of Muslims. The attacks of September 11, 2001 and the continued efforts of these extremists to engage in violence against civilians has led some in my country to view Islam as inevitably hostile not only to America and Western countries, but also to human rights. All this has bred more fear and more mistrust.

So long as our relationship is defined by our differences, we will empower those who sow hatred rather than peace, those who promote conflict rather than the cooperation that can help all of our people achieve justice and prosperity. And this cycle of suspicion and discord must end.

I've come here to Cairo to seek a new beginning between the United States and Muslims around the world, one based on mutual interest and mutual respect, and one based upon the truth that America and Islam are not exclusive and need not be in competition. Instead, they overlap, and share common principles—principles of justice and progress; tolerance and the dignity of all human beings.

I do so recognizing that change cannot happen overnight. I know there's been a lot of publicity about this speech, but no single speech can eradicate years of mistrust, nor can I answer in the time that I have this afternoon all the complex questions that brought us to this point. But I am convinced that in order to move forward, we must say openly to each other the things we hold in our hearts and that too often are said only behind closed doors. . . . There must be a sustained effort to listen to each other; to learn from each other; to respect one another; and to seek common ground. As the Holy Koran tells us, "Be conscious of God and speak always the truth." [Applause.] That is what I will try to do today—to speak the truth as best I can, humbled by the task before us, and firm in my belief that the interests we share as human beings are far more powerful than the forces that drive us apart.

Now part of this conviction is rooted in my own experience. I'm a Christian, but my father came from a Kenyan family that includes generations of Muslims. As a boy, I spent several years in Indonesia and heard the call of the azaan at the break of dawn and at the fall of dusk. As a young man, I worked in Chicago communities where many found dignity and peace in their Muslim faith.

As a student of history, I also know civilization's debt to Islam. It was Islam—at places like Al-Azhar—that carried the light of learning through so many centuries, paving the way for Europe's Renaissance and Enlightenment. It was innovation in Muslim communities—[applause]—it was innovation in Muslim communities that developed the order of algebra; our magnetic compass and tools of navigation; our mastery of pens and printing; our understanding of how disease spreads and how it can be healed. Islamic culture has given us majestic arches and soaring spires; timeless poetry and cherished music; elegant calligraphy and places of peaceful contemplation. And throughout history, Islam has demonstrated through words and deeds the possibilities of religious tolerance and racial equality. [Applause.]

I also know that Islam has always been a part of America's story. The first nation to recognize my country was Morocco. In signing the Treaty of Tripoli in 1796, our second President, John Adams, wrote, "The United States has in itself no character of enmity against the laws, religion or tranquility of Muslims." And since our founding, American Muslims have enriched the United States. They have fought in our wars, they have served in our government, they have stood for civil rights, they have started businesses, they have taught at our universities, they've excelled in our sports arenas, they've won Nobel Prizes, built our tallest building, and lit the Olympic Torch. And when the first Muslim American was recently elected to Congress, he took the oath to defend our Constitution using the same Holy Koran that one of our Founding Fathers—Thomas Jefferson—kept in his personal library. [Applause.]

So I have known Islam on three continents before coming to the region where it was first revealed. That experience guides my conviction that partnership between America and Islam must be based on what Islam is, not what it isn't. And I consider it part of my responsibility as President of the United States to fight against negative stereotypes of Islam wherever they appear. [Applause.]

But that same principle must apply to Muslim perceptions of America. [Applause.] Just as Muslims do not fit a crude stereotype, America is not the crude stereotype of a self-interested empire. The United States has been one of the greatest sources of progress that the world has ever known. We were born out of revolution against an empire. We were founded upon the ideal that all are created equal, and we have shed blood and struggled for centuries to give meaning to those words—within our borders, and around the world. We are shaped by every culture, drawn from every end of the Earth, and dedicated to a simple concept: E pluribus unum—"Out of many, one."

Now, much has been made of the fact that an African American with the name Barack Hussein Obama could be elected President. [Applause.] But my personal story is not so unique. The dream of opportunity for all people has not come true for everyone in America, but its promise exists for all who come to our shores—and that includes nearly 7 million American Muslims in our country today who, by the way, enjoy incomes and educational levels that are higher than the American average. [Applause.]

Moreover, freedom in America is indivisible from the freedom to practice one's religion. That is why there is a mosque in every state in our union, and over 1,200 mosques within our borders. That's why the United States government has gone to court to protect the right of women and girls to wear the hijab and to punish those who would deny it. [Applause.]

So let there be no doubt: Islam is a part of America. And I believe that America holds within her the truth that regardless of race, religion, or station in life, all of us share common aspirations—to live in peace and security; to get an education and to work with dignity; to love our families, our communities, and our God. These things we share. This is the hope of all humanity.

Of course, recognizing our common humanity is only the beginning of our task. Words alone cannot meet the needs of our people. These needs will be met only if we act boldly in the years ahead; and if we understand that the challenges we face are shared, and our failure to meet them will hurt us all.

[. . .]

Now, that does not mean we should ignore sources of tension. Indeed, it suggests the opposite: We must face these tensions squarely. And so in that spirit, let me speak as clearly and as plainly as I can about some specific issues that I believe we must finally confront together.

The first issue that we have to confront is violent extremism in all of its forms.

In Ankara, I made clear that America is not—and never will be—at war with Islam. [Applause.] We will, however, relentlessly confront violent extremists who pose a grave threat to our security—because we reject the same thing that people of all faiths reject: the killing of innocent men, women, and children. And it is my first duty as President to protect the American people.

The situation in Afghanistan demonstrates America's goals, and our need to work together. Over seven years ago, the United States pursued al Qaeda and the Taliban with broad international support. We did not go by choice; we went because of necessity. I'm aware that there's still some who would question or even justify the events of 9/11. But let us be clear: Al Qaeda killed nearly 3,000 people on that day. The victims were innocent men, women and children from America and many other nations who had done nothing to harm anybody. And yet al Qaeda chose to ruthlessly murder these people, claimed credit for the attack, and even now states their determination to kill on a massive scale. They have affiliates

in many countries and are trying to expand their reach. These are not opinions to be debated; these are facts to be dealt with.

Now, make no mistake: We do not want to keep our troops in Afghanistan. We see no military—we seek no military bases there. It is agonizing for America to lose our young men and women. It is costly and politically difficult to continue this conflict. We would gladly bring every single one of our troops home if we could be confident that there were not violent extremists in Afghanistan and now Pakistan determined to kill as many Americans as they possibly can. But that is not yet the case.

And that's why we're partnering with a coalition of 46 countries. And despite the costs involved, America's commitment will not weaken. Indeed, none of us should tolerate these extremists. They have killed in many countries. They have killed people of different faiths—but more than any other, they have killed Muslims. Their actions are irreconcilable with the rights of human beings, the progress of nations, and with Islam. The Holy Koran teaches that whoever kills an innocent is as—it is as if he has killed all mankind. [Applause.] And the Holy Koran also says whoever saves a person, it is as if he has saved all mankind. [Applause.] The enduring faith of over a billion people is so much bigger than the narrow hatred of a few. Islam is not part of the problem in combating violent extremism—it is an important part of promoting peace.

Now, we also know that military power alone is not going to solve the problems in Afghanistan and Pakistan. That's why we plan to invest $1.5 billion each year over the next five years to partner with Pakistanis to build schools and hospitals, roads and businesses, and hundreds of millions to help those who've been displaced. That's why we are providing more than $2.8 billion to help Afghans develop their economy and deliver services that people depend on.

Let me also address the issue of Iraq. Unlike Afghanistan, Iraq was a war of choice that provoked strong differences in my country and around the world. Although I believe that the Iraqi people are ultimately better off without the tyranny of Saddam Hussein, I also believe that events in Iraq have reminded America of the need to use diplomacy and build international consensus to resolve our problems whenever possible. . . .

Today, America has a dual responsibility: to help Iraq forge a better future—and to leave Iraq to Iraqis. And I have made it clear to the Iraqi people—[applause]—I have made it clear to the Iraqi people that we pursue no bases, and no claim on their territory or resources. Iraq's sovereignty is its own. And that's why I ordered the removal of our combat brigades by next August. That is why we will honor our agreement with Iraq's democratically elected government to remove combat troops from Iraqi cities by July, and to remove all of our troops from Iraq by 2012. [Applause.] We will help Iraq train its security forces and develop its economy. But we will support a secure and united Iraq as a partner, and never as a patron.

And finally, just as America can never tolerate violence by extremists, we must never alter or forget our principles. Nine-eleven was an enormous trauma to our country. The fear and anger that it provoked was understandable, but in some cases, it led us to act contrary to our traditions and our ideals. We are taking concrete actions to change course. I have unequivocally prohibited the use of torture by the United States, and I have ordered the prison at Guantanamo Bay closed by early next year. [Applause.]

So America will defend itself, respectful of the sovereignty of nations and the rule of law. And we will do so in partnership with Muslim communities which are also threatened. The sooner the extremists are isolated and unwelcome in Muslim communities, the sooner we will all be safer.

The second major source of tension that we need to discuss is the situation between Israelis, Palestinians and the Arab world.

America's strong bonds with Israel are well known. This bond is unbreakable. It is based upon cultural and historical ties, and the recognition that the aspiration for a Jewish homeland is rooted in a tragic history that cannot be denied.

Around the world, the Jewish people were persecuted for centuries, and anti-Semitism in Europe culminated in an unprecedented Holocaust. Tomorrow, I will visit Buchenwald, which was part of a network of camps where Jews were enslaved, tortured, shot and gassed to death by the Third Reich. Six million Jews were killed—more than the entire Jewish population of Israel today. Denying that fact is baseless, it is ignorant, and it is hateful. Threatening Israel with destruction—or repeating vile stereotypes about Jews—is deeply wrong, and only serves to evoke in the minds of Israelis this most painful of memories while preventing the peace that the people of this region deserve.

On the other hand, it is also undeniable that the Palestinian people—Muslims and Christians—have suffered in pursuit of a homeland. For more than 60 years they've endured the pain of dislocation. Many wait in refugee camps in the West Bank, Gaza, and neighboring lands for a life of peace and security that they have never been able to lead. They endure the daily humiliations—large and small—that come with occupation. So let there be no doubt: The situation for the Palestinian people is intolerable. And America will not turn our backs on the legitimate Palestinian aspiration for dignity, opportunity, and a state of their own. [Applause.]

For decades then, there has been a stalemate: two peoples with legitimate aspirations, each with a painful history that makes compromise elusive. It's easy to point fingers—for Palestinians to point to the displacement brought about by Israel's founding, and for Israelis to point to the constant hostility and attacks throughout its history from within its borders as well as beyond. But if we see this conflict only from one side or the other, then we will be blind to the truth: The only resolution is for the aspirations of both sides to be met through two states, where Israelis and Palestinians each live in peace and security. [Applause.]

That is in Israel's interest, Palestine's interest, America's interest, and the world's interest. And that is why I intend to personally pursue this outcome with all the patience and dedication that the task requires. [Applause.] The obligations—the obligations that the parties have agreed to under the road map are clear. For peace to come, it is time for them—and all of us—to live up to our responsibilities.

Palestinians must abandon violence. Resistance through violence and killing is wrong and it does not succeed. For centuries, black people in America suffered the lash of the whip as slaves and the humiliation of segregation. But it was not violence that won full and equal rights. It was a peaceful and determined insistence upon the ideals at the center of America's founding. This same story can be told by people from South Africa to South Asia; from Eastern Europe to Indonesia. It's a story with a simple truth: that violence is a dead end. It is a sign neither of courage nor power to shoot rockets at sleeping children, or to blow up old women on a bus. That's not how moral authority is claimed; that's how it is surrendered.

Now is the time for Palestinians to focus on what they can build. The Palestinian Authority must develop its capacity to govern, with institutions that serve the needs of its people. Hamas does have support among some Palestinians, but they also have to recognize they have responsibilities. To play a role in fulfilling Palestinian aspirations, to unify the Palestinian people, Hamas must put an end to violence, recognize past agreements, recognize Israel's right to exist.

At the same time, Israelis must acknowledge that just as Israel's right to exist cannot be denied, neither can Palestine's. The United States does not accept the legitimacy of continued Israeli settlements. [Applause.] This construction violates previous agreements and undermines efforts to achieve peace. It is time for these settlements to stop. [Applause.]

And Israel must also live up to its obligation to ensure that Palestinians can live and work and develop their society. Just as it devastates Palestinian families, the continuing humanitarian crisis in Gaza does not serve Israel's security; neither does the continuing lack of opportunity in the West Bank. Progress in the daily lives of the Palestinian people must be a critical part of a road to peace, and Israel must take concrete steps to enable such progress.

And finally, the Arab states must recognize that the Arab Peace Initiative was an important beginning, but not the end of their responsibilities. The Arab-Israeli conflict should no longer be used to distract the people of Arab nations from other problems. Instead, it must be a cause for action to help the Palestinian people develop the institutions that will sustain their state, to recognize Israel's legitimacy, and to choose progress over a self-defeating focus on the past.

America will align our policies with those who pursue peace, and we will say in public what we say in private to Israelis and Palestinians and Arabs. [Applause.] We cannot impose peace. But privately, many Muslims recognize that Israel will not go away. Likewise, many Israelis recognize the need for a Palestinian state. It is time for us to act on what everyone knows to be true.

Too many tears have been shed. Too much blood has been shed. All of us have a responsibility to work for the day when the mothers of Israelis and Palestinians can see their children grow up without fear; when the Holy Land of the three great faiths is the place of peace that God intended it to be; when Jerusalem is a secure and lasting home for Jews and Christians and Muslims, and a place for all of the children of Abraham to mingle peacefully together as in the story of Isra—[applause]—as in the story of Isra, when Moses, Jesus, and Mohammed, peace be upon them, joined in prayer. [Applause.]

The third source of tension is our shared interest in the rights and responsibilities of nations on nuclear weapons.

This issue has been a source of tension between the United States and the Islamic Republic of Iran. For many years, Iran has defined itself in part by its opposition to my country, and there is in fact a tumultuous history between us. In the middle of the Cold War, the United States played a role in the overthrow of a democratically elected Iranian government. Since the Islamic Revolution, Iran has played a role in acts of hostage-taking and violence against U.S. troops and civilians. This history is well known. Rather than remain trapped in the past, I've made it clear to Iran's leaders and people that my country is prepared to move forward. The question now is not what Iran is against, but rather what future it wants to build.

I recognize it will be hard to overcome decades of mistrust, but we will proceed with courage, rectitude, and resolve. There will be many issues to discuss between our two countries, and we are willing to move forward without preconditions on the basis of mutual respect. But it is clear to all concerned that when it comes to nuclear weapons, we have reached a decisive point. This is not simply about America's interests. It's about preventing a nuclear arms race in the Middle East that could lead this region and the world down a hugely dangerous path.

I understand those who protest that some countries have weapons that others do not. No single nation should pick and choose which nation holds nuclear weapons. And that's why I strongly reaffirmed America's commitment to seek a world in which no nations hold nuclear weapons. [Applause.] And any nation—including Iran—should have the right to access peaceful nuclear power if it complies with its responsibilities under the nuclear Non-Proliferation Treaty. That commitment is at the core of the treaty, and it must be kept for all who fully abide by it. And I'm hopeful that all countries in the region can share in this goal.

The fourth issue that I will address is democracy. [Applause.]

I know—I know there has been controversy about the promotion of democracy in recent years, and much of this controversy is connected to the war in Iraq. So let me be clear: No system of government can or should be imposed upon one nation by any other.

That does not lessen my commitment, however, to governments that reflect the will of the people. Each nation gives life to this principle in its own way, grounded in the traditions of its own people. America does not presume to know what is best for everyone, just as we would not presume to pick the outcome of a peaceful election. But I do have an unyielding belief that all people yearn for certain things: the ability to speak your mind and have a say in how you are governed; confidence in the rule of law and the equal administration of justice; government that is transparent and doesn't steal from the people; the freedom to live as you choose. These are not just American ideas; they are human rights. And that is why we will support them everywhere. [Applause.]

Now, there is no straight line to realize this promise. But this much is clear: Governments that protect these rights are ultimately more stable, successful and secure. Suppressing ideas never succeeds in making them go away. America respects the right of all peaceful and law-abiding voices to be heard around the world, even if we disagree with them. And we will welcome all elected, peaceful governments—provided they govern with respect for all their people.

This last point is important because there are some who advocate democracy only when they're out of power; once in power, they are ruthless in suppressing the rights of others. [Applause.] So no matter where it takes hold, government of the people and by the people sets a single standard for all who would hold power: You must maintain your power through consent, not coercion; you must respect the rights of minorities, and participate with a spirit of tolerance and compromise; you must place the interests of your people and the legitimate workings of the political process above your party. Without these ingredients, elections alone do not make true democracy.

The fifth issue that we must address together is religious freedom.

Islam has a proud tradition of tolerance. We see it in the history of Andalusia and Cordoba during the Inquisition. I saw it firsthand as a child in Indonesia, where devout Christians worshiped freely in an overwhelmingly Muslim country. That is the spirit we need today. People in every country should be free to choose and live their faith based upon the persuasion of the mind and the heart and the soul. This tolerance is essential for religion to thrive, but it's being challenged in many different ways.

Among some Muslims, there's a disturbing tendency to measure one's own faith by the rejection of somebody else's faith. The richness of religious diversity must be upheld—whether it is for Maronites in Lebanon or the Copts in Egypt. [Applause.] And if we are being honest, fault lines must be closed among Muslims, as well, as the divisions between Sunni and Shia have led to tragic violence, particularly in Iraq.

Freedom of religion is central to the ability of peoples to live together. We must always examine the ways in which we protect it. For instance, in the United States, rules on charitable giving have made it harder for Muslims to fulfill their religious obligation. That's why I'm committed to working with American Muslims to ensure that they can fulfill zakat.

Likewise, it is important for Western countries to avoid impeding Muslim citizens from practicing religion as they see fit—for instance, by dictating what clothes a Muslim woman should wear. We can't disguise hostility towards any religion behind the pretence of liberalism.

In fact, faith should bring us together. And that's why we're forging service projects in America to bring together Christians, Muslims, and Jews. That's why we welcome efforts like Saudi Arabian King Abdullah's interfaith dialogue and Turkey's leadership in the Alliance of Civilizations. Around the world, we can turn dialogue into interfaith service, so bridges between peoples lead to action— whether it is combating malaria in Africa, or providing relief after a natural disaster.

The sixth issue—the sixth issue that I want to address is women's rights. [Applause.] I know—I know—and you can tell from this audience, that there is a healthy debate about this issue. I reject the view of some in the West that a woman who chooses to cover her hair is somehow less equal, but I do believe that a woman who is denied an education is denied equality. [Applause.] And it is no coincidence that countries where women are well educated are far more likely to be prosperous.

Now, let me be clear: Issues of women's equality are by no means simply an issue for Islam. In Turkey, Pakistan, Bangladesh, Indonesia, we've seen Muslim-majority countries elect a woman to

lead. Meanwhile, the struggle for women's equality continues in many aspects of American life, and in countries around the world.

I am convinced that our daughters can contribute just as much to society as our sons. [Applause.] Our common prosperity will be advanced by allowing all humanity—men and women—to reach their full potential. I do not believe that women must make the same choices as men in order to be equal, and I respect those women who choose to live their lives in traditional roles. But it should be their choice. And that is why the United States will partner with any Muslim-majority country to support expanded literacy for girls, and to help young women pursue employment through micro-financing that helps people live their dreams. [Applause.]

Finally, I want to discuss economic development and opportunity.

I know that for many, the face of globalization is contradictory. The Internet and television can bring knowledge and information, but also offensive sexuality and mindless violence into the home. Trade can bring new wealth and opportunities, but also huge disruptions and change in communities. In all nations— including America—this change can bring fear. Fear that because of modernity we lose control over our economic choices, our politics, and most importantly our identities—those things we most cherish about our communities, our families, our traditions, and our faith.

But I also know that human progress cannot be denied. There need not be contradictions between development and tradition. Countries like Japan and South Korea grew their economies enormously while maintaining distinct cultures. The same is true for the astonishing progress within Muslim-majority countries from Kuala Lumpur to Dubai. In ancient times and in our times, Muslim communities have been at the forefront of innovation and education.

And this is important because no development strategy can be based only upon what comes out of the ground, nor can it be sustained while young people are out of work. Many Gulf states have enjoyed great wealth as a consequence of oil, and some are beginning to focus it on broader development. But all of us must recognize that education and innovation will be the currency of the 21st century—(applause)—and in too many Muslim communities, there remains underinvestment in these areas. I'm emphasizing such investment within my own country. And while America in the past has focused on oil and gas when it comes to this part of the world, we now seek a broader engagement.

On education, we will expand exchange programs, and increase scholarships, like the one that brought my father to America.

[Applause.] At the same time, we will encourage more Americans to study in Muslim communities. And we will match promising Muslim students with internships in America; invest in online learning for teachers and children around the world; and create a new online network, so a young person in Kansas can communicate instantly with a young person in Cairo.

On economic development, we will create a new corps of business volunteers to partner with counterparts in Muslim-majority countries. And I will host a Summit on Entrepreneurship this year to identify how we can deepen ties between business leaders, foundations and social entrepreneurs in the United States and Muslim communities around the world.

On science and technology, we will launch a new fund to support technological development in Muslim-majority countries, and to help transfer ideas to the marketplace so they can create more jobs. We'll open centers of scientific excellence in Africa, the Middle East and Southeast Asia, and appoint new science envoys to collaborate on programs that develop new sources of energy, create green jobs, digitize records, clean water, grow new crops. Today I'm announcing a new global effort with the Organization of the Islamic Conference to eradicate polio. And we will also expand partnerships with Muslim communities to promote child and maternal health.

All these things must be done in partnership. Americans are ready to join with citizens and governments; community organizations, religious leaders, and businesses in Muslim communities around the world to help our people pursue a better life.

The issues that I have described will not be easy to address. But we have a responsibility to join together on behalf of the world that we seek—a world where extremists no longer threaten our people, and American troops have come home; a world where Israelis and Palestinians are each secure in a state of their own, and nuclear energy is used for peaceful purposes; a world where governments serve their citizens, and the rights of all God's children are respected. Those are mutual interests. That is the world we seek. But we can only achieve it together.

I know there are many—Muslim and non-Muslim—who question whether we can forge this new beginning. Some are eager to stoke the flames of division, and to stand in the way of progress. Some suggest that it isn't worth the effort—that we are fated to disagree, and civilizations are doomed to clash. Many more are simply skeptical that real change can occur. There's so much fear, so much mistrust that has built up over the years. But if we choose to be bound by the past, we will never move forward. And I want to particularly say this to young people of every faith, in every country—you, more than anyone, have the ability to reimagine the world, to remake this world.

[. . .]

We have the power to make the world we seek, but only if we have the courage to make a new beginning, keeping in mind what has been written.

The Holy Koran tells us: "O mankind! We have created you male and female; and we have made you into nations and tribes so that you may know one another."

The Talmud tells us: "The whole of the Torah is for the purpose of promoting peace."

The Holy Bible tells us: "Blessed are the peacemakers, for they shall be called sons of God." [Applause.]

The people of the world can live together in peace. We know that is God's vision. Now that must be our work here on Earth.

[. . .]

Source: Barack Obama, "Remarks by the President on a New Beginning," The White House, http://www.whitehouse.gov/the_press_office/Remarks-by-the-President-at-Cairo-University-6-04-09/.

Index